THE NORTON/GROVE
HANDBOOKS IN MUSIC

PERFORMANCE PRACTICE
MUSIC AFTER 1600

THE NORTON/GROVE
HANDBOOKS IN MUSIC

PERFORMANCE
PRACTICE

MUSIC AFTER 1600

Edited by HOWARD MAYER BROWN and STANLEY SADIE

W. W. NORTON & COMPANY

NEW YORK   LONDON

Parts of this material first published in
The New Grove Dictionary of Music and Musicians®,
edited by Stanley Sadie, 1980

The New Grove and *The New Grove Dictionary of Music and Musicians*
are registered trademarks of Macmillan Publishers Limited, London

First published in the UK 1989 by
THE MACMILLAN PRESS LTD
Houndmills, Basingstoke, Hampshire RG21 2XS
and London
Companies and representatives throughout the world

British Library Cataloguing in Publication Data
Performance practice. — (The New Grove handbooks in
musicology).
1. Western music. Performance, 1450–
I. Brown, Howard Mayer, 1930 — II. Sadie, Stanley,
1930 — III. The new grove dictionary of music and
musicians
780'.903
ISBN 0–333–47404–X (hardback)

First American edition 1990

All rights reserved.

W. W. Norton & Company, Ltd.,
500 Fifth Avenue, New York NY 10110

ISBN 0-393-02808-9

Typeset by Footnote Graphics,
Warminster, Wiltshire

1 2 3 4 5 6 7 8 9 0

Contents

Contents

PART FOUR: THE 20TH CENTURY

Illustration Acknowledgements

We are grateful to the following for permission to reproduce illustrative material. (Every effort has been made to contact copyright holders; we apologise to anyone who may have been omitted): Bayerische Werwaltung der Staatlichen Schlösser, Gärten und Seen, Munich (cover); Civici Musei Veneziani d'Arte e di Storia, Venice (p.6); Fotografico della Soprintendenza per i Beni Artistici e Storici per le province di Bologna, Ferrara, Forli e Ravenna (p.9); Kunstsammlungen der Veste Coburg, Kupferstichkabinett (p.68; Inv. No. IX, 118, 106); Staatliche Kunstsammlungen, Kupferstich-kabinett, Dresden (p.98); Mark Lindley (p.187, figs.1a and b); after Mark Lindley (on pages 170–183 figs.1, 2, 3, 6, 7, 8, 9, 10, 11 and on page 187 fig.2); Stadtbildstelle, Augsburg (p.188, fig.3); Germanisches National-museum, Nuremberg (p.219); Statens Konstmuseer, Stockholm (p.297); Mansell Collection, London (p.327); photo Giraudon, Paris (p.347); Freies Deutsches Hochstift, Frankfurt-am-Maim (p.396); Mary Evans Picture Library, London (p.426).

Abbreviations

AcM	Acta musicologica	JVdGSA	Journal of the Viola da Gamba Society of America
AMf	Archiv für Musikforschung		
AMw	Archiv für Musikwissenschaft	MD	Musica disciplina
AMZ	Allgemeine musikalische Zeitung	Mf	Die Musikforschung
AnMc	Analecta musicologica	MGG	Die Musik in Geschichte und Gegenwart
AnnM	Annales musicologiques		
BJb	Bach-Jahrbuch	MJb	Mozart-Jahrbuch des Zentralinstituts für Mozartforschung
BMB	Biblioteca musica bononiensis		
BWQ	Brass and Woodwind Quarterly		
CSM	Corpus scriptorum de musica	ML	Music and Letters
DM	Documenta musicologica	M&M	Man & Music
DTÖ	Denkmäler der Tonkunst in Österreich	MMA	Miscellanea musicologica
		MME	Monumentos de la música española
EHM	The English Harpsichord Magazine		
		MMR	The Monthly Musical Record
EM	Early Music	MQ	The Musical Quarterly
EMH	Early Music History	MSD	Musicological Studies and Documents
FoMRHI	Fellowship of Makers and Restorers of Historical Instruments		
		MT	The Musical Times
		NMA	Neue Mozart-Ausgabe
GfMKB	Gesellschaft für Musikforschung Kongressbericht	NRMI	Nuova rivista musicale italiana
		PMA	Proceedings of the Musical Association
Grove 6	The New Grove Dictionary of Music and Musicians		
		PNM	Perspectives of New Music
GroveMI	The New Grove Dictionary of Musical Instruments	PRMA	Proceedings of the Royal Musical Association
GSJ	The Galpin Society Journal	ReM	La revue musicale
IMSCR	International Musicological Society Congress Report	RILM	Répertoire international de la littérature musicale
IRASM	International Review of the Aesthetics and Sociology of Music	RIM	Rivista italiana di musicologia
		RMARC	R[oyal] M[usical] A[ssociation] Research Chronicle
JAMS	Journal of the American Musicological Society		
		RMFC	Recherches sur la musique française classique
JAMIS	Journal of the American Musical Instrument Society		
		RRMBE	Recent Researches in the Music of the Baroque Era
JBIOS	Journal of the British Institute of Organ Studies		
		RMI	Rivista musicale italiana
JM	Journal of Musicology	SMA	Studies in Music [Australia]
JMT	Journal of Music Theory	VMw	Vierteljahrsschrift für Musikwissenschaft
JRMA	Journal of the Royal Musical Association		
		ZMw	Zeitschrift für Musikwissenschaft

Preface

'Early music', that is, music composed more than 40 years ago (to paraphrase Johannes Tinctoris, the 15th-century theorist who claimed no music written more than 40 years before was worth hearing), has been cultivated at various times and places in the history of the West. Most of the manuscripts containing the songs of the troubadours, for example, were copied out long after the music was composed. The Squarcialupi Codex prepared in the 15th century, some time after the death of Francesco Landini, was intended to celebrate the achievements of the musicians of Florence, evidently as a kind of historical record. By the second half of the 16th century, a number of musicians regularly performed music at least 50 years old. Sacred vocal music often stayed in the repertories of church and cathedral choirs for more than a hundred years. And in the late 18th and early 19th centuries, groups such as the Academy of Ancient Music and the Concert of Ancient Music in London organized performances centred partly around early English church music and partly around the music of Corelli, Handel and Purcell.

On the other hand, the idea that 'early music' should be performed 'authentically' – that is, in a way as close to the composers' original conception as it is possible to come – seems to have been new in the 20th century. Only since the first decades of the present century have scholars and performers alike studied systematically the way music was performed in the past. The discipline of performance (or performing) practice (*Aufführungspraxis*) was born partly through the efforts of German academics who founded the first Collegia musica in universities to perform the old music they studied, and partly through the single-handed efforts in England of Arnold Dolmetsch, the great polymath who believed deeply in the artistic achievement of the old composers and therefore built instruments and learned to play them by studying the treatises of the 17th and 18th centuries. Dolmetsch's book, *The Interpretation of the Music of the Seventeenth and Eighteenth Centuries Revealed by Contemporary Evidence* (London, 1915; new edition with an introduction by R. Alec Harman, Seattle and London, 1969), along with the more comprehensive surveys of past times, such as Robert Haas, *Aufführungspraxis* (Potsdam, 1931; repr. 1949), and Arnold Schering, *Aufführungspraxis alter Musik* (Leipzig, 1931) thus were the pioneering works that first set out the premises and assumptions with which we still operate and which first explained to present-day scholars and musicians how music was performed in earlier times.

In the last quarter of the 20th century, questions of performance practice, like so many other areas of scholarly inquiry that seemed much simpler 50 years ago, have grown ever more complicated. Performing musicians, for example, continue to expand their repertories backwards in time, and today there are many more groups specializing in ever earlier medieval repertories and many more medieval compositions heard in concert halls, churches and university recital rooms than anyone could have imagined 50 years ago.

Preface

Most recently, performers have begun to be interested in learning to perform the music of the late 18th and early 19th centuries 'authentically', that is, with instruments and playing techniques no longer in common use, and with the sort of balance of forces and arrangements of musicians familiar to the audiences who first heard the music. This new initiative to perform standard concert repertory in a way close to that envisaged by the composers will surely teach us something important about the sound of Mozart's, Beethoven's and Schubert's music, but it also raises new questions about the propriety of authenticity as an ideal, and about the nature of the discipline of performance practice. The nature of the discipline will change more and more as scholars come to realize that the advent of recordings has changed radically the way we can know about how music sounded in the past.

In short, the study of performance practice has become too extensive and too complicated for any one person to master the entire field. Two works attempt a comprehensive bibliography of studies on performance practice: M. Vinquist and N. Zaslaw, *Performance Practice: a Bibliography* (New York, 1971; supplements in *Current Musicology*, no.12 (1971), 129–49, and no.15 (1973), 126–36), and R. Jackson, *Performance Practice, Medieval to Contemporary: a Bibliographic Guide* (New York, 1987; annual supplements in *Performance Practice Review*). At the same time, it has scarcely yet established itself as a discipline within musicology, partly because relatively few academic scholars have engaged themselves directly with such questions, partly because the cooperation between scholars, performers and instrument makers necessary to debate meaningfully central issues is often difficult to organize, and partly because many scholars still mistrust studies that do not deal with the analysis and criticism of the great works by the great composers, or with philological or social issues that seem to them more central to our main concerns with the great issues of history.

The idea for this handbook of performance practice came about, then, from an awareness that the boundaries of the discipline of performance practice needed to be defined more clearly, and that no one person could do that satisfactorily. In preparing the book, we have kept in mind that we have hoped .to address both scholars and performers, although each group has different preoccupations and asks different sorts of question. The purely scholarly problem of finding out how music sounded in the past, for example, differs significantly from the aesthetic and practical questions that arise from the decision to offer earlier repertories to modern audiences.

In a sense, scholars and performers need opposite emphases: performers should learn that there are no simple right answers to most of their most pressing questions, however necessary it may be for them to find a single solution appropriate for a particular performance, and scholars that only through the study of performing traditions can certain kinds of questions regarding the nature of the written evidence be illuminated and that answers to certain of their questions can be reached with enough patient work, if sometimes by means of fairly circumstantial arguments. Both groups need to be reminded of their mutual dependence. We shall never really understand a repertory of music until we have learned how it sounds in performance, but good performances and 'understanding' alike depend heavily on archival, literary, iconographical, analytical and purely philological studies.

Preface

This handbook hopes to make clear the traditional areas of research into performance practice while at the same time raising new questions for study. Rather than providing performers with easy, prescriptive answers to complicated questions, the handbook aims to help them ask the right questions and give them some guidance as to how and where answers might be arrived at. We have tried to be suggestive rather than prescriptive, concentrating more on what we do not know than on what we do. The handbook aims, in short, at being comprehensive in the kinds of questions it offers to be answered, but without suggesting any single answer as correct. In that sense, we have conceived it as an attempt to bring up to date the best and most provocative essay on the central issues of performance practice yet published, Thurston Dart's *The Interpretation of Music* (London, 1954).

As in every other scholarly field, certain kinds of question dealing with performance practice are still very much open to debate, and it would be disingenuous to propose answers that are not yet clear. Dialogue is an essential part of the scholarly process. We have tried not to obscure matters under current debate, even at the expense of allowing some contradictory statements to stand from essay to essay. We have tried, too, to bring the discipline of performance practice up to date, by asking what its tasks are in the study of late 19th-century and 20th-century music. As far as we know, this is the first book to attempt an overview of performance practice for these later periods, a field of inquiry still very much in the process of being developed.

Although this book is issued in the *New Grove* handbook series, no part of it is derived from or based on material in *The New Grove Dictionary*; the entire text was expressly commissioned and written in the form in which it now appears.

H.M.B., S.S.

Chicago and London, 1989

PART ONE

The Baroque Era

CHAPTER I

Introduction

ELEANOR SELFRIDGE-FIELD

It was primarily in relation to the Baroque period that an interest in performance practice first developed. The middle decades of the 19th century brought forth a heightened historical consciousness that resulted in a sustained exploration of the repertory of earlier times. The now hackneyed phrase 'newly rediscovered' applied at one time to the music of Bach, whose long-forgotten sacred vocal music was revived by Zelter, Mendelssohn and others. A recognition that 19th-century media and methods of performance did not necessarily suit music of the 18th and earlier centuries developed only gradually. Our knowledge of how Baroque music was performed is provisional, for extensive research into forgotten repertories and their performance continues vigorously at the present time.

Three central features of Baroque music – its improvisatory aspects, the use of a basso continuo, and the emerging awareness of instrumental colour and variety – engender a large proportion of all questions asked about the performance of this repertory. These elements of performance all reflect the keen appreciation of spontaneity that marked the Baroque era but which is alien to the pursuit of fixed norms, a value of our own time. Furthermore, our historical perception of the period 1600 to 1750 as a unified whole has encouraged us to search for all-embracing answers where (for the most part) none exists, and where greater aesthetic value is attached to variety than to consistency.

Performers and composers

Musicians of the Baroque period were employed in a great variety of situations. Formal employment by a court or church often lasted a lifetime, although eminent performers and composers could be attracted to new positions if sufficient enticement were offered. Organists were often the most rigorously trained musicians in matters of musical theory and compositional technique. Like chapel singers, they were well schooled in counterpoint.

The rise of instrumental music and opera in the 17th century created a new class of musician whose primary emphasis was on technique.[1] These performers succeeded not, as organists did, by satisfying juries with their command of procedural concepts but by their ability to extemporize, to ornament or to evoke a desired effect. There is much evidence of a lingering tension between those who revered the propriety of the music as written and those who savoured the sound as heard in performance, but by the 18th century this ambivalence had been transformed into a self-nurturing dialectic

3

that found its final consummation in Bach's skill at extemporizing music of great contrapuntal complexity.

In the Baroque era female performers won recognition in an increasing number of places, although they were often celebrated collectively rather than individually. The *concerto delle donne* in Ferrara, and other small groups of female virtuose who flourished in the last decades of the 16th century, may have provided an important example. The all-female Venetian conservatories cultivated singers and instrumentalists who were hailed by dignitaries of many nationalities. It was, however, the opera stages of Europe that fostered the earliest musical superstars, both male and female. The early prima donna Faustina Bordoni and the celebrated castrato Carlo Broschi *detto* Farinelli were but two of Italy's significant exports to the theatres of London, Madrid, Dresden and elsewhere. By the 18th century, instrumental virtuosos also enjoyed great esteem, but their demonstrations were generally limited to a narrower public than those of opera singers since they were likely to exhibit their skills by invitation before monarchs or other dignitaries. Travel was a major element in the life of most virtuosos.

Choirmasters were responsible for providing a steady stream of new choral compositions and for maintaining musical personnel. Much of the 17th-century repertory for instrumental groups was composed by organists who, in many circumstances, also seem to have been responsible for rehearsing such groups. Chamber music, like opera, was usually directed from the harpsichord. Since both in sacred and in secular circumstances the composer was almost always involved in the performance of his music, there was no need for a conductor and little need for cues to tempo, dynamics or ornamentation in partbooks.

Up until the first half of the 18th century instrumental music was primarily viewed as an adjunct to vocal music. The ensemble sonatas that were interleaved with psalms in Vespers, and the organ toccatas used for the Elevation of the Host in masses, sensitized worshippers to the meaning of sacred texts and sacramental acts. Sinfonias (which became progressively longer over time) introduced operas and oratorios. Theorbo and lute solos filled the intervals of oratorios in Italy in the later 17th century,[2] while organ concertos provided the same function for English oratorio in the early 18th century.[3] Novel instruments – for example the chalumeau – seem repeatedly to have been used to highlight texts of a particular character. In vocal works, obbligato reed instruments (especially instruments that have never become standard members of the orchestra) often had some association with texts concerning death or mourning. Their timbre seems to have signified not the sorrow of earthly departure, however, but the beauty of the eternal realms to which the spirit, through death, gained access. Such is the intimation of the chalumeau obbligato in Vivaldi's oratorio *Juditha triumphans* (1716) and of the oboe d'amore in Bach's Cantata no.60, *O Ewigkeit, du Donnerwort* (1723). The possibility that untexted pieces with corresponding requirements were composed in some instances to introduce such works, and in others to take advantage of an unusual skill made available by a virtuoso, accounts for a significant number of pieces involving unusual instruments.

Instrumental music was often composed in the apprenticeship years of those who aspired to direct large chapels. A typical career path in sacred music led from the position of choirboy to organist, to assistant music director and finally to chief director. As a chorister one learnt to perform, as an organist to compose for keyboard and other instruments, as an assistant director to compose texted music, and as full *maestro* to combine all these skills in music for the most august occasions.[4] Direction of the music, in the modern sense of conducting, was unknown, although choirs could include designated beat-tappers and pitch-givers.

Composers who produced mainly instrumental music throughout their lifetimes were usually in court service. The violinist-composers of Modena – Uccellini and the Vitalis – provided the Este court with hundreds of instrumental pieces. Corelli, born mid-century into comfortable circumstances, found patronage in the courts of cardinals in Rome. He typified a new breed of composers who came from the ranks of virtuosos, especially violinists, and who devoted themselves entirely to repertories for their own instruments. Before him, there were few prolific composers who wrote only for instruments.[5]

Venues

When considering the venues where music was performed in the Baroque era it is necessary to recognize the dichotomy that existed between what was politically inspired and what was artistically motivated. The trend in contemporary architecture, guided by political interests, was toward grandiosity. This principally emanated from Rome, which acquired many of its palaces and piazzas in the 17th century, chief among these being Bernini's impressive piazza in front of St Peter's Basilica. St Paul's Cathedral in London, as rebuilt after the great fire of 1666, combined grace and a classical sense of hierarchical proportion in the enclosure of a large space. The illusion of non-enclosure was cultivated at Versailles, with gardens out of doors and mirrors inside. A sense of spaciousness was cultivated elsewhere in London, Rome and Paris with the rise of pleasure gardens and Arcadian pretexts for using them. While gardens provided none of the acoustical benefits of halls, serenatas and occasional works (Handel's Water Music and Fireworks Music, to name two famous examples) were written in considerable abundance for outdoor performance.

Inevitably, works written for large or not fully contained spaces could only be appreciated if they used large numbers of performers and powerful instruments. The trumpet sonatas composed for the church of S Petronio in Bologna – a church that would have been the largest in Christendom had its transepts ever been built – took advantage of an opportunity that did not exist in many smaller churches. This was an age of spectacular effects. S Petronio, which had existed since the 12th century, finally came into its own. The same might be said for Salzburg Cathedral, with the performance of a festival mass for 53 voices (formerly attributed to Benevoli, now credited to Biber) in 1682; this work stands as a paramount symbol of the colossal aspect of the Baroque aesthetic.

The dualism of the era is represented, however, by the fact that small spaces were also employed for certain purposes. The smallest may be the Holywell Music Room in Oxford, opened in 1748. Seating 200 persons, it

Teatro Grimani a S Giovanni Grisostomo, Venice, built by Tomaso Bezzi for Carlo and Vincenzo Grimani and opened in 1678 (renamed Teatro Malibran in the 19th century): engraving by Padre Vincenzo Maria Coronelli

was well suited to the chamber music which was already flourishing in English drawing rooms. Indeed, the Academy of Vocal Music, founded in 1726, originally met in the Crown and Anchor Tavern on the Strand to pursue its stated intention of 'restoring ancient church music'. Whole genres of Baroque music – solo motets, secular vocal solos with guitar or lute accompaniment, suites for harpsichord, and unaccompanied violin pieces – were created for spaces that were either intimately small or had exceptionaly fine acoustics. The revival of this repertory today confronts the musician with difficult choices; historically correct technique and instrumentation are ill suited to large halls and unfortunate compromises must sometimes be made in the interests of audibility.

The aspect of spatial context that varies most radically from today's model is represented by the theatre of the Baroque era. Almost universally, theatres were extremely small. The largest were comparable with the smallest cinemas of today.[6] The earliest public theatres, opened in Venice from 1637 onwards, had several tiers of boxes, most rented for a year, if not for a lifetime, by noblemen and other dignitaries. Temporary seating for one-time attendees could be provided on the parterre, but the front section of the ground floor was fenced off for the instrumentalists, too few to constitute a true orchestra. Ground-floor seats were considered unattractive because the necks of large instruments, such as cellos and theorboes, blocked the view. The stages in such theatres must have been extremely crowded, since they could include six or more singers, small choruses and dance groups, live animals when appropriate to the plot (hunters might, for example, pursue real game), and mechanically intricate sets. (The engineers who designed machines to enable gods to descend on clouds, waves to roll in from the ocean, and lightning to strike the unjust were as highly valued as composers and performers.)

Dynamics of performance

In the Baroque period the single event had a firmer identity than the individual composition.[7] Thus we may be able to say what resources were used in a particular work on a particular occasion, but to assume that the same resources were always used for the same work would be pure speculation. The resources of even the most traditional institutions varied from occasion to occasion. For example, at the church of S Petronio in Bologna in 1694 three violins figured in an ensemble of 12 for one feast and ten violins in an ensemble of 50 for a different feast. The works were by Colonna and Torelli in both cases.[8] At the Palazzo Bonelli in Rome in 1708 Alessandro Scarlatti's oratorio *L'Annunziazione* was performed with an orchestra of 11 and Handel's oratorio *La Resurrezione* with an orchestra of 48.[9] This difference in part reflected the contrast in subjects.

A fluidity of both numbers and personnel could characterize the successive performances of individual operas. Cavalli's operas were usually performed in Venice in the middle decades of the 17th century with a five-part string ensemble and a stable of continuo instruments (lutes, theorboes and harpsichords). But in Paris, where Cavalli's operas were highly regarded,[10] Lully's operas were performed with the 11 Petits Violons as well as two flutes, two oboes, bassoon, trumpets and timpani.[11] Casual reading of opera librettos that enumerate the instruments used in performance has led to occasional confusion between stage props and performing instruments. The trumpets of Cavalli operas were played by heralds on stage,[12] just as the 40 instruments allegedly heard in Pallavicino's *Nerone* were involved in a musical academy depicted on stage; in all probability there were only about ten instruments in the orchestra.[13] For the 17th century the question of the numbers of instruments used and their relative distribution can often be answered in only a very limited sense. The same variability pertains to the specific sequence of items within the work, since scenes were altered and arias substituted freely to accommodate changes of venue and cast. One can attempt to re-create the 1665 Venetian production of Cavalli's *Muzio Scevola* or the 1662 Parisian performance of *Ercole amante*, but not *Muzio Scevola* or *Ercole amante* as general entities, for the concept of the individual opera as the sum (or the statistical average) of its performances did not exist.

In the 18th century the questions become more subtle and perhaps more difficult because it is easy to assume that the more familiar external appearance of things represented the results that we now associate with those things. In Vienna virtually all the instruments of the modern orchestra were available in the 1720s and 1730s, the woodwinds having been greatly improved in the first decades of the century. Collectively they comprised a palette from which soloists, trios and small ensembles could be employed by turns. There is no evidence that they ever all played together as a single ensemble.[14]

Many instruments with now familiar names possessed sounds that are different from those of their modern counterparts and ranges more restricted than those of later times. In general they produced less volume and somewhat different tone qualities. The reed instruments had few keys (although there was rapid mechanical development as the 18th century progressed) and played in only a limited range of tonalities. The brass were still 'natural' instruments that were unable to modulate or transpose and were thus used sparingly except in their traditional role as processional instruments.

At the Cöthen court during Bach's employment there (1717–23) the total number of instruments, between 13 and 15, was relatively stable, but their specific distribution in both the string and the wind sections varied from year to year and from genre to genre (concerto, cantata, suite). Flutes (to which philosophers of antiquity and popes of the 17th century objected on moral grounds) joined the orchestra sooner in the Protestant northern part of Europe and later in the Catholic south. Trumpets were usually hired on a separate basis from orchestral instruments and were rarely integrated members of the ensemble. Churches retained instruments (like the cornett) into their obsolescence, while courts and theatres embraced the novel and sometimes the ephemeral (e.g. the chalumeau). Some instruments (e.g. the baryton) that joined the orchestra in the second and third decades of the 18th century were gone by the fourth and fifth decades, even though they may have returned in the age of Haydn and Mozart.

The context in which a work was created often bears upon the manner of its accompaniment, and in fact questions of accompaniment may affect the subtler considerations governing the arrangement and direction of perfor-

*The church of S Petronio,
Bologna, on the occasion of
the visit of James the
Pretender and his wife
Clementina Sobieski on 4
October 1722: painting by
Leonardo Sconzani (Bologna,
Archivio di Stato, 'Anziana
... insigna', xiii, f.37a)*

mers. In general, for example, the organ is preferable to the harpsichord in the accompaniment of church works, although well documented exceptions do occur. On specific occasions, such as Holy Week, harpsichords were used in the performance of lessons and perhaps of Passion scenes in Italian churches. To determine what other instruments should join in the accompaniment requires some consideration of time and place. Lute and organ, cello and organ, violone and organ, gamba and organ, and various combinations of these instruments were all accepted at different times and in different places.

In opera there were usually at least two harpsichords – one for the composer-conductor, who might accompany the arias, and one for the recitative accompanist. In some cases the accompaniment group might vary with the 'affect' of the aria. This flexibility in forming a variety of constellations of accompanying instruments from a galaxy known only by its outer dimensions persisted throughout the period and influenced the tendency of early Classical orchestras to have a wind cluster and a string cluster, each with its own keyboard accompaniment. It must have influenced the imaginations of composers who, alas, were often more reticent in giving specific instrumentation for continuo than for other parts. These questions about the number and kinds of instruments to use in accompaniment necessarily bear on what kinds of accompaniment parts should be played. A basso continuo characterized by many sustained notes suggests, in the absence of other information, an organ accompaniment, since the rapid decay time of a harpsichord requires the reinforcement of a string bass of some kind. But if some leavening of the effect is desired, a lute can be added to an organ continuo to simulate the effect of a harpsichord. Alternatively, a series of shorter note values may be substituted.

In the chamber repertory of the early 18th century one of the most conspicuous problems of accompaniment is to determine when a cello, gamba or violone might have been used (as many title-pages of the time seem to suggest) without a keyboard accompaniment of any sort. In the repertory for solo instrument and keyboard this question is transmuted at the end of the Baroque era, when the keyboard established itself as a soloist in its own right and the 'obbligato' could be a superfluous reinforcement of the keyboard treble. Such questions gain from the comparison of chronologically distinct repertories. In the same vein, the testimony of many printed partbooks and of some documents is that solo vocal music, following the models of the Renaissance, was sometimes accompanied only by lutes or theorbes in the first part of the Baroque era.

Sources of information

The sources of information that may be used to enlarge our knowledge of performance are extremely diverse. They include theoretical writings, journals and diaries, personnel records, iconographical objects and surviving instruments.

THEORETICAL WRITINGS Theoretical treatises are the most commonly consulted sources of the time. In the Baroque period there were principally two kinds of treatises – comprehensive but speculative works aimed at academicians and practical manuals aimed at the performer. Works of the first kind are likely to discuss the rules of composition (which may bear on the question of *musica ficta* among other things), to provide inventories or descriptions of existing (or at least of theoretically possible) instruments,[15] and to discuss mathematical and somewhat idealized historical aspects of music. The writings of Gioseffe Zarlino, from the second half of the 16th century, for example, are exemplary as speculative works but contain little that is of immediate value to today's performer. Michael Praetorius's *Syntagma musicum* (1615–20) and Marin Mersenne's *Harmonie universelle* (1636–7) are somewhat more helpful, partly because they provide illustrations of instruments then in use. Lodovico Zacconi's *Prattica di musica* (1592, 1622) is so practical in places that it delves into such matters as what makes a good *maestro di cappella*. In breadth and lofty inclination, the closest parallels in the 17th century are the *Musurgia universalis* (1650) and the *Phonurgia nova* (1673) of Athanasius Kircher, a German historian, theologian and Egyptologist through whom a distilled version of the writings of Zarlino was transmitted to the 18th century.

Practical guides, in contrast, give generous information on singing and playing techniques. The progressive changes of focus in works concerned with instrumental performance reflect the changing tastes and technology of the period. For example, a series of organ tutors such as Girolamo Diruta's *Il transilvano* (1593, 1609) and Adriano Banchieri's *L'organo suonarino* (1605), and collections of lute music with performance advice, such as Vincenzo Galilei's *[Il] Fronimo: Dialogo sopra l'arte del bene intavolare et rettamente sonare la musica* (1584), ushered in the period. Throughout the 17th century, tutors concentrated on a single instrument or family of instruments thereby reflecting their close connection with performance. Christopher Simpson's *The Division-Violist* (1659) is an important work of this type, for it documents not only the growing interest in consorts and ensembles but also the emerging recognition of instrumental music as a genre distinct from, yet still closely connected to, vocal music. *Musick's Monument* (1676), by Thomas Mace, addresses the needs of lutenists and theorbists. There were also tutors and selections of works for specific wind instruments, such as Bartolomé de Selma y Salaverde's *Canzoni, fantasie et correnti* (1638) and G. A. Bertali's *Compositioni musicali* (1645), both for bassoon. (During the latter half of the 17th century few such manuals were written.) While facsimile editions of many practical guides give today's performer access to information about playing technique, the availability of exact replicas of the instruments at issue is sometimes limited. Even when exact duplication of instruments is possible, subtle changes in the meaning of words over centuries may leave interpretations open to question.

Writings advocating a rhetorical approach to composition constituted something of a third stream in that they were speculative in their appeal to the authority of antiquity but practical in assuming an advisory tone. They were generally addressed to composers of vocal music. Rhetorical procedures for which musical equivalents were postulated included invention, elaboration, affirmation, refutation and conclusion.[16] Some theorists went beyond general recommendations to propose particular musical figures to convey quite precise meanings. Among such theories, which issued especially from north and central Germany, there is no fundamental consistency in the use of terminology. Efforts to systematize the teachings on *Figuren*, an activity to which much attention was devoted earlier in this century, are now regarded with caution.[17]

In general, the great tomes of the early part of the Baroque period, frequently consulted for clarification on matters of performance, help to exclude some possibilities, but they rarely offer straightforward advice of immediately practical help, since their authors were often closer to the ranks of philosophers than of musicians.

In the 18th century the instruments of today's orchestras and chambers began to take a more secure place in the general scheme of things. Manuals on the wind instruments were well served by the French, starting with Hotteterre's *Principes de la flûte traversière* (1707), a volume that deals with the recorder and the oboe as well as the flute and which was in wide circulation for half a century. Manuals of violin playing became extremely popular, particularly in the wake first of Corelli's sonatas and then of Tartini's concertos. Both repertories were so widely distributed, however, that treatises discussing them must be understood to reflect views that originated with the authors but which the composers themselves might not have recognized as appropriate. This factor increases the value of manuals that were written by composers, such as Tartini's undated *Regole per arrivare a saper ben suonar il violino* and Leopold Mozart's *Versuch einer gründlichen Violinschule* (1756).

The voice was perhaps the instrument most neglected by theorists. Caccini's *Le nuove musiche* (1601/2) includes a famous essay on the new singing techniques as a preface to a series of pieces for solo voice and figured bass through whose performance these skills can be developed. Particular elements of execution, such as the *trillo*, the *groppo* and the *ribattuta* are carefully distinguished from each other. Philosophically orientated treatises, such as Mersenne's, gave consideration to diction and pronunciation. Vocal technique was addressed in Bénigne de Bacilly's *Remarques curieuses sur l'art de bien chanter* (1668). The phenomenal growth in the popularity of opera generated treatises on singing, such as Pier Francesco Tosi's *Opinioni de' cantori antichi e moderni* (1723), which, like most of the literature generated by the conflict of ancient and modern, advocated the older methods. Jean-Antoine Bérard's *L'art du chant* (1755), responding to the growing spirit of scientific inquiry in the 18th century, offered anatomical explanations of tone production.

The principal focus of attention in practical manuals of the early 18th century was keyboard instruments, both as the mainstay of continuo practice and as an independent medium. Gasparini's *L'armonico prattico al cimbalo* (1708) and Heinichen's *Der generalbass in der Composition* (1728) were typical of the first and more traditional type, while the newer type was represented by François Couperin's *L'art de toucher le clavecin* (1716). As the Baroque period drew to a close, German writers came to dominate this field with works such as C. P. E. Bach's *Versuch über die wahre Art das Clavier zu spielen* (1753 and 1762) and Friedrich Wilhelm Marpurg's *Anleitung zum Clavierspielen* (1755). Tutors on continuo practice are devoted largely to keyboard figuration and the harmonic studies of the middle and later 18th century are an outgrowth of these. The most comprehensive survey of this kind of work remains F. T. Arnold's vintage study, *The Art of Accompaniment from a Thorough-Bass* (1931).

Some treatises written by performers with one instrument in mind contain advice that may be applicable in other contexts. This is particularly true of works that are concerned mainly with improvisation. Dalla Casa's *Il vero modo di diminuir* (1584) and Bassano's *Ricercate, passaggi, et cadentie* (1585/6) were studies of signal importance but of marked contrast in detail considering that both masters were cornett players at the ducal chapel of St Mark's, Venice. Such differences, which are clearly documented in the parallel editions of corresponding chanson elaborations in Erig's and Gutman's *Italienische Diminutionen* (1979),[18] only serve to suggest how broad was the scope for individuality even when time and place were constant. Their divergent ideas cast a long shadow over a number of decades. As late as the 1670s Bassano's approach can be seen to have been faintly echoed in a *Nova instructio pro pulsandis organis* by the monk Spiridion a Monte Carmelo.[19]

Despite such remarkable examples of continuity, performers who consult these works today should remember that the advice offered was generally intended for a well-defined and immediate circle. Authors did not perceive themselves as writing for posterity and they therefore often failed to document what was obvious to their peers but may be completely unfamiliar now. Most authors of practical manuals travelled little and knew of practices elsewhere only as much as they could deduce them by examining music itself. That, as today's performers are no doubt aware, was sometimes quite little.

In the final analysis, treatises and tutors leave many questions unresolved. Even when they can be interpreted unequivocally, it is almost never certain whether a particular composer or performer sought to prove a particular theorist correct. It is not at all clear how widely the bulk of the period's music and of its treatises were known. Few books or musical works survive in more than a handful of copies.

JOURNALS AND DIARIES Journals and diaries, formal correspondence and the monthly and weekly forerunners of modern daily newspapers all may contain comments on musical performances from time to time. Although they rarely offer specific advice, they sometimes select their material in ways that have revealing implications for repertory and performance practices. The English diarist Thomas Coryat, for example, in his description of the celebration of the feast of St Roche in Venice in 1608,[20] must have been referring to a performance of Gabrieli's forward-looking *Sonata per tre violini* (published posthumously in 1615) or to a work of similar characteristics. The diaries of Samuel Pepys in the later 17th century and the travel letters of Lady Mary Wortley Montagu in the early 18th are representative of voluminous sources which not only describe events but also give some sense of why they happened and how they were received.

From letters we may learn of the practical considerations that influenced the final result – why, for example, the arias of an opera were recast to suit a new singer or a change of venue. Such information is valuable in sparing us the effort of ponderous philosophical debate to explain the effects of such mundane occurrences as a head cold or a sprained ankle. Conversely, formal correspondence, which was particularly prevalent in France, sometimes serves to highlight philosophical considerations that influenced musical practices. The 17th-century correspondence of Mersenne with the Dutch composer and diplomat Constantijn Huygens[21] and with Descartes[22] might be cited as examples.

The forerunners of modern periodicals offered three distinct kinds of commentary on music – the glowing accounts of events, chiefly opera productions, in the Catholic press; the usually scathing accounts, also often of opera, in the Protestant press; and the noncommittal reports and notices, often of publications, in music magazines such as Mattheson's *Criticus musicus* (1722–5). *Le Mercure galant* speaks so often of sets and machines when describing Italian operas of the late 17th century that we may justifiably wonder whether the music was of any real consequence. The contemporary journal *Pallade Veneta*, on the other hand, comments so consistently on the use of instruments in oratorio productions, while failing to mention them in accounts of operas, that a performer might reasonably ask whether the ad libitum addition of instruments to oratorios with scores lacking specific indications is not appropriate. Such sources also enable us to determine how programmes of music were formed and how resources were deployed. Opinion may, of course, obscure fact. Joseph Addison's *Spectator* commentaries on Handel's *Rinaldo* (1711) concentrate so heavily on the distractions of the Italian language and staging techniques that little is revealed about the music. In general, the press reported what was novel without prejudice toward anticipated longevity or abiding value because the motivations for their criticisms were frequently political rather than aesthetic.

PERSONNEL RECORDS Records from courts and churches that itemize personnel according to dates of hire or retirement, or reveal rates of pay, have been of considerable value in sketching the general dimensions of choral and instrumental groups and in providing detail about the itineraries of peripatetic musicians. Thus with a minimum of effort one can establish rosters for the English, French and Austrian courts, the Italian churches, and various institutions both sacred and secular in Germany (and of course in other countries). These all serve as good outlines for giving an overall impression of affairs, and sometimes they give very complete detail for individual occasions. They cannot, however, provide a wholly adequate basis for making direct comparisons from year to year or from place to place at random for several reasons: (*a*) the records are often difficult to decipher and some names are incorrectly transcribed; (*b*) the apprentice system that dominated most of Europe meant that the names of the elderly were left on the books long after they had effectively retired and the names of young musicians who served, but who could not officially be hired until a vacancy was created by the death of a senior musician, were not recorded; (*c*) many staffs were organized into shifts whose responsibilities changed; (*d*) positions were sometimes sold, especially at the court of St James, without official note being made; and (*e*) in the case of instrumental music, particularly in the 18th century, it was common for one performer to serve in two capacities.

Thus in 18th-century Venice oboists were often flautists as well, while in Vienna oboists doubled as trombonists and in Paris those who played the horn also played the viola. This creates a problem of uncertain resolution in orchestrating scores on the basis of such records: a single term may designate both an instrument and the position occupied by a performer who played both this and another instrument.

A comparison of pay scales for individual players tends to suggest that by modern standards wind players were more cherished than fiddlers, but further examination sometimes reveals that they played on a greater number of occasions and that on a *per diem* basis pay scales were fairly uniform within a given performance environment. Only in the case of 18th-century opera was a class of highly paid superstars created. In general, therefore, payment information does not form a secure basis for inference about the actual deployment of available talents, although it frequently establishes the outer limits.

ICONOGRAPHICAL SOURCES The iconographical sources that are of value in the study of Baroque performance practice are as different from those of the Renaissance as the two repertories are different from each other. For the Renaissance, sumptuous paintings of careful composition and arguably reliable detail show arrangements of musicians and sometimes even display the music before them. In the Baroque period, painters turned their attention to subjects that were more fanciful, dramatic and introspective. Musicians are rarely represented other than singly, and the inclusion of a musician in the painting of a group was often allegorical. We can only rarely learn much from a literal 'reading' of Baroque paintings, not simply because the subjects may be allegorically or mythologically orientated but also because the painters themselves may be too little known to permit accurate interpretation of their works with regard to time or place.

As the period progressed there was a marked increase in portraiture and the major composers were well served by it. However, the reliability of such works in matters of detail is open to question since it is obvious that such representations were sometimes motivated more by a desire to flatter than to inform. Conversely, caricature, which satirized works that intended to flatter, is sometimes a telling source of information about the foibles of particular performers.

Many less celebrated kinds of iconographical evidence have proved of value, particularly in exploring the history of Baroque opera. Architectural plans for theatres have established that stages were often small. Lithographs and engravings give abundant details of the set designs and machines that were such a characteristic feature of opera performances.

Engravings in books of the period are sometimes useful in indicating how the moving parts, both of men and of instruments, functioned in performance. Dance manuals of the late 16th and early 17th centuries show postures appropriate to particular kinds of pieces. Treatises and journals may contain diagrams that demonstrate the working parts of instruments, although in certain cases these plans have proved to be slightly defective or incomplete when used as a basis for modern manufacture. Yet we owe the earliest illustration of the fortepiano mechanism to Scipione Maffei's diagrammatic description of an early Cristofori instrument in a 1711 issue of the learned *Giornale de' letterati d'Italia.*

SURVIVING INSTRUMENTS Surviving collections of instruments, on the other hand, offer much tangible help to the performer of Baroque music. There are many such collections, but among the most rewarding for Baroque enthusiasts are those of Brussels, Vienna and London; for Baroque string instruments, the Witten-Rawlins collection in Vermillion, South Dakota, is particularly noteworthy.[23] While certain aspects of an instrument's construction must be closely examined to determine whether they have been modified in subsequent eras, other aspects are virtually unalterable. The eight-foot-tall Venetian violone of *c*1600 in the Victoria and Albert Museum, London, for example, is a much more imposing instrument than many accounts of the violone as a class would lead one to expect, but because it has been modified, its value as 'evidence' for historical performance is uncertain. There are many variations on this kind of problem. In the case of bowed string instruments, the number of strings may have been altered; often the neck has been tilted and the bridge raised. Such changes, and complementary ones in the construction of bows, were usually motivated by the wish for greater volume.

Surviving bowed instruments may provide some insight into the lower dynamic levels of Baroque music but they are valueless in considerations of pitch. Wind instruments are of greater value here, for the dimensions that control pitch are largely unalterable. Small changes may be caused by expansion or contraction of the original materials of construction, and accumulated dust can distort the tone of string and wind instruments. Furthermore, the evidence that surviving winds provide cannot be extrapolated from one place, time, or species of instrument to another. Cornetts from *c*1600 that sounded a' at 460 Hz and oboes that sounded a' at 392 Hz a century later only add to the confusion already created by organ pipes of variable lengths (pipe lengths generally falling and pitches rising approximately in a northerly direction). The pitch and dynamic suggestions embodied in surviving ensemble instruments often become problematical when period string and wind instruments are used in combination.

Another class of historically informative 'instruments' from the 18th century is that of music boxes, musical clocks, barrel organs and other mechanically governed devices. In so far as the mechanical skills of the time permitted, these provide fairly precise information about relative pitch and rhythmic values. Some insight into absolute tempo values can also be gained by timing performances preserved in this way.

The modern reconstruction of instruments, which has been of enormous value in reviving a Baroque aesthetic, flourishes in equal measure as an art and a science. The problems modern makers confront sometimes bring new insights to the performer and the scholar. Thus, for example, the Charles Fisk Organ at Stanford University, an instrument completed in 1983 with duplicate pipes for 'meantone' and 'well-tempered' tunings, was designed to accommodate the multiple practices of the Baroque soloist; but in offering them simultaneously to today's ensembles it creates a corresponding need for 'push button' adaptability among collaborating instrumentalists and singers that was not a requisite of earlier times.

Introduction

Facing the music

The modern performer of Baroque music has access to music produced in response to a great range of stimuli and needs. The existing spectrum of editions ranges from the octave-laden 'piano' accompaniments provided by editors from the era of Brahms and rippling glissandos offered by editors of the early 20th century to 'compensate' for the awkwardness of the original music, to reputable modern editions which generally explain what elements of the original music have been altered and why. The unaltered facsimiles that are available in ever-increasing numbers leave the determination of tempo, dynamics and articulation to the performer. Scores of every kind are viewed less authoritatively today than they were a generation ago.

The performer of Baroque music will almost inevitably confront problems for which there is no definitive or widely accepted solution. At times he must be a technician, at times an interpreter and at times a creator, for many rules impinge on the alleged liberty with which he may present the music. His exploration of a specific group of works of one particular sort may ultimately be of value in ascertaining where and how a certain composer, or a certain repertory, consistently deviated from the norms suggested by sources external to the music. Matters such as articulation (including phrasing and bowing), ornamentation and, in the early Baroque, the treatment of *musica ficta*, are especially appropriate for such examination; despite a wealth of exact advice on these subjects in theoretical works, specific pieces sometimes refute their intellectually grounded precepts. Thus the performer must be the final arbiter in such matters.

At the same time, the performer must accept the responsibility of being an artist and an interpreter, not simply a technician and implementer of rules. Our increasing awareness that an infinity of rules purport to 'govern' the performance of Baroque music has sometimes obscured the essentially playful spirit of the age, replacing the exhilarating quest for novelty that often dominated the Baroque with a drive for precision and exactitude; this smothers the most fundamental possibilities for re-creating a sense of that part of the past to which the repertory belongs.

Baroque music strove to 'move' its hearers. The finer points of articulation and ornamentation, not to mention instrumentation and other basic matters, were part of the repertory of technique believed to be capable of achieving this end. This is a central truth towards which the novice and the amateur are sometimes more easily directed than the experienced professional.

Notes

[1] E. Selfridge-Field, 'The Canzona and Sonata: Some Differences in Social Identity', *IRASM*, ix (1978), 111–20.

[2] See for example the account of the performance of Giacomo Spada's *Santa Maria Egizziaca penitente* at the Ospedale della Pietà in Venice in 1687 in E. Selfridge-Field, *Pallade Veneta: Writings on Music in Venetian Society, 1650–1750* (Venice, 1985), 184, in which it is related that the singer Francesca, who took the role of Zosima in the oratorio and was known as a theorbist, 'carried the entire audience into ecstasies of admiration with the *galant* ricercate that she played on the lute' after the first half of the work.

[3] At least in the case of Handel, according to reports carried in the *Daily Postman*. Among many citations of the practice, a recent one appears in C. Hogwood, *Handel* (London, 1984), 159. The

17

particular works cited were *Saul* and *Il trionfo del Tempo e della Verità* in performances given in 1739. All of the organ concertos in Handel's op.4 and four of those in op.7 are associated with odes or oratorios (*Esther, Athalia, Deborah,* Samson, *Theodora, Alexander's Feast, The Choice of Hercules,* and *L'Allegro, il Penseroso, and il Moderato*). These works were performed in the 1730s, 1740s and early 1750s.

[4] While this is a composite career path to which few composers' lives exactly conformed, its general validity is established by many careers that followed this sequence without necessarily including every element in it. Giovanni Gabrieli and Henry Purcell exemplify many composers whose highest calling was as organist (at St Mark's Venice, and Westminster Abbey) but who exceeded the requirements of their respective posts by composing vocal as well as instrumental music. Schütz and Cavalli more nearly conformed, although Schütz bypassed any serious responsibilities exclusively as an organist. Telemann was already a Kapellmeister at 20 (in Sorau, now in Poland). Caldara's instrumental apprenticeship was served as a cellist rather than an organist. In short, there are many individual variations, but the general sequence of events is predictable.

[5] The modern historical view of most composers inevitably rests on music that survives. Much of the music of the Baroque era is lost. In addition, some that survives is ignored. Sweelinck, Frescobaldi, Rosenmüller and Torelli are but a few of the large number of Baroque composers currently regarded as instrumental specialists who in fact composed at least one volume of vocal music. In contrast to many composers of instrumental music whose lifetime corpus numbered only one or two volumes, Corelli was exceptional in leaving six volumes of published instrumental works without any reported vocal works.

[6] According to figures recently given by Myron Schwager in 'Public Opera and the Trials of the Teatro San Moisè', *EM*, xiv (1986), 388, the Teatro di San Moisè, in which Monteverdi's lost *Arianna* was given in 1640, measured 13 metres across at the stage end and 14 across at the rear; its length was 25 metres. It had 107 boxes. The Teatro di SS Giovanni e Paolo was both 50 per cent longer and 50 per cent wider.

[7] This is the general import of R. Strohm, 'Italienische Opernarien des frühen Settecento (1720–1730)', *AnMc*, no.14 (1976). The validity of this general thesis has been confirmed by many source studies of operatic material in recent years.

[8] A. Schnoebelen, 'Performance Practices at San Petronio in the Baroque', *AcM*, xii (1969), 92ff.

[9] See A. Morelli, 'Alessandro Scarlatti maestro di cappella in Roma ed alcuni suoi oratori', *Note d'archivio*, ii (1984), 144, and H. J. Marx, 'Die Musik am Hofe Pietro Kardinal Ottobonis unter Arcangelo Corelli', *AnMc*, no.5 (1968), 130.

[10] Cavalli's operas were, nonetheless, heavily revised to suit French taste. *Serse* (1660) was extended from three acts to five and acquired an overture by Lully; *Ercole amante* (1662) lasted six hours and concluded with a ballet comprising 20 *entrées*, J. R. Anthony, *French Baroque Music from Beaujoyeulx to Rameau* (London, 1973, rev. 3/1981), 51–2.

[11] On the opera orchestra of Lully's time see Anthony, ibid, 92–8.

[12] J. Glover, *Cavalli* (London, 1978), 111.

[13] Selfridge-Field, *Pallade Veneta*, 342.

[14] In 1721, a year in which the instrumental establishment of the court was substantially expanded, there were 30 violinists and viola players, seven cellists, three violone players and one gambist. It was in this year that the first baryton player was engaged (the position was rescinded in 1740). The wind players were 18 trumpeters, four trombonists, one horn player, nine oboists and four bassoonists. One cornettist was engaged until 1727 and a theorbist until 1731. There were two timpanists. For further information see E. Selfridge-Field, 'The Viennese Court Orchestra in the Time of Caldara' in *Antonio Caldara: Essays on his Life and Times*, ed. B. W. Pritchard (Aldershot, 1987), 125.

[15] One example of a theoretically possible instrument was the elaborate water organ shown in the third of Vitruvius's *Dieci libri d'architettura* (Venice, 1556), unnumbered page; the writing itself was from antiquity but the illustration was contemporary. Regrettably, it is omitted in the recent reprint of this work (New York, 1967).

[16] Of those who wrote on rhetoric the best known are Kircher and Johann Mattheson (*Der vollkommene Capellmeister*, Hamburg, 1739), but Bernhard, Heinichen, Scheibe and J. G. Walther also addressed the subject.

[17] See especially the writings of George Buelow on rhetoric and music in *Grove 6*, xv, 793–803, and on 'Johann Mattheson and the Invention of *Affektenlehre*' in *New Mattheson Studies*, ed. G. J. Buelow and H. J. Marx (Cambridge, 1983), 393–408, as well as W. Arlt, 'Zur Handhabung der "inventio" in der deutschen Musiklehre des frühen achtzehnten Jarhrhunderts' also in *New Mattheson Studies*, 371–91.

[18] *Italienische Diminutionen: die zwischen 1553 and 1638 mehrmals bearbeiteten Sätze*, ed. R. Erig and V. Gutmann (Zurich, 1979).

[19] B. Lamott, *Keyboard Improvisation According to 'Nova instructio pro pulsandis organis' (1670–ca.1675) by Spiridion a Monte Carmelo* (diss., Stanford U., 1980).

[20] Thomas Coryat, *Coryat's Crudities* (London, 1611), 251.

[21] *Musique et musiciens au XVIIe siècle: correspondance et oeuvres musicales de Constantin Huygens*, ed. W. J. A. Jonckbloet and J. P. N. Land (Leiden, 1882).

[22] *Lettres* (Paris, 1657–67).

[23] This collection, acquired in 1984 by the Shrine to Music Museum at the University of South Dakota, is especially rich in unaltered and little altered instruments by the Linarol, Tieffenbrucker, Sellas, Amati, Maggini, Stradivarius, Guarneri and Grancino families. At present there is no catalogue of the collection but preliminary information is available in *The Shrine to Music Museum: a Pictorial Souvenir*, photographed by S. R. H. Spicer (Santa Barbara, 1988).

CHAPTER II

Keyboards

PETER WILLIAMS

1: ORGAN

The nature of organ music

As soon as organs were appearing regularly (*a*) with separate stops, (*b*) with manual-departments differentiated according to certain conventions, and (*c*) with great regional variation in design, their builders, then their players and perhaps lastly their composers began to give suggestions as to how music transcribed, composed or improvised on the organ might be effectively 'scored'. Thus in the early 16th century it was a short step from Schlick's descriptive lists of stops and timbres to the suggestions for combining stops made in, for example, some contracts in Bordeaux.[1] By the end of the 16th century various sets of registrations were made throughout Europe.[2] Particularly interesting are Diruta's directions (1609),[3] for they show that choosing stops was not an arbitrary act but one that was part of the art of expressive playing; certain stops were used for certain music at certain moments in the service, and were thus played in a certain way, for example:

> mode IV (E-phrygian) – sad, *lamentevole* – Principale + tremolo, perhaps +
> Flute – for the Elevation of the Body and Blood

As is usually the case, such theorists as Diruta or Antegnati were merely expressing what had become conventional. Similarly, when Diruta (1593) noted the difference between legato and *détaché* touch (not so called) and assumed the former to be native to the organ and the latter to the playing of *balli* on harpsichord and spinet, he is reflecting a common understanding.[4]

But although the late 16th century must have seen the various aspects of keyboard technique become distinct and disparate, they did not become so suddenly or indeed entirely. It is probable that in our search today for authentic repertories and for clues as to how to play them, we are missing at least one crucial factor: the importance of improvised transcription. Perhaps 'improvised transcription' is itself an anachronistic term; we should rather see the organist of 1600, in each country and context (Protestant or Roman Catholic, sacred or secular, cathedral or parlour) as using any keyboard score or tablature he could get hold of as a kind of skeleton which he filled in according to the potential of the instrument to hand – few or many stops, one or more manuals, with or without pedal, all depending on what had developed in his area.

It is certainly clear that the following century or so was a period in which players and composers became more and more specific in their rubrics, often producing music requiring a type of organ so specific that it cannot be played on any other type. Yet the principle of 'improvised transcription' survived until at least Mozart's period, and only the 19th century, with the firm lines it drew between organ and piano music, and its *monumenta* series of categorized genres ('Bach's Organ Music', 'English Virginals Music' etc) gave the impression that there were 100 per cent clear categories to draw. One result of this is that 'transcription' eventually became a discredited kind of music; it was what the concert-hall organist did to an overture of Wagner in a programme for a popular audience unable to hear the work as the composer wrote it. Only gradually are today's organists becoming aware that they are perfectly entitled by precedent to arrange, for example, a pavan of William Byrd for an organ of two manuals. It would be more than the history of English organs justifies to take this a step further and register, for example, Byrd's cantus firmus pieces so that pedal reed (8' or 4') takes the melody; for such stops were unknown in England. But the one- or two-manual arrangement is justified.

Another result is that even in the familiar organ music of J. S. Bach, there are forgotten elements of 'improvised transcription'. The Schübler Chorales, for instance, were published towards the end of the composer's life in a kind of open three-stave score which the organist can lay out on three keyboards (manual/pedal) in more than one way, irrespective of the composer's own specification. Moreover, it is this same element of 'improvised transcription' that is responsible for what is to us the puzzling question 'are we to use two alternating manuals in the larger organ preludes and fugues of J. S. Bach?'. Copies do not say so, but the long tradition was for organists to use to advantage whatever potential their instruments had, and we must assume that organists did change manuals if they could. Even if manual-changing sometimes leaves a break or hiatus in the music, we cannot necessarily reject it until it can be shown without doubt that composers considered mono-chrome continuity more desirable than breaks and changes of colour. Rhetorical breaks well handled, and colourful changes strikingly made, seem particularly well suited to 'Baroque ideals'.

The nature of organ variety

By 1700 the instruments themselves and the context in which they played varied so much that a visitor to, for example, the Lübeck Marienkirche, St Paul's Cathedral in London, Saint-Gervais in Paris, Seville Cathedral, S Petronio in Bologna and the Franziskanerkirche in Vienna would barely have recognized a type of music-making common to all six. At present not enough is known about the history of organs to be sure whether all types derive from a common ancestor, though it is possible that the fundamental distinction between Italian and non-Italianate organs (like that between Italian and non-Italianate harpsichords) is part of the definition of organs. It reflects the split between the northern and southern branches of that part of Christendom that alone had church organs: the patriarchate of Rome. The south may always have favoured organs made up of separate ranks of pipes, ever since the little Roman bronze organs built even before the Emperor Constantine; the north, with its technologies developed by energetic and evangelizing Benedictines, may always have preferred multi-rank, noisy bell-substitutes audible around the town (as at Winchester in 980) or instigating the world's first public concerts in large buildings (as at Haarlem in 1480) or, in our modern period, drawing from composers vastly varied musical genres based, as no other music was, on a cosmopolitan array of styles and influences (as at Lübeck in 1680).

In Protestant Lübeck and London, the organs' raison d'être lay in the hymns. They introduced the hymns and metrical psalms: they may not always have accompanied them (this practice was still not uniform by Mendelssohn's period) but may well have played interludes between the verses or even the lines of each verse. They certainly played variations on the tunes during public recitals or during the service and in general they served to set the atmosphere for congregational participation by, for example, prefacing the service with suitable music. (Praeludia or voluntaries *after* the service were later to appear: J. S. Bach, for example, probably did not know them.) In the Catholic cities, on the other hand, the organ was always more of a quasi-precentor, 'replacing' parts of the Mass or Office chant with little fantasias of one kind or another based on the 'missing' chant. While the musical style, registrational colour and general *ton* of these contributions naturally differed between Seville, Paris, Bologna or Vienna – so much so as to have made it immediately possible to say which of the cities (so to speak) one was in – the principle was the same. In some cases, indeed, the Catholic and Protestant conceptions came together: an *alternatim* Vespers *Magnificat* in both Lübeck and Bologna may well have been very similar, though the organist in Lübeck is more likely to have played interludes that required pedal, reed stops and two manuals than his *confrater* in Bologna.

Such differences in organ-type and organ-potential were striking. There is nothing more 'vocal' and 'perfect' than the sound of a good Italian Diapason (open metal Principale at 8′ pitch); it is the basic sound of an organ and can play anything and everything, like the 8′ + 8′ strings of an Italian harpsichord. The Italian builders, and those few in other Mediterranean areas that imitated them, merely added more of the same kind if they needed a bigger sound. The tramontane builders, with that restless passion for technological development characteristic of the former Carolingian Empire, added manuals (shorter than the Italians' very often), extra bass pipes (the big pipes of organs gave the deepest man-made sounds in the world), and a large variety of pipe-constructions (tin, lead, wood, open, stopped, flute, reed, conical, cylindrical, square, even overblowing at the octave or twelfth). The results can still be heard in many extant examples: the French taste for piquancy and a certain brashness (easily debased, as it was by 1875), the Spanish taste for extremes of loud and soft, light and dark (a sensuous spectrum that made it possible to dispense with sophisticated music), the north German and Dutch assumption that organs are *the* means of making music and must therefore be enormously versatile (with many instrumental colours and a majestic totality from lowest to highest sounds), Austrian and Habsburg ambivalence in tonal requirement (so that both Italian 'vocality' and German majesty are attempted despite being irreconcilable). Against this background, the English contribution was puny, and yet its original inspiration – Italian organs, organ music and visual design of the 16th century – retained a few ideas acquired in Holland or Brittany and served to keep the English organ better suited than any other for the accompaniment of choirs and choral music (which either did not exist, or were not accompanied by organ alone, in the other cultural areas).

Fingering and pedalling

Although the organs of Lübeck, London, Paris, Seville, Bologna and Vienna looked and sounded different from each other, it is not difficult to imagine that the way the hands and feet were made use of by their organists – in short, the way they played[5] – must have been similar over the whole area and period. Establishing principles behind that similarity is not an easy task since the sources and theorists of music give patchy information; besides, composers no doubt differed in their techniques, and a fairly short acquaintance with, say, the fugues of Bach and Grigny, suggests they used their hands in their own way. To some extent, however, it is possible to be clear about the principles to be borne in mind for each repertory.

A phrase often met with today is 'old fingering', and many degree courses and summer schools of North America and Europe include instruction in what are claimed to be authenticated systems. Such authentication is drawn with more or less circumspection, from a few theorists (from Diruta to Rameau and even C. P. E. Bach),[6] from the sources of certain schools of keyboard music whose composers or copyists often wrote in fingering[7] and from suppositions based on what is known of fingerings in about 1500 and about 1800. From such different sources it is clear that certain general rules – or, rather, certain habits and conventions – obtained in the period from Byrd to Bach:

1. There was a willingness to use fingers pragmatically and to shift hand-position (rather in the manner of violin playing).

2. Chief interest was not in the 'long line' or legato touch but in the figuration and what an imaginative composer could do with it.

3. Certain customs arose from these general considerations and from the physical nature of the instruments (e.g. strong fingers such as 2 or 3 were used on strong notes; there was little crossing under or over of the thumb, etc).

Such principles lose their value when they become very specific (e.g. 'Frescobaldi did not use the right-hand thumb') or when periods are not properly distinguished (e.g. when Bach's early Weimar works are not distinguished from those that he composed much later in Leipzig).

Similar general points about pedalling can be made for the two particular repertories that required nimble use of the feet: the central and north German schools from Scheidt to Mendelssohn and beyond, and (to a much lesser extent) the Parisian school of c1675–1750. Towards the end of the 18th century some German books (e.g. Türk and Kittel)[8] began to describe pedalling techniques, and although they are concerned with music too much changed to relate directly to J. S. Bach or Grigny – their scales and exercises belong to the era of Czerny – they do indirectly imply some broad principles:

4. When the pedal has the role of an accompanying bass, the left foot plays mostly in the lower octave, the right in the upper.

5. When the pedal is more difficult (e.g. in the specifically virtuoso solos of big praeludia), the feet are played mostly in alternation by the front of the foot only (i.e. with toes not heels).

The player today could well begin from these three or five 'rules' even if (as, after all, is so often the case) the music concerned is not particularly taxing.

And yet 'old fingering' is often a phrase misused today in so far as there was no single 'old fingering' and a doctrinaire approach (quite at variance with the ineradicable pragmatism of good composers) can all too easily result from a belief that there was. One could make a similar point about the so-called 'Doctrine of single *Affekt*', which would have surprised a good composer of any country in 1700. Fingering is merely a means towards putting a piece of music into practice and is second to touch and articulation.

Touch and articulation

That fingering and pedalling customs relate directly to the kind of instrument concerned, even to its physical dimensions, ought to be obvious. For example, thumbs cannot achieve such versatility on the short keys of 1600 as they can on the long keys of 1800. As for pedalling, the short-keyed, wide-framed but short-compass pedalboards of Thuringia c1700 made it easier than is now appreciated for the left foot to remain with the lower octave, the right with the upper. The fact alone that the pedal barely had two octaves (c–a, C–a' and C–d' were all known compasses) would affect the way a player thought of the pedalboard and how to play it.

Despite the variety and scope of the repertory, from the fantasias of Sweelinck or toccatas of Frescobaldi to the partly extempore fugues of Mozart and even Schubert, there must have been some underlying principles for organ playing. These relate to the art of composition (in particular, composers' interest in creating figuration suitable for fingers pressing keys) and keyboard making (in particular, the manner in which key-action works and how it affects the behaviour of wind admitted to speaking pipes). If the composer's aims are grasped, and if the player has access to a relevant keyboard-action, then questions of registration, tempo, fingering, articulation and 'style' tend to answer themselves. Neither of these two conditions is easy to achieve; but it is probably easier to find suitable organs than to grasp 'composer's aims'. Yet essentially this is only a matter of the player studying the notes in front of him – not reading the treatises of Diruta or Mattheson but contemplating the notes composed by Bull or Buxtehude.

Every organist who has experienced it will know the subtle variety of touch that is possible on a well-made key-action, and there can be little doubt that the multi-manual organs of the period drew from the able player different touches and playing-styles for each manual – at Klosterneuburg (1642), for example, a ponderously sustained playing of the main manual (*Hauptwerk*), a firm and bright touch on the most frequently used manual (*Rückpositiv*) and a sprightly, fast and neat fingering of the top manual (*Brustwerk*). No music or theory-book of the time says so, but the organ itself inspires the player to such varied response and he would in turn select from the repertory suitable pieces for those responses. Many anachronisms and misleading impressions result, for example, from playing Bach's trios on a large Dutch organ of 1650. To understand fully, one must be very specific. Thus the earlier pieces of Bach, such as the C major Toccata BWV564*i*, could be interpreted as a dialogue between two manuals, the one 'sharper' and lighter (in action and registration, even in acoustic immediacy) than the other; while the later pieces, such as the E♭ Prelude BWV552*i*, are more homogeneous works in which long ritornello episodes could well pass to a second manual (in addition to the simple echo phrases specified by the composer) but one within the same organ-case and not registered very differently nor touched in a totally different way. It would also be faithful to the conditions taken for granted by the composer during the periods concerned if the earlier work were played at a higher relative pitch and with a more marked unequal temperament than the later – that is to say, on a different organ. The fact alone that a major praeludium is cast in E♭ major means that in 1739 (publication date of the third part of *Clavier-Übung*) the piece was very up-to-date. Very likely its original key was D major.[9]

For fine details of articulation, and thus of touch and fingering, the 'composer's aims' certainly have to be appreciated. In ex.1, the composer,

Ex.1
(a) Scheidt: Passamezzo (Var. 8)

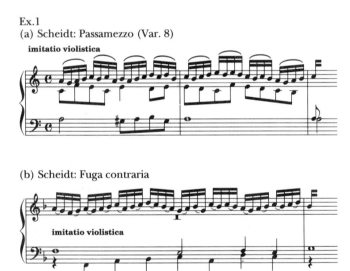

(b) Scheidt: Fuga contraria

Samuel Scheidt, made clear what he was doing: grouping off the semiquavers into fours (1*a*) and twos (1*b*), beginning on the beat and producing a slurred effect evidently known to German string-players, hence his term 'imitatio violistica' and his explanation in a postscript that slurs here are the same as bowing-marks (neither so called). Judging by similar bowing-slurs at certain moments in W. F. Bach's fair copy of the Six Sonatas for Organ, such effects remained familiar in central Germany. But the notation – the slur – did not become commonplace before the piano music of the later 18th century, and the organist himself must look at lines in the music to discover what the groupings are. Thus in ex.2, Bach begins a praeludium with a broken chord

Ex.2 J.S. Bach: Praeludium in A minor, BWV543

and eventually runs off into conjunct triplets. But not only do the latter, by their nature, imply a slurred touch as opposed to the relative *détaché* of the former: it ought to be clear to the player that the broken-chord *figura* is off the beat, while the triplet *figura* is on it. Of course, if the off-beat element is too marked in the playing (ex.3), it will offend an absolute – or what one has

Ex.3

etc

to assume to be an absolute? – about any performance gesture: that there is a point at which it is overdone and becomes an irritant. But therein lies the subtlety of the good performer; having found an appropriate instrument, and having seen for himself how the composer has created his lines, he knows how far he can afford to mark the distinctions and draw the attention of his listeners to it.

Since the player's aim is presumably to understand the nature of the music in hand and to rid his mind as much as possible of anachronism, he will have to assume that appearances are often deceptive. Thus, what appear to be scales or arpeggios in the music of Gibbons and Sweelinck, or of Handel and Bach, are not so – at least not in later senses. Seen through the eyes of Czerny-trained pianists – to whose ranks *all* modern keyboard players directly or indirectly belonged, until the younger generation of the last decade or so – a scale is a scale; but it is clear from even relatively poor sources (copies made by copyists not alerted to the finer points) that a distinction was made between, for example, simple scale-like embellishments in a variation (ex.4) and subtler runs distributed between the hands (which normally changed after the beat, not on it – see ex.5). Both exx.4 and 5 are taken from harpsichord works of Handel as left very ambiguous by the copyists; but the point is nevertheless clear and can serve as a useful starting-

Ex.4 Handel: Chaconne (Var.47) from Suite in C, HWV443

Ex.5 Handel: Prelude from Suite in D minor HWV449, bars 19–24

point for players anxious to look at figuration anew, that is, with the eyes of a composer. Here is where the truth of fingering lies: fingering produces a practical version of what the composer composed. Thus the thumbs may well have been used in some runs and 'scales' if, played on the beat, this served to mark that beat emphatically in a series or sequence of such figures. In such instances, repetition itself is an *affetto* in music.

Just as in many harpsichord sonatas of Scarlatti difficulties can often be resolved and fluent dexterity won by giving one hand a note awkwardly placed for the other, so in ex.6 it is perfectly possible to produce a fast, unbroken, glibly fluent line. But in both cases – the Scarlatti sonata, the Bach praeludium – the point would then have been lost. Glib fluency was not intended in such contexts. Art was not to hide art but to bring out (in the case of ex.6) a brief yet effective dialogue between the left and the right hand. It is in such details that rhetoric, in its true sense, emerges: not as a wide-ranging theory-book study for writers of the past and present, but as an art of performance in the detail of compositions.

Ex.6 J.S. Bach: Praeludium in E minor, BWV533

Notes

[1] See F. Douglass, *The Language of the Classical French Organ* (New Haven, 1969).

[2] See C. Antegnati, *L'arte organica* (Brescia, 1608/R1958); H. Klotz, *Über die Orgelkunst der Gotik, der Renaissance und des Barock* (Kassel, 1975); M. A. Vente, *Die brabanter Orgel* (Amsterdam, 1958, 2/1963); and P. Williams, *The European Organ 1450–1850* (London, 1966).

[3] G. Diruta, *Il transilvano, seconda parte* (Venice, 1609/R1978), iv, 22.

[4] *Il transilvano*, (1593/R1978), f.5v.

[5] The word 'play', gradually adopted in the various languages over this period, is itself one with a many-branched history, serving to remind us that words can be universally adopted without (or having lost) a precise meaning. An earlier example for 'playing' instruments is 'pulsare', the organist a 'pulsator'; contrary to frequent speculation, this never meant 'one who thumped the keys' since in classical Latin it is also used for lyre playing, for example. In the case of Baroque organ music, the 'playing' of keys can approach a form of game playing: the pleasure of shaping fingers around the opening of, for example, Buxtehude's D major Praeludium BuxWV139 does seem to justify the recent German term 'Spielfreudigkeit'.

[6] Diruta, *Il transilvano*; J.-P. Rameau, *Pièces de clavecin avec une méthode pour la mécanique des doigts* (Paris, 1724); and C. P. E. Bach, *Versuch über die wahre Art das Clavier zu spielen* (Berlin, 1753 and 1762).

[7] For example the English copyists, summarized in P. le Huray, 'English Keyboard Fingering in the 16th and early 17th Centruies', in *Source Materials and the Interpretation of Music*, ed. I. Bent (London, 1981), 227–57, and the Italian copyists, summarized in M. Lindley, 'Keyboard Technique and Articulation: Evidence for the Performance Practices of Bach, Handel and Scarlatti', in *Bach, Handel and Scarlatti: Tercentenary Essays*, ed. P. Williams (Cambridge, 1985), 207–43.

[8] D. G. Türk, *Von den wichtigsten Pflichten eines Organisten* (Halle, 1787/R1966), and J. C. L. Kittel, *Der angehende praktische Organist* (Erfurt, 1801–8).

[9] This point is not affected by the work having undoubted symbolic significance in its three flats (one of the many Trinity allusions in part 3 of *Clavier-Übung*). Both the *ouverture*-like prelude and the *alla breve* fugue of BWV552 would be much more likely in D major, in which the work is also more comfortable for the hands. Did the composer transpose it for this volume, like the C minor *Ouverture* transcribed into B minor for part 2 of *Clavier-Übung*?

2: OTHER KEYBOARDS

It must be a constant surprise to pianists and church organists of today that the several and very varied kinds of keyboard instrument available in 1600 – church organs, positives, regals, harpsichords, spinets, clavichords, *Geigenwerke* and almost any combination of these ('claviorgana') – are hardly ever distinguished in repertory-sources of the period, and that to some extent this continued to be true for another century and a half. That the question is left open for such works as *Das wohltemperirte Clavier* or the *Musical Offering* is a puzzle when one considers the very different touch, playing-method and sound of the various instruments. It is likely that the very specific requirements for keyboard music in the late 18th century were part of the startling contribution made by the piano-makers and piano-composers of that period; there came a point when piano, not harpsichord or organ, had to be used. Yet there had been a few much older parts of the repertory with similarly rigid requirements, such as French harpsichord music *c*1700. By the time of Beethoven's mature piano sonatas perhaps the only element of versatility remaining was that some buyers in Germany and Scandinavia may well have played them on the large clavichords of the period, problematic though the composer's directions for sustained pedalling would then have become.

What seems to distinguish one idiomatic keyboard repertory from another is the kind of expressiveness each attempts to convey. Clavichord expressiveness is not compatible or interchangeable with the expressiveness of organs or of harpsichords; a piece calculated for one kind of instrument's expressiveness will not suit another. It is hard to believe that texture – the number of notes in a chord or the amount of part-writing activity – demanded organ rather than clavichord, for no doubt notated keyboard scores were adapted according to circumstances, and all keyboard instruments must have seemed to belong to one category. And were the music concerned to be 'neutral', as in certain kinds of counterpoint, or less idiomatic, as in a piece transcribed from vocal or orchestral music (or one imitating the characteristics thereof), then there was in any case less of a problem, for the music immediately becomes more versatile and able to achieve its *affetto* by several means. Thus the homophonic skeletal version of the Granduca theme by Sweelinck (see ex.1) could be played – that is to say, idiomatically realized – on any

Ex.1 Sweelinck: Granduca theme

keyboard instrument, and in many cases one must suppose this versatility to have been intended (or assumed) by the composer. One *applies* the expressiveness and playing idiom characteristic of each instrument to such 'open' music; only when the composer already specifies such details (e.g. by spreading or breaking the chords in a manner typical of plucked-string instruments) is the choice reduced, the ultimate intention of all notational details being to reduce the performer's choice.

The separation of harpsichord from organ

The distinction drawn by Diruta in 1593[1] between organ and harpsichord playing is one of the earliest of such pointers, but it should not be overlooked that his aim was also to mark the differences in purpose and context of their respective music: *ballo* playing (harpsichord, spinet) on one hand, *missa* playing (church organ) on the other. The *détaché* harpsichord touch was characteristic of simple dance music, but it is difficult to see how even the most legato and sensitive organ-touch could be out of place for other kinds of harpsichord music, such as a good English pavan. In fact, characteristic of all the best harpsichord music – whether of London in 1600, Paris in 1675 or Leipzig and Madrid in 1725 – is that it welcomes a varying touch and 'style' even from bar to bar. Some instruments naturally respond better than others to such varied treatment, but studies of extant and well-restored English virginals of a somewhat later period (*c*1660) have shown that, though of course they did not specify the effect, the good English composers could have found instruments which would have responded to a varying touch. A good rectangular virginals or (imported) Venetian harpsichord could show how such composers as Bull or Byrd developed the older *balli* so as to produce variety of texture and thus expressivness; see ex.2.

Ex.2 Bull: Pavana from *Parthenia* (1612/13)

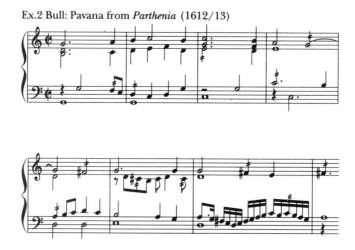

Diruta's distinction was a counsel of perfection, and no doubt church organists then, as now, often confused idioms and inappropriately brought in the secular *détaché*. Differences in timbre between instruments were not so readily confused. When the *intermedi* of 16th-century Florence used different keyboard instruments at different points in the entertainment, and when

Monteverdi followed the tradition in a few cryptic directions in *Orfeo*, one may also suppose that touch, timbre and method of basso realization also differed. In ex.3 the Messenger interrupting the pastoral revels presumably

Ex.3 Monteverdi: *Orfeo*

did so with a sustained organ chord after the rhythmic beat of the shepherds' dance. One can only speculate as to how the realization differed, and it could be, for example, that the right hand played coloratura divisions on one or the other instrument (like the lyra viol embellishments in contemporary English ensemble music).

The celebrated *brisé* or broken-texture style of French harpsichord music in *c*1650 may well have been given impetus, as commonly supposed, by lute and guitar playing in early 17th-century France, but it is clear from the English lute repertory that the *brisé* manner is not inevitable with lutes, and it is evident from the Italian keyboard repertory that broken textures were already assumed in certain contexts. The technique is, after all, as natural to keyboards as to lutes, and it hardly seems wild speculation to interpret some English ornament-signs as implying a *brisé* technique, optional as to its actual layout. Frescobaldi's remark on arpeggios may also indicate something of the kind: 'the beginnings of the toccatas are to be played slowly and arpeggiando ... not to leave [a feeling of] emptiness in the instrument, the chords are to be restruck according to taste'.[2] One may imagine the opening of the first toccata, when played on the harpsichord (*istromento*), to be something like ex.4. Although Frescobaldi did not find it necessary to say so, such *arpeggiando* on the harpsichord could well be very similar to that on the organ; the difference would be that the organ sustains and does not require the reiteration and repetition which makes broken textures so natural on the harpsichord. As a much later writer pointed out, 'The Art ... chiefly consists in rendering the Sounds of the Harpsichord lasting, for frequent interruptions of the Sound are inconsistent with true melody'.[3] Frescobaldi's actual notation was plain and therefore both economical and stimulating to the player; so it was for Froberger, many of whose chords (especially at the beginning) would turn out to be, when treated in the *arpeggiando* manner, very like those so carefully notated in open 'semibreves' by Louis Couperin. In fact, the French *prélude* notation gave the player less choice.

Two further natural differences between the repertories specific to organ and to harpsichord are firstly, that fast passage-work is more feasible on harpsichord than organ (not so much because the action is usually lighter

Ex.4 Frescobaldi
(a) Toccata Prima as written

(b) One possible interpretation

but because plucked strings speak so much more readily than even the smallest organ pipe), and secondly, that uneven or variegated textures are more naturally a part of the rhetoric of the harpsichord than organ (though there are exceptions to this, as in the opening *passaggi* of north German praeludia). Neither of these differences is total. In the first case, fast passage-work can have very similar effect on both instruments. For example, the grouping of four semiquavers (and thus the producing of many strong beats) in a virginals prelude of Gibbons or in an organ chorale of Scheidt have much in common; compare ex.5 with that of Scheidt in ex.1 of part 1 of this

Ex.5 Gibbons: Praeludium from *Parthenia* (slurs editorial)

chapter. In the second case, were a texture to be characteristically even, as in a three-or (better) four-part canzona or ricercar, then the differences in performance would be only incidental; the harpsichord might be faster, with a more varied touch and perhaps more *agréments* (including spread chords). Although theorists progressively mention more of these distinctions (pointing out, for example, that spread chords are not characteristic of organ continuo realization),[4] a full picture of how the differences were seen cannot be assembled from theorists. Theorists are sometimes wrong; arpeggiation can be very effective in organ continuo – for example, at a particular moment in recitative – even if German Protestant organists of 1711 did not care for it.

Other keyboard instruments: regals, clavichords, fortepiano

In Monteverdi's *Orfeo*, not only are chamber organ and harpsichord contrasted, but so is the regals; and from what Agazzari says, it could be assumed that a spinet or two might also have characteristic ornamentations to contribute to an ensemble, particularly (one imagines) at such moments as the final *moresca*. Spinets (including the *ottavini*) were like little harps, with the added advantage that they are so much easier to play; regals also had an advantage, namely the ability to play both sostenuto (thus serving as infernal little organs) and very rhythmically, even percussively. As fashions changed, and the tone of the regals lost popularity, its role in continuo-laying could be taken over better by claviorgan (harpsichord-with-organ), according to Mattheson.[5] One can hardly speak either of a totally different playing-technique or of a repertory for the regals, however, any more than one can for claviorgan or *Geigenwerk*. Yet both regals and *Geigenwerk* needed a particular approach to the question of touch; the shallow key fall and characteristic leverage of the short, back-hinged regals keys on one hand, and the peculiar bowed-string tone-production of the *Geigenwerk* on the other, must have required careful handling. Praetorius, for example, says of the regals: 'the harmony [harmoniousness?] is much more pleasing when one plays the music [chorale?] with great refinement, gravely and slow'[6] – from which one somehow suspects Praetorius to have had bad experiences of regals playing. 'Careful handling' was of course necessary for all the rare or unique keyboard inventions, of which the Florentine 'harpsichord-with-little-hammers' was only one.

It is difficult to determine how far the special nature of clavichord touch (less special, perhaps, in the earliest examples) and the frequency with which players in parts of Italy and Germany came into contact with the instrument produced a common understanding of clavichord playing and a notion of 'clavichord music' *per se*. This is for the simple reason that the instrument must chiefly have served in a secondary role: a cheap, portable, easily maintained substitute for spinets, harpsichords and chamber organs. The development of the clavichord's potential belongs to the north and central German *galant* composers of the later 18th century, who were also drawn to the fortepiano, *Tangentenflügel* and other discourse-imitating keyboards. For J. G. Walther in 1732,[7] however, the clavichord is still only 'the first *grammatica*' from which the player can proceed to other keyboard instruments. It must remain doubtful whether German composers of *c*1700, whose customers included clavichord owners, published their *Partien* or *Arien* with the clavichord in mind, even though various illustrations show clavichords playing both continuo and solo music. The view that, for example, the C major Prelude (and, some even claim, the Fugue) of book 1 of J. S. Bach's *Das wohltemperirte Clavier* was composed as clavichord music is speculative; even when such albums contain pieces that borrow elements particularly suitable to a particular instrument, it cannot be assumed that the composer was doing more than marshalling together the many instrumental techniques at his disposal. In the case of *Das wohltemperirte Clavier*, certain preludes seem to suit one kind of instrument in particular, their fugues another. There was, and is, no reason why harpsichords should not have been accommodating to idioms that also suited clavichord or church organ; but there was good reason why church organ or clavichord should not adopt some harpsichord idioms.

In the case of the fortepiano,[8] without doubt it was the *dolce* or *piano* tone that was the chief attraction to composers and players rather than its *forte* or even, perhaps, its crescendo and diminuendo. (Various kinds of evidence also suggest that the earlier 18th-century liking for Swells in English and Spanish organs was centred on its closed position, i.e. the attraction was its soft, distant echo.) Effects in L. Giustini's *Sonate da cimbalo di piano e forte* (Florence, 1732) include *piano*, *forte*, staccato, slurred appoggiaturas, *arpeggiato nell'acciaccature* (spread chords with slipped-in chromatic notes), *più piano*, *più forte*, sometimes with frequent change from one to other. To some extent, these can be imitated (or, to put it more correctly, they exaggerate effects already possible) on the harpsichord. In pure counterpoint the fortepiano is at a great disadvantage, since it cannot but play expressively. One can easily miss the desired evenness between the parts; this is true of the modern piano too, with which the virtuosos of today deal either by playing with a kind of neutral blandness or on the contrary by producing the kind of drama that Beethoven sensibly wrote into his fugues. Assuming the *Musical Offering* (1747) to have been composed with reference (or in deference) to Frederick's Silbermann pianos, one can imagine that the Ricercar *a* 3 allows for the new instrument most skilfully: high tessitura for the opening theme (*b'–a''*, where early pianos have a pretty, 'pearly' tone), crescendo-like episodes, *sforzando*-like entries, *galant* appoggiature (*Seufzermelodik*, including the very last cadence) and an astonishingly varied texture – all unique, even in the very special corpus of J. S. Bach's three-part keyboard fugues. Other Bach works to which the fortepiano is not inappropriate include several preludes in book 2 of *Das wohltemperirte Clavier* (B major, F minor and G major) and *Art of Fugue* (Contrapuncti 1 and 3). The more dramatic, *sforzando* rhetoric of the fortepiano equally suits the 'top-and-bottom' style of French music *c*1760. Perhaps only with such music did a specific piano technique emerge, including the gradual conviction that the 'sustaining pedal' (London, 1772) was an element so basic that both the piano makers and the piano composers had to master and conventionalize it. Earlier, the problem must have been (as it was with the *Geigenwerk*) to use the fingers as smoothly as possible, avoiding any lumpiness in scales, arpeggios and even-textured counterpoint, and to learn to distinguish by heaviness of touch how one played a melody above or below its accompaniment.

Some important harpsichord idioms

In practice, the chief 'schools' of harpsichord music are markedly different from each other: English 1600, Italian 1625 and 1725, French 1650 and 1700, Saxon 1725. One may hazard the guess that no other corpus of music in the period concerned has schools with so little in common between them. Perhaps the reason is that Italian keyboard music did not dominate its fellows as Italian vocal and string music did, hence the success of French harpsichord (but not organ) idioms in influencing so much of what happened elsewhere in the early 18th century, at least before the Italian-inspired *galant* idioms won the day in the middle of the century.

Much of the success of the English virginals school results from its being so vocal in inspiration: its tunefulness and its part-writing are worked out in keyboard terms. The motivic complexity of Byrd, or the melodic immediacy of Bull, are vocal in origin but keyboard-like in achievement. Preserving the identity of the motifs or *figurae* is important; thus in ex.5 above, the slurred fours are the raison d'être of the line, whether one plays it on a virginals or an Italianate 8.8 or 8.4 harpsichord, and however fast a tempo it seems to require. Certain textures, in particular the tune with accompaniment (see ex.6), do require a virginals which can preserve that distinction, i.e. one in

Ex.6 Anon: 'Tille valle Monye growe' from *Clement Matchett's Virginal Book*

which distinctive touch conveys the tune (legato) above the *ballo*-like accompaniment (*détaché*). Decisions on tempo have to remain conjectural, despite recent claims that dance tutors provide the answer; but the amount of detail in, for example, a good pavan tends to narrow the margin of choice. It is doubtful if two pavans in *Parthenia* are meant to have exactly the same tempo, and no amount of information from dance tutors helps the player to a quick understanding of music by talented composers at pains to develop textures, rhythms, patterns etc of their own, seductive though such external evidence may be to students 'desirous of learning'.

When dealing with problems of touch, fingering, articulation and tempo in English virginals music, the player should always bear in mind its vocal origins. A Tomkins pavan, for example, has much of the Anglican full anthem in it, such that one 'sings' the lines as the fingers play the keys. The divisions in a Tomkins set of variations do not interfere with the prevailing *melos* however one breaks up the figuration. Fingering and ornamentation are secondary considerations, indeed subservient: a means to an end only.

In the case of the Italian repertory typified by Frescobaldi, it is the freedom of interpretation that can cause problems to the player. Reference has already been made to Frescobaldi's remarks on *arpeggiando*; other hints given in the preface to his book of 1637 concern the beat (variable, unstressed; changing tempos), the make-up of the piece (sections can be played separately, cadences made at will), the marking of cadential trills or *passaggi* (a comma before the next chord, etc), tempos (rallentando· at cadences), the marking of distinct sections, touch (semiquavers 'somewhat *détaché*', *alquanto puntati* – at least, the second note of a pair), expression (passage-work shared by the hands, played *risolutamente*) and again tempo (to suit the spirit of the movement and the playing-style). Although the remarks apply equally to such music played on the organ, one can imagine that harpsichordists would draw particular conclusions, for example that arpeggiation could be very freely realized, or that tempo might generally be livelier. Certainly the composers of the next generation created a music of extravagant gestures (very chromatic or full of virtuoso passage-work) that indeed deserves the name 'Baroque'. It could well be that some of the more unusual effects in the sonatas of Domenico Scarlatti derive not from his Iberian experiences but directly from familiarity with the later manifestations of this Baroque idiom. For example, sudden pauses could come as much from older Italian toccata traditions as from dramatic Portuguese folk music; the right-hand/left-hand opening solo melodies, so characteristic of Domenico, were already known in the music of Alessandro Scarlatti (see ex.7) and are of a kind later described by Padre Martini; the famous

Ex.7 A. Scarlatti: Toccata seconda (*I-Nc* 34.6.31)

acciaccature chords were conventionally part of Italian continuo style, judging by examples in F. Gasparini's *L'armonico pratico al cimbalo* (Venice, 1708) and the manuscript *I-Rli* R I (see ex.8 for a sample perfect cadence).

Ex.8
(a) Written   (b) Played

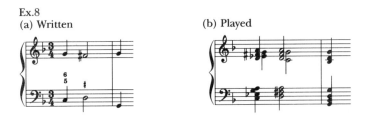

An important element in the Scarlatti idiom is the keeping to right- or to left-hand passages which would be much easier if shared between the two, see ex.9. In the case of the direction to play quick scale-passages with one finger (i.e. glissando), one must assume that, in all keys but C major, the appropriate sharps or flats have to be omitted; curiously, on the right kind of Italian harpsichord this causes no problems. Generally speaking, however, glib fluency – the apparently effortless virtuosity characteristic of the 19th century – is not required in such music; the rhetoric of the passages concerned (as in ex.9) will partly depend on the 'effort' that results from keeping to one hand what correctly belongs to it, since not only is there an inevitable break or pull-up as the hands seek their note but the harpsichord touch is affected by the speed and weight of the 'seeking' hand. In a certain sense, art here is not hiding art but drawing attention to it.

The use of hands in historically idiomatic ways is important in all schools

Ex.9
(a) D. Scarlatti: KK21, bars 15–22

(b) D. Scarlatti: KK26, bars 48–52

of composition, and remarks have been made in part 1 of this chapter on the dividing of passage-work between the hands in German and other toccata (praeludium) traditions. It is particularly important for the player to understand the nature of scales (and to a lesser extent arpeggios) in music before Beethoven.[9] In the English, Dutch, Italian and German harpsichord repertories, scale-patterns are not scales as such but lines built up of scale-motifs. Thus by dividing the line between the hands (as the original beamings suggest) and by producing not a smooth scale but a group of motifs, the opening of J. S. Bach's G major Partita is realized approximately as in ex.10. The expressing of motivic interest in such apparently simply scale-lines as that in ex.11 is not difficult, and is simply a matter of avoiding

Ex.10 J.S. Bach: Partita, BWV829, bars 5–8

[l,r indications editorial]

Ex.11 Handel: Allemande from Suite HWV436.i bars 13–16

any thoughtless *perpetuum mobile* feeling in the semiquavers by an artful placing of commas and sostenuto articulation. The best German composers have many such passages. At other times, there are indeed even-running scales in the later sense (see ex.12), and presumably it was the growing

Ex.12
(a) J.S. Bach : BWV903.i, opening

(b) D. Scarlatti: KK24, bars 4–5

popularity of these kinds of lines that helped to direct music towards later pianistic styles.

In conveying 'motivic interest', the player today should also try to understand, as from the composer's point of view, how lines came to be written. The problem for almost all keyboard players today is that they are not composers, or at least not composers of the kinds of music they will be playing. It is therefore difficult for them to appreciate that in such passages as ex.13 the triplets are so constructed that they emphasize the beat. Such an

Ex.13
(a) Handel: HWV436.iv

(b) J.S. Bach: BWV860.i

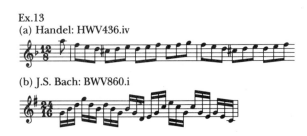

articulation as in ex.14 is very effective on the right kind of harpsichord, while in other triplet passages, the emphases seem to be elsewhere, i.e. off, not on, the beat (conjectural slurs in ex.15). The understanding of motivic or

Ex.14

Ex.15
(a) Handel: HWV433.v

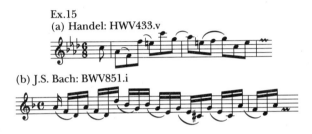

(b) J.S. Bach: BWV851.i

figural composition is the more practical side of *Figurenlehre* and is of far more importance to the player than its theoretical aspects (e.g. the theory that motifs or *figurae* are allusive, associative or symbolic in a supposed scheme of rhetoric). It is towards an understanding and thus an expressing of motivic interest that fingering ought to be directed.

Quite what is the most appropriate harpsichord for the earlier music of J. S. Bach and Handel (as for the better of their contemporaries, such as Buxtehude, Böhm and Kuhnau) is not yet certain; but it can be assumed to be more Italianate (in scaling, stringing in brass, case-construction, touch and tone) than the Flemish–French masterpieces of the 1730s onwards. Articulation can be very precise and varied on Italian harpsichords, less lingeringly sensual than on the Flemish–French; the result of this in, for example, book 1 of *Das wohltemperirte Clavier* is to produce 48 case-studies in figural articulation (preludes) and counterpoint by articulation (fugues). In the interests of variety of *Affekt*, diversity of key and versatility of contrapuntal texture, *Das wohltemperirte Clavier* (and the three-part Inventions) demands from the player an astonishingly full digital technique; almost any finger can find itself a strong (on-beat) or weak (off-beat) finger, a pivot, and a substitute, according to context. That the remoter keys, as such later theorists as C. P. E. Bach pointed out, did encourage more versatile use of the thumbs (and, as we might say, 'hand-shifting') is suggested when one compares the same piece known in different keys. A good example can be found in Handel, in the G major/E major Variations (see ex.16). The G major version allows a figural conception (i.e. the eight demisemiquavers are grouped 2 × 4) achieved by hand-shifted fingerings 1234 1234, whereas the E major seems well on the road to the Czernian conception of longer phrases (1 × 8) achieved by versatile use of fingers and thumbs.

Compared to the variety of technique required by *Das wohltemperirte Clavier*, the French School had a more limited, if colourful and sensitive,

Ex.16 Handel: Variations
(a)

(b) HWV430.iv

[Fingering & slurs editorial]

vocabulary. The melodic charm of Froberger and Louis Couperin is matched by a sensuous understanding of harmony that produced some of the most startling sounds of the 17th century, equalled only by Monteverdi and Purcell in quite different contexts. There is no mere eccentricity or wild experimentation in such passages as ex.17, experimentation as often admired

Ex.17 L. Couperin: Prélude in D minor

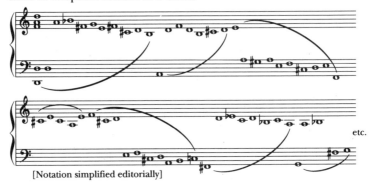

etc.

[Notation simplified editorially]

in some earlier Italian vocal and keyboard music, but a more basic notion of how triadic diatonicism could develop, with seventh and ninth chords, accented passing notes and so on. The French style at its best (as in Louis Marchand, or in F. Couperin's *Allemande à deux Clavecins* in A major) is a network of such effects, requiring leisurely tempo, delicate touch and a penchant for sostenuto harmonies. Particularly important to the French style is the correct understanding of the accented passing note or appoggiatura or *port de voix*: melodies (with or without the stylized ornament-signs) and accompaniments (often but not always notated *brisé* or sostenuto) are full of them, as are the viola da gamba, flute and vocal repertories of the time. The *détaché* or *marqué* effects naturally contrast with them, as in ex.18.

Ex.18 F. Couperin: *Les laurentines* from the Troisième Ordre

Ornaments

The easy availability of ornament manuals, and the sheer visual impact of notational signs in so much keyboard music (especially English *c*1600 and French/German *c*1700) can easily mislead the player today into giving them an attention out of proportion to their weight. Even in the lavishly equipped French systems of *c*1700 – when Parisian composers (like their colleagues in other arts and disciplines) were attempting to standardize all French creativity and orthography – it is not always clear exactly what an ornament-sign implies nor whether it implies a single, obligatory meaning at all. F. Couperin's famous remark could be taken as referring either to the most detailed, sophisticated alteration of his directions or to gross, ignorant distortion of them:

> I am always surprised, after the pains I gave myself to mark the ornaments ... to hear people who have learnt them without heeding my instructions ... my pieces must be performed as I have written them ... without adding to them or subtracting them.[10]

Two brief discussions follow, as examples (1) of one particular keyboard school with its own ornamentation, and (2) of a 'rule' fancied by more recent theorists to govern ornamentation in general.

 1. In the case of the English repertory *c*1600, little fresh light has been cast on the meaning of the signs in ex.19 (the last, with yet more complex signs, in

Ex.19

a few sources only), but the graphic character itself suggests that those three involve progressively more notes. Thus it is possible that for some copyists the single dash meant mordent, the double an upper-note mordent or trill, the triple dash a full-trill-with-turn etc; others may have used them far less specifically. In some cases the dashes must have drawn attention to a playing method (such as arpeggio or quasi-*sforzando*) or an articulation (a note so marked is the first of a pair of notes or a group or a phrase etc). Thus a galliard might have its hemiolas pointed out by 'ornament signs', as in ex.20. That the sources themselves vary so much (even by normal standards of source-variants) supports the idea that such signs often served as a kind of

Ex.20 Byrd: Galliard Mrs. Mary Brownlow from *Parthenia*

nota bene mark rather than as ornaments *per se*. On the other hand, Spanish ornaments of the period were to some extent formalized, Bermudo (1555) or Correa da Arauxo (1626) describing formulae which elevate the ornament sign to a kind of variation-shorthand, i.e. the little *figurae* become division-like motifs characteristic of vocal/instrumental embellishments of the time. In many a passage of English virginals music, the ornamentation (*coloratura*, *fioratura*) is written out, showing (among other things) how the English composers knew the upper-note trill (supposed in some books to be a later development); see ex.21.

Ex.21 Gibbons: Galliard from *Parthenia*

2. In attempting to understand the ornament signs in the music of J. S. Bach – i.e. in trying to establish for them, scattered over nearly five decades of composing, copying and recopying, a consistent system – various writers have suggested 'rules'. These include the 'parallels rule', whereby no ornament is to be so realized that it creates parallel fifths or octaves with notes already in the music. Thus, the argument goes, in ex.22, the first

Ex.22 J.S. Bach BWV140.iii

interpretation is correct, the second wrong. The problem with this 'rule' is that it is based on an observation made on paper or (even if some people do train themselves to hear the parallels) prompted by a theoretical understanding of what is happening in the parts. In any case, some parallels are only apparent. In the following example, it could be said that ex.23c makes 'outer

Ex.23 J.S. Bach: BWV830.v, bar 35

fifths'. But the second fifth is an accented passing-note of the kind not infrequent in the works of J. S. Bach and Mozart. Of course, ex.23b is still a reasonable way to understand the ornament, since it is a *tierce coulée* ('gliding or slurred third') of the kind admired in France; but ex.23c ought not to be rejected on the grounds of its supposed parallels. We cannot be sure that the composer was not leaving a choice here, or even nudging the connoisseurs (at whom so much of the various *Clavier-Übung* volumes was aimed) into making such observation for themselves. Music is not merely to be played; it is to be thought about, its grammar, rhetoric and meaning to be pondered. There are many examples of difficulties in the interpretation of the best keyboard music – ornamentation, registration, tempo, fingering – that come from our assumptions that the only thing to do with a piece of music is to play it, and that in a certain way only.

Notes

[1] G. Diruta, *Il transilvano* (Venice, 1593/R1978).

[2] Preface to *Toccate d'intavolatura di cimbalo et organo*, i (Rome, 1637).

[3] F. Geminiani, *The Art of Accompaniment* (London, 1756), i, 1.

[4] See for example J. G. Heinichen, *Neu erfundene und gründliche Anweisung* (Hamburg, 1711), 226.

[5] J. Mattheson, *Der vollkommene Capellmeister* (Hamburg, 1739/R1954), 484.

[6] M. Praetorius, *Syntagma musicum*, iii (Wolfenbüttel, 1619), 116.

[7] J. G. Walther, *Musicalisches Lexicon* (Leipzig, 1732/R1953).

[8] Specious though the distinction fortepiano/pianoforte is, the convenience of using the former for the piano of at least the 18th century is undeniable.

[9] Even in the keyboard music of Beethoven, the player today can quite miss details of the composer's inventiveness. For example, the two first entries of the soloist in the Concerto no.5 in Eb – firstly the opening arpeggios and secondly the chromatic scale running into the second exposition – are far more original than post-Czerny pianists would assume.

[10] Preface to *Troisié me livre de piéces de clavecin* (Paris, 1722).

CHAPTER III

Strings

PETER WALLS

1: THE VIOLIN FAMILY

Instruction manuals

Roger North speaks of techniques 'which may be knowne but not described'.[1] Some subleties are indescribable, and some – particularly in the 17th century – may have been kept as mysteries of the trade. It is not until the end of the period that treatises by virtuosos are addressed to players with more than amateur aspirations. Geminiani's *Art of Playing on the Violin* (1751) is the first, and it was followed by volumes from Mozart and Herrando (both 1756), L'abbé *le fils* (1761) and Tartini (1771). These can explain much about violin playing in the first half of the 18th century, but each must be used with a clear sense of its context (and hence of its limits). Geminiani, the pupil of Corelli, is often regarded as an exponent of an Italian violin tradition,[2] but by 1751 he had become fascinated with French music.[3] The hybrid character of his style led his admirer, Sir John Hawkins, to comment: 'It is much to be doubted whether the talents of Geminiani were of such a kind as qualified him to give a direction to the national taste'.[4] Geminiani may be a rather idiosyncratic guide, yet, almost by default, he is a prime influence upon the present generation of Baroque violinists.

It is difficult even to establish a context for some volumes. Giuseppe Tartini (1692–1770) was active as a teacher from 1728 when he established a school for violinists in Padua. His treatise, *Traité des agréments de la musique*, was published in Paris shortly after his death, but manuscript copies were already circulating. It is generally assumed that it must have been written before 1756 since Leopold Mozart refers in his *Violinschule* (1756) to Tartini's remarks on the augmented second trill as the teaching of 'a great Italian master'. But when exactly was this work compiled? How relevant is it to Baroque performance? In any case, is it all by Tartini, or is some of it (as Boyden suggests)[5] by pupils? And how do we reconcile, say, Tartini's advice (in the Letter to Signora Lombardini) to 'make yourself a perfect mistress in every ... part of the bow' with his puzzling injunction (in the 'Rules for Bowing') never to play near the point or heel?

Quite apart from broad definable differences in stylistic orientation, performers obviously had diverse ideas then, as now, on matters of technique and interpretation. Lenton (1693) almost gives up on the task of giving bowing guidelines because 'the humours of Masters being very Various ... what is approved by one would be condemned by another'. Tutors addressed to amateurs are often uninformative; many do little more than sketch the topography of the fingerboard and provide a few simple tunes. Speer (1697) concludes his instructions for the violin with the comment, 'a true teacher will be sure to show his student what remains: how to hold the violin properly, how to place it on the breast, how to manage the bow, and how to play trills, mordents, slides and tremolos combined with other ornaments'.[6] Worse still, when these writers do venture into technical matters their advice may be extremely suspect. Some, like Prinner (c1677) and Berlin (1744), are manifestly non-specialist since they were probably not string players and set out (like Speer) to give instruction in a whole range of musical instruments.[7] The problem is particularly acute for the lower strings; the first separate tutors for viola, cello and double bass appeared well into the 18th century; moreover, they were all written by that Jack-of-all-trades, Michel Corrette.

But these volumes are not without interest. Robert Bremner's *Compleat Tutor for the Violin* (c1750) is typical. It is addressed to beginners, and its eight pages of instruction tell us almost nothing useful about violin technique. But it includes a charming frontispiece of a violinist with portraits behind him of Corelli and Handel (an indicator of taste), a revealing one-page dictionary of musical terms, and a fascinating advertisement for musical accessories ('mutes or sordines' etc) sold by Bremner. In a rather oblique way it helps to fill out a picture of string playing in the period. Materials like this take their place alongside other suggestive (but equivocal) forms of evidence – paintings, observers' accounts of performances and the like.

Instruments

The violins, violas and cellos of the Baroque period are distinct in a number of basic features from their modern counterparts. The neck, generally shorter than on modern instruments, projects straight out from the body so that its upper edge continues the line of the belly's rim. The elevation of the strings over the bridge is achieved by a wedge-shaped fingerboard, which is, again, shorter than that found on modern instruments. Bridges were perhaps a little thicker, and slightly lower. The bass bar was shorter and lighter, and the soundpost thinner. Strings were of gut, although in the later 17th century gut wound with silver was used for the lowest string on each instrument. Violins and violas lacked chin rests (invented by Spohr about 1810) and cellos endpins (standard only from the late 19th century). The tone of all these instruments is brighter, clearer, less loud and less 'mellow' than that of their modern counterparts.

Such a summary – necessarily peppered with qualifying phrases and inexact comparative adjectives – may be useful enough; but getting beyond it is no easy matter. Throughout the period, all these instruments underwent change, which took place unevenly in different parts of Europe. Recognizing this makes the 'Baroque violin/viola/cello' a concept of convenience, or a serviceable generalization. The scarcity of instruments which have never been altered and the contradictions and approximations inherent in other sorts of evidence create many difficulties. The late 17th-century Talbot manuscript gives measurements for a whole range of wind and string instruments but its cryptic notes often undermine any sense of certainty: is 'thickness goosequill' for soundposts to be taken literally?[8] Another late 17th-century manuscript, the violin method attributed to Brossard, contains a few apparently detailed measurements, but these too are surprising. The bridge, for example, seems thinner rather than thicker than modern bridges: 'about a *demie-ligne*' (1.125mm) for the base, and the top should be 'thin, but not too much so or it will cut the strings'.

Accessories, rather than basic body dimensions, tend to be regarded as the defining features of Baroque instruments. But what are now accepted as standard body sizes for string instruments were not established until the first half of the 18th century, and for the music of the early Baroque period we ought to think in terms of a wider range. Sound ideals changed; the primacy of Stradivari instruments was not accepted until the late 18th century. In the early years of the century the sweetness of Nicola Amati and Jacob Stainer instruments was more appreciated.[9] Before 1700 violins and violas were constructed in small and large versions and bass violins with body lengths of up to 80 cm were not uncommon. In the mid-16th century Charles IX's set of 38 Andrea Amati instruments included both large and small violins.[10] Mersenne (1636-7) lists among the family of violins a contralto and an alto instrument and says that it is customary to add a fifth part, the *Quinte de violon*. These instruments, all tuned C-g-d'-a', were of different sizes. By the early 18th century the situation had changed. Parts were sometimes still designated 'alto viola' and 'tenor viola' (and used both alto and tenor clefs), but this was no more than an indication of register.

The word 'violoncello' – like 'violoncino' a diminutive – was attached to a smaller-than-usual bass violin with a body length of *c*75 cm which emerged in the 1660s in Bologna. The invention there of silver-covered gut C strings was crucial in this development. It is only in the late 17th century, and principally from composers associated with Bologna (Domenico Gabrielli, Jacchini, Fiorè) that a separate solo repertory developed. Large *basses de violon*, tuned B♭-F-c-g, were standard in France until the 18th century, and in 17th-century Italy instruments tuned C-G-d-a with bodies as long as 80 cm were used until, gradually, the violoncello proper took over. Various terms were used to describe these bass violins, but from about 1620 to 1700 the most common was 'violone'. The confusion surrounding this word is enormous, since after 1700 it became synonymous with 'contrabasso' (Corrette begins his double bass method with the words 'the double bass, which the Italians call *Violone*') and before 1620 it was applied to two bass members of the viol family, the 'violone da gamba', tuned a 5th lower than the normal bass and the 'violone del contrabasso', tuned an octave lower.[11] To complicate matters further, this early use of the term survived in the 18th century alongside later applications – it corresponds to descriptions given by Mattheson (1713), Majer (1732), Walther (1732), Eisel (1738) and by the notoriously unreliable Bonanni (1722). Bach's violono grosso or violone parts in the Brandenburg Concertos seem to require a six-string contrabass viol, although neither of the conventional tunings quite fits.[12]

Current practice suggests that a related pair of assumptions is being made:

first, that the contrabass member of an 18th-century string ensemble would commonly have been called a 'violone' (correct), and secondly, that this meant a double-bass viol (often not correct). The range of possibilities for this instrument of 16′ pitch was in fact wider. Early double basses tended to be large – again because of the length needed to produce a satisfactory tone from a plain gut string. One instrument attributed to Gasparo da Salò stands 2.4 m high and has a body length of 173 cm.[13] In the whole of the Baroque period and beyond, there was little consistency about the number of strings, or even whether or not frets were used.[14] Numerous musicians voiced their preferences for one disposition or another. Speer (1697) describes an instrument with three or four strings. Quantz (1752) writes that 'the so-called German violon with five or six strings has been justly abandoned'. Mozart (1756) comments that 'the double bass is commonly called the 'violone ... it usually has four, sometimes only three strings', and Corrette's method is described as being for instruments with '3, 4 or 5 strings'.

Non-standard members of the violin include the violino piccolo, a small violin (body length 28–31 cm) usually tuned a fourth above the normal violin although Bach (in Cantata no. 140 and Brandenburg Concerto no. 1) uses a tuning (mentioned by Speer, 1697) only a minor third higher. Monteverdi's 'violino piccolo alla francese' (among the instruments for *Orfeo*) seems to have been a boat-shaped pochette tuned an octave above normal.[15] The violoncello piccolo, which could be as small as 59 cm, had four or five strings tuned (C)–G–d–a–e'. Bach's Suite no. 6 BWV1012 is designated 'à cinq accordes' and was probably written for this instrument (although some nearly full-size five-string cellos survive). Bach wrote for violoncello piccolo in nine cantatas. The viola d'amore in the 17th century was a shallow, viol-shaped instrument with metal playing strings but no sympathetic strings. The 18th-century instrument is more familiar: viola-sized, viol-shaped and with seven playing strings (variously tuned) and seven sympathetic strings which run through the bridge and under the fingerboard.

Strings

This chapter is concerned primarily with instruments strung in gut. But metal stringing for violins was known, and liked, for a short time at the beginning of the Baroque period. Praetorius (1619) expressed the opinion that 'when brass and steel strings are used on these instruments they produce a softer and lovelier tone than with other strings'. Metal strings were sometimes also used on the theorbo and chitarrone.

There were various types of gut string. Exactly what 17th-century musicians understood by such terms as 'minikins', 'gansars', 'catlines', 'Lyons' and 'Pistoy basses' is not absolutely clear, but the vehemence with which these were variously recommended or condemned indicates that the distinctions were important. The present-day identification of the term 'catline' with strings twisted like rope is a hypothesis which, although it works well acoustically, is not based on secure historical evidence.[16]

By the early 18th century gut strings wound with silver were being used on various instruments. These appear to have been invented in Bologna in the mid-17th century. They must have reached England by 1664 since Playford advertised them then as a 'late invention ... which sound much better and lowder than common Gut Strings, either under the Bow or Finger'.[17] Because they allowed for an increase in mass without an increase in diameter (and consequent loss of flexibility), covered strings could produce good-sounding bass notes from a shorter vibrating length than pure gut strings of the same pitch. For the violin, this meant a more resonant and refined-sounding *G* string. For other instruments the consequences were even more drastic: the tenor-size viola and the two-headed, 12-course lute became obsolete. The invention was (as noted above) the *sine qua non* of the cello's development, and it made possible the addition of a seventh string to the French bass viol. All of this, needless to say, did not take place overnight, and there is some evidence that in certain parts of Europe (notably in Italy and Germany) violinists continued using pure gut *G* strings until well into the 18th century.[18] Speer (1697) implies pure gut stringing for violins, but mentions covered strings for violas in terms suggesting that inferior quality might explain why they were not universally accepted: 'There are also some viola strings wound with thin silver or copper wire from button makers. These strings almost rattle when played because of the wire, and such violas (because of their rattling strings) are called bassoon-violas [*Violae di Fagotto*]'.

French sources mention strings which are half-covered. Brossard (*c*1695) recommends them for the violin D string. Such strings are extremely resonant and mediate well between the covered G string and a pure gut A; they are, though, so rough beneath the fingers that shifting becomes difficult. Forqueray (*c*1767) advocates strings 'half wound with very fine wire' for the C (middle) string on the bass viol, with fully wound strings below and pure gut above.

The question of pitch standards is related to string types. Gut strings behave well at the arbitrarily selected Baroque pitch standard of $a'=415\,\mathrm{Hz}$, but some players experience chronic breakages if a high pitch is being used (a problem recognized by Praetorius, 1619).[18] But as we shall see (chapter VII), pitch standards varied widely, between about $a'=380$ and 480, in different parts of Europe and at different times. Ideally, string players would be happy to tune to, say, $a'=410$ for early 18th-century French music and somewhat higher than 440 for Monteverdi. J. F. Reichardt observed in 1776 that regional variation in pitch made it necessary to adjust string gauges:

> The strings for the instrument [violin] must be chosen according to the pitch of the orchestra. In an orchestra that tunes to a low pitch, like the Berlin one, for example, the strings must be much heavier than for one that tunes to Vienna pitch: the difference is important.[20]

Bows

Since the relatively few old bows which have survived are virtually all unsigned and undated, it is not a simple matter to link a particular model to a specific musical style (to come up with a 'Monteverdi bow' or a 'Corelli bow', for example). For the early period information about bows comes principally from paintings and dimensions estimated from these must be regarded as approximate. At the beginning of the 17th century, violin bows may have been as short as 36 cm (14″) with the hair leaving a high frog to meet the stick at the point. A clearly-defined bow head seems to have developed in the later 17th century.[12] By the end of the century bows were considerably longer. Lenton (1693) writes, 'let your Bow be as long as your Instrument' (about 61 cm) and Roger North described Matteis's bow as being two feet long (also 61 cm). Talbot gives two feet as 'the usual length of the Consort bow' but has lengths of up to 27″ (68.6cm) for 'the Bow for Solo's or Sonata's'. Before the domination of the Tourte design (perfected in the late 1780s) there was little standardization in length, wood or stick form. A few general characteristics can usefully be isolated, however. Baroque bows tend not to have sticks which curve in towards the hair, and have a graceful 'pike's head' or 'swan's bill' at the point. The band of hair is often little more than half as wide as on a Tourte model bow. Pernambuco, although used on some fine bows even in the 17th century, was not yet standard; ironwood and snakewood were used and Talbot's reference to a 'Bow of fine Speckled-wood' suggests that the latter may have been especially favoured. The ferrule (which keeps the band of hair flat as it leaves the frog) is not found on bows of this period; this has important implications for articulation – Baroque bows are not designed for modern *martelé* or *marcato* strokes.

There were various ways in which bow hair was given tension. Clip-in frogs were probably most common. (Since they cannot be adjusted, there are difficulties in achieving uniform tension with varying humidity; some makers now remedy this by supplying several frogs of slightly different heights.) The screw frog was used on some quite early bows, but was not standard.[22] Bremner (*c*1750) advertised violin and cello bows 'pillar'd or plane' and 'ditto with screws'; the screw was clearly seen as an optional refinement. ('Pillar'd' bows have fluted sticks for added strength and lightness.)

Violin technique

BOWING Basic bow grips are described in a number of sources. In the early Baroque period, the thumb was placed on the hair near the frog. The change to placing the thumb on the under side of the stick was initiated by the Italians. In France, the thumb-on-hair method persisted into the 18th century; it is the grip described by Montéclair (1711–12) (although he has the thumb pressing against the underside of the frog). Not until Corrette's *L'école d'Orphée* is the thumb-on-stick grip offered as an alternative (and it is still identified as an Italian practice). According to Roger North, Matteis persuaded the English 'out of that awkwardness'; yet in 1693, 20 years after Matteis's arrival, Lenton describes a grip with the thumb on the hair at the frog. The Italian bow hold may not have seemed such an obvious improvement to all who encountered it. Falck (1688) describes the French grip in terms of its positive qualities, saying that it produces a good deep stroke.[23] When conscientiously following the bowing principles of the Lullists, players should ideally be using a shorter, French-style dance bow and the bow grip that goes with it.

The Italian grip is carefully discussed in terms of the subtleties of tone production by Geminiani (1751), Mozart (1756), Herrando (1756) and L'abbé *le fils* (1761). What they discribe is very different from the prevalent modern bowing style. All insist that the parts of the body closest to the bow stick are the most active; flexible wrist and finger movements are vital, then a freely moving lower arm and, finally, an upper arm which will become involved only in the broadest strokes. L'abbé *le fils* (1761) comments on the flexibility of fingers which, he says, 'will naturally make imperceptible movements which contribute a great deal to the beauty of the sound'. A low elbow which allows the weight of the arm to be brought to bear in a relaxed way is important. Lenton (1693) advises players to 'hold not up your Elbow, more than necessity requires'. The most precise statement about elbow position comes from Herrando (1756), who also stresses the role of the wrist, and lower-arm movement:

> The right arm is raised naturally, the elbow separated from the body about the distance between the extended thumb and forefinger, without movement from the elbow up, for the movement must come from the elbow forward with freedom at the wrist and evenness in the bow.

Mozart, too, warns against a right arm that is held too high, and like Herrando refers his readers to the engravings in his treatise; the contrast in elbow positions between the 'good' and 'bad' pictures is marked.

The bow could be held some distance from the frog. Corrette (1738) claims that the Italians 'hold it three-quarters of the way down the stick'. Berlin (1744) says: 'imagine that the length of the bow is divided into three parts, and put your hand in the middle of the first part'. Geminiani advises players to use the whole bow 'from the Point to that Part of it under, and even beyond the Fingers', implying that the hand is not at the frog. Corrette, Herrando and L'abbé *le fils* all recommend tipping the bow slightly towards the fingerboard, but Mozart, typically concerned with achieving greater strength of tone, warns against this. For the same reason, he (and L'abbé *le fils*) advocate having the second or middle joint of the index finger (rather than the first joint) on the stick.

RULES FOR BOWING The earliest explanations of how to organize up- and down-bows enshrine the basic principle later to become known as the Rule of the Down Bow. Riccardo Rognoni (1592) gave a few rules in the introduction to his treatise on diminution. His son Francesco developed these in *Selva de varii passaggi* (1620). Zanetti (1645), like Rognoni, uses the letters 'T' (*tirare*) and 'P' (*puntare*) for down- and up-bows to produce down-bows on strong beats. Early violin bowing was not, however, just a matter of rather rudimentary note-counting. Francesco Rognoni gives expressive slurrings of up to 15 notes and deals with some advanced bowing techniques.[24]

The rule of the down-bow dominates French bowing in the 17th century. It is neatly summarized by Mersenne in 1636, and it forms the basis for the elaborately codified principles of Lully set out so fully by Muffat (1698). The most distinctive of the Lullists' ways of achieving a down-bow at the beginning of each bar is the use of a down-up-down/down bowing sequence in slow triple time as an alternative to the more facile down-up-up/down (ex.1). (To divide – *craquer* – the up-bow is possible at all but the very fastest of tempos.) Only fast courantes, gigues and canaries may be played with continuously alternating bows. Of the rapid ornamental notes found so often

Ex.1 Muffat (1698)

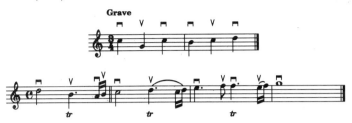

at the end of a beat in the opening section of a French overture, Muffat says only that they can be bowed separately, or slurred 'for greater sweetness'. His brief example throws the whole question back on to the performers' taste (ex.1). The 'Rules', which make so much sense of this Versailles-court dance-oriented style, are corroborated by other writers, notably Montéclair (1711–12) and Dupont (1718). Dupont, described on the title page of his treatise as 'Maître de Musique et de Danse', stands in a tradition of violinist–dancing masters going back to the origins of the instrument. Muffat himself stresses the need for a musician to have a knowledge of dance and claims that 'the majority of the finest string players in France understand this full well, so it is no miracle that they know so well how to find and keep the tempo'. The relationship between musical and choreographic patterns in French court and theatre dances of this period is subtle and not infrequently involves a kind of counterpoint between visible and audible rhythms. Awareness of this might well influence the way in which performers project musical phrase structures.[25]

The discipline of Lully's band was exceptional. Muffat stresses how little agreement could be expected elsewhere in Europe. Since the best informant on the bowing of the Lullists was an Austrian composer of (amongst other things) French-style orchestral suites, we might assume that the bowing principles travelled abroad with the compositional style. But to what extent? The imposition of French musical tastes on the Restoration English court is well documented. It seems right to approach, say, Purcell overtures (or pieces like the introductory symphony to *My Heart is Inditing*) with the rules in mind. Lenton's instructions (and those of other derivative English tutors) all serve the rule of the down-bow, and include the characteristic down-up-down/down triple metre bowing of the Lullists. The Rules may also be brought to bear on Telemann or Bach French-style movements, but these emerge from a later and much more eclectic musical environment than Lully's. The members of the Leipzig Collegium Musicum may have understood that a French overture would respond to a particular bowing style, but for them this would surely have been only one in a range of equally accessible styles. Hubert le Blanc's colourful *Défense de la Basse de Viole* (1740) strongly conveys a sense that the Italians' influence on violin playing in France involved not just a more convenient bow grip but a complete revolution in sound production: 'Playing in a new manner, the Violin was admired as it had not been since the time of Lully (when the bow-strokes were chopped up and the hatchet-stroke marked each bar or at least every phrase ...)'. The

Lullists' principles will clearly not get us far with the music of the Corelli-inspired composers of early 18th-century France (Anet, Mascitti, Leclair, Guillemain, Guignon, Rebel, Duval etc). More complex influences were at work and contemporary accounts delight in the lightness and fire of these violinist-composers.

Geminiani scorned 'that wretched Rule of drawing the Bow down at the first Note of every Bar', and in the examples specifying bowings (XVI, XVII and XXIV), he goes out of his way to ensure that the student will become equally adept at using up- or down-bows at the beginning of a bar. Tartini (1771) also recommended constant practice in bowing fast passages in different ways. For all this, the rule of the down-bow still exerted an influence. It lies behind Mozart's and Herrando's bowing instructions and reminiscences of the Lullists' principles can still be found in L'abbé *le fils*.

BOWING INFLECTIONS What seemed most important in the control of the bow? Bremner (1777) passes on an old (but plausible?) anecdote about Corelli's demands:

> I have been informed that *Coreli* judged no performer fit to play in his band, who could not, with one stroke of the bow, give a steady and powerful sound, like that of an organ, from two strings at once, and continue it for ten seconds.

This ability to play a long even stroke was, according to Muffat, one which transcended national boundaries. Montéclair, too, claimed that 'it is essential first of all to get used to playing up- and down-bows evenly from one end of the bow to the other without making the string produce an ugly sound'. His words are echoed by Corrette (1738), Geminiani (1751) and Mozart (1756). A basic element in producing a strong sound, however, is to make the string speak without a percussive consonant at the beginning of the note. According to Mozart:

> Every note, even the strongest attack, has a small, even if barely audible, softness at the beginning of the stroke; for it would otherwise be no note but only an unpleasant and unintelligible noise. This same softness must be heard also at the end of each stroke.

Controlled and strong tone production precedes and supports all nuanced bowing. Yet it is clear that the bow, to a much greater extent than in modern playing, became the primary source of expressive inflection. The malleable quality of a violin's sound is compared by Le Blanc (1740) with (among other things) clay on a potter's wheel. Roger North also has some fine images for bowing of a kind which he says the Italians brought to perfection:

> Learn to fill and soften a sound as shades in needlework, in sensation so as to be like also a gust of wind, which begins with a soft air, and fills by degrees to a strength as makes all bend, and then softens again into a temper and so vanish. And after this to superinduce a gentle and slow wavering, not into a trill, upon the swelling the note.[26]

Geminiani (1751) calls this kind of dynamically modulated bowing 'one of the principal Beauties of the Violin'.

There are a few more specific indications of how inflected bowing might be used (although these are almost all significantly later than similar indications in viol sources: see below, p. 69–71). Matthew Locke's storm music for *The Tempest* contains the directions 'lowder by degrees' and 'soft and slow by degrees'. Piani (*Sonate*, 1712), and Veracini (*Sonate accademiche*, 1744) have prefaces explaining the use of signs for a swell, a diminuendo and a combination of the two. The swell sign features in Geminiani's violin treatise, and in the earlier volumes *A Treatise of Good Taste* (*c*1746) and *Rules for Playing in a True Taste* (1749). These signs were taken up and used by other French and English composers. Geminiani's pupils, Festing and Avison, made extensive and generally straightforward use of them. Avison, for example, uses combinations of these marks to show a natural phrasing off at cadences (ex.2). Sometimes the swell sign seems to require a rather

Ex.2 Avison: Concerto grosso op.4 no.1 (1755), end of 1st movt

unspecific interpretation, an expressive accent perhaps. It occurs on many upbeats,[27] and the effect aimed at here is perhaps what Corrette describes in his cello method (1741):

> In all types of movements which one would call lopsided, it is necessary to emphasize the third note of each beat a little more with the bow – the first two executed a little more gracefully than the third, especially in the pieces in a slow tempo like *adagio*, *largo*, *andante*, affettuoso. Examples are the *affettuosos* of the sonatas of Mr Senaillé and Mr Aubert.

(Quantz says upbeats should be accented even in fast movements: 'In gay and quick pieces the last quaver of each half bar must be stressed with the bow'.) These run counter to what we might have expected from bowing principles designed to make down-bows coincide with first beats; but they widen the expressive possibilities in 18th-century repertory. Placing a first beat in the shadow, so to speak, of a swelled upbeat can be a fine affective gesture. Cupis, in his celebrated Menuet (*c*1742), uses large versions of these signs to indicate that the swell and/or diminuendo may be spread over several bars. William Hayes, Professor of Music at Oxford, was contemptuous of Geminiani's habit of giving very specific ornament and phrasing instructions to performers, claiming that he was 'paying his Brethren of the String but an ill Compliment'.[28] The attitude that, at best, explicit markings are patronizing may help to explain why they are found in relatively few scores.

SPECIAL BOWINGS The flexibility of wrist and fingers, so emphasized in the instruction manuals, is vital for special bowings, particularly for the various kinds of slurred staccato. Francesco Rognoni (1620) describes '*il lireggiare affettuoso*' (or simply '*con affetti*') as including a number of notes in one bow but using the wrist to make each note bounce. Walther has 'arpeggiando con arcate sciolte' written above broken-chord figurations and 'ondeggiando', indicating a slurred alternation between two strings (ex.3). These bowings

Ex.3 Walther: *Scherzi da Violino Solo* (1676), Sonata VIII

were used by other composers, although terminology is inconsistent. ('Ondeggiando', or French 'ondulé', in some sources means vibrato; when two notes of the same pitch – one stopped and one open – are alternated the effect is known as 'bariolage'.) Complex staccato bowings were closely associated with violin playing: Jean Rousseau (1687) remarks disdainfully that the *dessus de viole* is above such vulgar display: 'It is never necessary [on the *dessus*] to practice those passages called *Ricochets* ... which we endure so reluctantly in violin playing'.

Muffat (1698) describes as an ornament the *pétillement*, in which a run is made to 'crackle' in the same bow stroke. Piani's 'Avertissement' explains that a group of dotted notes under a slur are 'equal and articulated within the same bow stroke'. Geminiani notes the existence of this kind of bowing but expresses little enthusiasm for it; in Example XX of the violin method it is marked 'Particolare' ('Indifferent'). Herrando calls it 'picada' (pricking or biting) and gives examples in which it occurs only within an up-bow. In *L'école d'Orphée* (1738), Corrette gives examples of 'notes égales et articulées d'un même coup d'Archet', which always occur on an up-bow; in his cello method (1741), however, he has an almost identical exercise with up- and down-bows mixed. L'abbé *le fils* also extends the technique to down-bows. Many virtuoso examples appear in 18th-century sonatas. Castrucci (in his op.2 no.10 of 1734) has a group of 22 quavers with dots under a slur with the direction 'Tutti in un Arcata'.

CHORDS AND DOUBLE STOPS Double stops and chords appear early in the 17th century. Imitation of hurdy-gurdies seems to have inspired some of the early Italian uses – the 'La lira' section of Farina's *Capriccio stravagante* (1627) and Marini's *Capriccio in modo di un lira* (op.8, 1629). They become especially prominent in the works of late 17th-century German composers (Walther, Biber, Nicolaus Bruhns and J. P. Westhoff). The *locus classicus* of this kind of playing is the Bach set of solo violin sonatas. The absurdity of the so-called 'Vega Bach bow' has long been demonstrated, but the assumption on which it was based – that chords should be chords – is not dead. There are, in fact, numerous chords in 18th-century violin works which must be broken, not because of the characteristics of the bow but because of the way the notes lie on the instrument. Both Leclair *l'aîné* (renowned for his performance of chords and double stops)[29] and his younger brother wrote some four-note chords which necessarily use only three strings. Veracini has a number of such chords and the final chord of the 'Handel' Sonata in F major op.1 no.12 contains five notes. Julien-Amable Mathieu gives fingerings in his op.1 (1756) which demonstrate that he expected the bottom notes of a chord to be released in time for the player to re-use the same fingers for notes on higher strings (ex.4). In each of these cases, the player has no option but to make the chord ripple from bottom to top; the notes cannot be sounded simultaneously and sustained equally. All of this should perhaps encourage violinists to think of chords almost as if they were played on a lute rather than produced by a stream of air from a bellows. Indeed, the lute transcriptions of the Bach violin and cello suites (BWV995, 1000 and 1006a) suggest the possibility of looking towards lute and viol techniques when approaching these chordal and polyphonic works.

But, as always, the picture is not absolutely clear. Leblanc (first name unknown) has in a Sonata in E♭ |(c1767) a series of three-note chords together with the instruction 'Strike all three strings at once and always use a down-bow'. In op.4 no.6 Leclair *l'aîné* indicates that he wants three notes sounded together at the beginning of each group of oscillating notes. Contradictions like this open up a wide range of options: arpeggiated chords, struck chords (Quantz, 1752, describes both) and presumably the various possibilities which lie between these two extremes.

What to sustain in fugal movements poses a similar problem. It is clear that some note values are indications of part-writing rather than prescribed durations. Even in Corelli, it is impossible to sustain every note in an interlocking chain for its full written value and Geminiani's fingerings for fugal movements in his revised op.1 (1739) clearly indicate that he did not expect performers to sustain all notes for their full value.

LEFT-HAND TECHNIQUE There is no problem more basic, or more contentious, for Baroque string players than how to hold their instruments. The one thing that is certain is that there was no single accepted way. A number of paintings, in fact, depict several violinists, each holding his instrument differently, playing in one ensemble.[30] The methods currently in use may be broadly categorized as 'chin-on' (using some pressure from the chin on the right-hand, E string, side to steady the instrument) and 'chin-off' (allowing the violin to sit on the collar bone and supporting it entirely with the left hand). The latter seems more difficult at first, but has some advantages, not least that it allows the instrument to speak more openly without any muting effect from the chin (or chamois).

Ex. 4

(a) Leclair *l'aîné*. op.1 no.6 (1723), 2nd movt

(b) Leclair *le cadet*. Sonata no.7 (1739)

(c) Leclair *le cadet*. Sonata no.3 (1739)

(d) Veracini: *Dissertazione sopra l'opera quinta del Corelli*

(e) Handel (attrib.): op.1 no.12

(f) Mathieu: op.1 no.4 (1756), last movt

The options in the Baroque period were wider. Many players held their instruments beneath the collar bone. Playford (1654), addressing absolute amateurs, advocates this breast position, but so too does Geminiani. Understandably, this has provoked incredulity, particularly as it was thought that Geminiani's instructions were implicitly contradicted by a frontispiece to the first French edition (1752), showing a chin-on violinist. But this engraving was copied from the frontispiece to Herrando's treatise (1756) and attached to Geminiani's work only with the De la Chevardière & Frères le Goux edition (*c*1770). It has nothing to do with the 1752 publication and, in the meantime, we have no evidence to suggest that Geminiani didn't mean what he said.

Prinner (*c*1677) and Herrando (1756) both prescribe chin-on playing, although Prinner admits that there are famous virtuosos (Schmelzer, Biber?) who hold the instrument only against their chests.[31] Lenton (1693) and Veracini (1744)[32] both provide evidence for resting the instrument on the collar bone, but without chin pressure. Lenton presents his solution as a kind of *via media*:

> I would have none get a habit of holding an Instrument under the Chin, so I would have them avoid placing it as low as the Girdle, which is a mongrel sort of way us'd by some in imitation of the *Italians* ... The best way of commanding the Instrument will be to place it something higher than your Breast, your fingers round and firm in stopping.

The Italian responsible for the bad influence was Nicola Matteis who Roger North reports (with some amazement) held his violin 'against his short ribbs'. Mozart (1756) offers the breast position and an under-the-chin (although not necessarily chin-on) position as alternatives; he states a preference for the latter on the grounds that it is more stable when shifting. Corrette (1738) and Berlin (1744) open up the possibility of a basically chin-off hold, but one in which chin pressure is applied to facilitate shifting; according to Corrette, 'It is absolutely essential to put one's chin on the violin when shifting since that gives the left hand complete freedom, especially when moving back to first position'.

The crux of the matter – as Prinner, Corrette, Berlin and Mozart make clear – is changing positions. Unfortunately, most 18th-century writers sidestep the problem: they describe the notes available in upper positions, but not the techniques for exploiting them. However, Geminiani (1751) gives, albeit elliptically, all the vital clues for shifting without using the chin. The first step is to develop maximum independence between thumb and fingers. The exercises contained in Geminiani's ex.1 are excellent for this, particularly the scales given in 1E which encourage elastic fingers to work around a stationary thumb (ex.5). The next step is to leave the thumb behind

Ex.5 Geminiani (1751); Essempio 1E

when moving into higher positions 'till it remains almost hid under the Neck of the Violin'; as opposed to the method used in modern playing technique, the whole hand must not shift as a frame. The final and most difficult step involves the return to lower positions and here, too, Geminiani provides the essential information: 'in drawing back the Hand . . . the Thumb cannot, for Want of Time, be replaced in its natural Position; but it is necessary it should be replaced at the second Note'. Fingers shift before rather than after or with the thumb (which has been prepared for the shift, anyway, by being left behind). The rest can be worked out empirically. The support of the instrument depends upon the downward pressure of the fingers being counterbalanced by some upward support, normally provided by the thumb. In the moment of the thumb's being shifted back, the lowest section of the index finger takes over that support. At other times, the index finger may be held away from the neck of the instrument.

Mozart (1756) has the most systematic discussion of fingering principles. He encourages extensions (upward and downward) to avoid unnecessary shifts, and the use of the same fingerings for each unit in a sequential passage. Many fingerings found in 18th-century sonatas accord with this.

VIBRATO Lenton's remarks on holding the violin lead into a description of vibrato (the close shake); the two issues are related. Continuous vibrato (regarded now as an element in tone production) is difficult without chin support. Geminiani's injunction (suppressed by Bremner)[33] to make use of the close shake as often as possible needs to be considered alongside his instructions on holding the instrument (and with its immediate context, the section on graces, in mind).

Vibrato apparently passed in and out of fashion. Roger North calls it a 'late invention', but it was not new. Mersenne (1636–7) describes it and says that it 'is not used so much now as it was in the past'.[34] Walther uses an 'm' to indicate vibrato in *Hortulus Chelicus* (1688), but its sparing use would suggest that he thought of it as a very special colouring (ex.6). Muffat (1698) cautions against vibrato which interferes with good tuning (a concern emphatically reiterated by Bremner in 1777). Mozart's main theme (despite his quip about players who sound as if they have the palsy) is that 'Nature herself is the instructress thereof'; like Roger North, he links vibrato, varied in speed and intensity, with eloquent bowing inflections.

A related point: from about 1720 many composers began specifying the use of fourth fingers on e'' and by the middle of the century the preference for a stopped note over open strings was general. Tartini (1770), Corrette in his cello treatise (1741), and fingerings in sonatas by Leclair and others make it clear, however, that open-string trills were a normal part of the string player's technique.

SPECIAL EFFECTS In Marini's op.1 (1617) 'Tremolo con L'arco' is found at the head of a passage in minims. The character of the passage suggests that it would not respond to the juddering measured-semiquaver division of Monteverdi's *stile concitato* (introduced in *Combattimento di Tancredi et Clorinda*).[35] The word 'tremolo' has various meanings in the period, including 'vibrato'.

Ex.6 Walther: *Hortulus Chelicus* (1688), Preludio 1, opening

Farina, in the *Capriccio stravagante*, uses it in imitation of a tremulant organ stop. Here and in the Marini example, a gentle pulsation within a smooth bow stroke seems most appropriate. In 1688, Walther also imitates an 'Organo tremolante' using semiquaver oscillation between two strings written underneath a wavy line, suggesting that 'tremolo' and 'ondeggiando' (see below) are sometimes synonymous. Marini's use of slurs is also fascinating, but they are so few and idiosyncratic that it would be difficult to take anything more from them than encouragement to find ear-catching articulations, and not just in his works but in those of his contemporaries (Castello, Merula, Fontana, Rossi, Cazzati, Uccellini, Legrenzi and others).

A dramatic idea often served as the handmaiden for technical innovation. In *Combattimento*, for example, Monteverdi has tied minims marked 'forte-piano' and 'arcata sola' for the pathos-filled moment in which Clorinda requests baptism. The freshness of these effects stands out. Devices which can now be invoked with a simple, conventional direction are explained fully;

for the final long note (as Clorinda's soul floats to heaven) we have 'Questa ultima nota va in arcata morendo' ('This final note to be sounded in a dying bow'). A similarly full description of pizzicato (with two fingers) is given earlier in the piece: 'Qui si lascia l'arco, e si strappano le corde con duoi diti' ('Here, put down the bow and pluck the strings with two fingers').

This virtuosity was exported, partly through Italian violinists moving around Europe. Marini was Kapellmeister in Düsseldorf from 1623 to 1645, and Farina worked in Dresden with Schütz (who in turn had had two periods of study in Venice with Gabrieli and Monteverdi). Their influence can be seen in the works of 17th-century Austrian and German composers (Rosen-müller, Schmelzer, Biber, Walther and others). Unfortunately, it is in the eccentricities of these composers that the connections are most easily seen, but they were part of a more general cross-fertilization, a shared excitement in the possibilities of the instruments. Virtually every device in the *Capriccio stravagante* can be matched in Walther's *Hortus Chelicus* (except *col legno*, which was, however, used by Biber). Marini's use of scordatura in op.8 (1629) was taken up by Biber, notably in his 'Mystery' or 'Rosary' Sonatas. This 'mistuning' of strings creates strange, often haunting resonances as in the D minor tuning ($a'-d'-a'-d''$) of Sonata no.4 ('The Presentation in the Temple') or the C minor tuning ($a\flat-e\flat'-g'-d''$) of no.6 ('The Agony in the Garden'). (Walther scorned the use of scordatura in his preface to *Hortulus Chelicus*, but the general thrust of his argument – that he was above such cheap effects – seems somewhat disingenuous.) Biber's other technical eccentricities include the invention of snap pizzicato (to represent gunshot in *Battalia*) and using paper between the strings and fingerboard of the bass instruments to mimic a side-drum effect.

Ornamentation

The relevance of early Baroque diminution manuals for string players is made explicit by the Rognonis (1590, 1620). Violinists should also be familiar with Caccini's *Le nuove musiche* (1601/2), not just for the demonstration of *passaggi* but for its guidance on the *messa di voce*. The most basic way to approach the ornamentation of the central Baroque period is through the distinction between French and Italian styles, neatly summarized by Quantz (1752):

> The first requires a clean and sustained execution of the air, and embellishment with the essential graces, such as appoggiaturas, whole and half-shakes, mordents, turns, *battements, flattemens, &c.*, but no extensive passage work or significant addition of extempore embellishments ... In the second manner, that is, the Italian, extensive artificial graces that accord with the harmony are introduced in the Adagio in addition to the little French embellishments.

French ornaments are described in numerous sources, although few are written specifically with violinists in mind. (Muffat, 1698, again proves particularly useful here.) The applicability of ornaments given in, for example, keyboard sources is suggested by accompanied sonatas in which the string player is told to take over the ornaments marked in the harpsichord part.[36] Quantz makes the point that 'with good instruction the French manner of embellishing the Adagio may be learned without understanding harmony. For the Italian manner, on the other hand, knowledge of harmony is indispensable.' Three chapters of Quantz's treatise provide systematic instruction in this kind of free Italianate ornamentation, but the various written-out examples of ready-made spontaneity are even more fascinating. The best known are the 1710 Mortier and Roger editions of Corelli's op.5 'with the ornaments for the Adagios, composed by Mr A Corelli, as he plays them'. This seems to have prompted numerous musicians (particularly in England) to write out their own sets of graces for these sonatas.[37] Curiously, most of these embellished movements from op.5 are from the *sonate da camera* in the second part, as if the printed graces for the first six sonatas were taken as a challenge to complete the set. These graced versions vary widely in quality, and some of the more over-elaborate succeed in destroying the character of the movement (a danger noted by both Mozart and Quantz).

There are, of course, other models. William Babell's two books of *XII Solos ... With proper Graces adapted to each Adagio, by ye Author* (both c1725) were obviously written with the celebrated Corelli edition in mind. Barsanti published graces for his Sonata op.1 no.2 (London, 1726). Telemann's *Sonate methodische* (1728, 1732), as their titles suggest, had a didactic purpose and were advertised as being 'very useful to those who wish to apply themselves to cantabile ornamentation'.[38] The embellishments here, however, have a more *galant* cast than in the Corelli sonatas. The Tartini *Traité* gives extended instruction on florid cadenzas, but this, too, is a slightly later preoccupation. Often, very expressive models for free embellishment can be found from internal variation in slow movements by Handel or Vivaldi.

The viola

Quantz (1752) writes that a viola player should be a fine musician 'because he does not, I presume, wish to remain always a violist'. Given the thematically deprived character of many Baroque viola parts, this attitude is hardly surprising. There is, too, a paucity of solo repertory; Telemann's two concertos (one for two violas) and – especially – Bach's Brandenburg Concertos nos.3 and 6 are the brightest points in the instrument's 18th-century history. In 1770, William Flackton (1709–98) claimed that 'Upon Enquiry at all the Music Shops in London for Tenor Solos, none were to be found, neither was it known by them that any were ever published.'[39] The viola normally had no place in the trio sonata, although in Germany, Biber, Schmelzer, Antonio Bestal (c1605–1669) and D. Woja (d1680) advocated its use on the second violin line. Telemann's *Scherzi melodichi* (1734) are a set of seven trio sonatas for violin, viola and basso continuo.

The viola had more responsibility in the 17th century. Large ensemble music in France, Germany and – before Corelli – in Italy normally had two violas. While these were often no more than 'parties de remplissage' (parts to fill out the harmony) they occasionaly took on more interest, as in Rosenmüller's *Sonate da camera cioe Sinfonie* (1670) or Muffat's *Armonico tributo* (1701).

The place of the viola in concerti grossi is interesting. Before Corelli the ripieno group in the concerto grosso contained two violas, rather than two violins.[40] Between the composition of Corelli's op.6 in the late 17th century and their publication in 1714, the viola was deprived of some of its independence. Its fugal entries, always 'covered' by concertino cello, originally stood on their own, as a comparison of the fugue in the Sinfonia for the oratorio *S Beatrice d'Este* with its revision in op.6 no.6 shows. The attempt to make the published parts more versatile (playable as trio sonatas) led to the doubling, and perhaps in performing these works now the redundant cello entries should be restored to the viola alone. The inclusion of the viola in the concertino group from about 1730 on (a development usually attributed – wrongly – to Geminiani) did not result in a genuine increase in interest in the instrument; despite the designation 'obbligato', the violas remained 'little more than a dull Ripieno, an Accessory or Auxiliary, to fill up or compleat the Harmony in Full pieces of MUSIC' (to quote Flackton once again).

For all this, it must be said that – confronted with an apparently insignificant part – the viola player can transform an ensemble through imaginative dynamic and articulative pointing. There are, too, those places where the violist must subtly penetrate (as in Corelli's cadential figures, or – more obviously – in imitative entries). All this Bach obviously appreciated; according to Carl Philipp Emanuel, 'as the greatest expert and judge of harmony, he liked best to play the viola with appropriate loudness and softness'.[41]

The cello and bass violin

Holding a Baroque cello may not arouse the same controversy as holding a Baroque violin, but 18th-century sources suggest a similar diversity of approaches. There is, however, a mainstream here and the alternatives (possibly more relevant for larger bass violins) offer little to competent cellists. Nevertheless, just as chin-on Baroque violin playing is manifestly not unhistoric, there would be some justification for Baroque cellists opting for an endpin. Corrette (1741) outlines the basic position:

> The cello must be placed between the calves of the legs. Hold the neck with the left hand and slant it a little to the left side and hold the bow in the right hand. See that the instrument does not touch the ground, since that would dampen the sound.

Cupis (1772) explains that the reason the left side is brought further forward is to facilitate playing on the *A* string. Corrette mentions an endpin for supporting the instrument when played standing up, but Berlin (1744) advocates it for the normal sitting position as well, nearly 150 years before the device became standard. Crome (1765), too, recommends an endpin (and frets) but only as aids for beginners.

The cello bow is held with an overhand (or palm-down) grip like the violin bow, while viol bows are held palm up. But again, the picture is not absolutely clearcut. Muffat (1698), after describing French-style violin bow holds, writes 'gambists *and other bass-players* [my italics] differ in that they place their fingers between the hair and wood of the bow'. Berlin describes a viol-type bow grip, and although his five pages of rudimentary cello instruction ought not to be relied upon too heavily, he is presumably describing what he has seen. He admits that not all hold the bow in the same way and says that 'you can move the bow backwards and forwards as you wish'. These two statements are implicitly linked: violin bowing principles would work with one grip, viol principles with the other. Quantz (1752) also suggests that bow strokes could be organized either like a violin (the method favoured by Italian players) or like a viol, but he doesn't make it clear whether he is thinking of alternative grips. Even in 1770, Burney noted, 'It is remarkable that Antonio [Vandini] and all the other violoncello players here [Padua] hold the bow in the old-fashioned way with the hand under it'.[42] Viol players, from quite early times, may also have used a cello-style bow grip – at least, the violone player in the background of Jan Brueghel's *Allegory of Hearing* is bowing overhand.

Corrette (1741) describes three different bow grips, all violin-related. The first corresponds to the Italian thumb-on-stick grip, but his diagram shows the hand much further towards the middle. The other two methods are variants of the French grip; one with the thumb on the hair well up the bow, and the other with the thumb on the frog.

Various fingering systems were in use in the first half of the 18th century. Corrette and Crome avoid using the third finger in 1st position, and their principles seem based on violin fingering. But Corrette makes it clear that *basse de violon* players had used a fingering system in first position like that which is now basic cello technique. Lanzetti (c1760) and Baumgartner (c1774) give fingerings in 1st and 2nd positions which a modern cellist would find natural, although in 3rd position they frequently indicate whole-tone gaps between second and third and third and fourth fingers. Cupis (1768) uses a virtually modern fingering system. The thumb position was introduced by Corrette above 4th position. It is described by Baumgartner and others as being like the use of a *capo tasto* on a guitar.

The cello, like the viola, was not expected to embellish, although many players (even great ones, according to Quantz) offended by doing so. Solo parts, of course, were an exception; the cello soloist in Handel's op.4 no.3 is invited to take the same initiative as the violinist (ex.7). Instructions to cellists stress harmonic understanding. Quantz talks about dynamic inflection in terms of harmonic function; the note which defines a cadence as interrupted, for example, should be given particular emphasis whereas the bass notes in a perfect cadence can be played quietly. He develops these ideas further in the section addressed to the keyboard player. Here he constructs a harmonic–dynamic hierarchy: the more dissonant the harmony, the more emphatic its delivery should be. His Table XXIV shows an apparently matter-of-fact bass (full of repeated notes) transformed by chiaroscuro effects (ex.8). Playing continuo in recitatives presents special problems, and no absolutely clear guidelines can be given. Towards the end of the period, bass notes would not, on the whole, be held for the full length; they would be quitted in order to leave the singer more space for natural-sounding declamation. This, at least, is suggested by some surviving continuo parts (the 1736 *St Matthew Passion* parts, for example) and the advice of some

Ex.7 Handel: op.4 no.3, 1st movt

Ex.8 Quantz (1752): Table XXIV

theorists (contradicted by others). How far back such practices should be pressed is far from clear. The placing of cadential notes presents another problem; as a rule of thumb for 18th-century recitative, it seems best to sound these with the ending of the singer's phrase in opera and dramatic cantatas, but to delay them until the singer has finished in sacred cantatas. Such a convention is suggested by Heinichen and Telemann in their figured-bass treatises.[43]

The contrabass

There is some evidence from early in the 17th century that the violone del contrabasso may have been used in Italy and Germany to play the bass line an octave below its written pitch. Agazzari (1607) recommends 'keeping on the thick strings as much as possible ... frequently doubling the bass line at the octave below' while Schütz implies a similar approach in his *Musicalische Exequien* (1636).[44] Such an instrument does not however seem to have been standard until the very end of the 17th century and it has no place in 17th-century English or French music.

Little special attention is given to the techniques of playing 16'-pitch bass instruments until well into the 18th century. Mattheson in 1713 described it as 'labour fit for a horse'[45] and Corrette (1773) claims that a variety of bow strokes on the double bass is scarcely possible, since the instrument requires so much strength. Quantz (1752) is more positive about the instrument's potential. He recommends a basic detached and airy stroke, and his remarks imply an overhand grip:

> If a note is to be particularly stressed, the bow must be guided from left to right, since the bow then has more power to produce the stress. The short bow-stroke mentioned above applies only to notes that require majesty and liveliness. It does not apply to the long notes ... that are frequently intermingled in quick pieces ... Nor does it apply to slurred notes, which should express a flattering or melancholy sentiment; these the bass player must express in just as sustained and quiet a fashion as the violoncellist.

(Corrette describes the bow grip as being like that of the bass viol, although the frontispiece to the treatise shows a player using an unmistakably overhand bow hold.)

Various sources emphasize that the contrabass player should not attempt to play all the notes in a bass line but rather to underline the harmonically important ones. Corrette and Quantz give a number of examples illustrating this, and Pepusch writes:

> We must take care not to make any Quick-running Variation in the lower Notes of the Bass, no Instrument being able to perform them well ... This Error is however, daily run into, by giving divided Basses to be play'd on the *Violone* or *Double Bass*, which makes a horrid rumbling, whereas if the *Violoncello's*, and other *such* Bass-Instruments only, did play those Divided Basses, and the *Violone* or *Double Bass* play'd a Fundamental Bass under Them, made up of what the *Italians* call *Note Sostenute*, a much finer and more agreeable Harmony would ensue, for Every Note would be clear and distinct in every part of the Composition.[46]

Sets of 18th-century parts make it clear that often double basses played only in the ritornellos of arias or the tutti sections of concertos.

65

Large ensembles

The actual size of Baroque groups varied enormously. Mersenne comments that ensembles 'can be made of 500 different violins', but adds '24 are enough' and goes on to describe the composition of the Vingt-quatre Violons du Roi (6–4–4–4–6). Lully's Petite Bande, formed in 1656, reduced the number of string players to 16 (6–2–2–2–4).

In Italy, Corelli took part in some extravaganzas with up to 150 string players. The original performance of Lulier's *Santa Beatrice d'Este* (1690) had 76 strings (with Corelli leading). On the other hand, the op.6 concertos were performed in the 1690s in the church of S Marcello in Rome with a group of four violins, two violas, one cello and two players on the basso continuo line.[47] Muffat (1701), Quantz and Avison (both 1752) give guidelines for maintaining the right balance in ensembles of varying sizes.

None of the establishments in which Bach was employed maintained a large group of musicians. Prince Leopold in Cöthen employed 15, including a timpanist and a music copyist. (The Margrave of Brandenburg almost certainly had fewer; in the late 1730s there were only six musicians at his court.) By far the largest group ever regularly associated with Bach was the Collegium Musicum in Leipzig; its total membership of singers and instrumentalists seems to have been consistently about 40, a figure mentioned by Telemann, Mattheson and Gesner.[48]

The difficulty of achieving uniformity in bowing, ornamentation and articulation is a recurring theme in the literature of the period. Bremner (1777) took exception to Tartini's idea that violinists should practice bowing the same passage in different ways on the grounds that it would cause untidiness; uniformity depended on a shared acceptance of bowing conventions. Muffat (1698), Quantz (1752), Potter (1762) and others are adamant about this, although, as so often, their protests reveal that their ideals were not understood or shared by all. But many 18th-century parts (including those for works by Bach) specify simultaneously different bowings for the same line in different voices.[49]

Tuning

Hubert le Blanc (1740) imagines Leclair putting the arrogant Harpsichord and Organ in their place by reminding them that they play three-quarters of their thirds out of tune. While it is true that the violin can get closer to pure intonation than any keyboard instrument – where compromises are necessarily made – this is of limited relevance in an ensemble which includes a keyboard instrument. The first steps in adjusting to the temperament of the keyboard instrument is not to tune simply by taking an *a'*. While 18th-century circular temperaments have a number of pure fifths, those that lie between the open strings are almost always tempered. Werckmeister I has C–G–D–A (and B–F♯) a ¼-comma narrow, Kirnberger III has C–G–D–A–E (all the open strings) similarly narrow, and the milder Vallotti temperament (recommended by Tartini) has all of these (plus F–C and E–B) a ⅙-comma narrow. Quantz (1752) notes that violins should tune their fifths a little low (while making it clear that many did not bother to do so); he adds 'it is to be hoped that each person will tune his instrument truly by itself as well as consonantly with the harpsichord'. A practical way of doing this is to tune in fifths while harmonies containing those fifths are played on the keyboard. Mattheson (1739) notes with approval the scrupulous tuning of one Kapellmeister who forbade simultaneous tuning of the string instruments in his ensemble.

2: VIOLS

The viol, although its European history is not in fact longer than the violin's, has a richer share of late Renaissance repertory. The reasons for this may be social: Jambe de Fer (1566), giving the first clear description of the violin, is at pains to point out that it is not an instrument for the well-bred. Thomas Hoby, in his list of desirable accomplishments for a gentleman (appended to his 1561 translation of Castiglione's *Il cortegiano*), includes the playing of the lute, the viol 'and all other instrumentes with freates', a distinction which seems designed to exclude the violin. The result, particularly in England, is a less clearcut break in style and repertory between Renaissance and Baroque. Viol fantasias assimilated Baroque traits. Many of the mannered compositions of Coperario, William Lawes and Jenkins not only combine violins and viols but achieve an extraordinary and typically English blend of contrapuntal earnestness and Baroque flamboyance. By 1676 Mace could still write about matching up a 'chest' of viols although he lamented the changing tastes which were leading to the neglect of this fine music. For all this, Hely's *Compleat Violist* (1699) was written primarily for consort players and, more significantly, Purcell's viol fantasies were written around 1680. Roger North, in the early years of the 18th century, had fresh memories of this kind of playing. The English produced more than just superb consort music. Their development of lyra-viol technique (seen in the solos and duets of Ferrabosco and Thomas Hume) and of division playing made a considerable impact in Europe, particularly in France.

The viol fared least well in Italy. After Monteverdi it was rarely specified, and foreign observers noted its neglect. In 1640 André Maugars, while noting the popularity of the chordally orientated lirone, commented: 'As for the viol, there is no one at present who excels in it, and it is even played very little in Rome'; 20 years later, Thomas Hill wrote from Lucca: 'the organ and the violin they are masters of, but the bass-viol they have not at all in use, and to supply its place they have the bass violin with four strings, and use it as we use the bass viol'.[50] Handel included a concertante bass viol part in *La resurrezione* (Rome, 1708)[51] and in his cantata *Tra le fiamme*, but as a Saxon in Italy his usage stands out as an aberration. The viol was better appreciated in Germany. From Schütz to Bach, the viol had a satisfying role as a solo instrument and participated fully in the rich cantata and Passion repertory. But it is in France, from about 1680 on, that the Baroque viol attained its greatest heights. In 1685, De Machy produced his *Pieces de violle*, proudly claiming that they were 'the first to be published up until now'. A year later, the first of Marin Marais's five books of *Pièces* appeared, and numerous other collections followed. There is also a wealth of chamber music for the instrument.[52]

Characteristic scene of private music making in the 17th century: three singers accompanied by lute and bass viol: engraving, 'The Sense of Hearing' (1635), by Abraham Bosse

The viol, like other string instruments in this period, underwent gradual but significant structural changes. It acquired a soundpost and a bass bar like members of the violin family. The neck, which in Renaissance viols continues the line of the upper edge of the ribs, was set back at an angle. The ..ew sloping neck, replacing the wedge which formerly created the angle between neck and fingerboard, gave the strings greater elevation and allowed for a higher bridge.[53] Thanks, apparently, to Sainte-Colombe, the bass viol in France acquired a 7th string tuned to A' (for information on stringing, see above, p. 47–8).

Technique

BOWING Christopher Simpson's instructions for holding the bow are fundamental; they were plagiarized by Playford (1674) and recommended by Mace (1676). Simpson wrote (1659):

> Hold the Bow betwixt the ends of your Thumb and the two foremost fingers, near to the Nut. The Thumb and first finger fastned on the Stalk; and the second fingers end turned *in* shorter, against the Hairs thereof; by which you may poize and keep up the point of the Bow.

This grip is similar to that used by French viol players; it corresponds, for example, to the explanation given by Loulié (*c*1700). The technique of French Baroque playing clearly builds on that of the 17th-century English masters. Some writers (Mace, J. B. A. Forqueray) advised using the third finger on the hair of the bow in the interests of more subtle control of inflection. A great deal of stress is placed on flexibility of the wrist and arm. Loulié gives five different postures for the wrist, and describes minutely the way in which each is passed through in the making of a single stroke.

The principles of viol bowing run exactly counter to those of the violin family, a natural consequence of the underhand grip. This is recognized in the earliest treatise to consider both families of instruments. The up-bow (or, more literally, 'push bow') is naturally stronger than the down (or 'pull bow'). A number of writers from the late 16th century to the mid-18th give rules designed to produce up-bows in metrically stressed positions. Bars with an uneven number of notes cause most problems. Roland Marais (*c*1740) addresses these in 'The Manner of Playing Minuets on the Bass Viol'. His solutions are mostly obvious – 'there must be only two bow strokes to a bar, two crotchets up-bow and one down-bow' – but his remarks on movements in 6/8 show that underlining stress patterns was not the only consideration in bowing strategy. He recommends slurring quavers which move by step and detaching 'in the same bow-stroke with two little flicks of the wrist' those which do not. He gives a good sense of the way in which melodic contour can be thrown into relief by the bowing. Roland Marais also emphasizes that a bass player accompanying a *pardessus de viole* must match his bowing to the treble line.

According to J. B. A. Forqueray, 'it is the bow that arouses the soul'. While the basic bowing stroke produces a well-articulated, detached sound (Le Blanc speaks of the style of playing *pièces* 'tic-toc with airy strokes'), many more luxuriant kinds of inflection were described and are indicated in the music. Simpson (1659) talks about gracing 'by the bow',

69

as when we play Loud or Soft, according to our fancy, or the humour of the Musick. Again, this Loud or Soft is sometimes express'd in one and the same Note, as when we make it Soft at the *beginning*, and then (as it were) swell or grow louder towards the *middle* or *ending*. Some also affect a Shake or Tremble with the Bow, like the Shaking-Stop of an Organ, but the frequent use thereof is not (in my opinion) much commendable.

The *enflé* is described by Loulié (*c*1700):

[It] begins after the preparation – that is, after the moment of stillness which precedes the wrist movement at the beginning of the stroke; the string must not scratch, but it must be made to sound as quietly as possible at first, and then more and more strongly as the up or down-bow continues.

Marais indicates the *enflé* by an 'e' above or after a note (depending on the effect desired). It has been pointed out by J. A. Sadie that these marks were used (like swell marks in violin music) to emphasize notes on rhythmically weak beats, the highest notes of phrases, and the last portion of suspended notes (when the viol's note becomes dissonant with the bass), and to create musical sighs or sobs within a single beat.[54]

CHORDS Chordal playing, highly developed by exponents of the English lyra viol at the beginning of the 17th century, seemed central to French Baroque composers. De Machy (1685) went so far as to claim that *pièces d'harmonie* best suited the character of the viol and that simple melodic playing 'should be compared to a person who could play the harpsichord or organ perfectly with one hand: this simple playing might be attractive, but it could hardly be called harpsichord or organ playing'. Rousseau, however, took strong exception to this and vigorously defended the *jeu de melodie*. (Marais, in his 'Avertissement' to the *Pièces à une et à deux violes*, 1686, claims to provide for both kinds of taste.) Simpson and Mace both describe the bowing of chords; they emphasize that the lowest string should be sounded properly before the bow is moved across the other strings.

The basic approach to viol fingering allows for maximum resonance in chords or *batteries* (broken-chord figurations). The left-hand position is like that used on a lute (and quite unlike the position for a violin). The thumb stays at the back of the neck. Simpson and the older French players (like Hotman) positioned the thumb opposite the index finger, but the followers of Sainte-Colombe placed it opposite the middle finger to achieve greater flexibility in the use of extensions. The concept of holds or *tenues* is of prime importance. Fingers are to be left in place until needed for another note; this was partly a matter of economy (what Rousseau calls *tenues de bien séances*) and partly a way of achieving maximum resonance (*tenues d'harmonie*). Simpson (1659) sums up their function:

When you set any Finger down, hold it on there; and play the following Notes with other Fingers, until some occasion require the taking it off. This is done as well for better order of Fingering, that the Fingers may pass smoothly from Note to Note, without lifting them too far from the Strings, as also to continue the Sound of a Note when the Bow hath left it. Instances of these Holds (for so they are called) you have, where you see such a Stroke as this [Simpson's 'hold' sign] drawn from One to some other distant Note unto which you must hold it.

French sources use a square bracket to indicate the notes affected by a *tenue*.

Techniques for shifting and playing above the frets were developed. English virtuosos in the 17th century had moved above the seventh fret, but in France this development occurred later. Marais used the *petit manche* from 1717 on, and Forqueray used it extensively.

ORNAMENTS Apart from the division techniques so fully elaborated by Simpson, English and French viol sources describe and use a wide of range of ornaments. Many of these correspond to those found in keyboard sources, but there are some, particularly the various kinds of vibrato, that are of special interest to string players. As early as 1631, Pierre Trichet recommended the viol for its expressive vibrato:

> Also, it must be said that, after fine human voices, there is nothing so captivating as the affecting vibrato [*les mignards tremblements*] which can be produced on the fingerboard, and nothing so ravishing as the sobbing bow strokes [*les coups mourants de l'archet*].

The two-finger vibrato was described by Simpson (who calls it a 'close shake', the name given to ordinary violin vibrato). In France, this effect was known as *pincé, aspiration, flatement* or *flatté*. The various names given to one-finger vibrato – *langeur* (Loulié) or *plainte* (De Machy and Marais) – suggest its expressive potential. (Terminology, though, can be confusing: Rousseau's *plainte* is Marais's *coulé* and Loulié's *coulé* is Rousseau's *chute*.) Rousseau encouraged the use of one-finger vibrato wherever possible; De Machy, however, claimed that 'some people, speaking metaphorically, call it miaowing' (viol players, like violinists, were apparently not unanimous in feeling that vibrato could enhance a performance). There were other special viol ornaments: Marais's *coulé du doigt*, for example, involves sliding the finger from one note to the next, usually a semitone higher.[55]

The pardessus

The *pardessus de viole* was normally tuned $g–c'–e'–a'–d''–g''$ or $g–c'–f'–a'–d''–g''$ (a fourth higher than the treble consort instrument), although it sometimes lacked the bottom string. It enjoyed considerable popularity both as a solo instrument and as a member of chamber ensembles. Caix d'Hervelois's *Sixième livre* (1750) is devoted to the instrument; Dollé, Heudelinne, Marc, Barrière and Blainville also composed solos and duets for it. Rousseau has a chapter dealing with the *dessus* in his *Traité* (1687), and in the 18th century it was the subject of treatises, by (inevitably!) Corrette (1748), and Brijon (1766). Rousseau (1687), comparing the violin and the *dessus*, presents the latter as an instrument of great delicacy: 'Take care ... not to violate the character of the instrument, which shouldn't be treated like a violin whose role is to animate; rather, the *Dessus de Viole* is made to gratify'.

3: PLUCKED STRINGS

The lute family

The sense of continuity with a noble past is even stronger with the lute than with the viol. Lutes made in Bologna in the 16th century were sought after and imitated (albeit modified) throughout the Baroque era. Nevertheless, a number of developments with far-reaching implications gained momentum in the early 17th century. A movement away from the Renaissance tuning (G–c–f–a–d'–g') can first be seen in Antoine Francisque's *Le trésor d'Orphée* of 1600; by 1636 Mersenne could claim that 'it would take a volume of more than a hundred pages' to describe all the tunings currently in use. The old tuning in fourths gives primacy to linear considerations; the new tunings (like lyra viol tunings) were harmonically conceived. Mace (1676), in justifying a personal preference for the 'Flat French tuning', emphasizes the importance of achieving 'fullness of parts' in all keys:

> That Tuning upon any Instrument, which allows the Artist most Scope, Freedom, and Variety; with most Ease, and Familiarity, to Express his Conceptions most Fully, and Compleatly; without Limitation, or Restraint; throughout all the Keys; must needs be accounted the Best Tuning.

The 'New' D minor tuning (A–d–f–a–d'–f', also known as 'B-flat') became standard; together with the D major or 'B-sharp' (A–d–$f\sharp$–a–d'–$f'\sharp$) tuning, it is described in the Burwell Lute Tutor as 'most ordinary'. (In all tunings, the courses lower than the six indicated by the staff used in lute tablature move down in steps which are chromatically adjusted to suit the basic tonality.) The new, tonally orientated tunings go hand in hand with a new style in lute composition. The harmonically saturated *pièces* by René Mésangeau, the Gaultiers, Charles Mouton, Jacques Gallot and their contemporaries belong in quite a different world from, say, Dowland's fantasias. And the distinctive arpeggiation of their *style brisé* had an influence beyond the lute itself.[56]

Quite radical structural change took place in the lute, much of it beginning in the 16th century. The neck was lengthened and the number of frets tied around the fingerboard increased from seven or eight. Although Dowland (1610) says that those lutes 'which are most received and admired' have ten frets on the fingerboard, the Burwell tutor (c1670) and Mace (1676) give nine as the standard number. (Three more frets were glued to the belly of the instrument.) An expansion in the number of courses of strings accelerated in the early Baroque period.[57] In 1603 Thomas Robinson envisaged his readers having lutes of '14, 16, or 18 strings' (i.e. up to nine courses); by the 1630s, the 11-course lute had become established. In the next phase, a twelfth course was added, and on these instruments the lowest four were accommodated in a second peg box; each course was of a different length and passed over its own nut. This rather complex disposition became obsolete with the introduction of covered gut bass strings. The English persisted with the 12-course lute after its rejection in France; in the Talbot manuscript it is described as the 'English two-headed lute' while the 11-course instrument is called 'the French lute'.[58] The Burwell Lute Tutor notes that the French masters 'are returned to their old fashion, keeping only the small eleventh' and describes the 12-course instrument still espoused by the English as 'a bastard instrument between a lute and a theorbo'.[59] On 11-course instruments all but the bottom three courses could be stopped (although French Music never seems to need stopped notes on the eighth course).

By the beginning of the 18th century, 13-course instruments (often converted from 11-course) were being made in Germany. The strings were all accommodated within a single head but with the lowest two courses often passing over a 'rider' at the side of the pegbox which gave them an extra 5 cm or so in length. While such an instrument can give a good account of, say, the works of Silvius Leopold Weiss, it cannot easily cope with the solo lute works by Bach. Some of these, anyway, may have been intended for the lute-harpsichord.[60] In Italy, the new tunings were never adopted, but large 13- or 14-course lutes (with six or seven unstopped diapasons) appeared early in the 17th century; these instruments were variously called 'liuto attiorbato', 'arciliuto' or simply 'liuto'.

The larger members of the lute family are all, broadly speaking, products of the Baroque era. The earliest, the chitarrone, emerged in the 1580s as an accompanying instrument for the Florentine camerata. Chitarrone, theorbo and archlute have significant solo repertory, but they are first and foremost continuo instruments (and virtually all theorbo treatises focus on this).[61] For Mace this function was essentially what distinguished the theorbo from the 'Old English Lute' (the two-headed 12-course instrument). There is much inconsistency in the terminology used for larger members of the lute family and wide variation in their disposition, but the thing which separated the theorbo and chitarrone from the rest is that the top (in England), or top two courses (in Italy and France) were tuned down an octave, making the second or third course the highest in pitch. The terms 'chitarrone' (not used after the mid-17th century) and 'tiorba' (which, with its national variants, endured longer) both described instruments with 13 or 14 courses (and these could be either single or double, or a mixture of double stopped courses and single diapasons). In the early 17th century, metal stringing was sometimes used. The seven stopped courses are accommodated in a pegbox only slightly angled back from the neck, which supports an extension (sometimes spectacularly long)[62] leading up to a second pegbox. The upper six courses retained the older lute tuning, either in G or a tone higher. Baron (1727) mentions that in 18th-century Germany the D minor lute tuning was being used for the theorbo to enable players to change easily from one instrument to the other.

By the late 17th century, the term 'archlute' had come to designate a 14-course instrument tuned in G but without the theorbo's characteristic lowering of the top course(s). Robert Spencer points out that the archlute became a preferred continuo instrument, since it could realize late 17th-century bass lines which rose above the range for which the theorbo could provide harmony. Archlutes also had a shorter string length than theorboes (yet another benefit, it seems, of covered strings) and so allowed for greater left-hand mobility.

Lute technique

Baroque sources are in broad agreement about the position of the right hand. The little finger must be placed on the belly near or just behind the bridge, since this '*steadies the Hand,* and gives a *Certainty* to the *Grasp*' (Mace, 1676). It must not be lifted except momentarily in order to reach bass notes with the thumb. The Burwell Lute Tutor (*c*1678), thought to encapsulate the teaching of the Gaultiers,[63] describes the right-hand position in some detail:

> Your hand must lie upon the belly of the lute with the little finger only, which must be as it were glued unto it; and keep the thumb as much as one can leaning upon the bass. It must be before all the rest of the hand, marching as the captain of the fingers. That hand must be rising in the middle in the form of an arch, that you may not smother the strings.

Piccinini (1623) had recommended varying the distance of the hand from the bridge to achieve different tone colours, a point elaborated a century later by Baron (who nevertheless treats the little finger on the belly as vital).

Plucking with fingernails was mostly disapproved of. Piccinini (1623) is remarkable for his advocacy of nails which he said should be 'a little long, in front of the flesh, but not much, and oval in shape'. The Burwell Lute Tutor adamantly rejects the practice. Mace (1676) disapproves too, but admits that some players thought it the 'the Best way of Play'. He concedes that where a penetrating quality is needed, nails might be tolerated:

> I confess in a *Consort*, it might do well enough, where the *Mellowness* (which is the most *Excellent satisfaction* from a *Lute*) is *lost* in the *Crowd*; but *Alone*, I could never receive so *good Content* from the *Nail*, as from the *Flesh*: However (*This* being my *Opinion*) let *Others* do, as seems *Best to Themselves*.

Five years later, John Dryden satirized the playing of Richard Flecknoe for his use of nails:

> My warbling Lute, the Lute I whilom strung
> When to King *John* of *Portugal* I sung,
>   Was but the prelude to that glorious day,
>   When thou on silver *Thames* did'st cut thy way . . .
> Methinks I see the new *Arion* Sail,
> The Lute still trembling underneath thy nail.
>   As thy well sharpned thumb from Shore to Shore
>   The Treble squeaks for fear, the Bases roar.[64]

In 1723 Weiss made the interesting observation that, while the lute was normally played with the flesh, the theorbo and chitarrone were played with nails which 'produce in close proximity a coarse, harsh sound'.[65] As with Mace, there is a link suggested here between an appropriate brilliance of tone and musical function.

The old fingering principle of using a downward thumb stroke on accented beats and an upward index-finger stroke for unaccented beats seems to have persisted in runs until the later 17th century. The rules for this (from Robinson, 1603, on) parallel 17th-century explanations of the rule of the down-bow for violinists. The Burwell tutor explains that the third (ring) finger was no longer used for plucking (although in late Baroque and *galant* music it was to come into its own again). The traditional way of playing chords involved using the thumb for the bass note and the other fingers (in an upward stroke) for the upper notes. Mersenne (1636–7) describes chords played in one downward stroke of the thumb, or with all but the top note played by the thumb. These 'raking' methods were to become central in the broken-chord style of the French Baroque, normally, however, with the thumb playing the bass note and the index finger stroking the other strings.

Mace (1676) conveys a vivid sense of an old technique giving way to a more fashionable one:

> You must know, That the *Explanation of This last Example*, [in which chords are played with thumb and three fingers] ... is not the way, which is much used, in these days, (although I use It often, as you may do, upon occasion;) but the Fashionable way of Playing them, (now us'd) is *much more easie*; namely, only to hit the *Bass* with your *Thumb*, and *Rake* down all the other 3 *Letters*, with your *Fore-finger*, at the same time; and is the *General way* of *Playing* all other Full, or Fuller Stops.

Baron (1727) found this method of playing distinctively French and distasteful: 'They brush chords with their fingers as if they were scratching'. He saw the lute's capacity for producing a diminuendo within a chord as quite special:

> The lutenist can strike a chord very strongly and allow the tone to die away imperceptibly while arpeggiating, so that it becomes first louder, then softer, which cannot be done on the harpsichord without great affectation, since the player must hop from one keyboard to the other.

Left-hand lute technique has much in common with viol fingering. The concept of holds was outlined by Judenkünig in the early 16th century and is stressed by Baroque writers. Besard (1603) presents diminutions as an exception to the rule (since sustaining individual notes would blur passagework). He and Robinson (1603) describe *barrée* technique (although they do not use this term); in this, the index finger is made to lie across an entire fret, functioning like a *capo tasto* in the fingering of certain chords.

Ornamentation is a preoccupation of nearly all lute tutors; Diana Poulton remarks that 'tablatures in which the [ornament] signs appear suggest that probably more graces were added than in music for any other instrument'.[66] This is partly a consequence of the lute's limited sustaining power: 'a relish will help, both to grace it, and also it helps to continue the sound of the note his full time' (Robinson, 1603). Apart from descriptions in instruction manuals, a number of volumes of lute music are prefaced by explanations of ornaments.[67]

The guitar

The Baroque guitar is an important but still somewhat overlooked instrument.[68] It has a rich solo repertory and was a favoured continuo instrument. In England, in the late 17th century, its popularity rivalled that of the lute. Makers of the first rank, including Stradivari, turned their attention to the guitar, and few instrumentalists could claim to have been in such demand as Francesco Corbetta (c1615–1681), who was patronized by the Duke of Mantua, the Archduke Leopold Wilhelm in Brussels, Louis XIV in Paris and Charles II in London.[69]

The standard guitar had five courses, although the smaller four-course treble instrument (called the *chitarrino* by the Italians) was still used, particularly at the beginning of the period. The Baroque guitar's most characteristic feature is its re-entrant tunings, most typically *a–d'–g–b–e'* (all double courses except for the highest which could be a single string).

Re-entrant tuning ensures that the guitar has a distinctive literature; it facilitates such devices as the *campanelas* cultivated by Gaspar Sanz (*c*1640–*c*1710), where bell-like scale passages exploit the resonance of the five open notes which all lie within a major 6th. The fourth and sometimes the fifth course often had octave *bourdons* but then, according to Sanz (1674), 'there is not the least doubt that for playing with much delicacy, and to balance the voices, and to have variety in the *campanelas*, it is better to match each *bourdon* with a thin string'.[70] Where octave tunings were used, it was normal (according to Ruiz de Ribayaz, 1677) to place the higher-pitched string in each course uppermost so that it could be struck alone.

There are two basic right-hand styles. That known in Spain as *punteado* and in Italy as *pizzicato* catered for melodic playing. The *rasgueado* or *battente* (strumming) style is most characteristic of the guitar and brings with it a whole range of distinctive ornaments (such as the repeated-note *trillo* and *repicco*). The distinction is nicely summed up by Ruiz de Ribayaz (1677):

> One strums all at once with the right hand in playing *rasgueado*, strumming, be it downwards or upwards, with all the fingers [of the right hand] all the strings of the guitar ... and in playing *punteado* one must pluck the strings with the right hand, using the three fingers of it, which are the thumb, the index and the middle, although sometimes when a full chord is intabulated on four lines, one also uses the ring finger, but no more.[71]

Tablatures, like those for the lute, are associated with the *punteado* style; a special kind of tablature, known as *alfabeto*, was used for *rasgueado* playing (although lute-style tablature was adapted for this in France towards the end of the 17th century). *Alfabeto* has letters to indicate complete chords, and vertical lines above and below a continuous horizontal line to show upward and downward strokes of the hand; it could be used in conjunction with ordinary tablature.[72]

It is almost inevitable, in writing about performance practice, that early instrumental treatises, as direct written instruction, will assume a significance they may not always deserve. How much better it would be if the real giants of the Baroque period could speak for themelves rather than leaving us to work out what we can from their contemporaries who, all too often, were musicians of the second rank. Musical judgment might be stimulated by hints and puzzles retrieved from the past, but it cannot be abdicated in favour of a set of rules. The obviousness of the gaps and contradictions in 17th- and 18th-century performance practice sources should make that clear. There is a danger that a new and equally stifling orthodoxy might replace the old. Mahler's maxim, 'tradition is laziness', or Berg's that we should approach classical music as if it were new (and new music as if it were classical), seem apt in this context as exhortations never simply to accept conventions associated with performing particular works or playing in a certain style. But a chapter on Baroque string playing could perhaps leave the last word to Geminiani (1751):

> I would besides advise, as well the Composer as the Performer, who is ambitious to inspire his Audience, to be first inspired himself; which he

cannot fail to be if he chuses a Work of Genius, if he makes himself thoroughly acquainted with all its Beauties; and if while his Imagination is warm and glowing he pours the same exalted Spirit into his own Performance.

Notes

[1] *Roger North on Music*, ed. J. Wilson (London, 1959), 194.
[2] See for example D. Boyden, *The History of Violin Playing from its Origins to 1761* (London, 1965), 361.
[3] It has been suggested that Geminiani wrote the violin treatise years before its publication, but this seems most unlikely since the 1751 text can be seen evolving in his treatises of the late 1740s.
[4] *A General History of the Science and Practice of Music* (London, 1776/R1963), ii, 847.
[5] Boyden, *History of Violin Playing* [*HVP*], 361n.
[6] Translation by Howey: see list of sources. Some other English translations noted in the list of sources are used in this chapter without further acknowledgment. I am grateful to Dr Laurie Bauer for translating Berlin (1744).
[7] Prinner was, however, recommended by Schmelzer for a post vacated by Biber; see 'Prinner', *Grove 6*.
[8] See R. Donington, 'James Talbot's Manuscript – Part II' [on bowed string instruments], *GSJ*, iii (1950), 27.
[9] See Boyden, *HVP*, 195ff. For a detailed account of the distinctive qualities of individual makers' work, see Boyden, ibid, 31–42, 107–11, 194–202 and 317–19, and the entries on makers in *Grove MI*.
[10] See Boyden, *HVP*, 35.
[11] Both of these instruments had alternative names; Talbot calls the violone da gamba a 'double bass viol' and it was known in Germany as a 'Gross Bassgeige'. The violone del contrabasso was also called 'contrabasso di viola' (Monteverdi, *Orfeo*) and 'Gross Bass Viole de Gambe' (Praetorius). The violone da gamba was often used as a continuo instrument. The clearest account of this vexed area is given in two articles by Stephen Bonta: 'From Violone to Violoncello: a Question of Strings?', *JAMIS*, iii (1977), 64, and 'Terminology for the Bass Violin in 17th-century Italy', *JAMIS*, iv (1978), 5. See also Francis Baines, 'What exactly is a Violone?', *EM*, v (1977), 173.
[12] See J. W. Finson, 'The Violone in Bach's Brandenburg Concerti', *GSJ*, xxix (1976), 105.
[13] See E. Halfpenny, 'The Double Bass', *Musical Instruments through the Ages*, ed. A. Baines (Harmondsworth, 1969), 154.
[14] Corrette (1773) describes a fingerboard with frets, but adds a footnote acknowledging that some instruments lack them.
[15] See D. Boyden, 'Monteverdi's *Violini Piccoli alla Francese* and *Viole da Brazzo*', *AnnM*, vi (1958–63), 387.
[16] For information about strings see E. Segermann, 'Strings of the Violin Family – Summary of Historical Information', *FoMRHI Quarterly* (Oct 1982), and, for a persuasive contrary view of the meaning of 'catline', S. Bonta, 'Catline Strings Revisited', *JAMIS* xiv (1988), 38. See also Bonta, 'From Violone to Violoncello'. Dowland (1610), Mace (1676) and the Talbot manuscript give (limited) information on gut string types.
[17] This advertisement, from *Introduction to the Skill of Music*, is quoted in full by M. Lowe, 'The Historical Development of the Lute in the 17th Century', *GSJ*, xxix (1976), 24.
[18] See Segermann, op cit.
[19] String breakages must anyway have been much more routine than we now expect. This is certainly suggested by Aphra Behn's witty picture of violinists tuning; in 2.ii of *The Lucky Chance* (1686), she has Sir Feeble complaining, 'I hate that same twang, twang, twang, fum, fum, tweedle, tweedle, tweedle, then screw go the pins, till a man's teeth are on edge, then 'snap' says a small gut, and there we are at a loss again'.
[20] Quoted by A. Mendel, 'On the Pitches in Use in Bach's Time', *MQ*, xli (1955), 471.
[21] See Boyden, *HVP*, 114.
[22] A bow with the date 1694 etched on to the frog has a screw mechanism; see Boyden, *HVP*, 112–14.
[23] See Boyden, *HVP*, 249.
[24] See Boyden, *HVP*, 164ff, and I. Horsley, 'The Solo Ricercar in Diminution Manuals: New Light on Early Wind and String Techniques', *AcM*, xxxiii (1961), 29.

[25] This kind of effect is described by A. L. Witherell, *Louis Pécour's 1700 'Recueil de dances'* (Ann Arbor, 1983), chap. 10.

[26] *Roger North on Music*, 18.

[27] See P. Walls, ' "Ill Compliments and Arbitrary Taste?": Geminiani's Directions to Performers', *EM*, xiv (1986), 221.

[28] *Remarks on Mr Avison's Essay on Musical Expression* (London, 1753), 26.

[29] The *Mercure de France* (June 1738) credited him with being the first Frenchman to perfect this technique. A correction was published in August saying that the honours must be shared with Duval, Anet and Senaillé.

[30] P. Walls, 'Violin Fingering in the 18th Century', *EM*, xii (1984), 300, cites some of these and deals further with the issue of holding the violin and changing positions.

[31] See Charles Medlam's letter, *EM*, vii (1979), 561.

[32] See the frontispiece to his *Sonate accademiche* (London and Florence [1744]), reproduced in Boyden, *HVP*, pl. 30, and in Walls, 'Violin Fingering'.

[33] See R. Hickman, 'The Censored Publications of *The Art of Playing on the Violin*, or Geminiani Unshaken,' *EM*, xi (1983), 73. Significantly, he also omitted Geminiani's sentence (quoted above) about leaving the thumb behind in upper positions; this suggests that he thought in terms of a different way of holding the violin, one in which vibrato would no longer be self-regulating.

[34] This occurs in the section on lute ornamentation, but he provides a cross-reference to it when discussing violin graces.

[35] In *Madrigali guerrieri et amorosi* (1638).

[36] J.-J. Cassenéa de Mondonville, *Pièces de clavecin en sonates* (Paris, 1734); J.-B. Despuits, *Sonates pour un clavecin et une viele* op. 3 (n.d.).

[37] See D. Boyden, 'The Corelli "Solo" Sonatas and their Ornamental Additions by Corelli, Geminiani, Dubourg, Tartini and the "Walsh anonymous" ', *Musica antiqua Europae orientalis III: Bydgoszcz 1972*, 591, and 'Corelli's Solo Violin Sonatas "grac'd" by Dubourg', *Festschrift Jens Peter Larsen* (Copenhagen, 1972), 113; and H. J. Marx, 'Some Unknown Embellishments of Corelli's Violin Sonatas', *MQ*, lxi (1975), 65.

[38] See the preface to the edition by Max Seiffert (Kassel, 1968).

[39] From the preface to *Six Solos, Three for a Violoncello and Three for a Tenor* op. 2 (1770).

[40] See O. Jander, 'Concerto Grosso Instrumentation in Rome in the 1660's and 1670's, *JAMS*, xxi (1968), 168.

[41] *The Bach Reader* ed. H. T. David and A. Mendel, (New York, 1945, 2/1966), 277.

[42] *Music, Men and Manners in France and Italy* (1770/R1974) 70.

[43] J. D. Heinichen, *Der Generalbass in der Komposition* (Dresden, 1728); G. P. Telemann, *Unterricht im Generalbass-spielen auf der Orgel* (Hamburg, 1733). On the practice of using (or omitting) a bowed string instrument on continuo lines in the Baroque period, see Nigel Fortune, 'Continuo Instruments in Italian Monodies', *GSJ*, vi (1953), 10, and Graham Dixon, 'Continuo Scoring in the Early Baroque: the Role of the Bowed-Bass Instruments', *Chelys*, xv (1986), 38.

[44] See F. Baines, 'What Exactly is a Violone?', 174.

[45] Ibid, 175.

[46] *Short Treatise on Harmony* (1731), quoted in *Roger North on Music*, 153.

[47] The S Marcello records show that in the 1660s works by Stradella would have been performed with single players on ripieno and concertino parts. The practice of using more than one player for ripieno parts was introduced in the 1670s. See S. Harris, 'Lully, Corelli, Muffat and the 18th-century String Body', *ML*, liv (1973), 197. For further information on Roman orchestras see Jander, 'Concerto grosso Instrumentation in Rome'; and S. H. Hansell, 'Orchestral Practice at the Court of Cardinal Pietro Ottoboni', *JAMS*, xix (1966), 398. On Handel's opera orchestras see Winton Dean, 'A French Traveller's View of Handel's Operas', *ML*, lv (1974), 172. A. Carse, *The Orchestra in the 18th Century* (Cambridge, 1940), gives tables of various orchestral sizes, as do E. Selfridge-Field and N. Zaslaw, 'Orchestra', *Grove MI*.

[48] On the meaning of the word 'orchestra' to Bach see R. L. Marshall, 'Bach's *Orchestre*', *EM*, xiii (1985), 176. Two recent articles, both in *EM*, xvii (1989), throw further light on the size of instrumental ensembles associated with Bach: H. J. Schulze, 'Johann Sebastian Bach's Orchestra: Some Unanswered Questions, 13–16, and O. Landmann, 'The Dresden Hofkapelle during the Lifetime of Johann Sebastian Bach', 17–30.

[49] For examples of this in Geminiani's later works see P. Walls, ' "Ill Compliments" '.

[50] Quoted in W. H., A. F. and A. E. Hill: *Antonio Stradivari: his Life and Works, 1644–1737* (London, 1902/R1963), 110n.

[51] See J. A. Sadie, 'Handel: in Pursuit of the Viol', *Chelys*, xiv (1985), 3.

[52] See J. A. Sadie, *The Bass Viol in French Baroque Chamber Music* (Ann Arbor, 1980).

[53] See 'Viol', *Grove MI*, for a diagram illustrating the differences between Renaissance and Baroque viols. J. B. A. Forqueray still countenanced the use of a wedge in 1769 as a way of reducing the distance between strings and fingerboard.

[54] J. A. Sadie, *The Bass Viol*, 107.

[55] A helpful description of viol ornaments is given by John Hsu in *A Handbook of French Baroque Viol Technique* (New York, 1981).

[56] See D. Ledbetter, *Harpsichord and Lute Music in 17th-century France* (London, 1987).

[57] There are two excellent articles describing lutes in the Baroque period: M. Lowe, 'The Historical Development of the Lute in the 17th Century', *GSJ*, xxix (1976), 11, and R. Spencer, 'Chitarrone, Theorbo and Archlute', *EM*, iv (1976), 407. N. North, *Continuo Playing on the Lute, Archlute and Theorbo*, (London, 1987), prefaces his instructions on figured-bass realisation with helpful descriptions of instruments and tunings.

[58] See M. Prynne: 'James Talbot's Manuscript: IV. Plucked Strings – The Lute Family', *GSJ*, xiv (1961), 52.

[59] In quoting from this tutor, I use Thurston Dart's transcription, *GSJ*, xi (1958), 3.

[60] See Lowe, 'The Historical Development', 19, and U. Henning, 'The Most Beautiful among the Claviers', *EM*, x (1982), 482ff.

[61] See for example Fleury (1660), Bartolotti (1669), Delair (1690) and Dalla Casa (*c*1770).

[62] Praetorius (1619) illustrates a 'Chitarron' with an overall length of almost 200 cm; the chitarrone by Magno Dieffopruchar (Venice, 1608) in the Royal College of Music, London, is 195 cm. Baron (1727) mentions Roman theorboes which were 'also called chitarrones' as being 'seven feet, two inches in length'.

[63] See T. Dart, 'Miss Mary Burwell's Instruction Book for the Lute', *GSJ*, xi (1958), 6, and Robert Spencer's introduction to the facsimile edition of *The Burwell Lute Tutor* (1974).

[64] *MacFlecknoe*, 11.35ff. See Kathryn Walls, 'John Dryden on Lute Playing', *EM*, iv (1976), 491.

[65] Quoted by D. A. Smith, 'Baron and Weiss contra Mattheson: in Defense of the Lute', *Journal of the American Lute Society*, vi (1973), 52.

[66] 'Lute', *Grove MI*.

[67] *Livre de tablature des pièces de Mr Gaultier Sr de Neves et de Mr Gaultier son cousin*, ed. D. Gaultier (Paris, 1762/*R*1978); and Jacques Gallot, *Pièces de luth composées sur différens modes* (Paris, *c*1670).

[68] James Tyler's *The Early Guitar: a History and Handbook* (London, 1980) is an invaluable introduction to the instrument and its technique and repertory.

[69] For a detailed study of Corbetta and a transcription of his works see Richard T. Pinnell, *Francesco Corbetta and the Baroque Guitar* (Ann Arbor, 1980).

[70] Quoted by N. D. Pennington, *The Baroque Guitar in Spain* (Ann Arbor, 1981), 51.

[71] Translation from Robert Strizich, 'A Spanish Guitar Tutor: Ruiz de Ribayaz's *Luz y norte musical* (1677)', *Journal of the Lute Society of America*, v (1972); cited by Pennington, *The Baroque Guitar*, 59.

[72] It is beyond the scope of this essay to deal with two classes of instruments: those that were relatively rare (the *chitarriglia*, for example) and those that served almost exclusively a popular clientele (such as the cittern).

I am grateful to Julie Anne Sadie and Robert Oliver for reading through and making suggestions about the section on viols, and to William Bower for similar help with the section on plucked strings.

CHAPTER IV

Woodwind and Brass

ALAN LUMSDEN

Most of the information about Baroque performance practice for wind players relates primarily to the flute, although little distinction was made between the various wind instruments as regards articulation, ornamentation and musical expression. Baroque writers generally agree that the strength of articulation varies from instrument to instrument, but this is a difference of degree not of kind. In his *Compendio musicale* of 1677, Bismantova gives 'de' and 'der' for the recorder as opposed to 'te' and 'ter' for the cornett, but he also says that the cornettist should start on the recorder to acquire the basic articulation and fingering; thus the difference between the two tonguings was obviously a natural and almost instinctive hardening or softening. 30 years later, Hotteterre states that the flute is articulated very gently, the recorder slightly more than the flute and the oboe stronger still, while Quantz, in 1752, says that oboe and bassoon tonguing is very similar to that of the flute. As one might expect, the trumpet methods of Bendinelli (1614) and Fantini (1638) give the hardest articulation of all – Arbeau had made the point that a hard articulation is 'plus convenable au son guerrier'.

By and large, 17th-century indications of tonguing follow the principles of the previous century. Longer notes are articulated 'te' or 'de' while shorter notes are articulated by the alternation of a more forward with a less forward tongue – combinations such as 'tere', 'dere' and 'lere'. By the 1630s Mersenne and Fantini give examples of true slurred pairs (ex.1a and *b*

Ex.1 (a)   (b)

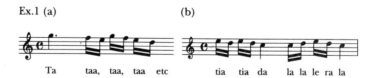

Ta   taa, taa, taa etc   tia   tia da   la la le ra la

respectively), although both regard tonguing as the norm. Fantini gives examples of the *trillo* – the rapid reiteration of the same pitch, a favourite vocal ornament of the early 17th century – saying that it is performed with the strength of the chest and articulated with the throat ('il trillo và fatto a forza di petto, a battuto con la gola'), while the *groppo*, or measured trill, is executed with a pointed tongue. Mersenne suggests the possibility of a slurred trill 'afin que la cadence en soit plus douce & plus amiable, & qu'elle

80

imite la voix & la plus excellente méthode de bien chanter' but stresses that it is the articulation which distinguishes the masters from the apprentices. While the syllabic underlay of Mersenne's examples is not always clear, it would seem that the alternation of syllables for dotted rhythms puts the weaker articulation on the beat and the strong articulation on the short note – the normal practice in French music of the early part of the next century (ex.2). One cannot talk of a 'French' style of articulation on the basis of this

Ex.2

Ta   ta ra   ra ra   ta   ta ra   ra ra

isolated example, but it is interesting that the only other significant information on the entire topic from the 17th century, Bismantova's *Compendio musicale*, gives no such 'French' articulation – but then neither are there any dotted-note figures in the musical examples. One example from Bismantova shows that long slurs in the notation were performed as a succession of slurred pairs (ex.3).

Ex.3

de   de, a, de, a, de, a, de

The French style of articulation in the early 18th century, as formulated by Freillon-Poncein and Hotteterre, is closely linked to the practice of *notes inégales*.[1] Generally speaking, the slower note values alternate 'tu' and 'ru' with the 'tu' on the main beat, but the faster note values, where dotted notes are written or implied, are grouped across the beat. Because no passage may start with 'ru', there are often two 'tus' in succession (ex.4 is by Hotteterre).

Ex.4

tu tu ru tu ru   tu tu   ru tu ru tu tu   tu   tu

By about 1735 this alternation of 'tu' and 'ru' was considered obsolete by Corrette, but Quantz, who was greatly influenced by the French school of flute playing, states that: ' 'Tiri' is indispensable for dotted notes; it expresses them in a much sharper and livelier fashion than is possible with any other kind of tonguing' (ex.5). According to Quantz, this kind of tongue stroke is 'most useful in passage-work of moderate quickness, especially since the quickest notes in them must always be played a little unequally'. For fast

81

Ex.5

ti ti ri   ti ri   ti ri   ti ri   ti ri   ti ri   ti ri   ti   ri

(and even) passage-work he recommends 'did'll', a form of double tonguing similar to the *lingua riversa* of the late Renaissance Italian writers. As he says: 'In its use 'did'll' is the opposite of 'tiri''. In 'tiri' the accent lies on the second syllable, in 'did'll' it falls on the first, and always comes on the note on the downbeat, the so-called 'good note'. 'Ti' is substituted for clarity after a rest, when notes of the same pitch are repeated or when large leaps occur (ex.6 *a*, *b* and *c*). This form of double tonguing persisted throughout the rest

Ex.6 (a)   (b)

ti tid'll did'll did'll di   ti ti tid 'll di ti tid 'll di

(c)

did 'll di ti tid 'll di ti tid 'll di ti tid 'll di ti

of the century; it is recommended by Mahaut (1759), Granom (1766) where it becomes 'toot-tle', Tromlitz (1791) where it becomes 'ta-d'll' and Gunn (1792) where it is variously 'diddle', 'teddy' or 'tiddy'. It should be emphasized that the 'modern' form of double tonguing, which consists of the alternation of tongue and throat ('te-che' or 'de-ghe') was a 19th-century revival of a practice known from as early as Ganassi in 1535. Its use in Baroque music should be confined to the rhythmic reiteration of the same pitch characteristic of music for brass instruments.

The significance of the various vowels used by wind players is still imperfectly understood. Although Ganassi (1535) gives examples using all the vowels, 16th- and 17th-century writers used mostly 'e' and occasionally 'a', while in the 18th century 'u' or 'i' are generally preferred. This may be related to the narrower bore of the later wind instruments, as Erig suggests, or it may be linguistic, with the Italians preferring 'e', the Germans 'i' and the French 'u'. It is also related to mouth resonance and embouchure, which varies not just between instruments but also between different registers of the same instrument. Both Bendinelli and Fantini mostly use 'i' on written *e″*, a note which needs to be lipped up on the natural trumpet, while long notes, particularly low ones, are mostly 'a'.

We have seen that the rather sparse information from the 17th century indicates that slurring in pairs was exceptional and was used almost in the nature of an ornament. This usage was also recommended by Hotteterre, who says: 'We must now pay attention to the *coulez*. These are two or several notes taken with the same tongue stroke; which is marked above or below the notes by slurs' (ex.7). However, there is much French music of the first half of the 18th century that contains many slurred pairs of notes to be played slightly unequally. This practice, called 'lourer' from the bagpipe known as a loure, was an attempt to imitate the drone instruments, such as the musette,

Ex.7

so popular in the Arcadian atmosphere of the court. (The practice of *notes inégales* itself may be partly due to the fact that the only way the musette could define the beat was by stressing and slightly lengthening it.) In 1728 the Abbé Démoz de la Salle described it as follows: 'Lourer is to express the notes slurred in pairs by slurring, caressing and rolling them in such a way that the notes are continuous, joined and connected (as in those playful airs for musettes, cornamuses and vielles), while perceptibly marking the first of each pair'.[2]

Longer slurs were performed equally so that the contrast between slurring and tonguing was one of rhythm as well as of articulation, although slurring in pairs was far more common in the early part of the century. Corrette gives examples of three- and four-note slurs but says that in still longer slurs the notes are articulated, the slur indicating that they are all to be played in the same breath.[3]

Fantini (1638) states:

> It must also be pointed out that wherever notes of one, of two or of four beats' length are found, they should be held in a singing fashion, by starting softly, making a crescendo until the middle of the note, and making a diminuendo on the second half until the end of the beat, so that it may hardly be heard; and in doing this, one will render perfect harmony.

Quantz states:

> If you must hold a long note for either a whole or a half bar, which the Italians call *messa di voce*, you must first tip it gently with the tongue, scarcely exhaling; then you must begin *pianissimo*, allow the strength of the tone to swell in the middle of the note, and from there diminish it to the end of the note in the same fashion, making a vibrato (*flattement*) with the finger on the nearest open hole.[4]

Le Blanc's eulogy of the flute playing of Michel Blavet records that: 'The flute was found to declaim better than the violin and to be better at doing the *sons enflés*, and making diminutions'.[5] This imitation of vocal technique was one of the most important expressive devices of wind playing throughout the Baroque period. It was usually combined with a finger vibrato known as a *flattement* in France and as an open shake beat or 'sweetning' (sometimes softening or lesser shake) in England. The anonymous 'Instructions and Tunes for the Treble Recorder' (*The Modern Music Master*, c1731) explains: 'The Open Shake beat or sweetning is by shaking your finger over the half hole immediately below the Note to be sweetned' and says: 'All descending long notes must be shook, ascending long notes sweetned'. Compare this with Bismantova, who says that all semibreves, minims and even crotchets as well as all dotted notes should be trilled. Since finger vibrato was always to the flat side of a given note it is natural to regard it as the converse of the trill. While there was a general desire to emulate the violin, Geminiani specifically says that on the violin vibrato should be used as often as possible but on the flute only on long notes.

All Baroque woodwind (apart from the recorder) were softer than their modern counterparts, and the flute was the softest of all. Quantz states that the viol player must play at normal strength when with the violin, cello or bassoon, less strongly with the oboe and very softly with the flute, particularly when in its low register. Quantz, as distinct from Hotteterre and Corrette, insists that the low register of the flute should be played more strongly than the high register. He also recommends that the oboist hold his instrument up to prevent the sound disappearing into his stand. On the other hand Bannister says that the hautboy is not much inferior to the trumpet, but adds that 'with a good reed it goes as easie and as soft as the flute'. This explains why, according to Haynes (see n. 11), there are at least 26 collections or separate trio sonatas for flute, oboe and continuo yet many more trio sonatas for oboe and violin than for flute and violin. As Avison says:

> The *Hautboy* will best express the *Cantabile*, or singing Style, and may be used in all Movements whatever under this Denomination; especially those movements which tend to the *Gay* and *Chearful*.... The German flute ... will best express the languishing, or melancholy Style.... With both these Instruments, the running into *extreme* Keys, the Use of the *Staccato*, or distinct Separation of Notes, and all irregular Leaps, or broken and uneven Intervals must be avoided.[6]

This characterization of the two instruments is the reverse of what we think today and may partly be explained on grounds of volume; as Quantz says, adagios are generally played softly as opposed to the more extrovert allegros. The Baroque conception of orchestral balance was quite unlike the one embodied in later practice, and in large orchestras the numbers of oboes and bassoons increased in proportion to the strings. The brass was even more prominent; in the works of Lully it was common for a single part to be played by nine trumpeters, while the open sound of the horn before the advent of hand-stopping needed no doubling to come through the texture. Eric Halfpenny pointed out that the cross-rhythms in the horn parts at the beginning of Bach's first Brandenburg Concerto are standard hunting calls and would have been played as such.

The recorder

The earliest Italian printed piece for recorder is Riccio's *Canzona* for two recorders and continuo of 1612. The recorder is also specified in Riccio's 1620 collection, which contains a *Canzona* 'La Grimanetta' for *Flautin e Fagotto con il tremolo* (an early use of this device), and in the collections of Picchi (1625) and Neri (1651). We know that the recorder was used both by the waits and in the Royal Wind Music in London, but little music written specifically for the instrument survives. From mid-17th-century Vienna there are two chamber works extant: the *Sonatella a 5 Flauti et Organo* by Antonio Bertali and the *Sonata a 7 Flauti* by Johann Heinrich Schmelzer. Schütz uses two recorders in the shepherd scene from the Christmas History (1664) while Biber's *Sonata pro tabula* for five recorders and five strings with continuo probably dates from the late 1660s. Jacob van Eyck's *Der Fluyten Lust-Hof*, a large collection of unaccompanied sets of variations for recorder in C appeared in Amsterdam between 1644 and 1649.

In France, Lully occasionally introduced the recorder into his orchestral scores; *Les amants magnifiques* (1670), for example, has a 'Ritournelle pour les flûtes'. This may have been the new Baroque model, made in three joints and with a range of two octaves and one note, first documented by Bismantova in 1677. Bismantova's instrument is in G, and it has been suggested by Castellani that the G recorder remained in use in Italy during the 18th century and that Bach's use of the Italian term 'Fiauti d'echo' for the fourth Brandenburg Concerto signified the G instrument;[7] in the transposed version for harpsichord, which is definitely for recorders in F, he uses the French term 'Flûtes à bec'.

The earliest English tutor for the recorder is John Hudgebut's *A vade mecum for the Lovers of Musick, Shewing the Excellency of the Rechorder* (London, 1679), but the new Baroque instrument itself had almost certainly been introduced into England by James Paisible, who arrived from France in 1674. By 1676 a character in a play by Sir George Etherege says 'you can be charmed by nothing but flute doux and French hautboys'. Purcell uses recorders in a number of vocal works and one purely instrumental piece, the Chaconne for three recorders and continuo. The newly fashionable public concerts seized on the new French instruments and the recorder became the favourite instrument of the gentleman amateur. Recorders were used for incidental music in the theatres, and concertos for small recorders became a feature of interval music in the 1720s and 1730s, while in the same period Handel used the recorder in 23 operas and oratorios produced in London. By the end of the 1730s in England, however, the recorder was totally superseded by the transverse flute.

The German repertory includes eight sonatas, two concertos, many trio sonatas and obbligato parts by Telemann, concertante parts in Bach's Brandenburg Concertos nos.2 and 4 and obbligato parts in about 20 cantatas and in the *St Matthew Passion*, also a trio sonata by C. P. E. Bach for bass recorder, viola and continuo. Vivaldi's op.10, a set of six concertos for transverse flute, was originally conceived for recorder, but the three concertos for *flautino* were probably for a piccolo rather than a high recorder.

The flute

Although the transverse flute is often depicted in paintings of the early and mid-17th century and there are occasional parts in large-scale concerted music, almost no solo or chamber music was written specifically for it until the very end of the century. The only exceptions are the works written by Thomas Morley and others for the English broken consort of the early 17th century, which include parts for a transverse flute, while the little alto flute in G is given as an alternative to the recorder in van Eyck's *Der Fluyten Lust-Hof*.

The redesigning of the flute focused on the standard tenor size in D, at the rather low pitch current in France at the time – Quantz says that the wind instruments 'owe their existence to the low pitch'. The new design developed within the Hotteterre circle around 1670 was made in three sections with a cylindrical head joint but a conical body. The conical bore meant that the finger-holes could be slightly closer together so that even at the lowest French pitch the D flute finger-holes fitted comfortably under the fingers. The sectional construction allowed for fine tuning of the finger-holes by undercutting, and the addition of a key to give $d\#$ made the instrument fully chromatic, although the cross fingerings for other chromatic notes were never as efficient as on other woodwind. Nevertheless, Schickhardt wrote sonatas in every key for the instrument, and Hotteterre and Quantz both consider keys such as B and F$\#$ major practicable if 'peu usitées'.

The early 18th-century French school of player–composers tended to concentrate on the lower part of the range, and even Quantz (1752) says that the flute should sound more like a contralto than a soprano and never takes it above e''' in his compositions. From about 1720 a four-jointed construction became the norm; this enabled alternative middle joints, the so-called 'corps de rechange', to be substituted for tuning purposes. Quantz recommends that for the adagio the instrument should be tuned sharp so that the player can play very softly and the converse for the allegro.

French flute music was mostly for small chamber ensembles, from the Marais *Pièces en trio* of 1692 (the frontispiece of which has the first illustration of the new design) to the Rameau *Pièces de clavecin* of 1741. The German school owed a great deal to French influence. Bach wrote nothing for the transverse flute before 1716 when he heard the great French player Buffardin, after which time he used it as an obbligato instrument in numerous cantatas and passions as well as one unaccompanied sonata, seven sonatas, two trio sonatas, the Triple Concerto, the B minor Suite and the fifth Brandenburg Concerto.[8]

Telemann's output for flute includes some excellent unaccompanied fantasies which go through the 12 most commonly used keys. Handel's sonatas op.1 were produced for the new public concerts which were a feature of London's musical life. While the D instrument was the standard size,[9] the *flûte d'amour* enjoyed a vogue in the late 1720s and early 1730s. Rameau consistently gives the flutes important parts. In his first opera, *Hippolyte et Aricie* (1733), there are 21 movements with independent flute parts, and from 1740, when Blavet entered the Opéra orchestra, the flute parts become very difficult, going up to g''' and sometimes with three or four flats. By this time the piccolo becomes almost a standard feature of Rameau's scoring.

The oboe

The word 'hautboy' in its various spellings was used for double reed instruments long before the Baroque oboe evolved in the middle of the 17th century. Nor was the Baroque oboe the only attempt to refine the shawm; the *deutsche Schalmey* which appeared at about the same time, was also made with a narrow bore and narrow reed (but still played with a pirouette) and, as Talbot says, was 'sweeter in sound' than the old model. Anthony Baines suggests that the *deutsche Schalmey* was a German attempt at a quick answer to the new French oboe, but Jeremy Montagu considers the German instrument may have preceded it. The Denner family made both, but from about 1720 even the German military bands changed over to oboes.

The oboe bore was only a little narrower than that of the treble shawm, but the steps at each joint give a much more irregular bore profile than the other woodwind. It was made one tone lower than the normal treble shawm and equipped with three keys, one for *c'* and duplicate *d♯'* keys for right- or left-handed players. By about 1760 the left hand above position was so universal that the duplicate key was omitted, and around this time the bore was narrowed still further, making overblowing easier. As opposed to the modern oboe with octave keys 'You should observe also to augment your breath little by little in ascending, and to squeeze the reed with your lips' (Hotteterre, 1707). Hotteterre also says that you rarely ascend higher than *d'''*, and although in some late works Bach takes it to *e'''*, *d'''* remained the normal upper limit for the whole of the Baroque period. Quantz says that the tongue strokes 'ti' and 'ri' can be used as on the flute (the opening of the reed being closed by the tip of the tongue), but that 'did'll' cannot.

The first appearance of the new instrument was probably in Lully's ballet *L'amour malade* (1657). A pupil of Lully, Georg Muffat, explains how oboes could be used in the concerto grosso:

> Should you have among your musicians judicious players of the *hautbois*, you may with success have the three parts of your trio, or concertino, played by two trebles and a bassoon in many of these concertos, or at least in some of their movements chosen with this in mind, taking care to choose those in keys, or to transpose them in keys, suitable to those instruments, and to put an octave higher or otherwise modify short passages which are out of their range.[10]

The solo repertory includes two sonatas and three concertos by Handel, concertos by Albinoni, Marcello and Vivaldi, the Bach Concerto for Violin and Oboe, concertos by Telemann (in C minor and F minor) and by C. P. E. Bach (in B♭ major and E♭ major). It is interesting that Handel's sonatas and concertos, as well as most of the important parts in the Bach cantatas, have a key signature of two flats. Bruce Haynes has suggested that it is entirely in keeping with the practice of transposing flute music up a minor third for the recorder to transpose sonatas for flute, violin or oboe, often written in keys uncomfortable for the oboe, down one tone.[11]

The bassoon

The words 'fagotto', 'dulcian', 'curtal' and 'bassoon' with their variants seem to have been used indiscriminately in the Baroque, so that 'curtal' could mean bassoon (and vice versa) while 'fagotto' could refer to either, or even to a bass shawm. We will classify those instruments in which the double channel is bored in one piece of wood as curtals, and instruments with separate joints as bassoons.

The curtal of the early 17th century was normally called *fagotto* in Italy. Although made in a number of sizes (used for example by Schütz), the bass curtal was by far the most common and was sometimes known as 'Chorist fagott' as it was used to give the pitch to the singers. By the 1620s it was also being used as a virtuoso instrument, particularly by Dario Castello, who wrote nine sonatas featuring it, while Marini in 1617 and Riccio in 1620 expect the curtal player to play 'con il tremolo'. All these parts stay within the range $C - d'$ and are obviously written for the standard two-key curtal, but the curtal player Fra Selma y Salaverde takes the instrument down to Bb which seems to indicate that some instruments had an extended bell section with a third key. Mersenne implies such an instrument and Baines has suggested that the Bb was necessary to match the cellos in Louis XIII's band. There are no surviving specimens of these transitional instruments and most of the rest of the mid-17th-century curtal repertory stays within the standard range of two octaves and a tone. A high level of virtuosity is required in the six sonatas of Bertoli (1645) (the first set of solo sonatas for any instrument), in Böddecker's *Sonata sopra La Monica* (1651) and in a number of chamber works by Schmelzer which also extend the range up to f'. Waterhouse suggests that the Vivaldi bassoon concertos, which consistently avoid Bb', might have been written for the curtal. Daniel Speer knew of no other bassoon in 1697 and his two sonatas for three 'fagotti' are curtal music at its most idiomatic. Although Eisel says it is no longer in fashion, in *Musicus autodidactus* (1738) he still gives a fingering chart for the curtal, which he calls 'Teutsche Basson'.

It is likely that the Hotteterre circle produced a true bassoon by at least the 1670s. James Talbot says that the French bassoon took over from the sackbut 'towards the latter end of K.Ch.2d'. An engraving by Christoph Weigel of 1698 shows an instrument maker, possibly Denner, making a two-key curtal with a three-key bassoon in four joints resting on the workbench. A fourth key was added by 1705 and this remained standard for the rest of the century. The bassoon was the natural bass to the French hautboy, and as with the oboe its use in the orchestra can often be inferred even when not actually specified. Whilst solo repertory is sparse, there are fine sonatas by Telemann (1728) and Galliard (1733), and Bach uses the bassoon as an obbligato instrument in a number of cantatas and in the 'Quoniam' of the B minor Mass, which takes the instrument up to a'. Burney speaks of Miller, the leading mid-18th-century bassoonist in London: 'the concertos at Vauxhall and the solo parts allotted him by Handel in his oratorios and concertos, always excited attention, were heard with delight, and justly applauded for the sweetness of his tone and neatness of his execution'. Handel uses two bassoons *soli* in the scene between Saul and the Witch of Endor (*Saul*, 1739) and in his last operas Rameau takes the bassoon up to bb'.

The chalumeau and clarinet

The chalumeau coexisted with the clarinet for a large part of the 18th century, and indeed for the first half of that century it had a much more significant repertory.[12] Bonanni, in his *Gabinetto armonico* (1722), says that 'it appears to be a modern derivative of the recorder to give a louder and more vigorous sound'. The four sizes of chalumeau listed by Majer in 1732 correspond in size to sopranino, descant, treble and tenor recorders, but as cylindrical stopped pipes they sound an octave lower. They were mostly confined to their fundamental range of an eleventh, whereas the early clarinet was viewed as a substitute trumpet, as its name implies, and was used mainly in its upper register.

It was only when composers started using the low register of the clarinet that chalumeaux became superfluous; in France this happened by mid-century, but in the German-speaking areas not until towards the end of the century. Telemann played the chalumeau and wrote many obbligato parts, usually for alto and tenor, while Graupner wrote for it in more than 80 cantatas and 18 instrumental works including five concertos. It was used for pastoral or amorous scenes in opera by composers such as Keiser (1710), Fux (1710) and Handel (1721), in Harmoniemusik by composers such as Molter and in divertimentos by composers as late as Dittersdorf.

While there is no doubt that Johann Christoph Denner was responsible for improvements to the chalumeau, his role as 'inventor' of the clarinet – basically by the addition of a speaker key – is less certain, although a very early three-key clarinet by him is described by Hoeprich.[13] While this type of instrument is capable of playing early concertos such as those of Molter (which concentrate on the upper register of the instrument) and Vivaldi, it was not until the second half of the century, when the five-key clarinet was developed, that the instrument became technically comparable to one-key flutes, two-key oboes and four-key bassoons. It is no coincidence that the development of the Classical clarinet was accompanied by an enormous increase in its use.

The trumpet

Throughout the 17th and 18th centuries the trumpet remained essentially unchanged; developments were confined to playing technique. Smithers makes the point that the Thirty Years War (1618–48) led to the stagnation of the other instruments, but that trumpets always flourish in time of war.[14] While military trumpets remained higher, Praetorius (1619) tells us that the court trumpet 'was lengthened . . . not too many years ago', and both he and Schütz composed for the trumpet in C. Variations in the pitch of German trumpets are graphically shown by Anthony Baines,[15] but for much of the Baroque period trumpets in written C or D were by far the most usual.

An instrument in C is capable of producing notes of the harmonic series as shown in ex.8. Only the most skilled players were capable of producing the

Ex.8

very highest notes; Johann Heinisch, arguably the greatest Baroque trumpeter, who was active at the Viennese court 1727–50 had parts written for him up to the 24th harmonic. Harmonics 5, 10 and 15 are somewhat flat, but the real problems arise with harmonics 7 and 14 which give pitches intermediate between a' and bb', and a'' and bb'' respectively; harmonic 11, which is almost exactly halfway between f'' and $f''\sharp$, and harmonic 13, which is actually nearer $a''b$ than a''. These out-of-tune harmonics, as well as other notes not in the series at all, needed to be lipped into tune, a practice that dates back at least to the tutor of Bendinelli (1614); indeed Fantini, the author of the first printed method for the trumpet (1638), was reputed to be able to play over the entire range of the instrument filling in *all* the gaps! Smithers[16] suggests that modern reproductions of Baroque trumpets do not respond nearly as well to such lipping as do the originals, but that with a correctly shaped mouthpiece notes such as a' and b' can be reliably produced by using minimal lip pressure and making use of changes in the back resonance in the mouth and throat while pushing the lower lip forward.[17] The trumpeter Vejvanovský uses such notes as $e'b$ and $c'\sharp$ as if to demonstrate just how far this technique could be taken, yet even a fine player like Sargent was taken to task by Burney for the unpleasant intonation of his sustained g'' (harmonic 11 on the D trumpet) in the obbligato in Handel's *Messiah*. The truth is probably that most lipped notes were glossed over quickly as passing notes between the in-tune harmonics, and as such were usually acceptable, particularly when played softly.

The addition of node holes to reproduction 'Baroque' trumpets in an attempt to bring these notes more into focus is analogous to adding valves to a handhorn – the tone and intonation may be more even, but something is lost in the process.[18] One of the main dangers in using such crutches is that it encourages the player to play at a much greater volume and, as Smithers points out, Bach often had as many trumpets in the orchestra as he had sopranos in the choir.

The *tromba da tirarsi* is met with only in the works of Bach. Apart from voice doubling in the final chorales of cantatas, it is normally used as a natural trumpet with the ability to change to a new harmonic series when necessary, rather than as a trombone moving position from note to note. The other exception to the normal straight trumpet, the *tromba da caccia*, is also associated with Bach, as the best representation of it is in the well-known portrait of Reiche, who served as Bach's first trumpeter at Leipzig. We can probably equate this with the *trombae brevae* specified by Vejvanovský in certain of his compositions, and with the Invention or Italian trumpet mentioned over a century later by Altenburg, who says that 'because of its greater coiling, [it] is a more convenient form, and merits highest consideration'. Fitzpatrick says that the coiled form helps the high register,[19] and Smithers notes that coiled trumpets are more easily controlled than straight.[20]

Bendinelli's method of 1614 contains some much earlier dated sonatas, one of which, from 1584, is probably the first piece of music for the trumpet in the clarino register, using exactly the same range $c'–a''$ as Monteverdi does in the Toccata from *Orfeo* in 1607. By 1638 Fantini is writing up to d''', a range never exceeded by Italian composers throughout the Baroque period, and rarely approached in the entire English trumpet repertory. Even Bach in the second Brandenburg Concerto goes no higher than this written note, although as it is written for trumpet in F this part has the highest pitch in the repertory up to that time (1721).

At the other end of the range, Fantini often goes down to the first harmonic for the last note of his early exercises, and Smithers claims that practising descending to these depths is an excellent aid to developing the high register. In the trumpet ensemble, however, the first harmonic, called *Flatter-Grob*, was, as Speer tells us, 'auf einem Quart Posaunen Mundstuck am besten, starcksten und leichtesten zu haben'. Above this the *Grob-Stim* and *Faul-Stim* reiterate the fifth of harmonics 2 and 3, while the *Mittel-Stimm*, sometimes called *toccata*, is based on harmonic 4 and the *quinta*, also known as *sonata* or more often *principale*, is based on harmonic 6. We learn from Praetorius that the second *clarino* and the *principale* should be able to read music, but most of the music was improvised using stereotyped formulae, discussed in Tarr's commentary on the Bendinelli method. Both Schütz and Praetorius suggest that the trumpeters should insert a *sonata* or *intrada* of their own at appropriate places and Praetorius warns:

> Since the trumpeters are in the habit of hurrying (particularly because the trumpets require a good deal of breath, which cannot be sustained very well at a slow pace), one should always accelerate the beat when the trumpets enter, otherwise they always finish their Sonaden too soon. Later the beat may be lengthened, until the trumpeters start in again.[21]

The music of the Baroque trumpet is discussed in great detail by Smithers, who includes an inventory of sources. Certain stylistic features are common to all countries throughout the Baroque period, with the technical limitations of the instrument dictating a brilliant style of writing based on short scale figurations and strong major triad formations. It is arguable that the idiomatic trumpet writing associated with the basilica of S Petronio in Bologna had a major influence on the development of the concerto grosso. Purcell used the trumpet only in the last five years of his life; his Sonata in D for Trumpet and Strings is very much in the tradition of the Bologna trumpet sonatas. In the cantatas and oratorios of Bach the trumpet is used to portray specific moods of praise and majesty, just as in the *Symphoniae sacrae* and Christmas History of Schütz, and this association of trumpet and voice reaches its culmination in 'The trumpet shall sound' from Handel's *Messiah*.

The horn

Early appearances of the horn in operas of Cavalli and Lully[22] are colourful insertions to depict hunting scenes; in Lully's *La Princesse d'Elide* (1664) the horn players actually dance on stage. A pair of horns is first used as an integral part of the orchestra in Keiser's opera *Octavia* (1705), produced in Hamburg while Handel was connected with the opera house there. Handel's use of horns in the Water Music (1717) marked their first orchestral appearance in England. Although crooks were known as early as 1703, Handel wrote for crookless horns and he takes his first player up to harmonic 16 (see ex.8 – the harmonic series of the horn sounds an octave lower than that of the trumpet). The solo repertory from the Dresden court library *c*1720–45[23] has florid passages going up to harmonic 24 and shows that the distinction between *cor alto* and *cor basse* was already well established in the double concertos which form a large percentage of Baroque horn concertos. The reason for the stratospheric writing is simply that horns were mostly played by trumpeters; many of the early orchestral parts are labelled horn or trumpet and Cato, a negro in the service of the Prince of Wales, was 'recon'd to blow the best French horn and Trumpet in England'.

During the first half of the 18th century the main development in playing technique took place in Bohemia, following a tradition established by Count von Sporck, who had two servants instructed in the art of horn playing after hearing the French *cor de chasse* when on the Grand Tour 1680–82. Among Bohemian players who worked at the Dresden court and contributed to the repertory mentioned above was Hampel, the first to systematize the technique of hand-stopping which marks the beginning of the Classical horn tradition. Fitzpatrick believes that Handel's horn players in London were also from Bohemia, but standards in France were obviously poorer; when *Dardanus* broke down in performance Rameau said 'it was the fault of the horns who were not at all in tune'.

Things improved, perhaps owing to the introduction of crooks, and Rameau writes much more idiomatic and sometimes virtuoso parts in his later operas. In general, however, horns were little used in France until mid-century and in Italy, although Vivaldi wrote two concertos for two horns and strings. Telemann's *Tafelmusik* (1733) contains a concerto for two horns, and the concertante parts in Bach's first Brandenburg Concerto are likewise for a pair of horns; the single horn obbligato in the 'Quoniam' of the B minor Mass may have been prompted by the horn obbligato in Hasse's opera *Cleofide* which Bach heard in 1731.

The cornett

'Of all wind instruments the most excellent for imitating the human voice, more than any other instrument, is the cornett. This instrument plays softly, and loudly, and in every key as does the voice.' Girolamo Dalla Casa, 'Capo de Concerti delli Stromenti di fiato, della Illustriss. Signoria di Venetia', as he styles himself on the title-page of his *Il vero modo di diminuir* (Venice, 1584), gives the two main reasons for the supremacy of the cornett in the early Baroque: its uncannily vocal quality and its wide dynamic range. Dalla Casa was hired to found the instrumental group at St Mark's in 1568; after his death in 1601 he was succeeded by Giovanni Bassano, who had joined the wind group in 1576 as a cornettist and who published a diminution manual only one year later than Dalla Casa. The two men thus worked together for a quarter of a century at a time when Giovanni Gabrieli was composing his *Sacrae Symphoniae* (published 1597). Is the written-out ornamentation in Gabrieli's second great collection of instrumental music, the *Canzoni e sonate* of 1615, an attempt to record the imaginative flights of his players or to curb their excesses?

The normal treble cornett had a basic range from *a* to *a''*. Fingering charts (e.g. Mersenne, 1636, and Bismantova, 1677) give a range up to *d''''* but in the solo literature *c'''* is rarely and *d'''* never used (the *d''''*'s in Monteverdi's Vespers of 1610 occur in the *Magnificat* which Andrew Parrott convincingly suggests should be performed a fourth lower than written).[24] The cornettino was pitched a fourth or a fifth higher and seems to have been used quite extensively in Germany and Austria; Schütz scores for it, and it is used in purely instrumental combinations such as cornettino, violin, alto trombone, bassoon and continuo by Weckmann, Schmelzer, Valentini and Fux. The mute cornett, a tone lower than the treble and with an integral mouthpiece, was occasionally used in mixed consorts, and the tenor cornett, a fifth lower than the treble, was combined with voices and mixed wind groups. It was rare for the different sizes of cornett to be employed together; throughout their history cornettos were nearly always used in the company of trombones.

The earliest solo sonata for the instrument is by Cima (1610), although the ornamented versions of chansons made by Dalla Casa (1584) can be considered as the first true solo repertory. In the early part of the 17th century there is a sizeable repertory of chamber music, mostly in combination with violin, trombone or occasionally bassoon. Later in the century they sometimes appear as alternatives to (or in dialogue with) trumpets; this seems to be principally a German usage starting with Schütz and including figures like Schmelzer and Tolar. But the greatest music for the cornett is in vocal works such as Monteverdi's *Orfeo* (1607), the Vespers (1610) and many works by Schütz. Its use in vocal music continued well into the 18th century; Telemann, in the cantata *Jesus wirst du bald erscheinen* of 1719, wrote for cornettino, and Handel (*Tamerlano*, 1724) for cornett, although both gave the newly-invented clarinet as a substitute. Bach used the cornett in 11 cantatas, including a cruelly sustained part going to d''' in Cantata no.118. He drew on the local Stadtpfeifer for his wind playing and their quality is attested by the fine works for the cornett–trombone combination from the late 17th century by Stadtpfeifer composers such as Speer, Pezel and Reiche. Similarly, the Royal Wind Music tradition in England produced some fine idiomatic cornett–trombone writing from John Adson (1621), Matthew Locke and Charles Coleman (1661).

The trombone

'On the sackbut it is very easy for an accomplished player to produce any note he please; it is so versatile that I do not know any instrument whatsoever with more musical scope and which can vary its notes so fittingly' (Pierre Trichet, *c*1640). The first slide position chart for the trombone, that of Virgiliano (*c*1600), shows that the same tenor-sized instrument was expected to cover alto and bass ranges as well, and while Praetorius describes the alto trombone he too says that alto parts are best played on the tenor instrument 'when this height is achieved on the latter with good embouchure'.

Most of the normal repertory has a' as its upper limit, but Praetorius mentions one Erhardus Borussus who had a range from A' to g'' 'and was able to execute rapid coloraturas and jumps on his instrument just as is done on the *viola bastarda* and cornetto'. The tenor instrument was pitched in A while the alto and bass instruments were normally in D; this tuning persisted until the end of the 18th century. Octave trombones (*trombone doppio*, *trombone alla ottava bassa*) were rare, and when one sees the length of the Oller instrument of 1639 now in Stockholm one can understand why. Mersenne shows a crook which could be used to convert a tenor instrument into a *Quart-Trombone* (i.e. a perfect fourth lower) 'so as to perform the bass in concerts performed with oboes' (i.e. shawms).

The word 'sackbut' and its variants used in England, France and Spain had no counterpart in Italian, but modern usage is to call any original or reproduction Baroque trombone a 'sackbut'. The most obvious distinguishing feature of early trombones is the small bell, funnel-shaped in the 16th century and with the flare gradually increasing during the 17th and 18th centuries; the change in bore profile is graphically shown by Baines.[25] Bore sizes tended to be smaller than in most modern instruments, and as with trumpets of the period, the stays are detachable – probably for ease of replacement in case of damage but also, perhaps, for acoustic reasons. It is hard to generalize about mouthpieces when the few authenticated originals show such diversity, but common features are a sharp shoulder to the throat and flat rims, like contemporaneous trumpet mouthpieces.

Like the cornett, the trombone was valued for its wide dynamic range. The fact that Agazzari (1607) says that when the trombone replaces the double bass in small consorts 'it must be well and softly played', and that more than half a century later Stradella writes on the score of *Il barcheggio* 'Tutti li Bassi con un Trombone solo, ma deve il Trombone sonare staccato assai e con poco fiato' implies that it was sometimes played louder than the musical context warranted. Mersenne says that if it is played like a trumpet 'This is deemed vicious and unsuited for concerts'.

From the early 17th century there is a wealth of church and chamber music including trombone, some of which has been mentioned in the section on the cornetto. One of the ornamented chansons from Rognoni's *Selva de varii passaggi* (1620) is marked 'per il Violone over Trombone alla Bastarda', but the earliest real solo is Cesare's *La Hieronyma* (1621). Among the numerous trio sonatas for violin or cornett and trombone those by Dario Castello (1621 and 1629) stand out both for musical quality and for the virtuosity of the writing, while Marini's *Affetti musicali* (1617) contains a trio sonata 'La Foscarina' which requires tremolo.

Two of Schütz's *Symphoniae sacrae* (1629) are for bass voice, four trombones and continuo and many of his other works with mixed instrumentation also have highly florid and imaginative trombone writing. Schütz frequently takes the bass trombone way below the staff, sometimes as far as G'; as Praetorius says: 'trombones ... sound the more grave and splendid the lower they are pitched'. Their use in the English Royal Wind Music was mainly with cornetts in the early 17th century and later with shawms; Talbot (*c*1695) says: 'Chief use of Sackbutt here in England is in consort with our Waits or English Hautbois. It was left off towards the latter end Of K.Ch.2d. & gave place to the Fr. Basson.' After the plague of 1630 few trombonists were hired at St Mark's in Venice, but they did not finally disappear from the complement until 1732. In Austria the tradition of florid trombone writing persisted; Biber (1644–1704) in Salzburg and Bertali (1605–69) and Schmelzer (*c*1620–1680) in Vienna were still writing works for violins and trombones such as were common in Italy half a century earlier. Later Austrian works, such as the settings of *Alma redemptoris* by Ziani and Fux, have concertante parts for alto trombone, a tradition leading to the spate of concertos for that instrument in the 1760s. It is surely no coincidence that the date of the first of them is 1762, the year in which Gluck first uses trombones in *Orfeo*.

The serpent

The serpent is reputed to have been invented by one Canon Guillaume of
Auxerre in or about 1590. It is described in great detail by Mersenne (1636),
echoed by Trichet (*c*1640), but there is little evidence of its use outside
French churches until late in the 17th century. Its six finger-holes are placed
in acoustically absurd positions in order that the fingers may cover them, but
it is perfectly possible to lip notes into tune over a wide range – Mersenne
gives two octaves and a fourth. He also says:

> the instrument is capable of supporting 20 very strong voices; it is so easy to
> play that a child of 15 can sound it as loudly as a man of 30. And the tone
> can be softened so that it will be suitable to join with the soft voices of
> chamber music, whose graces and diminutions it imitates; it can perform 32
> notes to the measure, although these ought to be avoided in polyphonic
> music, because it must be sounded simply in the part it undertakes to sing.

Westrup,[26] who unkindly says 'it is attractive neither to the eye nor to the
ear', gives details of its use in some French churches from the earliest years of
the 17th century. It was usually played by priests and used for the musical
education of the choirboys. Although Mersenne says that 'the true bass of the
cornetto is performed with the serpent, so that one can say that one without
the other is a body without a soul' and that it 'serves as bass in all sorts of
concerti', there is little record of its having been used in ensemble music until
the 18th century. In 1730 Bailey wrote of it as 'serving as bass to the cornet or
small shawm', and with the rise of Harmoniemusik it found a useful function
doubling the bassoon at the bottom of the ensemble. Orchestral use is rare; a
sinfonia by Perti has the bass staff labelled 'Violone o Tiorba, Violoncello,
Trombone, Bissone, Tiorba' (according to Hutchings 'Bissone' is a dialect
form of Serpent). Serpents are scored for in Handel's *Music for the Royal
Fireworks*, and notes on some Handel scores tell us for example that in 1749
the serpent was used in performances of *Samson* and *Solomon*.

Notes

[1] The subject is dealt with in some detail in B. B. Mather, *Interpretation of French Music from
1675 to 1775 for Woodwind and Other Performers* (New York, 1973), and in David Lasocki's
introduction to his translation of Hotteterre's *Principes de la flûte traversière* (1707). The
relevant exerpts from contemporary treatises are given in M. Castellani, *Del portar della lingua
negli instrumenti di fiato* (Florence, 1979).

[2] Mather, *Interpretation*, 39.

[3] Quantz's slurring practices are well discussed in M. Rasmussen, 'Some Notes on the
Articulations in the Melodic Variation Tables of Johann Joachim Quantz's *Versuch*', *BWQ*, i
(1966–7), 3–27.

[4] J. J. Quantz, *Versuch einer Anweisung die Flöte traversiere zu spielen* (Berlin, 1752, 3/1789/
*R*1952; Eng. trans., 1966), 165.

[5] Mather, *Interpretation*, 57.

6 Charles Avison, *An Essay on Musical Expression* (London, 1753), xxx.

[7] M. Castellani, 'The *Regola per suonare il flauto Italiano* by Bartolomeo Bismantova', *GSJ*, xxx
(1977), 76–85.

[8] The authenticity of some sonatas has been questioned: see R. L. Marshall, 'J. S. Bach's
Compositions for Solo Flute: a Reconsideration of their Authenticity and Chronology', *JAMS*,
xxxii (1979), 321–34.

[9] This is disputed in C. Addington, 'In Search of the Baroque Flute', *EM*, xii (1984), 34–47.

[10] Georg Muffat, Foreword to *Auserlesene Instrumental Music* (Passau, 1701); quoted in Strunk, *The Baroque Era*, 89–92.

[11] The best overall account of the Baroque oboe is given in J. Marx, 'The Tone of the Baroque Oboe', *GSJ*, iv (1951), 3–19. Measurements and construction details are given in E. Halfpenny, 'The English 2- and 3-keyed Hautboy', *GSJ*, ii (1949), 10–26, and 'The French Hautboy: a Technical Survey', *GSJ*, vi (1953), 23–34, and viii (1955), 50–59. See also A. Baines, 'James Talbot's Manuscript', *GSJ*, i (1948), 9–26. The most detailed information on fingering comes from B. Haynes, 'Oboe Fingering Charts 1695–1816', *GSJ*, xxxi (1978), 69–93. Reeds are dealt with in Haynes, 'Making Reeds for the Baroque Oboe', *EM*, iv (1976), 31–4 and 173–9; F. R. Palmer, 'Reconstructing an 18th-century Oboe Reed', *GSJ*, xxxv (1982), 100–111; and N. Post, 'The 17th-century Oboe Reed', *GSJ*, xxxv (1982), 54–67. The larger varieties of oboe are described in R. Dahlqvist, 'Taille, Oboe da Caccia and Corno Inglese', *GSJ*, xxvi (1973), 58–71. For repertory other than solo sonatas and concertos, the most useful source is B. Haynes, *Catalogue of Chamber Music for the Baroque Oboe 1654–c1825* (The Hague, 1980).

[12] See the following articles by Colin Lawson: 'The Chalumeau – Independent Voice or Poor Relation?', *EM*, vii (1979), 351–4; 'Telemann and the Chalumeau', *EM*, ix (1981), 312–19; 'Graupner and the Chalumeau', *EM*, xi (1983), 209–16; 'The Early Chalumeau Duets', *GSJ* xxvii (1974), 125–9.

[13] E. T. Hoeprich, 'A Three-keyed Clarinet by J. C. Denner', *GSJ*, xxxiv (1981), 21–32.

[14] D. L. Smithers, *The Music and History of the Baroque Trumpet* (London, 1973).

[15] A. Baines, *Brass Instruments, their History and Development* (London, 1976), 127.

[16] D. L. Smithers, 'The Baroque Trumpet after 1721: some Preliminary Observations', *EM*, v (1977), 177–83, and vi (1978), 356–61.

[17] See E. Tarr, 'Trumpet', *Grove 6*, for a good illustration of the differences between Baroque and modern mouthpieces.

[18] See M. Rasmussen, 'Bach Trumpet Madness', *Brass Quarterly*, v (1961), 37–40.

[19] See the letter 'Sounding Brass' by H. Fitzpatrick in *EM*, iv (1976) 347–55.

[20] Smithers, 'The Baroque Trumpet'.

[21] Translated in H. Lampl, 'Michael Praetorius on the Use of Trumpets', *Brass Quarterly*, ii (1958), 3–7.

[22] Discussed in R. Morley-Pegge, *The French Horn* (London, 1960).

[23] Described in M. Rasmussen, 'The Manuscript Kat. Wenster Litt.I/1–17b (Universitetsbiblioteket, Lund): a Contribution to the History of the Baroque Horn Concerto', *Brass Quarterly*, v (1962), 135–52.

[24] 'Transposition in Monteverdi's Vespers of 1610: an "Aberration" Defended', *EM*, xii (1984), 490–516.

[25] Baines, *Brass Instruments*, 112.

[26] 'Sidelights on the Serpent', *MT*, lxviii (1927), 635–7.

CHAPTER V

Voices

ELLEN T. HARRIS

Vocal performance practice in the Baroque era is not a unified subject but a series of issues and questions. One must acknowledge chronological, national and stylistic distinctions as well as differences of voice type and range. The music of Monteverdi, in other words, cannot be approached in the same way as that of Handel, despite the fact that both composers wrote Italian operas; the music of Bach and Handel must not be performed in the same manner, although the composers were exact contemporaries; Handel's cantatas should be performed differently from his operas or sacred music, and instructions appropriate to a soprano cannot be applied directly to a bass. There are no simple or definite answers to the questions of how Baroque music was sung, but tentative conclusions can be drawn from a study of the surviving sources.

Treatises on singing make up the most important source of information about Baroque performance practice, and many of these are now available in English translation (see Bibliography). Contemporary descriptions of singers and their vocal abilities provide a second source of information. These may often be found in letters and diaries of the time, but the most important are concentrated in the treatises of Quantz (1752), Mancini (1774) and Burney (1776–89). Contemporary satires, such as *Il teatro alla moda*, by Marcello (*c*1720), also offer valuable insights into performance practice.

From these sources one can learn that there are different styles (church, chamber and theatre) and various musical genres (such as recitative, aria and chorus), and that the various vocal ranges (soprano, alto, tenor and bass), as well as the various voice types (in the treble range: boy, adult female, castrato and countertenor), have distinct qualities. Chronological and national distinctions, on the other hand, need to be determined from context; they are generally not discussed by the theorists. Throughout the following discussion, therefore, specific chronological and national trends will be noted wherever they can be discerned, but the 17th and 18th centuries will be discussed as a unit, and the Classical era will also be touched upon to clarify Baroque practices. Indeed, because treatises tend to take a retrospective view, a number of important writings about Baroque music postdate the period. Mancini's treatise (1774) provides the best example of such a work. It need hardly be said that the most basic elements of vocal performance practice have never changed. In 1810 Domenico Corri,[1] like the Baroque

Opera performance at the court of Turin in 1722: engraving by Antoine Aveline after a drawing by Filippo Juvarra

authors before him, emphasizes that good technique and production are the essential parts of a good singing style (p.1):

> the vocal art affords various characters, – the sacred, the serious, the comic, anacreontic, cantabile, bravura, etc. etc. and though each style requires different gifts and cultivation, yet true intonation, the swelling and dying of the voice, with complete articulation of words, are essential to all.

General elements of good singing style

The four essential vocal qualities emphasized by Baroque authors will sound familiar to any modern singer: perfect intonation, good breathing technique, clear enunciation of the words and proper expression of the text. These requirements are generally the first to be discussed in the treatises, and they regularly form the basis for descriptions of good voices. Caccini (160/2),[2] the earliest author on Baroque singing, writes, 'Therefore, to proceed in order, thus will I say that the chiefest foundations and most important grounds of this art are the tuning [intonation] of the voice in all the notes' (p.382). Quantz begins his description of the famous castrato Senesino (né Francesco Bernardi; *d* 1759), 'He had a powerful, clear, equal and sweet contralto voice, with a perfect intonation',[3] and the soprano Francesca Cuzzoni (1698–1770) is described by Burney: 'Her high notes were unrivalled in clearness and sweetness and her intonations were so just and fixed, that it seemed as if it was not in her power to sing out of tune'.[4]

The treatises offer two correctives for bad intonation: proper breath support and careful attention to the learning of intervals. Bacilly (1668),[5] for example, argues that 'bad pitch' often is caused by 'ignorance of whole-steps and half-steps' and 'that a good knowledge of notes can greatly contribute to its correction'. He also emphasizes that the student 'will be able to sing without concern over his pitch, on condition that he sings the notes as much as possible from the diaphragm [*du fonds du gosier*], which is the sole guide to "correctness" in singing' (p.28).

Breath support was considered critical not only to good intonation but to good singing in general. Mattheson (1739)[6] declares that 'the first and most important abuse in singing may well be when through too frequent and untimely breathing the words and thoughts of the performance are separated, and the flow is interrupted or broken' (p.265). Caccini specifically links good breathing technique to the proper use of dynamics: 'a man must have a command of breath to give the greater spirit to the increasing and diminishing of the voice, to exclamations and other passions, as is related' (p.391). All the theorists agree that improved breathing technique can be taught, and Tosi (1723)[7] emphasizes the need for such instruction, 'because there are Singers who give Pain to the Hearer, as if they had an Asthma, taking Breath every Moment with Difficulty, as if they were breathing their last' (pp.60–61).

Nothing is more important to singing in Baroque music than the clear communication of the text; it is the fundamental axiom upon which Baroque music is based. At the very beginning of the period, Caccini writes that 'unless the words [are] understood', the singer cannot 'move the understanding' (p.378). Bacilly devotes one of the three main sections of his singing treatise solely to pronunciation. Tosi urges the study of vowel and consonant sounds (pp.25 and 58), and Quantz[8] gives similar admonitions. All emphasize that, as Quantz says, 'Only the voice itself and the use of words give singers preference over instrumentalists' (p.300).

The singer must be proficient in any language he sings, and he must not only pronounce the words correctly but also know what they mean. Bernhard (c1649)[9] writes (p.20) that the singer must know:

> the proper pronunciation of the words which he must set forth in song. Burrs, lisps, and other forms of bad diction must be eschewed, and a graceful, blameless manner of speech cultivated. In his mother tongue, [the singer] should certainly adopt the most elegant way of speaking, ... If, however, he is to sing in a language other than his mother tongue, then he must read that language at least as fluently and correctly as those people to whom it is native.

Proper pronunciation and understanding of the text will enable the singer to express its meaning and, as Caccini writes, 'to delight and move the affections of the mind' (p.382).

The proper expression of the text also depends on both musical and dramatic interpretation. Caccini (p.381) and Tosi (p.107) warn against singing all songs in the same style, without regard for whether the nature of the text is pathetic or agitated, and Bernhard (pp.21 and 25), Bacilly (p.34) and Tosi (pp.25–6) all warn against ruining musical interpretation with unseemly facial distortions and expressions. Bernhard writes (pp.21–2):

> The question may here be raised, whether a singer's face and bearing should reflect the affects found in the text. Thus let it be known that a singer should sing modestly, without special facial expressions; for nothing is more upsetting than certain singers who are better heard than seen, who arouse the expectations of a listener with a good voice and style of singing, but who ruin everything with ugly faces and gestures.

A singer should never hold the music before his face (Mattheson, p.247, and Tosi, p.61) nor mark time with the hands and feet by weaving from side to side (Mattheson, pp.246–7). Gesticulation should be kept to a minimum and be done gracefully. Bernhard suggests that in the singing of 'motets and the like, it is ... not proper to use even simple theatrical gestures' (p.22). As with many other aspects of Baroque singing, dramatic expression of the text appears to break down according to national boundaries. Mattheson writes that the French express the texts beautifully, but that the Italians 'frequently overstep the limits [of expression] and love the extremes' and the Germans tend to the unexpressive in singing, looking 'just as stiff and unemotional with the sad as well as the cheerful emotions' (p.136).

Vocal production

The quality of Baroque vocal production that differs most from modern singing techniques is the clear distinction of registers as defined by range. That is, all singers must negotiate a change in vocal production around e' or f' between what is generally known as the chest and head voice. Female singers have yet another 'break' or *passaggio* an octave higher. Modern singers diminish the differences between these various ranges or registers as much as possible by the use of a mixed production throughout the voice, but Baroque singers maintained the distinctions in tone quality by mixing their production only on the few notes over the break, thus ensuring a smooth passage. The Baroque emphasis on the different colours of the two or three vocal registers can be confirmed in many contemporary writings about singing. Unfortunately, however, the issue is clouded by a lack of common terminology. The head (or falsetto) voice is usually distinguished from the heavier, darker tone supported 'from the chest' by its clarity, lightness, and, sometimes, lack of support. It must be noted, however, that this terminology refers only to the male voice. The female voice lacks a true falsetto and contains a large middle register (spanning about an octave) that separates the chest and head voice. An awareness of these differences is implicit in most Baroque vocal tutors.

Some composers and tutors distinguish three registers, a practice which can be dated back to at least the 13th century and the theorists Johannes de Garlandia and Jerome of Moravia. Monteverdi (1638), for example, speaks of the voice as having 'high, low, and middle registers'.[10] Tosi identifies these (from bottom up) as chest voice, head voice and falsetto, and he declares that the 'full natural Voice' ends at the break between head and falsetto (p.24). On the other hand, Mancini (1774) equates head voice and falsetto, as some modern tenors still do.[11] According to this classification the break between the natural and 'feigned' voice occurs at the break between chest and head (at about e'), and this is undoubtedly what Caccini intended when he encouraged the male singer to use only the 'natural' voice and to avoid the falsetto, 'for from a feigned voice can come no noble manner of singing, which only proceeds from a natural voice' (pp.391–2).

These differences in terminology obscure what otherwise seems to be a clear development in the use of the registers during the Baroque era. At the beginning of the period, Caccini identifies two registers and counsels singers to avoid the falsetto by performing arias in keys suitable to their natural voice. In the mid-17th century, Bacilly continues to recognize two registers but implies that modern singers may choose to perform in one or the other. He writes (p.19):

> Some people are proud of their high voices, and others of their low tone, taking the view that a high voice is little more than a screech. Those who have natural voices scorn the falsetto as being artificial and shrill, while on the other hand falsetto singers are usually of the opinion that the beauty of a song is more evident when performed by the shimmering brilliance of their vocal type than when done by a natural tenor, which, although it ordinarily has better intonation, doesn't have the brilliance of the falsetto.

Although both authors speak of two distinct registers, they discuss the voice as if it can be limited to one. By and large, the music of the period spans a single clef (or eleven notes) and does not demand that the two registers be united (but see 'Voice types and choir sizes' below). However, it may also have been the case that 17th-century singers were specifically encouraged to use only one register in order to avoid the break in the voice, a problem that was not addressed until the 18th century. In their discussions of two registers, Caccini and Bacilly undoubtedly refer to the natural male voice. The female voice and the castrato are spoken of with much less frequency in the 17th century, but assuming that women and castratos generally sang in the range of the treble or soprano clefs, their 'natural' voices would be the middle range rather than chest. Still it would be relatively easy to avoid changing registers and thereby to avoid the break. In most 17th-century music, therefore, women and castratos could have managed well with a 'natural' tone, and men could have chosen between natural or feigned production by careful choice of key.

With the increased range of later Baroque music, the acceptance of the female virtuoso and, most importantly, the growing predominance of the castrato voice, vocal tutors needed to address the problem of vocal registers differently. Tosi is the first to discuss the unification of the natural with the feigned voice by a single singer.[12] He directly attributes the need for this development to the increased range of the music (p.23).

> A diligent Master, knowing that a [male] *Soprano*, without the *Falsetto*, is constrained to sing within the narrow Compass of a few Notes, ought not only to endeavour to help him to it, but also to leave no Means untried, so to unite the feigned and the natural Voice, that they may not be distinguished; for if they do not perfectly unite, the Voice will be of divers Registers, and must consequently lose its Beauty.

Mancini's discussion of this problem,[13] though 50 years later, does not differ appreciably (p.20):

> The voice in its natural state is ordinarily divided into two registers, one of which is called the chest, the other the head or falsetto.... Every [male] scholar, whether he be soprano, contralto, tenor or bass, can ascertain for himself the difference between these two separate registers. Have no doubt that of all the difficulties that one encounters in the art of singing, the greatest by far is the union of the two registers.

Both authors imply that the chest and head voices should maintain their distinctive qualities and should not be blended throughout the entire range. However, the singer, in moving from one register to the other, should conceal the break or 'jerk' by blending the four or five notes over the *passaggio*. Only very rarely was the chest voice carried to the top of the range. Mancini says 'there are rare examples in which one has received from nature the most unusual gift of being able to execute everything in the chest voice' (p.20). Tosi agrees, making a specific reference to the female voice: 'Among the Women, one hears sometimes a *Soprano* entirely *di Petto*, but among the Male Sex it would be a great Rarity, should they preserve it after having past the Age of Puberty' (p.24; see 'Voice types and choir sizes' below). Therefore, despite the fact that Tosi and Mancini use different terminology to identify vocal registers, they describe the same vocal practices and exceptions in their discussions of vocal production.

The blending of the passage between the chest and head voice while maintaining the distinctness of each register appears to have been an important quality of late Baroque singing, especially in the Italian style. It is not mentioned by French or German authors before Quantz, who confirms a different practice in those countries: 'Joining the chest voice to the falsetto is as unknown to [the German singers] as it is to the French' (p.336). Apparently French and German singers continued the older tradition of singing in one register as much as possible, using transposition (as suggested by Caccini) to facilitate this where necessary. Where the compositional range demanded vocal expansion beyond one register, the natural break was probably accepted, as it was in many voices well into the 19th century.[14]

The regular use of chest voice throughout the range, or, at least, the pulling up of a heavier sound into the head register, first appears after the Baroque period. At the end of the 18th century, for example, this type of production in the tenor voice began to elicit excited commentary. Michael Kelly (1762–1826), the famous English tenor who sang for Mozart in Vienna, is described as follows: 'His compass was extraordinary. In vigorous passages he never cheated the ear with feeble wailings of falsetto, but sprung upon the ascending fifth [from *d'* to *a'*] with a sustained energy that electrified the audience'.[15] And the French tenor Gilbert Duprez (1806–96) is said to have 'carried the "chest register" up to the tenor high "C"'.[16] In the Baroque, however, the two registers remained distinct despite an effort to cover the break. As Mancini writes (in a statement that at first appears paradoxical) a good singer will have 'united the two registers, which are in every one separated; in some a little, in some more' (p.39). That is, the registers, although united, remain distinct. Tosi is clearer. He identifies the use of two separate registers: 'Let the Master attend with great Care to the Voice of the Scholar, which, whether it be *di Petto* or *di Testa*, should always come forth neat and clear' (p.22). And he argues specifically against the use of the chest voice in the higher register:

> The practice of some few who teach solfeggio, obliges the student to sustain the semibreves with a voice forced from the chest to the highest notes, and finally it follows that day by day the [throat] become[s] more inflamed, and if the scholar does not lose his health, he loses the Soprano [range].[17]

Apparently, only an occasional female singer succeeded in using a full tone throughout the range.

The separation of the registers (blended only at the break) helps to explain other aspects of Baroque vocal production. For example, many of the theorists state the rule that volume should relate directly to range by having the voice produce high notes softly and low notes loudly. Mattheson gives a Latin 'rule which has already served for two hundred years, that each singing voice, the higher it goes, should be produced increasingly temperately and lightly: however in the low notes, according to the same rule, the voice should be strengthened, filled out, and invigorated' (p.266). Tosi writes 'that the higher the Notes, the more it is necessary to touch them with Softness' (p 19). Such stipulations make sense only if the high notes are sung lightly in head voice. Indeed, the change in vocal production during the Classical era not only brought the chest voice into the upper register, it also reversed the rule concerning volume. In 1791 William Jackson complained that 'instead of developing their voices so as to be soft at the top and full at the bottom, singers were achieving the opposite effect',[18] and in 1810 Domenico Corri taught (in the earliest instance of such instruction I have found) that the voice should increase in volume as it rises and decrease when descending (p.52). The use of the chest voice on high notes necessitated a different approach to volume as it relates to range.

The use of vibrato may also have been related to registral separation, for blending of the chest and head voices in the upper registers certainly increases the forcefulness of vocal production and the likelihood of a wider pitch alternation, or vibrato. However, the term 'vibrato' is not used in the Baroque, at least not in relation to the voice, and the Baroque term 'tremolo', which refers either to rhythmic pulsation or pitch variation, is not exactly equivalent. Some authors object strenuously to any pitch vibrato; some describe the pitch vibrato of less than a semitone as an ornament similar to a trill (where the pitch alternates by a semitone or whole tone); and some argue for continuous use of tremolo (which may not, however, refer to pitch variation at all but to rhythmic pulsation).

Bernhard clearly uses 'tremolo' as an equivalent for the modern term 'vibrato' and is the most emphatic of all Baroque authors in objecting to its use (p.14).

> *Fermo*, or the maintenance of a steady voice, is required on all notes, except where a *trillo* or *ardire* is applied. It is regarded as a refinement mainly because the *tremulo* [*sic*] is a defect... Elderly singers feature the *tremulo*, but not as an artifice. Rather it creeps in by itself, as they no longer are able to hold their voices steady. If anyone would demand further evidence of the undesirability of the *tremulo*, let him listen to such an old man employing it while singing alone. Then he will be able to judge why the *tremulo* is not used by the most polished singers, except in *ardire*.

Tosi also urges singers to learn to hold notes without vocal 'trembling'. Those who fail 'will become subject to a Flutt'ring in the Manner of all those that sing in a very bad Taste' (p.27). Certainly the Baroque separation of the vocal registers allows for a straight tone more easily than post-Classical methods of vocal production. Even in the Baroque, however, the vibrato was not entirely absent, despite the statements of Bernhard and Tosi.

A number of authors describe the pitch vibrato as an ornament to be used sparingly. Mattheson carefully defines the tremolo and trill as being related. The former 'is the slightest possible oscillation on a single fixed tone'. On the organ 'the wavering air itself performs the effect and no higher or lower keys are touched on the keyboard ... On violins the same trembling can also be accomplished on one tone within one bowing... Thus *tremolo* cannot be clearly indicated through notation'. The trill, on the other hand, 'consists in a sharp and clear striking of two adjacent or neighboring pitches, alternating one with the other as fast as possible' (p.270–71).

Mattheson's distinction between tremolo and trill closely resembles that made by Bacilly between 'cadence' and 'tremblement'. In his edition of Bacilly, Austin Caswell translates 'cadence' as 'vibrato', but in the following quotations, the French term has been reinstated. Both terms are treated in the section on ornamentation. Bacilly writes that 'a singer's *cadence* is [usually] a gift of nature', but that many people 'have an acceptable voice without having a *cadence* at all'. Some have '*cadences* that are [too slow,] too fast or sometimes too coarse, a quality which is commonly called *chevrottante* [wobbling or bleating]' (p.83). Bacilly distinguishes between the pretty voice and the good voice by saying that the former 'is very pleasing to the ear because of its clearness and sweetness, and above all because of the nice *cadence* which usually accompanies it'. Good voices may lack the natural *cadence*, but they have 'vigor, strength, and [the] capacity to sing with expression' (p.20). Bacilly later implies that the use of these terms may vary, depending on the gender of the singer, when he states that 'men have a vocal advantage of movement and expression over women although they have voices and *cadences* which are less beautiful' (p.83).

It is difficult to know how far to take Bacilly's apparent references to vibrato. But if it is true that women tended towards a natural vibrato more than men, then descriptions of Francesca Cuzzoni (*c*1698–1770) as having a 'natural warble' and a 'nest of nightingales in her belly'[19] may refer specifically to a natural vibrato in a voice that by all accounts was 'pretty', to use Bacilly's term, and excelled in pathetic airs. As early as 1592, Ludovico Zacconi suggests the continuous use of vibrato:

> the tremolo, that is the tremulous voice, is the true portal to the *passaggi*, and the means of mastering the *gorgia*: just as the ship is made to move more easily when already in motion.... This tremolo should be slight and pleasing; for if it is exaggerated and forced, it tires and annoys; its nature is such that, if used at all, it should always be used, since use converts it into habit; for this continuous motion of the voice helps and spontaneously encourages the movement of the *gorgie*, and miraculously facilitates the undertaking of *passaggi*; this movement of which I speak should not be undertaken if it cannot be done with just rapidity, vigorously and vehemently.[20]

The question of vibrato, therefore, remains vexing, especially because the term cannot be accurately defined in Baroque usage. That is, vibrato refers not only to the familiar pitch alternation that stems from the diaphragm, but can also mean a rhythmic pulsation without pitch variation that originates in the throat. The Baroque term 'tremolo' might well refer to either kind of vibrato, especially if one considers that the original meaning of 'trillo' was rhythmic pulsation on a single note. In this regard, it seems likely that the earlier references to 'tremolo', such as Zacconi's, refer to throat vibrato, making its continuous use more likely. On the other hand, Bernhard seems to be speaking of a pitch waver. In sum, it is only possible to conclude that a general prohibition, or at least a warning, against the continuous use of pitch vibrato existed in Germany and France in the 17th century. However, even pitch vibrato was probably used by some singers, especially women with light, pretty voices; perhaps Cuzzoni was one of these. Mancini makes no mention of vibrato, but as singers began pulling the chest voice up into the head register, pitch vibrato would have appeared naturally. Because vibrato is most frequently associated with women's voices, it may not be coincidental that the use of chest voice throughout the range is first attributed by Tosi to female sopranos.

Zacconi, in his description of vibrato, offers the most important prohibition when he warns against forcing, a warning also issued by all later Baroque theorists. In other words, one should not force the chest voice higher than is natural; one should not force the voice to sing loudly in high passages; and one should not force a vibrato. In the Classical era, however, a trend started towards the use of chest voice in the head register, a loud dynamic in high passages and continuous vibrato. But even in the Baroque era these vocal qualities existed in rare instances and were accepted.

Interpretation

Beyond good singing style and vocal production, the Baroque singer was trained to exercise great discretion in terms of articulation, dynamics, tempo, rhythm and ornamentation. Mattheson states the case for articulation succinctly by stating that one important defect in singing arises 'when one slurs what should be detached; and detaches what should be slurred' (pp.265–6; see also Quantz, p.122). Unfortunately, he does not elaborate. In general, however, the tutors imply that Baroque articulation was strongly marked. Slurring and legato phrasing were apparently reserved for cantabile singing and even then were used sparingly. Tosi writes: 'The use of the *Slur* is pretty much limited in Singing, and is confined within such few Notes ascending or descending, that it cannot go beyond a fourth without displeasing' (p.53; i.e. intervals of larger than a fourth should not be slurred).

Marked articulation was particularly important to the performance of divisions. Once again it is Tosi who states this most clearly (pp.52–3).

> Division, according to the general Opinion, is of two Kinds, the Mark'd, and the Gliding; which last, from its Slowness and Dragging, ought rather to be called a Passage or Grace, than a *Division*. In regard to the first, the Master ought to teach the Scholar that light Motion of the Voice, in which the Notes that constitute the Division be all articulate in equal Proportion, and moderately distinct, that they be not too much join'd, nor too much mark'd. The second is perform'd in such a Manner, that the first Note is a Guide to all that follow, closely united, gradual, and with such Evenness of Motion, that in Singing it imitates a certain Gliding, by the Masters called a *Slur*; the Effect of which is truly agreeable when used sparingly. The *mark'd Divisions*, being more frequently used than the others, require more Practice.

When attempting to sing marked divisions many singers apparently erred by adding a consonant before each note. Tosi writes (p.57):

> those [divisions] are likewise displeasing which are neither mark'd nor gliding; for in that case they cannot be said to sing, but howl and roar. There are some still more ridiculous, who mark them above Measure, and with Force of Voice, thinking (for Example) to make a *Division* upon *A*, it appears as if they said Ha, Ha, Ha, or Gha, Gha, Gha; and the same upon the other Vowels.

Mattheson writes, 'the mere ring, tone, or sound of certain syllables has its own burden, and diphthongs will [often] not emerge unharmed without being miserably hacked to pieces and dismembered into many ha ha ha, he he he, ei ei ei, etc.' (p.416). Indeed, Quantz ties this problem particularly to the German style of singing (p.336).

> Their disagreeable, forced and exceedingly noisy chest attacks, in which they make vigorous use of the faculty of the Germans for pronouncing the *h*, singing ha–ha–ha–ha for each note, make all the passage-work sound hacked up, and are far removed from the Italian manner of executing passage-work with the chest voice.

Quantz repeatedly speaks of performing vocal divisions with the chest voice. He writes that Senesino 'sang allegros with great fire, and marked rapid divisions, from the chest, in an articulate and pleasing manner'.[21] Since many, if not most, divisions for treble voice are written in the range of the head voice, Quantz's comments probably refer to articulation that derives from the diaphragm in contrast both to artificial articulation by syllable and to throat articulation. Quantz's apparent reference to diaphragmatic support in his use of the word 'chest' is clearer when he writes: 'every note of passage-work of this kind for the voice must be performed distinctly and stressed by a gentle breath of air from the chest' (p.124). This terminology is only confusing because diaphragm and throat production should not be equated with chest and head registers, as the repeated use of the term 'chest' might imply. Rather, production of divisions from either the diaphragm or throat relates directly to the distinction between diaphragm and throat vibrato.[22] As Zacconi states (see above), the singer who uses a continuous throat vibrato can easily produce divisions articulated from the throat, and although it demands a light voice, this style of production does result in great flexibility and facility. Quantz writes, 'a singer who articulates all fast passage-work from the chest can hardly produce it as quickly as one who produces it in the throat, although the former method, because of its distinctness is always superior to the latter, particularly in large places' (p.287).

These comments on articulation and the limited use of slurring all derive from the 18th century, and although it is almost impossible to extrapolate backwards, it is still useful to summarize the existing evidence. It would seem that slurring was reserved for adagios and cantabile airs, and that even there it was used with restraint. Allegros were distinctly articulated, but not detached, especially in divisions. In part, good Baroque singing style was probably articulated through the clear enunciation of the text.

Dynamics have been discussed in terms of the common Baroque stipulation that singers should sing their high notes softly and lightly and their low notes with more volume, a performing tradition that seems to be linked to the separation of the head and chest registers of the voice. Beyond this, however, a great deal of dynamic flexibility was practised. Crescendo and diminuendo on single long-held notes (*messa di voce*) was encouraged by all and abrupt changes of dynamics were discouraged. Bacilly writes (p.100):

> The proper technique, as I have already mentioned in the preceding article when I spoke of irrational changes of volume, is to increase the volume of the voice up to a certain point and then to diminish it little by little so that the resulting effect is a sort of surge and ebb.

Bernhard says, 'Care must be taken not to shift too abruptly from the *piano* to the *forte*, but rather to let the voice wax and wane gradually' (pp.14–15). The modern practice of sometimes maintaining individual phrases at a single dynamic level, or 'terraced dynamics', which apparently derives from an assumed transferral of the Baroque use of textual contrast between groups of varying size of timbre to dynamic use, has no sanction in the theoretical sources. Indeed, a contained change in dynamic level due to textural contrast does not necessitate, or even imply, a limitation to one dynamic throughout the phrase. Dynamic markings from the period illustrate the use of crescendo and decrescendo from Monteverdi to Leopold Mozart and beyond.[23]

Baroque tutors and singers offer practical as well as aesthetic advice in their discussions of dynamics and volume. Tosi warns the singer to 'regulate his Voice according to the Place where he sings; for it would be the greatest Absurdity, not to make a Difference between a small Cabinet and a vast Theatre' (p.150). Quantz gives specific directions to accompanists that are appropriate also to singers (p.275):

> To express the Forte and the Piano well, you must also note whether you are [performing] in a large place that reverberates, or in a small place, especially a tapestried one, where the tone is muffled; [or] whether the listeners are at a distance or nearby... In a large place that reverberates, you must not [perform] a Piano that immediately follows a loud and noisy *tutti* too softly, since it will be engulfed by the echo. But if the Piano lasts a while, you may gradually moderate your sound. In other situations you will do better to take the Piano just as it ought to be at the note where it is indicated. If, on the contrary, a Forte follows a Piano, you may [perform] the first note a little more strongly than the following ones.

The use of *piano* and *forte* in singing, however, 'must never be unduly exaggerated' (Quantz, p.274). Caccini criticizes those singers who take it as 'a general rule that in increasing and abating the voice, and in exclamations, is the foundation of passion, and who ... always use them in every sort of music, not discerning whether the words require it' (p.381). Bacilly warns against this 'great and widespread error which appears most frequently among provincial singers, which is that of singing softer now and then without any cause. The result is complete vocal inconsistency' (p.97). He even argues that because vocal music communicates a text it does not need as much fluctuation of dynamic as instrumental music to be expressive. Both Tosi (p.176) and Quantz (p.274) refer to dynamic changes as a kind of chiaroscuro (use of light and shade in painting) in music.

Like dynamics, tempo in Baroque music is to be treated with flexibility. In 1615, Girolamo Frescobaldi wrote of performing keyboard toccatas:

> This kind of playing must not be subject to the beat, [but should be performed] as we see done in modern Madrigals, which, in spite of their difficulties, are made easier by means of the beat, taking it now slowly, now quickly, and even held in the air, to match the expressive effect, or the sense of the words.[24]

Bacilly (pp.48–9) urges that singers be allowed to 'slow down the tempo in order to give themselves time to add *agréments*' especially in the sung gavottes where

> the dance meter is broken in order to give the air more refinement... It is completely unfair to criticize this style of performing by saying that the airs aren't danceable, as thousands of ignoramuses have done. If this were to be the intention of the performing singer, then his function would be no more than that of a viol.

He writes later 'that a variation of *mesure*, now slow, now fast, contributes a great deal to the expressivity of a song' (p.101). Like terraced dynamics, the so-called 'motoric rhythms' of Baroque music that result from a literal performance of the notes do not find corroboration in contemporary sources on singing, where the performer is regularly encouraged not to set a rigid tempo. 'Accelerando' and 'ritardando' may not appear as directions in the scores, but the treatises emphasize the importance of these effects in performance.

In rhythm as well as tempo, Baroque scores often fail to provide an exact notation, depending instead on conventions of performance, and, as a result, inequality, conflicting rhythms and double dotting are subjects that have caused much controversy. However, if the many comments on flexible tempo and rhythm in Baroque singing are taken into account, then the rhythmic conflicts or distinctions between parallel and simultaneous passages – in solo vocal music, at least – seem far less important than we, who are accustomed to an exact notational style, often make them. Rhythmic flexibility in performance eliminates many of the conflicts apparent in notation. As Caccini writes, 'there are many things used in good singing style that are written in one way but, to be more graceful, are effected in quite another'.[25] He then gives numerous examples. Clearly, rhythm was an important element of ornamentation. Just as ornamental pitches were rarely notated, so too rhythmic notation could be varied by the singer. As Bacilly writes of rhythmic notational alteration in the performance of the *port de voix*, 'This example can serve for all other cases so that it becomes evident that in the case of musical notation the music is printed one way but is performed in another' (p.67).

Tempo rubato provides a specific example of this practice. Caccini writes (p.391):

> I call that the noble manner of singing which is used without tying a man's self to the ordinary measure of time, making many times the value of the notes less by half, and sometimes more, according to the conceit of the words, whence proceeds that excellent kind of singing with a graceful neglect, whereof I have spoken before.

Caccini calls this style 'sprezzatura'. Tosi describes the practice in even more detail (p.156n):

> In this Place speaking of stealing the Time, it regards particularly the Vocal, or the Performance on a single Instrument in the *Pathetick* and *Tender*; when the Bass goes an exactly regular Pace, the other Part retards or anticipates in a singular Manner, for the Sake of Expression, but after That returns to its Exactness, to be guided by the Bass. Experience and Taste must teach it. A mechanical Method of going on with the Bass will easily distinguish the Merit of the other Manner.

To sing with rubato, the soloist must keep the beat exactly but alter the rhythmic values, slowing some, hastening others. The teacher will know when 'to anticipate the Time, knowing where to lose it again; and, which is still more charming, to know how to lose it, in order to recover it again (p.165). Burney writes of Cuzzoni that 'she had a creative fancy, and the power of occasionally accelerating and retarding the measure in the most artificial and able manner, what the Italians call *tempo rubato*'.[26]

Rhythmic flexibility is also a very important aspect in the performance of recitative. Very late in the period John Hoyle accurately described the practice of performing simple recitative in his *Dictionarium musica* (London, 1770): 'RECITATIVO: notwithstanding this sort of composition is noted in true time, the performer is at liberty to alter the Bass, and Measure, according as his subject requires; hence the Thorough Bass is to observe and follow the singer, and not the person who beats time'.[27] The rhythmic (and sometimes pitch) notation of a late 17th- or 18th-century simple recitative is a mere outline for a very free performance that expresses the text. Bernhard explains this as early as 1649 (pp.24–5).

> In the recitative style, one should take care that the voice is raised in moments of anger, and to the contrary dropped in moments of grief. Pain makes it pause; impatience hastens it. Happiness enlivens it. Desire emboldens it. Love renders it alert. Bashfulness holds it back. Hope strengthens it. Despair diminishes it. Fear keeps it down. Danger is fled with screams. If, however, a person faces up to danger, then his voice must reflect his daring and bravery.

In 1723 Tosi devotes an entire chapter to recitative. He distinguishes between church, theatrical and chamber recitatives: the first must display a noble majesty with fewer graces than in the other styles, but with freer cadences; the second must be acted 'in character'; the third is the most passionate. He criticizes many faults in the performance of recitative, which include whispering, hurrying and bellowing, but at his most exasperated he writes, 'To speak my Mind freely, yours and their Faults are unpardonable; it is insufferable to be any longer tormented in the Theatres with *Recitatives*, sung in the Stile of a Choir of *Capuchin* Friars' (p.72). In sum, the singer must not perform Baroque recitative either too quickly or too slowly, nor should he follow the exact rhythmic notation; probably normal speech patterns provide the best guide to both rhythm and tempo. Most importantly, as in all aspects of Baroque singing, the style of performance must be tied to the expression of the text.

Voice types and choir sizes

In discussing musical interpretation, differences between voice types are often overlooked. In the Baroque, however, important vocal distinctions were made by range and voice type that largely determine the kind of singer that should perform any particular piece or operatic role. Distinctions were made first of all by range. For example, in the early 17th century composers seem to have favoured tenors.[28] The castrato only began to appear regularly in operas after 1640, and the female virtuosos (such as Francesca Caccini and Barbara Strozzi) were usually limited to chamber rather than theatrical work.[29] The primary virtuoso roles in the *Orfeo* operas of Peri, Caccini and Monteverdi are all for tenor. This is remarkable only because the situation changed so quickly and abruptly.

By the middle of the 17th century the tenor voice was largely supplanted in Italy by the castrato. Tenors were often pushed aside into comic and often transvestite roles, such as the Nurse in Monteverdi's *L'incoronazione di Poppea* (1642). Although the tenor continued to be used in sacred music, Carissimi and Schütz frequently limited this voice to narration, and of Bach's 19 solo cantatas only one is for tenor (with nine for soprano, five for alto and four for bass). In French opera, the 'simple' tenor, as opposed to the *haute-contre* discussed below, maintained a lowly status throughout the 17th century and well into the 18th.[30] Handel used a tenor for the leading male role in the non-public *Acis and Galatea* (1718), but his setting of the important role of Bajazet for tenor in *Tamerlano* (1724) was perhaps the first milestone in the rediscovery of the theatrical and dramatic possibilities of the tenor voice. However, the tenor voice did not fully regain its importance in solo and operatic singing until the rise of comic and national opera in the late 18th century. Even in Mozart's three Da Ponte operas, most of the leading male roles are taken by baritones rather than tenors.

The bass voice, on the other hand, never enjoyed wide acclaim. Although the Florentine theorist Giambattista Doni (1635) placed it second only to the tenor voice, Giovanni de' Bardi counselled Caccini 'never to pass from the tenor to the bass, seeing that with its passages the bass takes away whatever magnificence and gravity the tenor, with its majesty, has bestowed'.[31] In 1668 Bacilly wrote (pp.22–3):

> considering the voice according to its musical range, using the musical terminology of Soprano, Contralto, Tenor, Bass, etc., we find that the higher voice ranges are more successful in effective performance even though all of the vocal ranges ought to be equally suitable for training. This is due to the fact that a greater number of the emotions or passions will appear to good advantage in the higher voice ranges than in the lower ones. The bass voice is suitable for almost nothing but the emotion of anger, which appears rarely in French airs. As a result, this voice range must be content with partsinging and doing the job for which nature seems to have destined it; i.e., singing the bass part rather than the melody.

Still, throughout the Baroque era there were exceptions to this severe judgment.

Giustiniani (1628) identifies three bass singers from the last quarter of the 16th century who 'sang bass with a range of 22 notes', and Caccini, despite Bardi's warning, wrote virtuoso bass arias for Melchior Palantrotti. Additional exceptions include the virtuoso bass songs by Henry Purcell for John Gostling and the virtuoso bass parts in Handel's Italian cantatas and dramatic works: *La resurrezione*, *Nell'africane selve* and *Aci, Galatea e Polifemo*.

Basses were more frequently used, however, in music that demanded less virtuosity and, for that reason, in countries where vocal writing was less florid. For example, basses were more popular in French and German opera. Raguenet (1702) identifies the use of the bass soloist as an important difference between French and Italian opera.

> Besides, our operas have a farther advantage over the Italian in respect of the voice, and that is the bass, which is so frequent among us and so rarely to be met with in Italy. For every man that has an ear will witness with me that nothing can be more charming than a good bass; the simple sound of these basses, which sometimes seems to sink into a profound abyss, has something wonderfully charming in it.... When the persons of gods or kings, a Jupiter, Neptune, Priam, or Agamemnon, are brought on the stage, our actors, with their deep voices, give 'em an air of majesty, quite different from that of the feigned basses among the Italians, which have neither depth nor strength.[32]

German opera, especially in Hamburg, also used basses frequently as elderly statesmen as well as comic servants and raging tyrants. Perhaps following the Hamburg tradition, Handel used the bass voice much more than contemporary Italian opera composers. However, one of his best bass singers, Giuseppe Maria Boschi, inspired the comment 'and Boschi-like be always in a rage',[33] which harks directly back to Bacilly's comments about the expressive limitations of the lowest register. Where basses were used frequently, as in French opera, their sound is described as 'simple' (Raguenet) or 'raging' (Bacilly). The exceptions were remarkable but rare.

Throughout the Baroque era the treble voice was preferred. Tosi and Mancini wrote their vocal treatises for sopranos, and the soprano voice was universally considered the best for passage-work and divisions. Bardi (c1578) writes, 'To make divisions upon the bass is not natural',[34] and all subsequent writers agree. The female soprano and the castrato (soprano or mezzo) prevailed because treble voices were best suited to rapid divisions and emotional expression. For this reason, the falsetto range of the adult male voice was also cultivated in the *haute-contre*, countertenor and falsettist and, of course, the boy treble was also highly prized. Perhaps in no other period was the treble voice so exclusively favoured. Music for castrato, *haute-contre*, countertenor and boy treble derives predominantly from the Baroque, and the cultivation of the male treble in its many forms is an important characteristic of the period.

Range was therefore very important to Baroque authors and composers. Each range has its known quality:

> a *Soprano* has generally most Volubility, and becomes it best; and also equally the Pathetick. The *Contr'Alto* more of the Pathetick than the Volubility; the *Tenor* less of the Pathetick, but more of the Volubility than the *Contr'Alto*, though not so much as the *Soprano*. The *Bass*, in general more pompous than any, but should not be so boisterous as now too often practised.[35]

It follows from the clear distinctions made between the ranges that it is inappropriate to transpose parts from one range to another, because, for example, an aria written for soprano would be composed differently from an aria for bass. Because of the preponderance of treble parts, however, and the disappearance of the castrato, many modern producers have assigned castrato roles either to basses who sing the vocal line an octave lower than written or to countertenors who preserve both the pitch and sex of the original part. Neither solution is musically or historically correct.

The castrato voice was prized for its power and flexibility. The high range was not considered effeminate but was compared to the trumpet and deemed especially heroic. Although it is difficult to assess the quality of this voice without living examples, it is well to remember that even the castrato passed through puberty, experienced a voice change and did not continue sounding like a boy treble. Tosi writes that it would be unusual for the castrato to preserve the ability to sing 'in chest' throughout the range after puberty, implying that even these singers resorted to falsetto. He writes about the male soprano: 'The Extent of the full natural Voice terminates generally upon the fourth Space, which is C [c″]; or on the fifth line, which is D [d″]; and there the feigned Voice becomes of Use' (pp.23–4). This vocal break may be why many castratos cultivated the mezzo range, and why a number of sopranos fell to mezzo as they became older.

The French *haute-contre* voice, the English countertenor, and the Spanish falsettist were all male singers in the same range, but the differences and similarities in the production of these voices remains confused. The apparent ability of the Spanish falsettists to sing in the high soprano range finds little parallel today, except perhaps among popular rock singers. The distinction between a *haute-contre* and countertenor seems to be that the former is a high tenor using head voice, and the latter a falsettist (the difference between, for example, Russell Oberlin and Alfred Deller). The countertenor and falsettist were used particularly in sacred choral music where the female voice was prohibited throughout much of the period. Their voices were very flexibile but lacked the power and drama of the castrato. Handel wrote for solo countertenor in his oratorios, but this voice rarely appeared on the operatic stage. On the other hand, the *haute-contre* was the premier male voice in French opera. During the 18th century Pierre de Jélyotte was as renowned as any castrato,[36] and the French treatise on singing by the *haute-contre* Bérard (1755) parallels the Italian treatise by the castrato Tosi (1723).

Women's voices were distinguished from male treble voices by having vibrato more frequently and by the ability to sing in chest register throughout the range. When Tosi writes that male singers rarely preserve the ability to sing entirely 'in chest', he seems to imply that the adult female voice resembled that of a boy. On the other hand, Raguenet, who openly disliked the castrato voice, described it as 'being perfectly like' a woman's. Certainly the female soprano voice was highly flexible and expressive. It is possible, however, that it lacked the power of the adult castrato voice.

The boy treble may have sounded something like the female soprano, as has been said. This is possible for two reasons: not only was the female soprano certainly a lighter voice than is generally heard in opera today, but boys' voices changed much later. Boy trebles frequently performed until 16 and as late as 18, allowing them more experience and greater physical development than today's boy trebles. It is thought that all of Bach's treble solos, with the exception of *Jauchzet Gott*, which may have been composed for Faustina Bordoni, were written for boys.[37]

Because of the multiplicity of voice types in the treble range during the Baroque, some of which cannot be duplicated today, performers frequently need to make choices about vocal quality. In assigning castrato roles, the historically correct decision is to use a woman. The countertenor voice was used in church and chamber, but was not a theatrical voice, making up in subtlety and beauty for what it lacked in passion and stamina. Not only is the female voice closer in sound to the castrato, therefore, but it was substituted for the castrato even during the Baroque era. Handel, for example, used women whenever he lacked a castrato. Indeed, sexual role reversal was never a problem in the Baroque. In the original production of *Rinaldo* (1713) the castrato Nicolini sang the title role, but the male role of Goffredo was written for a woman. In 1713 the opera was revived with Mrs Barbier singing Rinaldo; in 1717 the part of Goffredo was given to a castrato. Some female singers (such as Jane Barbier) specialized in transvestite roles. Even in the oratorios, Handel entrusted major male roles for treble to women rather than countertenors; for example, the title role in *Solomon* was written for Signora Galli, a mezzo-soprano. On the other hand, because of the prohibition against women appearing on the Roman stage, many female roles were written and performed by male castratos, some of whom specialized in female roles – such as Girolamo Bartoluzzi (*fl* 1719–24) and Andrea Martini (1761–1819).[38] Women and castratos frequently exchanged roles and played parts of both sexes. Castratos and countertenors were not similarly interchangeable.

Vocal transposition by octave in order to bring a castrato role into the natural male range was never a solution. This not only transfers an aria written particularly for one range into another, but frequently, with the mezzo-castrato roles, it moves the vocal line below the written instrumental bass line. For both reasons octave transposition is stylistically inappropriate to the music. Although some exceptions exist to the prohibition against simple vocal transposition, these generally involve a relationship between soprano and tenor; for example, Handel sometimes had a soprano sing 'Thy rebuke hath broken his·heart' and 'Behold, and see if there be any sorrow' from *Messiah*, both originally for tenor. In most cases, however, the transferral of a role from one range to another demanded rewriting of both the vocal line and accompaniment; Gluck's recomposition of the title role of *Orfeo* from soprano castrato range to *haute-contre* is an example. If Baroque operas were sometimes performed by all-male casts (as were Shakespeare's plays), then we should not hesitate today to produce Baroque opera today with predominantly or all female casts. From a historical point of view, range and vocal colour are far more important than sexual identity.

With choirs the problem is less severe. Almost all Baroque choristers were male, especially in sacred music (which women were frequently prohibited from singing), with boys singing the top part, boys and countertenors singing alto. By the end of the 17th century, women were sometimes associated with choirs as soloists, but they rarely performed as part of the choir. For example, Handel always used two or three female soloists in performances of *Messiah*, but the choir remained all male. In the *Dublin Journal* it was said of the first performance that 'the Gentlemen of the two Choirs, Mr Dubourg, Mrs Avolio, and Mrs Cibber...all performed their Parts to Admiration'.[39] The personnel lists from the Foundling Hospital for performances of *Messiah* in 1754, 1758 and 1759 all include three female soloists and a chorus consisting of boys (twice identified as six in number) and between 11 and 13 men.[40] Bach certainly did not use female voices in his choirs.

In sum, even if the original range of a vocal part is zealously preserved, it may remain difficult to determine or even to find the right vocal quality. Substitutes must be found for castratos, and must often be sought for parts originally written for male altos (countertenors, falsettists and *haute-contres*) and boys. In both solo and choral singing, this must be done with caution – with an awareness of Baroque attitudes towards vocal production and Baroque sensibilities about voice types. It can only be mentioned here in passing that in determining appropriate vocal types, pitch is yet an additional hazard (see Chapter VII).

The size of choirs in the Baroque is also a concern. In general, the number of singers ranged from as few as four to as many as 90. Many choruses were quite small. Most closing 'choruses' in Italian operas are nothing more than an ensemble of soloists, and Bach speaks of three or four to a part in four-part writing as ideal.[41] Mid-17th-century sources of oratorios do not generally distinguish between choruses (with multiple singers to a part) and ensembles of soloists,[42] but the oratory of S Marcello in Rome at various times used 12 or 20 voices – that is, four or five to a part.[43] Some choirs, however, were

Voices

much larger, especially in the royal courts. In 1645 the French royal chapel listed 26 singers: two boy sopranos, eight basses, eight tenors and eight countertenors.[44] By 1708 there were 90: 11 sopranos consisting of falsettists, castratos and boys, 18 countertenors, 23 tenors, 24 baritones and 14 basses.[45] In England at the beginning of the 18th century the Chapel Royal had 38 singers: 26 men and 12 boys; for the Coronation Anthems of 1727, 47 singers were used (about seven to a part).[46] French opera contained real choruses, as opposed to solo ensembles, and in 1713 the opera chorus at the Royal Academy of Music included 22 men and 12 women;[47] this is one of the clearest instances of the existence of female choristers during the Baroque, and it is not surprising that it occurs in secular, dramatic music. Baroque choruses varied greatly in size and balance, but women rarely sang in sacred choirs. The average chorus can be said to number about 30.

Although the part singer followed the same guidelines as a soloist in vocal production and interpretation, he was, of course, more restricted. Tosi offers good instructions to the ensemble performer in terms of volume, blend and vocal decorum (p.150):

[The singer] is still more to be blam'd, who, when singing in two, three, or four Parts, does so raise his Voice as to drown his Companions: for if it is not Ignorance, it is something worse. All Compositions for more than one Voice ought to be sung strictly as they are written; nor do they require any other Art but a noble Simplicity.

Notes

[1] D. Corri, *The Singer's Preceptor* (London, 1810).
[2] G. Caccini, *Le nuove musiche* (Florence, 1601/2), Eng. trans. in O. Strunk, in *Source Readings in Music History* (New York, 1950).
[3] As quoted by Winton Dean in 'Senesino', *Grove 6*, xvii, 130. The source of the quotation is the autobiography of Johann Joachim Quantz in F. W. Marpurg, *Historisch-kritische Beyträge zur Aufnahme der Musik*, i (Berlin, 1755), 197–250; a complete English translation may be found in P. Nettl, *Forgotten Musicians* (New York, 1951), 280–319.
[4] C. Burney, *A General History of Music* (London, 1776–89), ed. F. Mercer (London, 1935/R1957), ii, 737.
[5] B. de Bacilly, *Remarques curieuses sur l'art de bien chanter* (Paris, 1668/R1971; Eng. trans., 1968).
[6] J. Mattheson, *Der vollkommene Capellmeister* (Hamburg, 1739; Eng. trans., 1981).
[7] P. F. Tosi, *Opinioni de' cantori antichi e moderni, o sieno osservazioni sopra il canto figurato* (Bologna, 1723/R1968; Eng. trans., 1742, 2/1743/R1969).
[8] J. J. Quantz, *Versuch einer Anweisung die Flöte traversiere zu spielen* (Berlin, 1752, 3/1789/R1952; Eng. trans., 1966).
[9] C. Bernhard, *Von der Singe-Kunst, oder Maniera* (c1649), Eng. trans. in W. Hilse, 'The Treatises of Christoph Bernhard', *Music Forum*, iii (1973), 13–29.
[10] Claudio Monteverdi, *Madrigali guerrieri ed amorosi* (Venice, 1638), 'Foreword', as translated in Strunk, *Source Readings*, 413.
[11] See *Great Singers on Great Singing*, ed. J. Hines (New York, 1982), 123, about Nicolai Gedda and Jussi Björling.
[12] E. V. Foreman, *A Comparison of Selected Italian Vocal Tutors of the Period Circa 1550 to 1800* (diss., U. of Illinois, 1969), 34.
[13] G. Mancini, *Pensieri e riflessioni pratiche sopra il canto figurato* (Vienna, 1774, rev. and enlarged 3/1777), Eng. trans. in E. Foreman, *Masterworks on Singing*, vii (Champaign, 1967).
[14] See *Great Singers*, ed. Hines, 140.
[15] In J. Boaden, *Memoirs of the Life of John Philip Kemble* (1825), as quoted by R. Fiske, *English Theatre Music in the Eighteenth Century* (London, 1973), 270.

[16] A. Della Corte, 'Vicende degli stili del canto dal tempo di Gluck al '900' in *Canto e bel canto* (Turin, 1933), as quoted by Foreman, *A Comparison*, 5.

[17] As translated by Foreman, *A Comparison*, 34.

[18] William Jackson, as paraphrased by Fiske, *English Theatre Music*, 270.

[19] See Burney, *A General History*, ii, 736, 721n and 743n.

[20] As translated by Foreman, *A Comparison*, 113–14; see also C. MacClintock, *Readings in the History of Music in Performance* (Bloomington and London, 1979), 73.

[21] As quoted by Dean, 'Senesino', *Grove 6*, xvii, 130–31, from Quantz's autobiography; see also Nettl, *Forgotten Musicians*, 292.

[22] See D. Galliver, ' "Cantare con la Gorga": the Coloratura Technique of the Renaissance Singer', *SMA*, vii (1973), 10–18.

[23] See R. Donington, *The Interpretation of Early Music* (London, 1963/R1974), 482–5, for a summary of examples; see also W. Kolneder, *Aufführungspraxis bei Vivaldi* (Leipzig, 1955), 24ff, for lists of dynamic terms used by that composer (also reproduced in Donington, *The Interpretation*).

[24] As quoted in Donington, *Interpretation*, 432.

[25] As translated by H. W. Hitchcock, *RRMBE*, ix (Madison, Wisc., 1970), 50.

[26] Burney, *A General History*, ii, 737.

[27] As quoted in Donington, *Interpretation*, 427.

[28] N. Fortune, 'Italian 17th-century Singing', *ML*, xxxv (1954), 208ff.

[29] A. Heriot, *The Castrati in Opera* (London, 1956/R1974), 24. Recently Iain Fenlon, in 'Monteverdi's Mantuan *Orfeo*: Some New Documentation', *EM*, xii (1984), 163–72, has shown that the major female roles in Monteverdi's *Orfeo* were taken by castratos.

[30] J. R. Anthony, *French Baroque Music from Beaujoyeulx to Rameau* (London, 1973, rev.2/1978), 55 and 78–9.

[31] As quoted in Fortune, 'Italian 17th-century Singing', 209.

[32] F. Raguenet, *Paralele des italiens et des françois, en ce qui regarde la musique et les opéra* (Paris, 1702), as translated in Strunk, *Source Readings*, 475.

[33] James Miller, as quoted by Winton Dean in 'Boschi', *Grove 6*, iii, 74.

[34] As quoted in Fortune, 'Italian 17th-century Singing', 213.

[35] J. E. Galliard in his translation of Tosi, *Opinioni de' cantori*, 10–11n.

[36] See A. Pougin, *Un ténor de l'Opéra au XVIIIᵉ siècle: Pierre Jélyotte et les chanteurs de son emps* (Paris, 1905).

[37] See R. L. Marshall, 'Bach the Progressive: Observations on his Later Works', *MQ*, lxii (1976), 313–57.

[38] Heriot, *Castrati*, 160–61, and R. Strohm, 'Vivaldi's Career as an Opera Producer', *Essays on Handel and Italian Opera* (Cambridge, 1985), 135.

[39] O. E. Deutsch, *Handel: a Documentary Biography* (London, 1955), 546.

[40] ibid, 751, 801 and 825.

[41] *Bach-Dokumente*, i: *Schriftstücke von der Hand Johann Sebastian Bachs*, ed. W. Neumann and H.-J. Schulze (Kassel, 1963), 60.

[42] H. E. Smither, *A History of the Oratorio*, i (Chapel Hill, 1977), 244.

[43] ibid, 214.

[44] Anthony, *French Baroque Music*, 14.

[45] ibid, 15.

[46] Dean, 'Handel', *Grove 6*, viii, 92.

[47] Anthony, *French Baroque Music*, 91.

CHAPTER VI

The Performer as Composer

DAVID FULLER

In the 17th and 18th centuries, the collaboration between composer and performer, without which no music can exist that is not improvised or composed directly into its medium (like electronic music), was weighted more heavily towards the performer than at any time since and perhaps before.[1]

A large part of the music of the whole era was sketched rather than fully realized, and the performer had something of the responsibility of a child with a colouring book, to turn these sketches into rounded art-works. This was what the thoroughbass player had to do with the harmony of ensemble music; this was what the soloist had to do with his ornaments to the melody; and this was what everyone had to do with the written rhythms. (Sometimes even the sketch would not do. On 1 April 1785, the Italian tenor Giacomo Davide sang Pergolesi's *Stabat mater* at the Concert Spirituel in Paris. Davide, according to the review in the *Mercure*, 'did not embellish, he *created* the verset *Qui maerebat* ... constructing *in promptu*, on the given harmonies, a melody very different from the one that is written. ... Is this not a case where skill in execution happily replaces the weakness of the composition?'.)[2]

Forty years ago, Bukofzer wrote of a Baroque 'code of performance' that had to be 'known and observed in order that a faithful and undistorted rendition of the music be accomplished'.[3] No doubt some musicians still search for that code – a Rosetta Stone or an 'Enigma' machine to translate Baroque ciphers into the notes that would fill out those sketches as their author imagined them. They are encouraged by manuals and ornament tables (genuine Baroque as well as modern) which set forth rules of seemingly universal applicability into which the score need only be plugged to set their music aglow with authenticity. It is easy to dream this way about music at three centuries' remove, but draw near and the rules collapse in disorderly reality. We can get an inkling of how it really was by observing ourselves and our own music-making.

The closest modern parallel to the gap between Baroque notation and the sounding product is to be found in jazz. Like the Baroque player of chordal instruments, the jazz musician must be skilled at 'realizing' a chord shorthand, and like Pasquini's *partimento* player, or the players in Agazzari's 'improvising orchestra', he must be able to improvise melodic solos or take his part in an ensemble with nothing but such a shorthand to guide him. Like Simpson's division violist, he must be able to improvise diminutions on a tune or make a counterpoint to it; like Mersenne's singer of *airs de cour*,

117

C. P. E. Bach's clavichord player or Tosi's opera star, he must be able to vary a tune each time it is repeated; like any French Baroque musician he must know when passages of quavers are to be delivered 'straight' and when they should be 'swung'; and he must have at his command a rich vocabulary of ornaments to colour his performance and stamp it with his own personality.[4] His 'charts' and 'fake books' are no less laconic relative to the finished product than are Baroque scores. Of course, jazz is very different from the Baroque music that mostly concerns us today in the simplicity and uniformity of its basic structures and in its expressive aims. But in its need to supply a constant flow of fresh, appealing and saleable material to a diverse audience, it is as much a living art as was opera and concert music of the 18th century – and, relative to a smaller and more varied public, also that of the 17th. (Witnesses to the vitality of an art are the contemporary accounts of it: jazz is described in masses of personal, anecdotal and circumstantial particulars; compare these with Burney's account of Italian opera in London in his *History*. In neither case can we read what the music actually sounded like because it was assumed to be completely familiar.)

The paucity of penetrating studies of jazz makes it impossible to draw many lessons about earlier music from the parallels, but there are at least three aspects that can be observed by the modern student which will bring him up sharply against the reality of what it must have meant to experience Baroque music as a living art. The first is the diversity of jazz; a diversity so manifold that any illusion about a 'code' of performance must be dispelled. The diversity referred to here is not that of period or nation or even genre; it is the diversity from one group to the next, one day to the next, one neighbourhood to the next. For example, a jazz scholar has found distinct performing styles associated with the west and east sides of Buffalo (where this is being written) in the 1980s.[5] Montéclair, in 1736, wrote that in Paris in his time 'there is little agreement on either the signs or the names of the ornaments ... even the masters do not understand each other, and the pupil of one teacher understands neither the language nor the notation of another'. There is every reason to believe that this kind of diversity is a permanent feature of a living tradition; as early as 1549, Bermudo gave up on the *quiebro* – 'the fashion of playing them changes every day'.[6]

The second aspect is the ornamental one, and here the imaginative listener to jazz – particularly jazz singers – can learn much, not only about the range of diversity in personal styles of ornamentation, but also about the immense range of ornamental possibility that is open to the performer free of academic norms of tone production and technique. Since we know so little of how early singers sounded (and to a lesser extent, players on instruments like the violin, where many components of the sound are under the player's control), we must keep an open mind about the ornamental effects they actually produced, perhaps by experimenting with some ornaments of jazz musicians that are congruous with what we know of Baroque music. It is the rare singer of Baroque music, for example, who is able to sing with the contrast of 'straight' and vibrating tone that seems to have been a feature of singing in the 17th and 18th centuries, yet it can be heard any day in popular music on the radio. Appoggiaturas are common in jazz; it is instructive to hear how performers who have never heard the word 'appoggiatura' handle them. But

118

it is particularly the indefinable ornaments of tone-colour, articulation (particularly cut-offs), pitch-adjustment and dynamics in popular music-making that can open up new worlds to the classically-trained musician.

Jazz is chiefly known for the nature of its rhythm, but its most ubiquitous rhythmic characteristic is hardly ever mentioned in writings about the art. This is precisely because it is so ubiquitous that it is absorbed into the very meaning of the word itself. Nowhere in the 32 columns devoted to jazz in *Grove 6* is there a reference to it. But in a primer of jazz improvisation we find a note to students: 'In order to help get a swing feel play eighths as follows: [ex.1]'. If an arranger or band leader does not want this effect, he must ask

for it by specifying 'straight eighths'. The primer warns the student not to 'swing' quavers when playing rock. Clearly, the effect is a generic tag. All this has a precise parallel in the *notes inégales* of the French Baroque (discussed in detail later in this chapter). It is unlikely that French inequality sounded quite like a jazz solo in which the alternation of longs and shorts may be modified by anticipations and delays over a beat that is implicit but not expressed.[7] French inequality is known, nevertheless, to have been variable, it may often have been spontaneous, it had to be adapted to the style of the music and it must have been characterized by a range of nuance that, if not the same as in jazz, was sufficiently analogous for a modern Baroque musician to learn something from observing it.[8]

No musician who listens to these three aspects of jazz can harbour any illusions about a 'code of performance', or indeed any combination of notation and written description that would enable him to reproduce a performance he has not heard. But we need not stray beyond the perfumed world of 'early music' itself to shake our faith in codes. Nothing could be more different than the results obtained by Wieland Kuijken and John Hsu from the viola da gamba, by Gustav Leonhardt and the late Wanda Landowska from the harpsichord or by Anthony Newman and Harald Vogel from the organ.[9] Lesser musicians listen to these masters and form schools whose approach to the problems of Baroque scores has little to do with historical evidence and much to do with emulation; if there are codes, then they must be as diverse as the models we follow.

Perhaps the fundamental lesson that performers of early music can learn from jazz is to revise their expectations. The artists mentioned above (with the possible exception of Vogel) claim the whole Baroque repertory for their instruments as their territory: Kuijken claims Simpson and Forqueray; Leonhardt claims Frescobaldi and Duphly. Everybody claims Bach. They piece together the documents and fill the lacunae with interpretation and conjecture. The results are variable, the music they know best being most successful. The early music performer expects too much if he thinks he can penetrate a dozen contrasting styles to the same depth as the one-track musician. There are a few practitioners of Baroque music who do specialize, who do confine themselves to a narrow range of styles and who steep themselves, morning and night, not only in the music but in everything that engendered and surrounded it. Of course they master the documents, but far more importantly they let the music and the instruments teach them everything they can. And they produce and produce. It is they who come closest to the music of the past by duplicating, in a very real way, the experience of the old musicians who also lived with this same repertory. They go far beyond the point where they can explain what they do, and thus beyond the point where what they do could ever have been transmitted by written documents. They can, however, be roughly imitated, and it is with such imitation that the modern musician who wishes to become a good performer of early music is advised to begin.

In the Marciana library in Venice there is a little anonymous recorder method dated 1630 and called 'Everything you need to know to play the recorder'.[10] It makes the point at length that the real difficulty in learning to play a dance from the notes is getting the *andamento* or *aria* right – terms that might be translated 'the way it goes'. The best way is to listen to a master. It is only as an aid, as we learn under the heading 'Oservationi per facilitar l'aria della sonatta', that musicians use beats to keep time and tails on the notes to show which ones are more or less fast. Two centuries later, both Hallé and Meyerbeer remarked how mazurkas under the fingers of Chopin sounded quite strictly duple, though notated in triple metre, and how angry it made him to have this pointed out.[11] He felt and understood the metre to be 3/4, and even if the first beat was as long as the other two put together, it was 'still à trois quatre!' as he is recorded to have almost yelled at Meyerbeer. He knew how mazurkas went; he had heard them all his life, and their *aria*, or *andamento*, required an altogether different kind of 3/4 from a minuet, for instance.

Though Chopin's pupils and the readers of the recorder treatise might learn notes from the score, they learnt the manner of playing them by imitation. Once they learnt how dances 'went', the very idea of notation underwent a remarkable expansion in their musical consciousness: to the notes and the flags was added the title at the top of the page. The crotchets on a page with 'mazurka' written at the top no longer had the same value as crotchets on a page labelled 'minuet'.[12]

This perception of musical notation as comprehending the whole page – perhaps even the circumstances surrounding the performance of the music – is not unrelated to the Baroque understanding of 'style'. This is considered to be the sum of the characteristics of a class of music, as 'theatre', 'church' and 'chamber' styles, and it furnishes a key to the understanding of many problems of historical performance. It does not help the performer who has not had the luck to be able to imitate the right models, but it does, for example, answer the historical question of how a performer might have been expected to know that the different dotted figures of a French overture were supposed to be synchronized and exaggerated (if indeed they were) without the benefit of some 'code'.[13]

We can conclude this cautionary introduction by citing three anomalies of Baroque notation for which there can be no code of translation because the composers and theorists of the time had no clear idea of what they meant.

One is the habit of writing triplets in values one stage too small, as triplets of quavers equal to a minim (see cx.4 below). J. S. Beyer's singing method of 1703 illustrates them in 3/2 time, saying simply, 'Sometimes nine quavers are found instead of three minims'. A little later, 9/4 is derived from 3/2 (the source gives 2/3, but this is apparently a misprint) and 9/8 is derived from 3/4, with the values given as today. There is no effort to reconcile these two notations.[14]

The same book is equally vague on the subject of whitened quavers in 3/2, which are presented as an idiosyncrasy of 'some composers'. This notation, which is not uncommon in mid-17th-century Italian scores, was often imitated by French composers in the first half of the next century, usually in 3/2 but occasionally in duple metres. Several theorists describe it and all are agreed that flagged or beamed white notes are exactly the same as black notes with one fewer flag or beam; but no one can say why they are used and almost no one suggests any special significance. A method by Vague (first name unknown) dated 1733 mentions them and says they indicate 'une plus grande lenteur das les mouvements'. Modern explanations have been attempted, but they do not fit their use by composers.[15]

The final anomaly is where there are too many flags on flagged notes. French composers of the late 17th and early 18th centuries – the most celebrated being François Couperin – have caused endless controversy in the overdotting literature by their prodigality with flags and beams, especially after dots, where they suggest to the eye great exaggeration of the dotted effect. The theorists are silent, but one composer who used extra flags consistently on semiquavers said that 'one should not be frightened, they should be regarded as nothing but semiquavers'.[16] Occasionally one finds over-flagged notes continuing throughout a bar against normal values in another part (e.g. 12 apparent hemidemisemiquavers filling a 3/8 bar) in a context that virtually forbids their having any significance for rhythm or tempo.[17] Again, explanations have been attempted, but none is satisfactory and the powerful visual suggestion of overdotting remains in dotted figures.

The rest of this chapter will address those aspects of Baroque music whose demands on the performer are most obvious.

Thoroughbass

Of all the areas of Baroque performance, the most lavishly documented is thoroughbass playing. The 'Handlist' in Peter Williams's *Figured Bass Accompaniment* (Edinburgh, 1970) contains 60 titles from the 17th and 18th centuries devoted expressly to thoroughbass, but this is only a fraction of the treatises, both printed and manuscript, that treat the subject more or less systematically. Many of these are summarized or partly translated in F. T. Arnold's monumental *The Art of Accompanying from a Thorough-Bass as Practised in the Seventeenth and Eighteenth Centuries* (London, 1931/R1965). To a greater extent than any of the other aspects of Baroque performance requiring a substantial contribution by the performer, thoroughbass has been revived as a living art, and it is now taught as a separate subject in many music schools and practised as a speciality by professionals everywhere that Baroque music is regularly performed. This does not mean, however, that our knowledge is sufficient to permit the stylish performance of all repertories. Abundant as the old manuals are, the overwhelming majority are concerned exclusively with getting the chords right and with linking them properly, not with how to play them. They are rarely illustrated with written-out realizations, and such models as do exist are usually in four parts, designed merely to show the most correct handling of parts.[18] Moreover, they do not deal with the basic question of whether there should be any accompaniment at all in certain repertories. Bach's motets, which lack a figured bass part, have long been performed without continuo; it has only recently been established that motets were performed with harpsichord and string bass in Leipzig.[19] On the other hand, the overtures, dances and other orchestral pieces in French opera from Lully to Rameau, long assumed to require a continuo, are now thought to have been performed without accompaniment. Even in cases where an instrumental piece was repeated with vocal parts, the continuo would enter only with the voices.[20]

Though the normal, and probably most desirable, interpretation of 'thoroughbass' assumed the addition of chords or some manner of harmonic filling to the score, it appears to have been not uncommon for sonatas and cantatas to have been performed without any 'realization', the soloist being accompanied only by a cello or other melody instrument playing the bass part. Thus Burney, in his *Travels*, joined with Metastasio in lamenting the early 18th-century cantatas that had no other accompaniment than a harpsichord 'or' a violoncello with no obbligato instruments to obscure the beauties and hide the faults of the singing.

Thoroughbass lies on the border between notated and unnotated music. In principle, at least, it is partly notated; that is, the harmony is written in the score with figures, even if the actual notes to be played are not. The properly trained accompanist reads the figures as he would any notation, but they leave him with far more basic decisions and impose far more demands on his musical literacy than does staff notation; he must match the requirements of the figures against the rules of part-writing, and only then against all the needs of the music he is accompanying. Learning to accompany from a figured bass takes as much effort as learning to play at sight from staff notation. But the accompanist's problems do not end here. A great many thoroughbass parts have no figuring, and still another set of rules must be mastered in order to select the right chords. Even with the rules, the player to a large extent depends on his ear and his knowledge of the style, since the rules only hold for a range of probabilities, rarely yielding sure answers. Only after these skills have been mastered does the art of accompanying begin.

The variety of particular continuo practices described in the enormous body of source material can only be suggested here by a list of some of the choices that must be made by the conductor or accompanist. Fortunately, all of these are addressed in literature easily accessible to the modern player.[21]

Assuming that the decision to 'realize' the bass with at least one chordal instrument has been taken, one must choose:

1. Whether to double the bass with one or more melody instruments.
2. What instrument(s) and how many to use for the realization of the figures. The list of possibilities is long, of course, and evidently included the

octave spinet in domestic music-making even though its pitch might lie above the soloist.

3. How much of a rapidly moving bass part to play or realize with chords (Arnold devoted over 60 pages to this question). Related to this is the matter of repeated notes, moderately paced as in *Trommelbässe* or rapid as in operatic storm scenes, etc.

4. What register or position to choose for the accompanying chords.

5. Whether to double the melody or occasional notes from it so as to give the singer his next note, as in recitative, for example. (Opinion and practices differed.)

6. What texture to choose. Although three parts plus the bass was the point of departure for all late Baroque figured-bass accompaniment and was the texture chosen for learning the chords and part-writing, all possible textures were regularly used in harpsichord accompaniment whatever the figures seemed to demand, from no added notes at all (the bass alone being played) through doubling in octaves, thirds or tenths, to the maximum number of notes playable by ten fingers. The choice was governed by the style, period and nationality of the music and the size of the ensemble. Organ accompaniment avoided thick textures, which were in any case unnecessary because of the possibilities conferred by registration, and variety on non-keyboard instruments was limited by their playing techniques.

7. Whether to strike all the notes of the chords together, arpeggiate them (slowly, quickly, up, down or both), or whether to expand them into some appropriate figuration. This issue arises mainly in harpsichord acompaniment, and the theoretical sources that address the question generally recommend some kind of breaking. But it is clear from other accounts (e.g. J.-J. Rousseau's entry 'Accompagnement' in his *Dictionnaire*) that at least in Italian recitative of the mid-18th century, chords were struck all at once, loud and full, and not repeated. According to the same author the French style, on the contrary, demanded continual breaking.

8. Whether to introduce dissonant notes, or *acciaccature*. The practice seems to have been especially characteristic of Italian accompaniment in the first half of the 18th century.[22]

9. Whether to take dissonances in the figuring that double dissonances in the melody. A related question is whether one should accompany appoggiaturas and suspensions in the melody with chords containing the resolutions of those dissonances, thus anticipating the resolution and creating a clash with the melody. Kirnberger's realization of the Andante from the trio sonata in Bach's *Musical Offering* shows such clashes on all the written-out appoggiaturas.[23]

10. Whether to double fugal entries.

11. Whether to introduce graces, passages, or imitations of the melody; whether to improvise an obbligato counterpoint to it, as Bach is reported to have done. All these questions are addressed in the sources, and practices varied widely.

12. Whether to sustain long bass notes in recitative.[24]

13. Whether to delay cadences in recitative until the singer finishes his phrase.

14. Whether to avoid consecutive fifths and octaves in the accompaniment or between the accompaniment and the melody.

Ornamentation

If thoroughbass is the best-documented component of Baroque performance, ornamentation has been the most studied in the musicological literature. From Edward Dannreuther's *Musical Ornamentation* (London, 1893–5) to Frederick Neumann's *Ornamentation in Baroque and Post-Baroque Music* (Princeton, 1978), the number of books, parts of books and articles devoted to the subject in English, French and German is beyond counting. But like thoroughbass, the subject of ornamentatiura is still larger than either the literature or the documentation, and the practice remains obscure in certain important repertories, such as mid-17th-century opera. There is not even a handy guide to ornamentation for performers of Handel, at the time of writing. Unlike thoroughbass, ornamentation seems to generate passionate partisanship among those interested in early performance so that much of the more recent literature consists of protracted quarrels about a very few aspects of the subject: whether to begin trills with the main note or the upper auxiliary and whether short graces should precede the beat (i.e. whether they should anticipate the written rhythmic position of the note they embellish). Such writings can be enlightening when they uncover new evidence or question cherished but ill-considered assumptions, but their arguments are often self-serving and their conclusions predetermined. Since practical manuals on ornamentation are so abundant and accessible to the English-speaking reader, this essay will simply be a guide to the subject without attempting to impart any of its substance, except by way of example.[25]

The resources of ornamentation may be classified as follows:
1. Graces (ornaments, *agréments*, *Verzierungen*, *Manieren*, *Mordanten*, *abbellimenti*, *quiebros* etc).
(a) Additional notes in stereotyped figures. The principal ones (using terminology most likely to be familiar, even when English equivalents for foreign terms exist) are: *Anschlag*, appoggiatura, *coulé*, mordent, *Nachschlag*, *port de voix*, slide, trill, turn.
(b) Alterations, or shifts of the written note values: arpeggio, *suspension* (French), and various types of articulation, e.g. *aspiration* (French), *strascino* (Tosi; rendered as 'drag' by his 18th-century translator).
(c) Dynamic, colour and pitch ornaments: *messa di voce*, portamento, various kinds of vibrato.
2. Diminutions or divisions, paraphrase, variation.
3. Cadenzas, elaborations of organ points or fermatas.
Short groups of notes in variable patterns that decorate a note or paraphrase an interval lie somewhere between classes 1*a* and 2. They are called *gruppetto*, *passo*, *diminution* (French, in the singular) or nothing at all. The early 17th-century Italian vocal *trillo* (the breaking of a long note into rapid or accelerating repeated notes), characteristically applied to the penultimate note of a cadence, falls between classes 1*a* and 1*c*. There is some disagreement over its execution, and it may have resembled a dynamic vibrato (without pitch change) more than a succession of separately articulated notes. There are many other ornaments or graces, many combinations of the above (for example the rising appoggiatura followed by a mordent so common in French music, or the double relish of 17th-century English

instrumental music), and a bewildering variety of terms and signs for them.[26] In much music the graces that we know, from indirect evidence, to have been expected were indicated incompletely or not at all. Occasionally (especially in the 17th century) one encounters sets of rules for the addition of unmarked graces to a particular repertory, but these are rare. And as for the improvised embellishments, categories 2 and 3, the performer is cut entirely adrift from notation; he must depend upon his own experience and know-ledge not only for the shape of his ornamentation but for the decision when to introduce it and when to leave the score alone. Anyone who asks for a succinct and useful précis of the subject of ornamentation is asking for the impossible and useless; Baroque ornamentation is not, in any case, a subject by itself but an aspect of style, and it can be usefully approached only in connection with specific repertories and specific media, each instrument and the voice having its own particular possibilities.

For a very limited repertory of 18th-century music it is possible to gain a precise idea of ornamentation in actual practice. This is the music that is pinned on automatic instruments.[27] Most surviving instruments were made after 1750, but the style of ornamentation they preserve does not greatly differ from that of the second quarter of the century. What sets automatic instruments apart from all other sources for ornamentation is that every ornament is shown in context with all of its component notes; there is no room for interpretation or conjecture.

Aside from these rare examples, the repertory in which the performer has probably the least chance of going wrong, and consequently the one in which it is possible for the beginner to acquire the most accurate idea of what players of the period actually did, is French harpsichord music from D'Anglebert to François Couperin, particularly Couperin's. Couperin took great care with his notation; this would be clear from the engraving itself even had he not told us. Moreover Couperin, perhaps alone among Baroque composers, insisted that his pieces be played with the graces as marked, and he wrote a method that supplements what the scores reveal.[28] Finally, we have harpsichords from Couperin's lifetime which respond to our fingers substantially as they responded to his, assuring a delivery of ornamental notes similar to what he must have expected. A skilled and conscientious player of today will produce an effect upon one of these instruments that, if not precisely what any one particular French harpsichordist of the 1720s would have produced, can hardly differ from it – at least in the matter of ornamentation – more than would the playing of some other early 18th-century Frenchman.[29]

There are a few other repertories, most of them French, whose ornamenta-tion can be reconstructed with similar completeness. If we cannot be so sure of the effect of these graces, it is because the production of tone is more directly under the control of the performer than is that of a harpsichord, upon which the intonation, attack, loudness and timbre are all more or less completely determined by the instrument itself. Nevertheless, the music for solo viol, and again, especially that of one composer, Marin Marais, is notated with a care and complexity equal to that of Couperin's, and there are method books to fill in the gaps.[30] The graces of viol playing, however, include dynamic effects and pitch adjustments (glissando and two kinds of vibrato) that are not only more difficult to describe in words or notes than keyboard graces but depend for their effect partly upon the attack of the bow, about which there is currently sharp controversy. This controversy affects particularly the *enflé*, or swell upon a note, which some players use as the normal mode of attack, whether or not called for by a sign (in Marais, an 'e').

The gracing of the *air de cour* in the third quarter of the 17th century is not generally notated, but two method books exist for this repertory which treat the matter at such length and in such detail that little remains for conjecture.[31] Here, of course, to a much greater extent than in viol music, the effect of the ornaments will depend upon the performer's conception of early technique. The 70 pages that C. P. E. Bach devotes to embellishment (in the English translation of his *Versuch*) cover the subject exhaustively as it applies to his own and similar music for the clavichord, but although ornament signs are liberally applied to this repertory, there are fewer types ·and these are subject to a much wider range of interpretations than those of Couperin or Marais; much of Bach's chapter is devoted to the problem of how to read the same sign in different contexts. In both of these repertories, the performer, though guided, must make a decision concerning nearly every ornament.

This responsibility becomes heavier as the documentation becomes more generalized; that is, as it takes on the aspect of sets of rules or tables of signs and realizations. When signs are incomplete or lacking, two sorts of rules are needed: one to explain the types of graces and the other to tell where they should be used. The latter kind is much the rarer; one of the most detailed is Georg Muffat's explanation of Lully's orchestral style.[32] As so often happens, however, the documents are almost silent concerning the most important component – in Lully's case, the solo singing. We know only that Lully disliked improvised diminutions and that he was closely allied to Michel Lambert, the composer of *airs de cour*. But the hyper-refined and esoteric court air occupied a different stylistic world from the recitatives and plain little airs of Lully's operas; these would have lost whatever theatrical energy they possessed if covered in the intricate graces of the court air. A somewhat similar situation exists with respect to Italian opera from late Monteverdi to Cavalli and Cesti. Much is known of ornamentation in Italian airs of the early 17th century, principally from the preface to Caccini's *Le nuove musiche* (1601/2), though also from other Italian accounts and the many German singing methods based on them.[33] But the smooth bel canto of mid-century operas and cantatas is as different from early monody as Lully from Lambert and is as unlikely a vehicle for Caccini's *gorgia* as would be Lully's airs for the *agréments* and diminutions of Guédron and Boësset.[34]

English virginal music of the period between 1550 and 1650 occupies a special position in the spectrum of certainty regarding ornamentation. The music is lavishly supplied with signs (single and double diagonal slashes) but their interpretation is still largely a matter of conjecture. Furthermore, trills are often written out in this repertory and their relation to the ornament signs can only be guessed. Probably – as was the case with most ornament signs – their meaning varied according to context and the user (as has been suggested in a penetrating analysis by David Wulstan, who proposes a set of solutions).[35] The mid-17th-century English art of playing 'divisions' on a bass with a viola da gamba is well served by Christopher Simpson's *The*

Division-Violist (1659), which presented the first important table of ornament signs (see n.4).

For Italian opera of the period from Alessandro Scarlatti to the end of the Baroque we have the most influential singing treatise of the 18th century, Tosi's *Opinioni*, together with its English and German translations – the latter with extensive glosses by Bach's pupil J. F. Agricola. But although much of Tosi's treatise is devoted to ornamentation, he had nothing but disdain for singers who needed signs to tell them where to place ornaments or notes to show them what to sing; there is not one music example in his original Italian version and there are no detailed instructions. Nevertheless Tosi's singer was expected to be familiar with the appoggiatura convention in recitatives, to know how to place them – as well as the various trills, mordents and other ornaments – effectively in airs, and above all to be able to improvise fresh divisions and other variations every time he sang an air, whether in rehearsal or performance.[36] It is clear from Tosi's complaints and other accounts that much of what was heard in the opera house was in fact written out or at least planned ahead of time, and the same tired diminutions were apt to be trotted out indiscriminately whatever the piece; a few written examples have survived to show us what these were like.[37] Thus although the situation is not quite so bleak for today's singer of late Baroque opera as it is for opera of the mid-17th century, the requirement that ornamentation should be lavish and original coupled with the virtual absence of any help from the scores leaves him with a heavy burden of research, conjecture and experiment.

Italian string music is much better served than opera, notably by Tartini's important treatise on ornamentation from the mid-1750s, and also by the publication by Etienne Roger during Corelli's lifetime of what purported to be his manner of playing the slow movements from op.5 and by Geminiani's version of a complete sonata from this same collection.[38] Such examples of complete pieces with all the ornamentation except trills written out serve as valuable models for the performance of other music in the same style. The extravagantly ornamented versions of movements by Nardini and Tartini in Cartier's violin method of 1798 lie at the summit of ornamental complexity. Though their extreme luxuriance and their late date might seem to remove these from consideration as models for Baroque performance, a little-known French harpsichord publication by the cellist Jean Barrière shows that Italian ornamentation had reached a comparable level of richness by the late 1730s.[39] As Quantz's 457 examples of ways to ornament simple melodic progressions prove, this richness was not confined to string music but was a general feature of 'good execution'. Indeed, there is sufficient evidence to support the assertion that a performance of a non-French instrumental adagio of the middle decades of the 18th century embellished only with trills, mordents and the like is simply wrong and misstates the intent of the music.

Quantz, Tosi and other writers make clear the important distinction at this time between the 'essential' graces (*wesentliche Verzierungen*) and diminutions and 'extempore variations' (*willkürliche Veränderungen*). The graces must embellish any performance, whether or not they were indicated, while diminutions were often optional and when used ought always to improve on the original. The ambivalence of 18th-century musicians towards diminutions that suffuses Tosi's book is also reflected by Quantz: 'Almost no one who devotes himself to the study of music, particularly outside France, is content to perform only the essential graces; the majority feel moved to invent variations or extempore embellishments'. But later he states: 'Variations must be undertaken only after the plain air has already been heard', that is, one varies only repeats.[40] Tosi said the same of da capo arias. But composers themselves refute this caveat. The slow movements of Telemann's *Methodische Sonaten*, whose melodies are given both plain and with suggested embellishments, would seem to prove that pieces without repeats were also ornamented with diminutions, so that the 'plain air' was never heard at all (unless the whole movement was meant to be taken twice). This same style of embellishment can be found in Bach's transcriptions of Italian concertos, BWV972–87; here the originals are not given and so there can be no question of playing them without the 'variations'.[41] Handel's profusely ornamented air from the third harpsichord suite (1720) was printed with most of the essential notes of the air larger than the ornamental ones, but the plain version can still not be reconstructed from these so as to be performed;[42] this example also shows how the apparent tempo of a plain air may be radically slowed to accommodate diminutions.

It is clear that in Italy, Germany and probably England, 18th-century practice was much more lavish with ornamentation than the rather prim admonitions of some writers would seem to indicate; in fact their very caution is evidence of a general extravagance that probably needed to be curbed. When foreigners came to France they brought as much of their ornamental exuberance as they dared, but French Baroque style itself – the styles up to Rameau and probably including younger, far more Italianizing composers such as Mondonville and the composers of *opéra comique* – did not admit much in the way of diminutions; French melody and particularly French rhythm were too finely detailed and short-breathed.[43] Barrière had to write out his Italianate ornamentation because no Frenchman would have known how to inflate his meagre little tunes to the desired dimensions. It was doubtless a question of quality rather than size that caused J. S. Bach to write out diminutions; Scheibe's complaint (1737) that the complexity of Bach's notation was a hindrance rather than a help suggests that German musicians could have supplied them themselves.[44] But no doubt what the average musician might have played would have failed to please the master. For us, the result is a wealth of fine models to follow, especially when less-ornamented originals also exist to compare them with, as with the *doubles* in the English Suites.

The modern musician who follows these, or any other, models of diminutions in the music of any period is a rarity. Reverence for the score is too deeply ingrained, fear of criticism too acute and improvisation is seldom taught in conservatories. Free ornamentation, like any other improvisation, involves risks and requires constant exercise. That the improvisation of stylish diminutions can nevertheless be mastered, given a sufficient immersion in a single repertory, is proved every day in the realm of popular music. Specialization is the answer.[45]

It is impossible to leave the subject of ornamentation without some reference to the controversies of the last two or three decades. Of these, the most narrowly focussed and most sustained was the quarrel over the 'French trill': the rule that in the 18th century (and thus in Bach, for it is nearly always his music that is at issue) all trills began on the beat with the upper auxiliary. As a doctrine this can be traced back to Dolmetsch's 40 pages on the subject;[46] by the post-war period it had become a commonplace of writings on Baroque music and normal for specialists among performers, though far from universal among non-specialists. Then, in 1964, the *Musical Quarterly* printed the first of Frederick Neumann's articles questioning the supremacy of this kind of trill.[47] An answer 'in defence of the French trill' by Michael Collins appeared in 1973 and the matter was addressed subsequently from one point of view or the other by Donington and others.[48] Neumann's final and exhaustive word occupied 120 pages of his book on ornamentation. Central to the issue was the relevance to trills in general of Marpurg's definition of the trill as a series of appoggiaturas. The rigidly metrical analysis of trills implied by this definition (the auxiliary note having always to be sounded on a strong subdivision of the beat in order to maintain its quality of appoggiatura) was taken into Neumann's system of classification in such a way as to exclude any consideration of the ornament as rhythmically irrational, expressive or coloristic – indeed, such essential factors as the speed and clarity of execution, the length or the endings of trills played almost no part in the controversy. Everything hinged on whether the trill began with the upper or the main note and, to a lesser extent, whether or not it might begin before the beat. While neither side conceded an inch, the result of all the research has been a more flexible and better-informed approach to trills in general; though it must be admitted that we do not know any more that we did before the controversy began about how Bach played them.[49]

The other controversial subject was the rhythmic placement of various ornaments such as the appoggiatura, the slide, the mordent or the arpeggio. Post-Dolmetsch doctrine, stoutly buttressed by C. P. E. Bach, required that all of these be begun strictly 'on the beat', that is, simultaneously with the bass note that accompanied the principal note (the one bearing the embellishment), so that the principal note was delayed. This treatment, at variance with the normal modern practice of crowding the ornamental note or notes into the space between the main note and whatever precedes it (or delaying the bass along with the principal melody note), was first attacked by Neumann in *Acta musicologica* in 1969[50] and later, massively, in the 280 pages devoted to these ornaments in his book. The results were the same as for the trill.

A final controversial point affecting all ornaments except those of class 1*c* is whether or not they may introduce parallel fifths or octaves into the part-writing. The creation of parallels is often cited as a reason for avoiding interpretations that substitute an offending ornamental note for an inoffensive written one (as in certain on-beat appoggiaturas or trills beginning with the upper auxiliary). The sources rarely mention the issue, but those that do lie on both sides. Neumann's discussion distinguishes between what happened in practice, what was tolerated by the composer and what the composer desired. He concludes that the composer's wishes should dictate modern practice and that these desires must have been for the most correct part-writing'.[51] He does not address the question of whether ornaments whose main purpose is to lend colour, brilliance or accent are perceived as affecting the conduct of the parts.

Rhythm

By far the most controversial of all issues affecting Baroque performance is what is commonly called 'rhythmic alteration': the alteration of written rhythms by performers.[52] Strictly speaking, of course, all expressive fluctuations of tempo – all delays, all anticipations, all 'pressing forward' and 'holding back', all the rhythmic adjustments performers use to give prominence to a note or minimize its effect, to shape phrases, to produce surprise or tension (what Riemann called *Agogik*, or 'agogics')[53] – all these involve alterations of the written rhythms and are hinted at somewhere in Baroque sources. But they have not engaged the polemicists. As with ornamentation, the controversial issues are narrow and, at least on the surface, easily defined. They are three in number: whether or not to exaggerate dotted rhythms; whether or not to resolve clashes between binary and ternary rhythms; and how broadly to apply the French convention of 'inequality', or *notes inégales* (the rendition of pairs of equal values as long–short or short– long).

The quarrel over the first has been the bitterest and most protracted. Again, it was Neumann who unleashed it, this time in the *Revue de musicologie* in 1965;[54] he was reacting especially to Thurston Dart's pronouncement that nearly all dotted rhythms from the beginning of the 17th century to the end of the 19th should be exaggerated. The most sweeping statement to this effect in treatises of the 17th and 18th centuries was written in the mid-1750s in Berlin by J. F. Agricola, a pupil of J. S. Bach and Quantz, a collaborator with C. P. E. Bach and an ardent enthusiast for Italian opera: 'Short notes after a dot, either semiquavers or demisemi-quavers, or, in ₵, quavers, whether in fast or slow tempo, whether there are one or several, are always played very short and at the very end of their value'.[55] The same rule applied to reverse-dotting, or 'Lombard rhythm'; the short note at the beginning was to be similarly snapped. Since overdotting is now generally associated with French style, and especially with that of the overture, Agricola's pro-Italian, and even anti-French, bias should be noted; the passage occurs in his glosses to a translation of Tosi's *Opinioni*. Indeed, with the exception of one notable category of references, most of the recommendations of generalized, blanket overdotting are to be found in German sources of the second half of the 18th century and may apply chiefly to post-Baroque Italian and German styles – music now rarely performed, and even more rarely with overdotting. Dotted figures in French Baroque music are an exception, for these values equivalent to the short notes after the dots are subject to the convention of *notes inégales* (see below). These notes, which are in effect the second notes of unequal pairs whose first members are the dots, are shortened, the dots correspondingly lengthened and the figures thus overdotted (see ex.2).

It is also possible that dotted figures of the next lower order, that is, for example, dotted quavers and semiquavers where quavers are unequal, are

Ex.2

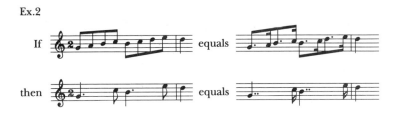

sometimes meant to be overdotted in French music to distinguish them from quavers written equal but performed dotted. But it is equally possible that such written dotting is a cautionary reminder of *notes inégales* in places where the composer feels his intentions may not be clear. A third possibility is that all the desired inequality is written out with dots, leaving equal notes to be played equal and the dotted figures to be played freely in whatever ratio of long to short best suits the expression of the passage.[56] Probable instances of all three of these cases are to be observed and it is very seldom that one can be sure which obtains in any given situation, since even the most careful composers seem to be highly inconsistent in their notation of dotted figures.

More ink has been spilled over the special case of the French overture than any other in the matter of dotting. One problem is that the overwhelming majority of French overtures are not French but German, and it is impossible to establish how much of French performing practice emigrated with the compositional style. As with the other controversies, the real interest is not French music at all but Bach and Handel. The few references to the performing style of French overtures in both French and German sources mention either the fire, majesty and energy or the effect to be produced by the execution of *tirades* (fast scale passages swooping up or down to the next long note). These were apparently to be played as rapidly as possible, at the last possible minute, but with each note separately articulated or bowed. A number of notes separately articulated, even if played with the greatest energy, will occupy a certain amount of time; probably more, not less, than the interval left after a strict dot of augmentation. A great deal depends on the speed of the beat, of course, and if the tempo of overtures was as fast as has recently been claimed,[57] then the issue of overdotting is an academic point.

When two parts have simultaneous dotted figures of different orders, as, for example, two dotted quaver–semiquaver figures against one dotted crotchet–quaver, the question arises whether the latter should be double-dotted to synchronize its quaver with the final semiquaver in the other part. Some French sources say an unequivocal yes.[58] The situation arises often, particularly in overtures, where playing the quavers in strict time tends to mask the effect of the shorter dotted figures by interposing a pulse between the dotted quaver and the semiquaver. Synchronization enhances the effect of energy; but where one order is derived from the other by rhythmic augmentation or diminution of the theme, as in Contrapunctus 6 of Bach's *Art of Fugue*, synchronization obscures the relationship.

The character of dotting in the performance of the best musicians was probably governed by the category of expression – the 'affection' – as determined by words (if any), or by standard stylistic classifications and symbols.[59] This admitted great variety, and the precise ratios of duration would have had to be coordinated with articulation, dynamics and the nature of the medium; but it did not mean *carte blanche*, and in particular it is unlikely to have admitted performances of overtures (such as those of *Messiah* or the Bach suites) 'in eight', as we used to hear them.

It has been argued (see n.13) that the synchronization of dotting in overtures would have imposed impossible demands on the performer's ability to interpret the notation of one part in relation to the others. But this takes no account of the total familiarity of the overture style to (for example) any German orchestral musician of the late Baroque period. He knew how overtures 'went', he could hear the rest of the ensemble and he played accordingly, whatever the notated rhythms.[60]

Clashes between binary and ternary rhythms in Baroque music are mostly of two kinds: even duplets against triplets and dotted figures against triplets or sextuplets. The issues are usually discussed only in relation to situations where the conflicting rhythms occur simultaneously in two parts, but changes from one to another in the same part can also be puzzling. The interpretation of proportional time signatures is beyond the scope of this article, but in so far as it affects binary–ternary clashes it should be noted that composers varied greatly in their own understanding of the archaic signs they used and were capable of inconsistency within the same composition.[61] More and more, as the 17th century progressed, the arithmetical meaning of the proportions was transformed into more or less vague indications of tempo.

Simultaneous duplets and triplets are not common in Baroque music, and theoretical comment is even rarer. A few sources from the second half of the 18th century stipulate that the duplets should be altered to fit the triplets (taking the second note of the duplet with the third of the triplet), and at least one theorist declares the clash to be a fault and recommends against writing it in a composition.[62] No tutor explains how to execute the effect (dividing the beat mentally into six and thinking of the triplet as $2 + 2 + 2$ and the duplet as $3 + 3$, although an analogous mental operation is applied by Quantz to the problem of overdotting: Eng. trans., p.67). Yet instances can be found where it is neither difficult to play, nor plausible to alter, the rhythms. In ex.3, the principal thematic idea is in quavers directed to be played evenly, then triplets are introduced against them in the middle of a phrase. Between 1733 and 1737 (cf Paris, Bibliothèque Nationale Vm[7]1881 and Rés. F. 455), however, the composer rewrote the piece and eliminated all two-against-three combinations.

One of the most famous instances of the persistent clash of triplets and duplets is furnished by Bach's chorale prelude 'In dulci jubilo' from the *Orgelbüchlein*; it is often cited as a case for adapting duplets to triplet rhythm (see ex.4a).[63] But it would be characteristic of Bach to have intended the repeated As in bar 3 to echo the six preceding As in diminution, an effect that would require them to be played evenly. Later on in the piece – curiously, at exactly the point where the double canon relaxes its rigour – he does not hesitate to write the duplets assimilated to triplet rhythm (see ex.4b).

A very much more common occurrence in Baroque music than simulta-

Ex.3

Ex.4(a) J.S. Bach: *In dulce jubilo*

(b)

neous duplets and triplets is the successive appearance of the two kinds of subdivision. This is particularly frequent in the 'divisions' of late Baroque arias in the Italian style, which often break into triplets after main thematic material in duple rhythm. But there are pieces that begin with a duple subdivision of the beat then quickly move into triplet rhythm, and this is sustained throughout the rest of the piece for all the figuration except the theme. The last movement of Bach's third organ sonata is such a piece. The question arises whether the duplets should not be altered in anticipation of the triplets to come, especially as later in the piece the duple theme is occasionally heard against triplets. No definitive answer is possible. The case would be stronger for altering duplets in the initially ternary fifth prelude from book 2 of Bach's *Das wohltemperirte Clavier* (ex.5), if Bach had not

Ex.5 J.S. Bach: 5th prelude from *Das Wohltemperirte Clavier*, book 2

(a) opening

(b) bar 18

written dotted figures against the ternary ones everywhere but for the theme itself. Yet at the one occurrence of this theme against sextuplets, even quavers produce a very uncharacteristic shift from a 3/8 to a 6/16 grouping of the accompanying semiquavers.

It has been argued that in the 16th and 17th centuries groups of three blackened breves, semibreves and minims were altered to duple anapaests or dactyls in a duple context, and that this treatment of triplets was extended to smaller values in the 17th century and even occasionally in the 18th. These conclusions have had little influence on modern performance, but they deserve to be explored and tested.[64]

Perhaps the most common clash of all is that between triplets and dotted figures. Again, it is the post-Baroque treatises that are most explicit on the subject, but they disagree; C. P. E. Bach and others assert that the second note of dotted figures occurring against triplets is to be played with the third note of the triplet, while Quantz and Agricola (the latter citing J. S. Bach as his authority) insist that the dotted figure must be played in its true time value or overdotted, that is, with its short note coming after the last note of the triplet. While this may be the right way to play some pieces, the great majority of scores, including ex.5, can hardly be played any other way than C. P. E. Bach's. A brief *querelle* on the subject occurred in 1959–60 in the pages of *Die Musikforschung*.[65]

In many cases, conflict between a ternary and binary subdivision of the beat is reflected in the time signature, sometimes with a combination of two signatures on the same staff as in ex.5, and sometimes with different signatures on the different staffs. In Variation 26 of Bach's *Goldberg*

Variations, the signatures of 18/16 and 3/4 are exchanged between the staffs as the figuration of running semiquavers and dotted quaver–semiquaver figures is exchanged between the hands; see ex.6. This variation also

Ex.6 J.S. Bach: Var.26 from the *Goldberg Variations,* opening

illustrates the very common occurrence in Baroque music of a dotted figure (or a series of them, as in 'Surely He hath Borne our Griefs' from Handel's *Messiah*) preceded by an even duplet of which the first value is either a rest or a note tied to something before and where the second value may be intended to initiate the dotted rhythm with a short upbeat equivalent to the note following the dot. To assert that all such upbeats should be shortened to conform to the rhythm in ex.7 is to deny composers of the Baroque period the

Ex.7

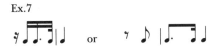

possibility of ever notating that rhythm, which does in fact seem to fit ex.6, especially with the ornamentation of the *Handexemplar.* Yet the majority of cases including 'Surely He hath Borne our Griefs' certainly require the shortened upbeat.

The French convention of *notes inégales* has been described in detail more than once in easily accessible articles by the present writer, and only a few general observations are needed here.[66] This convention, too, was the subject of a controversy initiated by Frederick Neumann in the mid-1960s, but although much confusion still exists, the subject no longer arouses the passions that it once did. That is partly because, as regards French music at least, it is the most richly documented of all Baroque practices after thoroughbass and ornamentation, and a great deal of that documentation is accessible in fascimiles, reprints and translations. No one any longer doubts the reality of the convention; what is questioned is the extent of its application.

A basic problem is the misconception that *notes inégales* involve, by definition, the alteration of evenly written values to long–short, or occasionally short–long, pairs. In fact, inequality was often written out in dotted figures; the commonest French term for 'to render unequal' was *pointer* (to dot), though *inégaliser* is also sometimes found, and there was no clear boundary between dotted rhythms, whether exaggerated or not, and *notes inégales.* The French were aware of this problem and sometimes tried to distinguish between written dotting (strict or exaggerated) and a gentler inequality, but there is plenty of evidence to prove that this distinction was rarely maintained by composers. I have already had more than one occasion to mention the organ book of Gigault (see nn.16 and 58). Here the inequality seems to have been written out, if not exhaustively, then with sufficient consistency to make it the most informative single document on the subject.[67] It is particularly valuable because it includes a number of instances of play between long–short and short–long inequality, and it shows a *Fugue poursuivie à la manière italienne* with a minimum of dotting, as one would expect from statements by the theorists.[68] Anyone who wants to observe authentic, applied inequality would do well to study Gigault.

Once it is recognized that inequality, namely a certain way of enlivening subdivisions of the beat (never the beat itself, and in the 18th century and duple metres, never the half-beat),[69] constituted a rhythmic *style* that might or might not be indicated by dotted figures, then this style can be observed in places other than France. The most striking and consistent use of written inequality occurred in English music from Locke and Purcell to the 1730s, and perhaps beyond. Several of the sarabandes in Richard Jones's harpsichord lessons of 1732 were dotted, as were countless other English pieces. A dotting traceable to French influence can be found in German and Italian music as well.[70] There are even scattered references to the dotting of undotted music. What we do not find, however, is sets of rules for inequality such as were common in French method books. A little French primer of about 1730, for example, devotes seven of its 24 tiny pages of text to rules for inequality in all the metres and another four to triplets and related rhythmic matters.[71] If English treatises mention dotting undotted rhythms at all, it is under the rubric of 'humouring'; that is, as an expressive nuance to be applied where needed, but not as a matter of principle.[72] German treatises sometimes toy with the subject in connection with explanations of 'good' and 'bad' (strong and weak) subdivisions of the beat, but their implications for performance are not clear. One notable German exception that does specify systematic inequality does so when describing Lully's orchestral style;[73] the only other exception is Quantz's famous and puzzling passage which lays down rules for inequality according to the common French model, though it makes no mention of French music.[74] But Quantz spent many years in Dresden under a French orchestra director and as a student and associate of a French flautist. It is possible that inequality was a local usage that Quantz associated with Dresden as much as with France (which he visited).

Possible local exceptions aside, we must assume that musicians outside France would not normally dot undotted passages and that composers who particularly desired the effect of *notes inégales* (or any other style of persistent dotting) would write dots. But they might not feel compelled to write out every instance, and one occasionally finds movements that begin with dotted figures, then continue undotted, as if the performer were expected to follow the principle, once shown, throughout the piece. As with upbeats to dotted figures, however, we must not deny composers the possibility of shifting in and out of dotted rhythm if that was their intention; the performer must make sure that there is not a plausible rationale for inconsistencies in dotting.[75]

The earliest reference to dotting undotted passages comes from a Franco-

Helvetian treatise of 1550 where it is already tied to the beat and its subdivisions.[76] For the next hundred years, however, inequality is described mainly in a few Spanish and Italian sources, and never so systematically as it was to be later. Both the long–short and short–long variety seem to have been an expressive resource of Italian monody and certain kinds of instrumental music. Ornamental passages with written dotting doubtless resemble what performers might have done with undotted passages in similar situations or improvised out of whole cloth.[77] German solo singing was closely modelled on the Italian monodists and may well have included dotting as an ornamental resource. But persistent dotting carried through a composition (in the manner of Gigault, for example) seems to have been rare until the second half of the 17th century.

Beginning in 1665, a rapidly growing number of French sources prescribe inequality as an ornament and increasingly as a requisite for proper performance. It had probably existed from the 16th century as an embellishment to diminutions as practised by singers, lutenists, keyboard players and (from the early 17th century) orchestral players, though there is little direct evidence.[78] On the other hand, the elaborate code from the 18th century that stipulated the note values that were to be treated unequally in every possible metre could only develop as the modern metrical system evolved out of the vestigial proportions of the late 17th century, so that before about 1700 one cannot be certain precisely what the implications of the signs C, ₵ and 2 were for inequality. Lully's overtures, for example, are variable in this regard (as Hotteterre noted in 1719); and Nivers, in 1665, recommended unequal quavers under the sign 'C'.

Even in the 18th century, theorists disagreed about ₵, 2/4 and 3/4 (which for some had Italian connotations, as opposed to the French 3), and there was wide divergence as to how the ratio between long and short was discussed, and even more disagreement over rules for the conditions under which normally unequal values should be rendered equal, as written. On this last point, Eugène Borrel assembled a list of contra-indications of inequality that has been copied and recopied to the great detriment of our understanding of this convention.[79] In reality, with the exception of its relation to metre in the 18th century, it was much less circumscribed by 'rules' than might appear either from modern accounts or from some unusually detailed sources. For every generalization that may seem to emerge from the perusal of these documents, there is at least one piece of evidence to refute it. One author, unfortunately unidentified, after having given instructions for inequality and dynamic accents on strong beats goes on to say that all this is only for learning; it is contrary to good taste and one should not play notes unequally unless their values are different. But the same sentence goes straight on to say that 'there are, however, many passages in a given piece of music' where one *should* play *notes inégales!*[80]

It has been frequently argued that inequality was a consequence of old playing techniques, and more specifically keyboard fingering and patterns of tonguing in wind instruments.[81] Sometimes such techniques are adduced to explain the origin of inequality, sometimes as proof that it must have been a feature of all music, not just French. There have also been attempts to explain inequality on the basis of French declamation.[82] In the first place, there is no necessary connection between playing technique and rhythmic unevenness unless the tempo is very fast or the player unskilled. Perfectly even subdivisions can be played with any technique, though it is true that the articulations that may result from fingering and tonguing patterns can sometimes give the illusion of inequality. Secondly, the groupings of notes resulting from old keyboard fingerings depend on the position of accidental keys (i.e. black notes on modern keyboards), leaps and so forth; more often than not, they fail to correspond to the long–short pairs described in the theoretical descriptions of inequality. Thirdly, some fingering systems count the second finger of the right hand as 'strong' and others, the third, so that the patterns produced by fingering differ according to the school of technique. Finally, and most importantly, inequality is first heard of in connection with vocal music, and throughout its history no distinction corresponding to the different media – voice, strings, winds, keyboard – was drawn in descriptions of the practice. Inequality was essentially a matter of rhythmic style, not performing technique, and it obeyed laws of metre and expression, not of fingers or tongue.

There are few musicians today who are not to some extent repelled by 'that deformity, devoid of logic, which consists in the unequal performance of equal quavers',[83] and one rarely hears *notes inégales* in anything like the ubiquity implied by the massive source material. Instead, we hear a kind of generalized rubato intended to clarify the metre and highlight important notes or events. This is not, however, confined to French music but has become commonplace for the whole body of Baroque instrumental music without distinction as to date, genre or national style (modern singers are less concerned with rhythm of any kind). Its salient characteristic is an exaggerated lengthening of the downbeat – sometimes every downbeat, no matter how clear it may already be from the harmony or other factors of its context. Further rhythmic distortions may emphasize dissonant or climactic notes, thematic entries or any feature the performer fears his audience may miss. Sometimes all sense of the beat, far from being clarified, disappears in a fog of nuance.

It is true that rhythmic liberties far beyond overdotting and inequality were cultivated in certain Baroque styles. The few mentions doubtless only hint at the wider reality. Frescobaldi insisted on all kinds of liberties in his keyboard music 'as we see practised in modern madrigals'; the *stylus phantasticus* of the German organists derived from him; the 'humouring' of English consort music introduced pauses and 'drags' (here, retards); the unmeasured preludes of the French lutenists and harpsichordists depended more or less completely on the player for rhythm; Rousseau is not our only witness that at the Paris opera 'music had no measure but that of gesture' (cf n.43); a late (but retrospective) French source advises us not to pay too much attention to the time signatures of a certain type of sarabande whose tempo varied in mid-course.[84] But the fact remains that we know virtually nothing of how Baroque musicians 'phrased' (the verb seems to appear in French around the middle of the 18th century); we do not know the kind or frequency of the retards they employed, nor (except in rare cases) do we know the precise nature of the other liberties they took even in music where we know that liberties were taken.

What is certain, however, is that the 'audible analysis' practised by modern players of Baroque music has nothing to do with *notes inégales* and cannot be justified as a rendition of it or a substitute for it. Any connection with old performance is purely speculative – which is not to say, of course, that it may not have corresponded exactly to the way some players performed.

Although 'agogics', articulation and dynamic nuance[85] are separate parameters of musical performance, they are interdependent and complementary in their effect on phrasing and expression, and they are always coordinated in good playing and singing. But the balance between them and the character of their interaction is different for every medium. It would doubtless be possible to make scientific studies of this interaction today, though no one seems to have tried; it was certainly not possible in the 17th and 18th centuries. Articulation and inequality received minute scrutiny in the treatises on barrel organs by Engramelle, but their effect on each other was not discussed nor were other rhythmic liberties (except – and that only briefly – retards).[86] Dynamics were not relevant to that medium. Modern studies of Baroque performance may transmit such data about these matters as are found in the sources, but they also do not attempt to gather them into a Riemann-like system – as perhaps they should not, since there would have to be different systems for each style and medium.

Musicians cannot escape the responsibility of the bar-by-bar decisions that must shape all performance, whether of Baroque or any other music. What can guide them? Now, as three hundred years ago, in ordinary performance these decisions are taken automatically, by analogy with similar situations in music previously studied or heard. But the automaticity must be acquired, and one can only repeat the advice given in the introduction to this chapter: begin by listening to those who have steeped themselves in one style, then immerse yourself in the same one until it becomes a part of you. Impractical advice, perhaps, for the professional who must seek jobs where he can find them, but there is no other way to find out how it really was.

Notes

[1] The question of where the Baroque era ends is one of the most delicate in the historiography of performance practice. This is due partly to the fact that nearly all of the most authoritative, comprehensive and lucid performance treatises of the 18th century postdate 1750: J. J. Quantz, *Versuch einer Anweisung die Flöte traversiere zu spielen* (Berlin, 1752, 3/1789/*R*1952; Eng. trans., 1966); C. P. E. Bach, *Versuch über die wahre Art das Clavier zu spielen* (Berlin, 1753 and 1762/ *R*1957; Eng. trans., 1949); F. W. Marpurg, *Anleitung zum Clavierspielen* (Berlin, 1755, 2/1765/ *R*1969 and 1970; Fr. trans., 1756/*R*1971); G. Tartini, treatise on violin playing, various titles, before 1756; pubd as *Traité des agrémens de la musique* (Paris, 1771); ed. E. Jacobi (New York, 1961; incl. Eng. and Ger. trans. and facs. of original It. MS, *I–Vc*); L. Mozart, *Versuch einer gründlichen Violinschule* (Augsburg, 1756/*R*1976; Eng. trans., 1948, 2/1951); J. F. Agricola, *Anleitung zur Singekunst* (Berlin, 1757), an extensively glossed translation of P. F. Tosi, *Opinioni de' cantori antichi e moderni* (Bologna, 1723/*R*1968; Eng. trans., 1742, 2/1743/*R*1969). The list could be expanded with further treatises by Adlung, Bérard, Bordet, Buterne, Choquel, Corrette, Denis, Dumas, Geminiani and Marpurg, still without leaving that same decade. Beyond 1760 are many others, though none bears great names like Bach and Mozart. The sheer weight and excellence of all this writing, much of it accessible in English for many years, has caused its influence, which is altogether out of proportion to the importance of the music of the same period, to flow backwards into the relative theoretical vacuum of the late Baroque and

attach itself to J. S. Bach and Handel. We simply do not know to what extent this is justified. As far as can be judged from a comparison of early 18th-century writings on performance with the great treatises of mid-century and later, there was no revolution in performance to correspond with the profound changes in compositional style that took place in the middle 50 years. But it is also true that we know virtually nothing of how Bach and Handel wanted their music to be executed. The importance of this music, the paucity of information about its performance, and the existence of a great mass of evidence of doubtful relevance have combined to engender a body of sectarian exegesis whose immensity only proves that there are no certain answers. In this chapter, the boundary of 1750 is ignored where it does not seem to be important.

Although no comprehensive bibliography of the matters treated in this chapter can be attempted, the citations in the notes have been chosen to provide a broad sample of sources and literature, especially items that themselves lead to further materials. The reader desiring access to recent specialized studies of any aspect of performance will find the classified indexes of *RILM* of the greatest help. The liveliest, most personal, most realistic insight into a Baroque musical mind available to English-speaking readers is to be had in *Roger North on Music*, ed. J. Wilson (London, 1959).

[2] C. Pierre, *Histoire du Concert spirituel, 1725–1790* (1900) (Paris, 1975), 193. Jefferson may have been present at this concert; he bought a ticket for the one two days later. It was apparently Davide as much as anyone who accustomed the late 18th-century Parisians to a style of singing festooned with those *notes multipliées* that they were already used to in instrumental adagios, where 'they would have been very surprised not to hear them' and without which the adagio 'would seem cold and bare' (ibid, p.194, after the *Mercure*, April 1786, 158ff).

[3] M. F. Bukofzer, *Music in the Baroque Era* (New York, 1947), 371.

[4] B. Pasquini, *Collected Works for Keyboard*, ed. M. B. Haynes, CEKM, v/7 (1968), has 29 sonatas for one or two keyboard instruments, notated as figured basses, to be turned into finished compositions by the performer, with only an occasional guide to the upper parts by the composer (see 'Partimento', *Grove 6*).

G. Rose, 'Agazzari and the Improvising Orchestra', *JAMS*, xviii (1965), 382–93; C. Simpson, *The Division-Violist* (London, 1659, rev.2/1665/*R*1955 as *The Division-Viol*); M. Mersenne, *Harmonie universelle* (Paris, 1636–7/*R*1963); C. P. E. Bach, *Sechs Sonaten ... mit veränderten Reprisen*, ed. E. Darbellay (Winterthur, 1976).

[5] Communication from James Patrick.

[6] M. P. de Montéclair, *Principes de musique* (Paris, 1736/*R*1972), 78; R. Parkins, 'Cabezón to Cabanilles: Ornamentation in Spanish Keyboard Music', *Organ Yearbook*, xi (1980), 5–16.

[7] Tosi's 'breaking and yet keeping time' as described by Roger North may have resembled certain rhythmic shifts in jazz.

[8] *The New Grove Dictionary of Jazz* treats the matter briefly under 'Beat', in terms remarkably reminiscent of the old French treatises, but with no reference to the parallel in *notes inégales*.

[9] W. Kuijken and C. Hogwood, 'On the Viol', *EM*, vi (1978), 4–11; J. Hsu, *French Baroque Viol Technique* (New York, 1981); G. Leonhardt, introduction to keyboard issue', *EM*, vii (1979), 452; H. Schott, 'Wanda Landowska', *EM*, vii (1979), 467–72; A. Newman, *Bach and the Baroque* (New York, 1985); H. Vogel, 'On the Interpretation of Baroque Organ Repertoire: some Remarks on the Relationship between Articulation and Fingering', *The American Organist*, xx (1986), 174. These represent recent points of view by some of the named artists, but the contrast in their styles of playing must be heard.

[10] 'Tutto il bisognevole per sonar il flauto da 8 fori', *I-Vnm* ital. IV 486, coll.9838.

[11] J.-J. Eigeldinger, *Chopin vu par ses élèves* (Neuchâtel, 1970, 2/1979), 110–11.

[12] These ideas are briefly developed in D. Fuller, 'You Can't Prove it by Notation: Thoughts on Rhythmic Alteration', *Diapason*, lxxii (1981), 3. See also D. Fuller, 'Rhythmic Alteration – if any – in Bach's Organ Music', *American Organist*, xxi (1987), 40–48.

[13] See the discussion of dotting (p.000) and also F. Neumann, *Essays in Performance Practice* (Ann Arbor, 1982), 106 and 161, who argues that no code of rhythmic alteration, applied consistently, could result in such synchronization and exaggeration and therefore that overtures must have been played as written.

[14] J. S. Beyer, *Primae lineae musicae vocalis* (Freiberg, 1703/*R*1977), 36 and 45. See also D. Fuller, 'More on Triplets and Inequality', *EM*, xv (1987), 384–5; and J.-B. Cappus, *Etrennes de musique* (Paris or Dijon, 1730–36), a facsimile of which by Minkoff is in preparation.

[15] White, stemmed, single-flagged notes were an alternative to the normal black stemmed semiminima (crotchet) from the mid-15th century; a white note with two flags was equivalent to a fusa (quaver). See W. Apel, *The Notation of Polyphonic Music* (Cambridge, Mass., 1942, rev.5/

1961), 6 and 87. D. Auriemma, *Compendio di musica* (Naples, 1622), 31, associates them with 'prolation', that is, perfect prolation, but assigns no significance to them other than the duple and quadruple divisions of the minim that are normal in this mensuration. See also K. Speer, *A Portuguese Manuscript of the Late Seventeenth Century, MS No. 1607, Loc. G, 7, Municipal Library, Oporto, Portugal* (diss., Indiana U., 1956), i, 13, where 'white quavers' seem to be used to distinguish normal crotchets from blackened (i.e. coloured) minimae, or minims. But in Couperin's *La langueur* (from *Folies françaises, Troisiéme livre de piéces de clavecin*, Paris, 1722, *Treiziéme ordre*), 'white quavers' are used with no connection to either perfect mensuration or coloration, in a metre marked '1/2' (one semibreve to a bar). The 'La Pierre' harpsichord book, *F-Pn* Rés. Vmd. 18 (1687–1730/*R*1984), has the same unmeasured prelude in three notations, one with single- and double-flagged white notes. The equivalences and the non-metrical context make it virtually impossible that the white notation should have any special meaning, unless it is a slower delivery.

[16] N. Gigault, *Livre de musique pour l'orgue* (Paris, 1685), ed. A. Guilmant, *Archives des maîtres de l'orgue*, iv (1902), 3. A fugue (p.142) has passages in notes with eight beams. J. O'Donnell, 'The French Style and the Overtures of Bach', *EM*, vii (1979), 340, suggested that Gigault's use of beams and flags was exponential: one for a quaver, two for a semiquaver, four for a demisemiquaver and eight for a hemidemisemiquaver (a system that allows three beams for triplets, five for quintuplets, etc). If Couperin got the idea of multiple beams from Gigault, he did not use them consistently.

[17] Couperin, *Pièces de violes avec la basse chiffrée* (1728), ed. L. Robinson (Paris, 1973), 'Passacaille ou chaconne', bars 177ff.

[18] A number of practical models for Florentine monody have been discovered by J. W. Hill, 'Realized Continuo Accompaniments from Florence c1600'. *EM*, xi (1983), 194–208.

[19] *Grove 6*, i, 811.

[20] G. Sadler, 'The Role of the Keyboard Continuo in French Opera, 1673–1776', *EM*, viii (1980), 148–57. Keyboard accompaniment in the tuttis of late 18th-century keyboard concertos has also been the subject of recent research: F. Ferguson, 'The Classical Keyboard Concerto', *EM*, xii (1984), 437–45. Four important monographs on continuo practices have recently appeared: L. Dreyfus, *Bach's Continuo Group: Players and Practices in his Vocal Works* (Cambridge, Mass., 1988); N. North, *Continuo Playing on the Lute, Archlute and Theorbo* (Bloomington, 1987); T. Borgir, *The Performance of the Basso Continuo in Italian Baroque Music* (Ann Arbor, 1986); and P. Rogers, *Continuo Realization in Handel's Vocal Music* (Ann Arbor, 1988).

[21] See Arnold, *The Art of Accompanying*; Williams, *Figured Bass Accompaniment*; and Williams, 'Continuo', *Grove 6*.

[22] P. Williams, 'The Harpsichord Acciaccatura: Theory and Practice in Harmony, 1650–1750', *MQ*, liv (1968), 503–23.

[23] Williams, *Figured Bass Accompaniment*, i, 85.

[24] See for example N. Harnoncourt, 'Notenschrift und Werktreue', *Musica*, xxv (1971), 564–6, and others on Bach's *St Matthew Passion*, one of whose sources has crotchets and crotchet rests for the continuo part of the recitatives instead of the usual sustained notes. Similar evidence for not sustaining the chords in recitative exists for 18th-century Italian opera.

[25] The most important and comprehensive study of 17th- and 18th-century ornamentation is Neumann's *Ornamentation in Baroque and Post-Baroque Music* (Princeton, 1978). Its tables, glossary, bibliography, superb index and wealth of examples make it an indispensable companion for the performer of Baroque music. A great deal of the text, however, is devoted to argument against modern doctrine concerning the beginning of trills and the rhythmic placement of short ornaments (discussed later in this chapter). The present writer's review of this work in *JAMS*, xxxiii (1980), 394–402, provides a context for the assessment of its more polemical aspects. The substance of the subject of ornamentation has been recently dealt with by Fuller in over 40 articles in *The New Harvard Dictionary of Music*, ed. D. M. Randel (Cambridge, Mass., 1986), and in *The Everyman Companion to Baroque Music*, ed. J. A. Sadie (London, 1990). With the exception of the classification of ornaments, an effort has been made here to avoid duplicating the content of these articles, to which the reader is referred for detailed information and additional bibliography.

[26] Robert Donington's article, 'Ornaments', *Grove 6*, revised in *Grove MI*, is an excellent summary of the subject. In general, it takes the opposite point of view from Neumann on controversial issues and provides a somewhat smaller table of ornament symbols as well as an up-to-date bibliography.

[27] See D. Fuller 'An Introduction to Automatic Instruments', *EM*, xi (1983), 164–6; G. F. Handel, *Two Ornamented Organ Concertos as Played by an Early Barrel Organ*, transcribed with commentary (Hackensack, 1980); and 'Analysing the Performance of a Barrel Organ', *The Organ Yearbook*, xi (1980), 104–15. See also Haendel, *Un enregistrement d'époque*: Erato ZL 30974 DT.

[28] Preface to *Troisiéme livre de piéces de clavecin* (Paris, 1722) and *L'art de toucher le clavecin* (Paris, 1716, rev. 2/1717); both available in several modern editions.

[29] For a comparative table of French harpsichord ornaments, see *Early French Keyboard Music*, ed. H. Ferguson (Oxford, 1966). See also Michel de Saint-Lambert, *Les principes du clavecin* (Paris, 1702/R1982), Eng. trans. and commentary by R. Harris-Warrick, Cambridge, 1984), and J.-P. Rameau, *Pièces de clavecin avec une méthode pour la mécanique des doigts* (Paris, 1724), ed. K. Gilbert with facsimile of the method (Paris, 1978), Eng. trans. in Rameau, *Pièces de clavecin*, ed. E. Jacobi (Kassel, 1958).

[30] M. Marais, *The Instrumental Works*, ed. J. Hsu (New York, 1980–); J. A. Sadie, *The Bass Viol in French Baroque Chamber Music* (Ann Arbor, 1981); C. Pond, 'Ornamental Style and the Virtuoso: Solo Bass Viol Music in France, c1680–1740', *EM*, vi (1978), 512–18; for a comparative table of ornament signs and extensive discussion of performance, H. Bol, *La basse de viole du temps de Marin Marais et d'Antoine Forqueray* (Bilthoven, 1973). Fascimiles of methods by Danoville, Jean Rousseau and Corrette are published by Minkoff, Geneva.

[31] B. de Bacilly *Remarques curieuses sur l'art de bien chanter* (Paris, 1668/R1971; Eng. trans., 1968); J. Millet, *La belle méthode ou l'art de bien chanter* (Besançon, 1666/R1973).

[32] K. Cooper and J. Zsako, 'Georg Muffat's Observations on the Lully Style of Performance', *MQ*, liii (1967), 220–45; others are: R. T. Dart, 'Recorder "Gracings" in 1700', *GSJ*, xii (1959), 93–4; Bacilly, *Remarques curieuses*; J. Hotteterre, preface to *Pièces pour la flûte traversière . . . Livre premier* (Paris, 1708/R1982), Eng. trans. in B. B. Mather, *Interpretation of French Music from 1675 to 1775 for Woodwind and other Performers* (New York, 1973), 82.

[33] H. Goldschmidt, *Die italienische Gesangsmethode des XVII. Jahrhunderts* (Breslau, 1892) and *Die Lehre von der vokalen Ornamentik* (Charlottenburg, 1907); G. Caccini, *Le nuove musiche* (Florence, 1601/2), preface translated by H. W. Hitchcock in RRMBE, ix (Madison, 1970); and in O. Strunk, *Source Readings in Music History* (New York, 1950), 377–92; M. Praetorius, *Syntagma musicum*, iii (Wolfenbüttel, 1619/R1958), 229–40, based on Caccini and also G. Bovicelli, *Regole, passaggi di musica* (Venice, 1594/R1957); J. A. Herbst, *Musica practica* (Nuremberg, 1642, 2/1653, 3/1658 as *Musica moderna practica*), based on Praetorius; C. Bernhard, *Von der Singe-Kunst oder Manier*, in J. Müller-Blattau, *Die Kompositionslehre Heinrich Schützens* (Leipzig, 1926, 2/1963), 31–9, based on Caccini for graces ('cantar alla Romana'); W. Mylius, *Rudimenta musices* (Mühlhausen, 1685), based on Bernhard; G. Falk (or Falck), *Idea boni cantoris* (Nuremberg, 1688), Eng. trans. by R. Taylor, diss. Louisiana State U. 1971), using Italian terminology like many other German methods. It should be pointed out here that this stemma is far from giving a balanced view of German ornamentation in the period preceding J. S. Bach, as is claimed by Neumann in *Ornamentation* in support of his efforts to separate the father from the doctrines of his son (see n.1). Three other, very different, ornamental styles operated in Germany simultaneously with that of Caccini: English chamber music, English and Dutch keyboard music (via Sweelinck), and French lute music. None of these is reflected in the theoretical literature, which deals overwhelmingly with vocal church music, and no modern study has attempted to assess them.

[34] Mersenne, *Harmonie universelle*, prints a number of ornamented versions of an air by Boësset, 'N'espérez plus mes yeux', *Livre sixième, De l'art de bien chanter*, 411–13; reproduced in H.-P. Schmitz, *Die Kunst der Verzierung im 18. Jahrhundert* (Kassel, 1983), 39–41, and superimposed in E. Ferand, *Improvisation in Nine Centuries of Western Music* (Cologne, 1961), Anthology of Music, xii, 107–9.

[35] *Tudor Music* (London, 1985), chap.6. See also R. Donington's article 'Ornaments' in *Grove 6*.

[36] For extended commentary on Tosi's approach to ornamentation and his historical position in these matters, see the essay by D. Fuller on ornamentation in *Everyman Companion to Baroque Music*, ed. J. A. Sadie (London, 1990).

[37] For 'an exhibition of all the furbelows, flounces, and vocal fopperies of the times', see C. Burney, *A General History of Music* (London, 1789), ed. F. Mercer (London, 1935), ii, 726; also reproduced in the essay mentioned in the preceding note. Examples of divisions sung by Farinelli, the supreme singer of the mid-18th century, may be seen in R. Haas, *Aufführungspraxis der Musik* (Wildpark-Potsdam, 1931), 185–7, Burney, *History*, ii, 831–8, and Schmitz, *Die Kunst der Verzierung*, 76–93. See also the bibliography to the article 'Castrato', *Grove 6*.

[38] See n.1. The ornamentations for op.5 are given in the complete edition of Corelli's works, ed. J. Joachim and F. Chrysander, vol.iii (1890); Geminiani's version is printed in Schmitz, *Die Kunst der Verzierung*, 62–9; see also D. Boyden, 'Corelli's Solo Violin Sonatas "Grac'd" by Dubourg', *Festskrift Jens Peter Larsen* (Copenhagen, 1972), 113–25. Roger North (*Roger North on Music*, ed. J. Wilson, 161) scoffed at the Roger graces, wondering 'how so much vermin could creep into the works of such a master'. See also B. Bismartova, *Compendio musicale*, Ferrara, 1677, *I-REm* Regg.E.41; facsimile (Florence, 1978).

[39] The Tartini movement with 17 different ornamented versions by Cartier is given in Schmitz, *Die Kunst der Verzierung*, 131–4. Cartier's *L'art du violon* is reprinted in facsimile (Geneva, 1973). According to Fétis, the violoncellist Jean Barrière studied in Italy in the late 1730s. Upon his return, he published six sonatas for *pardessus de viole* in the Italian *galant* style, five of which he transcribed for harpsichord with additional ornamentation written out apparently for the benefit of French players unfamiliar with the new idiom. The resulting publication, the first solo keyboard sonatas by a Frenchman, has been reprinted by Minkoff (Geneva, 1982).

[40] Quantz, *Versuch*, 136 and 139. Note that 'plain' here means without diminutions but definitely not without 'essential' graces.

[41] The original melody of an Adagio by Marcello can be compared to Bach's version in Schmitz, *Die Kunst der Verzierung*, 100–102, and Ferand, *Improvisation*, 128–9.

[42] Schmitz, *Die Kunst der Verzierung*, 102–3; see also E. Melkus, 'Die Entwicklung der freien Auszierung im 18. Jahrhundert', *Der Junge Haydn*, ed. V. Schwartz (Graz, 1972), 147–67.

[43] An issue little discussed is whether ornaments may be allowed to distort the beat. Method books that mention it at all seem to favour keeping time, but the rule may have been honoured in the breach. T. Jamard, *Recherches sur la théorie de la musique* (1769), 280f, compared the relative exactitude of the Italians to the practice of the French, who always beat time loudly but continually sacrificed it to ornaments. 'It must be admitted that in most of our French pieces, the measure is so little felt that musicians would get off continually if they consulted only their ears'. As with all such citations, one must guard against applying it to times very far removed from the writing unless other evidence corroborates it. Tosi complained bitterly against Italian singers who did not keep time.

[44] *The Bach Reader*, ed. H. T. David and A. Mendel (New York, 1945), 238.

[45] For an unusually practical (and in spite of the title, sensible and well-informed) guide to the improvisation of diminutions, together with a list of 181 models from 1535 to 1638, see A. Waldo, 'So you Want to Blow the Audience Away', *American Recorder*, xxvii (1986), 48–59.

[46] A. Dolmetsch, *The Interpretation of the Music of the XVIIth and XVIIIth Centuries* (London, 1915, 2/1946/R1969), 154–95. The separate appendix to this work, containing 22 illustrative pieces, was published without date by Novello, London. It is neither supplied with nor mentioned in the front matter of the modern reprint.

[47] Many of Neumann's articles on performance, including this one, have been gathered in his *Essays on Performance Practice* (Ann Arbor, 1982). Since some have undergone revision or expansion, it is to this collection that the reader is referred where possible.

[48] Donington gave careful consideration to Neumann's views on the trill and other matters to (to which he had access before publication) in *The Interpretation of Early Music* (London, rev. 3/1974), 620–40.

[49] A similarly inconclusive, though less contentious, controversy regarding Beethoven's trills occurred from 1976 to 1979 in the pages of *JAMS* and *MQ*, in which Robert Winter advanced the hypothesis that the first note of the trill should be chosen to be dissonant with the prevailing harmony, while William S. Newman argued for main-note starts as a general rule in Beethoven's maturity.

[50] 'Couperin and the Downbeat Doctrine for Appoggiaturas', *Essays*, 227–41.

[51] For arguments and citations on both sides of the issue, see Neumann, *Ornamentation*, 13–15. Rameau was one composer whose desires condoned parallel octaves. 'J'ai inséré deux Octaves de suite dans quelques-unes de ces derñieres piéces exprès pour desabuser ceux qu'on a pû prévenir contre l'effet de ces deux Octaves: et je suis persuadé que si l'on n'y consultoit que l'Oreille, on trouveroit mauvais qu'elles n'y fussent pas' (preface to *Nouvelles suites de pièces de clavecin*, [1739]).

[52] Perhaps three dozen articles or chapters on the subject have appeared since the mid-1960s. See the bibliographies to the articles 'Notes inégales' in *Grove 6* and 'Dotted Notes' in *The New Harvard Dictionary of Music* for a partial list.

[53] H. Riemann, *Musikalische Dynamik und Agogik: Lehrbuch der musikalischen Phrasierung* (Hamburg, 1884).

[54] *Essays*, 73–98. This version is a translation from the original French and was first published in *EM*, v (1977), 310–24. It was answered by the present writer and also, briefly, by Donington in the next issue of the same journal, pp.517–44. Neumann's response (*Essays*, 137–50) first appeared in *EM*, vii (1979), 39–45. Three further articles on the same subject are included in Neumann's *Essays*. See also J. O'Donnell, 'The French Style and the Overtures of Bach', *EM*, vii (1979), 190–96 and 336–45; G. Pont, 'Rhythmic Alteration and the Majestic', *Studies in Music*, xii (1978), 68–100, and 'French Overtures at the Keyboard: "How Handel Rendered the Playing of Them"', *Musicology*, vi (1980), 29–50.

[55] *Anleitung zur Singekunst*, 133–4. Quantz, *Versuch*, Eng. trans., 67, gives a similar rule with an exercise to obtain the effect. See also R. Falkener, *Instructions for Playing the Harpsichord* (London, 2/1774), 17–19: in the rhythm semiquaver–dotted quaver, 'touch the semiquaver as quick; or make it as short as you possibly can, and stay upon the dotted quaver as long as the time will permit you', and in dotted quaver–semiquaver–dotted quaver–semiquaver etc, 'you must make the dotted quaver as long as the time will permit and the semiquaver as short'.

[56] The inequality is entirely written out in Gigault, *Livre de musique*, and in a number of pieces by François Couperin, e.g. *La Mézangére*, *Second livre de pièces de clavecin* (Paris, c1716), tenth *ordre*.

[57] For example, 50–56 minims to the minute in such overtures as Variation 16 of Bach's *Goldberg Variations* or the first movement of his fourth harpsichord partita, according to J. O'Donnell, 'The French Style and the Overtures of Bach', *EM*, vii (1979), 190–96. This is roughly double the usual tempo for these pieces.

[58] Gigault, *Livre de musique*. Montéclair, *Principes de musique*, 23, presents a 'manière de concevoir et d'étudier la tenue et le point' that shows clearly the double-dotting of crotchets in a context of dotted quavers. See O'Donnell, 'The French Style and the Overture of Bach', 337, for further discussion and citations.

[59] For a discussion of dotted rhythm in relation to style and expression, see D. Fuller, 'The "Dotted Style" in Bach, Handel and Scarlatti', *Bach, Handel, Scarlatti: Tercentenary Essays*, ed. P. Williams (Cambridge, 1985), 99–117.

[60] The orchestra for a revival of Lully's *Atys* (Florence, Paris, Montpellier and Versailles, 1987) worked out dotting in rehearsal where necessary. The matter of synchronization required no special attention from the leader; the players simply listened to each other (communication from the orchestra leader, John Holloway). The conductor, William Christie, directed from a 'clean', unmarked photocopy of the 17th-century edition. The extreme richness and subtlety of the rhythms throughout the opera, which may be heard on a recording by Harmonia Mundi France, had little to do with notation and less with any 'code'.

[61] For discussions of this very difficult problem, see E. Darbellay, prefaces to Frescobaldi's works in *Monumenti musicali italiani a cura della Società italiana di musicologia* (Milan, 1977–); F. Hammond, *Girolamo Frescobaldi* (Cambridge, Mass., 1983), 226–7; P. Brainard, 'Concerning Proportion and Pseudo-Proportion in Seventeenth-Century Rhythm', paper given at the annual meeting of the AMS, Philadelphia, 1984.

[62] Hammond, p.227, and M. Collins, 'The Performance of Triplets in the Seventeenth and Eighteenth Centuries', *JAMS*, xix (1906), 281–328, take opposite points of view on the matter of two-against-three.

[63] e.g. Donington, *The Interpretation of Early Music*, 467, and Collins, op cit.

[64] In addition to the article by Collins cited in n.62, see his dissertation, *The Performance of Coloration, Sesquialtera, and Hemiolia (1450–1750)* (Stanford U., 1963), and 'The Performance of Sesquialtera and Hemiolia in the Sixteenth Century', *JAMS*, xvii (1964), 5–28. O'Donnell, *The Diapason* lxvii/1(Dec 1975), 5, printed a version of 'In dulci jubilo' inspired by Collins's researches in which all the triplets were changed to duple dactylic or anapaestic figures, with horrifying effect.

[65] Eta Harich-Schneider and Erwin Jacobi concerning dotted figures against triplets, in two articles, both entitled 'Über die Angleichung nachschlagender Sechzehntel an Triolen', *Mf*, xii (1959), 35–59 and xiii (1960), 268–81. See also Jacobi, 'Neues zur Frage, "Punktierte Rhythmen gegen Triolen" und zur Transkriptionstechnik bei J. S. Bach', *BJb*, xlix (1962), 88–96.

[66] In *Grove 6*, *Grove MI* (slightly revised with additions to the bibliography) and *The New Harvard Dictionary of Music*.

[67] Gigault, *Livre de musique*. To Gigault's apparently obsessive dotting the player is invited to add yet more dots 'pour animer son jeu'; and an allemande in another of his publications (printed in the modern edition on pp.xviii–xx) is designed to provide a model for adding *ports de voix*, which in the event amount to dotted diminutions of a dotted original. André Pirro, who

wrote the preface to the edition, attempted to reassure the reader appalled at all this dotting by invoking an undotted piece by François Couperin with the heading, 'les doubles croches un tant-soit-peu pointées', which he took as authorization to render Gigault's dots as no more than gentle accents. But a treatise on organ playing roughly contemporary with Gigault's music makes it clear that in certain types of piece at least (duos and trios, for example), the dotting, written or not, was to be as sharp as possible. See W. Pruitt, 'A Seventeenth-century French Manuscript on Organ Performance', *EM*, xiv (1986), 237–51. The issue of notated inequality has recently flared up in the *Journal of Musicology*: F. Neumann, 'The *Notes inégales* Revisited', vi (1988), 137–49; D. Fuller, 'Notes and *inégales* Unjoined: Defending a Definition', vii (1989), 21–8.

[68] pp.77–9 in the modern edition.

[69] ₵ could be either four rapid or two slow beats. In the former case, semiquavers were unequal and quavers equal; in the latter, quavers were unequal. Since the meaning of ₵ is rarely clear, the decision as to which values are unequal has to be taken on the basis of stylistic analogies with music whose beat is known.

[70] See Fuller, 'The "Dotted Style" in Bach, Handel and Scarlatti'.

[71] J.-B. Cappus, *Etrennes de musique*; see Fuller, 'More on Triplets'.

[72] On 'humouring' see J. Johnson, 'How to "Humour" John Jenkins' Three-part Dances', *JAMS*, xx (1967), 197–208. The many instances in English 17th-century music of pieces in different sources with and without dotting can be taken to suggest that the undotted versions might have been dotted in performance.

[73] Muffat; see Cooper and Zsako, 'Georg Muffat's Observations'.

[74] Eng. trans., pp.123–4. Inequality is stipulated for the same list of note values in the various metres as in the French manuals and in all but the fastest tempos (inequality applies to the normal allegro, as a reference on p.130 indicates). Unlike any but a very few French authors, however, Quantz relates the practice to the doctrine of strong and weak ('good' and 'bad') subdivisions of the beat. He also makes certain exceptions that are not found in French sources, notably fast vocal passages ('divisions', apparently) unless slurred, and groups of four or more notes under a single slur – the possible contradiction is not reconciled. But since no connection is made to national styles, Italian music is evidently included under the rules of the convention, whereas it is often excluded by the French. L. Frischmuth, *Gedagten over de Beginselen en Onderwyzingen des Clavicimbaals* (Amsterdam, [1758]), 52, specifies unequal semiquavers in allemandes and unequal quavers in courantes: 'even if there are no dots ... they must be played as if they were there'.

[75] A clear example of initial dotting meant to be continued is F. Dagincour, *Allemande La Couronne* from *Pièces de clavecin* (Paris, 1733), ed. H. Ferguson (Paris, 1969); a controversial one is the 'Domine Deus' from Bach's B minor Mass: see G. Herz, 'Lombard Rhythm in the *Domine Deus* of Bach's B-Minor Mass: an Old Controversy Resolved', *Essays on J. S. Bach* (Ann Arbor, 1985), 221–9; and Neumann, *Essays*, 51–3, for a sample of opposing views. Graham Pont has devoted much attention to Handel's inconsistent dotting: see his 'French Overtures at the Keyboard', 'Handel's Overtures for Harpsichord or Organ: an Unrecognized Genre', *EM*, xi (1983), 309–22, and 'A Revolution in the Science and Practice of Music', *Musicology*, v (1979), 1–66.

[76] L. Bourgeois, *Le droict chemin de musique* (Geneva, 1550/R1954). The bibliography to 'Notes inégales' in *Grove 6* gives a chronological overview of some of the source material.

[77] See for example F. Severi, *Salmi passaggiati (1615)*, ed. M. Bradshaw (Madison, 1981), *passim*.

[78] A sarabande in the hand of Louis Couperin, and therefore dating from before his death in 1661, has instances of an anacrusis of three rising semiquavers marked 'point cela' (dot that) or 'point'. See B. Gustafson, *French Harpsichord Music of the 17th Century* (Ann Arbor, 1979), ii, 284.

[79] *L'interprétation de la musique française de Lully à la Révolution* (Paris, 1934), 157; for critical comment see 'Notes inégales', *Grove 6*.

[80] *Nouvelle méthode pour apprendre à jouer du violon et à lire la musique* [?Toulouse, c1760], 29.

[81] Notably by Sol Babitz; e.g. *Rhythmic Freedom: a Historical Table in the Light of Wind-Instrument Tonguing* (Los Angeles, 1974); see also N. Powell, *Early Keyboard Fingering and its Effect on Articulation* (diss., Stanford U., 1956); and G. Houle 'Tonguing and Rhythmic Patterns in Early Music', *American Recorder*, vi (1965), 4–13.

[82] J. Chailley, 'A propos des notes inégales', *RdM*, xlv (1960), 89–91. Since inequality applied mainly to diminutions, which were sung to prolonged syllables, the argument is specious. Also,

Italian and Spanish are pronounced very differently from French, but analogous phenomena are described in treatises in those languages.

[83] C. Van den Borren, 'De quelques principes pour l'interprétation de la musique ancienne', *Musica viva*, i (Brussels, 1936), 53; the passage is translated in Fuller, 'Dotting, the "French Style", and Frederick Neumann's Counter-Reformation', *EM*, v (1977), 533.

[84] E. Darbellay, 'Liberté, variété et "affetti cantabili" chez Girolamo Frescobaldi', *RdM*, lxi (1975), 197–243. See also Hammond, *Girolamo Frescobaldi*, chap.15; Johnson, 'How to "Humour" John Jenkins' Three-Part Dances'; B. Gustafson, 'A Letter from Mr. Lebègue Concerning his Preludes', *Recherches sur la musique française classique*, xvii (1977), 7–14; *The Art of the Unmeasured Prelude*, ed. C. Tilney in preparation; P. Prévost, *Le prélude non mesuré pour clavecin* (Baden-Baden and Bouxwiller, 1987); Rousseau, 'Exécution' in *Dictionnaire de musique* (Paris, 1768); Cleret (first name unknown), 'Principes de musique nécessaires à savoir pour l'accompagnement', MS (1786) (*F-Pn* Rés. 2328), 405–6.

[85] The character of attack and release of the notes is an important aspect of articulation.

[86] M.-D.-J. Engramelle, *La tonotechnie* (Paris, 1775/*R*1971); also his essay on barrel organ pinning in Dom B. de Celles, *L'art du facteur d'orgues* (Paris, 1766–8/*R*1934–6 and 1963–6), part 4.

CHAPTER VII

Pitch

CARY KARP

Pitch is an audible sensation produced by some, but not all, vibrating objects. A tuning fork, for example, will produce a clear sensation of pitch, whereas many drums will not. The vibrating bodies which generate the sounds used in music – vocal cords, strings, columns of air etc – produce several frequencies simultaneously and the perceived pitch cannot necessarily be related to any single one of them.[1] If the pitch of a sound does not change as the higher partials are eliminated, the pitch can be described by the fundamental frequency.

Wind and bowed string instruments generally adhere to this model. If one of these sounds what is arbitrarily designated as an A with a fundamental frequency of 440 Hz, we can say that the pitch is A–440. The pitches produced by plucked strings and struck instruments will not necessarily remain unchanged as higher partials are eliminated. The most extreme example is the pitch of a bell, which often bears no direct relationship to any one of its many partial frequencies of vibration. In such cases a pitch designation can only be made by comparison with the pitch of a sound which is not affected by the removal of its higher partials. To avoid any confusion in this regard, all pitches will be notated below in the general form A–440. The designation 'A' will not be related to a specific octave.[2]

In situations where several musicians are to play 'in tune' with each other there must be agreement on a common pitch. This need involve little more than an informal consensus which allows everyone to play comfortably within the ranges of their voices and instruments. In other situations it may be necessary to use more formally established pitch references. This will require defining the pitch of at least one step of the scale in absolute terms. Any study of the history of musical pitch will deal largely with the development of such absolute pitch levels, and their subsequent adoption on an increasingly widespread basis.[3]

The documents which provide information on pitch can be divided into several groups, of which only a few will be considered in detail below. They are: written sources, including reports of direct measurements of frequencies of vibration; musical instruments and other pitch recording implements such as monochords, pitch pipes and tuning forks; iconographical evidence; and finally, notated music. Much of this will only be useful in determining pitch levels in relative terms. The names applied to pitch standards will be found solely in written sources. These names can be linked to absolute values if the reports of individual pitches fall reasonably together into broader standards.

There are at least vague references to absolute pitch dating from early in the 16th century. The entire body of documentary material dating from that time has pitch levels spanning an interval of no more than a fifth.[4] Since the concept of notated pitch names was established in vocal performance before the 16th century, the reported limits for pitch variation may be related to the basic range of the human voice.

This may, in part, account for the surprisingly uniform history that can be gleaned from the written record, which also suggests that our authorities shared a high level of understanding of the problem. There are inconsistencies, however, and these have generated controversy among scholars. One earlier reason for this was difficulty in understanding the pitch behaviour of surviving musical instruments in other than conjectural terms. This uncertainty is gradually diminishing as a result of the growing collective experience of those musicians, instrument makers, organologists and museum scientists who have specialized in the study and use of earlier types of instruments. As the body of information which they are providing increases, we can expect many of the remaining questions about historical pitch to be answered. Our interpretation of the written sources must, therefore, remain open to change. All material and comments presented here must be understood in this light.

Standardization

There are essentially two attitudes towards the standardization of pitch encountered during the 16th, 17th and 18th centuries. The first is that an instrument should be tuned to whatever pitch is most convenient for its player; hence Aaron, in 1523: 'the first matter which you must consider is setting the string called C, which is tuned to whatever level you please'.[5] Similar comments are found about instrumental and vocal ensembles, for example Ganassi's description in 1542 – in *Regola rubertina* (Venice) – of the means by which viol players can adjust their instruments to be playable at the pitch most comfortably used by singers.

The second attitude is that it is a source of confusion and discomfort for there to be a multiplicity of pitch levels, and that uniformity in this regard would be highly desirable. Praetorius in *Syntagma musicum*, ii (Wolfenbüttel, 1618, 2/1619/R1958 and 1980) states, 'For this reason a musician is subjected to great strain when the organs, positives, harpsichords, and other wind instruments, are not kept together at one and proper pitch', while Adlung (1783) writes:

> From where do we take the start of tuning, or how do we determine the pitch of the C? It is known that organs are not in agreement, so that the musician, in addition to his trumpet, always must carry several crooks if he is to play in more than one church ... It is therefore not unreasonable to wish that the organ makers were in agreement about this, and that they should have some rule according to which they were able to set a uniform bass and treble. However, this is as yet lacking, since what Sauveur has proposed has not yet come into practice.[6]

These remarks do not refer indiscriminately to the entire state of musical affairs. The instructions for ad libitum pitch selection most often refer to string instruments used individually or in small ensembles. A related, and often repeated, piece of advice is to tune a string instrument so that its highest string is close to the breaking point. For a given instrumental design this specifies pitch with some accuracy.

Many complaints about pitch variation relate to performance with organ. Consider an organ tuned to A–460 and located in an unheated church whose indoor temperature varies from 5°C to 25°C during the course of a year. Let us say that when the organ was tuned the temperature in the church was 15°C. This information is important since the speed at which sound travels through air is dependent on the temperature of the air. The pitch of the organ will therefore vary with the temperature of the church. On a day with an ambient temperature of 5°C its pitch will approach A–450 while on a 25°C day it will be near A–470. A local flautist called upon to perform with this organ at all times of the year would experience some anguish at having to deal with this pitch variability. The pitch of the flute would also vary with the temperature, but not as much as that of the organ since the temperature of the air within at least part of the flute is reasonably close to body temperature, whereas the air within the organ pipes is at ambient temperature. The net expense and inconvenience of having the entire organ repitched in anticipation of every larger change in temperature would probably be greater than that necessary for the flautist to acquire as many different flutes – or exchangeable middle joints for a single flute – as the battle with the organ's pitch might require.

An additional problem was caused by the need for a tuning mechanism which allowed the pitch of an organ pipe to be lowered. Lacking a convenient means for lengthening its pipes (which is far more difficult than shortening them) the pitch of an organ will of necessity climb each time the instrument is tuned. This is the basis of Praetorius's comment in 1619, 'The organs often also climbed still higher than their original pitches, as a result of much renovation and tuning'.

Thus even if two organs had once been tuned to the same pitch, they would diverge upon repeated tuning, with each climbing in pitch at its own rate. In historical practice, organs were allowed to climb until unacceptable pitch levels were reached, at which time they would be repitched by shifting all pipes up one position and making a new largest pipe for each voice. The organ was then retuned to the desired level. The difficulties involved in establishing uniform pitch standards for organs were indeed substantial.

The reasons for the delay in the development of pipe tuning devices lie outside the scope of this study. The technology applied to capping and tuning closed metal pipes was quite similar to that which was later employed for open pipe tuning slides. Organ makers may simply have ignored the wishes of musicians. It would, however, not be unreasonable to assume that the lack of organ pitch standardization was not felt to be as acute a problem as the authors with whom we are familiar seem to indicate. Not every comment made about the situation contains a value judgment, as this passage by Quantz (1752) reveals:

> Because the pitch according to which one tunes varies so much, so that a different one is used not only in every country, but also for the most part in every province and city, to say nothing of the harpsichord which in a single

town due to incautious tuners may be tuned now too high or then too low; about 30 years ago the flute was fitted with several middle joints. At that time one made ... two or three which, since the one always had to be shorter than the other, differed from each other by about a semitone.[7]

The number of extra middle joints for the flute was subsequently increased to as many as eight, spanning an interval in excess of a whole tone. The combined options of transposition and using different joints should have allowed for playing over a wide range of pitches. Other woodwind instruments are more flexible in pitch than are flutes. The selection of a crook or staple, and the design of the reed and mouthpiece can make substantial differences. However, multiple upper joints were not made exclusively for flutes. It may often be noted on surviving instruments that only one of a set of exchangeable joints shows signs of real wear. This suggests either that instrumentalists had a preferred home pitch from which they made occasional forays into varying pitches, or that players preferred other tuning techniques and transposition to the use of exchangeable joints. (The internal tuning of an instrument, and therefore its fingering, will differ with each extra joint.) The situation for brass instruments is mentioned in the above passage from Adlung. Quantz complains about the lack of pitch standard elsewhere in his book, and it is interesting that he does so solely with reference to the difficulties it causes for singers.

Difficulties inherent in the standardization of organ pitch did not necessarily cause similar difficulty in chamber contexts without an organ. This may be one reason why the standardization of organ pitch was not regarded as an acute problem. If chamber pitch is defined as a fixed interval from organ pitch then it will, of course, wander together with the pitch of the local organ. If chamber pitch is defined independently it could be quite stable. Trends towards standardization beyond the closed community of a town would follow as the musical styles and instruments of one area asserted themselves ever further afield. Given that both organ and chamber pitches could become stable at levels differing from each other by a convenient transposition interval, the need for an absolute convergence of these pitches would rarely be felt.

The current use of transposing instruments clearly demonstrates that there are substantial tonal reasons for not building all instruments at the same pitch. The range within which the design of an individual instrument can be modified to alter its pitch without losing its unique tonal identity is hard to determine, and is quite specific to that instrument. Keeping pace with a pitch that varies within a few Hz is not likely to ruin the basic characteristics of any instrument. Pitches a tone or more distant from each other are quite a different matter. In addition to tonal changes, there are significant design criteria which may be affected. For example, the strain that is placed on the body of a string instrument when it is tuned to ever higher pitches cannot be increased indefinitely. The structural modification which would be necessary to keep the instrument from collapsing, or its strings from breaking, can rarely be accomplished without modifying the sound which it produces. A second example can be seen in any keyless woodwind large enough for the fingers just to be able to reach all the finger-holes. Designing a version of the same instrument to sound one tone lower would require the use of at least one key. Since a key may require more space along the length of the instrument than does a simple finger-hole, other aspects of the instrument could require redesign, with a concomitant alteration of its sound.

The changes in tonal characteristics resulting from any such redesigning may, of course, be regarded as entirely desirable. Indeed, changes in pitch levels may be motivated by the wish to produce precisely this type of tonal change. An example of this may be found in the modern symphony orchestra where the desire for ever 'brighter' string sounds continuously pushes pitch levels upwards.

There is a lingering implication here that an idealized concept of an instrument's sound, coupled with a clear definition of the technical demands to be made of the instrument, will determine its ideal structure and, therefore, its optimum pitch. If the musical factors change more rapidly than the pace of instrument design then this optimum will not be attained. If a basic instrument design survives long enough in a stable musical environment one might expect to see it optimized, including a tendency towards its 'right and proper' pitch. When dealing with a number of tried and true designs, minor pitch adjustments to allow for standardization would do little damage. Redesigning for use at a pitch a semitone or more distant would not necessarily be without adverse tonal consequence. This leads to a major caveat for exponents of authentic performance. Instruments which have been modified to play at pitch levels other than those for which they were originally designed may not sound as they were originally intended. This also applies to similar changes made in the preparation of a reproduction instrument. This is not to say that successful repitching is impossible, nor that this invariably makes a difference. The basic question should, however, not be dismissed out of hand.

Writings: Praetorius

The first major studies of pitch in the modern musicological literature were conducted by Alexander J. Ellis and Arthur Mendel. In 1880 Ellis presented an annotated catalogue of documents relating to pitch dating from the early 17th century until his own day. He included a detailed study of tuning forks. In 1948 Arthur Mendel published a series of articles on pitch in the 16th and early 17th centuries, and in 1955 on pitch in the time of J. S. Bach.[8] These pioneering studies have served as a starting-point for virtually all work subsequently done on the subject. Although many errors have been found in their conclusions, their basic presentations of the historical evidence remain a useful source of general reference. An article published by W. R. Thomas and J. J. K. Rhodes in 1971[9] strongly questioned the manner in which Mendel dealt with the material presented by Michael Praetorius in 1618, and offered an alternative to Mendel's conclusions. This provided the impetus for a number of valuable studies of pitch in general and of Praetorius in particular. Mendel also renewed his interest in the subject, publishing his final study in 1978.[10]

Since then, a number of authors have done detailed work on many aspects of the history of pitch. The writings of Praetorius provide an extremely useful description of the pitches of his day and form the first truly detailed written record of this type. His work has therefore been fruitfully examined time and time again. Two basic approaches to its interpretation have emerged, and proponents of each viewpoint have not invariably been kind to each other in their respective publications. It is characteristic of all such writings that they present the source material as reasonably easy to interpret unambiguously. Indeed, it is easy to sketch a coherent relationship between the various pieces of information contained in Praetorius's writing. There are a few apparent contradictions in what he says, but these can often be resolved, or can at least be shown not to be of vital importance for the understanding of his work. Similarly, if he says something which is genuinely difficult to understand, he often describes the same matter in clearer terms elsewhere. The latitude with which he can (and at times must) be read has triggered exegetic debate. As a first case study in the history of pitch we may review this material.

Praetorius provides useful snippets of information about pitch at various places in the second volume of his *Syntagma musicum*. Each quotation will be given here, with its page reference.

> However, the 'Chor Thon' of our ancestors was initially one tone lower than it is now (it is still found on old organs and other wind instruments) but over the years it has been raised to its present level in Italy and England, and also in the ducal chapels of the German states. The English pitch may be a very little lower than this, which is noticeable on the cornetts, 'Schalmeys' or 'Hoboys' (as they call them) which are made there. There have been some who allowed themselves to raise our present pitch by yet another semi-tone: although it is not my place to correct this, nonetheless in my opinion it is so high that singers, especially altos and tenors, would find it very uncomfortable and often almost impossible to reach. For this reason it would be best to leave the previously mentioned pitch unchanged; because even that is often found too high not only for singers but also for string players: Violins, viols, lutes, pandoras and the like need exceptional strings to withstand such heights. For this reason, when one is in the middle of a performance, the top strings [*Quinten*] snap and the players are stuck. To allow the strings to stay better in tune, these types of string instruments are commonly tuned one tone lower, and the other instruments are played one tone lower. Although this causes difficulty for the inexperienced musician, it helps the voices of the vocalists and singers if they can make music one tone lower. (pp.14–15)[11]

Reference has thus far been made to a single pitch level which, over the years, has climbed one tone upwards from its original level to its present one, as used in Germany, Italy and, slightly lower, in England. There are those who wish to raise this pitch by yet another semitone, but this would have unfortunate consequences for singers and the players of string instruments. Indeed, many string players tune down one tone from this to keep their strings from breaking. Performance at this level is also easier for singers, and it causes no hardship to experienced players of other instruments who accordingly transpose downwards one whole tone. This lower level is the same as the old pitch which subsequently climbed and it is still to be found on certain old organs and other wind instruments. Thus instruments are found which have been pitched at both the old level and the new, but many of the latter instruments either retune or transpose to the lower of these. The reference to the difference between English and German pitches indicates that Praetorius regarded slight differences in pitch as noteworthy.

For this reason I am particularly pleased by the distinction whereby in Prague and many other Catholic chapels pitch is divided into 'Chor Thon' and 'Cammer Thon'. There the present common pitch, to which almost all our organs are tuned, is called 'Cammer Thon' and is used only for *musique de table* and festivities; it is then most convenient for the instrumentalists whether they play wind or string instruments...

'Chor Thon', however, which is a whole tone lower, is used only in churches, and then primarily for the sake of the singers... for which reason ... no harm would be done if all the organs were tuned and set one tone, or a second, lower: however, such a change would be impossible now in our German states, which therefore must remain at the common 'Cammer Thon' (which at the present time in most places is called 'Chor Thon'). (pp.15–16)[12]

Here we learn that the lower pitch is used only in churches, largely for the sake of the vocalists, while the normal higher pitch is nonetheless the one to which all organs are tuned. Since this means that the organist would be transposing whenever playing together with singers, it might make sense to repitch all organs one tone lower, which is simply impossible. The higher pitch is used on festive secular occasions, for which it is well suited to all instruments. Although the higher pitch is called choir pitch in most places, Praetorius prefers the terminology used in Prague where the term 'choir pitch' (*Chor-Thon*) refers to the lower level, that is, the one used for vocal performance in the church. He uses the term 'chamber pitch' (*Cammer-Thon*) for the higher pitch, which is also his organ pitch. Thus he knows of two pitches separated by a useful transposition interval of one whole tone. The lower level, choir pitch, is defined in terms of the higher level, chamber pitch. This in turn is the pitch standard to which the makers of organs and most other instruments tune their products. 'The *cornamusa*... are tuned exactly at Chorton, that is, one tone lower than our proper 'Cornetten' or 'Cammerthon'' (p.41).[13]

Here is at least one wind instrument which was directly tuned to the lower pitch. (The *cornamusa* are otherwise quite elusive and are not shown in Praetorius's drawings. Considering his earlier reference to a few wind instruments still being tuned to the older low pitch level, this may indicate that their basic design was older than that of the other instruments which he describes.) Praetorius equates cornett pitch with chamber pitch. In most other older German sources cornett pitch is regarded as the same as choir pitch. This is consistent with Praetorius's own statement that he does not follow conventional German terminology. In the first of the quotations in this section he refers to choir pitch in the more conventional manner, although he does this before explaining his preference for the Prague terminology and may be making a deliberate concession to popular usage. In any case, he is not entirely consistent in his terminology throughout his writing.

In England previously, and to this day in the Netherlands, they voiced and tuned most of their wind instruments a minor third lower than our present 'Cammer Thon', so that their F is D in our 'Cammer Thon' and their G our E. The excellent Antwerp instrument maker, Johannes Bossus, thus voiced and tuned most of the harpsichords and 'Symphonien', including the registers of pipes within them, in this pitch.

In fact, with this pitch one not only bestows harpsichords (as the understanding instrument maker knows) with a lovelier and more graceful

resonance than when they are divided according to 'Cammer Thon': but
also the flutes and other instruments are lovelier at this lower pitch than
when sounding at the usual one, and produce an almost entirely different
sound (since they are not as strident at this pitch). However, these
instruments would be very awkward to use in full ensemble and we are left
with the previously mentioned 'Chorm' and 'Cammer Thon'. In spite of
this, in Italy and other Catholic chapels in Germany, the pitch a minor third
lower is very much in use. (p.16)[14]

Another pitch standard has now been described: the one in use for most wind
instruments and for chamber keyboard instruments in the Low Countries.
This pitch is also widely used in Italy and in German Catholic chapels. It is a
minor third lower than Praetorius's chamber pitch and he finds that
instruments tuned to it sound far better than those tuned to his chamber
pitch. He regrets that it is awkward to mix these instruments in full
ensemble, for which reason their musical use is restricted to the previously
described choir and chamber pitches. The narrative continues with a not
entirely unambiguous description of Italian practice. In any case, it appears
that Italian organ pitch was a minor third above their instrument pitch and
thus at the same level as Praetorius's church organs. Singing at this pitch
does not only 'obscure understanding of the text'; vocalists using it 'may
rightly be regarded as unpleasant ... one crows, screeches and sings in a
high-pitched voice just like a shepherdess'. As a result, organists sometimes
transpose down a minor third:

> Initially these transpositions are rather sour and repugnant to both
> organists and other instrumentalists. However, as long as one is not
> discouraged by effort and spends time diligently practising, it will become
> very easy and it will be enjoyable to be able to put it into practice. (pp.16–
> 17)[15]

It is therefore unclear just what impediment there was to the use of the Low
Countries' wind instruments together with those of northern Germany. One
possibility is that the number of instruments made at Praetorius's choir pitch
was larger than has otherwise been indicated. For such instruments,
performing at a level a minor third lower than the organ pitch would not,
indeed, have been a convenient alternative.

> Nowadays when an organ maker tunes all the registers of an organ to the
> common 'Cammer Thon', most organs which are not too small and of
> limited compass will have their lowest C in the principal register of the 8'
> manual at the same pitch as is found on proper harpsichords and spinets.
> (p.17)[16]

The harpsichord and spinet were also tuned to the organ pitch. We know
little of the scaling of the harpsichords with which Praetorius was familiar.
The only full-sized such instrument he illustrates is of Italian type and is
labelled, 'Harpsichord, thus one fourth below "Chor Thon"'. (The question of harpsichord pitch will be discussed below.)

Praetorius also discusses the history of the organ during the centuries prior
to his writing. He provides a vague chronology of the age of various
innovations and speaks of at least one earlier period during which most
organs were a tone higher than his own organ pitch: 'Almost all the organs of
that time stood at one tone higher than our present "Cammer Thon"'

(p.116).[17] This contradicts his statement about organ pitch initially having been one tone lower than his own. Since he reports that lower-pitched organs still existed in his day, Praetorius was a first-hand observer of the lower pitch. His discussions of the pitches of specific organs from a much earlier period are based on fragmentary evidence.

Thus far the picture is reasonably clear. Praetorius's reference pitch was that of the organ, and of almost all other instruments, which he called chamber pitch. The pitch used for performance in church, at which only a few instruments were actually built, was one tone lower and Praetorius calls this choir pitch. This terminology differs from the one in widespread use, where the higher pitch is choir or cornett pitch and the lower is chamber pitch. A third standard, a minor third lower than his chamber pitch, was widely used for most instruments in the Low Countries. There is an English pitch just slightly lower than his chamber pitch, and the Low Countries' pitch is also used in some German situations and in Italy. The Italian organ pitch was the same as Praetorius's own.

A major point of debate in the modern literature is whether Praetorius used the terms 'choir pitch' and 'chamber pitch' to refer to two distinct pitch levels or to denote a single pitch level. It is hard to read his text in a manner which supports the latter contention. The nominal set of pitches with a cornett or choir pitch as the highest, followed by a chamber pitch one tone lower, and a second chamber pitch yet another semitone lower, is found in Germany throughout the 18th century. It remains to be seen if this uniformity of terminology has any counterpart in what we can determine about absolute pitch levels. Praetorius provides material which may give some indication of the absolute levels of what, to avoid further confusion, may be labelled his 'instrument' and 'performance' pitches. The most substantial evidence for the former may be found in the woodcut illustrations in his *Theatrum instrumentorum* published in 1620.[18] This contains astonishingly detailed scale drawings of many instruments, including those familiar from extant museum specimens. Although reference is made to instruments of types found in many different countries, it is probably safe to assume that those objects which were actually measured and drawn were obtained locally, and thus were built to Praetorius's pitch(es). On the reverse side of the title-page there is a six-inch measuring scale.

> This is the proper length and measure of one half shoe or foot according to the scale which is one quarter of the Braunschweig 'Elle', to which all the following drawings of instruments with the smaller scales included with them have been set.[19]

Many of the individual illustrations are provided with their own scales which were clearly drawn using the same scale as this reference one. Two original copies of both the second volume of *Syntagma musicum* and the *Theatrum instrumentorum* were examined side by side in the preparation of the present discussion. Comparing the individual scales with the master scale shows that the drawings were made setting one foot on them to either 10/12, 11/12, 13/12, 14/12, 15/12, 16/12 or 17/12 of one inch on the master scale. It is therefore likely that the basic layout of each plate was transferred directly from the master scale.[20]

The Brunswick elle (about two feet; an elle is the distance between the elbow and the fingertips) is preserved in a standard which predates the Thirty Years War, and is given as 570.7 mm. All direct measurements of the master scales found in various copies of the *Theatrum* thus far reported come up a bit shorter than exactly a quarter of this value. Most authors assume that the printed scale was prepared with absolute accuracy and that any discrepancy between its measured length and that of an exact quarter of its prototype can be explained by the paper of the book having shrunk subsequent to printing. They further assume that the degree of shrinkage of the page containing the master scale is identical to the degree of shrinkage of every other page in the book, and that this can be given by a single linear factor. (That is, every measurement need only be multiplied by a single constant amount to give the proper value.) It is, however, not possible to determine the accuracy with which the master scale was cut. Considering the difficulty with which two absolutely identical and accurate measuring scales can be found among present-day drafting implements, transferring an exact quarter of the Brunswick elle to a woodblock and maintaining its dimensions unaltered on to a printed sheet of paper would have been extremely difficult – as would have been the unerring transferral of these dimensions to each and every one of the woodcuts.

Even if this absolute accuracy is accepted, a further uncertainty in Praetorius's measurements relates to changes in paper dimensions subsequent to printing. Obviously, both the tolerances in the measurements and the characteristics of the paper must be considered before evaluating any data taken from the woodcuts. It was not possible to determine if the two copies of the *Theatrum* in Sweden were from the same impression, but it is quite likely that they were not. Side by side comparison of them revealed that the behaviour of the paper varied substantially from page to page, and that the dimensions of each page changed by different amounts along its length and breadth. Also, the discrepancies in the dimensions observed in the illustrations on either side of a single page were surprisingly large. This suggests that the dimensions of each block changed to different degrees between impressions, and/or that the paper was not dimensionally stable from printing on its one side to printing on the other. There is also no reason to assume that all paper-related dimensional changes are due to shrinkage and not to expansion.

To determine the extent to which the paper responded to changes in atmospheric conditions, the books were permitted to stabilize for several weeks in a room with a relative humidity of 35 per cent before any measurements were taken. The humidity was then raised to 55 per cent for a further month and the individual sheets were remeasured. The results revealed that there was no regularity in the changes which took place. The dimensions of many of the sheets remained unaltered, while both slight shrinkage and significant expansion were noted with others. The extent of the change on any sheet could be quite different along its length and breadth, the extreme case being an unchanged width and an increase of 0.5 mm in length. The largest change noted was an expansion of 0.8 mm in the breadth of one sheet. Thus the degree to which the behaviour of any one page can be extrapolated from another is severely limited. One final caveat is that the measuring scales may not be particularly accurate for measurements taken at right angles to them.

With all this in mind we may consider reports of absolute pitches which can be related to the objects illustrated in a few of the woodcuts. The first of these is Plate 9, which shows a set of recorders, 'Blockflöten, ganz Stimm-werk' (Recorders, a full set). The nine different sizes shown are the same as those mentioned on p.34 of *Syntagma*, consisting of one full set of eight different sizes, and a 'gar klein Plockflötlein' (very small little recorder). 'And a full set of this type can be imported from Venice for about 80 Thaler.'[21]

Instruments surviving in Verona, of the same general appearance as those in the woodcut, have been described by Rainer Weber who reports them to be pitched in the neighbourhood of A–450.[22] Bob Marvin reports museum instruments of about the size shown in the *Theatrum* to be between A–450 and A–460.[23] Paul Bunjes had a full set of facsimiles made of all the organ pipes shown in Plates 37 and 38; he reports their average pitch as being A–445 at 20°C.[24] It would be impossible to attempt any direct calculation of the pitches of the instruments shown in the *Theatrum*. On the basis of the reports considered here we may place the instrument and organ pitch in the interval between A–445 and A–460 with some bias towards the upper end of this range, since it has been observed in a number of surviving instruments.

Praetorius also provides explicit reference to the level of his performance pitch. In an appendix to *Syntagma* he writes:

> In this Second Volume mention has often been made of the proper Chor Thon. However, I have found that many places, including large and eminent cities, do not use the proper choir pitch standard [rechte Chor-mass] by which both the human voice and instruments must be guided. These places, and the grandest organs found there, use a pitch [Tonus] which is either too high or too low, and this is one of the primary defects of the organs. I have therefore considered diverse ways and means for how and in which form this can be remedied, so that the proper pitch and choir pitch standard is made known to all organ makers and organists. The organ makers can then be guided by this when voicing new organs, and could use it for renovating and correcting old ones. For this purpose a correct outline of the proper pitch standard is given below... providing the scale for a number of small pipes at the proper choir pitch standard, by which an entire just and pure octave can be built. This can be used, in addition to by the organ makers, also by the organists and 'Cantores' for tuning. (p.231)[25]

Praetorius has devised a pitch pipe which can be used by organ builders and others in need of a performance pitch reference standard. He then gives a drawing of the measurements of the pipes to be used in this device. This drawing is presumably to full scale. There is, however, no reference scale against which these measurements can be judged. Previous authors have assumed that the so-called shrinkage factor determined from the 1620 illustration of the *Theatrum* master scale could be applied to this 1618 woodcut published in *Syntagma*. Despite the fact that both these blocks were used for later continuous impressions of both books, it would now appear to be exceedingly unsafe to assume that they have any reliable dimensional correction factor in common. The pitch pipe drawing is immediately followed by:

> I also humbly regard there to be no better instrument for providing the proper pitch than a trombone, particularly as they once were, and still are

being made in Nuremberg. If the slide is extended from its end by the width of two fingers it produces an absolutely correct and just tenor A at the proper choir pitch standard. (p.232)[26]

References to trombone slides in floating first positions are found elsewhere. Unfortunately, the present reference is not easy to put into absolute terms. Praetorius's illustration of a 'rechte gemeine Posaun' (proper common trombone) in the *Theatrum* shows the instrument with two additional tuning bits, and it is therefore not possible to judge what his reference configuration was. Surviving instruments tested without tuning bits have been reported to speak at about A–460 which is not at odds with Praetorius's instrument pitch as thus far determined. With the added tuning bits, the trombone could presumably be played at all three of the pitch standards which Praetorius described.

Bunjes also had a full set of the small tuning pipes made and reported their pitches. He adjusted the measurements taken from the drawing under the assumption that the *Theatrum* master scale shrinkage factor was directly applicable to the illustration of the small pipes, and that the pipe drawing was otherwise absolutely accurate. The equivalent A pitches for each of the 13 tuning pipes differ, giving some idea of the precision of the drawing. Bunjes's values ranged from A–429 to A–440 at 20°C. However, the two C pipes in the drawing lie both close to each other and to the average value for all the pipes. This may indicate that the imprecision lay primarily in the way the intermediate pipes were drawn. Bunjes's C pipes are at A–434 and A–435 with an average for all pipes of A–434. His actual A pipe was at A–430. The 20°C reference temperature is useful for comparison with all modern direct measurements, which in lack of specific information may be assumed to have been made near this temperature. Praetorius's reference temperature is likely to have been lower. If we take it as 15°C, all the figures provided by Bunjes must be lowered by 4 Hz. The conversion from the reported pitches to their A equivalents was done using quarter-comma meantone temperament, which is the one used by Praetorius for tuning organs.

The applicability of a 'shrinkage correction factor' taken from one book and applied to another ought not to lead to entirely reliable results. Indeed, it is hard to see how it would be possible to interpret the Praetorius drawing in any genuinely useful manner. Despite this, a number of authors have calculated his performance pitch from it. A review of this work is provided by Dominic Gwynn,[27] who reports his own calculation of the average value of this pitch at 3 Hz higher than the one given by Bunjes (with reports by Thomas and Rhodes 4 Hz below Bunjes, and Ellis another 2 Hz lower). The Uppsala copies of *Syntagma* and the *Theatrum* are from a single impression and are bound together. The volume is in excellent condition and should be as reliable a source of raw data as any. It might therefore be useful to perform a similar calculation on the basis of this. It may be noted that there is virtually no difference between the dimensions of the small pipe drawings in it and in the Stockholm volume.

Both Gwynn and Thomas and Rhodes used a standard expression for calculating the fundamental frequency of an open organ pipe. This requires the use of a somewhat arbitrary 'end correction' factor which can have a range of values. Using the lowest commonly-accepted value together with the paper shrinkage factor taken from the *Theatrum* master scale, the Uppsala pipes give equivalent A pitches ranging between A–439 and A–455 at 20°C. The equivalents of the C pipes are at A–448 and A–450, the average pitch of all 13 pipes being A–449. The nominal A pipe is at A–445. If the end correction factor is set at its highest likely value, these results change substantially. The range is then from A–416 to A–433, with an average of A–426. If the reference temperature is reduced to 15°C, all these values must be lowered by 4 Hz. Using the correction factor assumed by Gwynn and a temperature of 15°C, the Uppsala drawing gives A–438, which is 8 Hz higher than the experimental value of Bunjes.

On the basis of all these figures it would be possible to argue credibly for Praetorius's performance pitch as having been anywhere between A–410 and about A–450. In doing so we would still be assuming that the drawing was absolutely accurate and would be ignoring the likelihood of the paper not behaving in anywhere near as predictable a manner as might otherwise be convenient. The uncertainty of the paper dimensions would provide further room for arguing the pitch higher or lower, as one might prefer.

Not much more can be said about this. If we accept that there was an interval of one whole tone between Praetorius's two pitches, there is little leeway in the way we can interpret all the evidence presented above. Assuming that it really is possible to determine these pitches on the basis of this material, both would have to be placed within the extremes of the range under discussion. There are not many ways to do this. If the higher pitch is taken in the neighbourhood of A–460 the lower pitch would be near A–410. Since there is more diversified evidence for fixing the upper limit than there is relating to the lower, there is no reason for avoiding this approach. The contention that Praetorius used only one pitch allows considerably more latitude in interpreting his work, although most of the writing supporting this view accepts the explanations of the pitch pipe drawing summarized by Gwynn, and largely dismisses the remaining evidence as unreliable. It might also be possible to revive Mendel's 40-year-old conclusions based on Praetorius's vocal writing, which puts his organ pitch at about a minor third above A–440. This would allow for accepting the pitch pipes at the upper limit of the range considered above, and would simply put more surviving instruments directly into his performance pitch than we might otherwise have expected. As will be seen, the A–460 and A–410 values figure prominently in the following discussion of 18th-century pitch, which may lend additional credence to the suggestion that they were quite close to the pitches referred to by Praetorius.

Formulating pitch

The first accurate reports of the pitches of musical instruments in absolute numerical terms come from the early 18th century. These values were determined by setting the pitch of a vibrating string equal to that of the pitch of the instrument being measured, and then calculating the frequency of the string. Marin Mersenne is generally credited with having been the first to observe experimentally the relationship between the frequency at which a string vibrates, the tension applied to it and its physical dimensions:

Harmonie universelle (Paris 1636–7/*R*1963; Eng. trans., 1957). This relationship became useful in more specific analytical terms in 1712, when Brook Taylor provided the first correct mathematical derivation of a vibrating string equation.

Taylor's formula was used by several 18th-century experimental workers to specify the pitches of musical instruments numerically. He reported the following experiments in 1713:

> I applied a quill to the crown wheel of my chamber clock, and making it fast to one of the of the clock [*sic*], I let the works run down for 7 minutes and by my Harpsichord I found the quill to sound Alamire in alt:, and by the works of the clock the quill struck 766 teeth per second. By which means the quill made 2 × 766 = 1532 vibrations per second. For in striking each tooth the quill goes once forwards and once backwards. Then with some wire which weighed 1 grain per foot, I made another experiment, hanging 10 ounces or 4800 grains to stretch it, and found it at 12.3 inches long to sound Alamire, two eighths below the former. So that this wire ought to strike the air 383 times per second. But according to my second theorem De Motu Nervi this wire made 383 vibrations per second, which agrees wonderfully with the experiment...
>
> I repeated the same experiment, and found that 2341 vibrations per second made Elami above the compass of my harpsichord. Which being a fifth above A, (the note in the former experiment,) that note should make 1561 (= 2/3 × 2341) vibrations per second, which is about 1/52 part bigger than in that experiment: a difference scarce worth regarding.[28]

It is easy to verify that Taylor's arithmetic is correct. Using the data from his second experiment together with other figures taken from the present-day reference literature allows the pitch of his harpsichord to be calculated at A–383.6. On the basis of his third experiment the pitch is A–390.2. If, however, his harpsichord were tuned with anything smaller than pure fifths (as is likely), this pitch would be slightly higher. The tension applied to this string was very low. Taylor reports several more experiments made with very long pieces of twine. Although he observed the same frequency upon repeated tests with samples of the same length and tension, the results could be significantly lower than his formula predicted. In his own words, 'Whence it appears that the more the string is stretcht the nearer it agrees with my calculation, as appears by the two experiments made with my clock'. The difference of about a third of a semitone between his two pitches may therefore be due to the low tension of the second experiment, although it is not clear if his third experiment was conducted with greater tension. The fact that Taylor regarded this difference as negligible suggests that the pitch to which he tuned his harpsichord may have varied within the same interval. In any case, it may be wise to accept this as the tolerance in pitches reported on the basis of calculations made with Taylor's formula.

In 1727 Leonhard Euler reported the frequency of a vibrating string which he measured with Taylor's formula: 'In choral instruments... the note called *d* sharp by musicians was found to have 559 vibrations per second'. In 1739 he reported another experiment which gave '392. Which pitch corresponds to that of the *a* on keyboard instruments'.[29] His results are both theoretically and arithmetically correct; he provides the formulae that he used and all his reference values in great detail. Recalculating his pitches using modern textbook equations and constants puts his choir pitch at A–395.7 and his 'keyboard' pitch at A–392.2. In 1762, Daniel Bernoulli wrote 'We applied the theory of M. Taylor, about the vibration of stretched strings, to determine the number of vibrations per second for each pitch. If a string is stretched until it sounds at choir pitch C, if one then examines the weight of this string, its length and the weight attached to it, one sees that it vibrates about 116 times per second: therefore a stopped 4′ organ pipe also produces about 116 vibrations of air per second'.[30]

Bernoulli may be repeating the results he had given 20 years earlier in a report about investigations dealing with the frequencies of vibrations of rods.[31] 'Which from data obtained from a simple hanging pendulum gives the same number of vibrations per second as that experimentally determined from choir-pitched instruments where the bass C corresponds to 116 vibrations per second'. This translates into a choir and organ pitch of A–390 or slightly lower depending on the temperament used. In 1775 Johann Heinrich Lambert reported in detail on the 1739 Euler and the 1762 Bernoulli experiments. He then provided the results of a similar experiment that he conducted himself: 'one finds N=830.5 for the note *a′*. From this follows . . . 124.6 for the note C so that instead of 117.6 or 116 vibrations, I shall find 124.6; this means that the pitches on my flute are about one semitone higher than those produced by the instruments which were used for terms of comparison in the experiment by Messrs. Euler and Bernoulli'.[32] Recalculating all of Lambert's figures gives a 'flute' pitch of A–415.3.

Another 18th-century source, Joseph Sauveur (1713), should be considered here. Although not specifically an application of Taylor's formula, it still involves the mathematical relationship between the physical dimensions of a string and the pitch that it produces. 'I took a white (=iron) harpsichord string . . . which sounded at "sub-bis PA" (Sauveur's new scale) or the bass C on the harpsichord which corresponds to the open 8′ pipe on an organ. One determines the value of the number of vibrations which this string makes in one second. Using article 48 one finds . . . 121 3/4 vibrations'.[33] The vibrating string equation derived and used by Sauveur was not as accurate as Taylor's. Recalculating his data with Taylor's formula gives a frequency of 121 Hz which, depending on the temperament used, translates into a harpsichord and organ pitch of about A–405. Sauveur also reported a pitch determined from a rather questionable measurement of the pitch of an organ pipe, first reporting a value equivalent to A–400, and later revising this to A–408. He was perhaps the first to suggest a numerical pitch standard for use in music. This was not derived from any specific musical practice, but rather from the numerical simplicity of using a power of the number 2. The recommended C–256 (about A–430) remains in use as 'physical' or 'scientific' pitch. It may be worth noting that many tuning forks have been made to the scientific scale, and it may not always be possible to distinguish them from tuning forks made for musical reference.

Two other reports of limited reliability may also be mentioned. Christiaan Huygens gave the pitch of a harpsichord in late 17th-century Amsterdam as equivalent to A–409. The same pitch was given by a tuning fork which belonged to the Flemish harpsichord maker Pascal Taskin. This was tuned in about 1780 to an oboe used in the Paris Opéra and/or the Chapelle du Roi.[34]

The pitches presented here come from different times and places in

The Baroque Era

18th-century Europe. There is a convenient and gratifying uniformity in several of these values. Taylor's, Bernoulli's and Euler's pitches are all close both to each other and to the minor third lower than A–460 pitch which may possibly be seen in the Praetorius data. This value is also close to what is currently termed 'low French' chamber pitch as determined largely on the basis of surviving woodwind instruments. Lambert's pitch will immediately be recognized as precisely the 'half tone below modern' pitch standard of the present-day Baroque revival, although the values just under A–410 are more common and may therefore better correspond to the 'mainstream' 18th-century chamber pitch

It is clear from work on the pitch standards implicit in the woodwind writing of J. S. Bach[35] that Bach's choir pitch was one tone higher than his chamber pitch, and that he at times may have used a second chamber pitch another semitone lower. This is entirely consistent with what the writings of his contemporaries would lead us to expect. A number of workers have reported direct measurements of the pitches of surviving double-reed instruments and flutes from that day. Most of these fall into two groups: one between A–410 and A–415, and the other near A–390. Although it is difficult to determine whether age may have altered the pitches of these instruments (in which case the reported pitches may be slightly high), the degree of uniformity is not likely to have been affected.

To the extent that modern players have developed the ability to determine the pitches of late 17th- and early 18th-century surviving cornettos in a reliable fashion, many of these would appear to be pitched near A–460. There is, however, a surprising degree of variability in the pitches of such instruments when measured by different workers. This, in turn, is hard to reconcile with the notion of the cornett determining a pitch standard. Similar problems arise when evaluating the pitches of brass instruments. Few brass instruments and cornetts survive with what are definitely known to be their original mouthpieces. Additionally, it may be difficult to determine the nominal pitch to which a brass instrument was made.

String instruments rarely provide information about the pitches to which they were tuned. Given data about the length of a string and the strength of the material of which it is made, one will be able to calculate the highest possible pitch to which it can be tuned. During recent years much effort has been devoted to determining the mechanical properties of stringing materials. On the basis of this it is possible to establish the likely maximum working pitches to which harpsichords and other strung keyboard instruments were tuned.[36] On the basis of both 18th-century and modern reports of the tensile strength of harpsichord wire it was shown that many 18th-century harpsichords are not likely to have been able to withstand tuning to levels much in excess of A–405. Subsequent work has shown that this figure may require revision upwards to about A–410. Some short-scaled instruments would appear to have been designed for use at choir pitch, at a maximum of about A–460. If an instrument not capable of withstanding more than A–410 is known to have been used in an ensemble tuned to a higher pitch, there is little alternative to concluding that it was tuned to a conveniently lower pitch from which the player then transposed. Considering the 18th-century references to harpsichord pitches near A–390, it would seem possible that this was a relatively common practice, at least with that instrument (cf the caption to Praetorius's harpsichord illustration).

Numerous 18th-century authors refer to a system with a high choir pitch, a chamber pitch one whole tone lower and a low chamber pitch one semitone lower still. In the contexts considered here it would seem justifiable to associate these with the clusters of observed pitches that focus to within 5 Hz on either side of A–460, A–410 and A–390. The individual pitches which do not lie quite so comfortably near any of these values can either be construed as fitting into this broad framework nonetheless, or may be assumed to belong to entirely separate pitch standards which cannot be derived from the summary evidence considered above. Indeed, it would be misleading and foolish to suggest extending the 460–410–390 values into the pitch systems of instruments, regions and times not discussed above.

Noticeably absent from the choir/chamber pitch system is a nominal standard one semitone below choir pitch. This is understandable in view of the need for a convenient transposition interval between choir and chamber pitches. There are, however, a number of references to pitch standards offset from each other by semitone increments. One such reference is by J. A. Silbermann (1772):

> there are many pitches to which organs are tuned. In all Germany the 'Cornet Thon' was previously common... Since, however, the highness of this pitch caused difficulty for singing, it was lowered by a semitone and called 'Chorthon'. This was subsequently lowered by an additional semitone, which was called 'Kammer Thon'. This pitch appears to be commonly and fully accepted, for all musical instruments are tuned to it. It is also called Italian pitch since it is used throughout Italy. Pitch in France was yet a semitone lower than 'Kammer Thon' and was called the French pitch, but is now seldom used.[37]

This and other comparable references are often dismissed as confused and unreliable. With the exception of the semitone difference between choir and chamber pitch, however, Silbermann's statement is remarkably similar to that made by Praetorius 150 years earlier. The only significant difference is that instruments are now commonly being built at the lower, rather than at the higher pitch. If the semitone interval is taken literally, we are confronted with a new German pitch level which may have been near A–435 and is therefore at least superficially attractive as a possible parent to our A–440 standard. If we accept that this report is confused, we have evidence of a decline in the clear terminological distinction between the various nominal pitches.

Late 18th century

The history of pitch standards during the 19th century can largely be documented with reference to tuning forks. The tuning fork is generally believed to have been invented by John Shore, an English trumpeter, in 1711. It was established as a precision device for measuring frequency in absolute terms when J. H. Scheibler published a description of his 'tonometer' in 1834.[38] Measurements have been made of the pitches of a number of famous 18th-century tuning forks, and these have been taken as weighty evidence of the pitches of that century. The most celebrated of these tuning forks are one said to have been used by Handel for the 1751 Foundling Hospital performance of *Messiah*, and another reported to have been used by the piano maker J. A. Stein. The former is at A–422.5 and the latter at A–421.6. The 422.5 fork can be associated with the organ at the Foundling Hospital, but it is not certain that it came into use there until long after Handel's death. The 421.6 fork has been connected with Mozart simply because he once purchased a Stein instrument. Largely on the basis of this it is assumed that there was a late 18th-century 'Classical' pitch near A–422.

Despite the highly tenuous character of this evidence there are advantages to assuming that there was a general tendency for (chamber) pitch levels to climb during the later 18th century. The pitches of the woodwind instruments of this period support this theory, as does the suggestion that the mass rebuilding of violins towards the close of the century was motivated by rising pitch levels among other things. This provides us with an alternative route towards an A–440 standard.

On the basis of tuning forks used in various opera houses and orchestras, pitch at the outset of the 19th century would seem to have generally been in the region of A–425. It climbed steadily through to the middle of the century when pitches exceeded A–450. In Paris, for example, the opera house pitch was A–423 in 1810, A–432 in 1822 and A–449 in 1855. A law was passed in 1859 which curtailed this development by stipulating a standard pitch of A–435. In London, singers protested against pitch levels near A–450 and Covent Garden adopted the French standard in 1880. The initial funding for what were to become the Henry Wood Promenade Concerts was given in 1895 under the specific condition that the pitch used for them be lowered to A–435.

The French standard was adopted at an international conference in Vienna in 1885. There was some misunderstanding about the A–435 pitch being dependent on temperature. As a result of this, the London Philharmonic Society adopted the standard at A–439 in 1896. The American Federation of Musicians adopted a standard of A–440 in 1917. The International Federation of National Standardizing Associations found that A–440 was the average value in use in 1939, and proposed this as a recommended standard. In 1955 the International Organization for Standardization (ISO) made the same recommendation. This was reaffirmed in 1975.

The climb in pitch noted from the outset of the 19th century is generally regarded as the result of a widespread desire to attain more brilliance and volume from the instruments used in the ever larger concert halls and opera houses. The structural modifications made to the violin at the end of the 18th century allowed the pitches of bowed instruments to climb. Wind instrument makers and musicians had a long tradition of adapting to various pitch levels. The hunt for increased brilliance would appear to have been reinitiated during the past few decades, as many symphony orchestras are now tuning to pitches several Hz above the nominal international standard.

The performer interested in the uncompromising re-creation of a piece of music as it was initially intended to be heard may have much difficulty both in determining the correct pitch level for a given such performance and in obtaining instruments tuned to it. Clearly, some degree of compromise will be required when dealing with this aspect of performance practice. A common reaction to this has been the dogmatic identification of largely unsubstantiated historical pitch levels and the equally unyielding adherence to them. A concept of 'modern old pitch' has arisen and musical instruments are marketed tuned to what is labelled the 'correct' Baroque pitch of $a' = 415.3$ Hz. Until recently this pitch level was arbitrarily applied to all old music. (Musicians who were party to the first attempts at the revival of authentic 18th-century performance in Germany claim that the A–415 tuning level was adopted simply because the viola da gamba used by an influential soloist of the day happened to sound best at that pitch.)

It would seem quite necessary for the performer to develop a clear sense of when the choice of pitch level is critical to a performance, and when a broader compromise may be tolerated. The historic record provides much useful information about general trends in the development of pitch standards, but little of this material provides an absolutely certain basis for the selection of specific pitches. It would be wise in most cases to regard pitch in terms of the nearest even 5 or 10 Hz figure, rather than with specious 1 Hz or 0.1 Hz precision. The latitude inherent in this approach will also provide some practical relief from the necessity for the use of instruments at many different pitches.

Notes

[1] The individual components are often referred to as the 'fundamental' and 'overtones', but are more properly termed 'partial frequencies of vibration'. The unit in which frequency is expressed is Hz (= Hertz, formerly 'cps' for cycles per second). There are no generally accepted units for the designation of pitch, which is a subjective concept that relates to frequency in the same way that loudness relates to amplitude. To avoid misunderstanding and potential error, the unit Hz will not normally be used with reference to pitch in this chapter.

[2] This is necessitated, if for no other reason, by the fact that a' is not within the range of many instruments, nor do transposing instruments tune their nominal A to, let us say, the nominal A of a tuning fork or an oboe.

[3] It should, however, be realized that by far the largest part of the music-making engaged in by humankind occurs without the slightest conscious involvement with absolute pitch levels or pitch standards.

[4] This interval allows for all the extremes in the interpretation of the basic data which have been proposed in the secondary literature. It is both possible and likely that the actual range of fluctuation was smaller still.

[5] '... bisogna che prima tu consideri la chorda ouer positione, chiamata C fa ut, con quella intonatione che a te piacera...' P. Aaron: *Thoscanello de la Musica* (Venice, 1523/R1969).

[6] 'Woher nehmen wir den Anfang des Stimmens, oder wie bestimmen wir die Tiefe des C? Es is bekannt, dass die Orgeln nicht überein sind, so, dass der Musikant nebst seiner Trompete stets etliche Aufsätze bey sich tragen muss, wenn er in mehrern Kirchen darauf blasen soll... Man wünscht deswegen nicht unbillig dass die Orgelmacher hierinnen einig wären, und dass sie eine gewisse Regel haben möchten, nach welcher sie einerley Tiefe und Höhe zu finden im Stande wären. Aber hieran fehlt es bis jetzo. Denn was Sauveur vorgeschlagen, ist noch nicht zu Stande kommen.' J. Adlung, *Anleitung zu der musikalischen Gelahrtheit* (Erfurt, 1758/R1953, 2/1783), 387.

[7] 'Weil aber der Ton, nach welchem man stimmet, so sehr verschieden ist; dass nicht nur in einem jeden Lande, sodern auch mehrentheils in einer jeder Provinz und Stadt, eine ander Stimmung, oder herrschender Ton eingeführet ist; zugeschwiegen, das der Clavicymbal, an

eben demselben Orte, durch unachtsame Stimmer, bald hoch, bald tief gestimmet wird: so hat man, vor ohngefähr dreyssig Jahren, die Flöte mit mehrern Mittelstücken versehen. Man hat ... zwey bis drey gefertiget, welche, weil immer eines kürzer als das andere seyn muss, sich damals ohngefähr um einen halben Ton von einander unterschieden...' J. J. Quantz, *Versuch einer Anweisung die Flöte traversiere zu spielen* (Berlin, 1752, 3/1789/R1952: Eng. trans., 1966, as *On Playing the Flute*).

[8] A. Mendel, 'Pitch in the 16th and Early 17th Centuries', *MQ*, xxxiv (1948), 28, 199, 336, 575; idem, 'On the Pitches in Use in Bach's Time', *MQ*, xli (1955), 332, 466.

[9] W. R. Thomas and J. J. K. Rhodes, 'Schlick, Praetorius, and the History of Organ Pitch', *Organ Yearbook*, ii (1971), 58; see also correspondence, iii (1972).

[10] 'Pitch in Western Music since 1500: a Re-examination', *AcM*, l (1978), 1–93; pubd separately (Kassel, 1979).

[11] 'Es ist aber der Chor Thon bey den Alten anfangs um ein Thon niedriger und tieffer gewessen, als jtzo, welches dann an den alten Orgeln und andern blassenden Instrumenten noch zu befinden: Und hernach von Jahren zu Jahren so weit erhöht worden, als er jtzo in Italia und Engellandt, auch in den Fürstlichen Capellen Deutschen Landes im gebrauch ist. Wiewol der Englische Thon an Instrumenten noch umb etwas, doch ein gar geringes niedriger ist, welches an ihren Zinken, Schalmeyen oder Hoboyen (wie sie es nennen) so daselbst gefertiget werden, zu vernehmen. Es seynd aber etliche gewesen, welche diesen jtzigen unsern Thon noch umb ein Semitonium zu erhöhen, sich unterstehen wollen: Welches, obs mir zu corrigieren zwar nicht gebüret, so ist jedoch meines ermessens solche höhe den Cantoribus vocalis Musicae, sonderlich den Altisten und Tenoristen sehr unbequem, und oftmals fast unmüglich zu erreichen. Darümb man es billich bei dem vorgesagten Tono bleiben lassen möchte; weil derselbige ohne das nicht allein vor die Vocalisten, sondern auch vor die Instrumentisten bei den Besaitteten Instrumenten, als Violini de Bracio und Violen de Gamba, auch Lauten, Pandoren und dergleichen, zum offtern zu hoch befunden wird: Denn es aussbündige Saitten seyn müssen, die solche Höhe erleiden können. Daher kömpts dann, wenn man mitten im Gesang ist, da schnappen die Quinten dahin, unnd ligt im Dr. Damit nun die Saitten desto besser bestimbt bleiben können, so müssen solche und dergleichen besaittete Instrumenta gemeinlich umb ein Thon tieffer gestimmet, und alsdann nottwendig mit den andern Instrumenten, auch umb ein Secund tieffer musicirt werden. Welches zwar den unerfahrnen Musicis Instrumentalibus schwer vorkömpt, den Vocalibus und Sengern aber an ihrer Stimm, umb einen Thon niedriger zu musicieren sehr viel hilfft', *Syntagma musicum* (Wolfenbüttel, 1618, 2/1619/R1958 und 1980; Eng. trans., 1962).

[12] 'Darümb lass ich mir mit der Unterscheidt, da man zu Praag und etlichen andern Catholischen Capellen, den Thon in Chor-Thon und CammerThon abtheilet, aus dermassen sehr wol gefallen. Denn daselbsten wird der jtzige gewönlicher Thon, nach welchem fast alle unsere Orgeln gestimmet werden, Cammer-thon genennet, und allein vor der Taffel und in Convivijs zur fröligkeit gebraucht; welches dann vor Instrumentisten, wegen der Blasenden, so wol auch Besaitteten Instrumenten, am bequembsten...

Der Chor-Thon aber, welcher umb einen gantzen Thon tieffer ist, wird allein in der Kirchen gebraucht: Und dasselbe erstlich, umb der Vocalisten willen ... Darümb dann ... nicht ubel getan were, dass alle Orgeln umb einen Thon, oder Secund tieffer gestimmet und gesetzt seyn möchten: Welches aber nunmehr in unsern Deutschen Landen zu endern gantz unmüglich, und demnach bey dem gewönlichen Cammerthon (welcher jtziger zeit an den meisten Ortern Chor-Thon genennet, und dafür gehalten wird) wol verbleiben muss' ibid.

[13] 'Die CornaMuse ... stimmen gleich ein mit dem Chorton, das ist, ein Thon tieffer als unser rechter Cornetten oder Cammerthon', ibid.

[14] 'In Engellandt haben sie vorzeiten, und in den Niederlanden noch anitzo ihre meiste blasende Instrumenta umb eine tertiam minorem tieffer, als jtzo unser Cammerthon, intoniret und gestimbt, also dass ihr F ist im Cammer Thon unser D unnd ir G unser E. Wie dann auch der vortreffliche Instrumentmacher zu Antorff Johannes Bossus die meisten Clavicymbeln und Symphonien, auch darein gemachte Pfeiffwercke, im demselbigen Tono intoniret und gestimmet.

Und ist zwar nicht ohne, dass man in diesem Thon den Clavicymbeln (wie verstendige Instrumentmacher wissen) ein lieblichern und anmütigern Resonantz geben und zuwenden kan, mehr, als wenn man sie nach dem Cammer Thon abtheilet; wie denn auch die Flötten und andere Instrumenta in solchem niedern Thon lieblicher, als im rechten Thon lauten, und fast gar eine andere art im gehör (sintemal sie in der tieffe nicht so hart schreyen) mit sich bringen. Aber solche Instrumenta sind in voller Music zu gebrauchen gar unbequem: und wird man nunmehr alleine bei vorgedachten beyden, als Chor- und Cammer-Thon verbleiben müssen.

Wiewohl auch in Italia und andern Catholischen Capellen Deutsches Landes jtzgedachter niedriger Thon in tertia inferiore gar sehr im gebrauch', ibid.

[15] 'Sintemahl etliche Itali an dem hohen singen, wie nicht unbillich, kein gefallen, vermeynen es habe keine art, könne auch der Text nicht recht wol vernommen werden, man krehete, schreye und singe in der höhe gleich wie die Grasemägde. Daher auch bisweilen im brauch, dass sie HypoIonicum Modum aussm C, wenn derselbe per quintam in F transponiret wird, noch umb eine tertz tieffer aussm D mit Orgeln, Positiffen und beygeordneten Instrumenten musiciernen: Ungeachtet dieser Modus fast besser als der andern einer, ohne fernere transposition, humanis vocibus musicirt werden könte, so wird doch solches eintzig und allein umb der Vocalisten und Senger willen also angestellt. Gleicher gestald wird auch HypoDorius umb ein Tertz niedriger aussm E musiciret. Welche und dergleichen Transpostiones einem Organisten sowol, als andern Instrumentisten anfangs zwar etwas sawer und weiderlich ankömpt: Aber wenn einer sich nun der mühe nicht verdriessen lest sondern mit fleiss ein zeitlang sich darinnen exciret und ubet, so ist und wird es ihm gar leicht, ja gleichsamb eine Lust zu practiciren und praestiren', ibid.

[16] 'Wann nun aber der jtziger zeit gewöhnliche Cammer Thon, vom Orgelmacher einer Orgel gegeben, und das ganze Werck darnach gestimmet wird; so ist mehren theils in Orgeln, die nicht gar zu gering und klein angestellt werden, das unterste C. im Principal des Manual Clavirs von 8. Fussen: Welcher Thon dann mit den rechten Clavicymbeln und Spinetten gleich uberein kömpt', ibid.

[17] "Es ... ist wie fast dir meiste do mahlige Orgeln umb einen Thon höher, als unser jetziger Cammerthon gestanden', ibid.

[18] 'M. Praetorius, *Theatrum instrumentorum* (Wolfenbüttel, 1620/R1958).

[19] 'Diese ist die rechte Lenge und Maß eines halben Schuhes oder Fusses nach dem Maßstabe, welches ein viertel von einer Braunschweiger Ellen: Und nach diesem sind alle Abrisse nachgesetzter Instrumenten, uffn kleinen Maßstab, so alzeit mit darbey gesetzt, gerichtet', ibid.

[20] The only obvious slip of the pen was made on one of two plates filled with drawings of organ pipes. This may be worth further examination since Praetorius's organ pipes will be considered in greater detail below. The error on the plate is that it has three half feet between the three-foot and four-foot marks on its illustrated scale (Plate 37). The basic scale units on both the organ pipe illustrations are, however, identical. Thomas and Rhodes suggested that the full length of the Plate 37 scale, which is labelled at 9 feet, ought to have been 10 feet, and that the entire scale was incorrectly divided. If this were so, the illustration would have been at a scale of one foot to one inch and could have been transferred from the master scale without any need for complex subdivision. Also, both adjacent organ pipe illustrations would then not have been drawn to the same scale, for which there is otherwise no apparent reason. It is more reasonable to accept that the scale was laid out correctly but subsequently mislabelled.

[21] 'Und ein solch ganz Stimmwerck kan auß Venedig umb 80 Thaler ohngefehr herauß gebracht werden', *Syntagma musicum*.

[22] R. Weber, 'Some Researches into Pitch', *GSJ*, xxviii (1975), 9.

[23] B. Marvin, 'Recorders and English Flutes in European Collections', *GSJ*, xxv (1972), 30.

[24] P. G. Bunjes, *The Praetorius Organ* (diss., U. of Rochester, NY, 1966).

[25] 'Djeweil in diesem Tomo Secundo, zum offtern des rechten Chor-Thons erwehnet: und ich befunden, das an vielen örtern, auch wol in sehr grossen und vornehmen Städten, und doselbst befindlichen herzlichen Orgelwercken, die rechte Chormaß, wornach sich die Menschen Stimmen, so wol als die Instrumenta richten müssen, nicht – sondern der Tonus derselben entweder zu hoch oder zu niedrig: Und solches einer von den fürnembsten Defecten der Orgeln ist. So hab ich uff allerley Mittel und Wege gedacht, wie und welcher gestalt solchem abzuhelffen, und einem jeden, so wol Orgelmachern als Organisten der rechte Tonus und Chormaß bekandt würde: Wornach ein Orgelmacher sich richten, die Newe Orgeln nach demselben intonieren, die Alten aber Renoviren unnd Corrigiren könte. Derwegen hierunter einen richtigen Abriß der rechten Chormaß setzen wollen ... Nach welcher Mensuer etliche Pfeifflin zur rechten Chormaß, durch eine ganze Octav, gar just und rein können gearbeitet werden: Deren sich, neben dem orgelmachern, auch die Organisten und Cantores zum anstimmen zugebrauchen.' (p.231) *Syntagma musicum* (see n.11).

[26] 'Auch halte ich vor meine Wenigkeit kein besser Instrument, den rechten Thor zuerfahren, als eine Posaune, sonderlich die vor der zeit und noch, zu Nürnberg gefertiget syen: Daß man nemblich den Zug um 2 Finger breit vom ende außziehe, so gibt es gar recht und just, in rechter Chormasse, das alamire im Tenor.' (p.232) ibid.

[27] D. Gwynn, 'Organ Pitch, Part 1: Praetorius', *FoMRHI Quarterly*, xxiii (1981), 72.

[28] 'De motu nervi tersi', *Philosophical Transactions*, xxviii [1713] (1714); MS, *GB-Cjc*, published

in J. T. Cannon and S. Dostrovsky, *The Evolution of Dynamics: Vibration Theory from 1687 to 1742* (New York, 1981).

[29] 'in instrumento chorali modo ... qui musicis audit ds' minuto secundo habere invenietur vibrationes 559 ... In 1739, he reported another experiment which gave '... 392. Huic autem sono congruere deprehendi in instrumento clavem signatam a'. *Dissertatio physica de sono* (Basle, 1727); repr. in *Opera omnia*, iii/1, 182. L. Euler, *Tertamen novae theoriae musicae* (St Petersburg, 1739).

[30] 'La Théorie de M. Taylor, sur les vibrations des cordes tendues, nous a mis en état de déterminer quel est le nombre de vibrations dans une seconde de temps pour chaque ton. Si l'on tend une corde jusqu'à la rendre consonne avec le C choral, si l'on examine ensuite le poids de cette corde, sa longueur & le poids qu'on y a attaché, on fait que cette corde fait environ 116 vibrations dans une seconde de temps: il faut donc qu'un tuyau d'orgue boché, long de quatre pieds de roi, produise pareillement environ 116 vibrations d'air dans une seconde de temps.' 'Recherches physiques, méchaniques et analytiques, sur le son et sur le tons des tuyaux d'orgues différement construits', *Mémoires de l'Académie royale des sciences* (Paris, 1762).

[31] 'Cum ex data penduli simplicis longitundine innotescat numerus oscillationum intra minutum secundum et cum etiam experimentis constet in instrumento musico ad tonam choralem composito sono infimo C respondere 116 vibrationes intra minutum secundum...' D. Bernoulli, 'De sonis multifariis quos laminae elasticae...', *Commentarii academiae scientiarum imperialis petropolitanae*, xiii (1741–3).

[32] '... on trouve N= 830.5 pour le ton a'. D'ou suit ... 124.6 pour le ton C de sorte qu'au lieu de 117.6 ou de 116 vibrations, je trouvai 124.6; ce qui fait que les tons de ma flûte sont plus aigus d'environs un demi-ton, que ceux des instruments qui ont servi de terme de comparaison dans les experiences de Mrs. Euler & Bernoulli.' J. H. Lambert, 'Observations sur les flûtes', *Nouveaux mémoires de l'Académie royale des sciences et belles-lettres* [1775] (Berlin, 1777), 13.

[33] 'J'ay pris une corde blanche de Clavecin ... Cette corde sonnoit le sub-bis PA ou le C-Sol-Ut du bas du Clavecin qui répond au tuyau d'Orgue de 8. pieds ouvert. On demande la valeur de s ou le nombre des vibrations que cette corde fait dans une seconde de temps. Par l'article 48. l'on trouvera ... = 121¾ vibrations.' 'Rapport des sons des cordes d'instruments de musique aux fleches des cordes; et nouvelle détermination des sons fixes', *Mémoires de l'Académie royale des sciences* [1713] (Paris, 1716).

[34] It may be wise to call attention to an alluring pitfall in this discussion. The numerical accuracy with which we can evaluate an individual surviving document of a reference pitch must not be confused with the certainty with which more widespread pitch levels can be determined. A tuning fork will reveal its own pitch quite unambiguously. If it is known to have been used to tune a specific harpsichord, we can safely draw conclusions about the pitch of that instrument – when tuned to the fork. We can only tenatively extrapolate from this the pitch of the orchestra in which this harpsichord at one time may have been used, or the chamber pitch of the city in which it was built. The analysis of individual pitch-producing implements may be at times legitimately be conducted in 0.5 Hz terms. The practical musical pitch levels to which these implements bear witness cannot generally be discussed with anything vaguely approaching that level of precision.

[35] B. Haynes, 'Johann Sebastian Bach's Pitch Standards: the Woodwind Perspective', *JAMIS*, xi (1985), 55; 'Questions of Tonality in Bach's Cantatas: the Woodwind Perspective', *JAMIS*, xii (1986), 40.

[36] Summarized in C. Karp, *The Pitches of 18th Century String Keyboard Instruments, with Particular Reference to Swedish Material* (Stockholm, 1984).

[37] '... vielerley thöne sind, worin die Orgeln gestimbt wurden. In ganz Teutschland ist vor diesem der Cornet Thon üblich gewesen ... Dieweil aber dieser Thon wegen seiner Höhe dem Gesang beschwerlich war, so machte man denselben einen ½ Thon tiefer und nannte ihn den Chorthon. Nach diesem wurde derselbe wieder um einen ½ Thon herabgesetzt, den man den Kammerthon nante. Dieser Thon scheint allgemein und vollkomen eingeführt zu seyn, denn alle Musikalische Instrumenten sind darein gestimmet. Man nennt ihn auch den Italiänischen Thon, weilen er in ganz Italien bräuchlich ist. In Frankreich war der Thon noch einen ½ Thon tiefer weder der Kammerthon, und hieß der Französische Thon, wird aber selten mehr gebraucht'. J. A. Silbermann, letter published in H. E. Rahner, 'Der Neubau der Stiftsorgel St. Blasien unter Abt Martin Gebert durch Johann Andreas Silbermann', *Archiv für Musikforschung*, ii (1937), 433.

CHAPTER VIII

Tuning and Intonation

MARK LINDLEY

Not all early music calls for fine nuances of intonation. Guido of Arezzo (*c*1000) prescribed a Pythagorean monochord scheme, that is, giving every whole tone the ratio 9:8, but it would be very naïve to think that in 11th-century plainchant every major third had to have the ratio 81:64 (= 9:8 × 9:8) and be a comma larger than a pure third with the ratio 5:4 (= 80:64). Craftsmanship and technology were not so refined.

They may have become so in some circles by the 14th century, but we have no proof. The ratios which Marchetto of Padua (1309) gave for dividing the 9:8 whole tone into 'minor' and 'major' semitones (18:17:16) contradict his own rule of thumb that the whole tone be divided into five, presumably equal, 'dieses'. He gave two of his dieses to what we today would call the diatonic semitones in ex.1*a*, and only one to the analogous interval in ex.1*b*. We should not interpret this too precisely, but take it as meaning that the diatonic leading notes were to be sung perhaps slightly higher than in equal temperament, and the chromatic ones distinctly higher.[1]

Ex.1 Marchetto: *Lucidarium musicae planae*, Tract. 2, chaps 6–7

In an anonymous 14th- or 15th-century prescription for organ pipes (*I-Ma* D 5 Inf.), septimal ratios are used for A♭ and E♭ (here I use short dashes for the fifths and fourths):

$$\overset{\displaystyle 9:7\quad \overset{\text{E}\flat}{}\quad 7:8}{\text{B}\flat - \text{F} - \text{C} - \text{G} - \text{D} - \text{A} - \text{E} - \text{B} - \text{F}\sharp - \text{C}\sharp}\underset{\displaystyle 9:7\quad \text{A}\flat\quad 7:8}{}$$

This A♭ and E♭ would sound quite sour if not retuned. Similarly, a number of 15th-century organ or clavichord prescriptions would make one of the diatonic fifths a comma lower than pure (D–A, A–E or E–B) – to such sour effect in the music of the day that a resourceful player might well indulge in some *ad hoc* tempering by adjusting the pipes or bending the tangents.[2]

Certain other 15th-century prescriptions are more promising; if taken literally they would yield the tuning scheme shown in fig.1. The fifths other than B–F♯ would be pure. B–F♯ would be a comma smaller, and thus sour, but all of the five sharps would make nearly pure thirds with the diatonic notes. It is this arrangement of 12-note Pythagorean intonation which the majority of extant 15th-century references suggest. (No one before 1500 is known to have put the Pythagorean wolf fifth at G♯ –E♭; and only one writer at C♯ –A♯.)

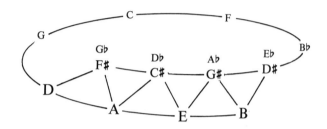

1 The tuning of the 12-note scale which seems to have been (judging by the treatises) the one most used in the early to mid-15th century. The lines indicate pure or nearly pure intervals, namely the thirds D–F♯⊢A♯⊢E–G♯⊢B–D♯ ⎸and all but one of the fifths and fourths. The other triadic intervals are impure by a comma – enough to make F♯ sour with B (except that in a 'Landini cadence' to C, the pure third D–F♯ may distract one from noticing).

Some 15th-century keyboard compositions and transcriptions seem to require this tuning. In ex.2 the anonymous composer has evidently exploited the contrast between the euphonious thirds with a sharp and the Pythagorean thirds which are juxtaposed with them at the beginning of bar 2 and the end of bar 5. The nervous beating of the Pythagorean thirds in bars 3–5 complements the melodic restlessness of the right-hand line, and so helps sustain a momentum to the cadence in bar 6. The piece ends with a sustained harmonic third, *d–f♯⊢d'*. (Other 15th-century keyboard music well served by this tuning includes the liturgical pieces in the Faenza Codex, and, in the Buxheim Organ Book, nos.19, 30–31, 126–8, 141, 153–5 and 180.)

Such contrasts were probably too subtle for unaccompanied voices to maintain systematically, and indeed the vocal mainstream of mid-15th-century music calls for well-fused triadic sonorities in the diatonic scale itself. No doubt the best singers could provide them, as they do today, and keyboard musicians felt obliged to find a way, namely some shade of meantone temperament, to have euphonious diatonic thirds in their music as well. Their experience with the sharps in Pythagorean intonation would have clarified the distinction between these and the old Pythagorean diatonic thirds. Conrad Paumann's music reflects this new development so well that if we were obliged to attribute the invention of meantone temperament to a famous musician, he might be the best candidate.[3]

Tempered intonation on keyboard instruments was referred to obliquely by Bartolomeo Ramos de Pareia in 1482 and by Franchinus Gaffurius in 1496,[4] and detailed tuning instructions were published in the first half of the

16th century by Arnolt Schlick (1512), Pietro Aaron (1523) and G. M. Lanfranco (1533).[5] Undiscriminating scholarship has yielded a fair amount of misinformation as to what kind of tuning they meant.[6] Ramos, Gaffurius and Lanfranco clearly intended a regular tuning, that is, with uniform good

Ex.2 Anon: Prelude (Buxheim Organ Book, no. 242)

fifths; but since Gaffurius excluded any enharmonic equating of flats and sharps, and Ramos and Lanfranco referred to the presence of a wolf fifth (for Ramos, C♯–A♯; for Lanfranco 50 years later, G♯–E♯), equal temperament is far less likely than some shade of meantone. But which? Ramos and Gaffurius give us no clues. Aaron's instructions, designed to supply the rudiments 'as easily as possible', are equivocal: the initial C–E was to be 'sonorous and just, i.e. as united as possible'; but C♯ was merely to be tuned a 'major third with A, and minor with E', and likewise F♯ in relation to D and A. According to both Schlick and Lanfranco, the major thirds were to be tempered larger than pure (as in figs. 2c, d and e), but to say exactly how much would have required a better mathematical grasp of tempered systems than anyone yet possessed. In 1558 Gioseffo Zarlino, *maestro di cappella* at St Mark's in Venice, published the first mathematically coherent model of a meantone temperament. Its major thirds were slightly *smaller* than pure, as shown in fig.2a. Later Zarlino introduced, as a new system (1571), the scheme represented here by fig.2b (where the zero stands for a pure major third).[7]

This was the only form of meantone temperament described by Costanzo Antegnati (1608), Michael Praetorius (1619) and Marin Mersenne (1636); and German scholars today apply the term 'mitteltönig' to it alone and assume that everyone in the 16th and 17th centuries used it. But the Renaissance term, 'participato', was applied to various shades of regular meantone temperament, as indeed was 'ton moyen' in the 18th century.[8] A modern keyboard performer of Renaissance music who wishes to use a

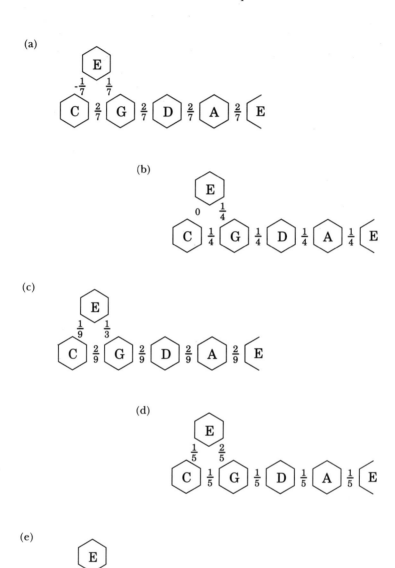

2 Tempering of the triadic intervals in some representative shades of regular meantone temperament. The fifths are tempered by the following fractions of a syntonic comma; (a) $2/7$, (b) $1/4$, (c) $2/9$, (d) $1/5$, (e) $1/6$. In these diagrams a positive number means that the fourth, major third or major sixth in question is tempered larger than pure (and the fifth, minor third or minor sixth smaller). In the first of the schemes shown here, the major thirds are tempered smaller than pure.

historically suitable tuning may choose any of the varieties of meantone temperament represented in fig.2, or any intermediate shade. I recommend that one judge by ear (with appropriate music and on an appropriate instrument, of course) the relative strengths and weakness of the extreme types in fig.2, and then choose an intermediate shade by ear.[9] In $^2/_7$-comma meantone the harmonic thirds and sixths are remarkably euphonious, but the leading notes are remarkably dull; in $^1/_6$-comma meantone the leading notes are more effective but the beating of some of the major sixths may sound rather nervous.

If the music has D♯'s as well as E♭'s, or A♭'s as well as G♯'s, the ideal solution, and generally the most feasible historically, is an instrument with split keys for a total of 13 or 14 notes per octave. Schlick (1511) did not favour this device, however; for music with A♭'s as well as G♯'s (he countenanced no D♯'s) he preferred an irregular scheme along the lines represented by fig.7a below.[10] It is difficult to determine whether this idea was much taken up in the 16th century.

Praetorius suggested (1619) that C♯ and *a fortiori* G♯ might be tuned slightly higher than in a regular meantone scheme; he said that although they must make pure thirds with A and E respectively, nevertheless the fifths F♯–C♯–G♯ must not beat so much as the other fifths. He said disapprovingly that some people even wanted to make C♯–G♯ pure. This would certainly prevent G♯ from making a pure third with E; but the pipes in question might 'draw' pure with one another (depending upon their layout on the soundboard) in the case of the lesser irregularities which Praetorius approved of. In either case, G♯ when not supported by an E major triad would gain a slight and perhaps welcome pungency as a leading note, but would not be raised enough to make a serviceable fifth with E♭ (as in Schlick's tuning).

Lute and viol players may sometimes have used a meantone temperament – the extant music of Schlick and of Luis de Milán suggests as much – but certain artistic depictions from as early as the late 15th century (see illustration) suggest equal semitones. In the first half of the 16th century some writers mentioned the use of all 'minor semitones' on the lute or viol (Giovanni Spataro, 1524; Martin Agricola, 1545); they undoubtedly meant the 18:17 semitone, which was soon acknowledged to yield, for all practical purposes, a very good equal-temperament fretting (Vincenzo Galilei, 1581; Mersenne, 1636; more obliquely Jerome Cardan, *c*1545 and 1571). Nicola Vicentino said in 1555 that 'from the time of the invention of the *viole d'arco* and the lute until now, people have played with the equal-semitone division', and that fretted instruments therefore never sounded in tune with keyboard instruments. Many late 16th- and early 17th-century writers made the same categorical distinction.[11]

Vincenzo Galilei referred in 1584 to certain 'gentlemen' – lute players, that is – who used extra little frets for the sake of unequal semitones. The pattern he gave of major and minor semitones is that of a meantone temperament. There is not much corroborating evidence, however, to suggest that extra frets of this kind were very much in use.

Everyone seems to have agreed that singers accompanied by 'artificial' instruments would match their tempered tuning, but different writers gave

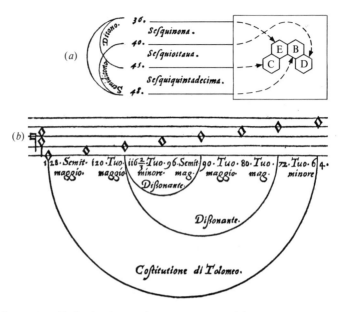

3 Two elements in Zarlino's theory of just intonation: (a) Ptolemy's 'diatonic-syntonic' tetrachord; (b) the dissonant wolf fifth among the diatonic notes on a normal keyboard instrument.

quite different accounts of the intonation of unaccompanied voices. Zarlino said that good singers when unaccompanied would adhere to the pure intervals of Ptolemy's 'diatonic syntonic' tetrachord (see fig.3*a*). He knew that in any diatonic scale of rigidly fixed pitch classes this would entail a dissonant wolf fifth (see fig.3*b*), yet he believed that the singers' capacity to intone pitches flexibly would somehow enable them to get around such problems without actually tempering. But Giovanni Battista Benedetti showed, in a letter to Cipriano de Rore, that if none of the intervals were tempered, the pitch level in any real music would constantly be shifting a comma up or down, and the cumulative shift would often be very great (see ex.3(a)). In 1581 Zarlino's former pupil Vincenzo Galilei said that even in unaccompanied singing the major third was tempered (though 'rather close

Ex.3(a)

to 5:4') and the whole tone made 'two equal parts of the said third'. In the 1590s, however, Simon Stevin declared that the octave is *naturally* divided into 12 equal semitones; and according to Giovanni Maria Artusi in 1603, certain obstinate 'modern composers' (Monteverdi) entertained a theory of intonation according to which the C♯–B♭ is 'neither a sixth nor a seventh, but sounds very well' and F♯–B♭ 'is a third' and is divided into a

Pythagorean whole-tone and two equal semitones as shown in ex.3(b). The resulting semitones are less than a cent larger than $1/12$ of an octave, so this amounted to a theory of equal temperament, though less radical than Stevin's. Given all these different views, modern singers of Renaissance music may as well forget about any particular system of intonation and be content to make a good ensemble with whatever instruments and other voices may be present.[12]

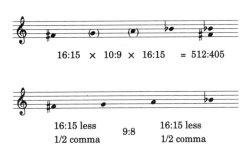

Ex 3(b) Monteverdi's theoretical diminished fourth and its division into a 9:8 whole-tone and two semitones each intended to be half as large.

$16{:}15 \times 10{:}9 \times 16{:}15 = 512{:}405$

16:15 less 1/2 comma   9:8   16:15 less 1/2 comma

In the 1640s a few theorists began to complain that certain musicians – most notably Frescobaldi – were advocating the use of equal temperament on keyboard instruments. Frescobaldi's *Cento partite sopra gli passacagli* might well have been played in equal temperament, if not on a harpsichord with a split key for middle C♯/D♭ as well as for G♯/A♭ and E♭/D♯. I imagine his pupil Froberger used equal temperament, as other tunings seem to me

Ex.4 Froberger: Courante in B minor (1st half)

175

less well suited to some of Froberger's music (see ex.4). There is a wealth of documentary and musical evidence, however, that players and organ builders converted for the most part from meantone to some irregular temperament – that is, with different fifths tempered by different amounts – and were won over to equal temperament only gradually during the course of the 18th century.

The irregular temperaments in question gave a variety of sizes to the various semitones and the various major and minor thirds. The semitones among the naturals were the largest, those at the back of the circle of fifths the smallest, the others intermediate, as shown in fig.4a. Similarly, the thirds were tempered least in the diatonic keys and gradually more in the more chromatic keys, as in fig.5. The fifths among the naturals were tuned more or less as in some form of meantone temperament, while those among the chromatic notes were larger. The simplest such scheme is that of the great Italian liturgical composer Francescantonio Vallotti (1697–1780), represented in fig.6b where the unit of measure for the tempering of the various intervals is the amount by which each of the fifths is tuned smaller than pure in equal temperament (see fig.6a).[13]

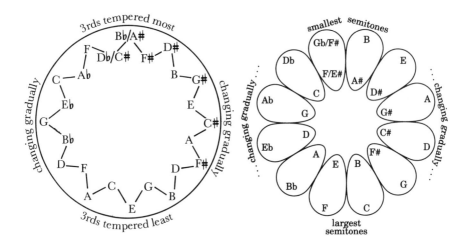

General pattern of 18th-century keyboard tuning: fig.4 the semitones; fig.5 the thirds and sixths.

(a)

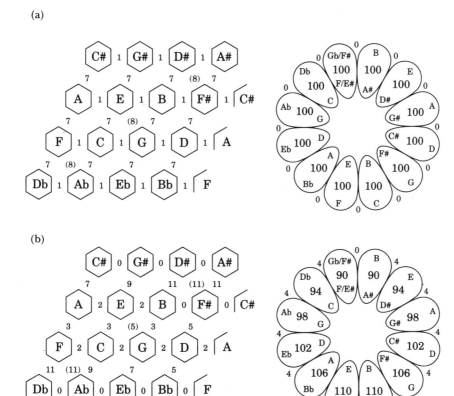

(b)

6 *(a) Equal temperament; (b) Vallotti's temperament. Here and in the remaining figures, the hexagon diagrams show by how many schismas the triadic intervals are tempered (one schisma = $^1/_{12}$ pythagorean comma or $^1/_{11}$ syntonic comma). The 'flower' diagrams show the sizes of the semitones and how they vary, in cents (one cent = $^1/_{1200}$ octave).*

Some 18th- and (in England) early 19th-century writings prescribe an irregular tuning with something of a wolf fifth, as in fig.7b–c.[14] Harmonically sophisticated music never sounds much in tune in this kind of temperament, but presumably a certain kind of musician used it at the time.[15]

In fig.5 the rubric 'thirds tempered most' is tilted to the left to allow for a peculiarity of the French style of irregular tuning:[16] it was customary to temper the fifths E♭–B♭–F slightly *larger* than pure, and perhaps also the old wolf fifth A♭–E♭, and consequently the whole tones and major thirds would increase in size more among the flat-laden keys than among the sharp-laden ones. For instance E♭–G was tempered distinctly more than in equal temperament, but A–C♯ distinctly less. This feature of the *tempérament ordinaire* seems to have originated from a misinterpretation of Mersenne's instructions (1636) for a regular meantone tuning, according to which B♭ was to be tuned 'forte' in relation to F, and similarly E♭ to B♭:[17]

177

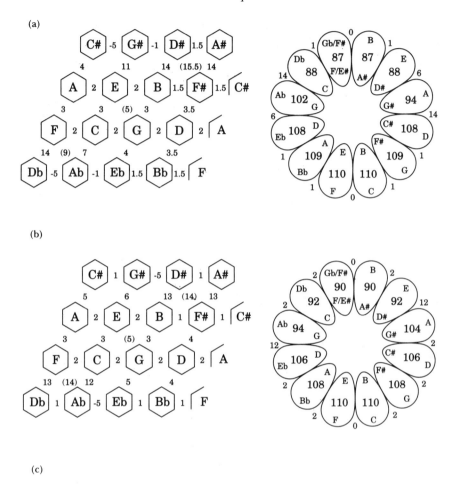

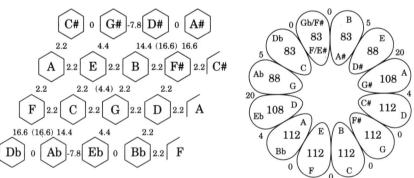

7 Three schemes with a wolf fifth rather less sour than in a regular meantone temperament or in Pythagorean intonation: (a) a modern reconstruction of Schlick's tuning; (b) a convenient approximation to Riccati's temperament (his wolf fifth was actually impure by 4.7 schismas); (c) Hawkes's proposal.

later writers reversed Mersenne's intention by applying the term 'forte' to the interval rather than to the note.

Fig.8 represents this style of tuning. Rameau said in 1726 that C–E must be altogether pure because 'la *Tierce majeure* ne frémit plus, si peu qu'on l'altère', and so the fifths C–G–D–A–E must be tempered by $\frac{1}{4}$ comma; but in 1737 he said that in practice the fifths were diminished only 'd'à peu-pres' $\frac{1}{4}$ comma. Etienne Loulié in 1698 described $\frac{1}{4}$-and $\frac{1}{5}$-comma meantone temperament and said the latter shade was 'more in use than any other'. Joseph Sauveur in his survey of regular temperaments (1707) said that 'in place of the major and minor (whole) tones *T t*, one must take a mean tone (*un ton moyen*)', and in the context of this postulate determined that the division of the octave into 43 parts, corresponding to $\frac{1}{5}$-comma meantone, was the best choice – partly because he reckoned its whole tone to be an arithmetic mean (*milieu arithmétique*) among the three major and two minor whole tones in his theoretical model of an untempered scale.[18] He said that the 43 division matched, better than did the 31 or 55 divisions (corresponding respectively to $\frac{1}{4}$- and $\frac{1}{6}$-comma meantone), the scale of a harpsichord which had been tuned 'très exactement', but that some tuners used 'some more piquant intervals, which thus may perhaps approach some of the other divisions'. These were presumably chromatic intervals, for a wealth of other documentary evidence shows that the *tons naturels* were tempered more moderately than the *tons transposez* and that in listening to keyboard music, musicians and connoisseurs could distinguish the various keys by ear even if the general pitch level were varied by a semitone or more.[19]

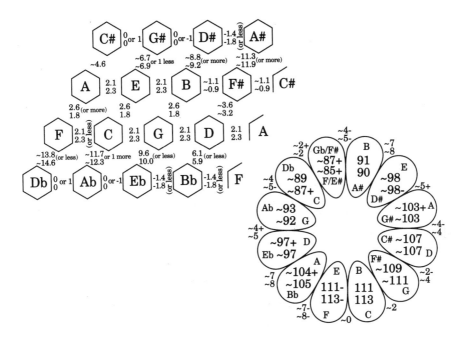

8 Approximate limits for the late Baroque 'tempérament ordinaire'.

Ex.5 d'Anglebert: Sarabande in D minor (1st half)

The corroborating musical evidence may be represented here by ex.5, the first half of a Sarabande by D'Anglebert, where the nuances of intonation among the chromatic notes help at certain moments to sustain the slow descent of the tune from its initial *d"* to its *a* at bar 12. In bar 3 the darkness due to the beating of the left hand's *bb* helps the inverted triad to match in weightiness the resonance of the *A* in bar 2. Similarly in bar 10 the beating of the *g♯* helps the E chord to sustain the harmonic tension generated in the previous bar. A sense of momentary repose at the outset of the second phrase is abetted by the moderate intonation of *B* as a leading note in bar 5, which then serves as a foil to the somewhat higher intonation of the *c♯* in bar 7 (as the outer lines prepare to 'cross' upon E, as it were, at bar 8); yet the *c♯* is intoned relatively lower than the ensuing *g♯*. Such elements of colour – a nice tuning of C♯ is particularly grateful to the style – are vital to D'Anglebert's music, which can be rather insipid without them, and no less so to the *pièces de clavecin* of François Couperin's maturity.[20] But Rameau's counterpoint plays less upon momentary vertical sonorities as his chromatic lines are less wayward and more obviously directed to a point of arrival; so his music is more congenial to equal temperament – which he endorsed in 1737 after having praised the nuances of the *tempérament ordinaire* in 1726.

French writers agreed that some keys were very heavily tempered – F minor being particularly 'melancholy' – and that a few keys, such as E♭ and A♭, were really too harsh to use at all. This would hardly do for Bach,[21] who used all 24 keys in his music and appears to have wanted none of it to sound harsh. An abundance of circumstantial evidence suggests that the tuning theorist whom Bach most respected was J. G. Neidhardt, who had advocated

Table 1 NEIDHARDT'S LOGIC

1724	range of tempering among the thirds (unit: 1/12 pyth. comma)	largest and smallest semitones (in cents); s.d. to 100	1732
	2-10	108; 94 s.d. 5.3	Village
Village	3-10	108; 94 s.d. 4.0	Small town
Small town	4-10	106; 96 s.d. 3.3	Large town
Large town	4-9	104; 96 s.d. 2.3	
Court	7-8	100; 100 s.d. 0	

equal temperament in 1706 but gradually over the next 25 years came to the view that while equal temperament 'will not very readily take last place', nevertheless a rather subtly unequal one was best for a large city, and progressively more unequal (see Table) for a small city and for a village. (This was presumably because music in more rural places would make less use of the extreme sharps and flats.) Fig.9a–b shows the schemes which Neidhardt recommended in 1726 for a small town and village respectively, and then in 1732 for a large and small town respectively. Fig.10a is intermediate between these two.[22]

Neidhardt was the first to give mathematically precise schemes combining not only tempered and untempered fifths, but also fifths tempered by larger

(a)   (b)

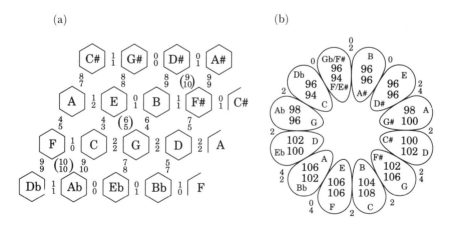

9 (a) the tunings which Neidhardt recommended in 1732 as well as 1724; (b) the tuning which Werckmeister recommended in 1680 for the 'chromatic genus' (and again in 1690) and which 18th-century writers associated with his name.

(a)

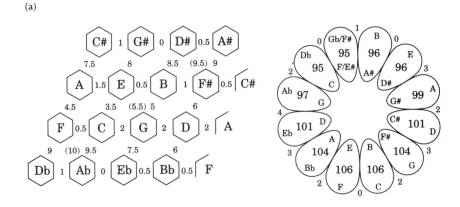

(b)

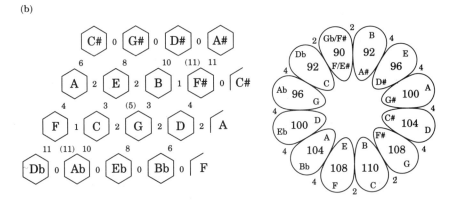

10 *(a) the average between Neidhardt's two schemes shown above; (b) an adaptation of Werckmeister's tuning to Bach's music by altering A, B, C and D.*

and smaller amounts; his object was surely not to say that some fifths must be tempered exactly twice as much as others, but rather to show a suitably gradual variation in the thirds and semitones. One need only compare his tunings in this respect with the scheme which Werckmeister introduced for chromatic music in 1681 (fig.9c) to see why Bach's associate Lorenz Mizler said of Werckmeister, 'As far as his temperament is concerned, it was the best at his time, but has been improved upon since the time of Neidhardt', and why Bach's son-in-law and musical protégé, J. C. Altnikol, said in reference to the Wenzelkirche organ at Naumburg rebuilt in the 1740s by Zacharias Hildebrandt (with advice from Bach), 'In tempering he (Hildebrandt) follows Neidhardt and one can modulate quite nicely in all the keys without giving the ear anything annoying to hear, which is the most beautiful for today's taste in music'.

My experience is that an organ tuned to Werckmeister's prescription will nicely suit the music of Buxtehude and his generation in Germany, but that for Bach's music the tuning can be improved by raising D and A 2 and 4 cents respectively and lowering C and B the same amounts. The result (fig.10*b*) is nearly as suave as Thomas Young's preferred tuning of 1801 (fig.11*a*). (Young mentioned another scheme – fig.11*b* – as second best; the one he preferred may be regarded as a compromise between this and Vallotti's scheme.)

Some modern writers[23] have said that the one or another of J. P. Kirnberger's proposals, with their pure major third C–E, must reflect Bach's way of tuning. But those proposals were roundly criticized by G. A. Sorge, who has every appearance of having known and approved of Bach's views on tuning; and Kirnberger himself was cited (by Marpurg) as saying on more than one occasion that Bach, with whom he had studied in the early 1740s, 'expressly enjoined him to make all the major thirds sharp'. Werckmeister, Neidhardt, Sorge and Barthold Fritz (whose tuning instructions were endorsed by C. P. E. Bach in the mid-1750s) all said that the thirds among the

(a)

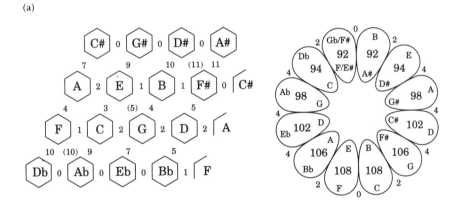

(b)

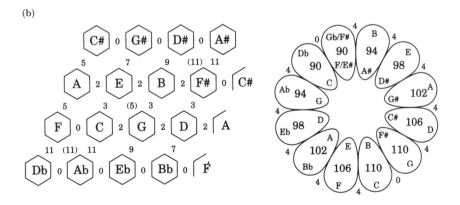

11 (a) a convenient approximation to Young's preferred temperament (his C–E was actually tempered by 2.75 schismas); (b) his other scheme, 'nearly the same'.

naturals must beat. So to let one or more of them draw pure would be contrary to the 18th-century German style.

Bach's music provides the best evidence as to whether he preferred a slightly nuanced tuning (*à la* Neidhardt) or equal temperament.[24] In *Das wohltemperirte Clavier* (part I of the '48') the different keys are in fact treated differently. The relatively neutral arpeggiation of the C- and G-major preludes is quite different to the sprightlier tunefulness and less solid vertical character of the A major prelude, and in a quieter, perhaps quasi-pastoral vein, the E major, and then, going a step further, the very expressive use of leading notes in the B major prelude. Among the preludes in minor keys, the increase in gravity from D to C to E♭ minor is of analogous significance. Any tuner who can accommodate and heighten these contrasts while keeping the extreme keys from sounding sour on the instrument to hand will probably dismiss the view that *Das wohltemperirte Clavier* 'must be performed with an equal-tempered keyboard'.[25]

Bach may perhaps have become more favourably inclined to equal temperament in the 1730s and 1740s. (I find it best for the six-part ricercar from the *Musical Offering*.) Yet some distinguished keyboard players late in the century were still using an unequal temperament.[26] Cramer's *Magazin der Musik* published a brief account of Clementi's tuning in 1784: 'C–E in the bass beating just a little high; E–G♯ very high; G♯–B♯ or A♭–A–C even higher'. In 1826 Pietro Lichtenthal, a Viennese physician, composer and musicologist (and a friend to Mozart), after defining an unequal temperament as one in which 'some fifths are quite pure and some are imperceptibly smaller than pure', declared that equal temperament 'cannot subsist, otherwise the keys would no longer have any character and one could just as well compose a nocturne in A minor and a military blare in A♭'. But Mozart's most distinguished former pupil, Hummel, took a different view in 1828:

> Sorge, Fritz, Marpurg, Kirnberger, Vogler and others…proposed various [tuning] systems…in earlier times, when people played clavichords, harpsichords and pianos with only two thin, weak strings for each note; but …those instruments are almost all out of use now, and pianos have been introduced in which every note has, not two, but three strings, [each] four or five times as thick and strong as then, [so] it is no longer as easy to carry out [the old] proposals, and one must use a temperament which is…easier and more convenient to tune…[since anyway] few of the many who now occupy themselves with tuning can exercise a sharp enough ear to distinguish exactly the fine nuances among the different chords in [an] unequal temperament.

Notes

[1] Details in J. Herlinger, 'Marchetto's Division of the Whole Tone', *JAMS*, xxxiv (1981), 193.
[2] This and the following two paragraphs are based on M. Lindley, 'Pythagorean Intonation and the Rise of the Triad', *RMARC*, xvi (1980), 6–61. Medieval prescriptions for organ pipe lengths are transcribed in K.-J. Sachs, *Mensura fistularum: die Mensurierung der Orgelpfeiffen im Mittelalter* (Stuttgart, 1970).
[3] S. Tanaka, 'Studien im Gebiete der reinen Stimmung', *VMw*, vi (1890), 61; M. Lindley, 'Stimmung und Temperatur', in *Geschichte der Musiktheorie*, ed. F. Zaminer, vi, *Musikalisches Hören und Messen in der frühen Neuzeit* (Darmstadt, 1987), chap.1.
[4] Details in M. Lindley, 'Fifteenth-century Evidence for Meantone Temperament', *PRMA*, cii

(1975–6), 37. See also E. C. Pepe, 'Pythagorean Tuning and its Implications for the Music of the Middle Ages', *The Courant*, i/2 (April 1983), 3.

[5] Details in M. Lindley, 'Early 16th-century Keyboard Temperaments', *MD*, xxviii (1974), 129.

[6] Most influentially J. M. Barbour, *Tuning and Temperament, a Historical Survey* (East Lansing, 1951, 2/1953/*R*1972), a brilliant work for 1932 when most of the research for it was completed.

[7] Details in Lindley, 'Stimmung and Temperatur', chap.3.

[8] Details in M. Lindley, 'Heinrich Schütz: intonazione della scala e struttura tonale', *Il flauto dolce*, xvii (1986).

[9] A general procedure for tuning any regular meantone temperament by ear is described in M. Lindley, 'Instructions for the Clavier Diversely Tempered', *EM*, v (1977), 18; specific instructions for $^2/_7$-comma meantone are in A. Bellasich *et al*, *Il clavicembalo* (Turin, 1984), 60, and for various particular shades of meantone temperament in the many current books and articles by G. C. Klop, H. A. Kellner, C. de Veroli, O. Jorgenson, J. Meffen, P. -Y. Asselin *et al*.

[10] Details in H. Husmann, 'Zur Characteristik der Schlicksen Temperatur', *AMw*, 24 (1967), 253; F. Hyde, *The Position of Marin Mersenne in the History of Music* (diss., Yale U., 1954) and Lindley, 'Early 16th-century Keyboard Temperaments'.

[11] This and the following paragraph are based on M. Lindley, *Lutes, Viols and Temperaments* (Cambridge, 1984) and 'More on Denis Gaultier, Söhne, Zarlino et al', *FoMRHI* communication 609 (April 1985).

[12] Details in Lindley, 'Stimmung und Temperatur', chap.3; 'Just Intonation', *Grove MI*; and 'Chromatic Systems (or Non-systems) from Vicentino to Monteverdi', *EMH*, ii (1982), 382.

[13] M. Lindley, 'La "prattica ben regolata" di Francescantonio Vallotti', *RMI*, xvi (1981), 45–95, describes (among other things) the effect of Vallotti's tuning in some of his music.

[14] Details in Lindley, 'Stimmung und Temperatur', chap.8.

[15] Perhaps William Croft? See J. Meffen, 'A Question of Temperament: Purcell and Croft', *MT*, cxix (1978), 504.

[16] Details in Lindley, 'Stimmung und Temperatur', chap.6. The tunings attributed to various French theorists in P. -Y. Asselin, *Musique et tempérament* (Paris, 1985) and 'Le tempérament en France au 18e siècle', *L'orgue à notre époque* (Montreal, 1982), 45, are arbitrary reconstructions.

[17] Details in M. Lindley 'Mersenne on Keyboard Tuning', *JMT*, xxiv (1978), 167–203.

[18] Details in Lindley, 'Stimmung and Temperatur', chap.5, and R. Rasch's introduction to his facsimile edition of writings by Sauveur (Utrecht, 1984).

[19] Details in R. Steblin, *A History of Key Characteristics in the Eighteenth und Early Nineteenth Centuries* (Ann Arbor, 1983).

[20] Earlier examples (by Marais and Louis Couperin) are discussed in Lindley, *Lutes, Viols and Temperaments*, 39 and 99.

[21] Details in M. Lindley, 'J. S. Bach's Tuning', *MT*, xxvii (1985).

[22] Another good 'modified Neidhardt' scheme is included among the various tuning instructions in W. Blood, ' "Well-tempering" the Clavier', *EM*, vii (1979), 491.

[23] Most notoriously H. Kelletat, *Zur musikalischen Temperatur, in besondere bei Johann Sebastian Bach* (Kassel, 1960).

[24] See C. Padgham *et al*, 'A Trial of Unequal Temperament on the Organ', *JBIOS*, iii (1979), 73, and J. Barnes, 'Bach's Keyboard Temperament. Internal Evidence from the *Well-tempered Clavier*', *EM*, vii (1979), 236.

[25] Thus R. Rasch in his 'Wohltemperirt en gelijkzwevend', *M&M*, xxxvi (1981), 264, and in his typescript, 'Does "Well-tempered" Mean 'Equal-tempered"?', for *Bach, Handel, Scarlatti: Tercentenary Essays*, ed. P. Williams (Cambridge, 1985), where the editor has changed his conclusions, however, to make them seem less contrary to mine.

[26] Details in Lindley, 'Stimmung und Temperatur', chaps.7–8.

CHAPTER IX

Keyboard Fingerings and Articulation

MARK LINDLEY

Why have the old keyboard techniques been more talked about than put into use? The answer is, presumably: because in taking up some early style of fingering, anyone with a good modern technique has deep-set habits to overcome and no longer feels at home with the instrument – a condition not only wanting in historical verisimilitude but also so annoying that the exotic appeal (which has to sustain the first stages of this kind of re-creation) is soured. Thus many of the best players have tended to forgo the best method of research, the mastering of pieces which are fingered throughout in the original sources, in favour of a selective reading of the old tutors, taking what they like – perhaps Diruta's placing of the wrist but not his fingerings, some of Santa María's scale fingerings but not his style of articulation, François Couperin's substitutions, certain remarks about the thumb from C. P. E. Bach etc – and saying that the more troublesome fingerings are less significant than a broad synthesis of this kind. This approach is now going out of fashion,[1] but for quite a few years it helped to preserve a naïve contrast between 'primitive' and modern. A closer look at the evidence suggests rather that there was a great variety of techniques in Germany, Italy, Spain and England during the 16th and early 17th centuries, and that early 18th-century playing was, like the music, as different from ours as from that of the Renaissance.

Ex.1 Summary of the rules for quick notes in Buchner's *Fundament Buch*

The oldest known fingering rules for fast notes, summarized in ex.1, are from a manuscript of Hans Buchner's *Fundament Buch*, dated 1551 (some 13 years after his death).[2] Did he really reserve 3 for weak notes, or is it only that none of these groups begins in the middle of a three-note span? Fortunately the manuscript gives the fingering for an entire piece. Here 3 takes all notes which have a mordent, and various minims weak or strong; but is generally reserved for weak crotchets, quavers and semiquavers. In

Ex.3 Buchner, 'Quem terra pontus', bb.15–18

Ex.4 Buchner, 'Quem terra pontus', bb.7–8

exx.2 and 3, the actual duration of the first bass note (which completes a
phrase) has to match the crotchet or quaver in the middle voice. If various
other minims are not also to be truncated drastically, the hand must perform
some rather novel gymnastics (see fig.1). Probably the semiquavers in
ex.4 want to be played with the back of the fingers facing left and the tips
touching the keys as shown in fig.2. Only a player quite at home with
manoeuvres of this kind can hope to distinguish between interesting fingerings and the mistake in ex.2, where the *c* was overlooked and the *c′* fingered
accordingly. The proper emendation is to play the octave with 5 and 1, like
all the other octaves; but *b* is still played with 3, as in the next bar.

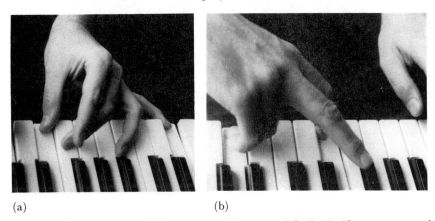

(a)   (b)

*1 Likely left-hand position (a) for the seventh in bar 5 of Buchner's 'Quem terra pontus'
(middle of the first bar of ex.2, opposite) and likely right-hand position (b) in the first half of
bar 10 of the same piece (middle of the third bar of ex.3, above).*

2 Likely points of contact with the keys in ex.4.

187

Ex.5 Erbach, Ricercar, bb.2–3 (r.h.), 6–7 (l.h.)

Ex.6 Erbach, Ricercar, b.13

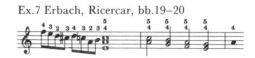

Ex.7 Erbach, Ricercar, bb.19–20

A ricercar by Christian Erbach is preserved with fingerings in a Bavarian manuscript of the 1620s. Once again, 3 has mostly weak quavers and semiquavers (ex.5), and here also one finds certain fingerings which even a German tutor might not explain (as in ex.6, where the 4 on *d'* entails a cadential rubato and a relatively deliberate articulation). A very high wrist as in fig.4 can facilitate some of the fingerings, such as $\frac{5}{4}$ for certain harmonic

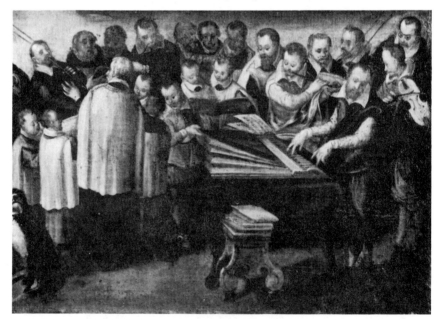

3. Detail of the painting 'Interior of Augsburg Cathedral' (1616) by Tobias Maurer in Augsburg Cathedral: Christian Erbach was cathedral organist at the time

thirds in the right hand (ex.7), not to mention the harmonic fourths so fingered elsewhere in the same piece.

In Elias Ammerbach's two sets of fingered exercises (1571, 1583), 3 is used on weak or strong notes indifferently (exx.8–9), and the left thumb is applied to the last note of certain groups (ex.9–10), even if it may be a chromatic note. The right thumb is not explicitly called for in any German Renaissance source. Ammerbach fingered most groups independently of each other, and often the same finger has the last note of one group and the first of the next.[3] The weak note may have been played with merely a finger motion, but the following strong note with a hand motion as well. Ammerbach may well have used a moderately low wrist as in fig.4.

In these exercises and in Erbach's ricercar, to slur all those notes which can most readily be slurred would often make a very silly, 'hiccuping' effect (see ex.11), so the phrasing is best achieved by shadings of articulation and tempo in a patina of marginal detachments. This is probably what the early tutors meant by terms like 'legato' and 'smooth'.

Our only 16th-century Italian source of information, part i (1593) of Girolamo Diruta's *Il transilvano*, prescribes that the wrist be 'a bit high' ('alquanto alto') to keep the hand and arm level. Diruta dwelt upon the importance of a quiet hand, relaxed as if caressing a child, except that in dances one might instead strike the keys, 'harpsichord-style'. He said the arm should guide the hand, and the fingers should be 'alquanto inarcate', which has been rendered by various translators as 'slightly', 'somewhat' or 'rather' curved.

Ex.8 Ammerbach, exercise (1583)

Ex.9 Ammerbach, exercise (1571), excerpt

Ex.10 Ammerbach, scale (1571, 1583)

Ex.11 Unlikely phrasing for part of ex.5

4. Title-page illustration (detail) to Elias Ammerbach's 'Orgel oder Instrument Tabulatur', 1571

5. Detail of the painting 'St Cecilia and St Catherine of Alexandria' (1566) by B. Carpi in the church of S Sigismondo, Cremona

Diruta was the disciple of a renowned virtuoso, Claudio Merulo, yet it is hard to extract a clear picture of contemporary practice from his book. He finds that in right-hand passages moving away from the body, 2 (with no notes to play) tends to become straight and still ('sforzato'), that the thumb also grows stiff under the hand, and that 5 rather draws in. He reports that many organists had accustomed the hand to these defects, to the detriment of their playing, but he does not say whether they were well-known performers or nonentities (see apropos fig.6). He reserves 3 for 'bad notes' ('note cattive'), but all the later Italian writers, including Banchieri in 1608, give the strong notes to 3 or are indifferent to the matter. Diruta reports that for scales the left hand should descend (2)3232 ... even though 'many eminent men' preferred to descend with 4, and that either hand should move towards the body (4)3232 ... even though many eminent men preferred to ascend with 1 and 2 in the left hand. He says bad notes which leap should be played with 3, adding that they can be played with 1 or 5 if the leap is larger than a fifth; but as none of his examples is fingered it is not clear whether a bad note before a large leap should ever be played with 3, nor whether a bad note after a leap might ever be played with 1 or 5.

Ex.12 (a) Anon., exercise (*Wegweiser*)

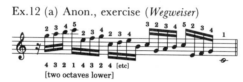

(b) A. Scarlatti, 'Toccata prima', bb.135–7

(c) Hartung, 'Fantasien zwischen die Sylben zu gebrauchen', beginning

According to Diruta, diminutions must be played 'cleanly, that is, not pressing a key down before the finger is lifted from the previous one, moving up and down at the same time'; however, his examples of diminutions include sevenths for which 2–5 would be the smoothest fingering not unmistakably contrary to his rules.[4]

One reason why modern players have trouble with these fingerings is that in bringing the right hand to the keyboard they habitually lead with the thumb rather than with the index finger. The early fingerings oblige us to orient the right hand with some finger other than the thumb. Ex.12 may show that this way of approaching the keyboard remained in currency during the 17th and early 18th centuries, as did the use, in appropriate circumstances, of the same finger for two successive notes in a tune (ex.13 and 38–9). Where one hand had to take two parts this was a very familiar technique

Ex.13 (a) Gibbons, Fantasia (cf, *MB* xx, 1), 6–5 bb. from end

(b) Dandrieu, Gavotte in D, bb.3–5

(c) F. Couperin, 'Les Ondes', 4th couplet, b.1 (r.h.)

(d) C. P. E. Bach, *Versuch*, tab.3, fig.61a

Ex.14 (a) Erbach, Ricercar, bb.15–17

(b) J. S. Bach, Fughetta, BWV 870a.ii, bb.30–33

(c) C. P. E. Bach, *Versuch*, tab.2, fig.66

throughout the 16th, 17th and 18th centuries (ex.14). Some tutors implied that each kind of harmonic interval or chord was always to be played with the same fingers no matter what the context. Such rules may have been over-simplified, but this aspect of the technique was at any rate simpler than a Romantic organist could conceive.

Ex.15 Gibbons, 'The King's Juell', bb.33–35

Ex.16 Bull, Prelude, b.4

Ex.17 Gibbons, Preludium (cf. MB xx, 2), bb.27–30

Ex.18 Anon., 'An easy one for a beginner' (*Lbm* 36661), bb.1–3

We have no 16th-century Spanish music with fingerings, but the rules given in four treatises and prefaces (Bermudo, 1555; Venegas de Henestrosa, 1557; Santa María, 1565; and H. de Cabezon 1578) show that scales were taken with various fingerings.[5] Bermudo prescribed 4321 4321 and 1234 1234. Cabezon, in his edition of the music by his blind brother Antonio, recommends to beginners: right hand up 343434, and down 323232; left hand up 4321 4321, but down 1234 3434. A preference for paired fingering away from the body is evident also in Venegas de Henestrosa's advice (again for beginners) that the left hand go up 4321 321, but down 1234 3434, and the right hand go down 4321 3 ... (or perhaps it might start with 5), but up 3434 (once 4 has been reached after starting from 1 or perhaps 2 or 3). Santa María's suggestions, some of which are summarized in Table 1, were the most elaborate; but for all fingerings alike he states the hand should point towards the keys to be played next and the finger which has just played should be lifted before the next one plays. So if the thumb followed 4 in a scale away from the body, the hand was turned outwards and the thumb would approach its key as 4 was just releasing its hold.

The English may have been the first to use 5 at the end of right-hand runs (ex.15). This was corollary to taking strong notes with 3 - a persistent habit (ex.16) which was, however, occasionally resisted to avoid a shift within a three-note span (ex.17). The left thumb was most often used instead of 3 in ascending scales (ex.18). Repeated notes would normally be taken with changing fingers (ex.19). (In the 18th century they were still usually played in this way, as in ex.20, and only sometimes with the same finger as in ex.21.)

Ex.19 Bull, Miserere, b.12

Ex.20 Hartung, Minuet, bb.1–2

Ex.21 D. Scarlatti, Sonata (KK 96), bb.140–44

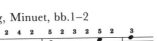

Ex.22 Anon., 'Courrante Lavigon', bb.66–68

A number of mid- to late 17th-century English manuscripts contain fingered music, but to assign a date to these fingerings would be so problematical that no one has distinguished much between 'early' and 'late' techniques among the virginalists.[6]

In north Germanic fingerings of the first half of the 17th century, 3 tends to take weak notes in the left hand but strong in the right (ex.22), with occasional exceptions for three-note spans (ex.23) or various other contingencies (as in ex.24).[7] In view of this, and of the contrary earlier traditions for the role of 3 in paired fingerings, we might expect to find many later examples of indifference, and we do (ex.25).

Ex.23 Anon., 'Courrante Lavigon', bb.36–41

Ex.24 Anon., Praeludium (attr. elsewhere to Bull), beginning

Ex.25 (a) Nivers, left-hand descending scales (1665 preface)

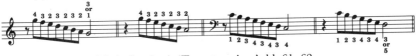

(b) A. Scarlatti, 'Toccata prima', bb.61–62

195

Ex.26 (a) Hartung, Menuet, bb.1–2

(b) Zipoli and anon., Minuet, bb.27–32

Ex.27 Dlla Ciaja, Toccata (1727, p.15), b.70

During the first half of the 18th century the main trend was to add new technical devices without rejecting the old ones,[8] so the fingerings were rather unsystematic and dependent upon the immediate musical context. Given a suitable occasion, 4, 3 or even 2 might cross beyond 5 (ex.26); 5 might cross over 1 (ex.27) or under 3 (ex.28); 2 and 4 might cross past each other (exx.29 and 31); the thumb might take a chromatic note (ex.30) or might not (ex.31), and scales might be rendered by an elaborate choreography of both hands (ex.32). It was in this context of nimble permutations that the old Spanish unpaired scale fingerings apparently began to be taken up outside Iberia in the 1720s: in Rameau's *Traité de l'harmonie* (1722, for slow bass notes as in ex.33), in a contemporary manuscript of Handel's G major Ciacona (ex.34), in Della Ciaja's *Sonate*, op.4 (1727), and no doubt elsewhere. Various tutors from 1730 on prescribed them (ex.35); Hartung in 1749 referred to 3434 and 3232 as 'that impoverished fingering',[9] and in 1789 Türk recalled that Friedemann Bach had been able to play, with only two fingers (3 and 4), 'certain runs straight-off and with an astonishing velocity'.

The effect of these developments upon articulation is not entirely clear. In 1735 Mattheson stated that a teacher should tell his pupil 'never to apply the next finger until he has lifted the previous one'. Marpurg in 1755 said that while slurring and staccato were usually indicated by signs in the music, the ordinary procedure, namely to lift the finger from the preceding key very quickly just before touching the following note, was never indicated because it was always presupposed. Dom Bédos in 1778 dwelt upon the necessity of little silences at the end of each note on any keyboard instrument, without which the music would be like an inarticulate series of vowels without consonants.[10] Czerny in praising Beethoven's legato referred to Mozart's 'chopped-up and clipped-off playing'. On the other hand, Duphly told Lord Fitzwilliam, some time after 1754, that in *le jeu françois* 'one must not quit one key until after having taken another'.[11] How then should we interpret Forkel's statement (1802) that J. S. Bach – whom he never heard play – had found a 'middle path' between too much legato and too much staccato, and so achieved 'the highest degree of clarity ('Deutlichkeit') in the playing of single notes as in the pronunciation of single words'?

Ex.28 Handel, Ciacona, var.11, bb.6–8

Ex.29 Zipoli and anon., Minuet, bb.9–10

Ex.30 Handel, Ciacona, var.13, bb.5–7

Ex.31 F. Couperin, 'Le moucheron', bb.14–15

Ex.32 Rameau, 'Les tourbillons' (1724), bb.36–37

Ex.33 Rameau, bass lines (1722, p.382*ff*)

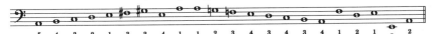

Ex.34 Handel, Ciacona, var.6, bb.1 and 7–8

Ex.35 Prelleur (*c*1730), exercise

Ex.36 Nivers (1665), 'Exemples du coulement des notes'

197

Some earlier French sources are of particular interest in this regard. In 1665 Nivers, discussing *distinction* and *coulement*, said it was very appealing to 'mark all the notes distinctly, and to slur ('couler') some of them' as a singer would do.[12] For instance, in a diminution or roulade of consecutive notes, one should raise the fingers 'soon and not very high', whereas for *ports de voix* and the like as in ex.36, one should still distinguish the notes but 'not raise the fingers so promptly: this manner is between distinction and confusion'. His illustrations of descending scales are shown in ex.25; for ascending scales he prescribed: right hand (1)23 4343 4; left hand (4)32 1212 1.

Ex.37 Rameau (1724), 'Expression de agréments', excerpts

Ex.38 Raison, 'Demonstration des cadences', excerpts

Ex.39 (a) Raison, *Messe du sixiesme ton*, 'Second Agnus', bb.33–36

(b) Raison, 'Second Agnus', bb.49–51

Ex.40 Saint-Lambert, Gavotte, bb.6–8   Ex.41 Dandrieu, Rondeau in C, bb. 14–16|

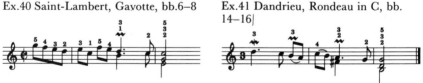

In a rubric to his 'Démonstration des cadences' (1688) Raison said that the *port de voix* should be executed with an overlapping legato; Saint-Lambert concurred in 1702, and Rameau in 1724 (ex.37). Some of the ornaments in Raison's table are fingered (ex.38), and with this guide one can tell how nearly every note in certain ornament-laden passages in his music was to be taken (ex.39). This French playing was as distinctive as the melodic style which it served.

Ex.42 Saint-Lambert, slurred arpeggiation

Ex.43 Dandrieu, 'Gavotte tendre' in C, bb.3–4

Saint-Lambert (1702, 1707) said the fingers should be curved to reach no further than the thumb, and advocated as quiet a hand as possible; his exact meaning can be seen by comparing ex.40 with ex.41. He proposed that to slur an arpeggiation be taken to mean that the each note be held through to the end as in ex.42, and Dandrieu adopted this proposal in 1713 (as in ex.43). Saint-Lambert also suggested that for a run of quick notes towards the body, the customary right-hand fingering, 3232, which he himself had prescribed, was less convenient than the use, by the right hand, of corresponding left-hand fingering, 2121; this idea seems to have been ignored.

In his influential *L'art de toucher le clavecin* (1716) François Couperin said that the old-fashioned use of $\frac{4}{2}$ for successive thirds could not render them legato ('n'auoit nulle liaison'); his playing of thirds is illustrated in ex.44. Sometimes Couperin used finger-substitutions (ex.45 – 'too often and without need' according to C. P. E. Bach (1753). Couperin's scale fingerings (ex.46) imply an anacrusis leading into each beat, like the other exercises in the same set (ex.47), but he often phrased within the beat as in ex.31 (or also ex.13*b*). His attitude to technical drills was equivocal; he had his pupils practice not only the *agréments* but also brief, progressive 'évolutions des doigts' (ex.47), and one of his pupils even learnt to trill in parallel thirds with one hand, but Couperin would not give himself 'la torture' to master such trills to his own satisfaction.

Rameau in 1724 said that 'the raising of one finger and the touching of another should be executed at the same moment'. He prescribed that ex.48 be played over and over 'with equality of movement', thus anticipating the 19th-century conception of the five-finger exercise as a thing of beauty.

Ex.44 F. Couperin, Passacaille, 4th couplet, bb.7–15

Ex.45 F. Couperin, Première prélude, bb.1–6

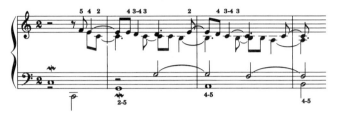

Ex.46 F. Couperin, 'progrès d'octaves'

Ex.47 F. Couperin, 'progrès de tierces; 'progrès de quartes'

Ex.48 Rameau, five-finger exercise

Ex.49 C. P. E. Bach, *Versuch*, tab.1, fig.18

According to Forkel the preliminary exercises which J. S. Bach gave to *his* pupils were cut from exactly the same musical cloth as the two-part inventions and the little preludes in Friedemann's notebook. Bach's pupils also had to practice, early on, all the ornaments in both hands – but apparently not scales, a considerable point of difference between his teaching and that of his son, Emanuel. Nor did Emanuel say of his father's technique, as the standard English translation of the *Versuch* would have it, 'I shall expound it here'; but rather, 'I take it here as a basis' ('so lege ich solche hier zum Grunde'). Whatever the exact relation, the chapter on fingering merits a closer reading than the many infidelities of the translation allow.[13]

Emanuel said that the thumb, which his father had promoted to the rank of 'principal finger', keeps the other fingers flexible because they must bend every time it presses in next to one or another of them. He said the fingers should generally be curved anyway (without saying how much), and the forearm should be a little lower than the keyboard. He gave a wealth of alternative scale fingerings (as in ex.49). Most of them fit his general rule that in moving away from the body the thumb should take a note directly after one or more chromatic notes, and moving towards the body should take a note just before one or more chromatic notes: thus for the left hand ascending in A major, he considered 21 321 432 'in most cases more useful' than 54321 321. (The latter, however, answers better to the rule which Kirnberger in 1781 attributed to J. S. Bach: that in most cases the thumb is placed before or after the leading note.) Such paired fingerings as Emanuel admitted, mainly 4343 and 2121, normally entailed, he said, the same technique that passing 3 or 4 over the thumb did: the longer finger crosses ('wegklettert') while the other 'still hovers over the key which it had depressed'. He declares that in scales with few or no accidentals, 4343 or 2121 would sometimes produce the smoothest effect, because without any chromatic notes the thumb has less ease to cross under. Fast thirds were to be taken mostly by one pair of fingers, but not slow ones; broken chords should sometimes be fingered differently from their unbroken counterparts (see ex.50), because 'clarity is always produced primarily by an even touch'; the fingering of ex.51a was to be used also for the analogous minor triads on C, C♯, F♯, G, G♯, B♭ and B; and that of ex.51b for the major triads on D♭, E♭, E, A♭, A, B♭ and B. Ex.51 suggests that even though the thumb was now the 'Haupt-Finger' the others could still do without it more often than one might suppose.

Ex.50 C. P. E. Bach, *Versuch*, tab.2, figs.54d and 55l

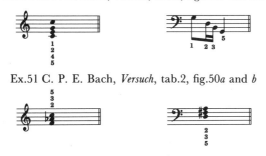

Ex.51 C. P. E. Bach, *Versuch*, tab.2, fig.50a and b

Ex.52 Chopin, Nocturne, op.9, no.2, bb.26–28

Ex.52 shows that this was also the case for Chopin, of whom Niecks reported: 'With one and the same finger he took often two consecutive keys (and this not only in gliding down from a black to the next white key), without the least interruption of the sequence being noticeable. The passing over each other of the longer fingers without the aid of the thumb . . . he freely made use of, and not only in passages where the thumb stationary on a key made this unavoidably necessary.'[14] When the current revival of Renaissance techniques has produced a generation of players to whom various styles of early fingering seem perfectly natural, it may be feasible to consider the value of such an eclectic mixture of old and new techniques on the fortepiano.[15]

Notes

[1] Representative of more recent trends are the section on fingerings in A. Bellasich *et al*, *Il clavicembalo* (Turin, 1984), 161–225; E. Fadini *et al*, 'La tecnica esecutiva degli strumenti a tastiera e del liuto nelle fonte storiche', *Praxis*, i (1983), 115–53; and the writings of M. Boxall, Q. Faulkner, M. Lindley, C. L. Lister, J. Rodgers, and B. Sachs and B. Ife cited below. Prophetic of these trends was A. Dolmetsch, *The Interpretation of the Music of the XVII and XVIII Centuries* (London, 1915, 2/1946/R1969), chap.5. For a learned polemic against them, see I. Ahlgrimm, 'Current Trends in Performance of Baroque Music', *Diapason*, lxxiii (1982), April.

[2] Buchner's rules are translated (and attributed mistakenly to an earlier source than the '1551' *Fundament Buch*) in B. Sachs and B. Ife, *Anthology of Early Keyboard Methods* (Cambridge, 1982).

[3] Ammerbach's 1571 exercises have often been transcribed, for instance in the works cited above of Sachs and Ife (who attribute them to the 1583 edition as well) and of Dolmetsch; the 1583 exercises are transcribed in M. Lindley, 'Ammerbach's 1583 Exercises', *EHM*, iii (April 1983), 59, and *The Courant*, ii (1984). The examples from Buchner, Ammerbach and Erbach are treated in detail in M. Lindley, *German Renaissance Keyboard Techniques* (in preparation).

[4] The most recent book-length treatment of Diruta is E. J. Soehnlein, *Diruta on the Art of Keyboard Playing* (diss., U. of Michigan, 1975). Of the many briefer ones see M. Boxall, 'Girolamo Diruta's "Il Transilvano" and the Early Italian Keyboard Tradition', *EHM*, i, (April 1976), 168, and 'New Light on the Early Italian Keyboard Tradition', *EHM* ii (October 1978), 71.

[5] For more on early Spanish fingerings see C. Jacobs, *The Performance Practice of Spanish Renaissance Keyboard Music* (diss., New York U., 1962) and the works of Sachs and Ife cited above and of Rodgers cited below.

[6] Two major studies have been P. le Huray, 'English Keyboard Fingering in the 16th and Early 17th Centuries', in *Source Materials and the Interpretation of Music: a Memorial Volume for Thurston Dart* (London, 1981), and M. Boxall, *English Keyboard Technique up to the Death of Henry Purcell* (diss., Trinity College, London, 1970). M. Lindley, 'Early English Keyboard Fingerings', *Baster Jb für Historische Musikpraxis*, xii (in preparation). Specialized writings include M. Maas, *Seventeenth-century English Keyboard Music, a Study of Manuscripts Rés. 1186 and 1186bis of the Paris Conservatory Library* (diss., Yale U., 1968); T. Koopman, ' "My Ladye Nevell's Booke" and Old Fingering', *EHM*, ii (Oct 1977), 5, and M. Boxall, ' "The Harpsichord Master 1697" and its Relationship to Contemporary Instruction and Playing', *EHM*, ii (April 1981), 178. For a substantial account of Renaissance fingerings in England and on the Continent see J. Rodgers, *Early Keyboard Fingering, ca. 1520–1620* (diss., U. of Oregon, 1971).

[7] For more on 17th-century German fingerings see C. L. Lister, *Traditions of Keyboard Technique from 1650 to 1750* (diss., U. of N. Carolina at Chapel Hill, 1979); S. Soderland, *Organ Technique, an Historical Approach* (Chapel Hill, 1980, rev. 2/1984), chap.5; M. Lindley, *German Renaissance Keyboard Techniques*; H. Gleason, 'A Seventeenth-century Organ Instruction Book', *Bach, the Quarterly Journal of the Riemenschneider Bach Institute*, iii/1 (1972), J. H. Baron, 'A 17th-century Keyboard Tablature in Brasov', *JAMS*, xx (1967), 279; and R. Jackson, untitled communication, *JAMS*, xxiv (1971), 318.

[8] Details in M. Lindley, 'Tecnica della tastiera e articolazione: testimonianze della pratica esecutiva di Scarlatti, Bach e Händel', *NRMI*, xix (1985), 21–61, of which a preliminary version appeared in *Bach, Handel and Scarlatti: Tercentenary essays*, ed. P. Williams (Cambridge, 1985), 207–43. An analogous perspective on contemporary violin techniques can be gained briefly from P. Walls, 'Violin Fingering in the 18th Century', and R. Stowell, 'Violin Bowing in Transition: a Survey of Technique as Related in Instruction Books c1760–c1830', *EM*, xii (1984), 300 and 317.

[9] The many excerpts from Hartung are one of the most valuable ingredients in I. Ahlgrimm, *Manuale der Orgel und Cembalotechnik* (Vienna, 1982).

[10] See also D. Fuller, 'Analysing the Performance of a Barrel Organ', *The Organ Yearbook*, xi (1980), 104, and, for an antidote, Fuller, 'French Harpsichord Playing in the Seventeenth Century – after Le Gallois', *EM*, iv (1976), 22.

[11] W. Mellers, *François Couperin and the French Classical Tradition* (London, 1950), 345.

[12] Details in W. H. Pruitt, *The Organ Works of Guillaume-Gabriel Nivers (1632–1714)* (diss., U. of Pittsburgh, 1969). See also Pruitt, 'Un traité d'interprétation du xvii siècle', *L'orgue*, no.clii (1974), 99.

[13] C. P. E. Bach, *Essay on the True Art of Playing Keyboard Instruments*, trans. W. J. Mitchell (New York, 1949/R1974). Q. Faulkner, *J. S. Bach's Keyboard Technique; a Historical Introduction*

(St Louis, 1984), is an excellent account; but see M. Lindley, 'Early Fingering: Some Editing Problems and Some New Readings for J. S. Bach and John Bull', *EM*, xvii (1989), 60.

[14] F. Niecks, *Frederick Chopin as a Man and Musician* (London, 1888), ii, 186. For more on Chopin's technique, see J.-J. Eigeldinger, *Chopin vu par ses élèves* (Neuchâtel, rev. 2/1979), and J. Holland, *Chopin's Teaching and his Students* (diss., U. of N. Carolina at Chapel Hill, 1973). The Henle editions of Chopin's music include some original fingerings in italics.

[15] See, for instance, *Selection of Studies by J. S. Cramer with Comments by L. van Beethoven*, ed. J. S. Shedlock (London, 1893). Information on 19th-century piano technique in general is to be found in R. R. Gerig's lovable *Famous Pianists and their Technique* (Washington, 1974). Some studies in early 19th-century organ technique are M. Schneider, *Die Orgelspieltechnik des frühen 19. Jahrhunderts in Deutschland* (Regensburg, 1941), and S. J. Schwartz, *An Examination of the Performance Practices for the Organ circa 1800 based on the 'Orgelschule' of J. H. Knecht* (diss., Stanford U., 1973). 19th-century organ techniques are placed in historical context in Soderland's work cited above. For more citations see M. Lindley, 'Early Keyboard Techniques: a Selected Bibliography', *EHM*, iii (April 1985), 155.

PART TWO

The Classical Era

CHAPTER X

Introduction

NEAL ZASLAW

Until recent decades, music composed after the passing of the generation of Vivaldi, Telemann, Rameau, Handel, Bach and Domenico Scarlatti was regarded as part of a continuous, living tradition maintained in our concert halls, opera houses, conservatories and homes by written and oral instruction. The music of the Classical period was seen as the beginning of a 'standard repertory', the performance of which required no special research or understanding beyond that imparted by the training offered in music schools. Thus the music of Gluck, Haydn, Mozart, Beethoven and Schubert – by its very familiarity and the apparent absence from it of unfamiliar instruments or enigmatic notation – aroused none of the need urgently felt by performers and scholars of earlier music to engage in research about historical performance practices. This complacency was aided and abetted by a powerful oral tradition. For example, many 20th-century pianists could say that they had studied with someone who studied with Leschetizky who studied with Czerny who studied with Beethoven who studied with Haydn who knew Mozart. Singers meanwhile studied with representatives of *bel canto* traditions claiming to trace their artistic lineage a century and a half before Mozart to Caccini. But this patrimony, while it had indeed been continually handed down from generation to generation, had not remained unchanged. On the contrary, it is now clear beyond reasonable doubt that each generation modified what it received from its teachers' generation until the manner of playing music of the Classical period had been altered almost beyond recognition.

In the face of a powerful consensus about how music of the period should be rendered, a consensus lacking for most earlier music, the known differences between modern concert conditions and instruments and those that musicians of the Classical period faced could be regarded merely with historical curiosity as a chronicle of handicaps since overcome through 'improvements' in technique and technology. The music of the Classical period had been given a spurious uniformity, both within itself and with music of the Romantic period: Gluck's *Orfeo* was known only in Berlioz's skilful conflation and reorchestration, his *Iphigénie in Aulide* only in Wagner's reworking; Beethoven's orchestration was as a matter of routine modernized by famous conductors; only a handful of Haydn's and Mozart's late works, especially those that seemed to adumbrate aspects of 19th-century music, were in the repertory; and the piano music of the period was known as rendered on instruments with strikingly different strengths and weaknesses from the pianos for which it was written, with an overlay of phrasing and articulation foreign to the music's style (however logical for the later pianos, performing techniques and styles).

Hidden beneath the spurious uniformity was a kaleidoscopic era of bold experimentation, in which the use of continuo declined but did not entirely vanish; pianos replaced harpsichords, flutes replaced recorders, clarinets upstaged oboes (at least as a favourite solo instrument); instrumental music first came to occupy a position on a par with vocal music, and German on a par with Italian; new systems of tuning were taken up; and – in the wake of the French Revolution and the Napoleonic reforms – the old patronage system collapsed, giving way to a new one requiring larger halls. This last transformation went along with changes in musical style, the total reform of woodwind and brass instruments, the rebuilding to new requirements of thousands of valuable old string instruments and the enlargement and reinforcement of the design of pianos as well as changes in styles of composing, playing and singing.

There are those who argue that attempting to re-establish lost performing practices of two centuries ago is probably impossible but in any case undesirable, and that the performing styles for 18th-century music which have been established in the 20th are the only ones valid for modern audiences. For them, the ensuing discussion is perhaps worse than useless. But for those who wish to know as much as possible about the original performance of the music they perform or study before making their own interpretative decisions, what follows may serve as a useful guide.[1]

The questions that must be answered to establish historically informed performances of music of the Classical period are the same as those for earlier periods: what instruments, playing techniques and vocal timbres to use; how to realize unnotated, partially notated or (from a modern standpoint) misleadingly notated aspects of the music; and the size and placing of forces as well as suitability of ambience and acoustic. If all of these are established, a modern performer may have the firmest possible foundation upon which to begin to construct an interpretation, which will involve learning how to render the style and content of Classical music in a broad range of affects by means of an apposite musical rhetoric.

Editions and notation

The end of the Classical period saw a revolution in the dissemination of music with the introduction of lithography, which enabled rapid, relatively inexpensive production of editions to such an extent that, according to one estimate, the amount of music published in the three decades between 1800 and the deaths of Beethoven and Schubert may have equalled all the music published in the previous three centuries from the advent of music printing just after 1500.[2] But even with engraving, a flood of music was published in the second half of the 18th century (and engraving continued to be used for the most elegant 19th-century editions). Published editions replaced manuscripts as the principal means of dissemination of music; none the less, the prevalent philosophy of making modern editions usually embraces autograph manuscripts as the main sources in preference to printed editions in chamber music and concert music, and in preference to attempting to reconstruct what text was actually followed in the theatre in opera. Musicians wishing to re-create performances of the period will want to take all the evidence into account, and will therefore require either editions that do this for them or facsimiles or other photocopies of the relevant manuscript and printed scores and parts, librettos, verbal descriptions, payrolls and other archival documents and contemporary pictures.

For the works of Haydn, Mozart, Beethoven and Schubert there are the series of complete works published by Breitkopf & Härtel in Leipzig in the 19th century.[3] These editions, repeatedly reprinted, have provided the basis of many of the full scores, miniature scores, vocal scores and parts found in music shops and in libraries. They were edited with a practical eye to late 19th-century performing conditions and often do not satisfy modern standards of editing in which all sources must be consulted (although not conflated) and editorial alterations distinguished from what is found in the principal sources. For some works the old complete-works editions adequately represent a reliable source and may be used for modern performance; for others they were based on a poor source or may contain inaccuracies or unacceptable, hidden editorial intervention.

Since the 1950s new complete editions of the works of Gluck, Haydn, Mozart, Beethoven and Schubert have been launched which, generally preferable to the old ones, should be carefully consulted before practice and rehearsal begins. Even with these excellent editions to hand, though, performers who specialize in music of the Classical period will discover that facsimiles of original sources often help to clarify performing decisions, for the new editions are, like all editions, necessarily a compromise with, or translation of, the originals. Even the finest modern editions are best used side by side with facsimiles.

Editions of this kind, which closely follow an autograph manuscript or other 'authentic' source and scrupulously distinguish between what is drawn from their sources and what constitutes editorial interpretation, are generally known as 'Urtext' editions. While the notion of allowing performers to make their own interpretative decisions by providing them with a version of a composition as directly from the composer as possible without intervening opinions is a defensible one, in practice it proves difficult to pin down. Composers did not always have a clear, fixed idea of what they wanted; sometimes they wished to allow leeway to performers; often changed circumstances led them to make new versions; and in all cases notation can convey only a part of what they may have had in mind. Besides, with all the conscientiousness and goodwill in the world, competent editors and performers will disagree about what the notation says, what it means, and what apparent errors of omission or commission need emendation. Performers seldom have time during rehearsals to resolve the inconsistencies and contradictions found in the original sources of most pieces and have a right to expect competent editions to do this for them. They are also entitled to expect to be informed of what changes were made, in case they find reason to disagree with the editor's decisions.

One of the clearest demonstrations from the Classical period of how slippery the concept of conveying the composer's intentions is can be found in the several so-called 'critical' editions of Mozart's piano sonatas. Even when based on the same sources, usually the autograph manuscripts and editions made with Mozart's consent, these excellent editions contain numerous divergences, especially in marks of articulation and expression. Further, some aspects of composers' manuscripts will not be conveyed by any kind of edition except high quality facsimiles – for instance, a passage where, in writing a long crescendo, Beethoven's growing excitement led to a gradual increase in the actual size of the notation.

One of the most controversial aspects of editions of music of the Classical period concerns the signs for staccato: the dot, the stroke and the wedge.[4] Some treatises and some editions of the period distinguish between them; others do not. Mozart and Beethoven use a range of symbols in their autograph manuscripts, but sometimes they elide into one another and it is often difficult to decide which is intended. This has led to the illogical suggestion that, if the distinction cannot consistently be maintained, it should be eliminated in modern editions.[5] It may be that Mozart and Beethoven, both excellent pianists, used their pen with the same varied touch as they used their fingers upon the keyboard. If so, perhaps an additional symbol is needed in modern editions, so that clear cases can be differentiated from ambiguously intermediate cases, which may indicate an intermediate degree of articulation of the music. In many passages the dot appears from the context to mean a light staccato and the stroke or wedge a heavier one; in others the stroke seems to single out a note or notes to be articulated differently from the surrounding texture. Here is another instance in which facsimiles remain indispensible.

With important composers of the second rank, for whom the great expense of a new complete edition may not be justified, publication of edited facsimiles provides a practical means of giving musicians access to a large repertory. This is best done not by tampering with the facsimiles, which risks unwittingly falsifying them, but either by marginal annotations or by editorial prefaces and critical reports, which draw attention to errors and inconsistencies in the original and explain any potentially puzzling notational symbols and abbreviations. The facsimile method of publication has already made available the previously largely inaccessible keyboard-centred music of Clementi, Dussek and a group of composers active in England, as well as a large sampling of opera scores and librettos, the keyboard works of C. P. E. Bach, and the complete works of J. C. Bach.[6]

Such a method cannot work in chamber and orchestral repertories, most of which survive only in sets of parts. For symphonies an ambitious series has published selections from the works of hundreds of composers, for the most part reproducing editors' quick and ready manuscript scores, along with prefaces several of which contain valuable performance practice information.[7] These serve well for preliminary study and performance but may not bear minute scrutiny as editions and may not be appropriate for use as the sole basis for supposedly definitive analyses or recorded performances.

In the day-to-day practice of teaching and performing the keyboard and chamber music of Haydn, Mozart, Beethoven and Schubert, critical or so-called 'Urtext' editions are gradually replacing older, heavily edited or insufficiently critical editions. The editions of such distinguished performer-pedagogues as Czerny, Busoni, Joachim, Schenker, Schnabel and the like remain a valuable record of musical thought and interpretation but can no longer serve as the basis for present-day performances. On the other hand, it is possible to rest too much faith in the clean, crisp, reassuringly pure and authoritative pages of so-called 'Urtext' or critical editions. The theory of such editions – the establishment of the composer's 'intentions' and their representation in as unencumbered a way as possible, with editorial intervention scrupulously distinguished as such – is (as we have seen) a will-o'-the-wisp. That no-one can know the composer's intentions, however complete and legible the sources may be, and that in any case intelligent musicians will disagree on how to render such intentions as may be ascertained, does not lessen the scholar's responsibility for providing better editions. Candour, however, demands the admission that even the very best recent editions will, in time, be found to embody the tastes and prejudices of their own times. Yet the distance often claimed to exist between so-called practical or performing editions and so-called scholarly or 'Urtext' ones shrinks in the face of the modern attitude to performance of early music as a speculative act of artistic, historical recreation. Increasingly, students, amateurs and professionals prefer not to have layers of interpretation placed between them and the music they try to understand; all are best served by scholarly editions with full, honest notes revealing the relationship of the edition to the sources, as well as what is known and what is responsibly speculated about relevant performance practices.

In the Classical period, soloists maintained the prerogatives of earlier periods to embellish, sometimes floridly, the music they performed. For the modern performer to recapture such freedom requires immersion in the music of the period, in order to have quantities of appropriate ornamental figurations in the ears and fingers (or throat) and to learn to avoid anachronisms. If the ornaments are to be something more interesting and more stylish than simple scales connecting melody notes, a firm harmonic grounding is essential. Helpful models are found in editions and manuscripts of the period in which the ornaments or variations of composers or of distinguished performers are preserved. Many arias and keyboard works as well as some songs and instrumental solos survive in ornamented versions, and some have been published in facsimile or modern editions.[8] The publication of more such examples of ornamentation is an important desideratum for an understanding of performance practices of the period.

Even with a first-rate edition in hand the question remains as to whether we can read the notation correctly. The amount by which a dot after a note lengthens it varies from one context to another. The instruments intended to be used for the line of a score labelled 'basso' depend on a number of circumstances. The 'missing' viola parts of Austrian church music may be missing only because we do not know how to derive them from the bass line. How often and in what style should cadenzas appear in concertos, arias or other genres? Should orchestral music as well as solo music be ornamented? Which notes should be stressed and which not? How long should notes be sustained? Such questions, which may be crucial to stylish performance, are rarely answered directly by the notation and must be investigated by other means.[9]

Treatises

The quantum leap in published music represented an attempt to satisfy the demands of a greatly expanded concert life and a steadily growing number of middle-class amateurs and connoisseurs, who wished to play and sing for their own edification or to have their children taught to do so. The increasing number of books of musical instruction were destined for the same consumers. Many of these books are rudimentary and of limited use to modern performers; others are detailed and even profound and, read carefully, of inestimable value towards the understanding of musical performance of the period. While no single book conveys all that one might like to know, the best of them taken together represent a vast body of information which has yet to be fully studied and evaluated.

The period begins with three major treatises representing mid-18th-century practice. Although the books by Quantz, C. P. E. Bach and Leopold Mozart deal ostensibly with the flute, keyboard and violin respectively, each covers many other aspects of musical practice. These works were widely read, reprinted, commented on, translated and plagiarized throughout the period; when the ten-year-old Czerny was brought by his father to Beethoven for lessons in 1801, Beethoven immediately dispatched them to purchase Bach's treatise (presumably the revised edition, completed just before Bach's death in 1788).[10] Marpurg's keyboard treatise has less authority than Bach's and is in any case heavily indebted to François Couperin's harpsichord treatise of half a century before.[11] One particularly thorough treatise on keyboard playing by an exact contemporary of Mozart's is Daniel Gottlob Türk's *Clavierschule*, which in effect updates Bach's treatise to the 1780s.[12]

Given the central position of Italian music in Europe, it is regrettable that the few Italian writings on music are relatively little known. The most important of them, with encyclopedic tendencies similar to those of Quantz, Bach and Mozart, is Francesco Galeazzi's *Elementi teorico-pratici di musica*, which while emphasizing violin playing deals with all of musical practice.[13] If Türk updates Bach and Galeazzi updates Mozart, then the flute treatises of Tromlitz and Lorenzoni perform the same function for Quantz, while at the same time leaning heavily on him.[14]

The revival of period instruments and their playing techniques has arguably outstripped the revival of comparable styles of singing. There exist a small number of 18th- and early 19th-century singing manuals, mainly French and German but also including a few in English and Italian, which offer a rich lode of information. But no single book about singing had a currency equal to Bach's, Mozart's or Quantz's. Since most instrumental instruction books of the period give good singing as the model, and as good singing generally meant Italian *bel canto*, recapturing that tradition is a prime necessity for understanding the music of the period as a whole and for reviving a broad range of attractive vocal music now languishing in neglect and incomprehension. The simple texture of the arias in the seemingly endless operas that poured from the pens of Cimarosa, Jommelli, Paisiello, Sarti, Traetta and other successful Italian composers – performer-orientated rather than composer-orientated works[15] – not only left room for but required extraordinary voices capable of sustained cantabile, coloratura fireworks, and flexible ornamentation. In the absence of such voices, these works must remain puzzling to modern ears.

A key Italian treatise is Giambattista Mancini's *Riflessioni practiche sul canto figurato*, an authoritative singing method, which is to the Classical period what Tosi's method is to the late Baroque and García's to the Romantic.[16] A valuable work is by Porpora's pupil Domenico Corri, his *The Singer's Preceptor*.[17] Tosi, Mancini, Corri and García represent the *bel canto* school of singing as it evolved from generation to generation; the tradition as viewed from Germany is lucidly presented by Hiller.[18]

The beginning of the 19th century saw a new development: the appearance of a type of treatise meant to serve a new type of institution: the conservatory. The first modern conservatory – that is, excluding the much older charitable conservatories of Naples and Venice – was founded in Paris (1795), followed by those in Prague (1811), Vienna (1817), London (1822), Milan and Brussels (1824). Whereas the older books of musical instruction were largely aimed at educated amateurs and connoisseurs or provincial music masters, these new methods are systematic courses of study for aspiring professionals, in which mechanical training for virtuosos through exercises and studies largely replaces philosophy about musical rhetoric and the communication of emotion.[19]

A crucial aspect of performance style in the understanding of the notation of the period 1750–1830 is the length to which notes are to be held. Early in the period, C. P. E. Bach wrote that the normal length of notes with neither slurs nor staccato markings is half their notated value. In the 1780s Türk criticized this, claiming that the correct length was approximately three-quarters of the notated value. At the end of the century, Milchmeyer and Clementi could claim that, in the absence of staccato marks, notes should normally be held to their full value.[20] (The shift to legato was not just a function of the fact that Clementi thought in terms of an English action piano: Milchmeyer and others writing with the Viennese action in mind agreed with him.) This evolution from a more detached style of playing to a more legato one means that in music from the beginning of the period the slurs are the most important marks of articulation whereas in music from the end of the period the dots and strokes indicating detached playing have acquired that role.

Literary evidence

Treatises provide information about many aspects of performance, including types of instruments, playing techniques and vocal timbres, and unnotated, partially notated (in modern terms) or misnotated aspects of the music. For more information on such matters, and hints about the size and placement of forces as well as suitability of ambience and acoustic, one may turn to other prose writings, including archival documents, letters, diaries, memoirs, periodicals, dictionaries and the like. Many of these have been discussed in scholarly articles and some are available in modern editions.

The autobiographies of Grétry and Dittersdorf, for example, provide, embedded in material of primarily biographical and sociological interest, anecdotes establishing performance practices.[21] Many travellers kept diaries in which items of musical interest appear, but Burney's are unparalleled in richness, for Burney represented an almost modern consciousness: a musician-scholar trying to record for posterity what he saw and heard while collecting the materials for a history of music. And the portions of Burney's history dealing with the period that he witnessed personally, from Handel to Haydn, are replete with descriptions of good and bad performances.[22]

The correspondence of C. P. E. Bach, Gluck, Kraus, Haydn, Beethoven and the Mozart family, contains valuable information about performance, although Bach's and Haydn's less so than the others.[23] Because the Mozarts travelled extensively, they observed many of the important musicians and musical institutions of their day; this makes their letters invaluable to understanding musical performance of the period.

The most important music dictionaries are Rousseau's in 1768 and Koch's in 1802, with Meude-Monpas weakly filling the breech in 1787.[24] These contain indispensible performance-practice information, although (like all sources) each must be considered as a product of its time, place and author: Rousseau the French-speaking partisan of Italian music, embroiled in controversy and hating fugues and most French music; Meude-Monpas the outsider who embraced cosmopolitan French culture, and Koch the conservative, provincial German Kapellmeister looking backwards near the end of a tradition. Two other dictionaries containing important information are difficult of access. These are Johann Georg Sulzer's *Allgemeine Theorie der schönen Kunste*, with musical entries by J. A. P. Schulz and J. P. Kirnberger; and Abraham Rees's *Cyclopaedia* with musical entries by Charles Burney.[25]

Verbal documents of course require interpretation just as much as do musical ones. An 'objective' document may, for example, report that there were 99 persons on the musical payroll of the Archbishop of Salzburg; even if it contains no errors, it will not necessarily reveal by what system of rotation the musicians may have served, whether the list includes extras, retirees, apprentices or political appointments of persons incompetent to perform. Conversely, in poorer courts small groups of musicians were regularly supplemented by students, amateurs, town waits or military bandsmen, none of whom will necessarily appear on a musical payroll. In short, even with such archival documents, the day-to-day musical practice still remains to be established by supplementary evidence, which can be done in part for Salzburg in the 1770s with the assistance of remarks in Leopold Mozart's letters. But such letters themselves require close reading, as the Mozarts', like everyone else, had their prejudices and blind spots, and they had to reckon with the Salzburg censor, who opened and read their letters.[26]

The same amateurs, connoisseurs and professional musicians for whom music and music histories were published also purchased periodicals. Thought-provoking musical information is sometimes found in non-musical periodicals, for instance, the *Journal de Paris* and *Mercure de France* in France, the *Gentleman's Magazine* and *The Times* in England, or the *Wiener Zeitung* in Austria. Such publications frequently contain announcements for and reviews of concerts, operas and new publications of music, as well as various polemics about musical taste and technique, that reveal aspects of performance. The 18th century also saw the rise of music magazines, in which musical information similar to that found in general periodicals occurs in concentrated form. Among the most important of these are the *Journal de musique* (Paris, 1770–7), the *Magazin der Musik* (Hamburg and Copenhagen, 1783–9) and especially the *Allgemeine musikalische Zeitung* (Leipzig, from 1799). Information about repertory and personnel is found in almanacs published in many cities towards the end of each calendar year to summarize musical and theatrical events of the old year and to provide liturgical and civic calendars for the new one.[27] Finally, the minutes and publications of learned societies also contain a surprising amount of information about music, some of it bearing on performance.[28]

Iconography

Pictures of musical significance range from the small engraved detail in a treatise, showing how to hold an instrument, to the large canvas portraying an event of political significance in which musicians took part. Leaving aside the illustrations in treatises, most of the iconographic evidence that can be brought to bear on questions of performance was created in the first instance to satisfy artistic, social or political ends rather than to provide realistic documentation of musical practice. Thus, even beyond any shortcomings of observation or technique that may have led an artist into inaccuracies, there are distorting forces at work in visual representations parallel to those mentioned above apropos prose sources. If, for instance, an illustrator was attempting to suggest the wealth and power of a ruler, he may have increased the splendour of an occasion of state by adding a row or two of musicians to the orchestra. If he was ill informed about music, he may have sadly misrepresented the forms of instruments and the postures of the musicians. Then, many drawings and engravings of performances prove on examination to have a satirical intent and, as such, must contain deliberate exaggerations. Furthermore, a large number of pictures inhabit fictitious or symbolic worlds and are evidence only for the artists' imaginations or for older art they may have copied.

A number of representations of musical performances in homes or theatres can be shown to contain a kind of time-lapse: that is, the artist, having only one opportunity to capture all aspects of an occasion, would telescope some of its important moments into a single image. Thus the fact, often remarked, that in many pictures of salon concerts people appear to be talking during the performance of music must be interpreted in light of accounts of such occasions that report careful listening followed by discussion of the music's merits.

Despite these potential pitfalls, many pictures contain reliable information about performance conditions. The most important categories of pictures include technical drawings in treatises, the collegium musicum concert (up to about 1770 only), opera performances, salon and other house concerts, official representations of occasions of state (such as celebrations of births of heirs to the throne, royal weddings, coronations and military victories) and portraits of music-loving families. Conspicuous by their rarity are pictures of public concerts, which were apparently considered less prestigious or less visually appealing than the other musical activities just mentioned. The rise of pictures of concerts coincides with the rise of the illustrated daily press, which does not belong to this period.

Rehearsal by a collegium musicum for the performance of a cantata 'Lobet ihr Knechte des Herrn': painting (c1775) from a family album in the Germanisches National museum, Nuremberg: the disposition of the musicians around the harpsichord illustrates the late Baroque placement

A number of illustrated histories, specialized monographs, dictionaries and encyclopedias of music and histories of specific instruments have made available a broad selection of illustrative materials.[29] An international effort is under way to collect, evaluate and catalogue pictures of musical interest.[30] The pictorial biographies of Haydn, Mozart and Beethoven, however, are for the most part devoid of pictures of music-making and provide almost no help in performing practice.[31] The often-reproduced painting of 'Haydn' leading an opera performance at 'Eszterháza' is mislabelled; it has no demonstrable connection with either Haydn or Eszterháza, although – unlike a number of 19th-century forgeries that have recently been given wide circulation by authors and publishers who should know better – it is a genuine 18th-century representation of a performance, perhaps at a small German court opera house.[32]

Society and venues

During the Classical period, churches in general gradually abdicated their traditional roles as leading patrons of new music. Although the masses of Haydn and Mozart were genuine liturgical music, in spite of complaints that they were too secular in character, some of the important sacred music of the period (for instance, Gossec's *Requiem* and Beethoven *Missa solemnis*) was a kind of religious concert music meant for ceremonial entertainment on occasions of state or for Lent and other times of year when opera was forbidden. In Austria, the Josephan reforms put an end to much concerted church music; there and elsewhere an assault upon the sources of the Catholic Church's wealth, which resulted from sweeping secularization in some countries, the Revolution in France and the Napoleonic reforms in countries he conquered, closed down or impoverished many ecclesiastical establishments that had long sustained concerted church music. Where such music was maintained, it often included not only mass and motet settings but sonatas, concertos, symphonies and sometimes even opera overtures and arias.

Although an increase in the number of public concerts and a gradual change in the status of the symphony from minor genre to major are evident as the period progressed, in many places opera houses maintained their primacy as the musical venues that enjoyed the most publicity, prestige and money. Towards the end of the period, *opera sèria* and *opera buffa* were giving way as distinct categories; and the vast enlargements of opera houses and the extension of opera seasons show opera to have enjoyed a kind of popularity that may be difficult to imagine nowadays. For most of the Classical period, however, the majority of theatres (and concert halls) were more modest in size, with audiences close to performers; this favoured a musical style that required a more agile, more nuanced and more articulate delivery than the delivery later developed for the music of Romantic opera, conceived for much larger auditoriums.

Public concerts rose as private and court orchestras declined. Large-scale concerts, whether public or private, usually had mixed programmes of orchestral (and sometimes choral) music and vocal and instrumental solos, especially arias and concertos. They were seldom devoted to a single performing medium or genre. Recitals in the modern sense were virtually unknown. Such programme planning would have seemed bizarre to music lovers of the period; modern programmes too might benefit from this catholicity. Chamber music and solo keyboard music, sometimes heard within large-scale concerts, formed, along with many kinds of songs, the backbone of domestic music-making. The private concerts held in middle- and upper-class homes could, at their best, be social-artistic events of real stature for which, for instance, the lieder and chamber music of the Viennese Classics written after 1780 was conceived.

Musical direction

At the beginning of the Classical period leadership from the harpsichord was the commonest form of musical direction for opera and some concerts, although the role of the leading violinist or concertmaster was always important and, in many concerts, more so than the keyboard player's. While continuo playing continued in some repertories and at certain institutions into the 19th century, long after bass lines had lost their tell-tale figures, the general decline in the need for continuo accompaniment brought with it a gradual demise of the keyboard director and the rise of the violinist director in his place. The forerunners of our baton conductors were the early 19th-century violin leaders who stood at the front of an orchestra or in an opera pit, violin in hand, and played less and less often while conducting more and more with their bows. The genres which clung longest to the keyboard continuo were choral church music (Bruckner's early masses still call for organ continuo); piano concertos, in which playing continuo in the tuttis was a form of conducting (and still required in all the concertos of Beethoven and Hummel, and probably of Mendelssohn and Chopin as well); and at least some portions of opera as long as *secco* recitative was still in use (*Il barbiere di Siviglia*, 1816, was Rossini's last opera requiring continuo).

Large-scale concerted church music and French opera long had their own traditions of direction. In church music, the coordination of instrumental groups, organs, vocal soloists and choirs, sometimes separated by considerable distances, demanded coordinating visual signals; the Renaissance practice of beating the tactus with a scroll of music paper was still followed in the Classical period for church music and oratorio. In French opera a 'time-beater' stood in the centre of the orchestra pit at the front edge of the stage with his back to the orchestra, beating time with a stick, apparently tapping it on the stage or music stand to create an audible as well as visual signal during the dances and choruses (but presumably not during recitatives and airs). This noisy practice, which so surprised foreign visitors to the Paris Opéra and the French court, is not mentioned after 1789. The best study of the direction and functioning of orchestras in concerts, theatres and churches remains Adam Carse's.[33]

In physics there is a well established way of working called the iterative solution. It consists of a series of ever-more-accurate approximations, employed for certain calculations that can never be definitively solved. Such approximations have been shown to yield results fully adequate to scientific

Concert in the home of the Countess of St Brisson, 1773: engraving by Augustin de St Aubin after Antoine Jean Duclos

progress. The same may be said of efforts to revive the performance practices of the Classical period: improved editions and greater knowledge of performing conditions enable thoughtful musicians to create performances ever closer to those of which the composers of the music might have approved. Such performances can be fully satisfactory both historically and musically without ever attaining the elusive and necessarily hypothetical goal of replicating performances of two centuries ago.

Notes

[1] For discussions of the advantages and disadvantages of a historically-informed approach to music, see N. Kenyon, ed., *Authenticity and Early Music* (Oxford, 1988).

[2] F. Blume, 'Musical Scholarship Today', in B. S. Brook, E. O. D. Downes and S. van Solkema, eds., *Perspectives in Musicology* (New York, 1972), 15–31, especially p.20.

[3] For a listing of *Gesamtausgaben* and other 'monumental' editions, see 'Editions, historical', *Grove 6*.

[4] See H. Albrecht, ed., *Die Bedeutung der Zeichen Keil, Strich und Punkt bei Mozart* (Kassel, 1957).

[5] R. D. Riggs, *Articulation in Mozart's and Beethoven's Sonatas for Piano and Violin* (diss., Harvard U., 1987).

[6] Clementi, *Collected Works* (Leipzig, 1803–19/R, 1973); J. L. Dussek, *Collected Works* (Leipzig, 1813–17/R, 1978); N. Temperley, ed., *The London Pianoforte School 1766–1860* (New York, 1984–7); H. M. Brown, ed., *Italian Opera, 1640–1770* (New York, 1977–83); D. Berg ed., *The Collected Works for Solo Keyboard by Carl Philipp Emanuel Bach* (New York, 1985); E. Warburton, ed., *The Collected Works of Johann Christian Bach* (New York, 1984).

[7] B. S. Brook, ed., *The Symphony 1720–1840*, 60 vols. (New York, 1979–86).

[8] Some are to be found in H. P. Schmitz, *Die Kunst der Verzierung im 18. Jahrhundert* (Kassel, 1955), and F. Neumann, *Ornamentation and Improvisation in Mozart* (Princeton, 1986).

[9] Answers to some of these questions are attempted in: G. Beechey, 'Rhythmic Interpretation: Mozart, Beethoven, Schubert and Schumann', *MR* (1972), xxxiii, 233–48; J. Webster, 'Violoncello and Double Bass in the Chamber Music of Haydn and his Viennese Contemporaries 1750–1780', *JAMS* (1976), xxix, 413–38; idem, 'The Bass Part in Haydn's Early String Quartets', *MQ* (1977), lxiii, 390–424; idem, 'The Scoring of Mozart's Chamber Music for Strings', in *Music in the Classic Period: Essays in Honor of Barry S. Brook*, ed A. Atlas (New York, 1985), 259–96; L. F. Ferguson, 'The Classical Keyboard Concerto', *EM*, xii (1984), 437–45; B. B. Mather, *Free Ornamentation in Woodwind Music* (New York, 1976); J. Spitzer and N. Zaslaw, 'Improvised Ornamentation in Eighteenth-Century Orchestra', *JAMS*, xxxix (1986), 524–77.

[10] C. P. E. Bach, *Versuch Über die wahre Art das Clavier zu spielen* (Berlin, 1753–62/R1957), trans. W. J. Mitchell as *Essays on the True Art of Playing Keyboard Instruments* (New York, 1949); J. J. Quantz, *Versuch einer Anweisung die Flöte traversiere zu spielen* (Berlin, 1752, 3/1789, R1952), trans. E. Reilly as *On Playing the Flute* (London, 1966); L. Mozart, *Versuch einer gründlichen Violinschule* (Augsburg, 1756/R1956), trans. E. Knocker as *A Treatise on the Fundamental Principles of Violin Playing* (Oxford, 1948).

[11] F. W. Marpurg, *Anleitung zum Clavierspielen* (Berlin, 1765/R1969), trans. E. L. Hays (Ann Arbor, 1985); F. Couperin, *L'art de toucher le clavecin* (Paris, 1716, 2/1717/R1969), trans. M. Robert (Leipzig, 1933).

[12] D. G. Turk, *Clavierschule: oder, Anweisung zum Clavierspielen für Lehrer und Lernende mit kritischen Anmerkungen* (Leipzig, 1789/R1962), trans. R. Haggh (Lincoln, Nebraska, 1982). Useful studies of the performance of the keyboard music of the central Classical composers are E. and P. Badura-Skoda, *Mozart-Interpretation* (Vienna and Stuttgart, 1957; Eng. trans. as *Interpreting Mozart on the Keyboard*, 1962, 2/1986); A. P. Brown, *Joseph Haydn's Keyboard Music: Sources and Style* (Bloomington, 1986); L. Somfai, *Joseph Haydn zongoraszonátái* (Budapest, 1979); K. Drake, *The Sonatas of Beethoven as he Played and Taught them* (Cincinnati, 1972); W. S. Newman, *Beethoven on Beethoven: Playing his Piano Music his Way* (New York, 1988); and C. Czerny, *On the Proper Performance of all Beethoven's Works for the Piano*, ed. F. Badura-Skoda (Vienna, 1970). The technique of the Classical period is surveyed in S. Rosenblum, *Performance Practices in Classical Piano Music: their Principles and Application* (Bloomington, 1988).

[13] F. Galeazzi, *Elementi teorico-practici di musica con un saggio sopra l'arte di suonare il violino analizzata, ed a dimonstrabili principi ridotta* (Rome, 1791). Violin tutors of the period are usefully summarized in R. Stowell, *Violin Technique and Performance Practice in the Late Eighteenth and Early Nineteenth Centuries* (Cambridge, 1985), which serves as a kind of sequel to D. Boyden, *The History of the Violin, from its Origins to 1761* (Oxford, 1965).

[14] J. G. Tromitz, *Ausführlicher und gründlicher Unterricht die Flöte zu Spielen* (Leipzig, 1791/ *R*1973); idem, *Uber die Flöten mit mehrern Klappen* (Leipzig, 1800/*R*1973); A. Lorenzoni, *Saggio per ben sonare il flauto traverso* (Vicenza, 1779).

[15] D. Libby, 'Italy: Two Opera Centres', in *Man and Music: the Classical Era* ed. N. Zaslaw and S. Sadie (London, 1989), chap.2.

[16] G. B. Mancini, *Riflessioni pratiche sul canto figurato* (Milan, 3/1777), trans. E. Foreman (Champaign, 1967); P. F. Tosi, *Opinione de' cantori antichi e moderni* (Bologna, 1723/*R*1968), trans. J. E. Galliard (London, 1742/*R*1987); M. Garcia, *Traité complet de l'art du chant* (Paris, 1847/*R*1985), trans. A. Garcia (London, 1924).

[17] D. Corri, *The Singer's Preceptor* (London, 1810/*R*1968 in E. Foreman, ed., *The Porpora Tradition*).

[18] J. A. Hiller, *Anweisung zum musikalisch-zierlichen Gesange* (Leipzig, 1780/*R*1976). For a bold attempt to explain bel canto technique, see L. Manén, *Bel Canto: The teaching of the Classical Italian Song-schools, its Decline and Restoration* (Oxford, 1987).

[19] F. J. Garnier, *Méthode raisonnée pour le hautbois* (Paris, *c*1798); L. Cherubini, *Solfège contenant des leçons* (Paris, 1799); J. X. Lefèvre, *Méthode de clarinette ... adoptée pour le Conservatoire* (Paris, 1802); L. Adam, *Méthode de piano du Conservatoire* (Paris, 1802, 2/1805); L. Cherubini, F. J. Gossec and E.-N. Méhul, *Méthode de chant* (Paris, *c*1802–3); E. Ozi, *Nouvelle Méthode de bassoon adoptée par le Conservatoire* (Paris, 1803); P. M. F. de S. Baillot, P. Rode and R. Kreutzer, *Méthode de violon* (Paris, 1803); J. L. Duport, *Essai sur le doigté du violoncelle, et sur la conduite de l'archet* (Paris, *c*1806); H. Domnich, *Méthode de premier et de second cor* (Paris, 1807). All *R*1974. Facs. of Garnier with trans. by P. Hedrick (Columbus, 1987). F. Devienne, *Nouvelle méthode théorique et pratique pour la flute* (Paris, 1794/*R*1984).

[20] M. Clementi, *Introduction to the Art of Playing on the Piano Forte* (London, 1801/*R*1974); J. P. Milchmeyer, *Die wahre Art das Pianoforte zu spielen* (Dresden, 1797).

[21] A. E. M. Grétry, *Mémoires, ou Essais sur la musique* (Paris, 1789–97/*R*1973); C. Ditters von Dittersdorf, *Lebensbeschreibung, seinem Sohne in die Feder diktiert* (Leipzig, 1801/*R*1967), trans. A. Coleridge (London, 1896/*R*1970).

[22] C. Burney, *The Present State of Music in France and Italy* (London, 1773/*R*1969); *The Present State of Music in Germany, the Netherlands, and United Provinces* (London, 1775/*R*1969).

[23] E. Suchalla, ed., *Briefe von Carl Philipp Emanuel Bach an Johann Cottlob Immanuel Breitkopf und Johann Nikolaus Forkel* (Tutzing, 1985); H. and E. H. Mueller von Asow, eds., *The Collected Correspondence and Papers of Christoph Willibald Gluck*, trans. S. Thomson (London, 1962); I. Leux-Heuschen, ed., *Joseph Martin Kraus in seinen Briefen* (Stockholm, 1978); W. A. Bauer, O. E. Deutsch and J. H. Eibl, eds., *Mozart; Briefe und Aufzeichnungen* (Kassel, 1962–75), trans. E. Anderson, *The Letters of Mozart and his Family* (London, 1938, 3/1985); E. Kastner and J. Kapp, eds., *Ludwig van Beethovens sämtliche Briefe* (Leipzig, 1923), trans. E. Anderson, *The Letters of Beethoven* (London, 1961).

[24] J.-J. Rousseau, *Dictionnaire de musique* (Paris, 1768/*R*1969), trans. W. Waring (London, 1779/*R*1975); J. J. O. de Meude-Monpas, *Dictionnaire de musique* (Paris, 1787/*R*1978); H. C. Koch, *Musikalisches Lexikon* (Frankfurt, 1802). See further J. Coover, *Music Lexicography* (Carlisle, PA, 3/1971).

[25] J. G. Sulzer, *Allgemeine Theorie der schönen Künste* (Leipzig, 1771–4); A. Rees, ed., *The Cyclopaedia; or, Universal Dictionary of Arts, Sciences, and Literature* (London, 1802–20).

[26] For the Mozarts' letters, see n.27; for Leopold Mozart's report, see 'Nachricht von dem gegenwärtigen Zustande der Musik Sr. Hochfürstlichen Onaden des Erzbischoffs zu Salzburg im Jahr 1757', in F. W. Marpurg, ed., *Historisch-Kritische Beyträge zur Aufnahme der Musik* (Berlin, 1757), iii, 183–98, trans. N. Zaslaw in *Mozart's Symphonies: Context, Performance Practice, Reception* (Oxford, 1989), Appendix A; E. Hintermaier, *Die Salzburger Hofkapelle von 1700 bis 1806: Organisation und Personal* (diss., U. of Salzburg, 1972); C. H. Mahling, 'Mozart und die Orchesterpraxis seiner Zeit', *MJb 1967*, 229–43.

[27] *Almanach musical* (Paris, 1775–83/*R*1972); *Calendrier musical universel* (Paris, 1788–9/ *R*1972); *Musikalischer Almanach für Deutschland*, ed. J. N. Forkel (Leipzig, 1781–8/*R*1974).

[28] A. Cohen, *Music in the French Royal Academy of Sciences* (Princeton, 1981); L. Miller and A. Cohen, *Music in the Royal Society of London, 1680–1806* (Detroit, 1987).

[29] Notably the *Musikgeschichte in Bildern* series: H. W. Schwab, *Konzert: Offentliche Musikdarbeitung vpm 17. bis 19. Jahrhundert* (Leipzig, 1971); H. C. Wolff; *Oper: Szene und Darstellung von 1600 bis 1900* (Leipzig, 1968).

[30] *Repertoire international d'iconographie musicale* (RIdIM).

[31] O. E. Deutsch, *Mozart and his World in Contemporary Pictures* (Kassel, 1961); L. Somfai, *Joseph Haydn: a Life in Contemporary pictures* (London, 1969); R. Petzoldt, *Ludwig van Beethoven* (Leipzig, 1976).

[32] L. Somfai, *Haydn: a Life*, 63, 229.

[33] A. Carse, *The Orchestra in the XVIIIth Century* (Cambridge, 1940/R1969). See also N. Zaslaw, 'Toward the Revival of the Classical Orchestra', *PRMA*, ciii (1976–7), 158–87, repr. in E. Rosand, ed., *The Garland Library of the History of Western Music* (New York, 1986), vii, 274–305; L. F. Ferguson, *Col Basso and Generalbass in Mozart's Keyboard Concertos: Notation, Performance Theory, and Practice* (diss., Princeton U., 1983); D. J. Koury, *Orchestral Performance Practices in the Nineteenth Century* (Ann Arbor, 1986).

CHAPTER XI

Keyboards

MALCOLM BILSON

Although harpsichords and clavichords were still very much in evidence during the latter part of the 18th century, this was the era of the emergence of the piano. The new instrument seems to date back to the 1690s, when Bartolomeo Cristofori built his first 'gravicembalo col piano e forte'. During the early 18th century many attempts were made in various parts of Europe to build pianofortes, but they do not seem to have challenged the supremacy of the harpsichord as the ideal concert keyboard, or the clavichord as the supreme instrument of personal expression, before the final third of the century.

It is difficult to ascertain how many pianos were in use during the first five or six decades of the 18th century. Incidents involving pianos are recorded in contemporary sources, but these may be more (or less) isolated than we may think given that nomenclature was often inexact. Giustini's *Sonate da cimbalo di piano e forte*, where there are dynamic markings in the score, are doubtless genuine piano pieces; these were published in 1732. The earliest public concerts on the pianoforte are generally thought to be those given by Johann Christian Bach in London during 1767 and 1768 (probably playing on a square piano by Zumpe). But there is evidence that one Johann Baptist Schmid was paid for a 'Concert auf dem Fortepiano' at the Burgtheater in Vienna as early as 1763.[1] It must be borne in mind, however, that the early piano was not only in name a 'gravicembalo col piano e forte'; harpsichord and piano were by no means as different as we think of them today. To the 18th-century musician they were but two versions of the same instrument, and they were no doubt often interchangeable. A few instruments survive with both mechanisms; one can simply 'shift gears' and go from harpsichord to piano, or vice versa. A further barrier to our clear understanding is the fact that the harpsichord, the piano and the clavichord were called by a variety of names, many of them ambiguous.

There are differences, nevertheless, between the early piano and the harpsichord, and these differences are reflected both in the diversity of the instruments that were built and in the variety of the music being written. The clear advantage of the piano over the harpsichord is its dynamic flexibility, but the very first pianos do not seem to have been able to compete with harpsichords for power and projection. It is likely that they simply did not sound as good; after all, harpsichords had existed and had been developed over some 300 years, while the piano was new. It is in fact harder to make a piano sound well; in a harpsichord the strings are lightly stretched over a rather delicate bridge and a thin soundboard, and they are plucked: such a mechanism can give enormous resonance from a minimum of input. A similar light-stringing method will not, however, support the blow of a piano's hammer; the string will flex like a rubber band. For strings to accept such a blow they must be thicker and must be pulled to greater tension over a heavier bridge and soundboard, such reinforcements were found to be injurious to the quality and quantity of tone produced. Furthermore, the geometry of a reliable piano action is very much more complicated and problematic than one for a harpsichord. All these problems were overcome, as we shall see, in the 1770s.

Several attempts have been made, particularly for the keyboard music of Haydn, to ascertain just which sonatas were primarily intended for which instrument. Beginning in the early 1780s, Haydn inserted dynamic markings into his scores, but a great deal of his keyboard music may nevertheless be played to good effect on the harpsichord. The Mozart sonatas, on the other hand, with the exception of some of the very early ones, are conceived in a musical language that is fundamentally inimical to the harpsichord. One must obviously look at the designation of instrument on the title-page, but even when this derives from the composer it does not necessarily indicate the best possible solution.

The music of Johann Schobert, for example, a German composer living in Paris at the time of the seven-year-old Mozart's visit to that city, shows a kind of lyricism and *galanterie* far better suited to the aesthetics of the new piano than the harpsichord. In the extract from a piano quartet given in ex.1,

Ex.1 Schobert: Quartet in E♭ major (1770), 1st movt, 2nd theme

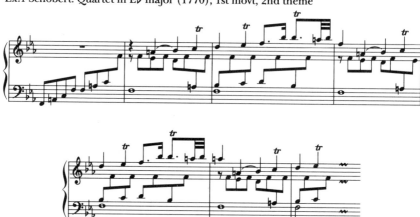

the ability to shape the melody of the right hand, and to play the left hand at a softer volume, make this passage, although playable on a harpsichord, more successful on a fortepiano; in spite of the fact that the title-page clearly states 'pour le claveçin avec accompagnements de deux violons et basse ad libitum'. (Here the string parts provide a simple harmonic background.)

It is clear that as Haydn's style evolved his interest in the fortepiano increased. In October 1788 he requested advance payment on a set of piano trios from the publisher Artaria in Vienna in order to purchase a fortepiano, and in 1790 he wrote to Marianne von Genzinger, to whom he had dedicated his Sonata in E♭ H xvi:49:

> I thought your Grace might turn over your still tolerable Flügel [i.e. harpsichord] to Fräulein Peperl and buy a new fortepiano...I know I ought to have composed this sonata for the capabilities of your instrument, but I find this difficult because I am no longer used to writing in that way.[2]

It is interesting to note that while Haydn's advance in keyboard style and idiom, from the modest divertimentos of the 1760s to the last three masterpieces written in London during 1794, shows the most acute awareness of possibilities of every new instrument, harpsichord-inspired material is always present (ex.2): note the *sforzando* octave in the bass, at *. Even

Ex.2 Haydn: Sonata in A♭ major, H XVI: 46 (1771), 1st movt, bars 49–51

Haydn's last sonata (in E♭ H vi:52), whose full opening chords are clearly conceived with the massive-sounding Broadwood pianos that he encountered in London in mind, still contains brilliant passage-work based on the harpsichord idiom (exx.3 and 4).

Ex.3 Haydn: Sonata in E♭ major, H XVI: 52 (1794), 1st movt, opening

Nevertheless, one cannot underestimate the importance of the fact that these instruments (and even occasionally the organ), were used interchangeably. When Mozart and his sister played his two-piano concerto K365 on two harpsichords in Salzburg, where no fortepianos were available, it was

Ex.4 Haydn: Sonata in E♭ major, H XVI: 52, 3rd movt, bars 65–70

perhaps not ideal, but the difference was not as great as a modern pianist would encounter when confronted with a harpsichord instead of a Bechstein. Tone-volume, touch and general aesthetics were far closer between the contemporary instruments.

Cristofori's pianos have not been seriously considered by revivers of early pianos, possibly because the repertory that would spur interest in them is lacking. However, they are remarkable; the action is extremely sophisticated (see fig.1*a*) and already possess the essential attributes of Erard's 19th-century action, with the exception of the double escapement feature. But the real emergence of the piano as a serious rival to the harpsichord must be placed in the 1770s, when the two most important builders of classical prototypes emerged: Johann Andreas Stein in Augsburg and John Broadwood in London, (see figs.1*b* and *c*). The difference between these two mechanisms, and the pianos in which they were housed, is the difference between two quite different philosophies of piano building which were to last a hundred years. It is reflected not only in the music of Haydn, Mozart and Beethoven, as opposed to the music of Field, Dussek, Cramer and Clementi, but also in the music of Brahms and Schumann as opposed to that of Chopin and Liszt: two different mechanisms for two different musical aesthetics.

The Viennese action or *Prellmechanik* ('flipping action', as Stein's mechanism and its later versions were called), is descended from the so-called 'primitive German' action in which each hammer is attached directly to the key. When the player depresses the key, the beak is caught under the escapement lever and causes the hammer to rise. When the hammer nears the string, the escapement lever trips back and the hammer returns to the key bed. The advantage of this mechanism is its extreme tactile sensitivity; the player is always in direct contact with the hammer. In the English action (from which the modern action is derived), the hopper pushes up the rear of the hammer until the set-off creates the escapement and the hammer returns. This is referred to as *Stossmechanik* ('pushing action'). Here the hammer is much further removed from the player's finger and the key-dip is greater and heavier, but more power is available and a fuller tone can be achieved than by *Prellmechanik*.

In addition to these mechanical differences, the English pianos were more massively built, and were triple strung quite early, whereas Viennese pianos were built more lightly and double strung at least two-thirds of the way up their five-octave range. The English pianos were louder and fuller, the Viennese clearer and cleaner and somewhat thinner in sound. A telling difference between the two was their method of damping. Whereas Viennese

(a)

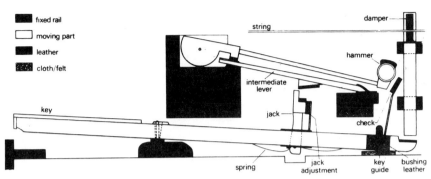

- ■ fixed rail
- □ moving part
- ■ leather
- ▨ cloth/felt

damper
string
hammer
intermediate lever
key
jack
check
spring
jack adjustment
key guide
bushing leather

(b)

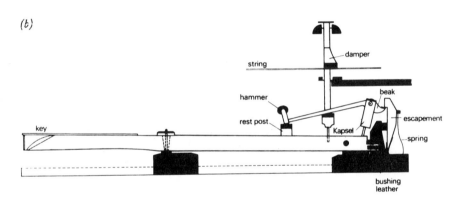

damper
string
hammer
beak
rest post
escapement
key
Kapsel
spring
bushing leather

(c)

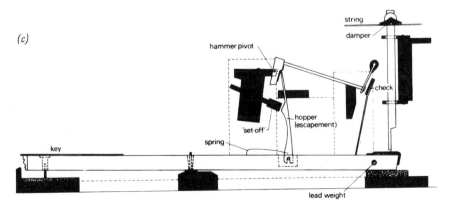

string
damper
hammer pivot
check
hopper (escapement)
'set off'
spring
key
lead weight

1 Actions of (a) a piano by Bartolomeo Cristofori, Florence, 1726 (Musikinstrumenten-museum, Karl-Marx-Universität, Leipzig); (b) a Heilman piano of c1785 showing the Prellmechanik (Viennese action) with escapement, believed to have been first used by Stein, from a Heilman piano of c1785 (private collection); and (c) an English grand piano by Broadwood, 1799 (Royal College of Music, London)

pianos had leather dampers for lightning-quick damping (quicker even than the felt dampers on modern pianos), English pianos had 'feather-duster' dampers that sat lightly on the strings and damped only modestly, leaving a long after-ring. In addition, English pianos boasted damper and shift pedals as early as the 1770s, whereas the Viennese pianos had knee levers for raising the dampers in most cases. Mozart's own concert instrument, built in about 1780 by Anton Walter and now in the Mozart Geburtshaus in Salzburg, seems to have had hand stops originally only for lifting the dampers – the knee levers were clearly added later to work the stops with the knee. (Could Mozart have bought the instrument and then asked for the knee levers to be added?)

What kinds of musical aesthetic do these two types of instrument represent? Are these merely different construction techniques, or is a different kind of musical expression involved?

In one of the most important and widely-read German treatises of the time, Daniel Gottlob Türk tells us:

> When notes are to be played in the usual manner, that is to say, neither staccato nor legato, the finger should be raised from the key a little earlier than the value of the note requires. If certain notes are to be held their full value, a *ten.* or *tenuto* is written over the note.[3]

Muzio Clementi, on the other hand, tells us:

> The best general rule, is to keep down the keys of the instrument, the FULL LENGTH of every note...When the composer leaves the LEGATO, and STACCATO to the performer's taste, the best rule is, to adhere chiefly to the LEGATO; reserving the STACCATO to give SPIRIT occasionally to certain passages, and to set off the HIGHER BEAUTIES of the LEGATO.[4]

The difference between these two approaches is striking. Sometimes a movement in a keyboard sonata by Mozart may have not a single dynamic mark, yet not one phrase of his music is ever without articulation slurs. Even in such works as operas and piano concertos, where he often sketched out first the treble line and the bass, leaving the rest to be filled in later, these slurs are ubiquitous. And the pianos being built in south Germany and Vienna were instruments that could readily realize this sort of musical aesthetic. With their small wooden hammers (occasionally round and hollow) covered with leather, the attack was immediate, and the 'singing' part of the tone set in only after a quick but pronounced decay. In addition, damping was instantaneous to permit the kind of articulation required by this 'speaking' aesthetic. The notion that music is like speech, and that it 'speaks' as one uses a language, means that clarity of meaning is achieved only through the proper use of inflection. In any language certain parts of speech are to be stressed, while others are to be virtually swallowed up (in English, for example, the only acceptable pronunciation of 'the house' is 'th' house' – 'thee house' would betray a foreigner). In the music of Mozart, Haydn and other Viennese composers, the slurs show an inflected group of notes; the treatises of the time tell us what they mean and how to execute them in terms of stressed and unstressed syllables. In ex.5 Türk would instruct us that each of the first three bars must be inflected to give what they would have referred to in the late 18th century as a 'sigh', with the third beat

Ex.5 Mozart: Sonata in F major, K332, 1st movt, opening

of each bar shorter and weaker than the first. Bar 4 also has a sigh, from f'' to e'', but it is ornamented (two quavers and a crotchet rather than two slurred crotchets); thus e'' must likewise be played softer and somewhat shorter. In ex.6 the first three notes are indicated by Mozart to be played detached, with

Ex.6 Mozart: Piano Concerto in A major, K488, 2nd movt, opening

emphasis on the first beat; beat four is somewhat less emphasized than beat one, but slurred through to beat six; in bar 2 the first beat is stressed and slurred to the second, which is detached (once again, a 'sigh') etc.

Such articulations as are shown in these two examples are rarely if ever heard in modern performance, and yet are at the very heart of the expressiveness of these passages. On a late 18th-century Viennese piano these come out easily and naturally; the slow development of tone of the modern piano makes them extremely difficult to realize.

The composers of the 'London Pianoforte School', and the piano builders in London in the late 18th century, on the other hand, seemed to strive for a quite different sort of musical language: one in which everything is done to 'set off the HIGHER BEAUTIES of the LEGATO'. Concentration here is on that very middle-of-the-tone, with heavier stringing, bigger and softer hammers with more layers of leather, and dampers that damped as gently as possible. The long slurs in ex.7 in fact conceal everthing Türk's admonitions would have the player bring out. This is a language that is not predicated on speech; indeed, it is one in which stress and release are deliberately

Ex.7 Clementi: Sonata in F major, op.33 no.2, 1st movt, bars 29–34

Ex.8 Dussek: Fantasy and Fugue in F minor, op.55, 2nd section

obfuscated. Dussek, it was said, put the pedal down at the beginning of the concert and took it up at the end. Thus a passage such as ex.8, written in 1804 and conceived for the full sound of the English pianos, would be pedalled throughout for as rich a tone as possible. There are no slurs here, but it is inconceivable that Dussek means to have each note played detached; the language is so far removed from that of C. P. E. Bach and Türk that even long slurs would be superfluous.

It may seem to us now, with hindsight, that the future lay with the London school of piano playing and that the Viennese Classicists, including in many respects, Beethoven, were relatively conservative and somewhat old-fashioned. It is however remarkable that Brahms, even in his very last piano works, written at the end of the 19th century, still used slurs to denote small groups of notes joined together in a tradition going directly back to Mozart, Haydn and Schubert (ex.9).

Ex.9 Brahms: Intermezzo, op.119 no.1, opening

Both the Viennese and the English pianos of the late 18th century differ from the modern piano in a number of ways. It seems clear that the Steinway firm was following the Anglo-French tradition when it invented, or rather compiled, the modern piano in the 1860s (Broadwood→Erard→Steinway is a very rough simplification). Several aspects of the modern piano make it unsuitable for the music of Clementi and Cramer, the most essential being the cross-stringing. In all modern pianos the bass strings cross the tenor strings, giving an extremely powerful but muddy bass. Many heavy chords which sound well on a Broadwood or Clementi piano acquire a thickness and turgidity on the modern piano that changes their character considerably. Furthermore, the composers of the London Pianoforte School used the pedals very sensually; the modern piano, with its greatly increased resonance, tends to change many long pedal marks of these composers from a gossamer veil into a smeary mush. The situation is more severe, however, with regard to the Viennese composers. Small inflections such as those in ex.5 above are simply not possible on a modern piano; the tone develops so slowly that to play the third beat of those first three bars softer and shorter results in a sort of hiccup. Anyone who has played or heard Mozart's keyboard music on a modern piano must have a somewhat distorted idea of the language, so at variance is it with the qualities of the later instrument.

But it is perhaps Beethoven's music that suffers the most when performed on the modern piano. One of the main reasons for this is that as well as a lack of articulation, virtually all performances on modern pianos are sorely lacking in the strong metric pulse considered of prime importance in all 18th-century treatises. Beethoven himself, in his annotations of the Cramer études for his nephew Karl, stresses metrical accent almost above any other performance consideration. The opening bars of the 'Waldstein' Sonata demand a rhythmic pulse and inflection without which the meaning of the passage seems very obscure. On a modern piano this is virtually impossible: the crossed strings blur the texture, the tone develops too slowly and the felt dampers are too smooth. What should be perceived as pup–pup–pup–pup–pup–pup–pup etc is reduced to buh–buh–buh–buh–buh–buh–buh.

One of the main expressive ingredients of Beethoven, and one taken most seriously by the best pianists today, is the *sforzando*. But the modern piano, with its great middle-of-the-tone, has no real *sforzando*; it has only loud notes. It is well recognized that the *fp* at the beginning of the *Pathétique* is problematic on a modern piano; indeed, there seems no adequate way to play it. (The main 'message' is the rapid decay of the first chord before proceeding.) But there are other passages equally dramatic not generally perceived by pianists. The *sforzandi* on *g♭"* in ex.10 are sharp accents, heightening the tension of the Allegro molto e con brio. Most modern performances barely pay lip service to these accents in order to preserve the

Ex.10 Beethoven: Sonata in C minor, *Pathétique*, op.13, 1st movt, 2nd theme

dynamic *piano*. When a modern pianist does make an accent, the result is a kind of swell (the short hairpin markings in parentheses are by the author), giving the entire passage a kind of 'heaving' quality which, though not at all unmusical, transforms the character from a heightened drama to a contrasting, more 'feminine' theme.

In ex.11a the first chord is not connected by a slur to the three following ones; hence there is no difficulty in perceiving each of the notes as *forte*. In ex.11b, however, there is a slur between the first two notes, this time *fffp*; a

Ex.11 Beethoven: Sonata in D major, op.10 no.3, 2nd movt

radical diminuendo is called for, one that will probably make the first chord last somewhat longer than a dotted quaver would warrant. Again, the rapid decay is the main expressive element; in performances on modern instruments one merely hears one loud note followed by three soft ones.

Similar misconceptions can occur for other reasons. The principal idea of the *perpetuum mobile* movement in ex.12 is the running semiquavers in the right hand at the beginning of the movement. (This is, incidentally, related to the main material of the first movement, a simple arpeggiation of a tonic chord.) These continuous running semiquavers are transferred to the left hand for the second theme (from bar 21). On a Viennese fortepiano they are perfectly lively and clear; the right-hand melody wavers unsteadily above them, and the main affect of the movement, one of breathless agitation, is increased. On a modern piano the left-hand semiquavers are in a murky register of the instrument; they are invariably underplayed, as a sort of background to the right-hand melody which is always given a kind of pathos.

Ex.12 Beethoven: Sonata in C# minor, op.27 no.2, 3rd movt
(a) bars 1–2

(b) bars 21–3

21

As was the case with the second theme of the *Pathétique*, this may be convincing musically, but it transforms Beethoven's intention of increased tension to one of clear contrast. The reader may object to the word 'invariably', but in over a dozen recordings of each of these pieces it has been impossible to find a performance on a modern piano that brings out what is surely there and what a sensitive 18th-century musician would have readily seen.

As we have seen, English pianos had pedals as early as the 1770s (a damper-raising pedal attached to the right front leg with a true una corda on the left). Viennese instruments usually but not always had knee levers for the damper-raising, and sometimes a moderator or celeste-stop (a cloth strip brought between hammer and string to create a special soft effect) operated by either hand or knee. There are no surviving Viennese five-octave pianos with pedals. After about 1800 both the English and the Viennese instruments expanded to six and six and a half octaves; the pedals on the English instruments are removed to a pedal lyre at the centre, in modern fashion, and on the Viennese pianos additional ones appear. Of primary interest here, however, is the question of just how much the damper pedal may have been used by either school of the 18th century. Pedal indications are grievously lacking before 1800, save in the music of certain Kleinmeister, but some inferences can be made on the basis of the instruments and the repertory. It seems clear that the English school strove for long lines and a full, even 'hazy' sound; this is easily seen by examining the music and the instruments. English pianos have poor damping at best, and the early adoption of pedals can only be a sign of striving for full resonance. The Viennese, on the other hand, did not adopt pedals, and used highly efficient dampers to cut off the tone quickly, right to the top of the keyboard. The abundance of small slurs in the Viennese repertory points to a desire for clarity and inflection between the tones that seems to be lacking in the piano music of the London school composers, and for which the English instruments were ill-suited.

The question of pedal usage in the Viennese repertory is the one least

likely ever to be conclusively solved. C. P. E. Bach, Mozart and Haydn did
not write pedal marks in their music (the 'Open Pedal' in the first edition of
Haydn's 'London' Sonata in C, H xvi:50 is a special case, and the meaning of
that nomenclature, if indeed it does stem from Haydn, is anything but clear).
C. P. E. Bach, in the second volume of his *Versuch über die Wahre Art das
Clavier zu spielen*, which appeared in 1762, states that

> the clavichord and the fortepiano are the most comfortable instruments on
> which to improvise free fantasies...The undamped register of the
> fortepiano is most pleasing, and if one but knows how to carefully control
> the after-ring, the most attractive of all in improvisation.[5]

One can imagine Bach playing a passage such as ex.13 completely un-
damped (the pedal indications in parentheses are by the author).

Ex.13 C.P.E. Bach: Fantasy in C major, bars 81–6

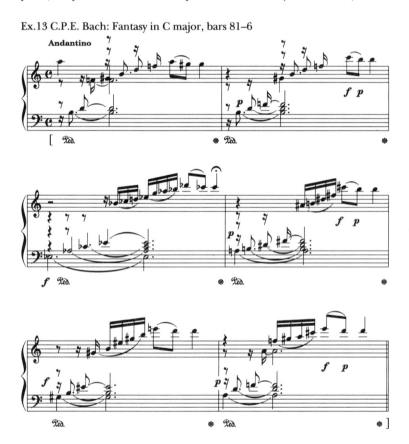

The sources that do speak of pedalling reveal that the dampers are to be
raised in 'harmonious passages', and whereas most of Mozart's keyboard
music is so carefully articulated by the composer that the raising of dampers
interferes with the music rather than enhances it, passages such as exx.14
and 15 may well have been quite heavily pedalled. The only passage in all
Mozart's keyboard music that cannot be played without the aid of a damper-

Ex.14 Mozart: Fantasy in D minor, K397, opening

Ex.15 Mozart: Concerto in C major, K467, 2nd movt, bars 23–6

Ex.16 Mozart: Sonata in D major, K311, 2nd movt, bars 86–93

raising device is the final bars of the second movement of the D major Sonata κ311 (ex.16).

Beethoven presents a rather special problem in regard to pedalling. Beginning in op.26 we find the markings *senza sordino* and *con sordino* (dampers off, dampers on) and, from the 'Waldstein' onwards, the standard English 'Ped.' and '✳'. But we know from many contemporary accounts that

Beethoven, even in his youth, had pedalled heavily; indeed, he was often criticized for it as it ran against the Mozartian ideal of clarity and precision. Studies by both William S. Newman and John Henry van der Meer have shown that Beethoven's allegiance to the Viennese piano ideal never wavered[6] even though he owned an Erard and a Broadwood, both of them gifts from the makers. Nevertheless, Beethoven seems to have been very much influenced in his piano writing by Clementi, Dussek and Cramer, and much of his music strongly reflects this influence. A passage such as ex.17

Ex.17 Beethoven: Sonata in B♭ major, op.22, 2nd movt, opening

seems to have no precedent in Mozart or Haydn; it is pure 'London' thinking, and would sound best heavily pedalled as indicated. I would also balance the hands almost equally, so that the left hand, rhythmically pulsating, is almost the main ingredient; the right hand floats above it, giving a feeling of gentle, expressive longing. This pianistic language has disappeared from our concert stages and recording studios, and yet it was one of the most important languages of Romantic musical thought in the early 19th century.

As well as demonstrating the significance of the English damping system as opposed to the Viennese, ex.17 serves to refute a current misconception: that the piano progressed from a 'primitive' state in Mozart's day to a 'fully developed' one in Liszt's (in his later years Liszt owned both a Steinway and a Bechstein). When restorers began working on early English pianos they were perplexed by the fact that they could not make them damp very well; eventually it was surmised that perhaps the English pianos had in fact damped with the kind of efficiency we now expect. But at that very time the Viennese were making dampers that were more efficient than the felt dampers used today; the English must have been aware of such dampers and could have easily produced them.

Conversely, the Viennese builders cannot have been ignorant of the fact that the English put pedals on their pianos; the lack of pedals on the Viennese instruments must indicate that they were not needed. When the need was felt (after about 1800) virtually every Viennese builder incorporated pedals into his instruments. Indeed, they seem to have wanted to outdo their English counterparts in the number and diversity of pedals, for it is not uncommon to find a Viennese piano fitted with six or seven.

Finally mention must be made of one important feature common to all 18th-century keyboard instruments – harpsichord, clavichord and piano alike: the striving for a light and responsive action. Virtually every source on keyboard playing – whether François Couperin in 1716, C. P. E. Bach in 1753, Türk in 1789 or even Hummel as late as 1827 – recommends a quiet hand in which the fingers alone control all manner of sensitivity and nuance. Examination of 18th-century instruments shows how much care was taken to provide the lightest and quickest actions possible. Many of the best builders carved wood out of each key rather than add lead counterbalances, giving the keys a feeling of immediacy, lightness and promptitude. The English instruments, both harpsichords and pianos, are somewhat less light than their continental counterparts; yet in 1827 Hummel still advises a light and quiet hand for those pianos as well.

By the mid-19th century, however, the tendency towards the fuller, louder pianos with ever greater carrying power and greater 'middle-of-the-tone' was in evidence among both the English (actually now the French, centred in Paris with the firms of Pleyel and Erard) and the Viennese. A bigger tone from any keyboard instrument is inevitably accompanied by a deeper fall and heavier feel to the key – a bigger hammer is travelling a greater distance to strike a heavier string. This will demand a different kind of technique, requiring stronger musculature. Thus it is that Adolph Kullak, in 1876, can speak of seven different kinds of touch, the last being the use of the entire upper arm. In the 20th century several schools of piano playing have developed in which a combination of the usage of arm weight and rotation of the arm supplant the usage of fingers altogether, in so far as that is possible.

The effect of this change in playing style on the language of the music being expressed can hardly be exaggerated. We only have to imagine a light hand operating basically through *Fingerspitzengefühl* as opposed to one sinking to the bottom of a deep and heavy key (a Steinway is approximately twice as heavy and deep as a Stein) to understand that the expressive language will be markedly different. The development of pianos and piano playing in the 19th century is directly connected to the phenomenon of larger halls for bigger audiences, and just as an actor will change not only the loudness of his speech but the speed and the weight as well in response to a larger hall, so the sound and the feel of pianos changed to accommodate this 'bigger' aesthetic.

The questionable notion that piano technique 'developed' during the 19th century seems to be widely accepted. Virtually every book on piano playing written in the last hundred years advances the argument that Mozart and Clementi, as the first great piano virtuosos, merely adopted the existing harpsichord technique of a quiet hand, with finger movement alone doing the work; it was not until later in the 19th century, the argument continues, that the full use of the upper arm was 'discovered'. It is clear, however, that technique changed with the corresponding change in pianos. Liszt could do things technically that Mozart could not have done, but this is because the pianos of Liszt's day were quite unlike those of Mozart's. The piano has not developed since Liszt: it is doubtful whether Vladimir Horowitz or Sviatoslav Richter can do things that Liszt could not.

The relationship between the musical message and the feel of the keyboard is a subtle but important one for interpretation. When the firm of Pleyel began to build harpsichords again in the late 19th century they tried to incorporate all the 'improvements' made to the piano since 1780 into their instruments. This meant, among other things, giving them deep and wide piano keys to assure the 'solid' feel of the modern piano. This solid feel was still present in the far more historical harpsichords being built in the 1950s by Hubbard and Dowd and others. It was not until the 1960s that a light and shallow action was more or less universally recognized as being important to teach the player the musical language.

No builder, from Stein to Steinway, has ever changed his pianos very much. Johann Andreas Stein built the same instrument from the 1770s until he died in 1792; Conrad Graf's instruments hardly changed from 1810 to 1840, and the Steinway company, which designed its piano in the 1860s, has not changed the instrument to the present day. (In each case there were endless refinements, but the basic recipe continued unchanged.) This is significant, for it points much more to a sense of changing aesthetics than constant improvement. Piano aesthetics were different in 1780 between England and Vienna, and they were different in Vienna between 1780 and 1870. To try to recapture the 18th-century language with 19th- or 20th-century instruments is to find oneself misguided on a number of central aspects of the music, for instruments are always a guide to a particular and individual musical culture.

Notes

[1] E. Badura-Skoda, 'Prolegomena to a History of the Viennese Fortepiano', *Israel Studies in Musicology*, ii (Jerusalem, 1980), 78.
[2] *Joseph Haydn Gesammelte Briefe und Aufzeichnungen: unter Benützung der Quellensammlung von H. C. Robbins Landon*, ed. D. Bartha (Kassel, 1965), 242.
[3] D. G. Türk, *Clavierschule, oder Anweisung zum Clavierspielen für Lehrer und Lernende* (Leipzig, 1789/R1962), 356.
[4] M. Clementi, *Introduction to the Art of Playing on the Piano Forte* (London, 1801/R1974), 8.
[5] C. P. E. Bach, *Versuch über die wahre Art das Clavier zu spielen*, ii (Berlin, 1762/R1957), 327.
[6] W. S. Newman, 'Beethoven's Pianos versus his Piano Ideals', in *Performance Practices in Beethoven's Piano Sonatas* (New York, 1971), 34–43; J. H. van der Meer, 'Beethoven et le pianoforte', in *L'interprétation de la musique de Haydn à Schubert* (Paris, 1980), 67–85.

CHAPTER XII

Strings

ROBIN STOWELL

The Classical era was a transitional period in string playing. The musical pre-eminence of Italy was challenged by other countries, especially by France. French acceptance of Italian idioms, styles and forms initiated dramatic developments in string performance, and these were further encouraged by the flourishing concert activity and (most notably) by the Parisian début of Viotti (1782), who established the technical and stylistic principles of the 19th-century French violin school. Musical education prospered with the foundation of the Paris Conservatoire (1795), which prompted the establishment of similar institutions in other capitals by its unprecedented consistency of instrumental instruction and by the publication of tutors for most instruments. Larger concert venues were required to accommodate growing audiences and the consequent demand for greater volume, together with changes in musical taste, led to remarkable developments in the construction and playing technique of instruments.

Extra volume and brilliance were chiefly produced by the greater tensions on string instruments resulting from a slightly higher playing pitch, by the use of a taller, thinner and more sharply curved bridge, and by an increase in the playing length of the strings. A narrower, longer, canted neck was introduced, mortised into the top block and tilted back to achieve the required string tension and to allow the longer fingerboard to follow the angle of the strings. A longer, more substantial bass-bar was introduced to reinforce instruments against the additional string pressure and to perform its significant acoustical function, and the soundpost was thickened. The length of the violin body was standardized at about 35·5 cm and the cello at 75–6 cm, but the equivalent viola measurement could be between 38 and 45·5 cm, while double basses varied in shape and size, as well as in their string complement and their tuning.

Gut strings were still the most commonly employed, but the more reliable and brilliant metal-wound strings were increasingly used, where appropriate, towards the end of the 18th century. Nevertheless, the violin E and A and the viola A and D strings were commonly made of gut well into the 19th century; cellists, too, normally employed uncovered gut for the upper two and silver- or copper-wound gut for the lower two strings. String thicknesses varied according to pitch, instrument size, situation and national or individual tastes.

The size, shape, weight, balance and general construction of bows also varied during the 18th century. With the gradual fusion of national styles and the demand for increased tonal volume, for cantabile and for a wider dynamic range, longer (and hence heavier), straighter bows derived from Italian models became the vogue (although many Germans, and most bass players, kept faith with convex types). Such bows required modifications in the height and curvature of the pike's head to allow sufficient separation of hair and stick. When, during the Classical period, sticks adopted a concave *cambre*, the 'hatchet' head was introduced for optimum separation between hair and stick at the middle (e.g. the 'Cramer' model bows, fashionable *c*1772–92). By the Classical period, pernambuco wood was the most popular, although snakewood, brazil wood and plum wood were still employed, and hair tension was generally regulated by a screw-nut attachment.

Early 18th-century violin bow lengths could vary anywhere between 61 and 71 cm but François Tourte (*c*1785) standardized the bow's dimensions, weight,[1] materials and design, making the hatchet head higher and heavier and redressing the balance by adding metal inlays to the nut. He also pioneered changes in the treatment and arrangement of the hair; he endorsed the contemporary trend of increasing both the amount and the width of hair, keeping it flat and even by securing it at the frog with a ferrule (probably invented by Louis Tourte *père*). This ferrule was originally of tin but later of silver. A wooden wedge pressed the hair against the ferrule to prevent the latter from slipping away, and a mother-of-pearl slide concealed the hair-fastening. John Dodd made a similar synthesis at about the same time as Tourte.

These modifications afforded string instruments greater volume, focus and brilliance, but only at the expense of the overtone structure; thus some of the relaxed clarity of the Baroque string sound was sacrificed. Universal approval of the new designs was slowly won; converted and original instruments, Tourte model, transitional and Baroque bows co-existed in most orchestras and uniformity of bowing technique was rare. It was not until the *Méthode de violon* (1803) of Baillot, Rode and Kreutzer that bowing technique using the Tourte model was examined in detail, and the full potential of Tourte's synthesis was not exploited until *c*1810 when its inherent power, expressiveness, suitability for cantabile playing, elasticity and other qualities could be brought to bear on instruments which had been modified in accordance with similar ideals.

The violin's importance as a solo chamber instrument initially declined during the Classical period, with the vogue for the keyboard sonata with accompaniment, but was preserved by such instrumentalist-composers as Gaviniès, Guénin, Paisible and Saint-Georges in France, Nardini, Pugnani and Boccherini in Italy, Giardini, J. C. Bach and Abel in England, Dittersdorf and Wagenseil in Vienna, and Mysliveček in Bohemia, before blossoming with the sonatas of Mozart and Beethoven, in which the 'accompanist' attained parity with the accompanied. The viola had no such repertory, only the works of Carl and Anton Stamitz, J. G. Graun, J. G. Janitsch and William Flackton gained prominence. Modern scholarship has shown that the Classical cello repertory began long before Beethoven.[2] There is also a wealth of chamber music for myriad combinations employing the cello in something other than an accompanying (or continuo) capacity; this includes Boccherini's quintets and the vast string quartet corpus. In these and in particular in the mature chamber works of Haydn, Mozart and Beethoven, the cello and viola gradually gained comparable status with the violins. In the orchestra the viola acquired some measure of parity with the other string instruments, though it was rarely stretched technically.

While the piano superseded the violin as the dominant concerto instrument, the violin could nevertheless still boast numerous mainstream concerto composers such as Johann, Carl and Anton Stamitz, Haydn, Michael Haydn, Lolli, Giornovichi, Woldemar, Viotti, Mozart and Beethoven. The viola's concerto repertory is largely drawn from Mannheim (Carl and Anton Stamitz and Holzbauer), Berlin (Benda, Graun and Zelter) and Vienna (Dittersdorf, Druschetzky, Hoffstetter, Hoffmeister, Mozart, Vanhal and Wranitzky). Significant cello concertos were composed by C. P. E. Bach, Wagenseil, Monn, numerous members of the Mannheim school, Bréval, Duport, Boccherini and Haydn. The Austrian bass school was pre-eminent in the late 18th century and Vanhal, Zimmermann, Haydn, Hoffmeister, Sperger and Dittersdorf provided concertos for the instrument.

Most string instruction books were designed to complement individual tuition. Few were comprehensive. Leopold Mozart's *Versuch einer gründlichen Violinschule* (1756), in its various editions, remained the most important German violin treatise well into the 19th century, while Galeazzi's two-volume *Elementi teorico-pratici di musica* (1791–6) (arguably the most significant late 18th-century Italian source regarding improvised ornamentation), provides a wealth of general information concerning technique and interpretation. Furthermore, the introduction and first four parts of Campagnoli's *Metodo* (?1797), provide systematic instruction regarding the use of the 250 exercises in Part 5. The ascendancy of the French school is witnessed by the progressive technical instructions within *Principes du violon* (1761) by L'abbé le fils, whose amalgamation of national styles was furthered by Corrette and Cartier,[3] and culminated in the *Méthode de violon* (1803) by Baillot, Rode and Kreutzer. The later, and inevitably retrospective, treatises of Mazas, Baillot himself and Habeneck[4] are also in parts relevant to Classical performance practice; Habeneck's work incorporates facsimiles of extracts from Viotti's unfinished elementary method.

The earliest viola treatises,[5] which appeared in France towards the end of the 18th century, are of little pedagogical value, but they were soon followed by the more substantial methods of Bruni (c1805), Gebauer (c1800) and Martinn (c1815).[6] Corrette wrote one of the first instruction manuals for the cello (1741),[7] and for the double bass.[8] His most notable successors included Lanzetti (c1760), Tillière (1764), Robert Crome (1765), Cupis (c1772), Baumgartner (1774), Gunn (1789), Müntzberger (1800), Bideau (1802), Bréval (1804) and Baillot, Levasseur, Catel and Baudiot (1804).[9]

The treatises consistently emphasize the importance of a relaxed and natural bearing when holding the violin, but there was no general agreement on the precise position to be adopted; it varied between those at the breast, at the shoulder or at the neck (each of these was recommended with a different degree of support and with the chin position varying from one side of the tailpiece to the other). L'abbé le fils recommended resting the chin on the left of the tailpiece, thus implying the chin-braced grip that had formerly been employed only to stabilize the instrument during shifts.[10] This afforded firmer support for the instrument and enabled it to be held horizontally at shoulder height and directly in front of the player at almost 90°. This allowed optimum freedom of left-hand movement and flexibility of bowing.

The elbow was generally positioned well under the middle of the instrument, much closer to the body than with the modern method. The wrist was turned inwards to avoid contact between the palm and the violin neck; the latter was not allowed to sink into the hollow between the thumb and index finger. The thumb, occasionally employed in multiple stopping, assumed a position either 'opposite the A natural on the G string'[11] or, for greater freedom of action and facility in extensions, 'more forward towards the second and third fingers than backward towards the first without projecting too far over the fingerboard.[12] The 'Geminiani grip' (ex.1) remained the

Ex.1

guide to correct hand and finger placement in 1st position, the hand and fingers generally forming a curve with the fingers well over the strings. Each knuckle was bent so that the top joints of the fingers would fall straight down on to the strings from the same height.

The viola was held in a similar way, although its greater weight and size generally caused the scroll to be positioned lower and it demanded greater stretches and pressure from the fingers. The cello, without its long endpin, was normally positioned between the knees with its weight supported on the calves, but some soloists used short wooden endpins and others preferred to stand, supporting their instruments on a chair or foot-stool. The high position of the instrument afforded by both methods allowed the left hand to exploit the full range of the fingerboard more freely than before.

Unnecessary finger activity was avoided. According to Leopold Mozart,[13] necessity, convenience and elegance were the reasons for using positions other than the 1st. Modern half- and 2nd positions assumed greater importance and most advanced violin treatises incorporated position-work up to at least 7th position (some extended to 11th position and beyond in supplementary study material). However, excessively high position-work was not unanimously sanctioned during the period because clarity of fingering was invariably difficult to achieve with a short fingerboard. Shifts were generally made where musically acceptable: on the beat or on repeated notes (ex.2), by the phrase in sequences (ex.3), after an open string (ex.4), on a rest or pause between staccato notes or after a dotted figure where the bow was generally lifted off the string (ex.5). If possible, one position was chosen to accommodate an entire phrase and extensions and contractions were invariably used (but harmonics rarely so) to avoid or to facilitate shifts (ex.6). The mechanics of shifting are sparsely documented, but the role of the thumb in leading the hand smoothly through the lower positions before adopting a comfortable position either beneath the neck or on the rib of the instrument was consistently emphasized. Positions were then established with the first finger, both for reasons of convenience and for security of intonation.

Ex.2 L. Mozart

Ex.3 L. Mozart

half position   whole position   half

Ex.4 L. Mozart

Ex.5 L. Mozart

Ex.6 L'abbé *le fils*

Upward shifts generally caused few problems for violinists and violists; if anything, they increased the instrument's stability against the player's neck; downward shifts, particularly without a chin-braced grip, invariably required the left hand to crawl back 'caterpillar fashion' from the high positions by means of skilful manipulation of the thumb, index finger and wrist. Like Leopold Mozart, most writers advocate small upward shifts, using adjacent fingers (23–23 or 12–12), rather than the bold leaps prescribed by Geminiani, Tessarini and Corrette (ex.7), though this naturally depended

Ex.7 Corrette

on tempo considerations and the speed of passage-work. With the exception of Galeazzi, large leaps (4321–4321) were favoured in descending passages, whatever the speed.

The benefits of scale practice were not fully acknowledged until the second half of the 18th century, following the treatises of Geminiani and Leopold Mozart. Thereafter treatises invariably included scales for the cultivation of accurate intonation, finger independence, elasticity and agility, together with strong finger action for tonal clarity and many bowing disciplines. Most writers adopted Leopold Mozart's approach to chromatic scales, which involved different fingerings for those written in sharps from those written in flats (ex.8). Geminiani's fingering, which employs one finger for each note and open strings when necessary (ex.9), was largely ignored by his immediate successors, even though it undoubtedly offered greater evenness, articulation and clarity.

Ex.8 L. Mozart

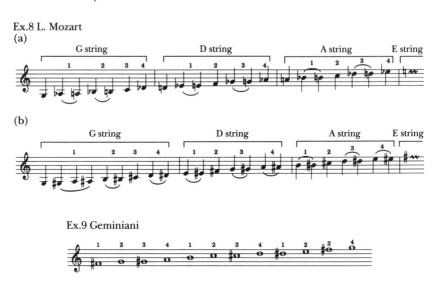

Ex.9 Geminiani

In the 18th century cello and bass fingering was derived from violin fingering with little consideration being given initially to the differences in size and playing position of these instruments. According to Corrette, the diatonic scale on all strings consisted of 1, 2 and 4 in the first two positions; 1, 2, 3 and 4 in the 3rd position; and 1, 2 and 3 in the 4th position. Chromatic fingerings also differed markedly from modern fingerings (ex.10), as did

Ex.10 Corrette

recommendations regarding shifting (ex.11); Corrette prefers the fingering shown in ex.11*b*). Thumb position was part of the mid-18th-century cellist's technique[14] (although Baumgartner prefers third finger extension to thumb

Ex.11 Corrette
(a)

(b)

position), but exploitation of double stopping and the higher registers was rare. However, John Gunn (1789), and cellists such as Cupis and Tillière, recognized the limitations of these fingerings and developed a system (eventually categorized by Duport in the early 19th century) which involved regular semitone intervals between one finger and the next, with the option of widening the interval between the first and second fingers to a tone. Initially, shifts were executed only with the first and fourth fingers, but the whole hand was eventually employed, shifting through three diatonic steps as appropriate.

There is conflicting evidence regarding the incidence of portamento when shifting. The systems described above rendered the use of portamento largely unnecessary; indeed, some writers reject it outright.[15] However, other sources, supported by certain notated fingerings (ex.12), suggest that

Ex.12 L. Mozart
(a)   (b)

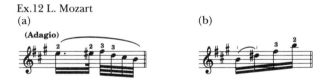

portamento was employed by some players, especially in solo contexts, either as part of the shift mechanism or as expressive devices.[16]

Although security of intonation was the prime consideration, performers began to cultivate uniformity of tone colour within the phrase. The higher positions were increasingly exploited for expressive purposes (Galeazzi provided violin G-string fingerings up to 8th position). Furthermore, sequences were played wherever possible with matching fingerings, bowings and string changes. Although open strings were sometimes necessarily employed in the execution of shifts, *bariolage*, double and multiple stopping, scordatura and suchlike, they were invariably avoided when stopped notes were technically viable: in descending scale passages involving more than one string (especially in slurred bowing), in trills (except in double trills where there is no alternative), appoggiaturas and other such ornaments and in most melodic or expressive contexts.

Despite Geminiani's exceptional recommendation of what was essentially a continuous vibrato in the approved modern fashion,[17] vibrato was generally used sparingly as an expressive ornament, particularly on long sustained or final notes in a phrase, at a speed appropriate to the music's dynamic, tempo and character. It doubtless had a more striking effect than the continuous variety practised today, even though the violin and viola vibrato movement, executed with the fingers and wrist but not with the lower arm, was necessarily somewhat narrower, tighter and less intense than its modern counterpart.

Although natural harmonics were exploited well before the Classical period, particularly in France (e.g. by Mondonville), their unanimous acceptance was slow owing to their 'inferior' tone quality.[18] The brief yet progressive survey by L'abbé *le fils* incorporates a minuet written entirely in harmonics (both natural and artificial), but it required virtuosos such as Jakob Scheller and Paganini to arouse public interest in harmonics and the techniques involved in their mastery.

Right-hand violin and viola pizzicato was executed either by adopting the normal violin hold and plucking with the index finger or by holding the instrument across the body and under the right arm, guitar-fashion, and plucking with the right-hand thumb. The thumb's fleshy pad proved ideal for sonorous arpeggiation of chords or for soft passages. Left-hand pizzicato, rarely used in the early 18th century, gradually became more popular and reached its zenith with Paganini and his successors.

Interest in the expressive potential of the bow, 'the soul of the instrument it touches' (according to L'abbé *le fils*), increased markedly. Vital to the fulfilment of such ideals was a natural and flexible bow hold. The close relationship between the manner of holding the violin (or viola) and the bow holds suggests that the right elbow was positioned close to but 'detached from the body' in a natural, unconstrained manner below the level of the bow stick.

Many factors influenced the bow grip of the mid-18th century: national style, musical demands, personal taste, the size of the hand and fingers and the balance (and hence the type) of the bow itself. The prevailing cantabile ideals and the increasing popularity of the sonata and concerto in France led to the demise of the thumb-under-hair 'French' grip in favour of the Italian method. Furthermore, L'abbé *le fils* implies that the hand was placed at the frog and not, as Geminiani, Corrette and Leopold Mozart had advised, slightly above it (*c*3–7 cm); Robert Crome clearly indicates the modern bow hold in his cello tutor (1765). The standardization of bow construction prompted a corresponding, if gradual, standardization of bow holds. Nevertheless, some cellists (notably J. G. C. Schetky) used the 'underhand' grip well into the 19th century and other performers, especially Germans, evidently held Tourte model bows in the 'old' manner some distance from the frog.

Contrary to modern practice, the thumb was kept fairly straight, allowing the bow to be gripped more securely without stiffness in the hand, fingers or wrist. Opinion varied regarding the thumb position, but normal practice was to place it opposite the second finger,[19] although positions between the index and second fingers, or between the second and third fingers, were also used.[20] The index finger was separated slightly from the others for the control of volume, by applying or releasing pressure as required (a manly tone was customary).[21] The second and third fingers, naturally rounded, merely rested on the stick, while the fourth finger aided balance when bowing in the lower half.

The recommendation of L'abbé *le fils* that the stick should be inclined slightly towards the fingerboard was endorsed by most of his successors, although some discouraged this practice, ostensibly because of its detrimental effect on tone quality. The fundamental short violin and viola bow stroke of the period was executed by only the wrist and forearm, but the upper arm and (in some cases) the shoulder were also brought into play for longer strokes; this upper-arm movement naturally was directed upwards and downwards but was never lateral. Suppleness of the wrist and fingers was thus of paramount importance (although no direct mention was made of the degree that the wrist should turn in towards the body). This was particularly important in the execution of smooth bow-changes and string crossing, for the natural stroke of most pre-Tourte bows was of an articulated, non-legato character (especially in the upper third). This was a direct consequence of their typical delayed attack (through only gradual take-up of hair), their lightness at the tip and because the early bow's balance point was closer to the hand. The player could vary the degree of articulation and modify the stroke by the application of nuances appropriate to the length of the note, tempo and the character of the music,[22] as well as by the regulation of bow speed, pressure and the point of contact (Leopold Mozart was the first to pinpoint the relationship between bow speed and volume). The *messa di voce* commonly adorned long notes, often with vibrato, and the so-called 'divisions' (the four types of nuanced bowings – crescendo, diminuendo, *messa di voce* and double *messa di voce* – categorized by Leopold Mozart[23] for the cultivation of tonal purity, variety of expression and mastery of bowing) were so much accepted practice that sustained strokes without nuance were exceptions rather than the rule.

The theory of terraced dynamics was relevant to string performance only for eçho effects, and the wide dynamic variation employed by, for example, the Mannheim orchestra more closely approximated to late 18th-century expressive practice. Furthermore, performing directions were more copiously and explicitly annotated in the late 18th century and the introduction of gerund forms into verbal indications[24] possibly implies an increasing vogue for more gradual modifications of tempo and expression, or at least a desire to systematize such gradations. Unlike modern staccato, the 18th-century staccato stroke[25] involved a 'breath' or articulation between notes somewhat greater than the articulation of the typical separate stroke. This articulation was invariably conveyed by lifting the bow from the string after each stroke, especially in slow tempos, and implied the use of a dry, detached stroke in the lower part of the bow, with some feeling of accent although not comparable to the sharp attack of the modern staccato. In fast movements, the bow necessarily remained on the string in the upper half, producing an effect similar to modern spiccato.

Few pre-Tourte bows were suited to such accented bowings as *martelé* or such effects as *sforzando*; these were used only rarely in the modern sense during the 18th century. However, such 'bounding' strokes as *sautillé*, spiccato and 'flying staccato' were occasionally employed in bravura passages. True legato bowing was achieved only by slurring. The capacity of the slur was enlarged substantially and slurred bowings (whether or not so notated) were increasingly exploited in the Classical period as a means of emulating the qualities of the human voice, especially in slow movements.

The execution of slurred staccato, confused somewhat by the variety and ambiguity of notation, was necessarily governed by the music's tempo and character. Dots above or under the notes in slow movements normally indicated an on-the-string execution rather like a portato; strokes above or under the notes were more common in faster tempos and generally indicated playing in 'lifted' style,[26] brief passages being executed in either up- or down-bow but longer passages normally being taken in the up-bow (ex.13).

The so-called 'Viotti' bowing (ex.14), the slurred tremolo and the portato strokes are all related to the slurred staccato. However the slurred tremolo (ex.15), the execution of repeated notes on the same string under one slur,

Ex.13 L. Mozart

down   up

Ex.14 Woldemar

Ex.15 Bailleux

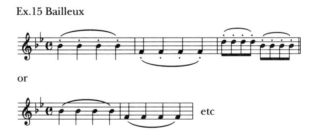

or

etc

was played either staccato (normally indicated by dots or strokes under a slur) or legato (implied by a slur alone). The expressive portato stroke, its articulations generally indicated by dots or lines above or under the slur, was mainly confined to slower tempos. *Bariolage*, the alternation of notes on adjacent strings (one of which is usually open) in either separate or, more usually, slurred bowing (ex.16), and *ondeggiando* (ex.17) (similar to the slurred *bariolage* but with a potential range over more than two strings), were also part of the Classical string player's bowing repertory. Furthermore,

248

Ex.16 L'abbé *le fils*

Ex.17 Gaviniès

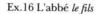

separate and slurred bowings could be mixed, especially in passages of double stopping, providing the performer with remarkable scope for flexibility and variety of bowing.

These bow-strokes represent merely a point of departure for the appreciation of an expanding and developing 18th-century technique, as some transitional bows were capable of all but matching the repertory of the Tourte model. The advent of the Tourte bow shifted the emphasis away from the articulated strokes, subtle nuances and delayed attack of most mid-18th-century models to a more sonorous cantabile style, with the added capability of a more or less immediate attack, *sforzando* effects and accented bowings and various 'bounding' strokes (spiccato, *sautillé*, ricochet etc.).

Phrasing, generally considered analogous to punctuation marks in language or breathing in singing, was given increased textual exposure, although few composers notated the balanced, complementary phrasing of the Classical period (the four-bar phrase formula was the most common) in their works. Nuances were applied (whether notated or not) to establish the 'peaks' and general contours of phrases, as well as their expressive content, and were also freely employed to highlight certain dissonances, ornaments, chromatic notes, cadences (especially interrupted cadences), *roulades* and suchlike.[27]

Bow apportionment according to tempo, the number of notes per stroke and their respective dynamic, value and accentuation, assumed greater significance, as did the prolongation of important notes within the phrase (for example, the first note of a phrase, a note that is longer or markedly higher or lower than its predecessor and dissonant notes within the phrase). The traditional rule of down-bow, which required rhythmically stressed notes to be played with the stronger down-bow and the unaccented beats with the weaker up-bow, still generally applied (although not so rigidly to the cello), especially in France and Germany. Furthermore, a flexible approach to dotted rhythms was characteristic of the 18th-century style (particularly in France), the dotted note invariably being lengthened and its complementary note shortened (ex.18) and played in lifted style.[28]

Polyphony was notated ambiguously throughout the period to clarify both the musical progression and the melodic and harmonic functions of the voice parts. Chords were spread either upwards or downwards, usually according to the register of the main melody note to be sustained (ex.19*a*), or played as arpeggios (ex.19*b*). Rapid upward spreading was the more common practice; this was generally taken in the down-bow (even successions of chords which

Ex.18 L. Mozart

(a)

down   up

At the dot the bow is lifted.

(b)

down   up

After the dot, the note following
it is long delayed.

Ex.19   (a)   (b)

etc

involved retaking the bow). Most players evidently held the lowest note a
little,[29] presumably to emphasize the harmonic progression, before sounding
the other chord members in a rapid cross-string movement.

Notes

[1] The bows were standardized as follows: violin, $c74$–5 cm and $c56$–60 g; viola, $c74$ cm and $c64$–
74 g; cello, $c72$–3 cm and 75 g.

[2] See for example the numerous works revived by Nona Pyron and published by Grancino
International; see also E. Cowling, *The Cello* (London, 1975).

[3] M. Corrette, *L'art de se perfectionner dans le violon* (Paris, 1782); J. B. Cartier, *L'art du violon*
(Paris, 1798, enlarged 3/1803/R1973).

[4] J. F. Mazas, *Méthode de violon* (Paris, 1830); P. Baillot, *L'art du violon* (Paris, 1834); F.
Habeneck, *Méthode théorique et pratique de violon* (Paris, c1840).

[5] M. Corrette, *Méthodes pour apprendre à jouer de la contre-basse à 3, à 4 et à 5 cordes, de la quinte
ou alto et de la viole d'Orphée nouvel instrument ajusté sur l'ancienne viole* (Paris, 1773).

[6] A. B. Bruni, *Méthode d'alto* (Paris, c1805); M. J. Gebauer, *Méthode d'alto* (Paris, c1800); J.J. B.
Martinn, *Méthode d'alto* (Paris, c1815).

[7] M. Corrette, *Méthode, théorique et pratique, pour apprendre en peu de tems le violoncelle dans sa
perfection* (Paris, 1741).

[8] see n.5.

[9] S. Lanzetti, *Principes du doigter pour le violoncelle dans tous les tons* (Amsterdam, c1760); J.B.
Tillière, *Méthode pour le violoncelle* (Paris, 1764); R. Crome, *The Compleat Tutor for the
Violoncello* (London, 1765); J.-B. Cupis, *Méthode nouvelle et raisonnée pour apprendre à jouer du
violoncelle* (Paris c1772); J. B. Baumgartner, *Instruction de musique théorique et pratique à l'usage
du violoncelle* (The Hague, 1774); J. Gunn, *The Theory and Practice of Fingering the Violoncello*
(London, 1789); J. Müntzberger, *Nouvelle méthode pour le violoncelle* (Paris, 1800); D. Bideau,
Grande et nouvelle méthode raisonnée pour le violoncelle (Paris, 1802); J.-B. Bréval, *Méthode
raisonnée de violoncelle* (Paris, 1804); P. Baillot, J. H. Levasseur, C.-S. Catel and C. N. Baudiot,
Méthode de violoncelle (Paris, 1804).

[10] J. J. Prinner, *Musicalischer Schlissl* (1677), is well in advance of its time in suggesting a chin-
braced grip.

[11] L'abbé *le fils*, *Principes du violon* (Paris, 1761/R1961), 1.

[12] L. Mozart, *Versuch einer gründlichen Violinschule* (Augsburg, 1756, enlarged 3/1787/R1956),
54.

[13] Mozart, *Violinschule*, 148.

[14] Corrette, *Méthode théorique et pratique*, describes the 4th position as 'thumb position' and
implies that some used the first finger instead of the thumb as a support.

[15] For example, B. Campagnoli, *Metodo* (?1797; Eng. trans., 1824), pt.iii, no.188.

[16] For example, J. Reichardt, *Ueber die Pflichten des Ripien-Violinisten* (Berlin and Leipzig,
1776), 35.

[17] F. Geminiani, *The Art of Playing on the Violin* (London, 1751), 8.

[18] See Mozart, *Violinschule*, 101.

[19] L'abbé *le fils*, *Principes*, 1.

[20] See J. B. Cartier, *L'art*, pt. i, art.6, p.1, and Baillot, *L'art*, 12.

[21] Mozart, *Violinschule*, 101.

[22] See Mozart, *Violinschule*, 262; J. J. Quantz, *Versuch einer Anweisung die Flöte traversiere zu spielen* (Berlin, 1752/R1952; Eng. trans., 1966), 239.

[23] Mozart, *Violinschule*, 102–5. These divisions were retained by early 19th-century writers and applied to Tourte model bows.

[24] 'Tempo and Expression Marks', *Grove MI*, iii, 562.

[25] Called *détaché* by many French writers, but this should not be confused with the use of the same term, from the early 19th century onwards, to describe a smooth, separate on-the-string stroke.

[26] D. Boyden, *The History of Violin Playing from its Origins to 1761* (London, 1965), 416.

[27] For example, the relevant dissonance might be stressed or even swelled and the resolution relaxed by means of a decrescendo.

[28] Mozart, *Violinschule*, chap.vii, sec.ii, paras.2, 3 and 4.

[29] Some went as far as holding it for almost its full value.

CHAPTER XIII

Woodwind and Brass

DAVID CHARLTON

The flute

Although the one-keyed conical flute remained in use throughout the Classical period, it is not appropriate for the modern player to employ it for all music up to, say, 1825. Yet the alternatives are also problematic. Pioneers of new keys were widely active by the 1780s, and three English makers had been adding keys for G$\sharp$, B♭ and F for 20 years before that.[1] About 1774 they added a foot joint for c' and $c\sharp'$. Mozart used these notes in his Concerto for Flute and Harp (1778); a six-keyed flute was heard publicly in Paris in 1781.[2] Some makers added b and $b♭$ during Beethoven's lifetime.

The eight-keyed flute was to become a quite long-lived system. It incorporated a closed c'' key, initially described by J.J.H. Ribock (1782), and a long duplicate F key. This existed from 1783 in Lüneburg and was publicized by Tromlitz (1785). The eight keys were thus D$\sharp$, two Fs, G$\sharp$, B♭, c'', with the foot joint c' and $c\sharp'$. Many mechanical 'improvements' flooded the markets of Europe from 1800 of which the most significant were perhaps the enlarging of the note holes in England, and the later inventions of Pottgiesser; he adjusted the position and size of the note holes and developed uses for that vital novelty, the ring-key (1824), which affected all woodwind.

None of these inventions, as Nancy Toff has pointed out, obviated the differences in tone quality inherent in flutes of the period.[3] Moreover, practical difficulties multiply for the modern player who uses the new keys. The flute's physical balance can be awkward, especially with a metal-lined head joint, and the position and technique of using the keys can seem almost to defeat the object of having them. The player cannot always rely on the mature 'roundness' of the Baroque flute and has to work to overcome problems of tone, especially low in the compass.

IDEALS OF TONE Writers up to about 1800 tend to accept a limitation of up to three sharps and two flats for flute music. For pre-classical France the information of De Lusse (c1760) is vital; that of Ribock (1782) concerning embouchure, bore, materials and keys is also generally available. In his extraordinary treatise of 1791, Tromlitz (whose work remains to be fully evaluated)[4] states that evenness of tone, in all keys and from note to note, with a 'bright, singing quality', was chiefly desirable; he describes certain scales in detail (chap.6). Devienne (1794, p.1)[5] disapproves of certain 'hard

252

sounds played strongly on low notes' like an oboe[6] as well as the tonal harm caused by the English foot joint. But he thought added keys very necessary in slow music on held notes like $g\sharp'$ or $b\flat'$. Hugot and Wunderlich (1804) gave
seven justifications for the four-keyed flute, stressing a new taste for strength: although 'essentiellement doux' the flute legitimately expressed 'un éclat, une force, une rondeur'; the same expressive range was mentioned by Fröhlich (1810–11).[7] By 1815 Nicholson[8] was advocating 'firm and brilliant Tone' as one of the first acquisitions of a player, plus 'varied modulation of tone' (p.3). A valuable account of the skills of Nicholson, Drouet, Rudall, Tulou, Berbiguier and others appears in James (1826, pp.153ff).[9]

ARTICULATION Flute tutors from Tromlitz (1791) to Berbiguier (?1818) make it plain that players were to apply varied and tasteful patterns of articulation to what they played. 'The principal point consists of knowing when to use [different patterns] with effect, and to be capable of choosing the different tonguing applicable to such a passage, in preference to another.'[10] Tromlitz (1791, pp.197–204) gives ten model versions of a two-bar phrase; though he counsels care in adhering to the composer's *Gedanken*, he also desires some variation within the spirit of the piece. But the vast extent of Tromlitz's exposition of tonguing syllables, which he conceived of as imitating the singer's art, implies that the modern player should study a rhetorical approach to interpretation (cf Schindler's account of Beethoven's similar approach). The syllables were adopted by Fröhlich (1810–11); the account by Warner can only be a beginning for the serious student.[11]

18th-century double tonguing is mentioned in the second of Catherine Smith's useful articles[12] but there is still much to be discovered; indeed, this was a controversial aspect of flute playing at the time. However, a continuity of technique ('tootle/tad'll') extends from Corrette (1740–41) through Tromlitz (1791), Wragg (1806), Fröhlich (1810–11) and Nicholson (1815), while Berbiguier (?1818) gives 'dou-gue'. Devienne (1794) and James (1826) rejected it altogether.

SPECIAL EFFECTS, VIBRATO AND EXPRESSION Emulation of string portamento was characteristic of some Classical flute playing, called by Tromlitz 'das Durchziehen' and by the English, 'glide'. Tromlitz prescribed it 'very seldom'; one suitable juncture was the lead-back to the refrain in a rondo (ex.1). Wragg (1818 edn.) recommended it strongly as 'being so much used

Ex.1 Tromlitz (1791), p.265

by the most celebrated Masters of the present day'; its purpose was a 'soft and soothing' blend from one note to another, achieved by sliding one or more fingers gradually on or off the hole. Glides were sometimes notated with a crescent moon sign and could cover different intervals[13] (see ex.2).

Finger vibrato continued in use throughout the period, called 'Bebung',

Ex.2 Nicholson (1815), p.39: from Duetto XXIII

'Vibration' or 'Sweetning'. Like Quantz, many Classical tutors prescribed vibrato in association with *messa di voce* as a standard ornament. Now, however, the swell typically covered a phrase of one or two bars' length. De Lusse (c1760) stands alone: although he used finger vibrato (sign: ƒ) his more normal vibrato was the 'tremblement flexible' (sign: ⌇) wherein the left-hand thumb 'rolled' the flute.[14] De Lusse also specified breath vibrato as an effective resource, done by pronouncing 'hou, hou' through exhalation. Associated with this was De Lusse's 'tac aspiré', notated, ƒƒƒƒ pronounced 'hu, hu', and confined to slow music. Moens-Haenen associates this practice with the typically Italian *tremulant/tremolo*. Although Tromlitz and Fröhlich rejected it, she finds a 'growing tendency for breath vibrato to replace finger vibrato' during the 18th century (p.55). The Vibration (sign: ⌇) was described by Nicholson (1815) as simultaneous finger vibrato with 'a regular swell and modulation of the breath ... exhaustion or panting with a regular decrease or diminution of the Tone' (p.22). Wragg (1818)[15] limits Vibration to occasional use in slow movements for 'much pathos and feeling' (p.67). The problem is judging whether to use it in French or Austro-German scores; their tutors ignore it.

The oboe

The two-keyed oboe was almost universal up to about 1800, but national variations in design existed. Some English and German instruments had a tapering of the bore.[16] Eight new keys were sporadically added to the oboe to c1825, though these were not used by all professionals (A. G. Vogt in Paris was content with four keys). Yet an eleven- and a nine-keyed oboe were procured for the Vienna Hoftheater in 1807–8.[17] Garnier (c1802) describes only the two-keyed oboe.

Oboe tone is crucially linked to reed design (see below) and it is thus impossible to reconstruct timbres on a historical basis. But the oboist using a two-keyed instrument is aware that $f\#'$, bb'' and $b\natural'$ were acknowledged as out of tune and that $c\#'$ was problematic. Choice of fingering is consequently a vital consideration. Bruce Haynes points to anachronistic modern fingerings adapted for $f\#'$, bb'', $b\natural''$ and c'''.[18] Tutors before 1800 counsel avoidance of E and even A major; the eb' key compromised between $d\#'$ and eb. One player's recent experiences of various tuning problems have been usefully described.[19]

Not until c1800, at a time when the oboe's range was extending upwards, was the left-thumb 'speaker' key added. By 1813 Choron[20] mentioned the general possibility of f''' (p.13). Koch (1802) noted that already 'many' oboes had the ab' key for the left-hand little finger, and (as a matter of course) described a key to assist the tuning of $f\sharp'$. Some oboes already had the $c\sharp'$ key. Five-keyed oboes are therefore appropriate for earlier Beethoven symphonies. Then keys for f', bb', c'' and a long one for $b\natural$ were introduced and all semitones now had their own air hole; the diagrams of Carse show this development well.[21] These keys aided tuning, equality of tone and air pressure, they aided soft playing in higher registers and made some passage-work easier to command. In earlier years technical deficiencies of key-work made it harder for the full benefits to be realized.[22] The 'Classical' oboe was at most a 'stabilized' version of the Baroque oboe.

TONE AND VIBRATO Burney's account of Carlo Besozzi should be quoted:

> Besozzi's *messa di voce*, or swell, is prodigious; indeed, he continues to augment the force of a tone so much and so long, that it is hardly possible not to fear for his lungs. His taste and ear are exceedingly delicate and refined, and he seems to possess a happy and peculiar facility of tempering a continued tone to different basses, according to their several relations.[23]

Changes in playing style are mentioned by Mozart; having admired J. C. Fischer's style in 1765, he criticized him severely in 1787: 'His tone is entirely nasal, and his held notes like the tremulant on the organ'.[24] But a London tutor states: 'The right Tone of the Hautboy should be even and clear, from the lowest Note to the highest, and not unlike the fine Tone produced by the ablest Bow from the Violin'.[25] G. F. Braun (1759–1824) thought 'Nothing is more offensive than an unnatural and overstrained forcing of the tones of the oboe', which ought to be 'delicate and impassionate' (1823).

Oboe tutors do not mention vibrato, with the possible exception of Garnier's 'frémissement de lèvres' (notated: ～～～), where it is discussed under tongued articulation; this was implicitly a legato technique a degree more sustained than: (the 'soft separation'). According to Moens-Haenen it was probably a continuous lipped vibrato.[26] Brod (*c*1826) asserted that 'almost all foreigners make [their reeds] stronger than we, also they make a hard, muted sound that misrepresents the instrument', while the French have attained a sound 'that most approaches the violin'. This seems to bear witness to the fact that 'Two entirely different ideals of oboe tone were being pursued in Europe, and two corresponding types of instrument were developing': the refined French with its narrower upper-bore, and the warm, robust German type, from *c*1810.[27]

REEDS The composition, dimensions and 'scrape' of early double reeds have often been written about and it is incumbent on the modern performer to research the subject in detail. Warner concludes that a change from wedge-like (tip *c*11 mm) to a narrow shape occurred *c*1780.[28] But shapes varied on an individual as well as national basis. The quality of cane is crucial, as is the 'scrape'. Extant reeds show a scrape of *c*15 mm and Garnier implies a shorter scrape than the modern habit, 'almost back to the binding'.[29] An article in 1830 outlines reed shapes and tones: Fischer's 'rather small' reed, Gries-bach's 'very large, strong' one (making a clarinet-like sound), Vogt's 'remarkably small, soft' reed (and 'thin' tone), etc.[30] According to *The Compleat Tutor*, small resistance is the main feature of blowing the lowest octave: 'The low Notes require little or no pressure on the Reed' (p.6).

The exact measurements, reed-making tools and techniques illustrated by Garnier (p.7) are discussed by Warner (n.28 above) and were adopted by Fröhlich (1810–11). Garnier's reed was 8 mm across, very similar to today's measurements; he gave detailed advice on adjusting new reeds by their response to certain pitches (p.8). The empirical approach of Jones (n.19), formed over two years of concert practice, is instructive. Much research still remains to be done and Bruce Haynes has called for assistance in updating and completing the bibliographical, graphic and other references to double reeds (and the location of surviving examples) published by him in 1981.[31]

ENGLISH HORN Oboe tutors regularly mention the english horn (or cor anglais), which existed in both curved and angled form and often with the pear-shaped end we recognize today. Laborde (1780, i/2, 266, 275)[32] actually lists both 'Taille de hautbois' and 'Hautbois de forêt', the latter with a 'more agreeable' sound than the oboe, 'less sonorous and more velvety'. Choron (1813) gave a range of *f* to *g″*, while Reicha (1816) took it to *bb″*. Chalon's tutor (c1802), illustrating a two-keyed curved english horn, allowed it a tone higher still.

Performance problems arise today through the unorthodox transposition schemes which musicians were apparently compelled to use because of the general rarity of instruments in this period. Parts by Haydn (*L'anima del filosofo*), Zingarelli and Mayr are notated diversely; those by Catel and Spontini are 'normal' to us.[33] Longyear says the english horn was 'extremely rare' in Germany at this time; even in France, Reicha's *Scène* was exceptional. The Italians made sporadic use of it in opera, at least, as did Weigl in Vienna in an ensemble of surpassing eccentricity.[34]

An important section on the english horn occurs in Brod's tutor (c1826); it is significant not least for its engravings of his new straight english horn with crook and his Baryton (pitched an octave below soprano oboe). Reeds for these are discussed and illustrated; the reed for the english horn was 8·5 mm across the tip.[35] Key-work echoed that of the oboe. Schubart (1806)[36] noted that english horn performance was very difficult because 'die vielen Klappen Schwierigkeiten in der Applicatur verursachen' (p.321).

The clarinet

The two- and three-keyed instrument was still known in the 1760s (*a′*, *bb′*, *e/bb* keys). The fourth key to be added was probably that for *ab/eb″*[37] and the fifth gave *f♯/c♯″*. This five-keyed clarinet flourished throughout the period. However a sixth key for either *c♯′/g♯″* or trilling *a′/b′* was used by some from around the 1790s.

Not only were semitonal trills usually impossible, but playing in keys with more than a single sharp or flat was often impractical. Thus players might have used a range of clarinets from low G to high F. Roeser (1764, p.2)[38] says the sopranino E and F instruments were too shrill for all except the noisiest pieces, and the G instrument was uncommon. The problem, particularly in French scores, is judging which to use; the choice was left to the player or perhaps director, and the part notated at sounding pitch. Printed tutors sometimes give extensive tables correlating orchestral key with type of instrument; some (e.g. Francoeur, 1772) outline the tonal character of each clarinet. Professionals evidently used various instruments, for one conductor (Blasius, about 1796) complained about the changing of instruments, especially in winter.

Written sources suggest increasing preference for centrally-pitched clarinets, e.g. in A, B, Bb, C and D;[39] English tutors suggest a B and a C instrument.[40] By 1785 the French were enjoined to forget the D clarinet (Vanderhagen, 1785); 10 to 15 years later Blasius and others describe basic use of two clarinets in C/B and Bb/A, altered by the variable joint called a *corps de rechange*. (Clarinets in C/B were ordered for the Vienna Hoftheater in 1782–3.)[41]

The occasional rubric 'Chalumeau' indicated that the passage was to be played an octave below written; it was cancelled by the word 'Clarinette'. Backofen (1802–3)[42] allowed the C clarinet in C, G and F major and their relatives, 'but only when the gentler nature of a piece does not make another [Bb or A] clarinet necessary' (p.34). Today we have a somewhat simplified impression of what was undoubtedly a varied world of timbre. The question of fingering is complex, and also potentially bears upon timbre. As Albert Rice suggests, 'A number of basic fingerings are shared. . . . A few fingerings, however, are peculiar to certain countries.'[43] Each player had his own techniques. An authentic approach to early clarinet playing on a five-keyed instrument would involve considering (*a*) commonplace musical figures deemed hard or impossible at the time; (*b*) exploiting or compensating for a weak tone on notes like *bb'*, *c#'*, *eb'*, *ab'*; (*c*) tonal differences between northern and southern European instruments (e.g. English ones gave a 'slimmer', perhaps brighter, tone than continental ones); and (*d*) various sizes of clarinet.

The clarinet was generally played reed uppermost in Italy, France, England and portions of Germany and elsewhere.[44] Articulation was then either by means of the tongue (Vanderhagen, 1799, and Michel, 1800, give both 'tu' for ordinary separation and 'té' for staccato), by means of a chest action, 'h' or 'ha', or a throat action.[45] Chest action is mentioned in Roeser (1764, p.12) and Lefèvre (1802, p.10)[46] and is described extensively by Fröhlich (1810–11), who alone considered its ideal proximity to the singer's art. Reed-below playing was developed in Germany and the Netherlands, perhaps with the teeth biting the mouthpiece, as asserted by Berr (1836, both tutors). Reed-above players had access to the highest notes, above *f'''* (Lefèvre gives *c''''* in 1802) and the ability to play leaps more quickly. Although reed-above technique cannot have precluded subtle and quiet playing, M (1808)[47] and Berr argued that reed-below gave the softest tone; 'very often just like a [glass] harmonica', stated M (cols.385–7). Much valuable research is waiting to be done here. Nowhere is vibrato mentioned in early clarinet literature; 'nuancing' (Lefèvre, 1802, pp.13–14) refers to 'giving more or less strength in beginning or ending' a phrase or note.

Lower-pitched clarinets

A variety of deeper-voiced clarinets existed in the Classical period; these generally await modern revival.

CLARINETTE D'AMOUR These were clarinets pitched in low A, A♭, G or F, often built with a globular bell and either a crook or curved barrel. (One in D is specified, mysteriously, in J. C. Bach's *Temistocle*, 1772.) 'There are at least 40 extant clarinettes d'amour which have from three to twelve keys, and date from *c*1750 to *c*1820';[48] their appellations included 'Douce-Klarinette', perhaps for their tone.

BASSET-HORN The basset-horn was developed and chiefly employed in Germany; about 14 survive from the 1760s and 1770s, with between five and seven keys.[49] Because its lower compass stretched to written *d* and *c*, and because it was pitched in low keys – mostly G and F but also E, E♭ and D – it required a curved or angled construction plus the use of an air-box.[50] This *Büch* or *Kasten* compacted three parallel lengths of tube inside a block of wood, which gave directly on to a flared metal bell. Various keys were added in the 1790s, some giving *c*♯ and *d*♯. With a new list of its music now available, there is considerable incentive for the modern player to revive this voice from the past.[51] It was played with reed above or below (Backofen, 1802, p. 37).

BASSET CLARINET[52] Developed in Vienna in about 1787, the basset clarinet eventually gave the (soprano) clarinet the downward extension to *e*♭, *d*, *c*♯ and *c*; it was made in C, B♭ and A. Mozart, whose incomplete basset clarinet quintet, K516*c*, dates from about 1787, the player Anton Stadler and the Viennese maker Theodor Lotz (who, in 1788, was credited with the instrument's invention) were well acquainted. Mozart's Clarinet Concerto (1791) was for a basset instrument in A, and had been sketched at about that time as a basset horn concerto in G.[53] By 1792 Stadler appears to have added further keys; a description of 1801 suggests that his basset clarinet pointed outwards in its lowest quarter, sounding 'like a French horn in the low notes'.[54] The modern player can have a regular clarinet extended and re-bored to give basset notes; this will improve the tone of the low (regular) portion of the compass. Reproduction basset clarinets are now commercially available.

REEDS (ALL CLARINETS) Backofen's information paints a picture of considerable variety: some players shaved their reeds to a fine wedge, others gave them a parallel thinness; some favoured a convex contour (in downward cross-section), others a concave one. The anonymous M (1808), who was a reed-below player, demanded so soft a reed that a player would experience 'far less strain' than in playing a flute, thus enabling two or more hours of chamber music to be undertaken. The same writer recommended 'broad' mouthpieces while mentioning that some clarinettists preferred 'the smaller ones' (cols.373 and 390–91). Modern players can experiment using a close lay and a soft reed and produce a smaller tone.

Bassoon

There is considerable evidence of the bassoon's diversity. There were national differences in style, local differences in the number of keys and individual differences in reed fashion. In general, the bassoon underwent a modification from four to seven or more keys, with concomitant exploration of higher notes; a fuller sound was sought than hitherto. But four-keyed instruments would not have been totally anachronistic even in the 1820s.[55] *B'* could not generally be sounded, except by 'lipping' *Bb'*

The closed keys for Eb and F♯ were added to the Baroque keys which provided Bb, D, F and G♯ in some places at least by the 1770s. By 1787 (Ozi) a left-hand key for *a'/bb'/b'* was described; by 1802 Koch, though omitting the key, added a new key for *c"/c♯"* and *d"*. William Waterhouse qualifies the position thus: 'Because of the lack of standardization of keywork or bore, no given set of fingerings would suit everyone; different notes were always out of tune... On French bassoons of the period many fingerings were different [to German ones].'[56] And in any case, in Eric Halfpenny's words, the bassoon's 'tonal character and overall capabilities have always depended more on the design of the tube and finger-holes than on its key-system'.[57]

The next keys were connected with Simiot of Lyons (*B'* and *C*), with Grenser and Almenraeder (*c/d/c♯'/d♯'*) and Almenraeder alone around 1820 (*bb*); but Müller (1825) independently described the addition of the same or analogous keys.

In England, from about 1770, bassoons lost their 'full and soft' quality in favour of 'greater sonority and clarity of speech' (see n.57). Ozi (1787)[58] observed that he himself used a Strasbourg instrument with wider than usual bore and crook which afforded a greater volume of sound (p.3). Bassoons from Dresden (especially Grensers) were internationally recognized and Germany was the scene of reforms in the 1820s described on p. 414. A pin-hole in the crook made its first appearance in the Classical period to assist tone production.

ARTICULATION AND PERFORMANCE Even in 1802–3 Ozi noted eight trouble-some pitches with their characteristics, noting the need for variant finger-ings (ex.3). Fröhlich (1810–11, pp.59ff), went through the compass in similar

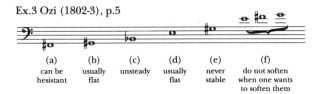

Ex.3 Ozi (1802-3), p.5

(a)	(b)	(c)	(d)	(e)	(f)
can be hesistant	usually flat	unsteady	usually flat	never stable	do not soften when one wants to soften them

detail. Ozi's treatise of 1787 emphasized the need to 'bring out' notated appoggiaturas; his later treatise agrees with Fröhlich about the tonguing syllable 'tu', hardest for wedge staccato, softer for a dot. To modern musicians Ozi's examples of ornamentation are apt to seem mannered (1802–3), but he judged them to possess a 'noble simplicity' (ex.4). The bassoonist, like other woodwind players, was expected to add phrasing to an unmarked sequence of notes (e.g. slurred pairs variously alternating with detached notes). For Fröhlich this endowed a certain speaking quality (p.52). Vibrato is not mentioned in tutors of this period.

Ex.4 Ozi (1802–3), p.13
(a) Written

(b) Played

REEDS Few early reeds survive to help the quest for authenticity.[59] A set of five English reeds (from ?c1800), recently described, has tips averaging 12·8 mm across, with 'a nice degree of arch'; 'the throats are very wide open, nearly as deep as wide just above the winding'.[60] Detailed and illustrated directions for fashioning reeds were published by Ozi in 1802–3. These have been described and edited by Warner,[61] who observes that Ozi's reed was both longer (c63 mm) and wider (c18 mm) than modern reeds, but also that such evidence is just 'a good beginning' in the matter of practical reconstruction. Fröhlich (1810–11), equally detailed in his information, illustrates two schools of reed-making, one producing reeds longer than the other but with the same width of tip. The Paris bassoon school adopted the former; others (unspecified) the smaller one.

The dangers of wrongly produced, forced tone in relation to reeds (with other notes on tone and phrasing) were discussed in 1820 by the leading player of the Prussian royal orchestra (Baermann, 1820).

CONTRABASSOON Contrabassoons are likely to be encountered only in music from Vienna, e.g. Haydn (*The Creation*), Mozart (Masonic Funeral Music K477/479a), and especially Beethoven (*Fidelio*, Symphonies nos.5 and 9, etc), who used two in his concert of 27 February 1814. It is likely that these were orthodox octave bassoons.[62]

The horn

Following momentous innovations around 1750, the horn began its 'early modern' phase of identity and technique, as Gerber explains: 'players sought further to fill in the gaps which occur in the natural scale of this instrument. This was especially the province of the second-horn-players, who already knew how to form the entire great bass octave with the hand about the year 1750'.[63] 'Hand stopping' is the name of the technique to which Gerber refers, whereby the player's hand (usually the right hand) changes its wrist angle in the bell and so causes a naturally produced note to be lowered by a semitone or a tone. The difficulty is that such 'stopped' notes are inherently muffled in timbre; when played loudly, however, they have a startling, brassy tone.

The important exponent of this technique was the Bohemian A. J. Hampel (or Hampl) who, as performer and teacher in Dresden, taught a generation of players how the horn could be a chromatic instrument. By 1753 or before

Hampel is said by Gerber to have designed a new horn specifically to accommodate the new playing style (Gerber originally credited the invention to 'an artisan at Hanau').[64]

This new horn, generally referred to as *Inventionshorn*, enabled the soloist's crooks to be inserted within the main circle of the tubing instead of being placed between this circle and the mouthpiece. The latter method caused the shape and balance to vary each time a new crook was used. However, in Vienna and Great Britain the older method was retained. The third component to be transformed, or at least codified, was the embouchure. With the new playing position and the decline of the clarino style, the wider Baroque mouthpiece rim gave way to a narrower rim. This derived from 'the general lessening of pressure which resulted from the availability of a chromatic scale in the middle register'[65] and in lieu of a 'trumpet' lay (two-thirds of the rim pressed against lower lip) came the new lay (two-thirds of the rim against upper lip, if not half-and-half). The fourth modification emerged when the bell was somewhat widened to take the hand, and the 'Baroque' tone became 'darker and fuller'.

The style-conscious musician today will be aware of the varieties of design and material used for mouthpieces[66] and the subtle differences of tone caused thereby. He will also be aware of regional differences such as the narrower bore and brighter sound of French (Parisian) horns. Fitzpatrick has described the practical effects of using early instruments and mouthpieces in some detail.[67]

Solo players tended to need the centrally pitched crooks (D, E♭, E, F) while orchestral players were required to use also more extreme crooks (low B♭ and C, high G, A, B♭, sometimes C). Thus orchestral players officially used the older system of 'terminal' crooking near the mouthpiece which assisted quicker changing. Yet there is evidence that in France around 1800 the younger players who were now specializing in the middle range of the instrument were beginning to use the 'wrong' crook: 'What happens? When a piece in B♭ turns up, instead of using the instrument proper to that key, they use the E♭ horn; they use the D horn if the piece is in A; and if it is in C, they are obliged to take the horn in F.'[68] Thus the brighter open notes conceived by the composer were transformed into stopped notes. Further, extempore octave transposition upwards by the second horn player ruined the part-writing and harmony.

In chamber and solo music, composers made increasingly liberal use of stopped notes; the exploitation of these stopped notes in the three E♭ concertos by Mozart has remained a *locus classicus* of hand-horn reference. Many wrote concertos and sonatas employing scalic, rapid figures. Beethoven's (written) A♭ scale for E♭ horn in the Adagio of the Ninth Symphony fell distinctly within current hand technique.

There is general agreement that a basic stylistic aim was to create evenness of tone throughout the horn's range between stopped and open notes. Total equality was inherently impossible. Charts edited from Domnich (1807), Fröhlich (1810–11) and Duvernoy (1802) are given by Morley-Pegge and Fitzpatrick to show recommended degrees of hand-stopping.[69] Domnich (p.5) states that evenness was assisted by some tempering of open notes by the hand. But it cannot be emphasized too much that the Classical horn was still an instrument characterized by the timbral purity of its open notes. It is just this eloquent quality that has become obscured by valve-horn technique. Furthermore, the horn in each of its possible crookings could be heard as a distinct instrument (the tubing could be anything from eight to 18 feet in length); French tutors describe the musical character of each in turn. This distinctiveness, too, has vanished in practice.

Vibrato is not discussed in horn tutors, but an Austrian writer in 1796 thought it could 'be produced on no other instrument with such expressiveness and vigour as on the horn'; the horn's richness of effect existed 'because of the roundness and fullness of its tone, and because of its vibrato'.[70] Further research is necessary on this topic, but this citation is highly suggestive. On the question of articulation Morley-Pegge reproduces the syllables 'daon' (attack), 'ta' (dry stroke) and 'da' (soft stroke) from Punto (*c*1794); this tutor was said by Punto to be originally by the great Hampel himself.

The trumpet

Just as pre-classical and early Classical symphonies sometimes exploited the horn's clarino register, clarino technique on the trumpet fell from use only gradually after 1750. It 'was developed to the fullest, especially in Vienna and its environs' by Michael Haydn, Reutter, Richter etc.[71] However, newer demands also arose for prolonged, soft notes in the orchestral context (especially in Vienna) and, as Edward H. Tarr suggests, for considerable endurance as required by Beethoven.

The actual instrument itself stayed the same. Altenburg (1795) used trumpets in D, F and G; the F could be crooked to E or E♭ and the D to C or low B♭.[72] However, Altenburg's treatise mentions many other things of importance to Classical practice: the three types of mute and their uses (p.85); the tonguing syllables (p.92); the necessity of imitating 'good players and singers' in phrase patterns (pp.96–7); extempore ornamentation (p.113); and the surprising fact that a teacher was supposed to have the mouthpiece for a new pupil specially turned to suit the pupil's lips (p.116). The embouchure was characterized by 'a tight closing together of the teeth and lips' and the mouthpiece lay more on the lower than the upper lip. The most accessible summary of the performance problems posed by such evidence, against the background of 20th-century assumptions, is offered by Baines.[73] The absence of French tutors is compensated for by relevant sections in Francoeur (1772), Vandenbroeck (1793–5), Choron (1813) and Reicha (1816).

CHROMATIC TYPES Western music, following the changes in horn technique, anticipated extensions of the trumpet's capabilities. Curved ('demilune') trumpets to allow hand-stopping were not uncommon, and the slide trumpet reappeared in late 18th-century Britain.[74] But Weidinger's keyed trumpet was the most important Classical invention of its type. This possessed between four and six keys and was pitched in D or E♭ (later also in G, A and A♭).[75] Weidinger (1767–1852) knew Haydn and probably inspired or commissioned his Trumpet Concerto (1796). The keys raised the pitch by ½,

1, 1½ and 2 tones respectively, so that a four-keyed model commanded chromatic range from *g* upwards. Dahlqvist, who has played modern reproductions, says not only that they possess 'good and nearly even tone', but that the normal E♭ trumpet used for the Haydn concerto 'does not come close to the tone of the keyed trumpet. A fluegelhorn would perhaps be the best substitute for the original instrument', failing a modern reproduction. The keyed trumpet 'is softer than ... the natural trumpet'.[76] Hummel's concerto of 1803, and a lost trio, were played by Weidinger. Though the instrument was unable to stand comparison with the new valved trumpet, Berlioz (1843)[77] said it was still used in some Italian orchestras (p.192); it still finds a place in Kastner (1844).[78] Important keyed trumpet solos occur in Rossini's *Guillaume Tell* (1829), Act 3, and Meyerbeer's *Robert le diable* (1831), Act 5, the latter calling for an instrument in A.

The trombone

Towards 1740 the trombone bell became more flared and the width of its tube was increased at the extreme end; there is some evidence that its mouthpiece became less conical and more cup-like.[79] Alto, tenor and bass instruments continued to be used, with differences according to locality. The trombone's traditional gentle tone probably predominated until 'the "military" got hold of the instrument' and coarsened it.[80] It was during the Revolutionary and Napoleonic wars that this process was initiated. It is interesting that, although chordal orchestral scoring or the doubling of choral voices was the norm, the use of a single trombone to double the orchestra's bass-line or that of a wind group had begun during the French Revolution with Mariotti.[81] The tendency to use a tenor trombone in lieu of the alto was supported by Fröhlich (1810–11) and others, who advised the use of a small mouthpiece in such circumstances: a larger-bore tenor and larger mouthpiece in lieu of a bass trombone was also advised.[82] But the alto instrument continued to be described, for instance by Catrufo (1832). We do not yet hear the finale of Beethoven's Fifth Symphony (for example) performed with conscientious regard to the timbre of its high alto trombone part.

Notes

[1] N. Toff, *The Development of the Modern Flute* (New York, 1979), 24–5. They were Pietro Florio, Caleb Gedney and Richard Potter.

[2] *Journal de Paris* (15 June 1781), 669; benefit concert for Mr Hartman.

[3] *The Development*, 41.

[4] J. G. Tromlitz, *Ausführlicher und gründlicher Unterricht die Flöte zu spielen* (Leipzig, 1791/ R1973).

[5] F. Devienne, *Nouvelle méthode théorique et pratique pour la flûte* (Paris, 1794).

[6] It is interesting to compare this with the following, a generation later: '[The flute] is, however, sometimes misemployed by players, in forcing it to produce a kind of trumpet tone, instead of its natural mellifluous sound': *The Harmonicon*, i (1823), 140.

[7] J. Fröhlich, *Vollständige Theorish-praktische Musikschule* (Bonn, 1810–11), from the 'vollen, klingenden Töne mancher wieblicher Sopran Stimme' to 'die reinen, eingreifenden Klänge der Harmonika'.

[8] C. Nicholson, *Nicholson's Complete Preceptor for the German Flute* (London, c1815).

[9] W. N. James, *A Word or Two on the Flute* (Edinburgh and London, 1826/*R*1982).

[10] *Berbiguier's Method of Instruction for the Flute* (London, *c*1827), 20, trans. from Berbiguier (*c*1818), 64.

[11] T. E. Warner, 'Tromlitz's Flute Treatise' in *A Musical Offering: Essays in Honor of Martin Bernstein* (New York, 1977), 261–73.

[12] C. Smith, 'Special Expressive Characteristics of the pre-Boehm Transverse Flute', *Woodwind World*, xiii/4 (1974), 26–34, and xiv/1 (1975), 11–24.

[13] Example from Nicholson (*c*1815), bk.2, p.39, Duetto XXIII. See Toff, *The Development*, 34, for Potter's sliding key system (1808) facilitating the glide effect.

[14] Two articles remain standard discussions of the subject: G. Moens-Haenen, 'Holzbläservibrato im Barock', *The Brussels Museum of Musical Instruments Bulletin*, xiv (1984), 1–60; B. Dickey, 'Untersuchungen zur historischen Auffassung des Vibratos auf Blasinstrumenten', *Basler Jb für historische Musikpraxis*, ii (1978), 77–142.

[15] J. Wragg, *Seventeenth Edition of Wragg's Improved Flute Preceptor for an Eight Key'd Flute* (London, 1818).

[16] P. Bate, *The Oboe: an Outline of its History, Development and Construction* (London, rev.2/1962), 45–6.

[17] Where in fact Haydn's earlier oboist Czerwenka was now leading player. On the Vienna instruments, see R. Hellyer, 'Some Documents Relating to Viennese Wind-instrument Purchases, 1779–1837', *GSJ*, xxviii (1975), 50–59, items 9 and 10. By 1827 a 13-keyed oboe was being ordered, with 3 *Motazionen* (item 16).

[18] B. Haynes, 'Oboe Fingering Charts, 1695–1816', *GSJ*, xxxi (1978), 68–93.

[19] D. Jones, 'A Three-keyed Oboe by Thomas Collier', *GSJ*, xxxi (1978), 36–43.

[20] A. Choron, *Traité général des voix et des instruments d'orchestre, principalement des instruments à vent, à l'usage des compositeurs; par L. J. Francoeur.... Nouvelle édition revüe et augmentée des instruments modernes* (Paris, 1813).

[21] A. Carse, *The Orchestra from Beethoven to Berlioz* (Cambridge, 1948), 402–3.

[22] Haynes, 'Oboe Fingering Charts', 79. Koch (1802) said the speaker assisted the quiet production of *e″*, *f″*, *f♯″*, *g″*. G. F. Braun (1823) said only six keys were used much and that 'too great a number undoubtedly injure the purity of tone'.

[23] C. Burney, *The Present State of Music in Germany, The Netherlands, and The United Provinces* (London, 1775/*R*1969), 46.

[24] Letter to his father of 4 April 1787, trans. E. Anderson: *Letters of Mozart and his Family* (London, 3/1985), 907.

[25] *The Compleat Tutor for the Hautboy* (London, *c*1790), 7.

[26] Moens-Haenen, 'Holzbläservibrato', 49–51.

[27] Bate, *The Oboe*, 57.

[28] T. Warner, 'Two Late Eighteenth-century Instructions for Making Double Reeds', *GSJ*, xv (1962), 25–33. A further relevant source is the article 'Faiseur d'instruments à vent' in *Dictionnaire raisonné universel des arts et métiers ... nouvelle édition*, ed. P. Jaubert (Paris, 1773).

[29] Extra differences would have occurred since players also made their own copper staples, which were bound with the same waxed thread used for attaching the reed. See Warner, 'Two Late Eighteenth-century Instructions'. F. J. Garnier *l'aîné*, *Méthode raisonnée pour le haut-bois* (Paris, 1802), 96, writes a 'Prélude pour ajuster un haut bois ou former une anche neuve par les intervalles les plus sonores', from which modern players might benefit.

[30] I. P., 'On the Oboe and Bassoon', *Harmonicon*, viii (1830), 192–3.

[31] B. Haynes, 'Early Double-reeds: Prospectus for a Survey of the Historical Evidence', *Journal of the International Double Reed Society*, ix (1981), 43–7.

[32] J. B. de La Borde, *Essai sur la musique* (Paris, 1780/*R*1972).

[33] See R. M. Longyear, 'The English Horn in Classic and Early Romantic Music', *Miscellanea musicologica: Adelaide Studies in Musicology*, ix (1977), 128–44. The editor of the opera in *Joseph Haydn: Werke*, xxv/13, considers that in 'Del mio core' a hypothetical oboe d'amore might have been intended: the part is for a B♭ instrument.

[34] i.e. the Concertante in E♭ for corno inglese, flauto d'amore, (keyed) trumpet, viola d'amore, keyboard, cello, glockenspiel and euphon. See R. Dahlqvist, *The Keyed Trumpet* (Nashville, 1975), 13.

[35] P. Hedrick, 'Henri Brod's *Méthode pour le hautbois* Reconsidered', *The Consort*, xxx (1974), 53–62, is an illustrated digest of this tutor. The term 'Baryton' in this connection does not appear in *Grove MI*.

[36] C. F. D. Schubart, *Ideen zu einer Ästhetik der Tonkunst*, ed. L. Schubart (Vienna, 1806).

[37] A. R. Rice, 'Clarinet Fingering Charts, 1732–1816', *GSJ*, xxxvii (1984), 17–18.

[38] V. Roeser, *Essai d'instruction à l'usage de ceux qui composent pour la clarinette et le cor* (Paris, 1764/*R*1972).

[39] L. F. Francoeur, *Diapason général de tous les instrumens à vent avec des observations sur chacun d'eux* (Paris, 1772).

[40] Anon, *The Clarinet Instructor* (London, *c*1780); and Anon, *New and Compleat Instructions for the Clarionet* (London, *c*1798).

[41] See the article by Hellyer, 'Some Documents', item 1.

[42] J. G. H. Backofen, *Anweisung zur Klarinette* (Leipzig, 1803).

[43] Rice, 'Clarinet Fingering Charts', 19.

[44] T. E. Hoeprich, 'Clarinet Reed Position in the 18th Century', *EM*, xii (1984), 48–55.

[45] D. Charlton, 'Classical Clarinet Technique: Documentary Approaches', *EM*, xvi (1988), 396–406.

[46] X. Lefèvre, *Méthode de clarinette* (Paris, 1802/*R*1974).

[47] M., 'Ueber die Klarinette', *AMZ*, x (1807–8), no.24 of 9 March, cols.369–75, and no.25 of 16 March, cols.385–91.

[48] A. R. Rice, 'The Clarinette d'Amour and Basset Horn', *GSJ*, xxxix (1986), 97–111.

[49] ibid, 102, with details of key fittings involved.

[50] Two recent articles must be read in tandem: R. Maunder, 'J. C. Bach and the Basset-horn', *GSJ*, xxxvii (1984), 42–7, and N. Shackleton and K. Puddy, 'The Basset Horn of J. G. Eisenmenger', *GSJ*, xxxviii (1985), 139–42.

[51] J. P. Newhill, *The Basset-horn and its Music* (Sale, Cheshire, 1983).

[52] Also called in the 18th century 'bass clarinet' or 'newly-invented clarinet'. The literature connected with Mozart's use of the instrument is quite extensive. For a concentrated marshalling of facts, see P. L. Poulin, 'The Basset Clarinet of Anton Stadler', *College Music Symposium*, xxii (1982), 67–82. Research on the instrument's early evolution is still continuing.

[53] As early as 1802 a critic complained that the publisher ought to have 'published it in the original version and to have inserted these [unauthentic] transpositions and alterations in smaller notes': *AMZ*, iv (1802), cols.411–13, taken from Poulin, 'The Basset Clarinet', 76.

[54] Later sources suggest the bell pointed 'somewhat sideways': Poulin, 'The Basset Clarinet', 79–81.

[55] As in Lichtenthal's *Dizionario* (1826), cited in L. G. Langwill, *The Bassoon and Contrabassoon* (London, 1965), 41.

[56] *Grove MI*, i, 185.

[57] E. Halfpenny, 'The Evolution of the Bassoon in England, 1750–1800', *GSJ*, x (1957), 30–39.

[58] E. Ozi, *Méthode nouvelle et raisonné pour le basson* (Paris, *c*1787).

[59] One is illustrated in full size outline in the article 'Bassoon', *Grove MI*.

[60] Length overall *c*68 mm; bottom ends fish-tailed. See M. Kirkpatrick, 'Register of Early Reeds: Bassoon Reeds in the Aylesbury Museum', *GSJ*, xxxiv (1981), 148–9.

[61] See n.28. Warner omits the admittedly more limited information in Ozi (*c*1787), 6–7.

[62] L. G. Langwill, 'The Double-bassoon: its Origin and Evolution', *PMA*, lxix (1942–3), 1–33.

[63] E. L. Gerber, 'Spörken' in *Historisch-biographisches Lexicon der Tonkünstler* (Leipzig, 1792), trans. H. Fitzpatrick in *The Horn and Horn-playing and the Austro-Bohemian Tradition from 1680 to 1830* (London, 1970), 226.

[64] i.e. in the *Lexicon* of 1792. The artisan is identified as J. G. Haltenhof by Fitzpatrick (*The Horn and Horn-playing*, 223). Gerber's identification of Hampel as inventor was in the *Neues historisch-biographisches Lexicon der Tonkünstler* (Leipzig, 1813), ii, 493; translation in *The Horn and Horn-playing*, 111. On p.223 n.5, Fitzpatrick says Hampel's design first appeared around 1750.

[65] Fitzpatrick, *The Horn and Horn-playing*, 160, also 88–9.

[66] ibid, chap. vi; also R. Morley-Pegge, *The French Horn* (London and New York, 2/1973), 101–2.

[67] Fitzpatrick, *The Horn and Horn-playing*, 137–8, and *passim*.

[68] H. Domnich, *Méthode de premier et de second cor* (Paris, 1807), p.vii.

[69] Morley-Pegge, *The French Horn*, 99; Fitzpatrick, *The Horn and Horn-playing*, 182.

[70] *Jahrbuch der Tonkunst von Wien und Prag* (1796), 193, trans. in Fitzpatrick, *The Horn and Horn-playing*, 180.

[71] E. H. Tarr, 'Trumpet'; *Grove 6*, xix, 220.

[72] J. E. Altenburg, *Versuch einer Anleitung zur heroisch-musikalischen Trompeter- und Pauker-Kunst* (Halle, 1795/*R*1972; Eng. trans., 1974); Altenburg calls the F the 'French' type but

Francoeur (1772), 55, says the E trumpet was usually used in preference. Use of the F trumpet grew in France towards 1800, where one also finds music for G and A trumpet, occasionally, from 1783. D. Charlton, *Orchestration and Orchestral Practice in Paris, 1789–1810* (diss., U. of Cambridge, 1973), 201.

[73] A. Baines, *Brass Instruments, their History and Development* (London, 1976), 22–5 and 32–5.

[74] ibid, 182.

[75] R. Dahlqvist, *The Keyed Trumpet and its Greatest Virtuoso, Anton Weidinger* (Nashville, 1975).

[76] ibid, 3.

[77] H. Berlioz, *Grand traité d'instrumentation et d'orchestration modernes* (Paris, 1843).

[78] G. Kastner, *Supplément au traité général de l'instrumentation* (Paris, c1844).

[79] P. Bate, *The Trumpet and Trombone* (London, 1966), 139. In France a conical bore mouthpiece was traditional and retained: Baines, *Brass Instruments*, 243.

[80] F. W. Galpin's opinion, reported in H. G. Farmer, *The Rise and Development of Military Music* (London, 1912), 64n.

[81] At the Théâtre Feydeau: D. Charlton, *Orchestration and Orchestral Practice*, 124–5. This idea adumbrated early Romantic practice. Mariotti's name is later found in English sources, up to at least 1836.

[82] Baines, *Brass Instruments*, 242–3. Unfortunately Baines overstates the thesis of early French abandonment of the bass trombone before 1800.

The author would like to express his particular thanks to Phyllis Clarke, Colin Lawson, Lesley Schatzberger and William Waterhouse for their generous advice in the preparatory stages of this chapter.

CHAPTER XIV

Instrumental Ornamentation, Improvisation and Cadenzas

ROBERT D. LEVIN

Until quite recently it was rare to hear a performance of Classical period music that went beyond the printed page. Within the last generation the desire for precise knowledge of earlier performance traditions has spurred the restoration of 18th-century conventions of embellishment and the use of historical instruments. The universality of improvised embellishment and cadenzas in the Classical era is confirmed in period reports of concert and opera performances and in contemporary histories. These practices have been discussed in detail within treatises and documented in composers' written-out embellishments of their own and others' unornamented musical texts.

It is germane to ponder why these three types of sources came into being. The reports and histories are the works of critics who were sufficiently confident in their artistic opinions to write voluminous evaluations of contemporary practice, find it wanting and define how things ought to be done. Such reports contain polemics that are at times similar to present-day reviews. While the authors of the treatises also desired to share their knowledge and improve artistic standards, their works are didactic and constructive, particularly in their presentation of specific examples. However, they also decry certain practices of performers of their time. As we shall see, both types of source inveigh against excessive improvisation and embellishment. This poses a quandary to the present-day reader: which is more 'authentic' – the allegedly tasteless excesses whose wide practice is confirmed by these writings, or the alternative, more conservative views of the critics and theorists? We shall consider the evidence provided by surviving musical examples below.

The third type of source poses no such problems. Documents of this sort – for example, surviving written-out embellishments by Haydn and Mozart – are due primarily to idiosyncratic circumstance. They were created not to illustrate aesthetic postulates, but to be performed. By showing what was actually done (as opposed to what some observers would like to have heard), they reveal the assumptions of the finest composers without the intermediary of contemporary abstraction. Such texts undoubtedly constitute the most precious information we have.

Reports and histories

We have noted that sources of this type record the reactions of individual critics without documenting exactly what contemporary performers did. (The discrepancy between these is easily demonstrated by listening to a recording made during a live performance, then reading a newspaper review of it.) Nonetheless, the learnedness and breadth of aural experience of the finest Classical critics – of vocal music as well as instrumental – is too valuable to ignore. Especially useful are *The Present State of Music in France and Italy* by Charles Burney (London, 1771) and *Le rivoluzioni del teatro musicale italiano dalla sua origine fino al presente* of Esteban de Arteaga (Stefano Arteaga) (Bologna, 1783–8, rev. and enlarged, Venice, 2/1785). Burney's perceptive observations were already recognized and quoted on the Continent during his lifetime; Arteaga's vast work comprises a remarkably thorough history and a critical analysis of period practice that is exhaustive in its attention to textual, dramatic and musical values.

Treatises

Among the numerous treatises dealing with performance practice from the 18th and early 19th centuries, some of the best known are: Leopold Mozart, *Versuch einer gründlichen Violinschule* (Augsburg, 1756/R1976; Eng. trans., 1948, 2/1951); Carl Philipp Emanuel Bach, *Versuch über die wahre Art das Clavier zu spielen* (Berlin, 1753 and 1762/R1957; Eng. trans., 1949); Giambattista [Giovanni Battista] Mancini, *Pensieri, e riflessioni pratiche sopra il canto figurato* (Vienna, 1774, rev. and enlarged 3/1777); Johann Adam Hiller, *Anweisung zum musikalisch-zierlichen Gesange* (Leipzig, 1780/R1976); Daniel Gottlob Türk, *Clavierschule, oder Anweisung zum Clavierspielen* (Leipzig and Halle, 1789, enlarged 2/1802/R1967; Eng. trans., 1982); Heinrich Christoph Koch, *Musikalisches Lexicon* (Frankfurt am Main, 1802/R1964, 2/1817); Johann Friedrich Schubert, *Neue Singe-Schule oder gründliche und vollständige Anweisung zur Singkunst* (Leipzig, 1804); and Ignaz Franz von Mosel, *Versuch einer Ästhetik des musikalischen Tonsatzes* (Vienna, 1813, 2/1910).

While the first two of these were written before the flowering of the Classical style, they exerted a lasting influence upon musicians of succeeding generations. C. P. E. Bach's treatise was admired by Mozart and Beethoven; Leopold Mozart's violin method went through several editions and was published in various languages throughout Europe. It should be emphasized that the Classical period treatises owe much in content to the Baroque treatises that preceded them, for example those by Tosi,[1] Marpurg,[2] Quantz[3] and Agricola.[4]

Of these treatises Mancini's offers advice but few written examples; the others offer a plethora of examples, clarifying what the writers meant. Their painstaking exposition of performance practice is indispensable; Bach's and Türk's precepts concerning fingering, Mozart's on bowings, Hiller's on the relationship between text and music or Mancini's on the use of the mouth while singing give the reader general knowledge that is applicable to Classical period music as a whole. However, C. P. E. Bach is the only author of this group whose music is likely to elicit the same respect from modern musicians as his writings; the disparity in proficiency between composers of Haydn's or Beethoven's level and those of Türk's and Koch's cannot be overlooked. Nor can the risk that exhaustive treatises often tend to the categorical and pedantic. One must not exaggerate the virtues of unexceptional embellishments and cadenzas to routine arias or instrumental pieces. The issue of taste – a word mentioned regularly by writers and composers of the period – is central; however, the taste of the master Classical composers is not necessarily identical in all respects with that of their writer contemporaries.

In addition to these source materials, there are modern treatises of performance practice. While most of the original treatises were written by composers and performers, the modern treatises are written primarily by musicologists. They are derived directly from the original treatises. What they lose for being second-hand reconstructions of a part-forgotten language, they compensate for by focusing on music of the major composers. Of these modern treatises, the following are especially valuable: P. and E. Badura-Skoda, *Interpreting Mozart on the Keyboard*, trans. L. Black (London, 1962); R. Haas, *Aufführungspraxis der Musik* (Wildpark-Potsdam, 1931); and F. Neumann, *Ornamentation and Improvisation in Mozart* (Princeton, 1986). All of these contain a blend of historical and aesthetic observations; the Badura-Skodas and Neumann also offer detailed practical suggestions. Haas's work provides a general historical survey of performance practice, including a brief treatment of non-Western and Greek music. He quotes a number of useful examples of Classical period embellishment. The remaining works are far more limited in scope: Neumann treats only music of Mozart, and the Badura-Skodas concern themselves only with Mozart's keyboard music. Nonetheless, they enumerate basic principles that have validity for much of Classical period music. Many of the Badura-Skodas' remarks concerning ornamentation and embellishment may be applied to vocal as well as instrumental music of the period, while those on cadenzas may be used as a basis for all instrumental cadenzas. Neumann's book treats both vocal and instrumental music. As a synthesis of the treatises and a broad source of knowledge of Mozart's works it is unlikely to be superseded. In addition, the *Grove 6* article 'Improvisation' has valuable sections devoted to 'The Classical period' and 'After 1800', while the article on cadenzas has sections on 'The Classical period' and 'Beethoven and the 19th century'.

The detail and attendant length of the treatment of embellishment and cadenzas in the treatises prohibits anthologizing the pertinent sections from them. The brief expositions that appear below include examples drawn from the sources discussed above.

Improvised embellishments

Anyone seeking to develop competence in prepared or improvised embellishments must have a thorough knowledge of the basic types (*Manieren*) and their execution.[5] These are discussed in C. P. E. Bach (pp.79–143), Badura-Skoda (pp.69–126), L. Mozart (pp.166–214), Neumann (pp.3–175) and Türk (pp.191–286). The length of these citations attests to the impossibility of treating the subject here.

It has been noted that composers' own embellishments survive for certain pieces because of the specific circumstances surrounding their composition. Works written for amateurs or students (who were not expected to have mastered the art of improvisation) were provided with embellishment. Works for virtuosos or for the composer's personal use could be left in a more sketchy state to be elaborated anew in each performance.

Türk gives the set of diminutions in ex.1 as a model for extemporaneous embellishment. Written-out instrumental embellishments may be found in numerous Classical works, especially at restatements of principal themes in rondos. Ex.2 shows an example by Beethoven. The elaborateness of these written ornaments attests to the preservation of the conventions of embellishment;

Ex.1 Sample embellishments by Türk

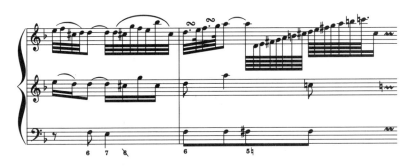

Ex.2 Two excerpts from Beethoven:
  Quintet in E♭ major for Piano and Wind, op.16 (1796), 2nd movt

however, these have been expropriated by the composer and removed from the domain of improvisation.

Mozart's mastery of progressive embellishment is shown by many of his instrumental rondos and is particularly noteworthy in those for piano in F major K494 and in A minor K511. The relationship between the texts he prepared for his own use and those he deemed necessary for the general public may be seen by comparing the autograph manuscript and the first edition of the second movement of the Piano Sonata in F major K332/300*k*, second movement (ex.3) and the third movements of that in D major K284/205*b*. (The printed edition of this work was apparently supervised by Mozart.)

It can be assumed, then, that restatements of a movement's principal

Ex.3 Comparisons between the readings in autograph manuscript and first edition of a Mozart piano sonata:
Sonata in F major K332/300K, 2nd movt

theme generically invite ornamentation, particularly in slow movements and rondos. It is worth noting that composers did not always write out such restatements; these were often signalled in the manuscript by da capo signs. Thus, the literal reprinting of the theme in modern editions creates an implication – not found in the sources – that the composer desired a note-for-note repetition of the opening music.

A special problem is posed by sonatas and other movements containing repeat signs. The repeats invite embellishment. When, as often occurs, the composer embellishes themes in the recapitulation of a sonata, he creates a significant contrast with the first, unadorned treatment of a given theme. The performer taking both repeats note for note in such a sonata movement runs the risk of destroying the illusion of spontaneity created by the written-out embellishment: first the audience hears a simple version of a tune twice; then an elaborated one which is also repeated. A possible solution is for the performer to create intermediate (or different) states of decoration so that an organic development of the initial ideas through its successive citations.

APPLICABLE REPERTORY In both vocal and instrumental music the most pertinent distinction is that between a work with a primary melodic line and one with a homogeneous texture. An aria, a solo piano work, a concertante sonata for piano and obbligato instrument, a string quartet with dominant first violin, a chamber work for a wind instrument and strings, an instrumental concerto – these are candidates for embellishment, depending upon how much is written out. It seems intrinsically impracticable for embellishment to be provided when more than one performer is assigned to a part, for example in a chorus or in orchestral string music. But there was little but common sense, then as now, to prevent an ensemble – whether single players in a chamber work or a larger band – from displaying the misplaced exuberance of simultaneous decoration. Indeed, in an account dated 19 December 1816 Louis Spohr (1784–1859) decries an orchestral performance conducted by himself the previous evening in Rome that was constantly marred by untrammelled embellishment by individual members of the orchestra. Spohr remarks that he specifically forbade the players to make any additions to the printed text, but acknowledges that ornamentation was second nature to them.[6] He cites the horns as converting ex.4*a* into ex.4*b*, and the clarinets as rendering ('perhaps simultaneously') ex.4*c* as ex.4*d*.

Ex.4

Admonitions against unwarranted embellishment appear to treatises throughout the period. C. P. E. Bach warns: 'many variants of melodies introduced by executants in the belief that they honour a piece, actually occurred to the composer, who, however, selected and wrote down the original because he considered it the best of its kind' (p.165). He elaborates his reservations elsewhere:

Ex.5
(a) Mozart: Clarinet Concerto in A major, K622, 2nd movt

*) a lead in is to be played here (see below)

(b) Mozart: Piano Concerto in C major, K503, 2nd movt, with sample embellishment

Today varied reprises are indispensable, being expected of every performer. A friend of mine takes every last pain to play pieces as written, purely and in accord with the rules of good performance. Can applause be rightfully denied him? Another, often driven by necessity, hides under bold variations his inability to express the notes as written. Nevertheless, the public holds him above the former. Performers want to vary every detail without stopping to ask whether such variation is permitted by their ability and the construction of the piece.

Often it is simply the varying, especially when it is allied with long and much too singularly decorated cadenzas, that elicits the loudest acclaim from the audience....Often these untimely variations are contrary to the construction, the affect and the inner relationship of the ideas – an unpleasant matter for many composers. Assuming that the performer is capable of varying properly, is he always in the proper mood? Do not many new problems arise with unfamiliar works? Is not the most important consideration in varying, that the performer do honour to the piece?... Yet, regardless of these difficulties and abuses, good variation always retains its value.[7]

Such documents confirm the value of taste and caution.

THE MOZART PIANO CONCERTOS Neumann is right to treat Mozart's piano concertos as a special case. Most of them were written for his personal use and contain passages that suggest he was using a sketch-like shorthand. The importance of these works justifies treating several of the cases in which the notated text may be incomplete:

1. Passages in which melodic and rhythmic activity sudenly slacken without obvious dramatic or expressive motivation. This is often the case in slow-movement sequences. Compare, for example, the two excerpts from Mozart concertos of ex.5.

2. 'Piano recitatives' in the slow movements, that is to say passages in which a melody in the right hand is accompanied by repeated chords in the strings. Such passages, relatively stark, are found in the concertos in D major K451; D minor K466; C major K467; C minor K491; D major ('Coronation') K537; and in B♭ major K595. We are fortunate that the composer's intentions about the performance of such passages are revealed in a letter to his father dated 9 (–12) June 1784. Regarding the recitative from K451, Mozart writes, '[Nannerl] is quite right in saying that there is something missing in the solo passage in C in the Andante of the concerto in D. I shall supply the deficiency as soon as possible and send it with the cadenzas'.[8]

Comparison between the ornamented version and the one in the autograph suggests how the recitatives from the other concertos were likely to have been performed by Mozart; see ex. 6.

3. Passages that are hardly more than sketches and require filling in with passage-work. Such partly notated passages exist in several of the Mozart piano concertos: K451 in D major, K482 in E♭ major, K595 in B♭ major and especially K491 in C minor. The sudden reduction in rhythmic speed of the solo, uncompensated for by activity in the orchestral writing, makes these stand out. Suggestions for filling in the gaps appear in Badura-Skoda,[9] Neumann[10] and within the NMA scores of the concertos, which identify these as editorial. While it is praiseworthy of the NMA to call the performer's attention to the need for these fill-ins, the solutions offered are often of debatable merit. Ex.7 is a passage from the third movement of K482 as it

Ex.6 Mozart: Piano Concerto in D major, K451, 2nd movt

Ex.7 Mozart: Piano Concerto in E♭ major K482, 3rd movt; suggested passage-
work by Heussner/Engel, the Badura-Skodas and R.D. Levin

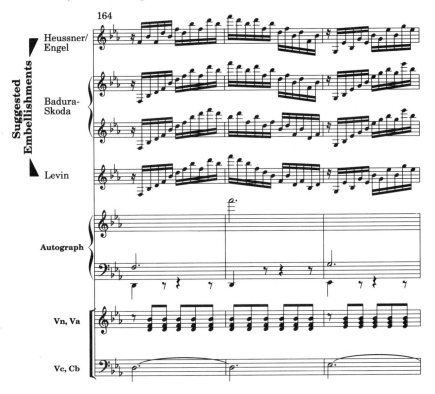

appears in the autograph, together with suggested fill-ins by NMA editors Hans Engel and Horst Heussner, by the Badura-Skodas and by the present writer.[11]

It is perhaps worth discussing the different versions in some detail:

> (*a*) While it would seem logical that Mozart's dotted minims delineate the outer extremes of the passage-work to be supplied, these are not strictly observed by Engel/Heussner or by the Badura-Skodas.
>
> (*b*) Neither Engel/Heussner nor the Badura-Skodas attempt to bring the descending portion of each arpeggio back to the register in which the next one is to begin.
>
> (*c*) The first of the Badura-Skodas' suggestions exceeds the upper range (*f'''*) of Mozart's piano. Mozart uses considerable melodic invention to disguise this absolute limit; to stray beyond it risks negating the value of his efforts.
>
> (*d*) Bar 168 of the Engel/Heussner solution is asymmetrical and awkward to play.
>
> (*e*) The passage-work codas of Mozart's concerto expositions and recapitulations normally culminate in a prolonged 6-4 chord before the final trill. Mozart usually underscores the 6-4 by interrupting the soloist's semiquaver passage-work with a quaver or an even longer value. The orchestral texture often changes at this point as well. The lack of rhythmic differentiation in Engel/Heussner and the first of the Badura-Skodas's solutions undercuts Mozart's change of orchestration and effect of the 6-4 itself.
>
> (*f*) In bar 172 of the Badura-Skodas's first solution, the accented *cb"* (second beat) contradicts the major-key tonality and the *c♮* in the next bar.

The Badura-Skodas and Neumann correctly caution that not all large leaps should be filled in as a matter of course. Such leaps are commonplace in arias of the period and are often mimicked in instrumental music. As a general principle they should be filled in only if greater rhythmic activity in the surrounding context offers persuasive evidence that the notated text is a sketch.

As implied above, it is recommended that embellishments should not exceed the instrumental range observed by the composer. This precept also applies to cadenzas.

Cadenzas

Although performers are becoming increasingly knowledgeable in stylistic matters, Classical works are still commonly heard with cadenzas whose style and content conflict with those of the work proper.[12] Modern cadenzas can be provocative,[13] and those of the Romantic era are of historical interest – particularly when they are the work of eminent composers.[14] However, it would be desirable for stylistically appropriate cadenzas to constitute the norm, rather than the exception, in today's practice.

A cadenza is less a prolonged virtuoso display than a decorated cadence, as denoted by the Italian word. The cadential formula begins with harmonic tension, created by the orchestral pause on the tonic 6-4 at the fermata. This seemingly arbitrary stop on the 6-4 is one of the elements of genius of the period. The interrupted cadential formula creates a dramatic gap, which the soloist bridges with improvisation and virtuosity, carrying the tension through to the final trill.[15] The tonic resolution brings on the re-entry of the orchestra.

The practice of including cadenzas within instrumental concertos was not universal. They are missing from most Parisian Classical concertos and symphonies concertantes, for example,[16] whereas few German concertante works omit them. Instrumental cadenzas of the period are not bound by the length limitation of vocal cadenzas – that of a single breath – even for wind and brass instruments where breathing is as relevant. It is illuminating to compare the lengths of a surviving cadenza and the movement to which it belongs. Mozart's keyboard cadenzas generally suggest a proportion of *c*10 per cent of the overall movement length.

Türk's rules for the construction of cadenzas are concise and valuable:

> 1. ...the cadenza...should particularly reinforce the impression the composition has made in a most lively way and present the most important parts of the whole composition in the form of a brief summary or in an extremely concise arrangement.
> 2. The cadenza, like every extempore embellishment, must consist not so much of intentionally added difficulties as of such thoughts which are most scrupulously suited to the main character of the composition.
> 3. Cadenzas should not be too long, especially in compositions of a melancholy character.
> 4. Modulations into other keys, particularly to those which are far removed, either do not take place at all – for example, in short cadenzas – or they must be used with much insight and, as it were, only in passing. In no case should one modulate to a key which the composer himself has not used in the composition. It seems to me that this rule is founded on the principle of unity, which, as is well known, must be followed in all works of the fine arts....
> 5. Just as unity is required for a well-ordered whole, so also is variety necessary if the attention of the listener is to be held. Therefore as much of the unexpected and the surprising as can possibly be added should be used in the cadenza.
> 6. No thought should be often repeated in the same key or in another, no matter how beautiful it may be.
> 7. Every dissonance which has been included, even in single-voiced cadenzas, must be properly resolved.
> 8. A cadenza does not have to be erudite, but novelty, wit, an abundance of ideas and the like are so much more its indispensable requirements.
> 9. The same tempo and metre should not be maintained throughout the cadenza; its individual fragments (those parts which are incomplete in themselves) must be skilfully joined to one another. For the whole cadenza should be more like a fantasia which has been fashioned out of an abundance of feeling, rather than a methodically-constructed composition.
> 10. From what has been said it follows that a cadenza which perhaps has been learned by memory with great effort or has been written out before should be performed as if it were merely invented on the spur of the moment, consisting of a choice of ideas indiscriminately thrown together which had just occurred to the player.[17]

We know the kinds of cadenzas Mozart and Beethoven envisioned for their concertos; many of these survive and are regularly played.[18] No composer left more written cadenzas than Mozart; it is interesting to compare his practice with Türk's precepts.

Ex.8 Mozart: cadenza to the 1st movt of the Piano Concerto in G major, K453

(a)

(b) first theme

(c) second theme

Mozart's cadenzas consistently display several important structural and rhetorical features. Most of these are present in his cadenza for the first movement of the Piano Concerto in G major K453 (see ex.8a). The typical Mozart cadenza is divided into the following sections:[19]

1. Introduction (optional): passage-work of a bar or more that provides a virtuoso springboard for what follows (missing in K453).

2. First section, often derived from the primary group. Care is taken to remove harmonic stability from quoted material. This is usually done by avoiding the root position tonic triad, whose presence would immediately destroy the tension of the initial 6-4 with fermata. Mozart often replaces root position tonic triads with a 6-4. Compare the quotation in the cadenza of the first theme of the first movement of K453 with its original form (ex.8*b*).

The first section leads to an arrival either on V^7 or on the tonic 6-4; this is often underscored by a fermata, and an optional bridge of passage-work leads to the second section.

3. Second section, often derived from the secondary group. Again the stability of root position tonic is usually avoided, and non-modulating sequences are sometimes made chromatic (or more chromatic). Compare the second theme from K453 (ex.8*c*) with its treatment in the cadenza.

Like the first section, the second culminates in a clear arrival, here on the tonic 6-4, elaborated by passage-work and a fermata. Sometimes the dominant note appears alone (with octave doubling), but it is clear that I_4^6, not dominant, is meant.

4. Conclusion: a flourish or running scale that prepares the trill, which ends the cadenza.

The melodic rhetoric of the cadenza appears to be exceedingly free; in fact motivic segments from the movement are often woven together with considerable adroitness. In ex.8 all motivic material is bracketed and its origin identified, revealing how little free material is employed. Nonetheless, an idiomatic cadenza does not depend upon the systematic quotation of themes. After an initial motivic citation, the cadenza to the Piano Concerto in A major K488 is virtually a free fantasia. Withheld harmonic stability, rather than thematic references, integrates the cadential gesture from the initial fermata to the final trill.

Passages outside the normal metre are not uncommon – note bar 34 of ex.8; but Mozart does not adhere to Türk's suggestion that stable metre be avoided. Regarding Türk's comments on modulation, Mozart commonly alludes to related keys,[20] or to keys borrowed from the tonic minor; as long as they appear briefly, these will not undermine the principal tonality. True modulations or stable alternation between root position tonic and dominant harmonies are rare as these vitiate the continuing tension.

Those seeking to study modern, stylistically idiomatic cadenzas to Mozart's concertos are referred to those of Paul Badura-Skoda,[21] Marius Flothuis[22] and the present writer.[23]

The generalizations above do not apply with equal validity to Beethoven cadenzas. Beethoven's concerto form differs from both Haydn's and Mozart's, and his harmonic and tonal vocabulary is in some respects wider. While his cadenzas may begin by quoting the primary group, then the secondary group, he does not feel bound to stay within the principal key and its related scale degrees. For example, the most commonly played cadenza to the Fourth Piano Concerto (in G major op.58), no.1, in 6/8 metre, starts in G major, quickly moves via E minor to C major, to F major, and to B♭ major for a quotation of the second theme. It remains in B♭ major for a considerable time; indeed it threatens to end there, arriving on the trill over the V^7 that normally marks the end of the cadenza. An interrupted cadence (to V_5^6 of G minor) momentarily reasserts tonal integrity; from there

Beethoven moves back to B♭ major, to A♭ major (Neapolitan key), and finally back to G (minor, becoming major). The length of time spent in B♭ major seems designed to erase the audience's memory of the orchestra's G major 6-4.[24] (Like Mozart, though, Beethoven avoids perfect cadences during the entire cadenza.)[25] Thus a performer wishing to improvise or prepare a cadenza for a Beethoven concerto would have fewer tonal constraints. This might seem easier, but the lack of firm guidelines makes the task more formidable.

Such distinctions between Beethoven's and Mozart's language are one of the reasons that Beethoven's cadenzas to Mozart's Piano Concerto in D minor K466 are problematic. Beethoven moves immediately to E♭ major, and then to B major and minor, creating conflicts with the conventions of Mozart's language (compare also Türk's point 4 above).

These considerations hint at a fundamental principle: one cannot attempt to write or improvise a cadenza without a precise command of the melodic, harmonic and rhythmic vocabulary of the composer. In analysing the relationship between a concerto and its surviving cadenzas it is possible to discern how one has spawned the other. The existence of as many as three separate cadenzas to certain of Mozart's concertos (e.g. the Piano Concerto in E♭ major K271) is a further stimulus to the imagination.

Ideally, the cadenza balances harmonic direction with moments of uncertainty, as the soloist negotiates a route to the perfect cadence that should sound extemporized, whether improvised or prepared (compare Türk's point 10).

Lead-ins (Fermaten)

Like cadenzas, lead-ins are signalled by fermatas.[26] Türk (among others) refers to lead-ins as *Fermaten* to distinguish them from *Cadenzen*. While cadenzas are prompted by the tonic 6-4, lead-ins are found at the soloist's first entry and at cadences before the statement or restatement of the principal theme in fast and slow movements alike, and are especially common in rondos. Thus they occur at half-cadences on the dominant triad or dominant seventh chord, and at perfect cadences in the dominant, mediant or submediant keys (less often, in the subdominant). They end at a second fermata or connect to the following music, in which case they are sometimes called *Übergänge*. Lead-ins can decorate consonant or dissonant arrivals.

Fermatas for lead-ins are found in solo and chamber works as well as in concertos.[27] In the treatises instrumental lead-ins display characteristics similar to vocal *Fermaten* (see chap.14 in this volume). Ex.9 shows Türk's sample lead-ins to the main theme from cadences in different related keys. These display a clear harmonic framework, particularly the one from E minor back to G major.

While a few of Mozart's lead-ins are ametrical (ex.10), the majority wholly or mostly remain in the metre of the movement. There is little need for motivic citation in ametrical lead-ins, but a number of the metrical lead-ins employ them, in which case the motif immediately preceding the fermata is often used. The length of Mozart's lead-ins varies considerably, from several bars to as many as 22 in the finale to the Piano Concerto in E♭ major K271, lead-in B.[28]

Ex.9 Sample lead-ins by Türk

While Mozart's instrumental concertos frequently call for lead-ins at cadences in related keys (compare especially the finales to the violin concertos), those in the piano concertos almost unfailingly start from an arrival at a dominant triad or seventh chord. Mozart often uses a harmonic progression, as in the first movement of the Piano Concerto in A major K488, that is essentially an elaboration of the V^7, until the resolution.

Ex.10 Mozart: lead-in to the Piano Concerto in C major, K415/387b, 2nd movt

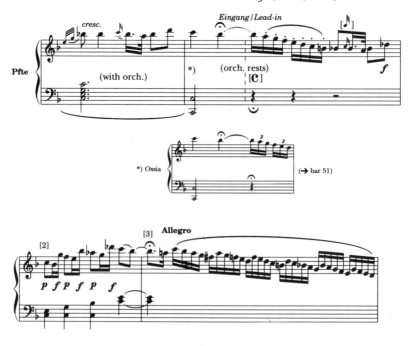

Free fantasies

Solo improvisation[29] has existed from the earliest times. By the Classical era such improvisation was carried out primarily by keyboard players, and only the most outstanding excelled at it. Dittersdorf declared that he could only stand hearing Mozart and Clementi, whose improvisation had been aped everywhere by incompetent imitators; above all he ridiculed flautists for attempting such solo fantasies in public.[30]

Bach's exposition of free fantasy concludes his treatise. He makes it clear that the key to successful improvisations of this kind is a solid knowledge of progressions and consistency of the harmonic rhythm. The ametrical fantasy that illustrates his points recalls many of his compositions.

Mozart's and Beethoven's improvisatory abilities were celebrated; their concerts frequently featured solo improvisation. While the fantasies by which Mozart is known are mostly metrical, there are two surviving ametrical pieces that are worthy of study. All are published in the NMA.[31] Beethoven's Fantasy op.77 is primarily metrical, though it contains several striking ametrical passages. Schubert's fantasies are metrical.

Keyboard improvisation was not limited to solo performances. Walther Dürr observes that the lack of piano introductions to many of Schubert's songs implies that the accompanist improvised a brief *Vorspiel*. Dürr theorizes that many of the piano introductions in the posthumous Lieder that are not provably composed by Schubert are derived from his improvisation; he characterizes these not as forgeries but as necessary complements (*Ergänzungen*) to the text in a printed edition for dilettantes.[32]

Continuo in piano concertos

There is considerable evidence that Classical composers expected the soloist to improvise from the bass – figured or unfigured – during the orchestral ritornellos of keyboard concertos.[33] 18th-century published editions of the keyboard part usually contain a figured bass during those sections, and

Mozart took the trouble to write 'col Basso' ('with the bass') in the left-hand staff of the keyboard part on virtually every page of the score when the soloist does not have an obbligato part. The reasons for this practice are still debated. Such concertos were normally conducted from the keyboard. It has been argued that the keyboard chords were to keep the orchestra together. It has also been suggested that the bass line was nothing more than a cue to prevent the soloist from getting lost.[34]

The Badura-Skodas present a balanced treatment of the question, pointing out the obvious differences in timbre between fortepiano and modern piano and between Classical and modern orchestral instruments. From this they adduce criteria for the discreet use of continuo in modern performance (pp.207–8). Neumann is more categorical, rejecting its use except on old instruments (p.255), and Charles Rosen states flatly, 'In the concertos of Mozart there is absolutely no place where an extra note is needed to fill in the harmony'.[35]

A central document in the controversy is an autograph continuo part to the Piano Concerto in C major K246. The Badura-Skodas argue that it shows how Mozart played continuo. Christoph Wolff argues that the realization reflects the modest abilities of the dilettante for whom it was intended,[36] while Rosen suggests that it was prepared for a performance without winds[37] – a view to which Neumann subscribes. More recently Faye Ferguson has given persuasive evidence that the continuo part was devised by Mozart for a performance of the concerto on two pianos.[38] It thus does not shed light on Mozart's own continuo playing.

While all aspects of improvisation inevitably involve questions of taste, the reinstatement of continuo hints at a deeper aesthetic conflict, from which present-day scholars are not immune. A strong objection to the use of continuo in modern performance, articulated forcefully by Rosen, is that it destroys the polarity between keyboard protagonist and orchestra.[39] This aesthetic objection reflects the Romantic view of the concerto as a heroic struggle between soloist and orchestra. However, that view is contradicted by acoustical and textural elements of Classical keyboard concertos. First, the fortepiano lacked the sheer power of modern grands; it could not equal or balance the sound of an orchestra playing at full volume. Second, the keyboard often accompanies the orchestra within solo portions of the concertos, whose texture ranges from absolute chamber music to occasional confrontations between soloist and ensemble.

Even if we leave aside the arguments for and against reinstitution of the practice, there is debate about how continuo was played in Classical concertos. Continuo is considered by some contemporary scholars to be a purely functional element of 18th-century music: the player merely marks each change of harmony by playing a chord.[40] This might be defensible if the only purposes of the device were to complete certain harmonies and keep the orchestra together. At the risk of challenging the Badura-Skodas, it must be said that purely chordal continuo playing contradicts both the tradition of thoroughbass and the treatises.

It is historically inaccurate to limit the function of continuo to the simplest harmonic underpinning. The figured bass is a product of the Baroque era, when polyphony was the primary texture. Quantz and C. P. E. Bach specifically suggest that the continuo player vary the number of upper voices and improvise linear and quasi-linear music when appropriate.[41] Thus continuo can be strictly chordal, in three or four parts; strictly linear, in three or only two voices; or a flexible integration of these. In all cases, however, part-writing remains primary. All thoroughbass textbooks[42] deal not merely with the interpretation of the figures but with their contrapuntal implications.[43] In any case, it is fallacious to reason that a composer was unconcerned with the qualitative presence of a chord merely because he did not write it down. Notated accompaniments were unnecessary because players were able to improvise them. As the fundament of keyboard improvisation the art of continuo playing requires the specialized ability to create elegant lines within chordal boundaries. Besides, a sensitivity to chord spacing has always been essential to the art of composition and to performance. Good pianists are well aware of this and weight the tones of chords according to their expressive power. The alert performer must regard the challenge of continuo in Classical concertos as a series of variable options: silence, chords, lines, mixtures of linear and vertical sonorities.

It should be obvious to historian and performer alike that the validity of a practice depends upon the skill with which it is carried out. Ornamentation is not an external process carried out upon a piece. The kinds of textural additions discussed above are most effective when they are fully organic to a work's expressive and dramatic content – indeed, when those without a score in front of them are unaware that anything has been added at all.

Notes

[1] P. F. Tosi (*c*1653–1732), *Opinioni de' cantori antichi e moderni, o sieno Osservazioni sopra il canto figurato* (1723/*R*1968; Eng. trans., 1742, 2/1743/*R*1969; Ger. trans. with commentary by J. F. Agricola, see n.4).

[2] The theoretical works of F. W. Marpurg (1718–95) span both performance and compositional practice; see H. Serwer, 'Marpurg', *Grove 6*.

[3] J. J. Quantz (1697–1773), *Versuch einer Anweisung die Flöte traversiere zu spielen* (1752, 3/1789/*R*1952; Eng. trans., 1966).

[4] J. F. Agricola (1720–74), *Anleitung zur Singekunst* (1757), incorporating a translation of Tosi.

[5] See C. P. E. Bach, *Versuch*, 79–86 and 149–50, cf also pp.87–143; however, these pages are mainly concerned with the execution of written ornaments rather than a treatment of embellishment to be supplied by the performer. The portions of the other treatises devoted to treatment of written ornaments are excluded from the page references below. Other sources to discuss the subject include Badura-Skoda, *Interpreting Mozart*, 177–208; Haas, *Aufführungspraxis*, 224–37, 242–5, 255 and 259; L. Mozart, *Violinschule*, 203–14; Neumann, *Ornamentation*, 230–56 and 275–81; and Türk, *Clavierschule*, 231–2 and 310–18. (Where appropriate, the page numbers refer to the English translation.)

[6] Spohr, *Selbstbiographie* (Kassel and Göttingen, 1860–61/*R*1954–5; Eng. trans., 1865/*R*1969), i.

[7] Bach, foreword to the first collection of *Sonaten mit veränderten Reprisen* (1760), quoted in Bach, *Versuch*, 166.

[8] *Letters of Mozart and his Family*, ed. and trans. E. Anderson (London, 3/1985), 880.

[9] See chap.8, 'Improvised embellishments', 177–96. This chapter gives examples of all genres of embellishment discussed above.

[10] *Ornamentation*, 240–56 *passim*.

[11] Neumann refers to this passage (p.240) but suggests no version of his own, finding those of the NMA and the Badura-Skodas 'very good'.

[12] While C. P. E. Bach does not deal with the cadenza *per se*, his remarks concerning the free fantasia are extremely valuable as a guide to harmonic shape and direction, *Versuch*, 430–45. Regarding keyboard accompaniment to a vocal or instrumental cadenza, see ibid, 384–6. See also Badura-Skoda, *Interpreting Mozart*, 214–34; Haas, *Aufführungspraxis*, 229, 237–8 and 243–5. L. Mozart does not treat the subject fully; however, he includes a few brief cadenzas in his treatment of embellishments (p.206). See also Neumann, *Ornamentation*, 257–63; and Türk, *Clavierschule*, 297–309, where the examples and discussion of poor cadenzas (pp.304–7) are illuminating and amusing.

[13] Recent cases include Sviatoslav Richter's performances of Benjamin Britten's cadenzas to Mozart's Piano Concerto in E♭ major K482, and Gidon Kremer's advocacy of the Alfred Schnittke cadenzas to the Beethoven Violin Concerto.

[14] For example, the cadenzas to Mozart's piano concertos in G major K 453 and D minor K466 by Brahms, to K466 and Beethoven's Third Piano Concerto by Alkan, to Mozart's piano concertos in C minor K491 by Saint-Saëns and in E♭ K482 by Britten.

[15] In piano concertos a dominant seventh chord is played under the trill by the left hand. In string concertos the soloist can create the chord through multiple stops. For wind and brass instruments the chord is implied.

[16] In Germany the final orchestral ritornello of the first movements to such works was sometimes recomposed to include a cadenza, as documented by the parts to numerous symphonies concertantes by Cambini in Münster.

[17] *Clavierschule*, 298–301.

[18] It had been assumed that Mozart's written-out cadenzas and lead-ins were designed for performance by others – particularly students. Recently Christoph Wolff has argued that Mozart intended these cadenzas for his own use (see 'Zur Chronologie der Klavierkonzert-Kadenzen Mozarts', *MJb 1978–9*, 235–46. Nonetheless, composer–performers of the period reputedly improvised their cadenzas. While these may have been more elaborate than those they wrote down, we have no proof that this is so; indeed, the technical demands of Mozart's and Beethoven's written cadenzas are at least equal to those in the concertos themselves.

[19] A more detailed discussion appears in Badura-Skoda, *Interpreting Mozart*, 216–34.

[20] Related keys are those whose tonic triads exist diatonically within the scale of the tonality: the related keys of C major are D minor, E minor, F major, G major and A minor; the related keys of C minor (taken from the natural minor scale) are E♭ major, F minor, G minor, A♭ major and B♭ major. Thus any of the keys just cited could appear briefly within a cadenza to a C major concerto. Of those derived from the tonic minor, III, iv and VI (here E♭ major, F minor and A♭ major) were most commonly used.

[21] For cadenzas to the first and second movements of the Violin Concerto in G K216, see Badura-Skoda, *Interpreting Mozart*, 296–8. Paul Badura-Skoda has also written a collection of cadenzas, lead-ins and embellishments to the Mozart piano concertos: *Kadenzen, Eingänge und Auszierungen zu Klavierkonzerten von Wolfgang Amadeus Mozart* (Kassel, 1967). They have much to recommend them, but – like some of the suggestions within *Interpreting Mozart* – do not entirely adhere to Mozart's language.

[22] Flothuis has written admirable cadenzas and lead-ins to the six piano concertos for which none by Mozart survive (Amsterdam, 1959, 1964). They are published in pairs: K466, 491; K467, 503; K482, 537. Neumann reprints the first movement cadenza to K491, *Ornamentation*, 261–3. Flothuis's cadenzas to the flute concertos in G major and D major K313-314/285c-d and to the Flute and Harp Concerto in C major K299/297c are also published, as are additional cadenzas by Flothuis to the violin concertos K211, 216, 218 and 219. Among the published cadenzas to Mozart's concertos these are probably the finest available apart from those by Mozart himself.

[23] Cadenzas and lead-ins for Mozart's five violin concertos by the present writer are published by Universal Edition, Vierra. Numerous cadenzas to Mozart concert and opera arias and concertos for wind instruments are at present unpublished.

[24] The alternative cadenza to this concerto – no.2, 'Cadenza (senza cadere)' (i.e. 'cadence [without making a cadence]') – modulates even more extremely.

[25] Nor is one reached even at the end of the cadenza; only in the tenth bar after it ends, within the concerto proper, is the perfect cadence reached. Beethoven experimented repeatedly with the music following the soloist's cadenza; cf also the Third Piano Concerto and the Violin Concerto. In the Fifth Piano Concerto ('Emperor') the cadenza is replaced by a solo passage that leads directly into the coda.

[26] Badura-Skoda, *Interpreting Mozart*, 234–40; C. P. E. Bach, *Versuch*, 143–6; Neumann, *Ornamentation*, 274; Türk, *Clavierschule* 289–96.

[27] While cadenzas are also occasionally present in the former genres, these are written out; see Mozart's Piano Sonata in B♭ major K333/315c and his Sonata for Piano and Violin in D major K306/300*l* (third movements).

[28] See NMA v/15, vol.ii, 123–4.

[29] C. P. E. Bach, *Versuch*, 430–45; Haas, *Aufführungspraxis*, 247–8.

[30] Dittersdorf, *Autobiography*, quoted by Haas, *Aufführungspraxis*, 247–8, and by Neumann, *Ornamentation*, 181–2.

[31] See NMA ix/27 (*Klavierstücke*, ii, *Einzelstücke*): no.2 ('Modulating Prelude (F–e), without K number; no.3 'Prelude in C', K284a (known as the Capriccio K395/300⁹; Appendix, no.1 'Fragment of a Prelude', K624/K³ 626a Anh. I/K⁶ Anh. C 15.11. The first and third of these are in fact a single piece.

[32] Forewords to Neue Schubert-Ausgabe, IV/1a–2a–3a–4a–5a, p.xiv: IV/6–7, p.xii.

[33] Badura-Skoda, *Interpreting Mozart*, 197–208; C. P. E. Bach, *Versuch*, 172–429. This reference, to virtually the whole of Part two of his *Versuch*, encompasses Bach's guide to 'Intervals and Their Signatures, Thorough Bass and Accompaniment'. While these are presented as general instruction in the proper performance of all works involving keyboard accompaniment, they obviously apply to the sections of a concerto in which the soloist is called upon to accompany the orchestra (Neumann, *Ornamentation*, 253–5). While Türk does not discuss keyboard continuo in concertos, he refers occasionally to the need for a good knowledge of thoroughbass in performing embellishments and performance in general; cf especially p.323 of his *Clavierschule*.

[34] The fact that Mozart's flute, oboe and clarinet concertos direct the soloist to play with the first violins during all ritornellos would seem to support this theory. It is difficult to believe that the soloist actually doubled the violin line in 18th-century performances; nor is there any evident musical value in doing so.

[35] *The Classical Style* (London, 1971), 192.

[36] Cf the foreword to NMA v/15, vol.ii, pp.vii–viii.

[37] *The Classical Style*, 193.

[38] Ferguson, 'Mozart's Keyboard Concertos: Tutti Notations and Performance Models', *MJb 1984–5*, 32–9.

[39] Rosen finds the modern use of continuo 'absurd' (*The Classical Style*, 193), arguing that Mozart in effect failed to realize that his music had outgrown the device. In this context Rosen asks, 'Does the composer know how his piece is to sound?', ibid, 195. Rosen thereby implies that his historical judgment should overrule Mozart's written performance directions.

[40] Rosen claims, 'The emphasis on the change of harmony is the only important thing – the doubling and the spacing of the harmony are secondary considerations', ibid, 194–5.

[41] See, for example, Quantz, *Versuch*, 251 (§4); Bach, *Versuch*, 173–7 passim.

[42] For example, Mattheson's *Grosse-General-Bass-Schule, oder der exemplarischen Organisten-Probe zweite, verbesserte und vermehrte Auflage* (Hamburg, 1731) and his *Kleine-General-Bass-Schule* (Hamburg, 1735); an excellent modern example is F. T. Arnold, *The Art of Accompaniment from a Thorough-bass as Practised in the XVIIth & XVIIIth Centuries* (London, 1931/R1965).

[43] Arnold would scarcely have required 918 pages for his treatise were it concerned solely with the picking out of the proper chords! Similarly, C. P. E. Bach's discussion of individual chords (*Versuch*, 198–311) makes part-writing a central priority.

CHAPTER XV

Voices

WILL CRUTCHFIELD

Sources

Among the sources for information about vocal practices of the past, instructional and theoretical works came to assume a new prominence through sheer quantity as the Classical period began and music publishing flourished. Between 1763 and about 1825 (after which the continuing Rossinian revolution begins to be reflected in treatises), there appeared in Europe at least 20 comprehensive vocal methods or critical studies written by respected authorities and containing extensive notated examples.

The last point is significant. In opera even more than in other genres it is necessary to assess the point of view behind contemporary accounts, because this theoretically impure art form has given rise to opposing polemical positions, not least on the questions of vocal style. The Classical era was a time both of operatic reform and of virtuoso vocalism. The latter art was cultivated with care, ambition and respect, while at the same time its more extreme manifestations found cogent and persuasive detractors. Almost every writer on the subject devotes a significant passage to questions of taste and judgment, balancing the claims of the composer and the virtuoso. A close reading of these discussions generally reveals not platitude but thoughtful argument and subtle difference of emphasis from writer to writer.

But without matching these accounts as closely as possible to detailed notation, it is impossible to determine what might have sounded restrained and what daring in Classical times – not to mention the idiomatic ways and means of carrying out standard ornamental procedures. Both admonition of restraint and exhortations to virtuoso exertion are (for us) vague almost to the point of irrelevance without a wide range of concrete examples. A consistent error of modern criticism has been to cite theorists' condemnations of ornamental excess in support of arguments against practices considerably more restrained than those advocated by the very same theorists. At the same time, editorial realizations of fermatas and other performance suggestions have often suffered from editors' insufficient familiarity with the surviving realizations from the period.

The Italian hegemony in vocal art was not seriously challenged within this epoch; as late as 1824 Richard Mackenzie Bacon wrote that 'the Italians are the only people who have cultivated vocal science with pre-eminent success. From them are deduced the few principles that are established in other countries'. It is only at first glance strange that most of the treatises –

especially those with informative musical illustrations – should be in English, German and French. In Italy, the oral tradition of instruction was strong and appropriate models were to be heard in every city. Elsewhere, the theorists are divided between expatriate Italians and native musicians who have mastered the Italian style (usually by study in Italy). The latter group are to some degree engaged in seeking independence from Italian principles at the same time as they are ostensibly describing the Italian-derived style; they tend to be especially cautionary about the virtuoso aspects of the Italian style.

It is thus simplest to survey Classical vocal style in the context in which it was taught: Italian music, principally operatic. We shall then return to note some of the divergences from this style when the native music of Germany, France and England was sung.

Domenico Corri (1746–1825) is probably the most valuable single theorist as far as the provision of practical examples is concerned, for several reasons. First, it was his avowed intention to provide what the modern scholar needs most: the details of execution that were normally left unwritten. These include the right-hand part of keyboard accompaniments (he seems to have been the first to publish songs this way in England, c1779) together with various indications of phrasing, accent, breathing, dynamics and ornamentation. Secondly, he was more reporter than advocate; though he consistently opposed extravagant ornamentation and shunned it in his collections (except in two examples specifically attributed to Catalani), his intent was clearly to show amateurs how professionals applied the musical conventions of the day. Thirdly, the approbation he received from his contemporaries recommends that he be regarded today as a central and tasteful representative of his time. Burney heard him sing and wrote approvingly; Bacon quotes at length from his 'very sensible and excellent treatise'; several of his pupils met with success (among them his daughter Sophia, who sang in the Haydn–Salomon concerts). Finally, his five collections of annotated songs and airs comprise the largest single body of such specimens from the period. The most important are the first (c1779), containing songs in Italian, almost all of them from operas performed in London within the decade and the last (1810), including music by Haydn and various other English and Italian works.[1] For the historian of the styles of the great Italian stars, Corri's insistent opposition to liberties taken by virtuosos makes him an insufficient source, but for modern revivalers of Classical practice, he seems a fairly consistent and reliable guide.

Other important works are those of Mancini (1774, 1777, the period's classic statement on vocal technique and aesthetics and a highly influential work, though sparing with specific examples), Hiller (1774 and 1780, practical and thorough), Lasser (1798), Celoni (before 1802, valuable as a document from an Italian still based at home), J. F. Schubert (1804, rich in specifics and sensitive to the stylistic shifts that were in the air), Lanza (1809 and c1817), Garaudé (1809 and 1811), Ferrari (1818), Roucourt (1821), Nathan (1823, rev.1836) and Bacon (1824, late enough to include an assessment of Rossinian style, but grounded in earlier values).[2]

Annotated performance materials are plentiful but difficult to study, since most remain unpublished (the compilation of early materials relating to

Haydn's *Creation* is a helpful exception).[3] Among the most valuable items are arias marked with performance indications by (or copied from those by) Mozart, Haydn and a number of minor Italian composers, and a vast number of manuscripts with embellishments added by distinguished music masters for their pupils. In London, following Corri's example, publishers began to issue arias with embellishments and nuances shown in small note-heads; both there and in Paris they also began to publish arias 'realized' with the performance devices of a particular famous artist on a separate staff. A broad survey of these sources makes it possible to distinguish the general practices of the period from the oddities or special cases that may be encountered in any single example.

Voice types

Musicians in the Classical era recognized the same four vocal types that had prevailed immediately before: soprano, alto, tenor and bass, with the first two belonging either to women or to castrated males. The decline of the castrato, both as an operatic presence and as a vocal model, is the central event of the history of vocalism in this period; when Haydn and Mozart began to write vocal music the castrato voice was still dominant in both roles, whereas by the time of Beethoven's maturity it was a freakish curiosity.

The subdivisions within and between the four basic voices made in later eras had not yet been adopted by composers and were only inconsistently described by vocal theorists. This does not, however, mean that singers with intermediate or otherwise unconventional ranges were not active. It is difficult to generalize about range, since it was uniformly understood that music would be transposed and adapted to suit the means of each performer, and consequently these adaptations generally passed without mention. For the purposes of the modern singer, two intermediate types that are not entirely self-explanatory require brief comment. A lower female voice was not usually called contralto unless the character in the opera was male. Several parts whose vocal tessitura is clearly lower than normal for a prima donna soprano (for instance Susanna in *Le nozze di Figaro*) were nevertheless always designated 'soprano'. A more troublesome case is the intermediate male voice, sometimes called baritone but occasionally also referred to as mezzo-tenor. Many tenor parts in Classical opera lie far lower than tenors today are generally expected to sing; Haydn's Orpheus, for example, dwells on *A* and *B♭, and some theorists describe the tenor range as beginning at G.* This was already characteristic of some Baroque parts (Handel's Bajazet, in *Tamerlano*) and continued through to the mature *opere serie* of Rossini.

That these singers could be considered tenors resulted from their cultivation of the head-voice upper extension that was then a standard part of the tenor's technical equipment and is almost never cultivated today. Some lower-pitched male voices could manage it, and could thus choose, to some extent, between tenor-clef and bass-clef roles. Several theorists distinguish baritone from bass partly by the former's softer and more delicate top range, a facet now not generally found in baritones. When Mozart revised the role of Count Almaviva for the Vienna performances, he took a tessitura that already lay high for a bass and moved it upwards, clearly with this low tenor voice type in mind. (Only part of the adaptation survives, and that only because, untypically, it occasioned some recomposition of the orchestral score.) Full tenors, meanwhile, are commonly described in treatises as ranging up to *d″* and *e″*, often with the specification 'in falsetto'. There is a particularly valuable Haydn letter telling how one tenor in an opera made a great effect with his falsetto on the G higher yet (*g″*), while another, attempting to imitate the first, displeased through his failure to join the chest voice smoothly with the falsetto. Few composers before Rossini wrote these high head-notes into scores, but they were clearly in use earlier. Bacon cautions that they be employed in passage-work, not sustained.

Technical aspects of Classical vocalism

Though an extensive discussion of vocal technique is beyond the scope of this book, certain aspects of it must be mentioned since many features of performance practice arise directly from the technical disciplines that were pursued. Italian vocalism was based (*a*) on the unification of the 'two registers', chest and head, into which 'the voice in its natural state is ordinarily divided' (Mancini); (*b*) upon the ability to spin the voice from *piano* to *forte* and back (*messa di voce*) on each note of the range; (*c*) upon the smooth joining of notes by 'gliding imperceptibly over the intervals' in between (*portamento di voce*); and (*d*) upon the mastery of a core group of basic ornamental devices including the appoggiatura, the trill, the *gruppetto* and the running scale or *volata*.

Any account of Classical performance style must begin with the acknowledgment that many Classical practices are impossible to achieve (or are obtainable only by awkward manipulation) except by means of a vocal discipline resembling that of the period. Singers today vary markedly in their ability to follow these practices, and since the instrument is a part of the artist's physique, a singer is even less able than an instrumentalist to shift technical procedures in the name of performance practice. The account given below aims to provide a simple description of the prevalent practices as far as they can be ascertained; each singer must judge the extent to which the adoption of the practices is advisable, and that judgment should be based at least as much on the level of technical assurance as on abstract stylistic and aesthetic considerations. When lack of restraint is criticized in modern revivals, the appropriate corrective for the performer lies less with theorists' criticism of excess (since hardly anyone has tried to revive the kind of vocalism they found excessive), than with Mancini's advice that it is better not to attempt an ornament than to sing it laboriously or indistinctly. ('Unless you can articulate every note as distinct as you could utter A, B, C, it would be highly detrimental to practice them quick', says Corri of his exercises.) Partly for this reason most of the examples shown in this article are chosen from the more conservative sources available.

Vocal vibrato is a thorny issue for the modern revivalist. Most pedagogues are agreed that a fully developed singer cannot continuously suppress his customary vibrato without some kind of unhealthy tension of the vocal mechanism. On the other hand it is certain that the degree of vibrato present in an artist's everyday singing is largely a matter of (subconscious) cultivation during training, and that during the history of Western artistic singing the steady trend has been towards the cultivation of stronger, wider and slower vibrato. This is observable even within our own century. There is little reason to doubt the supposition that in the Classical era, as before, a perceptible oscillation in pitch and intensity on a sustained note would have been thought undesirable. Mozart recalled in 1778 that Joseph Meissner 'had the bad habit of intentionally vibrating his voice', which he called 'contrary to nature', since 'the voice has its own natural vibrations'. Voluntary vibrato came to be specified as an occasional expressive device for particularly impassioned passages in the early Romantic era. No doubt the practice, like most others, came into use some time before it first appeared in notation (as Mozart's description suggests). The gradual transition to continuous vibrato took place during the 19th century and was a subject of much debate; it is discussed in Chapter XXI.

Recitative

All theorists agree that recitative is to be declaimed freely, with more regard for the stresses and accents of speech than for the notated rhythm, which should be 'loosened in such a manner that it resembles a perfect and simple spoken declamation' (Mancini). For the modern performer, accustomed to the conversational flow of naturalistic film acting, it is perhaps necessary to emend 'speech' to 'theatrical speech', as only in *opera buffa* was recitative typically described as rapid. The more formal and measured delivery of recitative in *opera seria* is attested to not only by written description ('con maesta propria degl'Eroi, e de' grandi soggetti', says Celoni) but by the more frequent punctuation with rests. Several sources attest that these rests were not likely to be sung through as often happens in modern revivals; additional rests were often added instead, and note values lengthened, as in Corri's examples from Handel, Gluck and others. This style was by no means thought of as inferior in communicative immediacy, and indeed was felt by many to be potentially the height of eloquence in singing.

Little or no ornamentation is advised for Classical *recitativo secco*; the *accompagnato*, being more 'sung', was more open to gracing. Hiller (1780) states that ornaments in *secco recitative* should be limited to occasional mordents and *Pralltriller*, but that 'so-called scenas, where an expressive aria is always preceded by a pathetic recitative', are an exception to that admonition. Mancini and others confirm this (though Mancini dissents from the prevailing view that chamber, church and theatrical recitative should be

Ex.1 Tarchi: *Mitridate* (1785) (ornamented copy in *I-Rsc*)

spo - sa, ti la - scio? Ah, non si - sto Ah, non re - si - sto Ad - dio

delivered differently). A consistent practice was the insertion of a brief melisma at the last cadence of a recitative (ex.1).

Schubert (1804) points out that when a fermata occurs on a syllable in recitative, 'appropriate free embellishments may be employed', but cautions that this should be avoided if the word in question expresses 'earnest wonderment or exhortation, or has a meaning in which embellishment can find no place', and gives as an example Donna Anna's 'Giura'. He also produces, for disapproval, a specimen of the 'pretty little things' that 'one often hears, especially in concerts': the first line of Vitellia's final scena from *La clemenza di Tito*, with a roulade of seven notes on the very first word and one of 20 notes at the end of the first line. Again, it is useful to see an example of precisely what a reformist critic meant by excessive ornamentation.

Courtly musicians, probably performing a cantata for solo singer accompanied by two violins, transverse flute and continuo: detail of painting, 'Interior in Gustavian Style with Musical Party' (c1779) by Pehr Hilleström in the National Museum, Stockholm

The prosodic appoggiatura

Appoggiaturas on all feminine line endings (line in this sense meaning not a complete poetic line but any vocal phrase followed by a rest or punctuation) were necessary in both forms of recitative as well as in concerted music; and these were not construed as 'ornament'. Increasingly during this period, appoggiaturas falling by intervals larger than a second were written out by composers, but it was assumed that these would be added when not written (Hiller, 1780, also asserts that the falling fourth can be sung either of the two ways shown in ex.2, and some other theorists add the possibility of using a lowered sixth degree for expressive coloration here. It was also assumed that all other feminine endings written on the same pitch, and approached by a falling third or second, by a unison or by any rising interval, would be sung with an appoggiatura at the interval of the second. The theorists are in complete agreement on this question where the word ends a line, but different theorists apply the appoggiatura with different frequency when dealing with words at the beginning or in the middle of a line. Ex.3 gives a sample excerpt of recitative with appoggiaturas written out, from Corri (*c*1779).

Ex.2 Hiller: *Anweisung* (1780)

Ex.3 Sacchini: *Perseo* (1774)

298

No Classical source suggests that there were exceptions to this practice or that these prosodic appoggiaturas were considered optional; some explicitly state that a note repetition – what critics today often call a 'blunt ending' – would have been heard as undesirable. However, one grey area emerges in the case of short fragmented lines or repeated rhythmic figures, such as the phrase 'voi ... sapete ... quel ... che fa' in *Don Giovanni*, Act 1, or the lines beginning with 'In mal punto ... son qui giunto' in *Le nozze di Figaro*, Act 1. Some period instrumental and vocal arrangements that otherwise specify appoggiaturas leave the 'blunt endings' in such cases. In general, though, where moderation in the insertion of appoggiaturas is advised (for instance by Mancini), this counsel must be understood in relation to the prevalent practice of adding further appoggiaturas – on masculine endings, in the middle of melodic phrases and on top of notes that already function as appoggiaturas – in addition to the uniformly required prosodic ones on feminine endings. Hiller (1774), for instance, gives many examples of appoggiaturas on masculine endings, but warns that monotony will result if too many are added.

These added (as opposed to required) appoggiaturas seem to have been most prevalent in music with German texts, perhaps because the language's relative paucity of feminine endings yielded fewer 'natural' appoggiaturas than were present in the Italian singing that served as a model. Another difference between German and Italian practice is that the former occasionally involved a 'divided appoggiatura' (ex.4), rarely known in Italian

Ex.4

sources. (In other contexts Germans often saw fit to indicate the anticipations effected by portamento with two notes, which the Italians did not indicate in notation and occasionally even deleted from German notation; thus it is possible that the written practice of the theorists differed more than did the actual practice of singers. Note, however, the presence at both divided and undivided forms in the keyboard transcription shown in ex.5.)

The appoggiatura from below is consistently mentioned or shown as a possible realization by Classical theorists. The preponderance of evidence suggests, though, that its use in *secco* recitative was uncommon, and that even in *accompagnato* and concerted music it was employed far less frequently than the appoggiatura from above. Modern editorial practice has probably overestimated its importance. Several theorists assert that the rising appoggiatura is made only at the interval of a semitone, and this is frequently the case (see ex.1), but whole steps and perfect fourths are also found. The suggestion that rising appoggiaturas were especially associated with questions finds strong support in early Romantic recitative; evidence on this issue in Classical sources is sparse, but Mozart tellingly confirms the rhetorical device in the 'letter duet' from *Figaro*, where Susanna sings 'sotto i pini' on a rising fourth and Mozart writes over her line 'domandando' – questioning. Occasionally described and often shown in musical examples are compound appoggiaturas of various kinds; some examples appear in exx.3 and 11. Many sources – including instrumental arrangements of vocal music – confirm that the appoggiatura was consistently observed not just in the recitative but throughout the concerted music of Mozart's operas (ex.5; ex.5*b* also shows the execution of elided syllables).

Ex.5
(a) *Don Giovanni,* from William Crotch's four-hand arrangement (*c* 1808)

(b) *Le nozze di Figaro,* from Crivelli (1824)

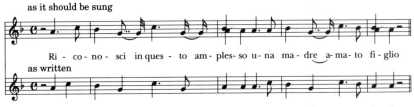

The aria

The da capo aria still held sway at the beginning of the Classical period, while the dominant form by the end of it was the cantabile–allegro 'rondò'; behind them ranged various kinds of arioso, canzonettas and cavatinas ('cavatina' at this time most often meant a cantabile aria without a consequent allegro or a da capo; in the 19th century, 'romanza' was the usual term for such a composition) and the genre pieces (siciliana, serenata). The mature Italian operas of Mozart are dominated by the shorter forms and the two-part rondò. Grand three-movement arias are also found, with the last movement corresponding to the allegro of the rondò and the first two (in either order) a cantabile and a moderato or allegro.

The da capo, associated as before especially with the castratos and the *seria*, tended to be a grand sonata-shaped aria with a cadenza in each of the three sections, light ornamentation in *A* and *B*, and virtuoso variation of *A'*. The principal differences from the high Baroque were that the cadenza was a more formal affair, introduced by a formulaic secondary-dominant preparation familiar to all through its use in Mozart's piano concertos, and that both compositional and performance interests were more and more concentrated in the *A* sections (with increasingly symphonic proportions), while the *B* was usually a slight arietta in contrasting metre (often 3/8). The return of *A* was frequently truncated, and eventually grand sonata-form arias without *B* sections or repeats emerged (the first two arias in Mozart's *Exsultate, jubilate*, for instance, are formally equivalent to *A* sections, but stand as complete arias).

Cantable and allegro styles

Theorists subdivide tempos and types of vocal movements in varying ways, but the principal distinction (other than that between recitative and measured music) divided cantabile from allegro. The former was a slowish movement, emphasizing flowing melody and simple accompaniment, headed with any tempo marking from Largo to Andante. It was generally the first movement of a two-part rondò; the allegro invariably stood last. Each had distinct manners of performance. The cantabile was sung legato, with portamento (Corri used small notes to suggest what was meant by this: ex.6), with *messa di voce* on sustained notes, and was more highly graced. The *gruppetto*, the appoggiatura (single or compound) and the *acciaccatura* were by far the most recurrent ornaments; little running passages often connected leaps or filled out long notes; syncopation, echo effects and 'division'-like passages were occasionally employed. The surviving Mozart-embellished arias (see ex.11 below for one of them) give representative examples of most of these devices; other typical lines of cantabile execution are shown in ex.7.

Ex.6 Haydn: 'She never told her love', from Corri (1810)

She   ne - ver told her love.   She   ne - ver told her   love.

The allegro proper was less subject to decorative ornament, largely by reason of its greater speed and stricter tempo. Passing notes, appoggiaturas and the like are found, but in less profusion, and unmeasured flurries of quick notes such as are commonly found in cantabile movements are rare in allegros. Staccato and syncopation are frequently employed as ornamental nuances, and running passages of measured semiquavers are often constructed on the outlines of melodies in longer note values (ex.8). Hiller (1780) explains the distinction: 'in slow and pathetic arias, slurred and drawn out [*geschleifte und gezogene*] ornaments are the most appropriate, just as thrusting [*gestossenen*] ones belong more to the allegro'.

Ex.7 Sarti: 'Lungi dal caro bene' from Corri (1810)

Ex.8 Cimarosa: 'Il mio cor' (Miss Jeffreys' copy)

In both styles, ornamentation generally involves adding notes of quicker rhythmic denomination than those in the score, rather than rerouting the existing semiquavers into another region of the voice or simply recomposing the melodies – a practice that has surfaced, and been criticized, in some modern revivals. One partial exception arises in the case of a rondò with recurring theme, where variation of the theme was expected and was sometimes quite freely creative. (Celoni, drawing a distinction between these and da capo arias, avers that 'Rondos ... have passages repeated more than once; one must therefore adorn them, and sometimes even alter them [*cambiarli*] in divers gracious ways, with which to increase their simple beauty'.)

At the end of the allegro, rather than a pause for cadenza, a repetitive stock cadence, in tempo, with continuous accompaniment generally appeared; this

Ex.9

too was subject to decoration. Over the course of the Classical period, the standard form gradually evolved from the type familiar in Mozart (ex.9, with embellishments from Corri) to the version that survived up to the time of Rossini and Donizetti (see chap. 21) which appeared as early as the 1790s in Italian music. There are some exceptions to the rule of ending in tempo; the Allegro of Leonore's aria in *Fidelio*, for instance, ends with a fermata, and a cadenza is clearly envisaged. But this was not typical.

Ex.10 Zingarelli: 'Cara, negl'occhi tuoi' variants of
Luigi Marchesi, transcribed by Vaclav Pichl (1792)

Many complete arias survive with variations attributable to specific singers or composers. In Milan in 1792 the important Czech composer Václav Pichl noted down and published the variants sung in different performances of Zingarelli's *Pirro* by the renowned castrato Luigi Marchesi. The very first line of the rondò 'Cara negl'occhi tuoi' (ex.10) gives some indication of what the theorists meant when they decried ornamentation that overwhelmed the original. (Other scribes, in Milan and Naples, preserved still further variations, related but distinct, by Marchesi for this aria.) Angelica Catalani, a natural soprano, was famous for her decorations later in the Classical period, and at least eight arias were published with her ornaments. As with Marchesi, we can see clearly that they represented a style considerably more florid than the conservative examples reproduced here.

For the da capo aria, Mozart himself left two invaluable examples with fully worked out *A* sections and repeats. One, for 'Ah, se a morir mi chiama' from *Lucio Silla* (1779, with truncated repeat), is excerpted in *Grove 4*[3] and given nearly complete in Neumann, *Ornamentation and Improvisation.*[5] (Examination of the entire score is worth while for showing what Mozart did not embellish.) Also from Mozart come embellishments for a da capo aria by J. C. Bach, 'Cara la dolce fiamma' from *Adriano in Siria* (ex.11). *A* and *A'* are shown complete, with cadenzas only for *B*, with multiple variants for the free incipit of *A*. Several observations arise from this pair of scores:

1. Passing notes and other small ornaments are introduced in the first statement and are increased during the repeat.

2. Appoggiaturas are made without exception on feminine line endings, and are often added elsewhere (note that their resolution is faster than implied by the crotchets of the original; this is also true of Mozart's realization of 'Non so d'onde viene' and of many theorists' examples.)

3. The cadenzas are short enough to be sung by an accomplished singer in one breath (see below).

4. The passage-work is not all in one rhythmic denomination, and prevailing semiquavers are often enlivened by a burst of demisemiquavers or uneven groups of quick notes.

5. The wide leaps in long notes in *Lucio Silla* are not embellished.

6. The prevalent idea in the variations is to increase the complexity and speed of figuration, not to alter melodic shape or tessitura; in general the idea of adding excitement through 'high' notes does not seem to play a part in the ornamentation, though the variants may rise higher than the original melodic line in the course of an ornamental figure.

7. Not only alterations of a pitch but also syncopation and phrasing are employed to vary the line.

8. Variations increase as cadences are approached.

Ex.11 J.C. Bach: 'Cara, la dolce fiamma' from *Adriano in Siria* with embellished versions by Mozart (Copy, in Leopold's hand, *A-Sm*)

Voices

sei____ E ne-gli af-fet - ti miei____ Co -

sei____ E ne-gli af-fet - ti miei____ Co -

sei____ E ne-gli af- fet - ti miei____ Co -

stan - te o - gnor sa -

stan - - - te o-gnor sa -

stan - - - te o-gnor sa -

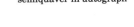

* semiquaver in autograph

rò Ca - ra la dol - ce fiam - ma dell'

rò Ca - ra la dol - ce fiam - ma dell'

rò Ca - ra la dol - ce fiam - ma dell'

al - ma mia tu sei E ne - gli af-fet - ti

al - ma mia tu sei____ E ne - gli af-fet - ti

al - ma____ mia tu sei E ne - gli af-fet - ti

probably
intended

307

The Classical Era

* omitted, presumably by mistake, in MS   (meant thus?)

MS lacks 'B' section but gives two cadenzas for it:

già cam - biò   già   cam - biò

già   [cam - biò]*

**♩. in MS
* text lacking in MS

Cadenzas and fermatas

The final cadenza in the da capo aria is symbolized in the written score by a fermata on the tonic, a trill on the supertonic and a final resolution on the tonic. The cadenza was inserted between the first two – that is, begun on the tonic and concluded with the written supertonic trill and its resolution. Most theorists agree that cadenzas should be sung on a single breath. This understanding should be tempered by two considerations: first, the rule is often stated together with an observation to the effect that infringements are frequent, once again raising the question of balance between conservative and liberal, or theoretical and theatrical, practice. Second, singers of the period (especially castratos) were trained to execute in a single breath passages that far exceed the capacity of most vocalists today. Thus a singer who wishes to perform 'authentically' in this regard may have to decide between authenticity of process (proceeding only as far as his breath span will permit, and perhaps striving to extend the latter by the discipline of cadenza-making) or of results (executing cadenzas of typical duration even though he may have to take extra breaths to do so). Mancini (1777) recommended the former approach to students. Ex.12 gives cadenzas from several sources, to supplement Mozart's in ex.11.

Among the principles to be observed in the many surviving Classical cadenzas are these:

Ex.12
(a) Mancini (1777)

Ad Libitum

A tempo   Adagio

(b) Hiller (1780)

(c) Mozart (*c*1778)

sa - rò   con - te

(d) Celoni (*c*1802)

1. The initial tonic is generally taken in the register shown in the score, though taking it in a different octave is not unknown. Beginning the cadenza on a note other than the tonic (i.e. the third or, as in the repeat of ex.11, the fifth above) is rare but again not unknown.

2. The inserted passage-work is not confined to the tonic 6-4 chord over which it appears, but rather modulates – usually to the subdominant, occasionally to the supertonic, submediant or even the dominant – and quickly returns; thus there may be a fair amount of figuration outlining II^7, or (less often) V^7, approaching the trill. (It is worth noting that the first example in a page of *bad* cadenzas in Türk's *Clavierschule*,[6] which contains much information applicable to singing, shows a cadenza that sticks closely to the 6-4 chord.)

3. The passage-work is formulaic but varied, and tends to include notes of more than one rhythmic denomination. (Mancini, 1774, seems to envisage the possibility of basing the cadenza on a motif from the aria, but this procedure is rarely described elsewhere and never, as far as I know, encountered in examples. More frequently, it is urged that the spirit or character of the cadenza should suit that of the piece.)

4. The final trill is taken in the register shown in the score, though here too octave displacement is not unknown. It seems likely that only cadenzas begun an octave higher than shown would have ended that way.

5. Resolution of the final trill was not limited to a simple *Nachschlag* but included – increasingly as the period progressed – brief dominant seventh roulades of varying prominence (usually eight semiquavers in Corri's examples) and compass (rising as high as the submediant or even, in a few instances, the leading note). These roulades sometimes included subsidiary trills along the way and were clearly forerunners of the dominant-founded cadenza that became popular early in the 19th century. Indeed, it is difficult to say where and how fast this shift took place. Schubert in 1804 is sceptical of the trend (he gives examples of 'die Mode' extending as far as 28 notes, and observes that 'it is easy to grasp that one can in this way discover still hundreds more trills, whereof each one may be more crinkly, motley and tasteless than the other'). But as early as 1792, in Martini, one finds a trill resolution of seven notes reaching up to the submediant. Ex.13 gives representative examples. By 1809 Lanza makes explicit the prevalence of the practice and its relation to the dominant cadenza: the short dominant roulades of up to eight notes are called 'Examples of various Conclusions to Shakes', while 'if there is a pause over the Note that has the shake, different decorations (which are called Cadences) are introduced *at the conclusion of the shake* [italics added], at the pleasure of the singer'. Lanza's examples for this latter practice start on a trilled supertonic, but otherwise resemble the dominant cadenzas of the Rossinian period.

311

Ex. 13
(a) Martini (1792)

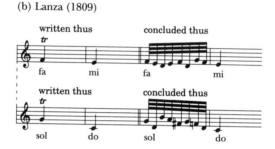

(b) Lanza (1809)

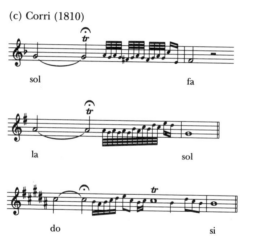

(c) Corri (1810)

Other fermatas

The two- or multi-part rondò generally lacked the da capo's formal cadenza in the tonic, but contained other fermatas (or, following the Italian usage, 'punti coronati') where the accompaniment was suspended while a vocal flourish was improvised or interpolated. (These could appear also in da capo arias, but did so less frequently, with one exception: the free, harmonically static open flourish on the tonic at the beginning of an aria – a hangover from the Baroque, and one that declined without ever quite disappearing during the Classical era. An example appears at the head of ex.11; numerous others are extant.)

The most significant denomination of fermata in Classical arias was associated with the end of a section in or on the dominant, where after a pause the music will resume in the tonic. (In the da capo aria, this function would generally have been discharged by an instrumental ritornello without pause.) Precisely where the fermata would stand, and what kind of interpolation would be sung, depended on several functional points. According to the style of writing, the roulade might come on the harmony preceding the actual dominant chord, on the dominant chord itself, or both. The close in the dominant might, at its most elaborate, have a full-scale cadenza indistinguishable from the final (tonic) cadenzas discussed below. More often, a pre-dominant fermata would stand on one of the commonly employed dominant preparations: the tonic 6-4, the secondary dominant in the second inversion or an augmented sixth chord (usually the 'Italian' sixth, sometimes the 'German'). Roulades on a fermata of dominant preparation are generally brief, sung on the single syllable on which the fermata stands.

When there is a fermata on the dominant preparation, it is always elaborated, and the following fermata on the dominant itself is occasionally left unadorned. When the dominant is in fact embellished, the type of roulade depends on what comes next. If the music is resumed by the accompanying instrument(s) alone, the roulade is rounded off on dominant harmony during the pause, and the seventh above the bass is present, if at all, only as a leading note to the dominant (as in exx.14*b* and *e*). If the voice resumes after the pause, the roulade expresses a dominant seventh or dominant ninth, and leads directly to the note of resumption (as in exx.14*f* and *g*). The latter type – much encountered – was known in various languages as a 'lead-in' (Ger. *Eingang* or *Eintritt*, Fr. *rentrée* or *conduit*, It. *conducimento* or *cadenza di ripresa*).

Ex.14

(a) Cimarosa: 'Il mio cor, gli affetti miei'
(Miss Jeffreys' copy, annotated, presumably by Sir John Stevens)

(Segue Allegro in F)

(b) Sarti: *Giulio Sabino* (1781; ornamented copy in *I-Rsc*)

(Segue Allegro in A)

(c) Mozart: *Le nozze di Figaro*

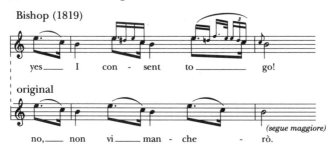

Bishop (1819)

yes___ I con - sent to _____ go!

original

no,___ non vi ___ man - che - rò.

(segue maggiore)

(d) Gluck: *Orfeo*, from Wrightson: collection of ornamented arias (1834–5)

nè   dal ciel

nè   dal ciel

(e) Lanza: 'The heart's first love'

sung

written

love re- mains for - e- ver re- mains for - e - ver

(Segue Allegro in E)

(f) Storace: 'Be mine, tender passion'

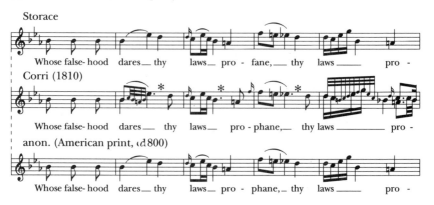

Storace

Whose false- hood dares___ thy laws___ pro - fane,___ thy laws _____ pro -

Corri (1810)

Whose false- hood dares___ thy laws___ pro - phane,___ thy laws _____ pro -

anon. (American print, c.1800)

Whose false- hood dares___ thy laws___ pro - phane,___ thy laws _____ pro -

314

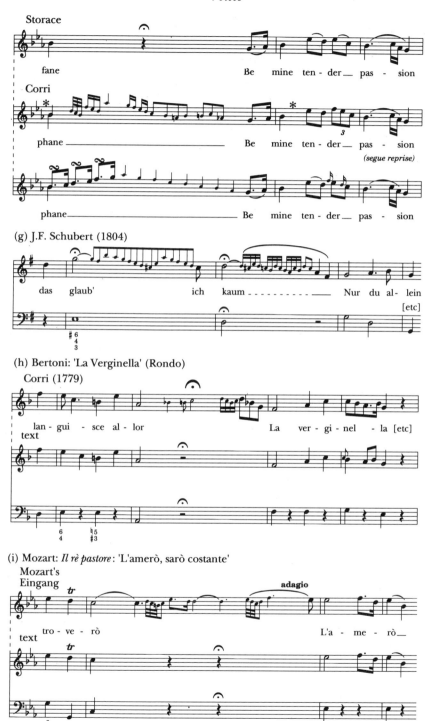

Storace

fane   Be mine ten - der — pas - sion

Corri

phane —————————— Be mine ten - der — pas - sion

(segue reprise)

phane —————————— Be mine ten - der — pas - sion

(g) J.F. Schubert (1804)

das   glaub'   ich   kaum - - - - - - - - - — Nur du al - lein

[etc]

(h) Bertoni: 'La Verginella' (Rondo)

Corri (1779)

lan - gui - sce al - lor   La   ver - gi - nel - la [etc]

text

(i) Mozart: *Il rè pastore*: 'L'amerò, sarò costante'

Mozart's
Eingang   *tr*   **adagio**

tro - ve - rò   L'a - me - rò —

text   *tr*

315

Occasionally, in rondò forms, one must make the *conducimento* from a key other than the dominant (generally the relative or mediant minor). This is usually done in the simplest possible way (exx.14*h* and *i*).

Towards the end of the Classical period, with the da capo aria out of circulation, the full cadenza in the tonic key makes a reappearance as a conclusion to the cantabile segment of the new two- or multi-movement aria which in earlier practice had usually ended in the dominant or on an unresolved dominant. The formal (secondary-dominant) preparation is absent; instead a simple subdominant (usually II^6) prepares the 6-4 chord, as in the arias of Handel. Both the 6-4 and 5-7 chords, and often the subdominant preparation as well, receive cadential roulades. These practices blend in with the beginnings of the Romantic period (for examples, see chap 21).

The *allegro* portion of the aria, though always involving some degree of repetition, did not invariably contain fermatas. When it did, however, the procedure was similar to those described above, with the understanding that an allegro of bravura vocalization would have correspondingly elaborate and brilliant fermata realizations.

Ensemble music

Several theorists stress the importance of exactitude and curtailment of liberties when two or more voices are singing together. Celoni writes:

> Duets, trios, quartets etc must be sung as they are written, and though it is permissible to vary this or that in the solos, in the remainder it is necessary to proceed with unanimity, and to play close attention to *forte, piano* and *pianissimo*; to smooth out, connect and separate [*spianare, legare e staccare*]; and this is to sharpen the expression, as I said above, and is scrupulously required in concerted pieces, in which appoggiaturas, trills and mordents are still permitted, but always with moderation.

Others emphasize that cadenzas for two voices or for voice with obbligato instrument (which was expected when the aria's accompaniment featured one) must be prepared in advance and are often written out by composers. Many examples survive, among them several for the duet of Susanna and the Countess in *Le nozze di Figaro* and for 'Ah perdona' from *La clemenza di Tito*.

Non-operatic and non-Italian music

Italian chamber and sacred compositions for voice in this period are little to be distinguished from operatic music in style, and few sources offer any specific examples to suggest a differentiation of performing manner. However, several assert, as a general principle, that sacred music is to be sung with more restraint and at slower tempos while domestic singing is described as being still more open to gracing and delicacies of style than singing for the stage.

Outside the sphere of Italian music it is a fairly safe generalization that the application of Italianate style decreased in proportion to the distance of the music itself from Italian models. This is true as regards both formal structure and the character of vocal and accompanimental writing. Germans noted with approval, and Italians with some grumbling, that sophisticated German accompaniments rendered vocal rhythmic freedom and ornamentation less appropriate. J. F. Schubert sensibly admonishes that 'Composition von Mozart, Haydn, Cherubini and Winter will bear fewer embellishments than those of Salieri, Cimarosa, Martin und Paisiello'. He also observes that 'Fewer embellishments are allowed in the church than in the concert or theatre'. Hiller gives a German sacred aria with full decorative apparatus – but it is an aria composed in italianate style. (Notable here is the ornamented version's strong resemblance to Mozart's personal style of passing melodic chromaticism, which is hardly to be found in ornaments dating from before Mozart's fame.) Large English and French arias graced on a similar scale are also readily found.

For the nascent German Lied we have only scant performance information; for the English theatre song and the French strophic air slightly more. Schubert's great interpreter Johann Michael Vogl ought perhaps to count as a Classical rather than a Romantic singer, since he made his Viennese Court Opera début in 1795 and came only as a veteran to the music with which his name is most directly associated today. Several examples of Vogl's interesting, dramatic and largely tasteful embellishments of Schubert survive;[7] they include the variation of cadences and small details in strophic songs; the application of trills, mordents, compound *gruppetti* and the like to the more operatic, large-scale songs; and a considerable amount of free, recitative-like treatment of metre.

French singers of the Classical period seem – on the basis of the fairly slender amount of evidence examined thus far – to have carried over from earlier generations a system of well-defined and differentiated ornaments (sometimes represented by symbols familiar from Baroque usage), to have preferred these to the bolder manifestations of italianate passage-work and cadential roulades, and to have applied them quite liberally to the ariettes and strophic songs that figure both in opera and in domestic song anthologies. Roucourt gives ornamental tables and sample realizations of songs.

In part because English publishers were quick to follow Corri's example, many English publications specifying vocal ornamentation exist for the latter part of the Classical period. Passing notes, trills and especially *gruppetti* are found in abundance even in simple English songs that lack the grander cadential points of music derived from Italian models. The decorations given in ex.15 are typical, and interesting as well for the particulars of dynamic shading.

Ex.15 Haydn: 'She never told her love'

Corri (1810)

original (Haydn)

Haydn: 'Sympathy'
Corri (1810)

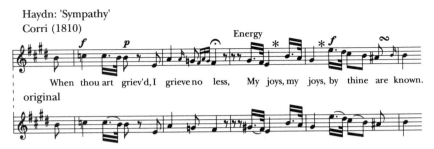

When thou art griev'd, I grieve no less, My joys, my joys, by thine are known.

original

In one type of English song about which questions often arise – that in which the voice is in octaves with the bass throughout – Corri implies, by the ungraced presence of Boyce's 'Hence with Cares, Complaints and Frowning' among ornamented neighbours, that the voice in such pieces did not take leave of the unison to add ornamentation. This is in contrast to songs in which the voice is doubled by a melody instrument over a conventional accompaniment. In the latter, the basic shape of the vocal melody is preserved, but not the strict unison – that is, the voice never ventures into descant or counterpoint, but does add passing notes and other graces without corresponding adjustment of the instrumental part.

Taste and judgment

Celoni's equation, in the passage cited above, of 'come è scritto' with the inclusion of small ornaments like trills and mordents is typical; for most theorists, these, along with the *gruppetto* and the portamento, seem to have been thought of as simply a part of tasteful execution, not as alterations. As a rule, annotated performance materials found in Italy lack indications of such ornaments and confine themselves to the larger devices such as cadenzas, altered passage-work and varied reprises. In this context, it is clearly wrong to read appeals to good taste, restraint and respect for what is written as calls for the 20th-century style of singing only the notes that appear in the score. Taste, in any case, can be exercised only within a framework of norms and standards, and is more a matter of the quality of the performer's intent and understanding than of the external details of execution. Judicious singers of one generation might habitually use a certain device that might happen to be employed only by the frivolous or vain artists of another; the device itself cannot be inherently tasteful or tasteless. This applies to musical perform-ance of all kinds, but it requires special emphasis in the case of singing because of the progressive tensions alluded to at the outset of this chapter, tensions that brings questions of taste and liberty to the forefront in operatic discussion. The performer interested in investigating period styles will have to arrive at an understanding of 'taste' that is free from the distorting 'purifications' carried out by later conductors and composers for their own good reasons.

Since the operas of Mozart loom so large in the modern singer's portion of Classical vocal music, a separate note on them may be useful. The approach to performance practice in these works is problematical, since anything resembling 'authentic' period style will necessarily, and for some musicians disturbingly, be quite different from the style in which we have all been accustomed to hearing them. There are strong reasons for entertaining the argument that our century's 'Mozart revival' has yielded a highly coherent and satisfying performance style that deserves to be respected and perpetuated.

Performers may find it useful to distinguish between aspects of performance practice that are necessary to make Mozart's scores musically and grammatically complete and those that fall into the realm of interpretation or soloistic liberty – even though such a distinction will be in some ways artificial, and certainly 'interpretation' plays a part in the way the 'grammatical' aspects are carried out. The category of grammatically necessary practices would include the prosodic appoggiatura and the fill-ins for fermatas. Those associated with the two-part rondò and the simpler aria forms are often called for in the Da Ponte operas (and, for instance, in the C minor Mass); only the *opere serie* have the old cadenza form treated in exx.11 and 12. The 'interpretative' class would encompass the niceties of cantabile execution, the variation of repeats and so forth – and these, arguably, are not necessary for a proper Mozart performance, even though Mozart himself would certainly have expected them. Much the same could be said of Haydn's oratorios: that they were in fact ornamented we know from many sources, but Haydn, like Mozart and Beethoven, was moving towards a different style, and the music – always excepting the fermatas – does not necessarily sound incomplete when ornamentation is forgone or kept to a minimum.

Notes

[1] D. Corri, *A Select Collection of the Most Admired Songs* (Edinburgh, c1779); Corri, *The Singer's Preceptor* (London, 1810).

[2] G. Mancini, *Pensieri e reflessioni pratiche sopra il canto figurato* (Vienna, 1774, rev. and enlarged 1777 as *Riflessoni pratiche sul canto figurato*); J.A. Hiller, *Anweisung zum musikalisch-richtigen Gesange* (Leipzig, 1774) and *Anweisung zum musikalisch-zierlichen Gesange* (Leipzig, 1780); J.B. Lasser, *Vollständige Anleitung zur Singkunst* (Munich, 1798); Celoni, *Grammatica, o siano regole de ben cantare* (Rome, 1810); J.F. Schubert, *Neue Sing-Schule oder gründliche und vollständige Anweisung zur Singkunst* (Leipzig, 1804); G. Lanza, *The Elements of Singing* (London, 1809–13); A. de Garaudé, *Méthode de chant* (Paris, 1810, rev. 2/1825); G. Ferrari, *A Concise Treatise on Italian Singing* (London, 1818); J.B. Roucourt, *Essai sur la théorie du chant* (Brussels, 1821); I. Nathan, *An Essay on the History and Theory of Music, and on the Qualities, Capabilities and Management of the Human Voice* (London, 1823, rev. as *Musurgia vocalis*, 1836); R.M. Bacon, *Elements of Vocal Science* (London, 1824).

[3] A.P. Brown, *Performing Haydn's 'The Creation'* (Bloomington, 1986).

[4] *Grove 6*, ix, 46.

[5] F. Neumann, *Ornamentation and Improvisation in Mozart* (Princeton, 1986).

[6] D. G. Türk, *Clavierschule, oder Anweisung zum Clavierspielen für Lehrer und Lernende* (Leipzig, 1789, enlarged 2/1802/R1967; Eng. trans., 1982).

[7] W. Dürr, 'Schubert and Johann Michael Vogl: a Reappraisal', *19th-Century Music*, iii (1979–80), 126–40; Neue Schubert-Ausgabe, iv/1a–2a–3a–4a–5a, pp.xiii–xiv, vi/6–7, pp.xi–xii.

PART THREE

The 19th Century

CHAPTER XVI

Introduction

D. KERN HOLOMAN

The 19th century – the age of symphony orchestra, heroic virtuoso and epic music drama – is close enough to our own for its traditions to be our common heritage. Our teachers' teachers were Cortot, Kreisler, Bernac and Mitropoulos, products of the great European conservatories of the preceding century. They in their turn were students of the luminous teacher-performers and teacher-composers of a tradition reaching back to the flowering of Romanticism. The proximity of the 19th century ensures that the central task in the study of its performance practice is to separate, among all the lore we have inherited, the practices that have survived unsullied from the past from those that have been corrupted by the vagaries of changing taste and fashion.

The proximity of the period also accounts for the enormous documentation of 19th-century musical life. What may especially distinguish this period from earlier ones is the size of the problem: the task of codifying and digesting all that there is to know is formidable. There are instruments to be found by scholars, rebuilt by craftsmen and mastered by performers; dozens of treatises and method books remain to be studied; many of even the central works of the repertory await modern scholarly editions (notably the operas of Rossini, Bellini, Donizetti and Verdi); while literally thousands of eyewitness accounts of performers and performances – newspaper reviews, lithographs, photographs, memoirs and recollections of every sort – have to be assimilated. Performance practice of 19th-century music is a study still in its youth.

It is important nevertheless to try to hear 19th-century music as the composer intended, using the instruments, tempos and phrasings specified in the score. In the case of the vast theatrical repertory it is important to see a work as it was first produced, with appropriate sets, costumes, machinery and, above all, a sense of grand tableau uncompromised by gratuitous gimmickry. For much of the century's music, reconstructing the conditions under which a masterpiece was first performed results in an unaccustomed intimacy of sound, delicacy of instrumental colour, and (in halls of appropriate size) warmth of expression. Balance of the orchestral choirs is often very different from what we are used to, and an obvious measure such as following the composer's metronome marks can immediately demonstrate how susceptible even the greatest works are to changing fashion. Roger Norrington's rethinking of Beethoven's Ninth Symphony, with its third movement taken at the prescribed minim = 60, is a successful attempt to restore the symphony to the 'humane, quicksilver thought-world of the Classical period, whose greatest progeny it is'.[1] His recent *Roméo et Juliette* of Berlioz has a remarkable texture, especially in the balance of brass and percussion and in the bowing strategies of the strings.[2] The lessons to be learnt from such experiments will encourage those at the helms of conventional orchestras and at the keyboards of nine-foot Steinways to adjust their conceptions of what such music was about.

Social change

The practice of 19th-century musicians was deeply affected by the rampant mechanization of western Europe. Machines descended from those of the 19th century still produce most kinds of music-making, and their prototypes are arguably the single most important source for the study of how music sounded then.

Railways, steamships and telegraph networks, in general use shortly after mid-century (Phineas Fogg made his 80-day journey in 1873, using all three), shrank what was widely thought of as the civilized world and appear to have profoundly altered perceptions of time and space. Notions of volume and size expanded in proportion to the new noise of industrialized urban life. The great pipe organs of Cavaillé-Coll[3] and his followers are one measure of this effect; industry rather more subtly begat the festival concerts with the massed performing forces common in that era.

Travel by steam-propelled conveyance offered new career possibilities as early as the century's second generation. Spohr and Weber travelled in similar fashion to the slow progress of Burney and Haydn before them. By the 1840s, however, with ever greater speed and comfort, the vagabondage of virtuoso performers was more or less universal. Liszt was on the road almost constantly in the early 1840s, reaching Portugal, England and Ireland, Turkey, the Balkan states and Russia – this last rapidly became an important locus for recitalists, especially during the Lenten theatre closings. (In the piety of his old age, when he again began to wander, Liszt insisted on second-class rail accommodation.) Berlioz's 1847 journey to Russia was made partly by sled; his second, in 1867, was from Paris to St Petersburg, via Berlin, entirely by train. By the 1860s it was not uncommon for rank-and-file orchestra players to make day trips by rail to augment each other's performing forces: the Karlsruhe musicians to Baden-Baden, for example, or Leipzig players to Dresden and vice versa.[4]

Five different orchestras of German-speaking musicians arrived in New York during the 1848–9 season, one of which, the 25-member Germania Musical Society, had considerable impact on the development of orchestral societies in the USA.[5] Jenny Lind was not the first operatic celebrity to make a tour of the USA, though her series was surely the most triumphant. In 1850–51 she gave nearly 100 concerts on the Eastern seaboard and as far as Havana, New Orleans and Cincinnati. Her way had been paved by musicians such as the violinist Sivori (1845) and two virtuoso pianists whose tours had preceded hers: Henri Herz (1845) and the 'lion pianist' Leopold de Meyer (1846), the latter selling European-made pianos as they went, like so much snake oil, and reaping profits of legendary proportions.[6] Giulia Grisi toured in 1854, and in the same year Mme Sontag succumbed to cholera in Mexico City. Thalberg arrived in the United States in 1856.

Among the Europeans to reach Rio de Janeiro were Thalberg, Gottschalk, Tamberlick and Mme Stoltz (who appeared in four Brazilian seasons for astonishing fees)[7]; the indefatigable American conductor Theodore Thomas numbered several European journeys among his almost ceaseless travels.[8] By the time that Dvořák sailed to the United States in 1892, regular voyages of musicians between the continents were nearly as common as aeroplane flights today, especially for conductors and opera singers.

Musical vagabondage of this nature created all manner of new demands for consistency in performance practice, among the most significant being the call for an international standard of pitch. (This was duly proclaimed, after the usual commission report, by Napoleon III in 1859; the resultant tuning contraption is enshrined today in the Musée Instrumental, Paris.)[9] Travelling artists required modern instruments and skilled instrumentalists when they arrived to perform, and often stimulated progress in cities and towns formerly content with indifferent standards. Business establishments responded quickly to the need for timely distribution of performance material and equipment. As early as the 1830s, a successful opera at La Scala would be required within a season or two in London, Paris, Vienna and St Petersburg (the commercial ramifications of this were quickly recognized, by the house of Ricordi in particular). Wagner's music reached Boston within a few months. Musical compositions, in short, strayed further and further from home, and the increasingly complex annotations in published music reflect these developments. By the mid-19th century, but not much before, the published full score of a work may be considered a reasonably precise indicator of the composer's intentions for its performance.[10]

Post-Enlightenment surges of revolution, imperialism and nationalistic pride resulted in marked changes in attitude towards public welfare. Education systems were greatly improved; the rise of the modern conservatories considerably elevated standards of performance. These institutions were high-powered descendants of the Italian conservatories of the 18th century, with courses of study for the instruments of the extended orchestra, and for composition, added to the customary courses for singers and violinists. Conservatories of considerable importance existed in Prague (1811), Paris (reorganized 1816), Vienna (1817), Leipzig (1843) and St Petersburg (1862).[11] Graduates of these conservatories formed generation after generation of technically secure instrumentalists, the best ones endowed with a healthy sense of enquiry and a determination to extend the technical possibilities of their instruments to the utmost. As the century progressed their teachers appear to have done much to establish what has become the standard repertory.

The singing schools and cathedral *maîtrises* faded away (except in England), the victims of modern secularism. In their place choral unions and the Orphéon movement prospered. Choral textures, often of six or eight parts, became correspondingly luxuriant. Women, mostly young, were encouraged to come out at night to participate in the work of the choral societies, and replaced boy choristers as sopranos and altos. The massed chorus of hundreds is symbolic of the 19th century's social values and aspirations.

Much has been written about the rise of the middle class – traditionally considered 'earnest, moral, not overly refined but still forward-looking' – and their buying power.[12] This general conception needs to be refined, but however we may choose to modify it this 'second aristocracy' unquestionably used its money to purchase entertainment. The arts became a point of contact between divergent social classes, for the remaining nobility was still passionate about the fine arts. But the taste of the middle-class parvenus may explain both the meretriciousness of much of the theatrical repertory and the volume of light fare that was included in the promenade concerts. In middle-class circles, the equestrian circus and pleasure garden were as inviting as the concert hall. Impresarios responded by giving concerts there, too, and the box office strategy was born.

Home music-making – *Hausmusik* – was similar to that of the preceding century. Properly bred young ladies still studied the piano and harp; aristo-cratic dilettantes still played the flute. Increasingly, a piano was to be found in the parlour of every tasteful family, and popular knowledge of the classical repertory was filtered through the medium of the *Trésor des pianistes* and similar collections. There apparently was not, as yet, a marked increase in leisure time. The successful business family seems to have worked long days in support of their entrepreneurial ventures. Yet music was more popular than ever, and a proper view of the performance history of, say, *Robert le diable* will not exclude the piano fantasies and the promenade quadrilles based on it.

Like universal suffrage, freedom of performance was an uncertain com-modity. Censors delegated with protecting the public morality demanded textual alterations that resulted in bizarre changes of characterization and plot. (Representatives of occupying nations, such as the Austrians in Italy, were the sternest censors, followed closely by the ecclesiastical lobby.) The versions of *Carmen, Boris Godunov* and *Un ballo in maschera* that were offered to the public, to cite only three examples, were moulded in some measure by the requirements of the censor. One significant role of performance practice research is to identify places where the composer's intent was adversely affected by the necessity of securing the censor's approval, and to restore if possible his intended reading.[13]

As the various independence movements in Europe gained momentum, music served as a potent political weapon. Nationalism in music is particu-larly interesting for its folkloric elements, expressed in terms not only of the Slavonic dance but also in texts like *Der Knaben Wunderhorn*. Performing the music of the later 19th-century demands an understanding of the *lassu* and *friss* and a good feeling for *cante hondo*. We should also be quick to sense the musical implications of common poetic images: the lone hurdy-gurdy player of the village band, for example, or the character attributes of Pierrot and his friends. Nationalistic music, a brisk confluence of elevated and popular styles, has a performance practice of particular complexity.[14]

The rise of the symphony orchestra and the invention of new instruments

Central to the musical life of the 19th century was the rise of the philharmonic societies and of the symphony orchestras. The most interesting of these were decidedly republican organizations, self-governing bodies led by committees whose meetings were often tempestuous and who paid scrupulous attention

Opening concert at the Queen's Hall, London, 1893, with the organ designed by A. G. Hill

to their pension funds and to the welfare of their widows and orphans. The Paris Société des Concerts du Conservatoire was founded in 1828, inspired by curiosity about Beethoven's music; the Philharmonic Society of New York and the Vienna Philharmonic Society both trace their origin to 1842. The same period saw the flourishing of the Leipzig Gewandhaus Orchestra under Mendelssohn from 1835. Concerts sponsored by the Philharmonic Society in London can be traced to 1813 (as can the Vienna Gesellschaft der Musikfreunde), though it was the last years of Smart's reign and the beginning of Costa's in the 1840s that gave most impetus to the development of a London orchestral style.

Characteristic of these orchestras was a clear breach with continuo practice, public concert series supported by subscription and leadership by a true conductor. The princely and royal court-theatre orchestras, like those in Berlin and St Petersburg, soon followed suit; in Berlin the Philharmonisches Orchester was founded in 1882. The Amsterdam Concertgebouw Gezelschap was founded in 1883. In America, three important orchestras were founded by the end of the century: in Boston (1881), Chicago (1891) and Philadelphia (1900).[15]

For the most part, modern orchestral practice is no livelier than the minor galleries of a museum of natural history (though it is surely no less interesting). The orchestra of the 19th century was, by contrast, a youthful institution, full of energy and not yet constrained by precedents. Spohr experimented in the late 1810s with his *Taktirstäbchen* ('directing baton'),[16] and along with Weber gave rise to modern conducting and to discussions of the proper role of the composer–conductor. By contrast, Spontini and others conducted with a baton held in the centre, and all manner of stamping of the floor and tapping on candle-racks was considered by many to be the only successful way to coordinate a performance.[17] (Berlioz's *victime du tack* is a prompter who expires from the mental agony of baton strokes on his box.)[18]

Orchestral seating arrangements were as varied as conducting techniques.[19] The members of the Gewandhaus orchestra stood to perform. Placement of the ensemble changed from orchestra to orchestra, house to house and work to work; choruses might be placed in front of the orchestra, and the conductor was sometimes to be found in the centre of his forces, surrounded by assistant conductors and mirrors. Flexibility in placing the force is *de rigueur* for 19th-century music. The practice of doubling in the wind section gained momentum as the century progressed, though from early on four bassoons were commonplace in many orchestras.

The philharmonic societies were adventurous in their choice of repertory as well, at least in the first half of the century. The thrill of discovering Beethoven dominated orchestral imaginations for a quarter of a century; the extent of Schubert's greatest accomplishment as an orchestral composer remained unknown, though it was the subject of widespread speculation. Orchestras devoured the music of Onslow, Moscheles and Cornelius, sometimes more readily than that of better composers. But by the 1850s this spirit of adventure was clearly on the wane. Old Masters began to dominate concert programmes much as they do today. Those planning the repertory bowed to the public enthusiasm for Weber and Mendelssohn (and for a few others) by offering their works season after season. Enthusiasm for novelty slackened as the decades passed, and the leadership in promoting new music largely shifted to more progressive organizations.

Such corrupt practices as the borrowing of favoured movements (for instance the Allegretto of Beethoven's Seventh Symphony) for insertion into other works came under increasing critical attack and eventually declined. So too, for the most part, did the habit of transposing arias into keys favourable to the star singers. Yet compromise was the rule of the day; thickly-scored works were routinely performed by ducal orchestras of 30, and english horn and harp parts were played on the clarinet and piano without a second thought.

The addition of piccolos, english horns and contrabassoons to the orchestral force vastly enhanced the symphonic palette. But an equally sweeping change in the sound of orchestras resulted from improved mechanisms for the traditional instruments. These innovations had the effect of improving the abilities of the players, particularly with regard to the new spectrum of keys and the vivid melodic configurations that the progressive composers increasingly required.

An excellent case in point is the improved clarinet, an instrument which, at the close of the 18th century, had already made a quantum leap from the five- and six-key instrument of Mozart and Haydn's associates to the 13-key clarinet used in the concertos of Spohr and Weber. In time the mechanism perfected by Klosé and Buffet in the late 1830s and early 1840s – called the 'Boehm system' by analogy with the relatively primitive structural improvements to the flute (1832) by the Munich maker of that name – was in general service.[20] Adolphe Sax, quite apart from his other accomplishments, was as successful in popularizing the new key mechanisms as anyone; soon they were extended to all the woodwind instruments.[21] From the same period come piston and rotary valves for brass instruments. The first of these were products of Silesian artisans in the 1810s; by the end of the 1820s, piston-valved brass were common in Paris, and rotary valves of increasing technical perfection were widely used by mid-century.[22] (Viennese practice still favours rotary-valved brass.)

A true chromatic harp was made possible by Erard's double-action pedal system of 1810.[23] Composers began to require a battery of percussion instruments assembled from diverse civilizations: remnants of janissary practice such as the Jingling Johnny or *pavillon chinois*, the 'antique' cymbals of old Pompeii and the simple assembly of straw-and-wood described so charmingly by Saint-Saëns (in the score of *Danse macabre*) as a xylophone. But the new sonority to be found in the percussion section that most characterizes the 19th century is the peal of bells: bells for the *Symphonie fantastique*, bells in the Kremlin, a bell machine for *Also sprach Zarathustra*, cowbells for the Alpine Symphony. (For *1812* Tchaikovsky had in mind all the church bells of Moscow, cued by the blast of a cannon from the Kremlin; he had to be content with a peal from Uspensky Cathedral.)

The wholesale conversion of string instruments into the high-powered models now almost universally used resulted in a dramatic change in string sonority. It is thought that less than a few dozen good violins escaped remodelling for volume, a process that lengthened necks and fingerboards, heightened bridges and permitted increased tension of the metal strings.[24]

The widespread adoption of the Tourte bow, developed in the late 18th century, completed the modernization of the violin; all of the superb instruments of Vuillaume were fashioned in the new style.[25] A similarly radical change in brass sonority was produced when the problem of the lowest brass instrument was resolved in favour of the German tuba – such an ideal solution that earlier scorings for serpent, ophicleide and the like seemed to many to beg for rewriting with the tuba in mind.

These developments are the more interesting in that the best among them resulted from collaboration between players, builders and composers, all firmly committed to the belief that modern technology would result in perfection. The modern orchestra was more or less identifiable by the time of the symphonies of Brahms and Mahler. With its mechanically sophisticated and visually attractive instruments, the extended symphony orchestra became the vehicle for the entire repertory. This development poses what I have referred to above as the central problem of 19th-century performance practice, for to manage Mendelssohn's orchestral works with the Brahms-Mahler aggregation raises some important issues and to try the *Symphonie funèbre* or *Les troyens* with such a force invites disaster. A really authentic 19th-century orchestra requires a collection of saxhorns, violas d'amore, a heckelphone or two and any number of other instruments that even the most avid concert-goer of today would fail to recognize.

Innovation also affected the sound of that most mechanically complex of musical instruments, the grand piano. By the maturity of Beethoven and Schubert pianos of conventional black and white keys and foot-pedals had begun to look, if not exactly to sound, like the modern grand. The simple action of the enlarged (six-and-a-half-octave) Viennese piano of Graf and Stein was favoured in central Europe for most of the century, though the London instruments of Broadwood and Clementi (later Collard & Collard) had their share of admirers. The double-escapement action patented by Sébastien Erard, on which the sensations of the mid-century industrial exhibitions were based, offered the possibility of much faster key repetition than before and is said to have permitted some of the most flamboyant characteristics of the 'Paris' technique of Thalberg and Liszt. The iron frame introduced by Hawkins of Philadelphia allowed a greatly increased string tension and a correspondingly greater volume, at the expense (it was held) of some degree of nuance. The concept of over-stringing made it possible to construct a grand piano small enough for the parlour, and a number of successful experiments in designing upright and square instruments contributed to the same end.[26]

Because the piano had become the favoured domestic instrument, its potential market was immense. This invited the better manufacturers to plan mass production schemes for cleverly organized factories. Steinway & Sons was founded in New York in 1853, the same year as Bechstein in Berlin and Blüthner in Leipzig.[27] By the 1867 Paris Exhibition the American makers had all but conquered the trade. Piano mania among consumers reached its peak just before World War I; afterwards the car and the record player were preferred signs of status.

The gadgets and gimmicks of industrialization were endless. Patents were issued left and right. For every mechanism that worked, a hundred did not;

for every medal garnered by an ambitious exhibitor, there is a laughing-stock like the piano-violino or a dead end like the giraffe.[28] Inventors sometimes failed to realize that the simplest solutions are usually the best. Maelzel's metronome (1815), for example, shows a certain perfection of simplicity, the product of scientific observation of two centuries before.

Visionary thinkers, naturally enough, focussed their ingenuity on the problem of reproducing music with mechanisms more sophisticated than the revolving cylinder and pins that had operated music boxes and barrel organs for centuries. Automated instruments powered by punched paper, in the manner of Jacquard's loom, seemed worthy of attention. Interest in automation proved ephemeral, but the player pianos of the 1890s represent remarkable change in the preservation of musical sounds of the past.[29] They are the first definitive records of what a musical performance sounded like. This was especially true of reproducing player pianos like the Pianola and the Welte-Mignon of 1904, where the nuance of performance by specific artists could be captured. (The first piano rolls, by contrast, were cut by technicians following a printed score.) Mahler and Debussy are among the great artists who cut piano rolls before the advent of acoustic recording. A reproducing pipe organ built by the Welte firm in Freiburg, the Welte Philharmonie (c1908), was favoured by Eugène Gigout and Max Reger (1912–13).[30]

Edison's tinfoil phonograph (1877) was the most perfect of experiments, reaching back to Léon Scott's phonautograph of 1857; in the same year as Edison produced his invention Charles Cros deposited a theory of recording technology with the French Academy.[31] Recording techniques were rapidly improved with the introduction of the wax cylinder (1885) and of the laterally-recorded flat disc (1888). Edison Home Phonographs and Victor Talking Machines were in mass production by the first decade of the 20th century. Electrical amplification became practical after World War I, by which time sound recording was big business. The advent of sound recording and, later, of radio broadcasting, afforded vast numbers of people their first opportunity to compare and contrast multiple interpretations of the same work. Recording had its implications for scholarship as well: such machines were adopted almost immediately by pioneer ethnologists.

Despite Edison's well-publicized attempts to record a Handel Festival performance of *Israel in Egypt* – in the Crystal Palace in April 1888[32] – the technology of recording through a horn did not favour orchestral music. Piano music (recorded by Brahms, Pugno and Grieg, among others) was barely satisfactory; organ music was not even that. (It is said, however, that a good recording was made of Alexandre Guilmant playing the organ of the 1904 Universal Exhibition in St Louis – the instrument now in the Wannemacher department store in Philadelphia.) It was different with solo instrumentalists, who could get close enough to the recording apparatus to achieve good results. Joachim and Sarasate, for example, left recorded performances.[33]

For the operatic voice, acoustic recordings are documents of considerable value. The first Othello and Iago (Maurel and Tamagno) made records; Caruso's 1902 recording of 'Vesti la giubba' sold a million copies. Nellie Melba recorded in 1904; in 1905 Adelina Patti – the greatest Violetta of her day, one of the era's most highly-paid artists and a singer well known to Verdi, who praised her 'purest style of singing' and her 'incomparable performance' – recorded two Bellini arias in the 56th year of her career.[34] Lionel Mapelson's cylinders of Metropolitan Opera performances were recorded from the prompter's box, so that he became the world's first record pirate.[35] Acoustic recordings are thus documents of a practice that extends well back into the 19th century. Recent scholarship has begun to re-evaluate their implications for modern performance.[36]

Venues

Democracy bred a delicate relationship between public enterprise and the vestiges of courtly patronage. In principle, the privately produced concert, following the example of the Viennese academy concert, was the discovery of the age; in practice, few musicians were wholly free of the need for what is now called external funding.[37]

The remaining dukes and princes proudly maintained the trappings of their courts. It was an interlocking nobility: the Grand Duchess Maria Pavlovna of Saxe-Weimar was sister to Nicholas, Tsar of Russia, whose tsarina was sister to the King of Prussia. This network could exercise enormous influence on the repertory by making their likes and dislikes known to each other by way of syrupy notes and gifts to their favourites: cash gratuities, gold snuff-boxes and membership of legions and orders. The blind Prince of Hohenzollern-Hechingen resolutely maintained his tiny orchestra through thick and thin, even when he lost his principality in the wake of 1848. The Prince of Detmold-Lippe was not too proud to take part in performances beside his several daughters; the Prince of Brunswick built a considerable musical establishment around the string-playing Müller dynasty and had an excellent music publisher, Leibrock, at hand.

It was these minor nobles, spiritual descendants of Lichnowsky and Lobkowitz, who kept the best traditions of musical patronage alive. Weimar and Futurism would have been as impossible without the Grand Duchess Maria Pavlovna as it would have been without Liszt; Bayreuth would have been unthinkable without Ludwig of Bavaria. The major monarchs, by contrast, were preoccupied with global concerns; they left such business to their huge but not especially imaginative bureaucracies.[38] Queen Victoria did not exert much personal influence on musical performance, nor did the monarchs of France; the Austrian emperor and Prussian king were slightly more active, but seldom with the passion to be found among the counts and dukes.

The great nations provided the wealth of their capital cities and the inexhaustible civic pride of their burghers and merchants who planned and built such houses as the Concertgebouw (1888) and Boston Symphony Hall (1900). They sponsored the philharmonic societies, bought season after season's worth of subscriptions, and often bequeathed their seats to their heirs.

The great nations also sponsored the international trade fairs which disseminated the latest innovations in technology across the seas. The Great Exhibition of 1851 in the Crystal Palace had a gallery devoted to musical instruments, copiously documented in official catalogues and penny guide-books.[39] (The pipe organ built for the Crystal Palace by Henry Willis was later transported to Winchester Cathedral for the use of Samuel Sebastian Wesley.) The London exhibition was followed by Napoleon III's reasonably successful attempt to rival it, the Paris Exhibition of 1855 in the Palais de l'Industrie on the Champs-Elysées. Important trade fairs to exhibit musical instruments included the Paris International Exhibition of 1867, the Phila-delphia Centennial (1876), the Paris Centennial Exhibition of 1889 (of Eiffel Tower fame) and the World Columbian Exhibition in Chicago in 1893. Ceremonial music, most of it insignificant, was composed for the fairs, and there were often huge festival concerts associated with them. New sounds from exotic lands were heard; it was at the Paris centennial, for example, that Debussy first admired the Javanese gamelan.[40] Equally intriguing sounds of the American jubilee and gospel song were reaching European ears at this same time.

Music lovers in *sociétés* and *Vereine* produced festival concerts of consider-able note. The Lower Rhine music festivals of 1818–67 are a conspicuous case in point;[41] the festival concerts in England (Birmingham, the Three Choirs Festivals) and America were fast becoming an established form of musical event. Beethoven's statue in Bonn was unveiled in June 1845 during the course of a festival that would appear to have been unmatched in the number and distinction of its participants.[42] Partisans of the Artwork of the Future had their own congresses. Nations celebrated with musical festivals when they bridged the rivers between them, then toasted their victories over one another with equally harmonious fervour.

As much good music as ever was available in the salon. The *Liederabend* and *matinée* or *soirée musicale* thrived. The salon served, moreover, as a place for discussion concerning performance. Many of the era's brilliant undertakings – resurrecting great works of the past, for example, in performance and publications – arose from informal conversations in these domestic circumstances.

Scores and other written evidence

As in any other period of music history, the materials used by the musicians themselves are critical primary evidence of their practices. Manuscript parts and conducting scores from the 19th century exist in abundance, at least in those houses fortunate enough to have been spared fire, invasion or removal to a new building. A complete set of manuscript material associated with the origin of a musical work is usually as good a record of its early performance history as of its compositional genesis. Players liked to sign and date their parts; alterations to the musical text bespeak the decisions made while preparing the work for its première, the compromises reached between composer and performers, and – perhaps most interesting of all – the lessons learnt by the composer from the players. Their number alone tells us a good deal about the size of performing forces. Original manuscript parts usually resolve dilemmas arising from printer's errors or other interruptions in the transmission of the composer's intention to the printed page. They are also uniquely able to shed light upon certain processes of revision in theatrical works. Assessment of such materials – without which there would be neither a Paris *Don Carlos* nor a viable *Benvenuto Cellini* – is one of the most intriguing tasks of modern musicology.

Another goal is to assure the preservation of these collections. Space is at a premium in the densely urbanized areas where the great orchestras and opera companies were born. The tidy are driven by an urge to discard things, and even the least practical-minded of archivists can see the folly of attempting to store every relic of a society given to generating countless tons of paperwork. But for performance practice research one copy of each part is scarcely better than nothing at all: it is the whole set that tells the complete story.[43]

Examples of other useful manuscript sources include the notebooks in which singers kept track of their cadenzas, as in the case of the albums of Mme Cinti-Damoreau.[44] Composer-teachers often corrected or amplified published editions of their works for their students, as in Jane Stirling's copies of Chopin.[45] Even autograph albums can be useful, since albumleaves often provide details on a specific performance just concluded, and they always give a musical passage by which an artist hoped to be remembered.[46]

From the late 1830s or so, lithography, a cheap process for generating multiple parts, did much to standardize performance material for certain works and began to curb the transmission of successive generations of scribal errors. Copper-plate engraving approaches perfection; the elegant work of the engravers (most of them women) for Breitkopf & Härtel, Richault and Rieter-Biedermann has had few rivals, before or since.[47] Networks for international distribution of published music were excellent; treaties between nations and agreements among publishers led first to a protection of the author's rights, and then to the seeds of international copyright for music.

In short, musical texts of the 19th century are often remarkably good. Engraved first editions carefully overseen by the composer remain superb sources and the ready availability of cheap photo-reprints of these (i.e. Dover scores and Kalmus parts) makes them the choice for many performers today.[48] For better or worse, the new critical editions notwithstanding, performance of the central repertory is still based almost exclusively on the 19th-century Breitkopf & Härtel editions and their descendants. Lore about their errors (often inaccurate lore at that) circulates informally among conductors and players. The enterprise of providing simple lists of corrections to famous scores and parts would be a worthwhile one for musicology.

The 19th century is also the period of *la musique à bon marché*:[49] penny editions sold to the masses in music shops, forerunner of this century's colour-printed sheet music. A sure measure of the success of an opera or symphonic work is the number of transcriptions, potpourris, and *extraits* it fostered. Editions for home performance took account of the instrumental combinations in vogue, so that it was common practice to modify one basic arrangement with alternative obbligato parts for flute, violin or cello. These editions were generally rushed through the press in order to respond to the intense public demand for tunes from the latest successful theatrical performances.

In recent years the discovery and circulation of production books for operas, their *mise-en-scène*, has generated considerable excitement among performers and scholars alike. These are accounts with diagrams and descriptive text of an opera's staging down to such minutiae as the gestures of the chorus. Most of the known manuscript books are in Parisian archives. Of the few published editions, the most intriguing are surely the *disposizioni sceniche* for Verdi's operas, published by Ricordi, *c*1856–1893. Eight have been traced (apparently there were nine), including an exceptionally detailed treatment, in 111 pages, of *Otello*.[50] The performance practice of Verdian opera is arguably the most carefully documented in all music, particularly when the vocal style preserved by the early recordings is taken into account. Without denying freedom of choice to modern theatre it can nevertheless be strongly argued that there is little excuse for ignoring issues of authenticity in productions of Verdi.

Music criticism and music scholarship

The 19th century was a period of the most universal dissemination of the written word so far: reasonably priced books and periodicals reached huge numbers of the population at almost every level of literate society. Whereas bibliophiles like Thomas Jefferson expended vast amounts of time and money to purchase books through diligent international correspondence, less conscientious readers fifty years later could assemble collections of similar size from shops a few steps away. Celebrity performers could afford to publish, at their own expense, short runs of their memoirs and treatises. The better books on music went through successive editions in a matter of months, and a few were immensely profitable to authors and publishers alike. There appears to have been an insatiable demand for readable discourse on music.

Of the composers, it was Berlioz who wrote the most perceptive of all the century's musical autobiographies (published 1870), though those of Spohr (1860–61) and Wagner (1869–81) are worth study.[51] The recollections of performing artists are refreshingly informative by comparison with today's ghost-written fan material; the memoirs of the tenor Gustave Roger, for example, have much to say about Meyerbeer's sweeping control over his productions, of backstage life at the opera house and of the conditions of his breathless tour of the British Isles with Jenny Lind.[52] Dozens of memoirs by articulate bystanders are worthy of attention, for example Eduard Devrient's recollections of Mendelssohn (1869) and Chorley's *Thirty Years' Musical Recollections* (1862).[53] The travel diary as a genre remained in vogue. The best of these books are teeming with information on the membership, habits and quality of the European ensembles.

But for our purposes the most remarkable trend in music publishing was the burst of method books, many of them still in use, for the century's newly improved instruments. The étude book as propounded by Czerny and Hanon[54] was envisaged as a vade-mecum for building technical virtuosity. (In that respect the masterworks which Chopin, Liszt and Debussy called études are, on the whole, uncharacteristic.) Many of the best tutors for orchestral instruments were written by members of the Société des Concerts du Conservatoire, like Arban's ('famous') trumpet method and Klosé's method for clarinet.[55] Such books as these played a major role in the palpable and widespread growth of technique in all 24 keys, leading to hitherto unknown levels of mastery. The quest for virtuosity is a constant of the era.

The early treatises on orchestration were a product of the same ideal. The Frenchman Georges Kastner wrote what is arguably the first of these (1837); next came Berlioz's (1843, later revised and expanded by both Weingartner, 1904, and Richard Strauss, 1904–5). Rimsky-Korsakov's treatise (1913, posthumous) is the last by a major composer before Piston, but good books on orchestration were compiled by such others as Gevaert (1863, 1885), Ebenezer Prout (a primer in 1876, a two volume study in 1898–9) and Widor (1904).[56] In the course of their expositions, they illuminate many issues of performance practice, among them orchestral placement, the tone quality expected of the instruments, how they were generally played, what was possible and what the writer thought needed to be improved.

As the craft of conducting developed into a true profession, theories of the conductor's art emerged. Berlioz was again the pioneer (1855); then came writings by Wagner (1869) and Weingartner (1896), and many lesser studies.[57] Berlioz naturally insisted on the conductor's responsibility to follow the composer's intent; some of the later conducting treatises of the century favour audacious schemes for modernizing works to suit the large symphony orchestra. Most of them agree, however, on the necessity that the conductor should use a full score (violin parts and abbreviated scores had formerly been employed) and baton, and on the value of leaving basic decisions of performance to a single musical executive.

Admirable music journalism – I hurry past the gossip and fashion magazines – appears to have grown from a succession of Viennese magazines and the Leipzig *Allgemeine musikalische Zeitung* (1798). Two important enterprises of the 1820s, A. B. Marx's *Allgemeine musikalische Zeitung* (1824) in Berlin and Fétis's *Revue musicale* (1827) in Paris, set the stage for the great music papers of the next decades: Schumann's *Neue Zeitschrift für Musik* (1834) and Schlesinger's *Gazette musicale* (1834; amalgamated in 1835 with the *Revue musicale* to become the *Revue et Gazette musicale*). Both offered critical writings about new music and were diligent in recording positive developments in the concert hall and opera house. In London *The Musical World* (1836) and the venerable *Musical Times* (1844) offered strong competition to the criticism found in the daily papers; the same generation produced the *Gazzetta musicale di Milano* (1842), *Le monde musical/Muzïkal'nïy svet* (St Petersburg, 1847) and, a little later, *Dwight's Journal of Music* (Boston, 1852).[58]

The good literary journals and newspapers took care to engage qualified writers to cover musical performances. Sometimes these were gifted composers; E. T. A. Hoffmann, Weber, Schumann, Berlioz, Liszt, Wagner and Debussy all wrote excellent music criticism.[59] Composer-critics, in particular, were sensitive to details of performance and often mention these in their notices, sometimes even discussing the nature of a particular artist's style of ornamentation. In any event, newspaper journalism is more accurate as to what was actually played than the printed programmes, and it is our chief source for understanding how performances were received by the public. A vast amount of such journalism survives: over fifty periodicals in Paris regularly sent correspondents to concerts and opera; nearly a hundred writers there were pleased to style themselves *feuilletonistes* on the musical arts.[60] One could not complain that the public was uninformed.

Articulate professional critics, unburdened by the urge to compose music, grew in number. Among these were Henry Chorley and J. W. Davison in London, H. F. L. Rellstab in Germany, and surely the most influential critic of the late 19th century, Eduard Hanslick (1855–1904), who wrote for the Vienna *Presse* and *Neue freie Presse*.[61] No one was barred from criticism for lack of professional credentials, and cultivated amateurs sometimes produced fine work. Heine wrote excellent reports from Paris to the *Augsburg Allgemeine Zeitung*;[62] George Bernard Shaw's criticism (1888–94) is highly regarded. Novelists from George Sand and Balzac to Tolstoy were also acute observers of the musical scene.

Curiosity about music of the distant past was intense. One of the remarkable accomplishments of 19th-century thought was to bring an approximation to the sounds of 'early music' before a large public. Mendelssohn's performance of the *St Matthew Passion* (1829) was but one revival of music a century old that also encompassed Scarlatti, Couperin and (in the early 1860s) Gluck. Fétis, in his Concerts Historiques (from 1832 in Paris; from 1839 in Brussels), systematically surveyed portions of the earlier repertory in concerts built around themes. Though sung in minims by large choruses, the music of Palestrina came to be widely admired, largely as a result of Baini's seminal work (1828). Brahms conducted a repertory that included Morley and Schütz as well as a great deal of Palestrina, Handel and Bach.[63]

Another result of such curiosity was the Bach Gesellschaft (1850) and *Gesamtausgabe*, the list of whose promoters and subscribers (Jahn, Spohr, Liszt, Brahms) still seems as fine a catalogue of the century's intellectual engagement as there is. Chrysander's Handel edition began to appear in 1859, the Mozart edition in 1877. Living composers, too, dreamed of collected editions of their works. By the last quarter of the century the idea of collecting the monuments of a nation's music had taken firm hold; the *Denkmäler deutscher Tonkunst* began to appear in 1892, followed shortly by the *Denkmäler der Tonkunst in Österreich* (1894).

These editions, together with such enterprises as Köchel's catalogue of Mozart (1862), Nottebohm's of Beethoven (1868), the work of the great lexicographers, and the beginnings of the notion of definitive biography all mark the birth of the discipline of *Musikwissenschaft*. The German tradition comes down to us from A. W. Ambros and Kiesewetter through Chrysander, Spitta and Guido Adler.[64] The French were, properly enough, interested in music of earlier times; the work of Coussemaker, Choron and Bottée de Toulmon introduced the study of plainchant, the music of the trouvères and troubadours, Machaut and the Netherlanders.[65] At the centre of these accomplishments is – once more – Fétis, whose ability to conceptualize the principles of a coherent music history (as in his explanation of the unities of the Netherlandish style for example) would be reason enough to admire him, but who moreover staunchly supported early music in performance, the concept of anthologies and the propriety of what is now called ethno-musicology.[66]

Discovering the music of the past, in any systematic way, affected composers more quickly than performers. Mastery of the performance of early music is the accomplishment of this century. But it was *Musikwissenschaft* that surely inspired the very notion of striving for authenticity in performance practice.

Iconography

The best 19th-century painting occupies itself with landscape and legend to such a degree that musical subject matter of a contemporary kind is uncommon. Notable exceptions to this rule are the wonderful canvases of Degas (1834–1917), showing the post-Romantic ballet in exquisite detail.

In contrast, forms of illustration new to the century depict the various activities of music-making in great depth. Mass-circulation illustrated newspapers are the most useful iconographic source of all for the 'look' of 19th-century music. It is always worth while to study halls, audiences and performers as they are depicted therein. For example, the papers published drawings of the memorable tableaux from operas, and these illustrations are as interesting for what they show of the blocking of singers as for their documentation of the décor. The musical subject matter of one picture newspaper, the Paris *Illustration*, has been critically indexed.[67]

Daguerre's picture of Liszt is usually dated 1841; the daguerreotype of Chopin is from 1849, with the famous portrait of Robert and Clara Schumann dating from the following year.[68] The heyday of photographic portraiture was reached by the mid-1850s, concurrent with the founding of the [Royal] Photographic Society in 1853 and the Société Française de Photographie of 1854. The photographs of Berlioz, Liszt, Meyerbeer, Wagner and, among performers, Ole Bull, David, the Dreyschocks, Ernst, Joachim and Gottschalk give that generation a presence in our mind's eye that is in some respects more thrilling than the sounds of the old recordings. But except for portraits of opera stars in their costumes, and for such curiosities as the photograph of Bottesini with his three-stringed double bass, they reveal little about performance practice.[69] Some experimental panoramic views of festival concerts are preserved; most other indoor photography of performances came after the turn of the century.[70]

Renderings of sets and costumes are well preserved for much of the century and most of the major repertory. It was a golden age of theatre decoration;[71] by the dawn of the 20th century, noted artists were frequently engaged to provide costumes and sets. Indeed, ballet of that period, from *Petrushka* to *El sombrero de tres picos* and *Le boeuf sur le toit*, is a considerably more attractive example of artistic collaboration than anything Wagner managed to arrange.

In most respects we are not especially dependent on iconography as a source for how 19th-century music was performed; we know of instrument design and numbers of musicians and the like from more direct sources. But it is worth observing here that the vast majority of 19th-century music is to some degree pictorial. Convincing interpretations of its imagery are impossible without a feeling for the contemporaneous landscapes and panoramas, for the grandeur of Nature as the artists saw it, for the immense aspirations of the age – attitudes that should affect both the scope and the pace of our performances. By the same token, a knowledge of the imagery of Romantic poetry is fundamental to making good 19th-century music.[72]

Introduction

Despite the proximities noted at the beginning of this chapter, our time is sundered from Romanticism by three decades of global war and monumental economic hardship from 1914. The mutations of common practice from, let us say, the 1850s to the present are quite substantial when taken collectively. Moreover 19th-century music is a succession of distinct repertories, each with its own particular customs of performance. The distance between Beethoven's Third Symphony (1803) and Brahms's Third Symphony (1883) is greater than the interval separating the *St John Passion* (1723) from *The Creation* (1798), or Willaert's first motets (1539) from Monteverdi's Vespers (1610).

It is unlikely that the historical performance practice movement will produce ophicleidists in the way that it bred shawm players; such instruments were, at best, transitional. But to insist on the difference between piston cornets and ordinary trumpets, to put a stop to the blatant filling in of natural brass parts and the incessant tinkering with poor Schumann, to curb (where appropriate) our passion for orchestral doubling, to follow the composer's metronome marks – all these are simple enough steps in the journey towards authenticity.

We should experiment more readily with orchestral placement and choral mix, with size and balance, with phrases and bowing. We might profitably attempt to evaluate the varying norms of Viennese custom versus that in Leipzig or Paris or London. In the theatre, we should attempt to discover all we can of the circumstances in which operas were conceived and most authentically produced.

Then there is the century's enormous repertory still to be rediscovered. Who has seen Daudet's *L'arlésienne* with Bizet's original score, or heard but a fraction of the corpus of chamber music and song that has been left to us?

One final admonition. Our fast-paced and sterile society rehearses, performs and packages the masterworks of this rich corpus of music in routine and predictable readings. A better performance practice would result from forcing ourselves to recall the passions of the time, the veneration of virtuosity, the willingness ever to linger, dwell and reminisce. It was, after all, the century of grandeur in musical enterprise, not just a time when music got louder and faster and more businesslike. Negotiating the compromise between past and present is as necessary for 19th-century music as it is for that of the Middle Ages.

Notes

[1] 'Performance Note', accompanying the recording: *Beethoven: Symphony 9*, with the Schütz Choir of London and the London Classical Players conducted by Roger Norrington.

[2] *Roméo et Juliette* and the *Symphonie fantastique* were offered on period instruments by Norrington and his forces during the 'Berlioz Experience' of March 1988. The *Fantastique* was released as a compact disc (1989).

Robert Winter has published discographies of other 19th-century music recorded on old instruments, see 'Performing Nineteenth-century Music on Nineteenth-Century Instruments', *19th Century Music*, i (1977–8), 163–75; 'The Emperor's New Clothes: Nineteenth-century Instruments Revisited', *19th-Century Music*, vii (1983–4), 251–65. On acoustic recordings made by 19th- and early 20th-century artists, see notes 33–5.

The documentation which follows in the remaining notes is based on a not especially scientific scan of the vast literature on 19th-century musical performance. I hope to be forgiven for dwelling on sources I have encountered in the course of my own work on the century's music, particularly work of the last several years; I mean merely to suggest avenues for further study, not necessarily to establish a definitive bibliography.

[3] See F. Douglass, *Cavaillé-Coll and the Musicians: a Documented Account of his First Thirty Years in Organ Building* (Raleigh, 1980); and H. Klotz, 'Cavaillé-Coll, Aristide', *Grove 6*.

[4] Berlioz's August concerts in Baden-Baden, 1856–63, were usually supplemented by musicians who arrived by train from Karlsruhe and occasionally from Strasbourg; sometimes the Baden musicians went to rehearse in Karlsruhe, where picnic lunches would be set for them in the gardens. As early as 2 February 1842, Berlioz had made the round trip by train from Leipzig to Dresden and back in a single day.

[5] See H. F. Albrecht, *Skizzen aus dem Leben der Musik-Gesellschaft Germania* (Philadelphia, 1869); and H. E. Johnson, 'The Germania Music Society', *MQ*, xxxix (1953), 75–93. See also I. Kolodin, F. D. Perkins and S. T. Sommer, 'New York', *Grove AM*.

[6] See for example R. Allen Lott, *The American Concert Tours of Léopold de Meyer, Henri Herz, and Sigismond Thalberg* (diss., City U. of New York, 1986).

[7] See the entries on Rosine Stolz in *Grove 6* and in *Baker's Biographical Dictionary of Musicians* (New York, 1900, rev. 7/1984 by N. Slonimsky), 2217; see also the entry 'Rio de Janeiro', *Grove 6*.

[8] See R. F. Thomas, *Memoirs of Theodore Thomas* (New York, 1911/R1971).

[9] See 'Paris, le 24 février [1859]. Rapport présenté à S. Exc. le ministre d'Etat par la commission chargée d'établir en France un diapason musical uniforme (Arrêté du 17 juillet 1858)', *Moniteur universel*, xxv (Feb 1859), 221–2. Berlioz's essay on the matter is found in *A travers chants* (1862), ed. L. Guichard (Paris, 1971), 307–17. See also U. Leone and P. Righini, *Il diapason: Storia e vicenda della sua normalizzazione* ([Turin], 1969).

[10] On some ways in which Urtext editions of earlier works from the century may be 'suggesting to the modern performer meanings that the composer did not intend', see Nicholas Temperley's review of entries in *Grove 6* on 'Notation' and 'Performing Practice', *19th-Century Music*, v (1981–2), 164–5; and W. Schenkman, 'Beyond the Limits of Urtext Authority: a Contemporary Record of Early Nineteenth-Century Performance Practice', *College Music Symposium*, xxiii (1983), 145–63.

[11] On Prague: *150 let pražské konservatoře* ('150 Years of the Prague Conservatory'), ed. V. Holzknecht (Prague, 1961). Paris: T. Lassabathie, *Histoire du Conservatoire impérial de musique et de déclamation* (Paris, 1860); C. Pierre, *Conservatoire national de musique et de déclamation: Documents historiques et administratifs* (Paris, 1900); also H. de Curzon, 'History and Glory of the Concert Hall of the Paris Conservatory, 1811–1911', *MQ*, iii (1917), 307–19. The Vienna Conservatorium was founded by the Gesellschaft der Musikfreunde: see C. F. Pohl, *Die Gesellschaft der Musikfreunde des österreichischen Kaiserstaates und ihr Conservatorium* (Vienna, 1871); R. von Perger and R. Hirschfeld, *Geschichte der k.k. Gesellschaft der Musikfreunde in Wien* (Vienna, 1912). Leipzig: K. Whistling, *Statistik des Königlichen Conservatoriums der Musick zu Leipzig, 1843–1883* (Leipzig, 1883); O. Günther, *Das Königliche Conservatorium der Musik zu Leipzig, 1843–1893* ([Leipzig], 1893); L. M. Phillips, jr, *The Leipzig Conservatory: 1843–1881* (diss., Indiana U., 1979).

[12] W. Weber, 'The Muddle of the Middle Classes', *19th-Century Music*, iii (1979–80), 175. See also Weber's *Music and the Middle Class: Social Structure of Concert Life in London, Paris, and Vienna, 1830–1848* (London, 1975).

[13] See for example R. W. Oldani, '*Boris Godunov* and the Censor', *19th-Century Music*, ii (1978–9), 245–53. L. A. Wright, in 'A New Source for *Carmen*', *19th-Century Music*, ii (1978–9), 61–71, describes the Parisian censorship process at some length; see especially 66–8.

[14] See for example M. Beckerman, 'In Search of Czechness in Music', *19th-Century Music*, x (1986–7), 61–73.

[15] Short historical sketches and bibliographies concerning all these orchestras are to be found in *Symphony Orchestras of the United States: Selected Profiles* (Westport, Conn., 1986), and *Symphony Orchestras of the World: Selected Profiles* (Westport, Conn., 1987), both ed. R. R. Craven. The best general study of orchestral practice of the time remains A. Carse, *The Orchestra from Beethoven to Berlioz* (Cambridge, 1948).

The major literature on the orchestras founded in the 19th century is as follows:

Leipzig: A. Dörffel, *Geschichte der Gewandhausconcerte zu Leipzig* (Leipzig, 1884/R1980–81); E. Creuzburg, *Die Gewandhaus-Konzerte zu Leipzig, 1781–1931* (Leipzig, 1931).

Paris: A. Elwart, *Histoire de la Société des Concerts du Conservatoire impérial de musique* (Paris, 1860); A. Dandelot, *La Société des Concerts du Conservatoire de 1828 à 1897* (Paris, 1898).

New York: J. Erskine, *The Philharmonic-Symphony Society of New York: its First Hundred Years*

(New York, 1942); H. Shanet, *Philharmonic: a History of New York's Orchestra* (New York, 1975); *Early Histories of the New York Philharmonic*, ed. H. Shanet (New York, 1979; includes reprint monographs of Henry Edward Krehbiel, James Huneker and John Erskine).

Vienna Philharmonic: W. Jerger, *Die Wiener Philharmoniker: Erbe und Sendung* (Vienna, 1942); H. Kralik, *Die Wiener Philharmoniker und ihre Dirigenten* (Vienna, 1938; rev. 4/1960).

London: M. B. Foster, *History of the Philharmonic Society of London, 1813–1912* (London, 1912); R. Elkin, *Royal Philharmonic: the Annals of the Royal Philharmonic Society* (London, 1947).

Vienna Gesellschaft der Musikfreunde: F. Klein, *Geschichte des Orchestervereins der Gesellschaft der Musikfreunde von 1859–1934* (Vienna, 1934).

Berlin: F. Herzfeld, *Berliner Philharmonisches Orchester 1882–1942* (Berlin, 1943).

Amsterdam: S. A. M. Bottenheim, *Geschiedenis van het Concertgebouw* (Amsterdam, 1948); G. K. Krop, *Concertgebouw orkest in diamant* (Amsterdam, 1949).

Boston: M. A. de Wolfe Howe, *The Boston Symphony Orchestra, 1881–1931* (Boston, 1931/ R1978).

Chicago: P. A. Otis, *The Chicago Symphony Orchestra* (Chicago, 1924); C. E. Russell, *The American Symphony Orchestra and Theodore Thomas* (New York, 1927).

Philadelphia: F. A. Wister, *25 Years of the Philadelphia Orchestra* (Philadelphia, 1925).

[16] L. Spohr, *Selbstbiographie* (Kassel and Gottingen, 1860–61), ii, 87; Eng. trans., *Autobiography* (London, 1865/R1969), ii, 81.

[17] I summarize early conducting practices in D. K. Holoman, 'The Emergence of the Orchestral Conductor in Paris in the 1830s', *Music in Paris in the Eighteen-thirties*, ed. P. Bloom (Stuyvesant, NY, 1987), 387–430. See also the chapters 'Conducting' and 'Conductors' in Carse, *The Orchestra from Beethoven to Berlioz*; G. Schünemann, *Geschichte des Dirigierens* (Leipzig, 1913); and E. Galkin, *A History of Orchestral Conducting* (New York, 1988).

See also W. A. Bebbington, *The Orchestral Conducting Practice of Richard Wagner* (diss., City U. of New York, 1984), which concludes with a superb bibliography.

[18] Berlioz, *Les soirées de l'orchestre* (Paris, 1852; Eng. trans., 1956, 2/1973); ed. L. Guichard (Paris, 1968), 155–71.

[19] See J. Westrup, E. Selfridge-Field and N. Zaslaw, 'Orchestra', *Grove MI*, with an interesting comparative table. See also G. Harwood, 'Verdi's Reform of the Italian Opera Orchestra', *19th-Century Music*, x (1986–7), 108–34, which includes several useful diagrams and comparative tables.

[20] See N. Shackleton, 'Clarinet', *Grove MI*; see also P. Bate, 'Boehm, Theobald', *Grove MI*.

[21] See M. Haine, *Adolphe Sax (1814–1894): sa vie, son oeuvre et ses instruments de musique* (Brussels, 1980). In general, on matters concerning 19th-century Belgian instrument manufacture, see the astonishing work of M. Haine and N. Meeùs, *Dictionnaire des facteurs d'instruments de musique en Wallonie et à Bruxelles du 9ᵉ siècle à nos jours* (Brussels and Liège, 1986).

[22] See P. Bate, 'Valve', *Grove MI*.

[23] A. Griffiths, 'Harp, §9: The Double-action Harp', *Grove MI*.

[24] See D. D. Boyden, 'Violin, §I, 5: Since c1785', *Grove MI*, and the bibliography cited at the end of the article.

[25] See D. D. Boyden, 'Tourte', *Grove MI*; also R. Millant, *J. B. Vuillaume, sa vie et son œuvre* (London, 1972).

[26] See various authors, 'Pianoforte, §I, 5–8', *Grove MI*, with numerous illustrations, and the bibliography at the end of the article. E. M. Frederick, in 'The "Romantic" Sound in Four Pianos of Chopin's Era', *19th Century Music*, iii (1979–80), 150–53, compares four instruments from his collection: a Viennese grand of the 1820s by Hasska, an English grand of c1830 by Stodart, a French grand by Pleyel of c1845 and a London Erard of 1856. See also n.28.

[27] See C. A. Hoover, 'The Steinways and their Pianos in the Nineteenth Century', *JAMIS*, vii (1981), 47–89; also T. E. Steinway, *People and Pianos: a Century of Service to Music* (New York, 1953), and A. Loesser, *Men, Women, and Pianos* (New York, 1954).

[28] See E. M. Good, *Giraffes, Black Dragons, and Other Pianos* (Stanford, 1982), especially the chapter 'Some Odds and Dead Ends'. The giraffe is pictured on pp.108 and 111, and in *Grove MI*.

[29] F. W. Holland, 'Player Piano', *Grove MI*.

[30] Record set *Orgues & Organistes français en 1930* (Paris, 1981), 5 discs. Programme booklet by J.-M. Nectoux, J.-M. Fauquet and J.-M. Louchart.

[31] See D. E. L. Shorter and J. Borwick, 'Sound Recording, Transmission and Reproduction', *Grove 6*.

[32] An engraving of Edison and his equipment in the Crystal Palace is reproduced in *Grove 6*, xvii, 575.

[33] Among records currently available are *Joseph Joachim: Complete Recordings* (1903), Pearl 804; *Pablo de Sarasate: Complete Recordings* (1904), Opal 804; and, of Kreisler's early recordings, 1904–28, Concertos of Bach and Mozart (Pearl 132), Brahms and Bruch (Pearl 250/1) and his own works (Pearl 233). Nikisch's 1913 recording of Beethoven's Fifth Symphony is said to be the prime example of Wagnerian conducting left to us: *Arthur Nikisch Conducts the Berlin Philharmonic Orchestra* (Perennial 2001) and *100 Jahre Berliner Philharmoniker, Frühe Aufnahme, 1913–1933* (DGG 2740 259).

[34] *Francesco Tamagno: Complete Recordings* (1903–4), Pearl 208/9; and *Greatest Arias* ('Nun mi tema' from *Otello*, 1904), Pearl 164. A complete edition of Caruso's recordings is being published by RCA, ARK 1–2766 etc. Melba is to be heard in Tosti's 'La serenata' (1907) on *Echo of Naples*, Pearl 219; in 'Des larmes de la nuit' from Thomas's *Hamlet* (1910) on *Greatest Arias*; and in arias by a number of composers (1907–21) on Pearl 180. Patti may be heard singing Arditi's 'Il bacio' (1905) on *Echo of Naples* and in the 'Air des bijoux' from Gounod's *Faust* (1905) on *Greatest Arias*.

On Caruso's recordings, see J. Freestone and H. J. Drummond, *Enrico Caruso: his Recorded Legacy* (London and Minneapolis, 1960); A. Favia-Artsay, *Caruso on Records* (Valhalla, N.Y., 1965); and J. R. Bolig, *The Recordings of Enrico Caruso* (Dover, Delaware, 1973).

[35] Record set: *The Mapelson Cylinders, 1900–04: Complete Edition Recorded during Performances at the Metropolitan Opera House* (New York: Rodgers and Hammerstein Archives of Recorded Sound, Performing Arts Research Center, the New York Public Library at Lincoln Center, 1985), programme booklet by D. Hall, D. Hamilton, T. Owen *et al*, R&H–100.

[36] See W. Crutchfield, 'Vocal Ornamentation in Verdi: the Phonographic Evidence', *19th-Century Music*, vii (1983–4), 3–54.

[37] On Clara Schumann's concerts, for example, see P. S. Pettler, 'Clara Schumann's Recitals, 1832–50', *19th-Century Music*, iv (1980–81), 70–76. On the concert series, see J. Cooper, *The Rise of Instrumental Music and Concert Series in Paris, 1828–1871* (Ann Arbor, 1983).

[38] On how this worked in Paris, see P. Bloom, 'Berlioz and Officialdom: Unpublished Correspondence', *19th-Century Music*, iv (1980–81), 134–46.

[39] See *Great Exhibition of the Works of Industry of All Nations, 1851: Official Descriptive and Illustrated Catalogue* (London, 1851); *Hunt's Hand-book to the Official Catalogues: an Explaining Guide* (London, 1851); *Exhibition of the Works of Industry of All Nations, 1851: Reports by the Juries* (London, 1852).

[40] See R. Mueller, 'Javanese Influence on Debussy's *Fantaisie* and Beyond', *19th Century Music*, x (1986–7), 157–86. Malou Haine and Nicolas Meeùs give an exceptionally comprehensive bibliography of the industrial exhibitions, 1803–1939, in their *Dictionnaire des facteurs d'instruments*, 745–51.

[41] See C. H. Porter, 'The New Public and the Reordering of the Musical Establishment: the Lower Rhine Music Festivals, 1818–67', *19th-Century Music*, iii (1979–80), 211–24. See also K. Whistling, *Der Musikverein Euterpe zu Leipzig, 1824–1874* (Leipzig, 1874). For the 1987 Annual Meeting of the AMS (New Orleans), Glenn Stanley read a paper entitled 'A Prelude to Bayreuth?: the Theory and Practice of the German Music Festival, 1810–1848' (*Abstracts*, 46).

[42] Described by Berlioz in 'Fête musicale de Bonn', *Les soirées de l'orchestre*, ed. Guichard, 411–32.

[43] I treat the migrations of one significant collection in 'Orchestral Material from the Library of the Société des Concerts', *19th-Century Music*, vii (1983–4), 106–18. This number of *19th-Century Music* is devoted to 19th-century French archives, embracing papers delivered to a work-group at the 13th Congress of the IMS in Strasbourg in August and September 1982. The other papers are J.-M. Nectoux, 'Music in the Archives of the Paris Churches', 100–03; E. Bernard, 'A Glance at the Archives of Some Parisian Orchestral Societies', 104–6; M. E. C. Bartlet, 'Archival Sources for the Opéra-Comique and its *Registres* at the Bibliothèque de l'Opéra', 119–29; P. Bloom, 'Academic Music: the Archives of the Académie des Beaux-Arts', 129–35; and H. R. Cohen, 'The Nineteenth-century French Press and the Music Historian: Archival Sources and Bibliographical Resources', 136–42.

[44] See A. Caswell, 'Mme Cinti-Damoreau and the Embellishment of Italian Opera in Paris: 1820–1845', *JAMS*, xxvii (1975), 459–92. The most significant contemporary treatment of vocal ornamentation was in M. Garcia, *Traité complet de l'art du chant* (Paris, 1840), rev. and trans. as *Garcia's Treatise on the Art of Singing* (London, 1894). For the 1987 Annual Meeting of the AMS (New Orleans), Will Crutchfield read a paper entitled 'The Prosodic Appoggiatura from the Time of Mozart to the Present Day' (*Abstracts*, 58).

[45] Fryderyk Chopin, *Oeuvres pour piano; Fac-similé de l'exemplaire de Jane W. Stirling avec annotations et corrections de l'auteur (ancienne collection Edouard Ganche)*, introduction by J.-J. Eigeldinger; preface by J.-M. Nectoux (Paris, 1982); see especially the 'table des annotations musicales' in the indices at the end of the volume.
On the matter of Chopin editions in general and Jane Stirling's collection in particular, see T. Higgins, 'Whose Chopin?', *19th Century Music*, v (1981–2), 67–75. Higgins has written a good deal on performing Chopin, as for example in his article 'Tempo and Character in Chopin', *MQ*, lix (1973), 106–20.

[46] See for example B. Friedland, 'Gustave Vogt's Souvenir Album of Musical Autographs', *Notes*, xxxi (1974), 262–77.

[47] On Breitkopf & Härtel, see R. Elvers, *Breitkopf & Härtel 1719–1969: ein historischer Überblick zum Jubiläum* (Wiesbaden, 1968); O. von Hase, *Breitkopf & Härtel: Gedenkschrift und Arbeitsbericht* (Wiesbaden, 1968). On Rieter-Biedermann, see H.-M. Plesske, 'Rieter-Biedermann, Jakob Melchior', *Grove 6*. On the Parisian publishers, see C. Hopkinson, *A Dictionary of Parisian Music Publishers, 1700–1950* (London, 1954), and 'Histories of French Music Publishers' in Hopkinson, *A Bibliography of the Musical and Literary Works of Hector Berlioz* (Edinburgh, 1951, rev. 2/1980), 194–200.

[48] The matter of what needs re-edition and what does not was the topic of a round-table discussion at the 1982 Smith College conference on Paris in the 1830s. See P. Bloom, 'Postface: Directions for Further Research', *Music in Paris in the Eighteen-thirties*, 611–13, notably 612.

[49] See A. Devriès, 'La "Musique à bon marché" dans les années 1830', in *Music in Paris in the Eighteen-Thirties*, 229–50, and the bibliography cited therein.

[50] See for example D. Coe, 'The Original Production Book for *Otello*: an Introduction', *19th Century Music*, ii (1978–9), 148–58. In his first footnote, Coe summarizes scholarship concerning the *disposizioni sceniche* as published by Ricordi from around 1856 to 1893. These *disposizioni* were first discussed at the 1969 International Congress of Verdi Studies at Verona and Parma; see especially A. Cavicchi, 'Le prime scenografie del Don Carlo', *Atti del 2° congresso internazionale di studi verdiani: Parma 1971*, 516–24. They were first listed systematically by Martin Chusid in his *Catalog of Verdi's Operas* (Hackensack, N.J., 1974).
For the French *mise-en-scène*, see H. R. Cohen and M.-O. Gigou, *Cent ans des mise en scène lyrique en France (env. 1830–1930)* (New York 1986) and the bibliography they cite in their Introduction, pp.xix–xxxiv. For the 1987 Annual Meeting of the AMS (New Orleans), Janet Johnson read a paper entitled 'The World of the Stage and the Staging of the World: Opera and Production Practices in Early Nineteenth-century Paris'; Rebecca S. Wilberg read a paper entitled 'The *mise en scène* at the Paris Opéra (1821–1873): Spectacular Effects in the Works of Meyerbeer' (*Abstracts*, 46–7). At the Indiana University conference 'Romantic Revolutions', in March 1988, M. E. C. Bartlet read a paper on 'The *mise en scène* of *Guillaume Tell*'.

[51] L. Spohr, *Selbstbiographie*. H. Berlioz, *Mémoires* (Paris, 1870; ed. and Eng. trans. by D. Cairns, 1965, rev. 3/1975). R. Wagner, *Mein Leben* (privately printed, 1869, 1875 and 1881), 1st authentic edition (Munich, 1963; Eng. trans. by A. Gray and ed. M. Whittall, 1983).

[52] G. Roger, *Le carnet d'un ténor* (Paris, 1880).

[53] E. Devrient, *Meine Erinnerungen an Felix Mendelssohn Bartholdy und dessen Briefe an mich* (Leipzig, 1869; Eng. trans., 1869/*R*1972). Chorley's *Recollections* (London, 1862/*R*1984); see also his *Music and Manners in France and Germany* (London, 1841/*R*1984).

[54] See Czerny's *Complete Theoretical and Practical Pianoforte School*, op.500 (1839); his *School of Extemporaneous Performance*, (op. 200 and 300) sheds considerable light on 19th-century improvisational practice. C.-L. Hanon, *Le pianiste-virtuose* (Boulogne sur mer, 1874).

[55] In addition to the famous *Méthode de violon* (Paris, 1803) of Baillot, Kreutzer and Rode, see such works as J.-L. Tulou, *Méthode de flûte* (Mainz, *c*1835/*R*1965); H.-E. Klosé, *Grande méthode pour la clarinette à anneaux mobiles* (Paris, 1844); H. Brod, *Méthode* [oboe] (Paris, 1835) (the great oboist Gustave Vogt left a tutor in MS); E. Jancourt, *Grande méthode pour le basson* (Paris, 1847); J.-J.-B. Arban, *Grande méthode complète pour cornets à pistons et de saxhorn* (Paris, 1864); P.-J. E. Meifred, *De l'étendue, de l'emploi et des ressources du cor* (Paris, 1829), and *Méthode de cor chromatique ou à pistons* (Paris, 1840); T. Labarre, *Méthode complète pour la harpe* (Paris, 1844). See also G. Bottesini, *Metodo completo per contrabasso* (Milan, *c*1865). The definitive tutor for the 15-key German bassoon is C. Almenraeder, *Fagottschule* (Mainz, 1843). See also F.-J. Fétis and I. Moscheles, *Méthode des méthodes de piano* (Paris, 1840).
From Vienna there were Hummel's *Ausführlich theoretisch-practische Anweisung zum Pianoforte Spiel* (Vienna, 1828/*R*1929), and Spohr's *Violinschule* (Vienna, 1832/*R*1960). See also, concerning Carl Czerny, n.54.

[56] G. Kastner, *Traité général d'instrumentation* (Paris, 1837), and *Cours d'instrumentation considéré sous les rapports poétiques et philosophiques de l'art* (Paris, 1839, rev. suppl. 1844); H. Berlioz, *Grand traité d'instrumentation et d'orchestration modernes* (Paris, 1843; rev. 2/1855, Eng. trans., 1856); F.-A. Gevaert, *Traité général d'instrumentation* (Ghent, 1863; rev. as *Nouveau traité d'instrumentation* (Paris and Brussels, 1885); E. Prout, *Instrumentation* (Boston and London, 1877/R1969), and *The Orchestra* (London, 1897/R1972); C.-M. Widor, *Technique de l'orchestre moderne* (Paris, 1904; rev., enlarged 5/1925; Eng. trans., 1906, rev. 2/1946). See also A. Carse, *The History of Orchestration* (London, 1925/R1964), and 'Text-books on Orchestration before Berlioz', *ML*, xxii (1941), 26–31.

[57] H. Berlioz, *Le chef d'orchestre* (Paris, 1856; Eng. trans., 1917). R. Wagner, *Über das Dirigieren* (Leipzig, 1869; Eng. trans., 1887/R1976); also trans. by R. L. Jacobs in *Three Wagner Essays* (London, 1979). F. Weingartner, *Über das Dirigieren* (Leipzig, 1895; Eng. trans., 1906/Rn.d.); also in *Weingartner on Music and Conducting* (New York, 1969). See also n.17, above.

[58] Of these, the Leipzig *Allgemeine musikalische Zeitung*, the Berlin *Allgemeine musikalische Zeitung*, the *Neue Zeitschrift* and *Dwight's* are widely available in reprint and/or microform. See also J. M. Barbour, 'Allgemeine Musikalische Zeitung: Prototype of Contemporary Musical Journalism', *Notes* v (1948), 325–37; and I. Fellinger, *Verzeichnis der Musikzeitschriften des 19. Jahrhunderts* (Regensburg, 1968).

[59] Hoffmann's music reviews are listed in the bibliography at the end of G. Allroggen, 'Hoffmann, E(rnst) T(heodor) A(madeus)', *Grove 6*, viii, 618–26, see especially 623–4. For Weber's criticism, see *Sämtliche Schriften von Carl Maria von Weber: Kritische Ausgabe*, ed. G. Kaiser (Berlin and Leipzig, 1908) and *Carl Maria von Weber: Writings on Music*, ed. J. Warrack (Cambridge, 1981). On Schumann, see *Gesammelte Schriften über Musik und Musiker* (Leipzig 1854, 4/1891/R1968); *The Musical World of Robert Schumann: a Selection from his Own Writings*, ed. and trans. H. Pleasants (New York, 1965); and L. Plantinga, *Schumann as Critic* (New Haven, 1967/R1977). Berlioz's best critical articles are found in his three collections: *Les soirées de l'orchestre* (Paris, 1852), ed. Guichard (Paris, 1968), *Les grotesques de la musique* (Paris, 1859), ed. Guichard (Paris, 1969); and *A travers chants* (Paris, 1862), ed. Guichard (Paris, 1971); a complete edition of his *feuilletons*, ed. H. R. Cohen, is in preparation. On Liszt, see *Gesammelte Schriften*, ed. L. Ramann (Leipzig, 1880–83). On Wagner, see *R. Wagner: Gesammelte Schriften und Dichtungen* (Leipzig, 1871–3 and 1883), summarized in *Grove 6*, xx, 139–40; on p.140 see also the subdivision 'Anthologies, Other Editions'. On Debussy, see principally *Monsieur Croche et autres écrits*, ed. F. Lesure (Paris, 1971, rev. 1987; Eng. trans., 1976).

[60] Cohen, 'The Nineteenth-century French Press', 136–42, outlines the general issues relating to this research and gives many useful particulars and suggestions of avenues for further research. Berlioz, in a manuscript list of tickets to be given away for his first performances of *Roméo et Juliette* in late 1839, lists more than 50 representatives from some 26 papers (*F-Pc*, *Papiers divers de Berlioz*, no.4).

J. Pasler, in '*Pelléas* and Power: Forces Behind the Reception of Debussy's Opera', *19th-Century Music*, x (1986–7), 243–64, treats the critical reception of that great work, giving a superb summarizing table of the Paris press in May–July 1902.

[61] The several collections of Hanslick's criticism, notably including *Vom Muskalisch-Schönen* (Leipzig, 1854; Eng. trans., 1957/R1974) and *Geschichte des Concertwesens in Wien* (Vienna, 1869–70), are summarized by Eric Sams at the end of the *Grove 6* article: 'Hanslick, Eduard'; much of it is available in reprint. See also *Eduard Hanslick: Music Criticisms, 1846–99*, ed. and trans. H. Pleasants (Baltimore, 1963), a revised edition of a selection first titled *Eduard Hanslick: Vienna's Golden Years of Music, 1850–1900* (New York, 1950).

[62] Heine's *Lettres confidentielles* are most convenient of access in *Heinrich Heine: Historisch-kritische Gesamtausgabe der Werke*, ed. J.-R. Derré and C. Giesen, xii/1 (Hamburg, 1980). On Shaw, see principally *Music in London, 1890–1894* (London, 1932/R1973) and *London Music in 1888–1889 as Heard by Corno di Bassetto* (London and New York, 1937/R1961).

[63] See V. Hancock, 'Brahms's Performances of Early Choral Music', *19th Century Music*, viii (1984–5), 125–41; and 'The Growth of Brahms's Interest in Early Choral Music, and its Effect on his own Choral Compositions', in *Brahms: Biographical, Documentary and Analytical Studies*, ed. R. Pascall (Cambridge, 1983), 37–40.

[64] A. W. Ambros, *Geschichte der Musik* (Leipzig, 1862–82/R1968). R. G. Kiesewetter, *Geschichte der europäisch-abendländischen oder unsrer heutigen Musik* (Leipzig, 1834/R1972; Eng. trans., 1848). Friedrich Chrysander, Philipp Spitta and Guido Adler founded the *Vierteljahrsschrift für Musikwissenschaft* in 1885; see also Chrysander, *Georg Friedrich Händel* (Leipzig, 1858–67), and

344

Spitta, *Johann Sebastian Bach* (Leipzig, 1873–80; Eng. trans., 1884–5/*R*1951). Adler's accomplishments include the general editorship of DTÖ and HMw.

[65] C.-E. de Coussemaker, *Scriptorum de musica*, an edition of four volumes of early music theory (Paris, 1864–76/*R*1963), to supplement M. Gerbert, *Scriptores ecclesiastici de musica sacra potissimum* (St Blasien, 1784/*R*1963); also *Drames liturgiques du moyen-âge* (Rennes and Paris, [1860]/*R*1975), and editions of the work of Adam de la Halle and of Flemish folksongs. Choron's leadership in the movement to restore the use of plainchant can be seen in his pamphlets *Considération sur la nécessité de rétablir le chant de l'église de Rome dans toutes les églises* (Paris, 1811) and his *Méthode élémentaire de musique et de plain-chant* (Paris, 1811). A. Bottée de Toulmon, *De la chanson en France au moyen-âge* (Paris, 1836), *L'art musical depuis l'ère chrétienne jusqu'à nos jours* (Paris, 1836) and *Instruments de musique en usage au moyen-âge* (Paris, 1838).

[66] See R. Wangermée, 'Fétis, (1) François-Joseph', *Grove 6*.

[67] *Les gravures musicales dans L'Illustration, 1843–1899* (Quebec, 1983).

[68] The daguerreotype of Liszt is given in *Grove 6*, xi, 33; of Chopin in iv, 298; of Robert and Clara Schumann in xvii, 844.

[69] The photograph of Bottesini is reproduced in *Grove 6*, ii, 92; see also the 1892 photograph of the snowflakes from the first performance of Tchaikovsky's *Nutcracker* in *Grove 6*, v, 206; and a 1913 photograph of Nijinsky in *L'après-midi d'un faune*, *Grove 6*, v, 209.

Stunning collections of photographic portraiture have been assembled by James Camner for Dover Publications: *The Great Instrumentalists in Historic Photographs* (New York, 1980), *Great Composers in Historic Photographs* (New York, 1981), *Great Conductors in Historic Photographs* (New York, 1982).

[70] See for example N. Wild, *Décors et costumes du XIXe siècle*, i, *Opéra de Paris* (Paris, 1987), a catalogue of the holdings there.

[71] See for example two Dover picture books: *The Decorative Art of Léon Bakst* (New York, 1972), including designs for *Daphnis et Chloé*, *Schéhérazade* and *L'après-midi d'un faune*; and *Picasso: Designs for 'The Three-Cornered Hat' (Le Tricorne)*, ed. P. Migel (New York, 1978).

[72] And even some argot. See C. von Canon, 'Zwirnknäulerl: a Note on the Performance of Johann Strauss *et al.*', *19th Century Music*, ii (1978–9), 82–4.

CHAPTER XVII

Keyboards

ROBERT WINTER

The most important fact about the Romantic piano is that it was many pianos. Between 1800 and about 1890 the piano underwent a surge of growth and technological development unsurpassed in the history of Western instruments. Musically, the 19th century was epitomized by colour, and the great variety of keyboard instruments produced represented the efforts of numerous builders to meet composers' and players' demands for a seemingly infinite variety of tonal palettes. As in most revolutions, there were leaders (among both builders and composers); the following survey is based upon their achievements.

In 1800 the Viennese fortepiano, for which the young Beethoven wrote works like the 'Moonlight' Sonata, differed little from that encountered by Mozart in the workshop of Johann Andreas Stein in the late 1770s. It generally had a length of about 215 cm and a width of about 97 cm. The range was five octaves, from F' to f'''. It was double strung to about a', then triple strung to the top, with the bottom octave in brass and the remainder in soft iron. The total tension on the frame was a moderate 1500 kg. The instrument itself weighed less than 70 kg. Two knee levers (replacing the hand stops of the 1770s) underneath the keyboard provided all of the tone-colour options: the lever on the right raised the dampers (one for each of the 61 notes), while the one on the left activated the moderator (a cloth strip brought between hammer and string to create a special soft effect). The action was the Viennese or *Prellmechanik* (flipping action).

Not even Beethoven could have foreseen that over the next two decades this instrument – still housed in a harpsichord case – would grow considerably in size and weight. Unlike individual string or wind instruments, the piano was harmonically and contrapuntally self-sufficient; there was no need for a keyboard family of varying sizes. Variant forms emerged, but they were inspired by marketing strategies and by considerations of space. While the dimensions of the violin have changed very little since the end of the 18th century, the dimensions of the piano were limited only by the expanse of keyboard which could be negotiated by a single player. Given the physics of piano design, especially the desirability of the longest possible bass strings, it would have been feasible to build an instrument 300 or even 400 cm long. The confinement of a grand piano's length to about 274 cm (only today's Bösendorfer Imperial is longer, by about 20 cm) was dictated more by space limitations in private residences than by the restrictions of concert halls. (This was not true, for example, of 19th-century organs.) An

346

'Schubert Abend bei Joseph von Spaun': sepia drawing by Moritz von Schwind in the Historisches Museum, Vienna: Schubert is at the piano, with Vogl on his right and Spaun on his left

instrument too large for a sitting room in a mid-century residence seems to have had little appeal for the emerging class of enthusiastic amateur pianists.

Since the developments in the Viennese fortepiano[1] took place in relative isolation from those in England and France, it makes sense to trace them independently. Although the growth of the Viennese instrument in size between 1800 and 1820 was unprecedented, there were no fundamental changes in the technology. A host of experiments with tone-modifying devices took place between 1810 and 1830, but these did not necessitate a revision of the basic design.

Although many composers contributed to the expansion of the Viennese instrument, the output of Beethoven provides the most reliable guide to its stages, contrasting markedly with the work of Schubert and other contemporaries. Until 1803 Beethoven's keyboard music remained within the five-octave compass of Mozart. His Piano Sonata in G major op.14 no.2 (1798) does call for an $f\sharp'''$ in bar 41 of the first movement, and there are some instruments from this period that add both $f\sharp'''$ and g'''. To judge by the survival pattern of several hundred instruments, however, the extensions in range occurred in discrete phases. The first encompassed the fifth up to c''''. With this expansion came an increase of about 20 kg in weight, caused largely by sturdier framing members to absorb the extra tension, now at almost 2000 kg. Virtually all Viennese instruments from this period retained the dual knee levers.

Beethoven's 'Waldstein' Sonata op.53 (late 1803–1804) demands not only an instrument with a compass up to a''', but one with a heftier tone as well. Though he had already called for a range to c'''' in the finale of his C minor Concerto (bars 346–9), Beethoven's first sustained exposure to the expanded instrument may have taken place when he received a grand on 6 August 1803 from the French maker Sébastien Erard. Rather than knee levers, it had four pedals in an unusual configuration: lute, dampers, moderator and shift (left to right). Not only did it employ the English grand action, but it differed substantially in other respects from Viennese instruments. Because of a bridge placed closer to the rim and a less efficient damping system, its tone was both more harp-like and hazier (not surprising features to find on an instrument by a harp manufacturer). Already in 1796 Beethoven had remarked to Streicher that 'so far as the manner of playing it is concerned, the pianoforte is still the least studied and developed of all instruments; often one thinks that one is merely listening to a harp'.[2] The English-style instrument from Erard can only have deepened his dissatisfaction.[3]

Whether Beethoven conceived the 'Waldstein' in 1803–4 because five-and-a-half-octave instruments were now available, or whether builders like Erard (or, in Vienna, Walter, Streicher and others) were responding to the demands of composers who wished to compose a 'Waldstein', is impossible to determine and is ultimately irrelevant. What is clear is that composers were in close and continuous contact with instrument makers.

The next stage in the development of the Viennese fortepiano was the further extension of the top octave to f''''. At present we know little about the exact construction dates of extant six-octave instruments. Discounting the cadenza to the finale of the piano version of the Violin Concerto op.61, Beethoven's first serious use of the new range dates from the late autumn of 1808, as he was completing the two piano trios op.70. The first of this pair, the 'Ghost'

Ex.1 Beethoven: Piano Trio in E♭ major, op.70 no.2, 4th movt, bars 329–35

Trio, as well as the first two movements of the second, in E♭, remain comfortably within the five-and-a-half-octave range. The finale of the E Trio has what might be construed as a careless *e''''* in bar 67, but in bars 330–32 there is a passage that unmistakably demands the larger range; see ex.1. Even more dramatic passages are found throughout his 'Emperor' Piano Concerto from the next year (ex.2).

The six-octave instrument was considerably larger than either the five- or five-and-a-half-octave models. Its weight approached 120 kg, with a length of *c*225 cm and a width of *c*123 cm. On most six-octave instruments the knee levers had been replaced by foot pedals. While the damper was retained (generally as the right pedal), the moderator was replaced on most pianos by a shift mechanism that moved the entire keyboard to the right. In some instruments the full shift meant that the hammer struck only a single string; hence the designation in Beethoven's music, 'una corda' (or, if the pedal were depressed only part way, 'due corde').

Many Viennese instruments from the period 1810–30 employed up to four additional pedals for tone modification. The familiar moderator was sometimes divided between two pedals (Conrad Graf serial no.423). One series of leather tongues was activated by one pedal; the second pedal pushed the mechanism in further to engage a superimposed series of shorter tongues, whose two combined layers muted the sound even more. There was the

349

Ex.2 Beethoven: Piano Concerto in E♭ major, op.73, 1st movt, bars 215–17

'bassoon' stop, in which a piece of cylindrical parchment (often filled with birdshot) rested on the tenor strings, producing a buzzing or jangling sound. The 'Turkish' stop activated a small bell and struck a soft mallet to the underside of the soundboard each time it was depressed (these functions were sometimes divided among two pedals). Although there are no instances in the music of either Beethoven or Schubert where such effects are specifically demanded, they are called for occasionally by Dussek (e.g. in the finale to his Sonata in D major op.45 no.3). Their vogue may have been restricted largely to the plethora of battle pieces that accompanied the Napoleonic wars and their aftermath. Nevertheless, their presence on so many surviving instruments (including those of the finest quality) suggests that they were used quite freely.

Most important, with all of the plain-wire unisons now triple strung, total string tension averaged 3000–4000 kg, twice that of instruments built only a few years previously. This produced a correspondingly larger sound, but it also explains why so few six-octave instruments survive in playing condition. Whether builders in the period between 1800 and 1820 were aware of the magnitude of increase in string tension is uncertain; no design records from this period have come to light. But the reinforcement technology remained the same as it had in five and five-and-a-half-octave instruments. Apart from a small iron brace between the wrest plank and the belly rail, the tension was absorbed by an all-wooden frame. In virtually all surviving instruments this proved too great a burden, with wrest planks taking on the characteristic upward bow that lifted most of the strings off the bridge. We do not know how long this process of deformation took to unfold, but the problem must have been obvious by the 1830s when Viennese builders began adding iron bars between the wrest plank and stringing plate. The problem facing both restorers and replica makers today is how to either reverse or to prevent structural damage without altering the essential sound characteristics of these instruments.

The final extension of range during Beethoven's lifetime had occurred by November of 1816, when he published his A major Sonata op.101 (1816).

With the development of wound bass strings[4] the Viennese instrument added the five notes down to C'. Twice at crucial junctures of the finale (at the retransition and at the end of the coda), E' serves as a conspicuous dominant pedal, labelled 'Contra E' at the retransition in both the autograph and first edition. All four of the remaining sonatas, as well as the Variations on a Theme by Diabelli op.120, make use of this extended bass range. The tension on the most heavily strung instruments built by Graf during this period reached 6000 kg. In spite of his obstinate refusal to add reinforcing bars (he sold the business in 1842, about the time when bracing became structurally mandatory), Graf's instruments proved to be among the most stable, aided by a layered construction (from the bottom up) and careful joinery. His structural frame members were built of oak rather than of the softer wood of fir or spruce, producing pianos weighing as much as 150 kg.

Schubert's use of range was not only more conservative than Beethoven's but was also calculated to avoid extremes that might preclude performances on smaller instruments. Seven of the nine sonatas begun between 1815 and 1817 (including two of the three completed ones) remain within a range of five and a half octaves at a time when Beethoven had been demanding the heavier six-octave instrument for years and had begun writing specifically for the six-and-a-half-octave instrument. Schubert's most ambitious work of this period, the A minor Sonata D537, completed in March 1817, presumes the six-octave instrument in terms of both range and general sound. The same is already true of the Rondo in E major D506, from December 1816.

With minor exceptions this was to be the extent of Schubert's exploration of range. The only piano work of his to require the six-and-a-half-octave instrument is the finale of the Sonata in A minor D784 (February 1823), whose primary group closes with an arpeggiated Neapolitan chord in contrary motion; see ex.3a. Without the D' the passage obviously loses its impact. More characteristic of Schubert is his avoidance of the extended low register. In the first movement of this same sonata, for example, the E' is specifically omitted; see ex.3b. A similar avoidance of the low register marks two passages in the otherwise forward-looking and virtuoso 'Wanderer' Fantasy of 1822, D760 (cf bars 66–7, 149). Sometimes the sidestepping of this newly available lower range involves not just octave doublings, but also motivic modification, as in ex.4. It is impossible to establish whether

Ex.3 Schubert: Sonata in A minor, D784
(a) 3rd movt, bars 24–5

(b) 1st movt, bars 17–21

Ex.4 Schubert: Sonata in D major, D850, 2nd movt, left hand, bars 42-4 (second group in the Exposition); 134-6 (second group in the recapitulation)

exposition:

recapitulation:

Schubert initiated such a change in the recapitulation because he was working on a six-octave instrument or whether he made a selfconscious decision to keep the entire sonata within its capabilities, but considerations of range almost certainly influenced his decision. Except for a single E' in each of the slow movements of the sonatas in G major D894 and B♭ major D960, all of the late sonatas (as well as the *Impromptus* and *Moments musicaux*) observe this same restriction.

The keyboard music of V.J. Tomášek (1774–1850) and J.H. Voříšek (1791–1826) demonstrates equally varied responses to the growth in range. Voříšek never exceeds six octaves, and a *Sonata quasi una Fantasia* op.20, composed the year before he died, remains within five and a half octaves. Two of Tomášek's *Tre Allegri Capricciosi di Bravura* op.84 (1818), however, call for six and a half octaves. Although few five-octave instruments were built after 1800, five-and-a-half, six- and six-and-a-half-octave instruments continued to co-exist into the 1830s. Indeed, the only contemporary illustration to come down to us of Schubert at a piano is Leopold Kupelwieser's water-colour of 1821, 'Party Game of the Schubertians'. The absence of foot pedals in this picture rules out all but a five- or five-and-a-half-octave instrument. A pen-and-ink drawing by Mortiz von Schwind from the same year of Schubert's living quarters in the Wipplingerstrasse shows an even clearer illustration of what is almost certainly a five-octave instrument. The vast majority of Schubert's songs fit such a keyboard.

Among the Viennese Classicists, it was Beethoven who continually pushed the piano to its limits of range and expression. This was surely the context for the remark attributed to him by Karl Holz: '[The piano] is and remains an inadequate instrument'.[5] If the attribution is accurate, it probably had as much to do with the composer's deafness as with the Viennese instruments themselves. Beethoven's enthusiasm for the six-octave Broadwood received by him in June 1818 was derived more from his pleasure at being honoured with a gift than from his opinion of the instrument; its compass ($C'–c''''$) was too small for most of the piano music he composed after it had been received, and he could not hear it.

The infrequent pedal indications in Beethoven's music (even rarer in Schubert's) have led many modern pianists to conclude that he must have pedalled far more extensively. Beethoven's most prominent pupil, Carl Czerny, claimed that the composer 'made frequent use of the pedals, much more frequent than is indicated in his works'. However, Czerny, who studied with Beethoven between the ages of ten and twelve (several years before foot pedals became common on Viennese instruments) and saw the composer perform on numerous occasions, published his recollections more than four decades after his initial study. He does not specify whether his remark refers only to the damper pedal, or to the moderator and other pedals that became common after 1810. Czerny's viewpoint almost certainly reflected the changing tastes of the 1840s.

The vast majority of Beethoven's printed markings are consistent with the directives for use of the pedal by authors of keyboard tutors from Louis Adam to Johann Nepomuk Hummel. Adam, whose *Méthode de piano* appeared in Paris in 1802, guiding generations of students at the Paris Conservatoire, advised that 'the large [*grande*, damper] pedal is to be employed only during consonant harmonies, when the melody is very slow, and where the harmonies do not change'.[6] Writing in 1827, Hummel argued:

> although the true artist does not need to use any pedals in order to touch his listeners, it is an injustice to reject them entirely. For that which lifts the dampers and that of the shift can sometimes be used to advantage in varying the effect; but they are to be used principally in slow movements, and in passages where the harmonies do not change too quickly. The other pedals are superfluous, having value neither for the performer nor for the instrument.[7]

Hummel's final remark was doubtless directed at the battery of tone-modifying pedals common to Viennese instruments in the 1820s. But his basic advice concerning the use of the damper pedal had changed little from that of Adam.

A great deal of misunderstanding has arisen about this repertory because of the poor results that ensue when Beethoven's literal markings are applied to our modern instrument in modern concert halls. The acoustical spaces in which music was performed during the first half of the 19th century were more reverberant than those of the present day – sometimes considerably more. This reverberancy meant that passages in moderate or fast tempos did not sound either clipped or dry without raised dampers. The modern instrument was conceived in terms of continuously raised dampers; its relatively slow attack and long sustaining power benefit from the overtones generated by the sympathetic resonance of many freely vibrating strings. The fortepiano, on the other hand, was designed with a self-contained tone. Its quick attack and rapid decay neither required nor benefited particularly from sympathetic resonance. By definition, then, the transference of forte-piano techniques to our modern instrument is problematic.

The same is true of the shift mechanism (*Verschiebung*) found on most six-octave and larger Viennese instruments. Beethoven's specific directions in the slow movement of his Fourth Piano Concerto (composed in 1806, but first published and performed in August and December 1808) are further evidence that six-octave instruments (most of which were fitted with a shift) first became widely available in 1808. Such explicit directions, as in the slow movement of the B♭ Sonata op.106, remained scarce, but there is some internal evidence, especially in the music of Schubert, that it could be used at the marking *pp*. While the autograph of the D major Sonata D850 contains no indication at the *pp* portion of the second group of the slow movement (bars 50ff), the first edition directs the passage to be played *mit Verschiebung*; see ex.5. Such an addition was almost certainly made by the composer, perhaps at the proof stage.

Ex.5 Schubert: Sonata in D major, D850, 2nd movt, bars 51–2

mit Verschiebung
[una corda]

The six-and-a-half-octave instrument for which Beethoven wrote his late sonatas was considerably larger than that of Mozart. Yet because the size of the hammers remained relatively small, the fall weight of the action was not dramatically heavier than on five-octave instruments. It was for this type of piano that the youthful Robert Schumann wrote his *Papillons*, *Davids-bündlertänze*, *Carnaval* and other piano cycles. Although Schumann was born a full generation later, Beethoven's instrument differed only slightly from the one presented by Graf (serial no.2616, built in 1839) to Robert and Clara as a wedding present in 1840.

In one respect the highly praised instruments of Graf signalled a victory for the 'Romantic' wing of Viennese piano building over the 'Classical'. The latter had been represented by the slender, curved models of Johann Andreas Stein, the former by the beefier, more squared-off instruments of Anton Walter. Stein's nephew André Stein carried on his uncle's design in the larger six- and six-and-a-half-octave instruments, and was joined by builders such as Georg Haschka and Josef Dohnal. In an effort to reinforce the case without adding excessive weight, these makers adopted a continuously curved bent side. They also strung their instruments lightly. The tone was clear, silvery and delicate, with considerable variation between registers. It is no accident that these instruments incorporated the largest number and variety of tone-modifying pedals.

Graf took Walter's case reinforcements and applied them even more rigorously to the newer, larger instruments,[8] producing grands with a darker, richer tone. A few builders like Joseph Brodmann and, later, his pupil Ignaz Bösendorfer (whose first instruments date from 1828) attempted to forge a balance, reinforcing their angular cases modestly and keeping the stringing relatively light. Tone-modifying pedals are found on almost all of the instruments by Brodmann and the first batch by Bösendorfer. But by the mid-1830s, when Liszt is reported to have admired Bösendorfer's instruments for their durability, his cases were, if anything, more massive than those of Graf.

The instruments of Nannette Streicher (*née* Stein) provide another example of this evolution. Her early five-and-a-half-octave instruments resemble those of her father in many respects. By the time the firm of Streicher produced its first six-and-a-half-octave instruments (presumably around 1816), their cases, stringing and slightly heavier actions were modelled on those of Graf, although not even Streicher seems to have been able to rival Graf for the care he invested in the construction of cases. Beethoven's personal enthusiasms probably played a role in Streicher's development. It was for this 'Romantic' Viennese instrument that Schumann and the young Brahms composed.

The 1839 Graf presented to the Schumanns was about 10 cm shorter than the longest instruments from the 1820s. It still included four pedals, two of which operated the split moderator (the 'bassoon' and 'Turkish' stops were now gone). Its only increase in range was the addition of $f\sharp''''$ and g'''' at the top (much like the additions to the five-octave instrument in Mozart's day). This was sufficient to accommodate virtually all of the keyboard music Schumann would ever write, including the Piano Concerto in A minor op.54 (1841–5). In fact, his first four opuses of piano music, composed between 1829 and 1832, do not exceed six octaves, and a number of well-known pieces (the *Arabeske* op.18, for example) fit the five-octave compass. Many others do not exceed c'''' in the treble. Schumann's exploitation of the treble range is far more conservative than either Beethoven's or Schubert's. The most ambitious work Schumann was ever to compose in these terms is the Fantasy in C op.17 (1836–9), whose middle movement exploits the entire upper register to g''''. Its Langsam finale contains the earliest recorded instance of a $B\flat''$, suggesting that seven-octave instruments (with a range from A'' to a'''') were becoming available about this time (see ex.6).

Ex.6 Schumann: *Fantasie*, op.17, 3rd movt, bar 32

Schumann's reluctance to explore range was more than compensated for by his contributions to Romantic tone colour. Although pedal indications in opp.1–5 are sparse and traditional, by the time of the *Davidsbündlertänze*

op.6 (1834–6) these are supplanted by the general marking 'Pedal', presumably a directive to apply the damper pedal freely. With op.9 it becomes Schumann's normal marking. Several stylistic factors contributed to his increased reliance upon the damper pedal. The frequency of octave doublings in both the melody and bass made the attainment of a true legato difficult without assistance from the dampers (see ex.7).

Ex.7 Schumann: *Kreisleriana,* op.16 [no.2], bars 21–8

Most important, Schumann's rich harmonies – marked by strong, filled-out dominants or applied dominants in root position and first inversion – invited the enrichment of sympathetic resonance. The Baroque-like rapidity and regularity of the harmonic rhythm in Schumann's music makes the pedalling pattern of most passages marked by 'Pedal' obvious.

The primary interest of most pianists in solo literature masks the circumstance that most 19th-century performers participated in a great deal of ensemble music. Here the choice of instrument plays a decisive role in matters of balance and projection. Anyone who hears an inspired performance of a Beethoven, Schubert or Schumann chamber work for piano and strings on period instruments comes away with a transformed sense of what this music is about. Once string players or singers realize that they do not have to push their tone to (and beyond) natural limits, the wide, constant vibrato, ubiquitous since World War II, is naturally eased. Equally important, once keyboard players realize that they are not (to paraphrase Gerald Moore) 'too loud', they can begin paying attention to the dynamic and articulation markings in the score. Of the countless examples that could be adduced, a representative one is the opening of Schumann's 'Ich grolle nicht' from *Dichterliebe* (1840, ex.8). The tenor (or high baritone; this cycle victimizes both) begins in the lower end of his range, sandwiched between bass octaves and full three-part chords in the right hand. The sustaining power of the modern piano smothers even the most resonant voice (sensitive

Ex.8 Schumann: *Ich grolle nicht*, bars 1–4

pianists all but drop out in the second half of bar 1, but the musical effect is greatly diminished). The transparency and rapid decay of any Viennese grand before 1850 allows the voice to shine through; moreover, the pianist can supply the first- and third-beat accents cleanly and crisply.

It is no accident that the two other great keyboard composers of Schumann's generation wrote music of a very different kind. The 'modern' pianistic styles of Fryderyk Chopin and Franz Liszt were made possible by the further development of a competing type of instrument. The 'English' piano had grown up in England and France simultaneously with the rise of the Viennese fortepiano. In London it was built and cultivated by Muzio Clementi, as well as by the firm of John Broadwood & Sons. In some areas it had been a pioneering instrument, as with the introduction in the 1790s of foot pedals (English pianos restricted themselves from the beginning to damper and shift). It introduced the range from E' down to C' before exceeding c'''' in the treble.[9] Hummel acknowledged the virtues of English instruments in 1828, though his preference for the Viennese is scarcely disguised:

> The German [i.e. Viennese action] is the easiest to play and responds most readily to the hands; it is capable of every nuance . . . The English action, however, must be acknowledged to have durability and fullness of tone. Nevertheless this instrument does not allow the same facility of execution as the German; the touch is heavier, the key sinks much deeper, and, consequently, the return of the hammer upon the repetition of a note cannot take place so quickly . . . this mechanism is not capable of such numerous modifications as to degree of tone as ours . . . Powerfully as these instruments sound in a chamber, they change the nature of their tone in spacious halls; and they are less audible than ours when associated with complicated orchestral accompaniments; I believe that it is precisely the thickness and fullness of the tone which is the cause.[10]

Without fully comprehending the acoustics, Hummel had identified the different objectives of Viennese and English makers. The Viennese instrument had a thinner soundboard, especially in the treble area, producing a quicker, brighter response but a correspondingly more rapid decay. Its hammers consisted of hard wooden cores covered by a few thin layers of leather, as opposed to the slender cores and generous felt coverings introduced into English pianos around 1830 (before 1830 the English had employed thicker layers of softer leather as hammer coverings). The hard, light Viennese hammers greatly accentuated the upper partials, producing the silvery brilliance so often associated with these instruments, but also contributing to the short tone life. The heavier, spongier English hammer activated the string more slowly, thereby eliminating many of the upper partials, but producing a more lasting tone. There is some evidence that the Viennese iron wire was less elastic than that used by the English, which would have accentuated the characteristics outlined above.

Finally, there is the greatly misunderstood matter of the striking point.[11] The widespread belief that this settled early in the development of the piano between a seventh and a ninth of the sounding length is belied by any Viennese or English instrument before 1865, and by many Viennese instruments to the end of the century. Early English builders had relied heavily upon harpsichord design; many had received their early training building harpsichords. The plucking ratio (the striking distance measured from the nut/the total sounding length of the string) on harpsichords ranged up to one seventeenth, or higher and similarly high ratios are encountered on Erard, Clementi and even Broadwood pianos from this period. The striking point on Beethoven's Erard varied from one-ninth to more than one-twentieth; that on his Broadwood varied somewhat less.

Most Austrian and German makers, on the other hand, were initially trained in organ building (Stein, for example), where no such prescriptions applied. Viennese instruments between 1810 and 1840 characteristically employed striking ratios of less than a seventh to a twelfth, with the lowest ratios throughout the singing range from g to c'''. All other things being equal, a string struck nearer its centre will produce more fundamental than one struck nearer its end; it will also respond more quickly and require less energy to activate. This accounts for the relatively light hammers on Viennese instruments before 1840. As already noted, however, the hammer design on the Viennese instrument also encouraged more upper partials at the expense of fundamental. This was intentionally compensated for by the striking point, producing a tone rich in both fundamental and upper partials, but with relatively weak representation by the middle partials.

It might seem that the early English piano arrived at a similar profile through reverse means: its hammer construction encouraged the fundamental, while its striking point favoured upper partials. But in practice the heavier, more resilient hammer produced a more resonant, lasting tone in spite of the striking point. The duration of the tone was further encouraged by a purposely inefficient damping system. The 'fullness' of tone on English instruments referred to by Hummel was something of an illusion, but one that exerted its power over most contemporary composers and performers.

Chopin began his career on the kind of piano with which Beethoven had finished his. His two Vienna sojourns in 1829 and 1831 afforded him ample opportunity to experience the best Viennese instruments, including a Graf reportedly placed at his disposal for a concert in 1829. The first two of the nocturnes op.15, the four mazurkas op.17, the Scherzo in B minor op.20, the

Andante Spianato and Grand Polonaise op.22 and the Waltz in A minor op.34 no.2 are among the works probably composed on these instruments. Yet their clear, woody tone was not ideally suited to the novel textures Chopin was introducing. His decision to move to Paris was made for many reasons, but the predominance of English-style grands in the French capital was probably an important factor.

Chopin performed on both Pleyels and Erards during his infrequent public appearances, but his home instrument was a Pleyel (a grand and an upright), and he appears to have favoured them. In spite of his revolutionary style, he was most comfortable with the more conservative design of Pleyel. The instruments built by Ignace Pleyel during the 1830s and 40s differed in small but important respects from those of Broadwood and Erard in the 1820s. Until late in the 19th century Pleyel retained the single-escapement English grand action. It had undergone numerous refinements since being introduced at the end of the 18th century, and in Pleyel's instruments was regulated for a light fall weight and minimal after-touch. His hammers now had a felt core, and after 1840 they may have been entirely of felt. The period of transition is difficult to pinpoint, since many instruments that originally had felt inner layers with a leather outer layer were replaced with felt in subsequent rebuildings. The wooden core was needle-shaped, even in the bass, to allow for a thicker covering and a more resilient attack. The mass of the hammer remained light, especially in the treble, where contact with the string was a point rather than part of a curve.

Following Broadwood's lead, Pleyel had smoothed out striking-point ratios but had retained considerable variation in the last one or two octaves. On a typical Pleyel grand from the 1840s, the bass and tenor hover around a ninth, while the alto and soprano up to g'' proceed to an eighth. The remaining treble enlarges the ratio gradually to a ninth at c'''', a tenth at c''', an eleventh at eb'''', and up through a thirteenth at g''''. This escalation in the treble, coupled with the rapidly decreasing size of the cylindrical hammers, produces the increasingly silvery, ethereal quality so congenial to many of Chopin's best-known melodies. Hence the F minor Fantasy op.49 hovers around c'' in bars 74–5, c''' in bars 76–7 (first half), and then reaches its melodic apex on c'''' in the second half of bar 77 (ex.9a). Each of these registers projects a different sonority. The variety is further enhanced at the final statement of the theme in bars 244ff, where it is pushed to near the top of the available range (ex.9b).

Ex.9 Chopin: Fantasy in F minor, op.49

(a) bars 74–7

(b) bars 243–4

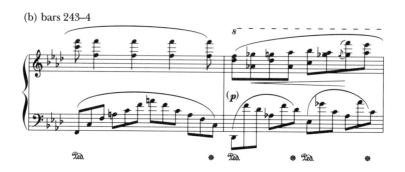

Nearly all the Pleyel grands that survive from Chopin's period in Paris are about 206 cm long rather than about 244 cm, now the standard with Erard and Austrian makers. Their tone is transparent and delicate, suiting perfectly Chopin's directives for the damper pedal, such as the dreamy, veiled effect of the coda to the Db major Nocturne op.27 no.2 (see ex.10*a*).

Ex.10 Chopin: Nocturne in Db major, op.27 no.2
(a) bars 66–71

(b) bars 75–6

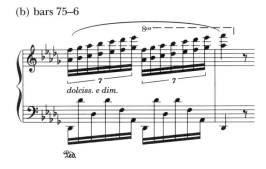

The registral split between the grace notes and the melody notes creates a polyphonic effect unattainable on the modern piano. The final bars contain an exquisite example of coordination between register and dynamics (ex.10*b*). The diminuendo that can only be faked on a modern instrument can scarcely be avoided on the Pleyel.

Chopin's pedal indications are remarkably numerous and precise. They form an essential part of the compositional process. It is not simply that passages played without Chopin's directives are drier than they ought to be; many simply cannot be understood. The wave-like ebb and flow of the Etude in Ab major op.25 no.1, for example, is predicated upon the sympathetic resonance of many simultaneously sounding strings. Its phrase structure depends directly upon the precise notations for the damper pedal.

In the C♯ minor Nocturne op.27 no.1 the dynamic contour of the opening phrase – with its characteristic blending of modes – is dictated by the overtones produced from the raised dampers (see ex.11). While *e″* is weakly

Ex.11 Chopin: Nocturne in C# minor, op.27 no.1, bars 1–5

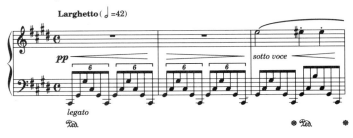

represented in the overtone series, $e\sharp''$, the fourth overtone, is amplified considerably by the $c\sharp$ heard twice each half bar in the bass (anyone can test this by depressing silently either melody note and playing the $c\sharp$; no sympathetic resonance occurs on the e'', whereas the $e\sharp''$ blooms). Chopin's explicit awareness of this relationship is revealed by his pedalling in bar 3, where the change occurs a quaver early to catch the $C\sharp$ as well, adding extra intensity to the first appearance. The hairpins in bars 3 and 5 are a natural by-product of the pedalling, down to the double appoggiatura on $c\sharp''$-$b\sharp''$. In any tuning known to Chopin (including, but probably not limited to, equal temperament), the overtones of the major seventh (against the d in the bass) are stronger than those of the minor seventh, contributing to the pathetic, dying quality of the Neapolitan harmony. After 1830 such coordination between pedalling and phrasing in Chopin's music is the rule rather than the exception.

The subtle blending of overtones came naturally to a composer whose style was built upon independent voices that, when parallel, moved in operatic thirds and sixths rather than orchestral octaves. The primary colours of Schumann's music, on the other hand, mirror perfectly the tone qualities of Viennese instruments. The famous left-hand opening of the Fantasy is sufficiently distinct to maintain its forward impetus; the right-hand octaves are clear and focussed. On a contemporary Pleyel the same opening comes across as flat and hollow, the melody octaves limp and lifeless. Conversely, the rarefied exploitation of register in Chopin's music can only be approximated on a contemporary Bösendorfer or Schweighofer.

When only ten years old, and on his first visit to Paris, Franz Liszt had his first Erard piano placed at his disposal. This bringing together of virtuoso builder and virtuoso performer seems predestined. The bond between Liszt and the firm that served him so well as a child remained strong for the rest of his life. While there is no question that, at least up to the 1860s, the instruments built by Erard most suited Liszt's pianistic style, his first allegiance was to quality instruments of whatever manufacture. During his long and distinguished career he either owned or endorsed instruments by Erard, Breitkopf & Härtel, Boisselot, Tomaschek, Chickering, Bechstein, Bösendorfer, Broadwood and Steinway. By no means were all of these firms on the cutting edge of technological development.

But it was the instruments of Erard that dominated design innovation between 1820 and 1855.[12] If Erard's instruments before 1820 are any guide, he was an unlikely spokesman for the Romantic piano; yet he set out determined to make whatever changes were necessary to bring the piano into line with a new brand of pianism. These innovations came neither quickly nor easily. Moscheles is reported to have commented in 1835 that 'in the matter of fullness and softness of tone, there was something yet to be desired'.[13] Erard's experiments were frequently made at the expense of practical exigencies. In 1826 he advertised a concert in London, at which Liszt was the featured performer, to be played upon a seven-octave instrument (C'-c'''''). At that time no keyboard music exceeded f''''. The instrument does not survive, but in matters of regulation and tuning it was reported to be extremely unstable.

Erard persevered. An instrument that he presented to Mendelssohn in

1832 was described by Moscheles as 'magnificent'. But within a few years it had begun to deteriorate. Rather than repair it, Erard insisted in 1838 upon providing Mendelssohn with a new instrument. Mendelssohn responded, doubtless sincerely:

> A thousand thanks, my dear friend, for your kind letter and all the trouble you have taken about the piano...and it is only now, since I enjoy the happiness of playing on an instrument so full and rich in tone, that I realize how hard I should have found it to accustom myself to any other.[14]

The apparent improvements noted by Mendelssohn show how far the builder had come in satisfying the needs of a Liszt. The celebrated action of Erard – he patented a double-escapement design in 1821 – had to be modified many times before it became more reliable than fragile. The reasons for its progressive adoption are generally misunderstood. It had nothing to do with the ability to repeat notes rapidly. This was not a prominent feature of Liszt's (or even Thalberg's or Pixis's) technique. Moreover, any well-regulated instrument built by Walter, Streicher or Graf could repeat notes with equal facility. It had little to do with the inherent quickness of a double-escapement action; nothing works more quickly than a well-regulated Viennese action built before 1840.

It had everything to do with *scale*. The double-escapement action triumphed for the same reason that horses do not exceed 17 hands. A horse at 15 hands is a marvel of engineering; the same horse at 25 hands would self-destruct. As far as propelling lightweight hammers is concerned, the Viennese action cannot be improved upon. But as instruments grew in size, as the tension on the strings increased dramatically, and as the amount of energy needed to activate a string increased exponentially, the high energy-expended-to-work-accomplished ratio of the Viennese action sealed its own fate. The fall weights on the Streichers and Bösendorfers from the end of the century are more than half again as much as those on a contemporary Erard. A double-escapement action with the intermediate wippen offered the player desperately needed leverage. The sheer size of the newest instruments (Erard was building 254 cm models by 1850) demanded a new technology, which Erard cheerfully delivered. To the end, advocates of the Viennese action (employed by Bösendorfer until shortly before World War I) lamented the loss of directness and intimacy; their grief was genuine and justified, but in real life there was no alternative short of developing a race of giants.

The action was by no means Erard's only accomplishment. In 1808 Sébastien Erard patented the agraffe, the metal stud at the keyboard end with a hole through which the string passes. In 1838 Pierre Erard patented the harmonic bar used in the treble. Both of these devices held the string more firmly in place than the conventional nut pin, while also providing a cleaner stopping point. Greater string tensions now became possible. Erard's hammers were more massive, and the total tension on his instruments 40–50 per cent greater than that on a contemporary Pleyel, approaching 12,000 kg on the largest models. Erard's unique under-damping system was more efficient and clean than Pleyel's English system.

But Erard's most important contribution to piano sound was a decisive

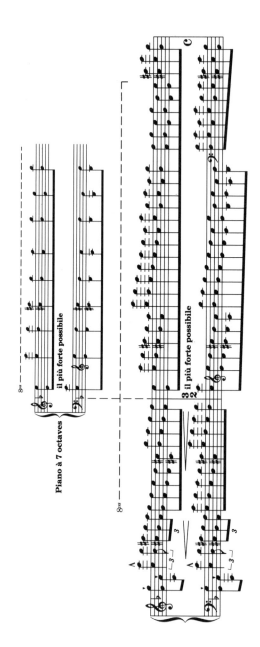

Ex.12 Liszt: *Mazeppa*, bars 27–28

move in the direction of uniform striking points. By 1850 Pierre Erard had arrived at a design whereby the range from the lowest bass A'' to a'' in the mid-treble employed a constant striking ratio of about 1:8·5, providing a more powerful, even tone than any previous instrument. Then came a very gradual ascent to a tenth at $d\sharp'''$, and to an eleventh at g'''', the treble thereby maintaining a modicum of registral differentiation. Erard's hammers were larger and harder than those of Pleyel, producing a more brilliant sound. All of these developments led a jury, headed by Sigismond Thalberg, at the Crystal Palace Exhibition of 1851 in London to describe the 254 cm Erard concert grand as 'an instrument of great power, fine quality of tone, and delicate mechanism in the action'.

Having been the most progressive maker until about 1850, Erard now consolidated a design that remained unchanged until the end of the century. He took a decisive stand against the principle of cross- or over-stringing patented in grands by Steinway in 1859. The issue has been consistently confused in the literature, with cross-stringing described as a device to maximize the length of bass strings. In practice, over-stringing lengthens strings by only an insignificant amount, but it does move them away from the rim towards the heart of the soundboard. Piano tone, as already observed, is affected by the nature of the striking material, the striking point and the properties of the wire. But it is also affected by the point on the soundboard at which the bridge is attached. Two factors are at work here. The first is the manner in which individual notes are distributed over the soundboard. If they are spread evenly over all the available space then the tones will be distinct and of varying colours – rounder towards the middle, more brilliant and penetrating near the rim. With many strings activating the same area, the tone is collectively more powerful (much as a gymnast bounces higher at the centre as opposed to the edge of a trampoline) but also less distinct. Erard chose to maintain his straight-strung (as it was called) design because he valued clarity and brilliance more than maximum resonance.[15]

During the 1840s makers began to introduce felt hammer coverings, eventually standardized at two or three layers. Into the 1890s Erard retained hammer cores covered in many thin layers, entirely of leather to about 1840, and later of leather and felt. The fuller but also spongier sound made possible by sheets of felt appealed as little to him as cross-stringing. Finally, Erard steadfastly refused to modernize his manufacturing processes. The multi-layered hammer coverings could be installed only by hand. The same was true of the iron frame reinforcement, involving as many as six bars, a stringing plate, individual agraffes, harmonic bar and numerous smaller pieces at the wrest plank – all custom fitted and requiring dozens of screws.

Liszt embraced Erard's innovations with enthusiasm, pushing the instrument to its limits of range and endurance. The fourth of the Transcendental Etudes, *Mazeppa*, composed some time during the 1840s, has a passage calling explicitly for the seven-and-a-third-octave instrument, with treble to c''''' (ex.12). It is not known whether Liszt altered the passage at about the time the set was published in its third revision in 1852, or whether the expanded instrument was available even earlier. No datable instruments from the 1850s with this added treble survive, but it is likely that Erard led the way.[16]

At the same time, Liszt's B minor Sonata (1852–3) was defining the lower register, as in the three accented *A″*s that close the transition in bars 81–7 of the exposition (ex.13). The only instruments capable of producing more than a dull thud here were those manufactured by Erard, or by his major American competitor before 1860, Chickering of Boston.

Ex.13 Liszt: B minor Sonata bars 81–8

Liszt's music claims the entire compass of the piano for its domain. In terms of technique this can be seen in the Transcendental, Concert and Paganini Etudes, but in orchestral terms (Liszt's youthful transcription of Berlioz's *Symphonie fantastique* was said to rival an orchestral performance in colour) it is most evident in the string of operatic paraphrases that Liszt set down from 1831 on. The harp-like figure from the introduction to the *Rigoletto* paraphrase (1851), given in ex.14*a*, is a good example of the

Ex.14 Liszt: *Rigoletto* paraphrase
   (a) bars 14-16

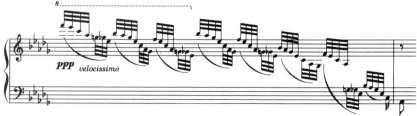

(b)

(c)

delicacy that could now be achieved with brilliance. Another favourite device was to have a tenor melody surrounded by a veil of accompaniment. The vestiges of register in the treble made possible the clarity of passages like that in ex.14*b*. If Schumann is a composer of octaves, and Chopin one of sixths and thirds, then Liszt is the champion of both, as ex.14*c* shows. In short, Liszt's music required an instrument of both power and clarity. More than any other instrument of the mid-century, the Erard supplied both.

Although the career of Brahms unfolded almost a generation after that of Schumann, Chopin and Liszt, and although the keyboard works of his maturity were written at a time when Steinway had vanquished all competitors, it should perhaps come as no surprise that the characteristic sonorities of Brahms's music were created for, and on, the Viennese instrument. With the exception of a solitary *ab′′′′* in the coda of the finale to the F minor Sonata, none of the keyboard works up to the Paganini Variations of 1861 exceeds the range of the 1839 Graf which Brahms knew at the Schumanns', and which Clara presented to him in 1856. These included works on the scale of the C major Piano Sonata op.1, and the D minor Piano Concerto op.15. If anything, the thick, closely-spaced sonorities in the music of Brahms demanded the clarity and register definition of straight-strung Viennese instruments even more than those of Schumann (ex.15).

In spite of the formidable technical demands of the larger works (including, but not limited to, the Paganini Variations), there is an intimacy and sweetness in Brahms's keyboard music that was well served by the Viennese action he persistently refused to abandon. Brahms finally presented Clara's piano to the Gesellschaft der Musikfreunde in 1873. The decision may have been hastened by the gift of a seven-octave Streicher grand presented to him around 1869 by the builder (serial no.6713). This was the instrument on which Brahms wrote the character pieces of opp.116–19 in 1892. Although

Ex.15 Brahms: Piano Sonata in F minor, op.5, 2nd movt

Streicher now employed heavier hammers with inner coverings of felt, the outer layer remained leather. The wooden bracing was stouter than that on instruments built before the middle of the century, though reinforced by only two longitudinal iron bars rather than the six that were now standard on Erards. In spite of this, the tension on the Streicher frame was nearly equal to that on the French instrument. Streicher, however, had not joined the movement towards uniform striking points; indeed, it was the higher overall average and the greater variation that maintained the characteristic quick decay and registral variety among late 19th-century Viennese pianos.

Like Schumann before him, Brahms wrote to the most sonorous of these registers, the tenor and alto. Works like the Ballade in B minor op.10 no.4 do not exceed *f* ♯″. Of the 20 pieces in opp.116–19, seven do not exceed in the treble the *f*‴ available to Mozart, and another nine do not surpass the *c*‴′ inadequate for Beethoven more than eight decades earlier. Brahms extended Schumann's near continuous use of the damper pedal, though he also specified detailed pedallings befitting the transparency and delicacy of the Viennese instrument; see ex.16.

Ex.16 Brahms: Intermezzo in E♭ minor, op.118 no.6

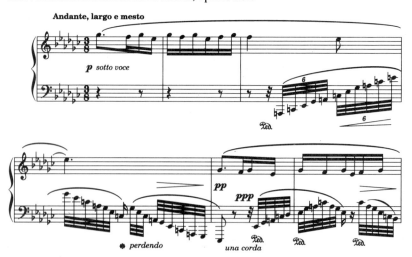

Because its basic design has gained such universal acceptance in our own day, and because relatively little modification has occurred since the late 19th century, the modern Steinway concert grand is viewed by the lay public and professionals alike as the culmination of a century and a half of progress. It is therefore easy to forget that virtually all of the Steinway innovations (including the middle sostenuto pedal, patented by Montal in 1862) involved the modification, standardization, manufacture and marketing of known technologies. Around 1860, in America, Steinway brought together a number of elements that are by and large retained in instruments being manufactured worldwide today. The overriding objective was a powerful, long-lasting, even and homogeneous tone (the sostenuto pedal represented an effort to compensate for some of these qualities). As a musical goal, this was neither original (Erard and Bechstein, for example, both worked towards this goal) nor universally shared (Chickering, Bösendorfer and Erard all rejected over-stringing). What set it apart was the single-mindedness with which these aims were pursued, first by Heinrich Steinway (1797–1871), and then by his sons Henry (1831–65) and Theodore (1825–89). During his years in the USA Theodore, the most gifted designer and craftsman among the Steinways, took out more than 40 patents, ranging from the cupola metal frame to the duplex scale.

Felt hammer coverings, for example, had been patented by Henri Pape in 1828. Other makers, such as Pleyel and Chickering, were using felt in layers by the 1840s. In the 1870s Steinway introduced a two- (and sometimes one-) piece covering that could be installed on all hammers in one swift operation by a hydraulic machine. The result was a strain of felt that was considerably harder yet more resilient and rounded at the striking point than anything produced before – and, not incidentally, cheaper in the long run to manufacture. Similarly, the one-piece cast iron plate upon which cross-stringing was erected grew out of a musical aim, but it also substantially reduced Steinway labour costs.

The Steinways worked continually to improve the leverage advantage in their double-escapement actions, necessary to activate their heavier, more massive hammers. This resulted in significantly more after-touch (the amount a key can be depressed after the hammer goes into check) than on contemporary Erards. The campaign for uniformity also extended to fall weights. Before 1850 many instruments sported a fall-weight ratio from bass to treble of nearly 2·5:1. By the end of the century Steinway had reduced this to 1·5:1, accomplished in part by adding lead weights to the hammer side of treble keys. The heavier hammers and greater leverage, in combination with over-stringing, led to a thick, highly crowned soundboard and massive bridges.

In the area of striking ratios the Steinways were not pioneers. An ebonized full sized grand from 1883 in the Kunsthistorisches Museum, Vienna (serial no.50,000), varies only slightly from the pattern established by Erhard around 1850. The soprano register, beefed up by heavier, harder hammers, now carries its full, even sound to the very top. It was an instrument such as this that Liszt praised in the last year of his life for its 'magnificent result in volume and quality of sound'. He prefaced his remark by professing ignorance of the piano's inner workings, and it would be reckless to assume that

369

the elder statesman's enthusiasm amounted to a wholesale shift of allegiance.

In fact, the only major keyboard composers before 1930 who could have written any music with the modern Steinway sound in mind were Alexander Skryabin, Sergey Rakhmaninov, Sergey Prokofiev and Béla Bartók – and they probably cut their pianistic teeth on older models. Of this group, only Rakhmaninov enjoyed a continuing relationship with the Steinway firm. Both Debussy and Ravel were said to prefer Erards or Bechsteins (neither of which included the sostenuto pedal) to Steinways. By 1870, the intimate and fruitful relationship between Mozart and Stein, Beethoven and Streicher, Chopin and Pleyel, Liszt and Erard was largely a thing of the past.

The triumphs of Steinway & Sons at the Paris Exposition of 1867 and thereafter can be attributed to their skilful integration of new manufacturing technologies, facilitated by a New World climate open to innovation. The Steinways proved that the introduction of steam-driven power saws for preliminary cutting, of power tools for machining, of cast-iron plates, of machine-installed felts – of assembly-line procedures, in short – did not lead to compromises in quality.[17] If some disputed the musical superiority of their product, no one could argue with their success at manufacturing and marketing it.

I have discussed the growth of the piano in primarily musical terms, but there were also powerful social forces at work. The 19th century opened with a household instrument which, by the end of the century, had evolved into a full-fledged concert instrument. The introduction of public concerts and the solo piano recital (popularized by Liszt in the 1840s) spurred a steady growth in the number and size of concert halls. Some of the most famous – such as Steinway Hall in New York, Bechstein [Wigmore] Hall in London, and the Salle Pleyel and Salle Gaveau in Paris – were built by piano manufacturers. At the beginning of the century Beethoven played for a few hundred listeners; by the end of the century Bülow was performing for thousands. A Graf might be the most appropriate piano for a Schubert *Impromptu*, but a performance where the furthest listener is hundreds of feet away in a dry hall is another matter. This acoustical dilemma is bound to haunt those who advocate a revival of historical pianos, for unless they pay equal attention to the listening environment such experiments are not likely to produce many converts.

Most of the pianos manufactured in the 19th century were not grands, much less full-size grands. More than 80% of Steinway's production in the 1880s was uprights, a design that the firm both legitimized and used to push the cumbersome square to extinction (the last squares were made about 1890). There is no evidence that major composers for the piano wrote with anything other than the largest grands in mind, and for this reason they must occupy centre stage. But the majority of 19th-century piano music belonged in the salon, where amateurs devoured the *Spaziergänge* of Stephen Heller on instruments of every size and type. Our cultivation of Beethoven, Schubert, Schumann, Chopin, bits of Mendelssohn, Brahms and chunks of Liszt is unrepresentative from a historical point of view. Without abdicating the responsibility to exercise aesthetic judgment, we must remain open to new sources of repertory from an enormously varied century (the Alkan revival of the mid-1960s provides a model).

Programming is an equally valid component of Romantic performance practice. We know too little about the manner in which programmes were planned and executed in the 19th century, though there would be little to gain from a literal revival of contemporary practices. But the traditional 20th-century piano recital, which often traverses two or three centuries in chronological order, may be equally inappropriate. There is considerable evidence that composers like Chopin and Schumann published integrated opuses that are freely excerpted today; we should at least know their reasons for doing so before disregarding them.

A final word of caution concerning Steinway and its technological spin-offs – Bechstein, founded 1853; Blüthner, 1853; Grotrian, German continuation of the original Steinway line, about 1865 – is in order. While it is true that after 1860 there were no fundamental innovations in piano design, it would be a mistake to assume that the sound of the modern piano has remained unchanged for 125 years. Minor modifications in scaling, stringing, sound-board and action design have continued, and account for significant variations in touch and sound among different makers (American as opposed to European, for example) as well as differences among varying years of the same make.

Two other components on older instruments of so-called modern design are critical because they are replaced most frequently: wire and hammer coverings. Between 1867 and 1893 the breaking point on common gauges of steel piano wire increased 19 per cent to 44 per cent, with the most dramatic increase in the thinner, treble wire.[18] While it is common to assume that this development produced an improvement, it was only in fact a change. Higher average breaking points may well have resulted in less breakage, although the most significant cause of breakage was lack of uniformity. But the higher its breaking point the less elastic wire becomes, and this produces a correspondingly harder and more brilliant – or, to some ears, brittle – tone.

A parallel development has occurred with hammer coverings. If the felt originally found on instruments like the 1892 Steinway concert grand in the Smithsonian Institution is any guide, then coverings made since World War II are more compacted and less resilient. Lacquers and other solvents used since the 1950s to harden hammer coverings further are additional evidence of this trend, most pronounced in popular music. It is a safe guess that many of the instruments that were originally constructed between 1870 and 1920 but which have now been rebuilt and produce a tone quality that is judged inferior to newer models, have been betrayed by the inappropriate replacement parts with which they have been supplied. The same reservations concerning wire are even more applicable to instruments built in the first seven decades of the century.

As modern technicians and players know, there is still more than enough mystery about what goes into a successful instrument. In terms of resurrecting the actual sounds and colours of the Romantic piano, we are in the 1980s at the same point as the harpsichord revival was in the early 1950s. Whether the movement (if that is indeed the right term) chooses to build upon the advances made with the five-octave fortepiano – superb replicas of which are now fairly common – will depend upon the tenacity of individual builders and restorers (whose potential market is greater than that for harpsichords), as well as upon the commitment of performers to the highest standards of professionalism. Finally, it will depend upon a dramatic shift in the perception of writers and commentators away from an oversimplified view of straight-line progress to a more complex picture of shifting musical tastes.

Notes

[1] The term 'Fortepiano' remained in common usage in Vienna until about 1815. In that year Franz Schubert began referring to it as a 'Pianoforte', while Beethoven – in a fit of post-Napoleonic xenophobia – advocated the German expression 'Hammerklavier'.

[2] *The Letters of Beethoven*, ed. and trans. E. Anderson (London, 1961), i, 25–6.

[3] Beethoven's purported dissatisfaction with the heaviness of the action on his Erard (see W. Lütge, 'Andreas und Nannette Streicher', *Der Bär*, iv (1927), 65) had more to do with its feel. In fact, the fall weights (the amount of weight it takes to move a hammer through let-off into check) of comparable English and Viennese instruments at this time are virtually equal. Because of its escapement mechanism, however, the English action had considerably more after-touch than the simpler Viennese action.

[4] The English had been using wound strings on squares since the 1760s. However, such strings were open-wound and under light tension. Around 1816 the Viennese builders either developed or gained access to a close-wound string (copper over iron) that could withstand up to 100 kg of tension without the buzzing lamented by English builders. Without this technology, the Viennese instruments would have remained bottomed at F', because a brass wire a half step lower on E' (especially with $a' = 415$–30) produces only a dull thud.

[5] The source of the remark is a letter sent by Holz to a Frau Linzbaur, and first quoted by L. Nohl in *Beethoven, Liszt, und Wagner* (Vienna, 1874), 112. The letter does not survive, and Holz's recollection would have been made as many as 45 years after the remark was made. Even if it is accurate, the larger context of the remark is Beethoven's desire to compose an annual oratorium and a string or wind concerto, 'assuming that my Tenth Symphony (C minor) and my Requiem are already completed'. This is not very solid ground upon which to summarize Beethoven's view of the piano.

[6] L. Adam, *Méthode de piano* (Paris, 1802), 219.

[7] J. N. Humme, *Ausführlich theoretisch-practische Anweisung zum Piano-forte Spiel* (Vienna, 1828/ R1929), 460.

[8] Even though Graf received a license to build pianos under his own name in 1805, the vast majority of the authenticated instruments that survive have a compass of six and a half octaves (from the very end of his career, some have the added $f\sharp''''$ and g''''). He must have produced quantities of five-and-a-half and six-octave models as well.

[9] The English were even less prepared than the Viennese for the rapid rise in string tension that accompanied increases in range. The framing of any Broadwood built in Beethoven's time is haphazard and flimsy. Rather than failing at the wrest plank, most French and English pianos from before 1830 suffer a more fundamental distortion of the cheek (the outward curve at the treble end of the keyboard), known as 'cheek cock'.

[10] Humme, *Ausführlich theoretisch-practische Anweisung*, 462.

[11] See Robert Winter, 'Striking it Rich: the Significance of Striking Points in the Evolution of the Romantic Piano,' *JM*, vi (1988), 267–92.

[12] Upon Sébastien's death in 1831, he was succeeded by his nephew Pierre. However, if the focus is on sheer invention rather than development and implementation, then at least an equal nod must go to Erard's countryman Henri Pape, who patented the use of felt for hammer coverings in 1826 and over-stringing in uprights in 1828. Neither of these became general practice until several decades later.

[13] C. Moscheles, *Life of Moscheles*, trans. A. D. Coleridge (London, 1873), ii, 106.

[14] *Letters of Felix Mendelssohn to Ignaz and Charlotte Moscheles*, ed. and trans. F. Moscheles (London, 1888), 175.

[15] It is still commonplace to describe Erards as 'thin-toned' (the 'Erard' entry in *Grove 6*), but this seems to be a modern article of faith with little acoustical basis. In practice, the sound of a concert Erard from the 1850s or 1860s is, while less full, more penetrating and piercing than that of a modern Steinway or Bechstein.

[16] Apart from the ill-fated 1826 Erard already cited, it is not clear when the additional third to c'''' became commonplace. The earliest documented example is a Chickering grand from the

year 1863 in the author's collection, and a Steinway grand (no.13547) from 1864 in the Yale University Collection of Musical Instruments. None of the dozens of Erards before 1875 that I have examined have it, though this may be an accident of survival. The use of these three additional notes has remained a rarity into the 20th century.

[17] More than two-thirds of the work would still have been done by hand; it was the fact that almost a third was not that set the Steinways apart from their European counterparts.

[18] A. Dolge, *Pianos and their Makers* (Covina, 1911), 126. Modern breaking points are another 15 to 20 per cent greater than those quoted by Dolge.

CHAPTER XVIII

Organ

WAYNE LEUPOLD

Touch

Keyboard musicians of the 18th century took great pride in their ability to assign an appropriate touch or touches to each composition depending on its mood and texture, whether or not the music was so marked (C. P. E. Bach, 1753). Crisp and distinct playing was the custom in passages using notes of short duration, and legato playing was used in slow sustained passages, with all degrees of gradation existing between these two extremes.

Organists in the late 18th and early 19th centuries continued to use the four basic 18th-century keyboard touches:

> 1. *Ordinary.* The lifting of a finger from the preceding key *very* shortly before the following one is played (Marpurg, 1755); the raising of one finger as the next is lowered, resulting in an almost imperceptible silence between the notes; an articulated or loose type of legato neither detached nor slurred (Türk, 1789). This was the primary and most common touch during the 18th century and was normally used when no directions were given.[1]
> 2. *Staccato.* A detaching of notes up to as much as half their value – indicated by dots or wedges.[2]
> 3. *Legato.* A smooth uninterrupted stream of sound where not the slightest separation occurs – indicated by a slur or a term such as 'legato', 'sostenuto' or 'lié'.
> 4. *Legatissimo.* An overlapping of notes, particularly in broken or arpeggiated chords, where the notes are held down as long as possible or until the chord changes – usually indicated by slurs.

GERMANY Throughout the 19th century the ordinary touch, which allowed for a great many subtleties, continued to be employed by many German organists when no directions for touch were given, particularly in moderate and fast tempos. Mendelssohn is known to have played in a wiry, crisp style, phrasing with all manner of subtleties of touch. Rinck (op.121, 1839) used this 18th-century touch together with older fingering techniques (e.g. long fingers over shorter fingers, the use of the same finger on adjacent keys) and little finger substitution. The primary touch of A. Hesse, a student of Rinck, was also the ordinary one. At the end of the Romantic era a great variety of slightly articulated touches, usually not indicated, were used for the sake of clarity (for example by A. Haupt, in 'Accentuation ...', 1882). K. Straube (1873–1950) often played in a *leggiero* manner and had a detailed system of five different touches to achieve clarity and phrasing when working with the opaque sound of the large, late Romantic German organ.

The desire for a greater expressiveness in music (a reaction to the 'strict' or 'learned' contrapuntal style) and the development of the orchestra encouraged new styles of homophonic composition for the organ in mid- and late 18th-century Germany. These changes led to new and more detached styles of playing (advocated by Schröter, Vogler and Knecht, among others): to the *galant* style of simple, finely nuanced periodic melodies supported by light-textured accompaniments, which required considerable detached playing and to the fiery, brilliant orchestral style which required imitations of the sounds and articulations of individual orchestral instruments as well as the full orchestral ensemble ('Sturm und Drang').

As early as the mid-18th century there began a long tradition of true legato playing by some organists. It first appeared in chorale playing. Wiedeburg (1765) and Laag (1774) both recommended that all notes common to successive chords should be tied when playing chorales, and Guthmann (1805) and F. Schneider (1830) advocated the use of double finger substitution to achieve a more legato style. As a general practice during at least the middle and late Romantic periods (1850s–1940), chorales and hymns were usually played in a very legato manner everywhere, with the tieing of all common notes and, varying between individual sources, of most or all repeated notes.

Certain organists also advocated a more legato style in general. Knecht (1795–8) states that legato is the style best suited to the organ and advises against crossing longer fingers over short fingers. Werner (1807) states that one finger should never be used successively on different keys since this interrupts the sound; for Werner, everything depended on a connected and even touch, for which he strongly recommended finger substitution. F. Schneider (1830) gives many examples of single and successive (double) finger substitution; Gebhardi (1837) does the same in both slow and fast tempos. Schütze (1839) presents a systematic and consistent use of single and double substitution in all exercises, chorales and actual organ music. In organ music written during the first part of the 19th century, slurs often appear in only the first few bars to indicate the use of legato throughout and to indicate how certain recurring motifs should be phrased (Türk, 1789). As the century progressed it became more common for composers to supply the slurs and phrase markings throughout the composition. The legato touch came to be called for more and more until it gradually replaced the ordinary as the most common and normal touch, even when slurs or directions were not present (Merkel, op.177, early 1880s). This was partly due to the influence of the legato style of piano playing in the 19th century. However, during most of the century in Germany, the degree of legato that organists employed created different schools of playing.

Legatissimo continued to be used by German organists throughout the 19th century either to create a crescendo or to bring out a particular melodic line. In some instances it was written out in conventional notation (e.g. Mendelssohn, Thuille, Liszt, Reubke and Reger) and in others it was only indicated by a slur (e.g. Brahms, Liszt and Brähmig) or by a direction such as 'legato possibile' (Thuille), 'legatissimo' (Reubke) or 'molto legato'. In the late 19th and early 20th centuries a type of *legatissimo* touch was cultivated by some organists where the notes of the melody were very slightly overlapped to achieve a more intense and expressive legato, simulating a singer's or string player's portamento (e.g. K. Straube), or where all the notes of successive chords were slightly overlapped to create a *sotto voce*, *misterioso* or clouded effect.

FRANCE French organists during the first half of the 19th century continued to use the ordinary touch, with longer fingers crossing over shorter, as the norm. Legato was only employed when indicated by slurs or a direction, e.g. 'lié' (Miné, c1836; Fessy, c1845). Jaak Lemmens can be said to have created a new French ideal of good organ touch by his recitals in Paris between 1850 and 1854 and by the publication of his *Journal d'orgue* (1850–51). In both he made extensive use of finger, thumb and pedal substitutions, glissandos, legato finger crossings and adopted the tieing of notes common to successive chords. By 1858 his French student C. Loret had published exercises and compositions for legato playing and was teaching this new technique at the Niedermeyer School in Paris. Thus the change from ordinary to legato as the normal touch occurred in France during the 1850s and 60s. However, Lemmens and his students, Guilmant and Widor, are known to have used and taught all manner of subtly articulated and detached touches for clarity, particularly in toccata-like compositions (Widor, 1914).

ENGLAND In England during the 1830s both the ordinary and the 'new' legato styles were in use, although W. T. Best (1853) continued to advocate a touch with little or no finger substitution into the second half of the century. During the 1860s and 70s legato became the regular touch for most organists (Archer, 1875; Stainer, 1877).

AMERICA During the first half of the 19th century in America certain but limited aspects of the older system of fingering (the same finger playing consecutive notes; Loud, 1845) and touch (different touches appropriate for different styles of music and different registrations; Taylor, c1800; Zundel, 1851) continued to be used. During the 1850s the legato touch became the new ideal (F. Schneider, American edition, 1851; Zundel, 1860), although organists continued to use a variety of non-legato touches to achieve clarity (Lemare, 1910; Eddy, 1917).

The practice of not raising the notes of the final chord in a composition of soft character precisely together, but instead releasing them in rapid downward succession allowing the bass or pedal note to linger the longest, developed in Germany (Volckmar, 1858), England (Archer, 1875) and America (Buck, 1877; Dickinson, 1922). By the early 20th century this effect was sometimes augmented by gradually changing the hands to a softer manual, beginning with the right hand, and then by closing down the expression pedal as the notes were successively released (Clarke, 1908).

Slurs

SINGLE SLURS The slur sign originally was a sign used in violin music to indicate notes to be played with the same bow stroke. In organ music of the late 18th and early 19th centuries, slurs were used to specify a legato touch for specific notes under or over the slur within the phrase, in a context in which the ordinary touch was the normal touch for all other notes. As time passed, slurs tended to become longer and longer, eventually developing into longer phrase markings. From the mid-19th century onwards the longer phrase markings assumed more the function of simply delineating the shape of the entire phrase but in the context now of legato as the normal touch. Different types of slurs exist in organ music from the Romantic era. (*a*) The short articulation slur placed around two, three or four notes indicates that they are to be grouped together in a legato manner with the last note shortened to create an articulation silence. The first note of the slurred group is usually accented. (An exception seems to have been a trill with a written-out termination whose slur ends before the note that follows. In such cases the termination is joined without any break to the following note.) (*b*) A phrase-member slur, longer than an articulation slur, delineates a phrase member, which should be separated within the phrase by very short articulation silences. The short articulation slurs and the longer phrase-member slurs often compliment each other in the same phrase. (*c*) The longer phrase mark indicates a musical phrase (a complete musical idea) played in a basically legato manner with the last note usually shortened to create an articulation silence. (*d*) Legato slurs each last only one bar and indicate a legato touch throughout a fairly long section usually without any articulation at the end of each slur (Czerny, 1839). This practice, carried over from the late 18th century, continued until about the middle of the 19th. (*e*) The *legatissimo* slur indicates the *legatissimo* touch (discussed above) where one or more notes in a broken or arpeggiated chord are to be held down as long as possible or until the chord changes. (*f*) Harmonic slurs, used in French organ music from the late 19th century and into the early 20th, show harmonic groupings but are not meant to indicate any articulation at the end of a slur in the basic legato touch. In such music, actual phrase endings are often indicated by the use of short rests for the purpose of articulation. Unfortunately, in some cases it becomes very difficult to differentiate between the various possible meanings of a slur.

DOUBLE SLURS Occasionally double slurs were used to indicate a combination of various touches (Türk, 1789). There are examples in the music of Knecht, Vogler and Guilmant, where very subtle subgroupings of notes, indicated by short slurs, are placed within longer phrase markings.

Pedalling

During the late 18th and early 19th centuries two systems of pedalling were used in Europe and America: the 'simple method', which was the alternating use of only the toes of both feet (heels raised high) anywhere on the pedalboard, and the 'artificial method', which was the alternating use of the toe and heel of each foot, but with the left foot used exclusively in the lower octave and the right in the upper. Some organ tutors also describe a third system, the 'mixed method', where both toes and heels are used but each foot is not confined to only one octave (Kittel, 1803; Rinck, 1818; F. Schneider,

1830; J. André, 1834). More complex pedal techniques also developed in Germany during the first half of the 19th century. Rinck's op.124 (1839) includes examples of pedal substitution between the toes, between the toe and the heel of the same foot, and the playing of thirds with the toe and the heel of the same foot. None of these techniques appear in his earlier method, op.55 (1818–20). Lemmens (1850–51, 1862) advocated a much greater use of the heels and the manipulation of both feet together as one unit with four potential points of contact. Widor encouraged the use of the heels as much as the toes. As finger substitution and glissandos were introduced on the manuals, pedal substitution and glissandos also became a part of pedal technique. In England and America by the 1890s the maximum use of the heels was advocated to facilitate the manipulation of the several expression pedals with the toes (Lemare, 1910; Eddy, 1917).

Rhythm

CONSERVATIVES AND LIBERALS Most musicians from the Romantic era can be placed within one of two schools of thought concerning various aspects of performance style. The conservatives found inspiration in the past, particularly in the Baroque period, and favoured a straightforward approach to tempo with little use of rubato. Conservative organists included the Bach students, J. C. H. Rinck (in his later years), J. Schneider, J. G. Schneider, A. Hesse, Mendelssohn and his circle, Rheinberger and his circle, Merkel, A. Haupt, Brahms, Lemmens, Loret, Guilmant, Widor, Saint-Saëns and Gigout. The liberals advocated more exploitation of the emotional element and made much greater and freer use of rubato. Organists of this persuasion included Vogler, Knecht, Rinck (in his early years, including op.55), Liszt and his circle, including Reubke, Straube, Reger, Lefébure-Wély, Franck and his students, including Tournemire, Bonnet and Lemare. However, all performers, including the conservatives, used rhythmic freedom to at least some degree; it was the amount and the frequency of its use that distinguished one group from the other.

RUBATO Two types of rubato were used by keyboard musicians throughout the Classical and Romantic eras: (1) free (or structural) rubato, where the melody and the accompaniment deviate from a strict tempo simultaneously (ritardando and accelerando); and (2) melodic rubato, where the accompaniment keeps strict time and the melody is allowed to fluctuate, at times rushing ahead or dragging behind in an expressive 'vocal' manner with the two parts periodically coinciding at structurally important points. Both types of rubato were employed to single out certain individual notes, groups of notes or even larger sections in the music for emotional purposes. Such points of stress could include high or low notes, dissonances, unexpected harmonies, modulations, approaches to climaxes, departures from climaxes and the end of phrases. The use of both types of rubato became more frequent as the era progressed, although free rubato seems to have been used more frequently than melodic.

During the course of the era, free rubato came to be regarded as an increasingly important part of the performer's art, particularly by the liberals. The terms 'ritardando', 'rallentando', 'accelerando', 'rubato' and 'espressivo' were all used to designate the use of free rubato, although organists also freely employed it where there was no direction (Widor, 1901). 'Tenuto' was also used as a sign for a slight holding of a note or chord (Hull, 1911). Widor, in addition, employed 'sforzando' to indicate an accent by a slight elongation (a chronometric alteration). The term 'crescendo' or its sign (the 'hairpin') also came to imply accelerando, particularly in association with a rising line and vice versa. 'Decrescendo' or its sign (the 'hairpin') also came to imply a ritardando, particularly in association with a descending line or at the end of a phrase and vice versa (Reger, op.30, 1899; Riemann and Armbrust, 1890). In much organ music, particularly that from Germany (including Reger), 'crescendo' and 'diminuendo' meant the addition or subtraction of stops respectively, while the 'hairpins' pertained to the use of the expression pedals. Thus free rubato became increasingly tied to dynamics. Wagner, in his theory of tempo modification, advocated that the basic tempo be continually adjusted so as to present each theme in its proper character, and that this continual modification be done gradually. Thus every mood or theme had its own tempo which, if taken to its ultimate, results in a liquid, rhythmic flow unhampered by any regularity of pulsation, a tempo dominated by expression with the conscious attempt to obscure the bar-line.[3] In the organ rolls he made, Reger uses a fairly even tempo in his own chorale preludes, but in his own free works he often greatly varies the speed according to different textures and sections. Recurring sections or textures always receive the same appropriate tempo.

Volckmar (1858) gives examples of both types of rubato in playing organ music. Notated examples of melodic rubato can be found in César Franck's *Fantaisie* in A, 1878 (bars 63–86, 184–7 and 230–56). Unnotated use by organists of the late Romantic period is recorded on organ rolls by Eugène Gigout (1912, *Andantino* by Chauvet, *Minuetto* by Gigout), the 78 rpm recording of the Andante of Franck's *Grande pièce symphonique* by Charles Courboin (c1935), and reminiscences of Clarence Dickinson's playing (up to the early 1940s). Melodic rubato also led to the tradition at the end of the Romantic era of not playing the hands together, thereby dissipating over-accented metric accents; this creates, often in conjunction with the harmonic idiom, a feeling of suspension a yearning, churning, plastic, indistinct effect.

The liberals, particularly Liszt and his circle, also played in a tradition of freedom towards the printed page. They deleted and added notes and even whole passages of music to printed scores, both of their own music and that of others. A striking example of this tradition by an organist can be heard in Alfred Sittard's 78 rpm recording of Liszt's *Ad nos, ad salutarem undam*.

RHYTHMIC THEORIES The 18th-century concept of articulation was based on the grouping of notes according to their place in the metrical structure (the bar). Accents were metrically conceived through a hierarchy of the primary divisions (beats) of the bar in the following order of stress (strongest to weakest): first, third, second, fourth. In a three-beat bar the hierarchy was first, second, third. In the early 19th century this system of emphasis was even extended to small rhythmic levels such as four semiquavers within the beat. This rhythmic system continued to be used by many musicians, particularly the more conservative organists, throughout the 19th century (Hauptmann, 1853). These organists used touch and articulation, at times in conjunction with free rubato, to phrase in this manner, particularly in polyphonic music. As late as the 1880s A. Haupt's playing was full of accentuation and phrasing by his 'dwelling slightly upon the primary part of each measure, or more properly upon the first notes of every well-defined phrase'.[4]

As the era progressed the melodic shape and its own natural dynamic curve, rather than the metre, increasingly began to dictate the rhythmic stress (Lussy, 1874, 1883, 1903). The bar-line became less important as the indicator of points of metric, and therefore dynamic, stress. Theorists concluded that the phrase assumes its most natural shape by beginning softly and logically increasing in volume until it reaches its emotional high point or climax (the point of greatest stress or accent), usually near or at the end of the phrase. Thus each phrase is clearly delineated by a dynamic curve which culminates in a single dynamic peak. This climax is to be achieved not only through dynamics but also by agogic emphasis (irrational prolongation, free rubato) (Westphal, 1872, 1880). Since the point of greatest stress is usually near or at the very end of the phrase, the large metric unit that is created is basically iambic in character (weak–strong). The dynamic curve of a basic iambic character then was extended to all levels from the larger units of the phrase and the period down to the short motif. To create this basic iambic unit at the level of the bar, the motif began towards the end of each bar and was extended with a legato slur and a slight crescendo over the bar-line (Riemann, 1884, 1886, 1903). At the level of the beat, the upbeat was slurred with a gradual crescendo (and possible rhythmic elongation) into the downbeat. The objective of this anacrustic concept of phrasing was to create an illusion of greater rhythmic movement.

Thus a complete reversal occurred from the 18th century, with its primary emphasis on rhythm, to the late 19th century, with its primary emphasis on melody. The older metrical scheme of accentuation where the rhythm of the metre (basically trochaic in character) determined the melodic shape was replaced by the basic shape of the melody (considered to be primarily iambic in character) now determining the rhythm (accentuation) through its use of natural, graduated dynamic curve and rubato. 19th-century organists, particularly the liberal school, quickly embraced these new concepts of phrasing and rhythm. Examples can be found in the organ works of Liszt, Brahms and Reger, and in the upbeat phrasing principles of Lemmens, Widor, Guilmant and Schweitzer.

Tempo

There is some reason to believe that at the beginning of the 19th century the extreme tempos of today did not exist as we now know them. However, as the Romantic era progressed the tendency to exaggerate tempos to extremes increased. During the late Romantic period (post-1885) in general, and among liberals throughout the entire era, virtuosos cultivated and composers often indicated very fast tempos. Some 19th-century organists, particularly the conservatives (e.g. Rinck, 1818–20) opposed this general trend and cautioned against taking their music too fast. A. Haupt played J. S. Bach's Fugue in G minor (BWV542) at quaver = 50. Reger admitted that his tempo markings were often too fast and his organ compositions should be taken slower than indicated. Frequently when Widor played, his tempos were considerably slower than the published metronomic indications, for he always demanded that everything should be heard clearly. Widor also lowered the metronome speeds in later editions of various movements of his organ symphonies. For him the smallest note values should guide the selection of the speed. When a group of rapid notes occurs unexpectedly in a composition of calm character and slow note values, Widor recommended slackening the tempo a little, to breathe for an instant, and then resume speed. Franck, Widor and Guilmant were against a flashy, virtuoso style of playing and instead advocated controlled, broad and dignified tempos. For many German organists the stops chosen determined the tempo, as some speak more quickly than others. As regards slow tempos, the late Romantics often followed Wagner's ideas that regarded the adagio as the most expressive tempo of all; consequently, at the end of the era, compositions in slow tempos increasingly tended towards infinite expansion.

Registration

The organ had certain basic design characteristics and registration procedures which were found in all countries during the Romantic era: (*a*) Unless otherwise specified the 8′ foundation tone was always to predominate and form the basis of any manual registration, and 16′ tone formed the basis of the pedal registration. In Germany, England and America organists were intensely interested in the various combinations of two or more 8′ stops, if necessary, using manual couplers to create many subtle differences in colour (E. F. Richter, 1868, 3/1885); writers of the time likened it to mixing pigments on the painter's palette with the four basic stop families – diapasons, flutes, strings and reeds – being considered the primary colours (Truette, 1919). Examples of frequently used combinations of different families of tone include: flute 8′ and string 8′ (for cantabile pieces, this was very common); soft reed 8′ with an additional soft flute 8′, string 8′ or flute 4′ (for a gentle solo); diapason 8′ and flute 8′ (for a fuller, rounder tone); and diapason 8′ or string 8′ and a flute 16′ (for a serious effect). (*b*) Organs had fewer mixtures and of lower pitch. (*c*) The tremolo continued to be used, but until the 1880s it was used only with the Vox humana or for short solo passages. (*d*) New scaling systems were devised during the late 18th century in Germany culminating in a codification by Töpfer (1855) called the 'Normal Scale'; this was quickly adopted in Germany, France and England. It was a non-variable scaling causing a reduction in the scaling variety but creating a very homogeneous and full effect, with weightiness in the bass, brightness and a singing quality in the treble, and a dynamic evenness throughout the rank with a slight tendency for an increase in intensity as one goes up the keyboard. Thus the top note of any chord will be the most prominent. (*e*) The 'Barker lever' was introduced in the 1830s and 40s, which enabled instruments to have a lighter key touch, just as precise and almost as intimate as the tracker touch, no matter how large the instrument.

EARLY ROMANTIC PRACTICES IN GERMANY: 1770s–1840s During the early period three types of instrument were in use in Germany: older Baroque instruments; 18th-century instruments constructed according to Silbermann's principles of design; and instruments with innovations such as Vogler's simplification system. The number and proportion of 8' stops and manual 16' stops increased with 8' principals beginning to appear on each manual. In the late 18th century, conservative composers and performers favoured the older types of instruments, while the liberals sought new directions for organ design and registration to enhance the instruments' effectiveness in rendering the new styles of the time (the *galant* and the fiery, brilliant orchestral manner). To achieve extreme and sudden dynamic contrasts, inspired by the developing orchestra of the time, some organs were even built with two separate pedalboards, each controlling different ranks (e.g. Paulskirche, Frankfurt, 1833). Vogler redesigned organs to function as an orchestra, with each family of sounds being placed on a different manual (though these were not intended to literally imitate orchestral sounds). Two of his ideas had an influence lasting throughout the entire era: a much greater use of mutation stops to create a fuller sound in general and to create resultants, especially in the pedal; and the reduction in the number of reeds, high pitched flue stops, and high pitched mixtures, but not the complete elimination of all mixtures.

Many writers cautioned that the choice of stops should to some extent be determined by the tempo. Slow speaking stops are best suited to *adagio*-like and cantabile execution, and should be avoided in full organ and fast pieces. Prompt speaking and bright stops are better for fast playing. Others, foreshadowing things to come, stated that there should be a greater number of 8' stops than stops at other higher pitch levels, and that when higher pitches were added there also should be a proportional increase in the number of 8' stops. Türk (1787) recommended taking 8' stops as the standard, using two or three of them to every 16', 4', 2⅔', 2' or mixture. 16' manual flues were frequently used to give gravity and to mitigate even further the intensifying effect of the upperwork (Kittel, 1801–8; Knecht, 1795–8). Thus already in the late 18th century there was an orchestra-orientated tendency towards deeper, darker tonal colour. Throughout the early and middle periods (1770s–1880s) fugues were played throughout on a full organ sound, including manual 16' flues. Zang (1804) also gives this direction for toccatas, fantasias and 'pompous' preludes.

Dynamic markings usually indicated a change of manual or registration, particularly among the conservatives. Rinck (1818) lists three groups of stops: soft stops, loud stops (omitting mixtures, Cornet and Sesquialtera) and full organ. He states that *piano* passages may be played on the secondary manual using a Flöte 8' or Gedackt 8' (op.55, 1818; op.74, 1823) or Gambe 8' (op.74), and *forte* movements may be played full organ (op. 55, 1818) or on the *Hauptmanual* using a few 8' stops, one 16' stop and one or two 4' stops (op.74). Mendelssohn also defined this practice in the preface to his sonatas, op.65 (1845): *ff* – full organ; *f* – play on the Great without some of the most powerful stops; *p* – soft 8′ stops combined; *pp* – soft 8′ alone; Pedal – always soft 16′ and 8′ stops. Two of Kittel's most frequently suggested soft registrations for preludes in free style are firstly Viola da Gamba 8′ and Grossgedackt 8′, and secondly Flöte 8′, Quintatön 8′ and Lieblich Gedackt 8′. Reeds were not usually used alone, their sound being considered too harsh, but instead were combined with an 8′ principal or flute. Schmoll states that when the Principal 8′ or 4′, Viola da Gamba 8′ or Vox humana 8′ was indicated each should be strengthened proportionally with several suitable gedackts and flutes. Adlung (1768) states that full organ consists of principals 8′, 4′, 2′ and 1′, quints, terzes, mixtures and for gravity the flutes 16′, 8′ and so on, omitting the softer stops that merely rob wind from the others. The mixtures can be omitted if less brilliance is desired. If it is to be more penetrating, draw the stops of the other keyboard in the same manner and couple them together. The Pedal should have a gravity which is produced with flutes and principals 32′, 16′, 8′, Violone 16′, reeds 32′, 16′, 8′ and higher pitches if available; if not, the normal manual couplers can be used. Throughout the Romantic era in Germany, mixtures were usually employed only when the full organ sound was desired or designated. Composers (e.g. Rinck) often doubled the pedal lines in octaves to achieve the desired weight and gravity and to compensate for weak pedal divisions (common in this early period) and often the existence of only one pedal coupler (I to Ped.).

Vogler and Knecht, both liberals who wrote and improvised programme music on the organ, advocated frequent registration changes as a means of varying expression. Knecht described how to register a crescendo on the organ: first a 16′ stop (*pp*), then one 8′ stop (*p*), slowly one by one more open 8′ stops, followed by 4′, 2′ and 1′ stops, the reeds and finally the Mixture. This was the basic order of the addition of stops in Germany to achieve a crescendo throughout the Romantic era, with the exception that most later writers suggest beginning with a very soft 8′ stop before the first soft 16′ stop. The conservatives of the early period, however, preferred to achieve a crescendo or diminuendo by increasing or decreasing, respectively, the number of voices in the actual musical texture rather than by altering the registration.

MID-ROMANTIC PRACTICES IN GERMANY: 1850s–1880s In the mid-Romantic period the German organ continued to develop in the same direction as it had begun in the early period, becoming even larger and with an even greater variety of 8′ sound. The presence at all pitch levels of mutations left no gaps in the overtone series and, coupled with the abundant 8′ and 16′ sound, this created a full and rich effect with a tremendous amount of weight and gravity without muddiness (the tonal hallmark of the entire era in Germany). Complete principal choruses, each beginning at 8′ (16′ in the Pedal) but including only low pitched mixtures (often with terzes), which did not break as often in the treble, were present on each manual, except the Echo division. Even relatively small instruments usually contained a variety of manual 16′ flue stops spread over the manuals. On large instruments Manual I would have a principal 16′ and then the Pedal would contain a 32′. When registrating, no holes or breaks were allowed in the overtone series unless specified by the composer. Composers (e.g. Bönicke, 1861) often called for manual registrations of 16' and 8' flue stops with no higher pitched ranks.

Manual divisions were graded according to strength: I – *ff*, the heaviest and loudest division with wide-scaled principals; II – *mf*, with narrower-scaled principals; and III – *p*. The pedal stops were separated into strong and weak groups; sometimes there were two pedalboards, one for each group of stops. The demand for dynamic variation continued to develop and stimulated the invention of a variety of devices. One of these, the staged crescendo mechanism, brought on all the stops of the organ in a small number (four to seven) of set stages. For example, the Ladegast organ in Merseburg (1853), which was closely associated with Liszt, had a crescendo mechanism of only four stages plus *pp* and tutti controls. At most, only one manual (usually the third) was enclosed, and this division was usually small with few or no reeds. The expression pedal was an unbalanced hitch-down mechanism which, unless left open, would return to the closed position once the player's foot was removed. The conservatives (e.g. E. F. Richter, Rheinberger, Haupt, Merkel and A. Hesse), in the majority at this time, attached little significance to swell effects. Crescendo and diminuendo markings begin to appear in German organ music chiefly after 1860. Only occasionally was a single céleste present (on the enclosed division), and there were very few orchestrally imitative stops.

Registration and manual changes usually continued to be indicated by dynamic markings. Below is a summary of the explanations of registration directions indicated by dynamics drawn from the 20 organ sonatas, published between 1869 and 1907, by the arch-conservative J. Rheinberger:

ff – full organ; full organ of Manual I
f – full organ without reeds
mf – Principal 8' (and sometimes 4') of Manual I; full organ of Manual II; the soft and medium stops of Manual I
p – two or three soft stops; a pair of soft 8' and 4' stops; a few soft 8' and 4' stops; soft 8' and 4' stops of Manual II, perhaps also of Manual I; Gamba 8' or Salicional 8' and Dolce 4'
pp – Gamba 8', or Salicional 8', or Aeoline 8', or Dolce 8'; Salicional 8' and Dolce 4'; a soft stop; 8' stop alone; on manual II
ppp – the softest 8' stop
The Pedal always was to be of corresponding strength.

Some composers continued to designate registrations in three gradations: soft stops (*sanfte Stimmen*), loud stops (*starke Stimmen*) and full organ (*volles Werk*). Riemann (1888) suggests soft 8' flute stops open or stopped for soft stops; a larger number of stops, especially principals, foundations and flutes in combination with some reeds for loud stops; and all but the very weakest stops for full organ. However, he qualifies the use of full organ by stating that enormous masses of sound should be used only for certain short passages, never for the performance of a long piece. E. F. Richter (1868, 2/1885) gives four types of moderately loud registrations: (1) principals and flutes 16', 8' and 4', with or without Rohrquint and deep Cornet, (2) the above plus 5⅓'s and 2's, (3) all of the above plus cornetts and quints, except high ones, and (4) all of the above plus all reeds. (Note the absence of mixtures.) Riemann

(1888) gives the following order for adding stops to achieve a crescendo: a soft 8' flue stop, progressively more 8' flues, Principal 8', Oktave 4', Flute 16', Quinte 2⅔', reed 8', Oktave 2', Mixture, all remaining stops. A louder crescendo can be achieved by coupling other manuals and drawing on stops in the same order. The crescendo was to be very smooth (a foreshadowing of things to come). As greater volume was desired successively higher and lower pitches were added, but the 8' fundamental sound on the manuals (16' in the Pedal) always was to continue to be the most prominent pitch line.

During the mid-Romantic period, the dominant playing style was that of the conservatives, who sought to return the organ to its classic function as a basically polyphonic instrument. However, from the middle of the century a new circle of liberals developed around Liszt who desired to expand the expressive power of the organ through a greater exploitation of its resources: faster tempos, greater use of crescendos and diminuendos, extreme dynamic contrasts through sudden manual changes and a more active use of the varied tonal palette of the organ. They sought to make the organ as expressive as the orchestra and thus continued the ideals of the liberals from the early period. By the end of the 19th century this tendency led to the development of the late Romantic German organ and its unique playing style.

LATE ROMANTIC PRACTICES IN GERMANY: 1890s–1940 In the 1880s and early 1890s a great many mechanical innovations and improvements occurred on German organs, which made them much more flexible to manipulate. Different types of electrical action came into being, which allowed the console and the pipes to be placed apart. Gradually more of the instrument was enclosed in chambers with Swell shutters. The *Rollschweller*, a register crescendo mechanism in the form of a revolving drum with between six and twelve stages was developed and, when augmented with hand registration, this allowed organists to achieve very smooth and graduated crescendos and diminuendos. German reeds had always been smoother and less fiery than French, so that their addition or subtraction fitted smoothly into the gradual dynamic changes of the whole ensemble. The desired aim became for the changes to be so smooth that one did not notice individual stops coming on or going off.

Thus organ playing in Reger's time was characterized by constant, occasionally rapid but more commonly gradual, dynamic changes coupled with frequent (and at times significant) tempo modifications and rubato playing. Reger often wanted his fugues to begin slowly and then gradually to increase in tempo and volume. His aim in using a very wide range of dynamic indications from *pppp* to *ffff* (usually with manuals coupled) was to achieve a sensitive, deeply-felt performance with great dynamic precision. Straube always performed Reger's music with all unison manual and pedal couplers on. For small crescendos he used the expression pedal, while for bigger dynamic changes he used the *Rollschweller*. Thus Reger's music was basically played on one sound with the employment of the *Rollschweller* for dynamic changes. Dynamics were often used for architectural reasons. Performers developed a very refined sensitivity to shades of colouring, with 8' and 4' stops freely mixed to achieve blendings of mellow tone. Examples would include a narrow 8' stop combined with a wide 4' stop; Gedackt 8', Voix céleste 8' and Spitzflöte 4'. Célestes also became prevalent and popular. Straube particularly liked the sound of the Quintedina 16' together with the Gedackt 8' on the third manual of the Ladegast organ in the Leipzig Conservatory.

EARLY ROMANTIC PRACTICES IN ENGLAND: 1800–1840s At the beginning of the 19th century English organs had few or no pedals. Up to 1850 when they were present, they were usually of G' compass and controlled only one set of large-scale, lightly-blown wooden pipes, designed solely to provide a deep-toned bass to the manuals. On most organs the manuals were also of G' compass and rarely contained any 16' stops. The Swell was enclosed in a Swell box but was of incomplete range at the bottom. As a result of Mendelssohn's trips to England in the 1830s and early 1840s and his urgings that organs should be built that could play the organ works of J. S. Bach, larger organs began to be built during the 1840s that had C' compass pedalboards of at least two octaves. Thus in the mid-19th century many variations in the bottom compass of various manual keyboards and the pedalboard could be found on English instruments. Basic registrational practices of the late 18th century as discussed in Marsh (1791), Blewitt (?1795) and Linley (c1800) continued through this early transitional period (e.g. Hamilton, 2/1842).

MID-ROMANTIC PRACTICES IN ENGLAND: 1850s–1880s Due at least in part to German influence, larger organs that began to assume present-day manual and pedal compasses began to be built in England during the mid-Romantic period. These were characterized by rich, singing diapason choruses, imitative solo stops and brilliant reeds, which in the enclosed Swell division produced an effect of great splendour. Contemporary sources indicate that English registration practices were similar to German practices of the time (Best, 1853; Hiles, 1876, 2/1878, 3/1882; Archer, 1875; Stainer, 1877). Frederic Archer gives the following list of stops to produce different desired dynamic levels:

ppp – Dulciana [8'].
pp – add Lieblich Gedackt 8'.
p – add Hohlflöte [8'] and Viola da Gamba 8'.
mf – add Diapasons 16' and 8', and 4' Flute.
f – add all flue work, up to Fifteenth.
ff – add a portion of the mixture work and a soft Reed.
fff – add all the Reeds and remainder of the mixture work.[5]

He also gives the following definitions of general registration directions frequently used by English composers of the day:

'Swell with Oboe' (or Sw. Reed) .... Swell Manual, with the 8'
Flue work and Oboe [8'].
'Swell without Oboe' .... 8' Flue work only.
'Swell with Reeds' .... add all the other Reeds.
'Full Swell' .... Draw the whole of the stops
in this manual.

It will be seen that the 8′ and 16′ flue work is always implied, and the stops actually mentioned are those that limit the extent of the power required, for instance

'Gt. Full to Fifteenth' .... The whole of the Flue work,
(or simply to 15th)   16′ pitch to 2′.
'Flue with Mixtures' .... add Sesquialtera and
                                                                                            Mixtures.
'Full' .... Draw the whole of the Gt.
                                                                                            Organ stops.

Archer considered the most legitimate large organ tone to consist of Diapasons 16′ and 8′ with all the other 8′ flues plus similar stops of the Swell so that a crescendo and diminuendo could be produced when desired. In the Swell he recommended adding the Oboe 8′ to the flues before adding any 4′ stops. When arranging a gradual increase of tone, 4′ stops should be added to those of 8′ in the proportion of two to three, afterwards drawing 12th and 15th, mixtures, and finally reeds. Note that the mixtures here precede the reeds, differing from the German order. This actually is a continuation of 18th- and early 19th-century English practice. Also departing from the German practice of the time, Stainer (1877) recommends certain registration changes in the performance of fugues, reserving the full power until the climax and playing the episode sections on a different manual or with a strongly contrasted tone quality.

EARLY ROMANTIC PRACTICES IN AMERICA: 1800–1850s Until the 1850s in America, organs exhibited gentle, clear tonal characteristics and the style of performance strongly reflected late 18th-century English influences (Taylor, c1800; Loud, 1845; Beckel, 1850). Most descriptions of crescendos indicate that on the Great the mixture was added before the reeds (Loud, 1845; Schneider, 1851; Zundel,[6] 1851) similar to the English practice of the time.

MID-ROMANTIC PRACTICES IN AMERICA: 1860s–1880s During the mid-Romantic period more American organists began to travel to Germany for their musical education, and German organ builders began to influence the design of new American organs. In the 1860s and 1870s American instruments became more assertive and capable of considerable power and brilliance. In the 1870s much larger organs began to be built, which had bold, bright principal ensembles. During the 1880s and 90s, 8′ sound began to dominate the ensembles with a thicker, heavier quality, with more contrast between loud and soft stops and with greater dynamic control of the enclosed divisions. Emphasis was placed more on blending sounds and on a grand body of sound. Mutation stops became less frequent.

Eugene Thayer gives the following suggestions concerning the *quality* of combinations:

1. If the music is solid, dignified or noble, it follows that the Organ tone [diapason tone] should be chosen.
2. If bright and cheerful or melodious, the Flute tone should predominate.
3. If soft or meditative, the String tone is best adapted.
4. If very bold or brilliant, the loud Reed tone should predominate. The soft Reed tone is chiefly for music of a plaintive or pathetic character.

5. For music that is very grand or imposing, the Organ tone [diapason tone] and loud Reed tone combined are best.
6. For pieces that are rather soft and at the same time cheerful and bright, a combination of the String tone and Flute tone should be used.
7. The Full Organ is best adapted to music of the most decided character. It should be the voice of majesty, grandeur and sublimity.[7]

Elsewhere Thayer states that when a particular tone quality is specified this is not to imply that the combination is to be played exclusively with that quality, but only that the particular tone quality should predominate. This is in keeping with the general mid-Romantic practice in German, English and American registrations of including stops from various families of tone rather than the use of 'pure' organ tone from only one family of sound.

George E. Whiting, in the introduction to his *20 Preludes, Postludes etc.* (1877), lists the following registrations for the dynamic markings in the collection:

Great Manual

pp The softest register in the manual – Dulciana, or Dulciana and 4ft Flute. (The stop[d] Diap. should not be used for 'chorus playing', that is, when both hands are on the lower part of the keyboard.)
p The Gemshorn or a very soft *open* Flute (Melodia, Clarabella, or Doppel Flute – the Höhl Flute should be classed with the stop[d] Diap.).
mp The Gamba ('Bell Gamba') and stop[d] Diap., or Gamba stop[d] Diap. and 4ft Flute.
mf All the 8ft stops except Gamba and Reeds.
f All the 8 and 4ft except Reeds – and perhaps to 12th & 15th when the organ is softly voiced.
ff The Full Gt. without Reeds, or in some cases the Full Gt. including Reeds without mixtures.
fff The Full Organ.
The 16ft manual stops (Bourdon, Double Diap., Double Trumpet &c.) are not to be used unless they are mentioned in the music, except in the *ff* or *fff* effects.
In the Pedal part 16 and 8ft stops are always intended to be used (the 8ft either by coupling to the manuals, or by an independent Ped. stop) except where marked '8ft' or by the name of some 8ft Ped. register. The 16ft Ped. should usually be either a Bourdon or a Double Dulciana.

Swell Manual

ppp The softest 8ft register – Viol d Gamba, (Dulciana) or Viol d Gamba and one soft 4ft stop (Violin or 4ft Flute).
pp Open and stop[d] Diap[ns], or Oboe (Hautboy) and 4ft Flute, or Oboe alone.
p The same as the last, with the Swell box slightly opened.
mp Cornopean (Trumpet) and stop[d] Diap., or open Diap. and octave.
mf The 'Full Swell' (closed).

LATE ROMANTIC PRACTICES IN ENGLAND AND AMERICA: 1890s–1940s As early as the 1850s in England, municipal hall organs became popular and this helped to usher in an era when secular music, both original and transcribed for the organ, became part of many organists' repertory. Thus began a period when the organ became very popular among the general public and can be said truly to have reached the common man.

In both England and America the 1880s and thereafter saw the advent of new actions which made use of electricity, and witnessed the continuous introduction of new mechanical accessories to assist the organist in the manipulation of the instrument. These innovations made the organ more versatile and responsive and allowed greater degrees of expressiveness. Progressively more divisions were put under expression so that in America by World War I most of the instrument was usually enclosed in expression boxes (with the possible exception of the Great and the Pedal). Beginning in the 1880s balanced Swell pedals and more efficient Swell shade actions allowed the performer to produce accents and *sforzandi* as aids to rhythmic drive for more vital music-making (Lemare, 1910; Dickinson, 1922). All of these changes were manifestations of the ideal that the late Romantic organ should be able to imitate the expressive range of the orchestra.

A preoccupation with colour, the blending of stops and the desire to expand the organ's tonal palette as much as possible resulted in the creation of many new stops, some inspired by contemporary orchestral instruments. The voicing tended to be very smooth and refined. The upper harmonic development of individual stops, and of specification designs except in string tone, was reduced and wind pressures were raised to add power and to project more tonal colour. String tone was developed in much greater variety, and it became more frequently used both as a solo colour and as an ensemble sound in its own right. The brightness of some strings was developed to the point that at times they came to serve the function of adding brightness in the ensemble formally assigned to mixtures. Entire divisions of strings were built and célestes became very common. 32' stops also became very popular. Hull lists six families of colour (given here in a crescendo order, according to the wearing qualities on the ear): gedackt tone, flute tone, diapason tone, clarinet tone (includes Oboe and Vox humana), trumpet tone and gamba tone.[8] Such an expansion from the hitherto traditional four families of tone colour represented a new emphasis on different types of flute tone and soft solo reed tone (some of it from new imitative orchestral stops).

Usually English organists drew a gedackt or flute with gamba tone, which Hull cautioned must be used sparingly since it is the keenest of all the colours and suggests very human sentiments. Some writers, however, also suggested using families of stops in purity, without mixing colours, and then contrasting these pure colours: flutes against strings in the upper register, flutes or strings against diapasons in the lower register, a flute against a reed, or a heavy body of all the reeds on one manual against all the diapasons on another (Lemare, 1910; Hull, 1911; Dickinson, 1922).

Changes in registration became more frequent, whether or not indicated in the score by the composer. In the late 19th century many American organists advocated changing registrations at the beginning of each phrase in slow movements. By the 1920s frequent changes occurred within each phrase, coupled with sensitive and constant use of the expression pedals (McCurdy, 1931). Hull gives the following rules for changing registrations:

> Any rules on the manner of applying tone colours must be of the most general nature and consequently subject to very considerable qualification in many instances.
> (*i*) The quality of foresight, so eminently useful in the ordinary conduct of life, should be always exercised in the matters of colour arrangement. Both outlines and details of colour should be carefully worked out and

decided upon before the commencement of the piece, taking care to give the various colours to those passages which are most grateful to them.

(*ii*) In many pieces there will be a climax of tone and colour which should be carefully worked up to, and away from, but it does not follow that the feeling of climax is necessary to all pieces.

(*iii*) Each phrase, or period, should as a rule have some slight change of colour or shading. Certainly the same phrase should not be repeated without some difference in colour treatment. Occasionally the idea of response in colour may be made by quite short figures or even by chords.

(*iv*) Violent contrasts should be avoided except for dramatic purposes, and even in elaborate pieces of many changes and tints there will always be some principal contrast in tone-colour round which the other contrasts and variations appear to group themselves.

(*v*) In using either shading or contrast, the new tone should be used *just after* and not immediately before an accented beat; that is, the tone should not be changed in the course of a phrase (feminine endings for an apparent exception to this rule).[9]

Often the normal position of the Swell shutters was closed. Volume and colour changes were accomplished by the addition or subtraction of stops while the Swell shutters were used primarily for accent purposes. There was a delight in achieving very gradual crescendos and diminuendos in the sound mass by a very refined use of Swell shutters so that the actual addition or subtraction of stops would not be noticed. For a crescendo this was accomplished by pulling back on the Swell shutters at the exact moment that one or more new stops were added. The box would then be opened and the process repeated with each new addition. A second way was to use two or more expression boxes simultaneously, fading from one to another with each successive change of stops. The build-up could be so smooth on these instruments that the effect was of a blooming of the sound, and of an expansive, almost limitless crescendo. E. H. Lemare is known to have added stops in the following order in a crescendo: all 8' couplers on, Gedackt 8', soft strings 8', louder strings 8', Vox humana 8',[10] Flute 4', soft reeds 8', diapasons 8', louder reeds 8', then gradually the upper work. Thus the strings built up and then the soft reeds began; smooth reeds (Cornopean and French Horn) functioned to reinforce and broaden the tone and to introduce the diapasons; diapasons additionally were used as large strings. Soft mixtures were intended to blend with the strings while any large mixtures were only used as the top of a large ensemble. Lemare did not like the crescendo pedal but instead favoured the achievement of crescendos and diminuendos through the coordinated use of pistons, hand registration (when possible) and the manipulation of the expression pedals. He rarely used the Principal 4' and mixtures unless 'capped' by a reed 8'. Super couplers were used in solo work not as a substitute for mixtures. For Lemare, sub- and super-couplers were most useful to create big chords on soft string-tone stops, when only one hand is available, and new and differing shades of colour. Lemare stressed that stops should be added at points in the music that will enhance the phrasing. There should never be the slightest pause when changing stops.

The late Romantic organ was conceived as a vast palette of tone colours which could be swelled, diminished, mixed and used in many different ways, all with the intent of heightening the expressiveness of the music. Coupled with these new means of expression there developed a new sense of freedom to allow the individuality of the player to come forth in interpreting music on these instruments. Thus the early 20th-century late Romantic organ and performance style in England and America can be seen as the final and fullest development of the expressive ideals first posited by the late 18th-century German liberals (e.g. Vogler and Knecht).

EARLY ROMANTIC PRACTICES IN FRANCE: 1789–1840s In this period of transition organs tended toward a thicker sound, increased loudness, new means for greater expression, and easier mechanical control. Older and new registration styles co-existed in France. As late as 1840 Classical French registration practices and terminology were given in the preface to a set of new mass versets (Fétis, 1840) and to an organ method (Fessy, 1845). However, the newer Romantic style registration practices of Germany were also known through the French publication of several German organ tutors in translation (Martini, c1804, from Knecht, 1795–8; Werner, French trans. by Choron Rinck, op.55, 1818–20, French trans. by Choron).

MID-ROMANTIC PRACTICES IN FRANCE: 1840–1940 The French Romantic organ began to develop in the 1840s, largely through the efforts of Cavaillé-Coll. Significant characteristics of this new organ included: (*a*) wide-scaled foundations creating a rich, full 8′ sound and consisting of a minimum of a Montre (principal), Gambe (string), Flûte harmonique (open flute) and Bourdon (stopped flute),[11] (*b*) excellent harmonic flutes, (*c*) good string-toned stops, (*d*) high pressure reeds of fine, brilliant quality, differing in power rather than in quality,[12] (*e*) imitative orchestral reeds, (*f*) coupling mechanisms which allowed the entire organ to be played from one keyboard, resulting in enormous crescendos and diminuendos, (*g*) the enlarging of the *Récit* to a sizeable division enclosed and under the control of an expression pedal, and (*h*) a consistency in the broad principles of basic tonal design and control so that composers always knew exactly what they were writing for. Probably because of this last feature most French organ music contains carefully indicated registrations.

French organists did not like 'kaleidoscopic' stop changes. They preferred continuity of tone colour and resisted the aesthetic of presenting the organ as a 'pseudo-orchestra'. For Widor the choice of registration was always determined to achieve a clarity of playing, while a change of registration only should result from the nature and plan of the composition. Modifications of sound should be the consequence of either a punctuation of the text or a developmental episode and should be proportionate to the importance of the punctuation or episode.

Normally only one division, the *Récit*, was enclosed in a Swell box (very occasionally a second division).[13] At first Cavaillé-Coll's expression pedal was a hitch-down mechanism which, when the foot was removed, only allowed for open, closed or one-half open. Beginning in the late 1870s he began to use a balanced expression pedal. Directions for the use of the expression pedal were indicated by dynamic markings: *f*, crescendo and the 'hairpin' for open and *p*, decrescendo, diminuendo and the 'hairpin' for closed.[14] In French organ music the use of the expression pedal was more for architectural line than for emotional expression; breadth and simplicity of treatment were the norm (Goodrich, 1917). Widor, Guilmant and Gigout all cautioned against the excessive use of the Swell box; similarly many writers and performers recommended that the Voix céleste and Voix humaine be used sparingly. In each division Cavaillé-Coll grouped various ranks on to one of two different chests; the foundations (*jeux de fonds*) on one and the reeds, mixtures and mutations (*jeux de combinaison*) on the other. Each chest had a separate valve (*ventil*) activated by a foot control for admitting air only when required. This system of dividing the stops on each manual into two groups, each with its own wind control, made it possible for the organist to prepare a registration, which would however sound only when the respective *ventil* was activated.

Through the use of couplers, *ventils* and the expression pedal, the French organist was able to achieve a very smooth and gradual crescendo. With slight variations sources give the following basic plan (Schweitzer, 1906; Goodrich, 1917). All manuals are coupled at unison pitch, and the *Récit* box is closed. Begin on the *Récit* with foundations 16', 8', 4' (and 2'). Go to the *Grand Orgue* with the *Positif* foundations already on and therefore coupled to it. Add the *Grand Orgue* foundations by the use of the *Grand Orgue ventil*. The *Récit* box is now opened or may have been opened at a previous time. Close the *Récit* box as the reeds and mixtures of the *Récit* are added by means of the *Recit* reed *ventil*. Gradually open the *Récit* box. Successively add the reeds and mixtures of the *Positif* and then the *Grand Orgue* by means of their respective reed *ventils*. Finally activate sub- and super-octave couplers. All additions should be made on strong accents. A decrescendo would be accomplished in basically the reverse order.

Although the voicing of French organs of the early 20th century exhibits somewhat the general tendencies of the late Romantic organ aesthetic (strings becoming narrower and brighter, flutes becoming broader, and principals (montres) becoming less bright), the organ in France never progressed to a true late Romantic stage of development as it did in Germany, England and America.

Notes

[1] J. S. Bach and a significant number of keyboard musicians including organists in the second half of the 18th century executed the ordinary touch by pulling the fingers across the keys (a stroking of the keys) rather than a vertical finger motion. Piano methods throughout the 19th century indicate that this stroking motion of the fingers continued to be employed for the execution of this touch.

[2] Many composers in both the late 18th century and the 19th (e.g. Türk, Widor and Guilmant) used wedges to indicate an even more extreme detachment than dots, a *staccatissimo*, where the note might receive as little as one quarter of its value.

[3] See J. Bonnet's organ-roll recording of his own *Romance sans paroles*, op.7 no.8.

[4] A. Haupt, 'Accentuation in Organ Playing', *MR*, xxii (1892), 207.

[5] *The Organ* (London, 1875), 53.

[6] Elsewhere, Zundel (1860) recommends adding the reeds before the mixtures (the German practice). Zundel had studied in Germany with J. C. H. Rinck.

[7] *The Art of Organ Playing*, pt.iii, op.60 (Boston, Mass., 1913), 6–7.

[8] *Organ Playing: its Techniques and Expression* (London, 1941), 141.

[9] ibid., 166–8.

[10] The link for Lemare between the softer strings and the softer reeds was the Vox humana 8′.

[11] Usually there is a difference in tonal quality between the fonds of each manual (*Récit* fonds, fluty; *Positif* fonds, stringy; and *Grand Orgue* fonds, full and rich).

[12] The reed(s) of each manual would be of increasing power in a progression from the *Récit* to the *Positif* and finally to the *Grand Orgue*.

[13] Widor favoured on a three-manual organ having two manuals under expression.

[14] However, Schweitzer (1906) does state that *crescendo poco a poco* in an increase leading in a short time to *fortissimo* means that the player, when he has permitted the full manual III to develop with the foundation stops of the first two manuals, should introduce at the climactic strong accents the mixtures and reeds of the other manuals and of the pedals.

CHAPTER XIX

Strings

ROBIN STOWELL

The late 18th-century explosion in amateur music-making, concert activity, publishing and systematic musical instruction,[1] coupled with developments in bow and instrument construction, prepared the stage for the touring virtuoso. Paris was the centre of string playing in the early 19th century; its traditions were fostered by Viotti and continued by his numerous French violin disciples (especially Baillot, Kreutzer, Rode and Habeneck) by influence or direct instruction, as well as by successors such as Alard (teacher of Sarasate) and cellists such as Duport, Levasseur, Baudiot, Norblin and Chevillard. The Conservatoire, where regular orchestral concerts were given from 1828 onwards under Habeneck's direction, was central. French influence spread quickly to other countries, notably Belgium; the Brussels violin school was instituted by Bériot (a pupil of Viotti and Baillot) and continued by Vieuxtemps, Léonard, Wieniawski,[2] Thomson and Ysaÿe; the cello school was established by Duport's pupil Platel and continued by Servais and Jules de Swert. Other branches of the French violin school flourished in Vienna, with Böhm (a Rode pupil) and his pupils Ernst and the Hungarian Reményi as chief representatives; in Norway, the leading violinist, Ole Bull, was largely a product of French training; and in Prague, Viotti's pupil Pixis and the latter's pupil Kalliwoda prepared for the later more systematic instruction of Ševčík, whose exercises based on the semitone (rather than the diatonic) system led to significant technical advances.

Although the Italian string school was in decline, it expired with a flourish, notably with the virtuoso skills of the violinists Lolli, his pupil Giornovichi, Paganini and Bazzini, the cellist Piatti and the bass players Dragonetti and Bottesini.

Musicians of the conservative German violin school (Spohr,[3] his pupil David, and David's pupil Joachim were the main 19th-century figures) admired Paganini's technical facility, but deplored such exploitation of technique for commercial rather than for artistic ends. David played a vital advisory role in the composition of Mendelssohn's Violin Concerto and Joachim in Brahms's, and both contributed numerous editions of 18th-century repertory which provide insights into their technical and interpretative ideals. The rise of the German cello school, prompted initially by Romberg and Kraft, centred on Dresden and the teaching of J.J.F. Dotzauer, whose pupils included Kummer, Schuberth, Voigt and Drechsler.

Distinctions between schools of playing became less well defined during the century; teaching methods and playing styles invariably intermingled, as exemplified in the musical background of Leopold Auer, whose fundamental training, though firmly based on the teachings of the French school, was so cosmopolitan – taking in Budapest, Vienna, Hanover and St Petersburg – and subject to so many influences (Kohne, Dont, Joachim) that he cultivated a flexible pedagogical approach which elicited the best from his pupils (among them Heifetz, Elman and Milstein).

The early development of the Romantic violin concerto was modelled on the work of Beethoven and the French school, but was fired with more virtuoso ideals (notably the concertos of Spohr, Bériot, Vieuxtemps and Paganini). The form blossomed from c1850 onwards in the hands of Mendelssohn, Brahms, Bruch, Tchaikovsky, Dvořák, Saint-Saëns, Wieniawski and Lalo. Only Rolla's works and Berlioz's 'symphony' *Harold en Italie* stand out in contemporary viola concerto repertory, but the cello boasts 'mainstream' concertos such as those by Schumann (op.129), Brahms (double concerto op.102), Dvořák (op.104) and Saint-Saëns (opp.33 and 119), together with Tchaikovsky's *Variations on a Rococo Theme* (op.33) and Strauss's *Don Quixote* (op.35). Dragonetti and Bottesini provide the most significant works of the bass concerto repertory.

The mid-19th century was the era of small concert works (e.g. Saint-Saëns's opp.28 and 83 and Chausson's op.25), salon pieces, caprices, études, character pieces (romances, élégies), national dances and ephemeral arrangements of popular themes. These last were mostly derived from opera and were presented as fantasies, variations or potpourris by such violinists as Paganini, Sarasate and Ernst. The more 'classical' types of chamber music also flourished, the sonata for violin and piano and cello and piano remaining particularly popular. The string quartet was nurtured in Vienna by the Schuppanzigh and (later) Hellmesberger Quartets and flourished in the second half of the century after a comparatively lean post-Beethoven period. Many other chamber genres and combinations were also cultivated. Prevailing virtuoso trends considerably affected orchestral writing for strings with such composers as Berlioz, Weber, Tchaikovsky, Wagner and Strauss demanding dramatic technical advances, especially from the lower string parts.

Violin treatises generally incorporated fuller technical and interpretative information than before,[4] especially those emanating from the Paris and Brussels Conservatoires by Baillot, Rode and Kreutzer (1803), Mazas (1830), Baillot (1834), Habeneck (c1840), Alard (1844), Bériot (1858), Dancla (c1850) and Léonard (1877).[5] Contemporary Italian violin treatises are negligible, but the German school prospered in the wake of Leopold Mozart with works by Guhr (1829), Spohr (1832), David (1864), Wilhelmj (1898), Courvoisier (1899) and Joachim and Moser (1902–5).[6] Other violinists credited with technical and pedagogical developments include Dont, Schradieck, Sauret and Ševčík.

Viola treatises were less abundant, but those of Bruni (c1805), Martinn (c1815), Brähmig (c1885) and Klingenfeld (1897) are noteworthy.[7] Duport's *Essai sur le doigté du violoncelle* (c1806–19) laid the foundations of cello virtuosity, particularly as regards fingering, but Bideau (1802), Baillot, Levasseur, Catel and Baudiot (1804), Bréval (1804), Baudiot (1830), Chevillard (c1850) and de Swert (c1890) made important French contribu-

Quartet recital at the Berlin home of Bettina Brentano (von Arnim; seated listening): Joseph Joachim plays first violin, Graf Flemming, cello, and probably Woldemar Bargiel, second violin: watercolour (1855) by Johann Carl Arnold in the Goethemuseum, Frankfurt am Main

tions,[8] Dotzauer (1832, 1836, 1837 and 1870), Kummer (1839), Romberg (c1840) and Banger (1877) were prominent German theorists[9] and Piatti (1878), Quarenghi (1877) and Braga (1878) represented the Italian school.[10] Fröhlich (1829), Bottesini (c1860) and Simandl (1874) wrote the most significant bass treatises.[11]

The various modifications in string instrument construction[12] were implemented gradually over a substantial transitional period (c1760–c1830) and so instruments were in a state of flux at the beginning of the Romantic era. However, the exterior body outline of the violin family remained substantially unaltered during the period despite attempts to 'improve' it with the use of such unlikely materials as earthenware, glass, leather and *papier mâché* and the introduction of such designs as Chanot's guitar-shaped violin, Savart's trapezoid violin, Ritter's *viola alta*, Woldemar's *violon-alto* and Vuillaume's enlarged violas. Spohr's chin rest (c1820) altered the appearance of the violin (and eventually the viola) slightly; the endpin, introduced by A. F. Servais c1860, did the same for the cello. The chin rest, made of ebony, was initially placed directly over the tailpiece, but the normal position today on the left of the tailpiece was standard by c1850. String materials changed little, the upper two strings of each instrument normally being of uncovered gut (possibly also the violin D) and the lower two of wound gut, most commonly with silver, brass or plated copper.

Universal approval for the Tourte bow was won slowly. Many French makers (e.g. Persois, Eury, Henry, Peccatte) regarded it as their ideal, but others persisted with pre-Tourte designs well into the 19th century. An assortment of bows (and a diverse vocabulary of bowstrokes and styles) co-existed at the beginning of the century, but gradually the Tourte model's superior ability to fulfil the prevailing aesthetic and expressive aims was acknowledged. Later modifications to the Tourte model include the addition of the underslide to the frog, the indentation of the frog's channel and track in the bow, the combination of rear and upper heel plates into one right-angled metal part[13] and a tendency for sticks to become more heavily wooded, with a consequent increase in weight, in order to achieve greater tonal sonority. The slimmer head and different camber of Voirin's design, which offered a stick of greater strength and lighter weight, achieved some popularity c1850, with such makers as Lamy, the Thomassins and Bazin, but Tourte's design eventually regained its supremacy.

In the late 19th century a different 'German' bow type, named after Simandl, co-existed with the Tourte model bass bow (nicknamed 'French' or 'Bottesini' bow), and in some areas, notably England, the convex 'Dragonetti' bow. This was a hybrid of cello and viol models with hatchet head and concave camber, but with marked separation of hair and stick at the frog.

A noble and relaxed posture remained the violinist's and the violist's goal: an upright head, feet normally in line but slightly astride, and body weight distributed with a slight bias towards the left side. The seated position involved bending the right wrist and elbow rather more, turning the right leg slightly inwards (to avoid contact between knee and bow when bowing at the point on the upper strings) and supporting the left leg (and hence the body weight) on a footstool, thereby enabling the trunk to remain erect. Cello posture changed little, but the introduction of the endpin (*c*1860) offered greater security, mobility and resonance.

The chin-braced grip on the left side of the tailpiece was most common but it was not universally approved by violinists and violists at the beginning of the period. Even Spohr's chin rest was positioned over the tailpiece. The resulting higher scroll and 'horizontal' position of the instrument offered greater facility of execution. Some licence was allowed when seated; the scroll was invariably lowered to facilitate straight bowing, and some performers employed a shoulder pad to increase security and comfort and to avoid raising the left shoulder.[14] The left hand was gradually relieved of its semi-supporting role and the common right-arm position (closer to the player's side than formerly), required that the instrument should incline more to the right for optimum bowing technique on the lowest string; Baillot prescribes an angle of 45°, Spohr 25°–30°. The 'Geminiani grip' persisted as a guide for left hand, wrist, finger and elbow placement in 1st position (Courvoisier is one of the few who opposed this), but players strove for easy elbow manoeuvrability and flexibility of the hand position to cope with new technical demands. An advanced thumb position was employed by many (notably Paganini) for greater mobility and facility in extensions.

Economy of finger movement still persisted, but finger activity was related more to tempo with the fingers remaining on the strings as much as possible in fast passages. In slow or moderate tempos, redundant fingers were allowed to fall independently from a height sufficient to articulate notes clearly (especially in slurred passages), freeing the hand for easier cultivation of vibrato.

Modifications to instrument design (especially the length of the fingerboard), confirmation of the more stable chin-braced violin grip and ever-increasing demands on finger technique ensured the exploitation of the entire range of hand positions on string instruments (Baillot gives the whole violin range as four and a half octaves). Shifting proved less precarious; classical theories regarding where to shift were somewhat relaxed and emphasis was placed on the odd-numbered positions; cultivation of the semitone shift facilitated achievement of the prevalent legato ideal. Sureness of intonation was paramount, but timbre and tonal uniformity were highly prized. Baillot demonstrates how the timbre of every instrument, and each of the four strings, can be modified in imitation of other instruments, and Spohr advocates the exploitation of higher positions for expressive and tonal purposes.[15] *Una corda* playing reached its zenith with the extravaganzas on the G string by Paganini; sequences were played wherever possible with matching fingerings, bowings and string changes, and differences in string timbre were veiled where appropriate.[16] Although 19th-century standards of viola playing were variable (Berlioz, and later Wagner, complained about the general technical incompetence of orchestral violists), viola and cello technique developed along similar lines, if more slowly; the cellist's thumb became a vital playing member and, as with the other string instruments, a prime agent in a more refined shifting mechanism.

Baillot acknowledges the interrelationship between fingering, the player's hand position and musical intentions. He distinguishes between sure fingering, fingering for small hands and expressive fingering relevant to selected composers. The last category includes Kreutzer's frequent shifts on all strings for brilliance of effect, and Rode's more uniform tonal characteristics, incorporating *ports de voix*.[17] Baillot's discussion of *ports de voix* and expressive fingering[18] provides clues to the mechanics of shifting. Anticipatory notes (unsounded) indicate the method of shifting, the stopped finger sliding forwards (or backwards) in order to be substituted by another finger. Spohr endorses this,[19] especially for rapid shifts involving leaps from a low to a high position in slurred bowing (ex.1) (without glissando effect), and gives a further example of a fast shift (ex.2) in which the highest note is a harmonic. Stopping the bow momentarily during the shift also helped to make shifting inaudible (ex.3), as many writers desired. Nevertheless,

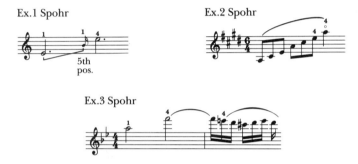

Habeneck and Baillot allow the tasteful introduction of portamento,[20] especially in slow movements and sustained melodies when a passage ascends or descends by step. In these cases they advise that the portamento should be accompanied by a crescendo and diminuendo respectively (ex.4).

Bériot[21] uses signs to indicate three types of *port de voix*: *vif*, *doux* and *traîné* (ex.5a, *b* and *c*). Paganini regularly employed glissando with great effect, both for showmanship (ex.6) and for cantabile execution of double stopping (ex.7). Exploitation of the glissando and portamento as an 'emotional connection of two tones'[22] (invariably in slurred bowing and with upward shifts), to articulate melodic shape and emphasize structurally important notes became so prevalent in the late 19th century that succeeding generations reacted strongly against it.

Paganini was one of the most remarkable exponents of extensions and contractions which were commonly employed to avoid formal shifts. He was evidently able to stop a three-octave span with ease and some of his fingerings render the recognition of a definite concept of positions practically

Ex.5 de Bériot

(a)

(b)

(c)

Et   c'est   moi —   qui   le   livre — au —   bour - reau

Ex.6 Paganini: Var. 1 from the 'Moses' Variations

Sul G

etc

Ex.7 Paganini: Caprice 21

3rd & 4th strings

Amoroso

Ex.8 Guhr

impossible (ex.8). The violin fingered octave technique ($\frac{1}{3}-\frac{1}{3}-\frac{1}{3}$), discussed for the first time by Baillot,[23] gradually found favour because of its greater clarity, accuracy and less frequent displacements of the hand than the $\frac{1}{4}-\frac{1}{4}-\frac{1}{4}$ fingering. The scale retained its important position as a technical discipline. Especially notable is Spohr's violin fingering system for three-octave diatonic scales in which the root position of a four-note chord of the key of a scale effectively determines the finger-position for the start of that scale. Spohr thus begins all scales with the second finger, except, of course, those commencing on *g*, *a♭* and *a*. Geminiani's chromatic fingering was largely ignored in formal scale contexts by 19th-century violinists – the 'slide' fingering was preferred (ex.9) – but its principle was acknolwedged in isolated passage-work (ex.10).

Ex.9 Habeneck

Ex.10 de Bériot

The selective employment of vibrato at speeds appropriate to the musical context continued, surveys of the period designating it an ornament used to emphasize certain notes, to articulate melodic shape or to assist in cantabile playing. The more stable chin-braced grip freed the left hand to cultivate a more fluid violin and viola vibrato, although viola (and the finger and wrist cello) vibrato tended to be slower and less intense than that for the violin. Spohr distinguishes four types of violin vibrato – fast, for sharply accentuated notes; slow, for sustained notes in impassioned melodies; accelerating for crescendos; decelerating for decrescendos – and demonstrates their sparing application (ex.11).[24] Baillot expands the vibrato concept to include three types of 'undulated sounds': a wavering effect caused by variation of pressure on the stick (used as early as the 16th century to imitate the tremulant of the organ), the normal left-hand vibrato and a combination of the two. He recommends that notes should be begun and terminated without vibrato to achieve accuracy of intonation (ex.12) and he provides examples of Viotti's vibrato usage (ex.13).[25] The use of vibrato became less selective towards the end of the century, thus prompting the kind of continuous vibrato (introduced, according to Flesch,[26] by Kreisler) practised today.

Paganini was foremost in using harmonics to their fullest potential and his introduction of artificial harmonics in double stopping was innovatory. Chromatic slides, single trills, trills in double stopping and double trills, all in harmonics, together with some interesting pseudo-harmonic effects, were included in his repertory, and he extended the range of the G string to cover at least three octaves.[27]

Right-hand pizzicato techniques changed little in the 19th century, particularly with regard to bass string instruments for which it was an indispensable effect, but Berlioz recommends violinists to pluck with the second finger and even suggests using the thumb and the first three fingers as plucking agents for variety in certain rapid pizzicato passages (ex.14).[28]

Ex.11 Spohr: Adagio

Ex.12 Baillot

Ex.13 Baillot (Viotti: Violin Concerto no.19)

Left-hand pizzicato, one of the most striking ingredients of Paganini's style, was also sometimes combined with right-hand pizzicato or simultaneously combined with bowed notes.

Scordatura gradually lost popularity during the 19th century, although it never became obsolete. Mazas, Spohr, Bériot, Prume and Winter were among those composers who employed the device, but Paganini was undoubtedly its most prolific exponent, using it to simplify his music, to add tonal brilliance and to reproduce, on open strings, harmonics which would normally have to be stopped.

The normal bow grip of the period involved placing the thumb at the frog, although some players (Mazas, Bruni, Paganini and Dancla) employed the old 'Italian' grip for optimum balance with the hand rounded naturally and

Ex.14 Berlioz

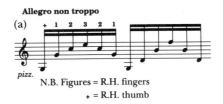

N.B. Figures = R.H. fingers
+ = R.H. thumb

the thumb a short distance from the frog, even with Tourte bows. The thumb was evidently slightly bent (although Baillot explicitly states: 'Avoid bending the thumb'),[29] and it was normally placed opposite the second finger[30] or between the second and third fingers.[31] Unlike their 18th-century counterparts, writers warn against separating the index finger from the others on the stick and advocate a combination of thumb, index finger (on or near the middle of the second joint) and wrist-joint pressure on the bow.[32] Inclination of the bow was accepted practice, but the degree of inclination was modified to suit the instrument, the string thickness and the desired musical effect. In violin and viola playing, the elbow took up a position closer to the body than formerly, necessitating a characteristically high, supple wrist position, especially when bowing at the heel. Although the upper arm was invariably used in long strokes (but less so than today), especially in cello playing, the fingers and wrist were the focal members in cantabile bowing. Variation of hand weight and finger pressure on the stick proved vital when changing bow, especially at the heel.

The usual 'overhand' grip was employed with 'French' bass bows, but the 'Simandl' and 'Dragonetti' types were grasped endways, meat-saw fashion, the palm enclosing the frog, the fourth finger below the hair/slide and the thumb resting on the stick (above) and acting as pressure agent.

With the rise of the virtuoso and the dissemination of the Tourte bow the full modern vocabulary of bow strokes began to emerge. Baillot's survey,[33] unique in the way it integrates bow speed and articulation, is the most extensive catalogue of violin bowings from the first half of the century. Baillot classifies bow strokes in two basic categories according to speed: slow or fast (a classification few modern players would endorse). He also admits a 'composite' stroke which adopts elements of slow and fast strokes simultaneously. The fundamental fast strokes were the *détachés*, which could be 'muted' (*mats*) – on-the-string strokes articulated by wrist and forearm (*grand détaché, martelé*, staccato); 'elastic' (*élastiques*) – mostly off-the-string strokes exploiting the resilience of the stick (*détaché léger, perlé, sautillé, staccato à ricochet*, flying staccato); or 'dragged' (*traînés*) – composite, on-the-string strokes (*détaché plus ou moins appuyé, détaché flûté*).

The Tourte bow was better suited than its various 18th-century counterparts to the execution of slow, smooth strokes and accented bowings.

Accented bowings comprised *saccadé* ('a sudden jerk of the bow given to notes, generally in twos or threes', ex.15),[34] *fouetté* and the straightforward accents that were employed at the beginning of some trills or arpeggios and in certain syncopated passages (ex.16), as well as for dramatic and expressive effect. The lifted bow stroke played a less prominent role, ex.17a being executed generally with the bow on the string, its movement checked

Ex.15 Baillot (Viotti: Violin Concerto no.24)

All the *sf*'s on the 1st and 3rd notes must be played mellowly, with a slightly longer bow.

Ex.16 Baillot (Beethoven: Quartet no.6)

Ex.17
(a)   (b)

momentarily (usually for no more than a demisemiquaver's duration) between the notes and the second note sounded through gentle wrist movement (ex.17b). *Bariolage* and the 'Viotti' and 'Kreutzer' bowings still remained in the repertory of slurred strokes and other specialized bowings such as tremolo, *col legno*, *sul ponticello* and *sulla tastiera* were increasingly employed.

Bowing indications and articulations were more thoroughly annotated during the period, ostensibly to avoid ambiguity of interpretation. However, inconsistent use of signs, notably the dot and wedge (a dot generally required an on-the-string and the wedge an off-the-string articulation), imposed extra responsibility on performers to interpret the music faithfully. With the general trend towards enlarging the capacity of the slur, bow apportionment and a general appreciation of the interdependence of bow speed, pressure and contact point (together with their combined effect on tonal quality and volume) became paramount for convincing execution. Habeneck illustrates how irregular bow apportionment relates to bow speed and the desired effect (ex.18).[35]

Ex.18 Habeneck

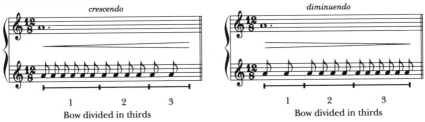

but arpeggiation of chordal progressions was less common than formerly. Open strings were generally sounded (where possible) in multiple stopping for greater sonority, and the left thumb was sometimes brought into play for certain chord shapes.

The less yielding qualities of the Tourte bow resulted in differing approaches to multiple stopping. Three strings could be played simultaneously (by pressing on the middle string in a down-bow at the frog), but only in *forte*, or if 'broken', as in ex.19*a*. Four-note chords were also 'broken', perhaps 2 + 2, commencing either before or on the beat, 3 + 1 or 2 + 1 + 1 (ex.19*b*). A down-bow was normally employed, even for consecutive chords,

Ex.19

(a)

(b)

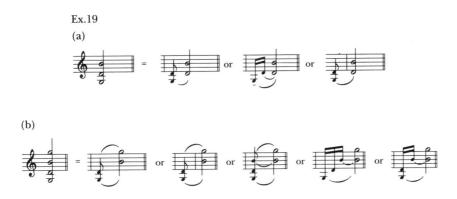

but arpeggiation of chordal progressions was less common than formerly. Open strings were generally sounded (where possible) in multiple stopping for greater sonority, and the left thumb was sometimes brought into play for certain chord shapes.

Composers tended to indicate their intentions more precisely. Cello notation was standardized to include the bass, tenor and treble clefs, but examples of music written in the treble clef for transposition an octave lower still persisted in the late 19th century (e.g. Dvořák, Bruckner). Much of the solo bass repertory is notated at pitch, but orchestral music for the instrument is written an octave higher than actual pitch. Although special signs were employed only rarely to clarify phrasing, nuances, indicated in greater profusion, played a significant role. Habeneck provides some interesting general rules: long notes should be 'spun out'; ascending phrases should crescendo; descending phrases should decrescendo;[36] any note foreign to the harmony, placed on the strong beat of the bar or on the strong part of the beat, must be emphasized if it is of any length; any modified note foreign to the scale of the prevalent key must be emphasized (ex.20). Baillot's

Ex.20 Habeneck

survey of phrasing concentrates particularly on the technique of 'phrasing off', making a diminuendo on or just before the last note of a phrase.[37] The subtle divisions of the bow, though not exclusive to pre-Tourte models, played only a small part in the wider 19th-century spectrum of expressive bowing. Bériot, for example, includes them in his method, but emphasizes that expression must embrace a whole phrase, deploring the practice of swelling the sound towards the middle of each stroke.[38] Significantly, the term 'bow division' took on a different meaning in the 19th century, referring to the actual division of the bow into parts (middle, upper third etc) for the classification and technical description of bow strokes. The rule of down-bow remained a guiding force in bowing throughout the century, although it was subject to modification for tone production and articulation purposes.

The trend for more prolific and precise interpretative indications (invariably involving qualification of the initial description of character, tempo or, as French writers broadly expressed it, *accent*) did not make the player's initiative redundant in the task of producing a faithful, expressive and convincing performance. Tempo markings were open to ambiguity and personal interpretation, while metronome indications were not necessarily reliable. Baillot, Rode and Kreutzer classified sound quality, movement, style, taste, genius of execution and precision as the chief expressive means.[39] Precision involved rigorous time-keeping, allowing at the same time for some freedom of expressive effect within the 'outlines' of the pulse. The chief means of this freedom was tempo rubato, a species of ornament with a definite structural function. It was applied to four different expressive techniques during the period: a natural flexibility of the prescribed rhythm within a constant tempo, after which the ensemble between melody and accompaniment was restored; the modification of dynamics and/or the displacement of natural accents (resulting, for example, in unaccented 'strong' beats of the bar); the expansion of the bar(s) to incorporate more notes than the time signature theoretically allows and a flexible, yet rhythmically controlled performance of these passages; or flexibility of tempo by arbitrary, unwritten accelerandos or ritardandos. 'Often a beautiful disorder is an artistic effect', remarks Baillot,[40] and such tempo flexibility invariably extended over a whole movement.

The theory that every melodic idea had an optimum tempo[41] encouraged performers to cultivate tempo differentiation within movements, articulating the structure by creating pockets of tempo, thematic and harmonic stability (for example, the two subject groups of a conventional sonata-form movement) and instability (development sections or developmental codas may incorporate tempo fluctuation to heighten tension). Liszt lends his support to this idea (1870): 'time and rhythm must be adapted to and identified with the melody, the harmony, the accent and the poetry'.[42]

Notes

[1] Following the social changes occasioned by the French Revolution and the establishment of the Paris Conservatoire (1795), similar teaching institutions were founded in other musical capitals.

[2] A Polish violinist, Paris-trained under Massart, but influenced by the Belgian school, Wieniawski later disseminated the teaching of the Belgian school in Russia.

[3] Spohr modelled his playing on the French school and on Rode in particular.

[4] Violin treatises are generally more detailed regarding general string performance practice than viola, cello or bass tutors.

[5] P. Baillot, P. Rode and R. Kreutzer, *Méthode de violon* (Paris, 1803); J. F. Mazas, *Méthode de violon* (Paris, 1830); P. Baillot, *L'art du violon* (Paris, 1834); F. Habeneck, *Méthode théorique et pratique de violon* (Paris, c1840); D. Alard, *Ecole du violon* (Paris, 1844); C. A. de Bériot, *Méthode de violon* (Paris, 1858); C. Dancla, *Méthode élémentaire et progressive*, op.52 (Paris, c1850); H. Léonard, *Méthode de violon* (Paris, 1877).

[6] C. Guhr, *Ueber Paganinis Kunst die Violine zu spielen* (Mainz, 1829); L. Spohr, *Violinschule* (Vienna, 1832/R1960); F. David, *Violinschule* (Leipzig, 1864); A. Wilhelmj and J. Brown, *Modern School for the Violin*, (London, 1898); K. Courvoisier, *The Technics of Violin Playing on Joachim's Method* (London, 1899); J. Joachim and A. Moser, *Violinschule* (Berlin, 1902–5).

[7] A. B. Bruni, *Méthode d'alto* (Paris, c1805); J.J.B. Martinn, *Méthode d'alto* (Paris, c1815); B. Brähmig, *Praktische Bratschenschule* (Leipzig, c1885); H. Klingenfeld, *Viola School for Violin Players* (Leipzig, 1897).

[8] D. Bideau, *Grande et nouvelle méthode raisonnée pour le violoncelle* (Paris, 1802); J.-B. Bréval, *Méthode raisonnée de violoncelle* (Paris, 1804); P. Baillot, J. H. Levasseur, C.-S. Catel and C. N. Baudiot, *Méthode de violoncelle* (Paris, 1804); C. N. Baudiot, *Méthode de violoncelle* (Berlin, 1830); P. A. F. Chevillard, *Méthode complète de violoncelle* (Paris, c1850); J. de Swert, *The Violoncello* (London, c1890).

[9] J.J.F. Dotzauer, *Violoncellschule*, op.165 (Mainz, 1832), *Violoncellschule für den ersten Unterricht*, op.126 (Vienna, 1836), *Schule des Flageolettspiels*, op.147 (Leipzig, 1837), *Praktische Schule des Violoncellspiels*, op.155 (Hamburg and Leipzig, 1870); F. A. Kummer, *Violoncellschule*, op.60 (Mainz, 1839); B. Romberg, *Violoncellschule* (Berlin, c1840); G. Banger, *Praktische Violoncellschule*, op.35 (Offenbach, 1877).

[10] A. Piatti, *Method for the Violoncello* (London, 1878); G. Quarenghi, *Metodo di violoncello* (Milan, 1877); G. Braga, *Metodo per violoncello* (Milan, 1878).

[11] J. Fröhlich, *Kontrabass-Schule* (Würzburg, 1829); G. Bottesini, *Metodo completo per contrabasso* (Milan, c1860); F. Simandl, *Neueste Methode des Contrabass-Spiels* (Vienna, 1874).

[12] See Chapter XII.

[13] J. Roda, *Bows for Musical Instruments of the Violin Family* (Chicago, 1959), 53.

[14] P. Baillot, *L'art du violon*, 16, is one of the first writers to recommend use of a shoulder pad.

[15] ibid, 140–44; Spohr, *Violinschule*, 195.

[16] Habeneck, *Méthode théorique et pratique*, 103–6.

[17] Baillot, *L'art du violon*, 146–9.

[18] ibid, 152–5.

[19] Spohr, *Violinschule*, 120–21.

[20] Habeneck, *Méthode théorique et pratique*, 103; Baillot, *L'art du violon*, 152–5.

[21] Bériot, *Méthode de violon*, 237.

[22] C. Flesch, *The Art of Violin Playing* (New York, 1924), i, 29.

[23] Baillot, *L'art du violon*, 152.

[24] Spohr, *Violinschule*, 175–6.

[25] Baillot, *L'art du violon*, 137–9.

[26] Flesch, *The Art of Violin Playing*, i, 40.

[27] Guhr's *Ueber Paganinis Kunst* provides the most detailed survey of harmonic effects.

[28] H. Berlioz, *A Treatise on Modern Instrumentation and Orchestration*, trans. M. Clarke (London, 1882), 21.

[29] Baillot, *L'art du violon*, 12.

[30] Spohr, *Violinschule*, 25.

[31] Baillot, *L'art du violon*, 12.

[32] For example, Baillot, *L'art du violon*, 15; Mazas, *Méthode de violon*, 6.

[33] Baillot, *L'art du violon*, 97.

[34] ibid, 125.

[35] Habeneck, *Méthode théorique et pratique*, 101. Habeneck here divides the semibreve into quaver values; the closer the quavers are placed, the slower the bow speed should be.

[36] Baillot adds an exception to this rule for very high notes, which must, on the contrary, be played softly to prevent them sounding harsh.

[37] Baillot, *L'art du violon*, 163–4.

[38] Bériot, *Méthode de violon*, 124.

[39] Baillot, Rode and Kreutzer, *Méthode de violon*, 158–65. Baillot included the survey verbatim as Part ii of *L'art du violon*, adding only a brief introduction.

[40] Baillot, *L'art du violon*, 137.

[41] Termed 'tempo modification' after R. Wagner, *Gesammelte Schriften und Dichtungen* (Leipzig, 1871–3 and 1883), viii, 287–308.

[42] As quoted in 'Performing Practice', *Grove MI*.

CHAPTER XX

Woodwind and Brass

DAVID CHARLTON

The flute

This period is not to be regarded as the musical domain of the Boehm flutes (or indeed of any 'Boehm' woodwind). As J. L. Voorhees has aptly said, 'From about 1830 to 1930 there was no universally accepted "standard" flute ... until the end of World War II there always existed at least one important school of flutists which did not use Boehm system instruments'.[1] Today's player seeking historical possibilities of interpretation must take account of the widespread and continued use of variants upon the 'old system' conical flute; Boehm flutes were slow to be adopted in Germany and were banned from certain German orchestras until 1914. In England there was no smooth transition, and even by 1906 they were not common either in Italy or in Russia.[2] The tone of the ordinary Romantic, non-Boehm instrument was sometimes, according to Hogarth (1836),[3] 'metallic, strong and piercing ... it no longer possesses the attributes of the "soft complaining flute"' (p.148). Metal was in fact used to counteract pitch rise which occurred when playing, and pitch adjusters were standard accessories. Makers adapted single features of Boehm's designs to conical flutes, for example the Card, the Carte, the Rockstro, the Pratten and other 'systems'.[4] Raised lip plates were experimented with, though they were by no means used on all later 19th-century flutes.

The leading player of the Stuttgart orchestra in 1842 used 'an ancient instrument that leaves much to be desired in point of purity of tone and unhampered execution of the higher notes', and he also extemporized embellishments.[5] Tulou (c1835) held to a recent ten-keyed model.

Boehm created two main flutes, both influential. The 1832 model was conical, with newly invented rod-axles. It stimulated important models developed by Buffet, Coche and Dorus (1838/9) that took into account players' conservatism in fingering. Coche (1838) claimed that this flute assisted soft playing as well as providing superior strength, fullness and evenness between notes. Boehm's more revolutionary design, now universal, dates from 1847. The totality of new thinking that created it should emphasize for us the radical departures in technique, tone and response that set it apart from past models: absence of finger-holes; cylindrical form permitting more air vibration; metal construction permitting more consistency, vibration and resonance; 'parabolic' curve inside the head joint; very large holes for ease of tone production at acoustically optimum points; and redesign of the mouth hole and its surround, eliminating 'the hissing common to the old embouchure'.[6] Boehm was acutely aware of the new flute's tendency to hardness and shrillness and to being overblown, and this raises the issue (for us) of a possible distinction by Romantic players between orchestral and chamber practice. Lindsay (1828)[7] specifically equated the evolution of large tone holes with 'the intention of increasing the power of the instrument for Orchestral effect' (p.2), which implies that Boehm's 1847 instrument would have been considered too loud for earlier chamber music.

ARTICULATION AND EXPRESSION Romantic flute tutors (and indeed those for other woodwind instruments) contain ample and still unresearched information on proper execution of the appoggiatura, trill, turn and other ornaments. Until *c*1860 there was general agreement that the wedge staccato signified the shortest notated form of staccato; it is never in itself defined as an accent. The dot signified separation, not always staccato; dots beneath a slur signified soft tonguing, and the slur was as understood today. English tutors specified or implied 'too' as the tonguing syllable; Tulou (*c*1835) gave 'tu' for the normal stroke, with 'du' for the *louré* style. For double tonguing, 'tootle' or 'tu-que' were used.

The articulate tutor by Lindsay (Part ii, *c*1829) is alone in suggesting the routine use of expressive rubato (p.78), but its eloquence and the praise which Part i received in respect of interpretation make the following extract more noteworthy: 'In passages of excitement or rising passion (which are generally of the ascending series), requiring animation and energy, the time should be rather accelerated; and in those of subdued feeling or depression ... the time should be correspondingly retarded'. The Glide and Vibration (see pp.253–4) were no longer expounded by Radcliff (1873) when he revised Nicholson's tutor, and on the Continent no secure information about the practice of vibrato is available. Nicholson's ornately embellished style of playing was already deplored by James (1826, p.158)[8] but his explanations of the trill and articulation were in fact taken over by Radcliff in 1873.

Tulou (*c*1835) stressed technical facility and the mastery over alternative fingerings. His own 'exquisite neatness' of playing was remarked upon by Hogarth (1836), as was the significantly less full tone of German players. The 'son pathétique et sentimental' was an essential and traditional tonal criterion for Tulou, and one that led him to reject Boehm's instrument.

The oboe

The design of Austro-German instruments of the period was stabilized by the acceptance of Sellner's 13-keyed oboe, which added extra levers for B♭, F and D♯. The classical 'warmth' and blending qualities remained. The French embarked on a series of reforms. Brod's tutor describes the tonal difference between France and elsewhere (see p.275) and was in favour of an eight-keyed oboe. In the 1830s he established the half-hole plate for the left-hand first finger. Under the Triébert dynasty boxwood fell to cocuswood, keys were made efficient, an *f*♯' ring-key was perfected, rod-axles were used, and a second octave key (for use from *a*″ upwards) and a *c*♯/*d* trill key were added (*c*1848). Triébert's 'Système 4', used at the Conservatoire around the mid-century, had 15 keys. Further refinements were added to *c*1880.

In England A. M. R. Barret also developed an improved oboe, partly as a reaction against the reform of Boehm, 'which diminishes the compass and changes entirely the quality of tone'.[9] This oboe had 14 keys; by 1862 Barret had evolved (with Triébert's help) a markedly original key-system.[10] In Italy there existed 'two native systems peculiar respectively to the Conservatoire of Milan and to the St Cecilia Conservatoire in Rome'.[11]

BOEHM OBOE The true 'Boehm' oboe with its wide bore, large holes and unorthodox appearance, made a loud sound and had some success in Spain. The adaptation of Boehm fingering key-work to the traditional oboe occurred *c*1880.[12]

TONE AND PERFORMANCE Berlioz (1843)[13] calls oboe notes lower than *g'* or higher than *e"*, 'flaccid or shrill, harsh or piercing, and all of fairly bad quality' (p.104); he noted many impossible trills, generally involving a tone rather than semitone. Wind tutors in the Romantic period contain abundant information concerning phrasing, articulation and expression, all deserving assessment. Brod's and Barret's tutors (1826–30, 1850) prescribe a swell for each ascending phrase and a fade for each descending one. Sometimes a tutor shows how a celebrated piece was performed; a phrase from *Der Freischütz* illustrates Brod's on-beat acciaccaturas (ex.1). Sellner (*c*1837) introduces

Ex.1 Brod (1826–30), p.26
  (a) Written   (b) Played

variable articulation for the oboe: 'ti' (hard), 'di' (softer) or a soft, exclusively lip-controlled impetus. Barret (p.5) outlawed breathing through the nose, and like others, he bears witness to an accepted freedom of expression for appoggiaturas, and a general consensus concerning 'the manner of executing small notes ... when there are several before a principal note ... in order to arrive in time on the principal note' (p.9). Modern players may find greater differences in these areas between present-day practice and that in 1850, than in perceptible ideals of tone production. Furthermore, certain orchestral wind players indulged in extempore embellishment even in the 1840s.[14]

Vibrato is not mentioned in oboe tutors, nor by Berlioz in his letters describing music-making in Germany.

REEDS Very detailed information on reeds is found in Brod (1826–30), summarized in English by Hedrick,[15] in Sellner (*c*1837) and in Barret (1850), who illustrates a 'recent invention': a mechanical cutter and gouger. Brod's reed tip was 7 mm wide, and it was scraped back to between 10 and 12 mm.

ENGLISH HORN Improvements to key-work and body construction are found in French and German instruments; but curved and angled examples survived, particularly in southern Europe. Berlioz (1870) found few German orchestras with acceptable players. Before the use of rod-axles and ring-keys, practical fingering problems may have prompted the creation of a smaller instrument pitched a fourth below the soprano oboe; this is one explanation of the key (G) of Donizetti's English Horn Concerto, and certain other early Romantic scores;[16] another is the substitution of the tenoroon, or miniature bassoon.

The clarinet

The advance guard of the clarinet profession had developed several addition-al keys by about 1810. The most important systems were based on that by Iwan Müller (who moved to Paris c1811) with its 13 keys and 'much better intonation through more carefully placed holes';[17] ex.2 makes clear what the

Ex.2 Berr (1836), *Traité*, p.2

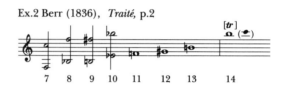

new keys did. Klosé (1843)[18] called his system 'une révolution totale ... étudié par un grand nombre de personnes'. Müller's aim was to establish an omnitonic instrument, but it was never realized in practice; instruments in A, B♭ and C were standard in England[19] and France,[20] and were ordered in 1837 for the Vienna Hoftheater.[21]

While Müller's ideas were adopted in southern Europe (Austria, Italy etc), 'English makers made a rather different 13-key clarinet'[22] and in 1824 William Gutteridge issued a 'No.1 Imperial Patent Clarinet' with 16 keys, making figures such as those in ex.3 possible in legato style.[23]

Ex.3 Gutteridge (1824), pp.2f.

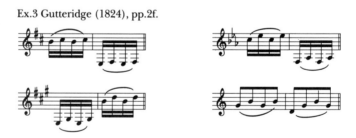

Important 'pre-Boehm' tutors were written by Frédéric Berr (1836), a Mannheim virtuoso who was Conservatoire professor in Paris from 1832 to 1838. Even using the Müller keys, Berr advocated special fingerings to obtain sharp leading notes.[24] He also advocated the occasional use of changing fingering on a given (held) note, and described the imitation (by others) of string portamento after the manner of the flute Glide or *Durchziehen*: 'some instrumentalists draw back bit by bit the fingers placed over the holes'

(*Méthode*, p.62). He himself approved more modest emulation of string technique, presumably akin to Willent-Bordogni's advice to bassoonists (see pp.415–16). The style-conscious player of today will recall that the great virtuosos of the earlier Romantic period mostly used varieties of the 13-key instrument: Johann Hermstedt,[25] Thomas Willman[26] and Müller himself. Heinrich Baermann used a 10- and a 12-keyed clarinet.[27] Performance ideals of the time are summed up in the exhortations of Müller's treatise (1825): the player should practise using violin music, should treat the clarinet like other instruments, and should practise to become fluent in all tonalities (he includes an exercise in C♭ major).

KLOSÉ, BUFFET AND BOEHM In 1839 the maker Buffet exhibited in Paris a clarinet related to the Boehm system; presumably it used ring-keys in some form. Not until 1844 did he and Hyacinthe Klosé (Berr's successor at the Conservatoire) patent a ring-key clarinet, later styled as 'Boehm clarinet' but not designed by Boehm. This model 'differs hardly at all from that of 1843' which had 17 keys and six rings.[28] It succeeded in reducing cross-fingerings and creating new duplicate fingerings. But whilst making fingering generally easier, it did not challenge the Müller system in the wider world until c1900. The Müller system was in turn improved by ring-keys as early as 1845.

REEDS AND REED POSITION Around 1830 English players usually used reed-above position (Metzler, c1830) and Longyear has stressed the longevity of this technique in Italy. Nevertheless, doubts remain concerning Verdi's expectations.[29] Müller played with reed below but bit on the mouthpiece, something Berr outlawed as professor. Müller (c1825)[30] and Blatt (c1828) approved of both reed-above and reed-below techniques; Müller also illustrated the newly invented metal reed fastener (opposite p.37) to replace the traditional thread. Reed-making is also shown. Berr's *Traité* justifies reed-below technique in some detail and reports that Baermann's *pianissimo* with reed below, in 1817–18, was of a type 'totally unknown' in France at that time. S. T. Blatt (1841–2) added much to Berr's information on reeds and embouchure. Klosé (1843) recommended a new and broader shape of mouthpiece: 'Formerly thin and narrowed off at the top, mouthpieces almost always forced the player to lose air at the corners of the mouth' (p.2), whereas the newer, wider sort would help produce a larger sound.

TONE AND TECHNIQUE With the consolidation of (German) reed-below technique in Paris, and the influence of French methods abroad, some degree of uniformity may have emerged in northern Europe during the Romantic period. Later tutors take the quality of tone for granted, and do not mention vibrato. As with the oboe, it is the nuances of taste and style betrayed in those tutors that suggest that the differences between then and now were greater than the similarities.

LOWER-PITCHED CLARINETS The basset-horn found limited popularity in the Romantic era as a solo instrument (Mendelssohn composed two *Konzert-*

stücke opp.113 and 114 for it with clarinet and piano) but its manufacture was not taken up importantly until the 1880s.[31] Alto clarinets were made, Simiot's model gaining official approbation in 1827 and Müller (1825) giving a chart for the 13-keyed alto, whose sounding range was A to f'''.[32] Bass clarinets gained in musical importance particularly from opera scores such as Meyerbeer's *Les Huguenots* Act 5 (1836) and Donizetti's *Dom Sébastien* (1843), which included two instruments. But no single design of bass clarinet was accepted until Adolphe Sax's 1838 straight design in B♭ with covered holes, little changed in essence to the present day. Kastner (1844) described its tone as 'plein de douceur et de majesté' (pp.7–8). Berlioz (1843) said that the bass clarinet reed was 'un peu plus faible et plus couverte' than those of other clarinets (p.148).

The bassoon

George Hogarth (1836) wrote of the current 15-keyed instrument in England: 'Many of the notes are false, and can only be corrected to a certain extent by the skill of the player. The under part of the scale is too low... some of the lower notes are dull and muffled'. Presumably this characterized the sound which 'gave way, towards the middle of the nineteenth century, before the Savary invasion'.[33] Savary's and Jancourt's instruments in France represent an essential point of reference: 'As regards the size and placement of tone-holes on the extension bore – that beyond the six basic finger-holes – and the almost cylindrical non-flaring bell, [the 'French' bassoon] has remained in its essentials very close to the archaic bassoon'.[34] 'French' bassoons consequently differ significantly in sound from the now common German type; and because the former was the standard instrument in England and many other countries throughout the Romantic period, it is vital to be aware of its timbral significance.[35]

Berr (1836) illustrates a Savary 16-keyed bassoon, noting that 'most' players used a 13-keyed model; indeed Simiot's company was marketing nine-key models even later.[36] Berlioz (1843) noted many trills that were still impossible. Eugène Jancourt (1847) included charts for 16- and 17-keyed bassoons (top extremities of e'' and f'' respectively). His collaboration with the makers Triébert and Savary improved evenness of tone and ease of production without greatly altering traditional fingerings. Even his chart (inserted ?1875) for a 19-keyed bassoon with ring-key mechanism denies any basic fingering change; the new keys improved notes such as $c\sharp'$ and d', and an added key for the crook hole helped stabilize the low register and permitted it to be played more softly.[37]

Carl Almenraeder's reform of the bassoon spanned two decades (he died in 1843), but in spite of his importance 'bassoons of the conventional type continued to be in demand well into the latter half of the century'.[38] He made sophisticated improvements to both key-work and to the notes A, a', he added slur/trill facilities for $A/B\flat$ and $F\sharp/G\sharp$, and he altered the size and position of certain holes – especially B♭, E and C. With J. A. Heckel (from 1831) Almenraeder developed the use of rod-axles and other modern devices; by 1843 he described an 18-keyed model, chromatically ranging from $B\flat'$ to $b\flat''$. Heckel and his descendants developed the modern (German) bassoon;

after 1877 Wilhelm Heckel (1856–1909) 'undertook a radical change in the bore', not to mention numerous other influential changes.[39] Today's player may well be using an instrument totally unknown to Romantic as well as Classical composers, German as well as non-German. Obviously this has the widest implications; we are in danger of losing a host of tonal qualities that Berlioz (1843) can only begin to suggest in his descriptions: 'Its sonority is not very great, and its timbre, absolutely without brilliance or nobility, leans towards the grotesque' (p.128).

BOEHM 'Improved' bassoons with holes re-sited and all holes operated by keys were commonly experimented with, from 1825 (Charles-Joseph Sax) through Adolphe Sax's metal model (1851), via Triébert and Boehm (exhibited 1862) to Haseneir in Germany and Tamplini in England.[40] All were doomed to defeat by cost, conservatism and the excessive distortion of traditional bassoon tone.

ARTICULATION AND SPECIAL TECHNIQUES For whatever reason, Romantic bassoon tutors are unusually informative about styles of playing now totally disregarded – styles probably applicable to other wind instruments. Berr (1836) considers types of articulation; the basic ones are as for those described above in the section 'Flute: articulation and expression'.[41] The new ones bear on accentuation: notes under a chevron are played *fz*, as were notes marked with a short accent; chromatic notes were to be accented more strongly than their succeeding resolution. Syncopated notes were to be emphasized by shortening the preceding on-beat note. The same points recur in Willent-Bordogni's tutor (*c*1844). Berr's illustration of cutting short ('throwing off') the last of a rising slurred group of two or more notes was echoed by Almenraeder (1843, p.51). The latter gave tonguing syllables 't' (stronger) and 'd' (weaker), echoed by the 'tu' and 'do' of Willent-Bordogni and the 'tu' and 'du' of Jancourt (*c*1847).

An expressive hesitation within the phrase is described by Berr (1836, p.23), shown with a comma (ex.4), and supported by even more striking

Ex.4 Berr (1836), iii, p.23

examples – in a tutor approved by the Paris Conservatoire – by Willent-Bordogni (ex.5).

Imitation of vocal or string sliding technique (cf the flute Glide and Berr's description of clarinet practice, pp.412–13) was explained both by Almenraeder (1843, p.67) and Willent-Bordogni (*c*1844, p.77).[42] Chiefly used in cantabile music, this effect covered both major and minor seconds (ascending or descending) and larger intervals, being related explicitly to the *port de voix* by both authorities. The example from Willent-Bordogni shows the repetition of the second of a pair of notes (as against the first in the Baroque

Ex.5 Bordogni (1844), p.76
(a) Written

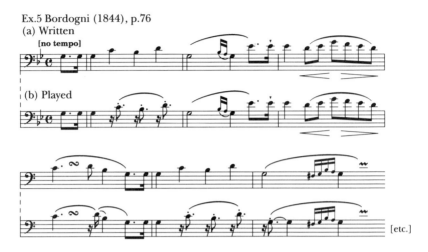

port de voix), and specifies that the tongue should strike the palate for the first of the ornamental repeated notes (ex.6). Almenraeder (1843) gives more detailed fingering involving sliding the fingers across the holes. He also gives examples of extempore ornamentation and asserted (p.72) that varied articulation was to be used as a means of expression. The interpreter, Almenraeder and other Romantic authors state, has the job of promoting the spirit of the piece by deciding (as traditionally) where to apply various moods, even though no composer's instructions are necessarily visible, e.g. *pathétique*, *furioso*, *flebile*, etc (p.115).

Ex.6 Bordogni (1844), p.77
(a) Written

VIBRATO Almost alone among Romantic woodwind tutors, those for bassoon discuss vibrato. Berr (1836, p.21), 'Vibration du son', appears to rule out breath vibrato in favour of finger vibrato.[43] Almenraeder insists on only very exceptional selective use of finger vibrato; the norm is 'to produce beautiful sounds, either soft or loud, without vibrato (*vibration* in the French text), in getting louder or softer' (p.69). Finger vibrato was to be applied to a longer, held note; the following pitches were most suitable on the bassoon: *d, f♯, g, g♯, b♭, b, c', d', e', f', f♯', a', b', c", c♯", f", g"*. Jancourt (*c*1847, p.44)[44] discusses finger vibrato (only), also giving suitable pitches and an applied musical example; for him, 'its effect is lost as soon as it appears to be

416

calculated'. It is interesting that Almenraeder's phraseology suggests that all woodwind instruments used finger vibrato.[45]

REEDS Hogarth (1836) noted that 'English performers, in general, use stronger reeds than foreigners, with a corresponding difference in the quality of their tone', even though a 'strong, thick reed', while lending strength, also 'prevents the attainment of smoothness and flexibility'. Berr (1836) corroborates this exactly: the English cannot play quietly, while the Germans, with 'very strong' reeds, produce 'disagreeable sounds'. French bassoonists 'use reeds of all sorts'. Almenraeder (1843) illustrated and discussed reed-making (pp.122–7). The widest part of the tip is shown as 17 mm across, with a length of *c*70 mm. He favoured Spanish cane. An extant French reed dating from *c*1860 is 61 mm long.[46]

CONTRABASSOON AND OPHICLEIDE Many experiments were carried out to create a more powerful contrabassoon than the Classical octave bassoon. Certain such instruments entered the military bands of the world, but no standard orchestral instrument emerged before that of Triébert and Marzoli, *c*1860. Before 1863, for example, the Conservatoire concert society in Paris substituted the ophicleide, a practice regarded by Berlioz (1843) as quite standard.[47] Heckel's contrabassoon, as known today, was not perfected until 1879 and only then did Wagner score for it, i.e. in *Parsifal* (1882), though he had used the ophicleide, and indeed the serpent, in *Rienzi*.

It is therefore generally impossible to be certain which kind of contrabassoon, if any, the Romantic orchestra used in a given case. Berlioz (1870) described the confusion in some German orchestras in the 1840s on the part of bass-horn players who called their instrument 'contrabassoon'. A major lacuna in our perception of the 19th-century orchestra is caused by the absence of the ophicleide (a bass keyed bugle) from our aural consciousness. It was ubiquitous and fairly standardized in its V-shaped form. Though it shared much the same range as the bassoon, its timbre was unique among orchestral instruments. Further comments on the ophicleide are found below in the discussion of the tuba.

The horn

In an age when mechanization and the consequent invention of many new instruments produced such a revolution in the individual sonorities of the orchestra, the horn did not radically alter. Today's type of double horn, in particular, had not yet been devised. Valves were long used as a complement to, not replacement of, hand-horn technique. They were applied to the horn before any other instrument and were first announced in 1815.[48] Two were originally used. By 1825–30 the valve principle had been applied to the trumpet, the cornet and the trombone. Each was affected differently in respect of musical utilization and character.

The valves served to direct the airstream through additional lengths of tubing, so producing a semitone, tone or tone and a half below the pitch blown. On the horn, terminal crooks were retained to preserve the character of the music especially when crooked low or high.[49] In his *Supplément*, of

1844, Kastner implied that players were substituting open sounds by the use of valves for the stopped sounds intended by a composer. The purpose of valves 'was only to assist defects in certain stopped notes on the ordinary [hand] horn relative to intonation, sound quality and difficulty of perform-ance'. The best compromise was to have two natural and two valved horns in an orchestra (p.28). The standard valve-horn tutor (Meifred, 1840)[50] explicitly described the difference between stopped and open notes as that which made the horn a superior instrument to the ophicleide or bugle (p.2). Valves were (*a*) to provide missing notes, e.g. *e, g♯, a, b♯*; (*b*) to improve tuning of certain notes such as *f♯'* and *a''*; (*c*) to make dull notes sonorous, while keeping those which were slightly muted, and so agreeable; and (*d*) to give leading notes their proper character (p.1).[51] Any modern player with the courage to revive 19th-century technique would find Meifred a sure guide and would gradually discover that modern orchestras have lost subtleties of colour and balance in the process of becoming louder and more standard-ized. Berlioz, in fact, objected to the brassy forced sound, especially on high notes, that was common in German horn playing (1870, pp.271 and 277).

The mid-century saw a reaction in Vienna against hand-stopping.[52] In *Lohengrin*, Wagner used the earlier method of specifying many 'crook' (i.e. valve) changes in succession, and expecting hand-horn technique between one instruction and the next; but when he addressed horn playing in the introductory notes to *Tristan und Isolde*, he allowed the players complete freedom on the understanding that the E and F crooks were usually intended.[53] By about 1860 technique was in a transitional and confusing state; in 1864 the valve horn was even banned from Paris Conservatoire teaching, and in 1865 Brahms conceived the horn part in his Trio op.40 for natural instrument, while other late Romantics pursued the line Schumann had taken in giving the instrument ever more idiomatic valve-horn parts.

In all the foregoing, questions of embouchure should be remembered. Two-thirds of the mouthpiece rim rested against the upper lip, but in a pressured manner. 'It is upon the greater or lesser pressure of the mouthpiece on the lips, and upon the latter's calculated tightening or releasing, that depend the performance and accuracy of all notes, low, high and intermedi-ate', states Dauprat (1824, p.15).[54] Dauprat's three-volume work is monu-mental in its coverage and detail, containing much historical matter relevant to Romantic interpretation. Performance problems within single major works are analysed, for example; it is here that we see how the clarino phrase in the second movement of Haydn's Symphony no.51 in B♭ was actually played (vol.iii, p.28).

The trumpet

Although valve trumpets were introduced during the 1820s, they did not yet oust natural instruments from the orchestra. But Berlioz and Kastner, for example, agreed that valve trumpets could be as good in tone, and by 1843 the former reported that in Germany natural trumpets had been 'almost completely superseded' and only the popularity of the valved cornet in Paris kept them out there (1870, p.319).[55]

The field of early valved brass and its performance and tone-colour has

hardly begun to be adequately researched. While we know that the traditional long trumpet, crooked from E or F down to C, was used up to the
mid-century, the advent of the short Bb trumpet began shortly after in parts
of Germany.[56] (Britain and France showed greater resistance to it.) But even
in Germany, the short Bb instrument had a markedly different character
from that of today because of the significantly narrower bore and mouthpiece;
indeed, it was to fall victim to the requirements of homogeneity and power.[57] In
addition, French brass, 'relatively narrow-bored by German standards', varied
distinctly in tone from one instrumental family to another.[58]

Trumpet writing in early German Romantic symphonies is traditionally
diatonic; yet in Schumann's Fourth Symphony valve instruments already
seem to be idiomatically handled. But such observations do not solve
problems of authentic tone, for it is easy to forget that 'there are marked
differences of colour between trumpet crookings (whether on natural or on
valve instruments)'[59] and that a now-forgotten effect may thus have been intended. There is also confusion in the literature about the instruments
intended by Wagner under the designation 'bass trumpet'.[60]

Cornets

Perhaps surprisingly, Berlioz approved of the mixed establishment of the
French Romantic orchestra, in which two natural trumpets sat by two valved
cornets so that 'the piston cornets which can provide all the intervals, and
whose timbre is not too dissimilar from that of the trumpets to be assimilated
into the ensemble, are then sufficient to complete the harmony' (1843,
p.189). But heard alone, the same instruments were condemned by the same
writer – and others – as intrinsically vulgar in sound (p.197).

The complicated relation between cornet crooking and tone, from the
orchestral point of view, was clarified by Kastner; he ruled that the cornet
should never be crooked in the key of the piece. A complicated transposition
situation in his *Traité* (1837) was resolved in the *Supplément* (1844) where all
cornets sound below written pitch.

In the Romantic period the cornet possessed a narrow, conical mouthpiece
that produced a 'rounder and more velvet sound' than the commonplace cup
mouthpiece of today.[61]

Trombone and tuba, with a note on Sax

The decline in use of the alto trombone was matched by the invention in 1839
of a thumb-valve-operated double Bb/F instrument. This Leipzig trombone
was copied by other makers as it gave access to C, and had other
advantages.[62] However, in *Der Ring des Nibelungen* Wagner demanded a
contrabass instrument reaching to E', an octave below the tenor trombone.
The quiet exploitation of trombone pedal notes (fundamentals sounding Bb'
and below) in the 'Hostias' of Berlioz's *Grande messe des morts* (1837) was
widely taken up.[63] And trombones in the Romantic orchestra were obliged to
lend voice to an unprecedented range of textures and dynamics, sometimes
taking a primary melodic line.

The valved trombone, like the ophicleide, was an everyday instrument in
the 19th-century orchestra that is now unheard. (They were made in all sizes

and to different valve systems.) One adverse consequence of this is that 'the chromatic scale figures which abound in the storms of [Verdi's] *Aroldo* and *Otello* ... inevitably sound like glissandi on modern instruments';[64] the same might be said for countless other scores. Kastner, in his *Supplément* to the *Traité*, said that players were better in tune on the valve instrument, though the slide one is inherently capable of more accurate intonation (p.42). Berlioz (1843) appreciated their capacity to trill but not their inability to play pedal notes (p.224). The difficulty of finding written evidence in researching this area of performance practice is self-evident.

The history of the orchestral tuba began in 1835 with Wieprecht's new 'tuba', which descended to sounding F' and was, according to Kastner, 'formidable' (1837, p.48). From this instrument stemmed innumerable upright and other tuba types. By 1842 Berlioz was praising the tubas then common in Prussia, especially when doubled in octaves: 'full and vibrant and well matched with the timbre of trombones and trumpets, to which it serves as a true bass' (1870, p.335). Adolphe Sax developed the whole range of bugle/tuba types.[65] In France, though, the ophicleide remained standard until around 1860 (as in England); moreover it has rightly been said that (for example) the two ophicleides in Berlioz's *Symphonie fantastique* ('Dies irae'), or the solo in Mendelssohn's *A Midsummer Night's Dream* overture, or Wagner's writing in parts of *Rienzi*, cannot be replaced by a tuba in terms of balance and character.[66]

The 'Cimbasso', the part in Italian scores found below the trombones, has recently been the subject of debate.[67] Its meaning apparently varied from (earlier) the bass-horn, to the ophicleide, to the bass trombone (later Verdi), to a thin-bore tuba by Rampone.

The 'Wagner tubas' are 9' and 12' bass tubas of medium bore, played by horn-players with their own mouthpiece. They first appeared in *Das Rheingold* (performed 1869), scored in four parts.

Valved brass thus opened the way for the expansion of this orchestral family to the status of a self-sufficient section; but conservatism protected the average orchestra from radical organic change between 1825 and 1885. In this connection the remarks of François Lesure are telling:

> No-one would, in any case, dream of denying that in the short term [Sax] modified the equilibrium of orchestral sonorities ... But the essence of Sax's impetus doubtless lies elsewhere: towards military music and working-class musical societies – areas that musicologists persistently consider as unworthy of their attention.[68]

Opera orchestras were those where new masses of brass tone chiefly existed; aside from the Wagner orchestra already mentioned, the Paris Opéra orchestra already in 1847 began to use Sax and his instruments as stage and supplementary forces, beginning with 20 extras in Verdi's *Jérusalem*.[69]

Notes

[1] J. L. Voorhees, *The Classification of Flute Fingering Systems of the 19th and 20th Centuries* (Buren, 1980), 9.

[2] N. Toff, *The Development of the Modern Flute* (New York, 1979), 76–7.

[3] G. Hogarth, 'The Flute', *Musical World*, iii/36 (18 Nov 1836), 145–50.

[4] Toff, *The Development*, chap.3.
[5] *Mémoires de Hector Berlioz* (Paris, 1870; ed. and Eng. trans. by D. Cairns, 1969), 277.
[6] Toff, *Development*, 68.
[7] T. Lindsay, *The Elements of Flute-Playing*, i (London, 1828).
[8] W. N. James, *A Word or Two on the Flute* (Edinburgh and London, 1826/R1982).
[9] A. M.-R. Barret, *A Complete Method for the Oboe* (London, c1850, 2/1862), 1.
[10] P. Bate, *The Oboe: an Outline of its History, Development and Construction* (London, 1956, rev. 2/1962), 66ff.
[11] ibid, 77.
[12] ibid, 73–4. Also K. Ventzke, *Boehm-Oboen* (Frankfurt, 1969), reviewed in *GSJ*, xxiii (1970), 137–8.
[13] H. Berlioz, *Grand traité d'instrumentation et d'orchestration modernes* (Paris, 1843).
[14] Berlioz, *Mémoires*, 281 and 305. Perhaps these chastening German experiences inspired the banal embellishments for oboe added by the character Somarone to the 'Epithalame grotesque' in *Béatrice et Bénédict*. The whole question is reviewed in J. Spitzer and N. Zaslaw, 'Improvised Ornamentation in Eighteenth-century Orchestras', *JAMS*, xxxix (1986), 567–71.
[15] P. Hedrick, 'Henri Brod's *Méthode pour le hautbois* Reconsidered', *The Consort*, xxx (1974), 53–62.
[16] R. M. Longyear, 'The English Horn in Classic and Early Romantic Music', *Miscellanea musicologica: Adelaide Studies in Musicology*, ix (1977), 141. Important operatic solos in French opera, e.g. Meyerbeer, *Robert le diable* (1831), Act 4, use 'modern' notation.
[17] P. Weston, 'Müller, Iwan', *Grove 6*. Müller pioneered the use of stuffed pads over countersunk note holes. See F. G. Rendall, *The Clarinet* (London, 1954, rev. 3/1971 by P. Bate), 90, as well as I. Müller, *Méthode pour la nouvelle clarinette et clarinette-alto* (Paris, 1825).
[18] H. E. Klosé, *Méthode pour servir à l'enseignement de la clarinette à anneaux mobiles* (Paris, 1843), Introduction.
[19] *Metzler and Son's Clarinet Preceptor* (London, c1830).
[20] G. Kastner, *Supplément au traité général d'instrumentation* (Paris, c1844), 38, n.3.
[21] R. Hellyer, 'Some Documents Relating to Viennese Wind-instrument Purchases, 1779–1837', *GSJ*, xxviii (1975), 50–59.
[22] C. Rendall, *The clarinet*, 92.
[23] W. Gutteridge, *Introduction to the Art of Playing on Gutteridge's New Patent Clarinet* (London, 1824), 2ff.
[24] F. Berr, *Méthode complète de clarinette* (Paris, 1836). See D. Charlton, 'The Berr Clarinet Tutors', *GSJ*, xl (1987), 48–52.
[25] With a design 'Very much after the style of Müller. The extra keys were fully described by Spohr in the foreword to the first published edition of the [first] concerto, by Kühnel in 1810': P. Weston, *Clarinet Virtuosi of the Past* (London, 1971), 82–3.
[26] A 13-keyed instrument after Müller by Thomas Key, described in Weston, *Clarinet Virtuosi*, 103.
[27] ibid, 118, says a 10-keyed boxwood one. But A. Vanderhagen, *Nouvelle méthode pour la clarinette moderne à douze clés, avec leur application* (Paris, [1819]), actually prints an engraving of Baermann's 12-keyed instrument as used on his Paris tour in 1817–18, complete with telescopic barrel.
[28] Rendall, *The Clarinet*, 97–101, with detailed comparison of Boehm and Müller systems on p.100.
[29] R. M. Longyear, 'Clarinet Sonorities in Early Romantic Music', *MT*, cxxiv (1983), 225–6. This article draws misguided conclusions concerning tone, but helpfully concludes that reed-below technique was probably authentic for Verdi both on account of his low writing and since Austria ruled Milan until 1859. A letter mentioning Willman's fine (reed-above) *pianissimo* is in *Harmonicon*, x (1832), 168.
[30] I. Müller, *Méthode pour la nouvelle clarinette et clarinette-alto* (Paris, 1825). See also D. Charlton, 'Classical Clarinet Technique: Documentary Approaches', *EM*, xvi (1988), 396–406.
[31] Rendall, *The Clarinet*, 134–5. Kastner gives the Cor de Bassette (in F) a section in the 1844 *Supplément* to his *Traité*, 40–42, its written range being *c* to *d'''*.
[32] Simiot's approbation was from the Académie des Beaux-Arts, to which Müller in 1813 had also presented an 'alto clarinet' earlier called by him 'corno di bassetto'.
[33] E. Halfpenny, 'The Evolution of the Bassoon in England, 1750–1800', *GSJ*, x (1957), 31.
[34] W. Waterhouse, *The Proud Bassoon* (Edinburgh, 1983), 'The French Bassoon'.
[35] The more so since French players are tending towards 'German' bassoons.

[36] Waterhouse, *The Proud Bassoon*, item 12. Mackintosh (*c*1840) gives a chart only for the six-keyed bassoon, lacking *B'* and *C#*.

[37] L. G. Langwill, *The Bassoon and Contrabassoon* (London, 1965), 61.

[38] Waterhouse, *The Proud Bassoon*, 'The German Bassoon'. For Almenraeder's publications, 1822–43, see 'Bassoon', *Grove MI*. Berlioz, *Mémoires*, 346, commented that at least in Germany (in the 1840s), a bassoon in tune was 'sadly rare'.

[39] Langwill, *The Bassoon*, 54. Details of German developments, pp. 49–57. Rubber and other material linings to the inner walls of the butt were evolved by different makers from *c*1870.

[40] L. G. Langwill, 'The "Boehm" Bassoon: a Retrospect', *GSJ*, xii (1959), 63–7; Langwill, *The Bassoon*, 64f; and Waterhouse, *The Proud Bassoon*, 'Boehm and others'.

[41] C. Almenraeder, *Fagottschule* (Mainz, 1843), 47, calls ⌒⌒⌒ articulation 'Portamento', whether slow or fast.

[42] J.-B.-J. Willent-Bordogni, *Méthode complète pour le basson à l'usage des Conservatoire [sic] Royaux de Musique de Paris et de Bruxelles* (Paris, *c*1844).

[43] He is very brief: 'Lorsqu'on veut faire vibrer le son les lèvres ne doivent pas participer aux divers mouvemens des doigts'.

[44] E. Jancourt, *Méthode théorique et pratique pour le basson* (Paris, *c*1847).

[45] (1843, p.68): 'One also makes use, on wind instruments with finger-holes, of a type of ornament...'.

[46] Waterhouse, *The Proud Bassoon*, item 39.

[47] Constant Pierre, *La facture instrumentale à l'Exposition universelle de 1889* (Paris, 1890), 29ff; after 1863 the contrabassoon proper was used by Saint-Saëns, Reyer, Thomas, Massenet etc; there is some evidence that Saint-Saëns intended the contrabass sarrusophone to be used where his score says 'contrebasson'.

[48] In *AMZ*; translation and original text in A. Baines, *Brass Instruments, their History and Development* (London, 1976), 206f. See 'Valve', *Grove MI*, for a summary with diagrams of 19th-century valve systems. R. Morley-Pegge's *The French Horn* (London, 2/1973) devotes chap.3 to valves.

[49] G. Kastner, *Traité général d'instrumentation* (Paris, 1837), 47.

[50] P.-J. E. Meifred, *Méthode pour le cor chromatique ou à pistons* (Paris, 1840).

[51] See Morley-Pegge, *The French Horn*, 109–13, for detailed considerations of performance practice in this style.

[52] Baines, *Brass Instruments*, 220.

[53] Morley-Pegge, *The French Horn*, 107–8, gives a translation of the whole passage.

[54] L. F. Dauprat, *Méthode de cor-alto et cor-basse* (Paris, 1824).

[55] Berlioz criticized the old 'piston' trumpet (1843, p.277) in favour of the 'cylinder' type, i.e. the Prussian valve or 'Berliner-Pumpe', adopted by Sax.

[56] E. H. Tarr, 'Trumpet', *Grove 6*, xix, 222. See Baines, *Brass Instruments*, 232, for another summary of the confusion. Most recent research in Germany and the USA concerns the early valve.

[57] Baines, *Brass Instruments*, 234, gives a particularly vivid if subjective description of its response.

[58] C. Bevan, *The Tuba Family* (London, 1978), 156.

[59] J. Wheeler, review in *GSJ*, xx (1967), 107–8. This is an interesting and probing response to P. Bate's *The Trumpet and Trombone* (London, 1966). See also the same author on Schubert's high trumpet writing: *GSJ*, xxi (1968), 185–6.

[60] Baines, *Brass Instruments*, 237–9.

[61] ibid, 229–30.

[62] However, it drowned the tenor and alto trombones when doubled with a second bass trombone used in place of an ophicleide: Berlioz (1870) in Berlin, 319.

[63] Berlioz's footnote to this passage reads: 'Ces notes graves de trombone ténor sont peu connues, même des exécutants; elles existent cependant, et sortent même assez aisément lorsqu'elles sont ainsi amenées'.

[64] J. Budden, *The Operas of Verdi*, ii (London, 1978), 49.

[65] For tables of concordance between types of tuba and nomenclature by nationality, see Bevan, *The Tuba Family*, 24–35. 'Saxhorns' are simply a family of 'valved bugle-horn, or flügel horn', ibid, 101. For a fuller explanation of the saxhorns in relation to the operatic repertory, see *Berlioz: Les Troyens*, ed. I. Kemp (Cambridge, 1989), appendix C.

[66] Bevan, *The Tuba Family*, 65–7 and 134.

[67] Baines, *Brass Instruments*, 251; Bevan, *The Tuba Family*, appendix B, 212–14, including also

information on the bass-horn; R. Leavis, 'More Light on the Cimbasso', *GSJ*, xxxiv (1981), 151–2; A. Myers, 'Fingering Charts for the Cimbasso and Other Instruments', *GSJ*, xxxix (1986), 134–6.

[68] From the Préface to Malou Haine, *Adolphe Sax (1814–1894), sa vie, son oeuvre et ses instruments de musique* (Brussels, 1980), 10.

[69] Haine, *Adolphe Sax*, 97–8. The same players were also used in Meyerbeer's grand operas, in Gounod's *Faust* and Verdi's *Don Carlos*.

CHAPTER XXI

Voices

WILL CRUTCHFIELD

Many factors converged during the Romantic era to alter vocal performance style more rapidly and markedly than at any time since the rise of opera. Theatres grew in size as court opera declined and commercial opera flourished. Orchestras were enlarged, and what was at the beginning of the 19th century still 'the accompaniment' grew in importance and complexity to the point that it could in some cases dominate the aural texture of an opera. At the same time the role of the conductor was dramatically expanded. The line between solo and ensemble style was blurred, since the conductor began to take some role in influencing the soloists and could also now bring unified 'soloistic' nuance to the ensemble. The standard aria forms, in which so many aspects of vocal style were rooted, ceased to evolve and were discarded almost completely by the end of the period. German opera took on a powerful life of its own in the first half of the century; by the end of the second half, proud national repertories had sprung up in all the east European nations. Parisian grand opera flourished and began, with the works of Meyerbeer, to be exported regularly. The primacy of Italian singing was not dislodged, but was severely shaken. Scientists began to attempt explanation of the phenomenon of 'voice', and scientific theory influenced pedagogy. Composers, cut loose from court positions, wrote and published operas for wide circulation, with the result that more frequently than ever before, professional singers were performing music that was not written specifically for their voices.

In simplest terms, there were two main results: (*a*) the need to cultivate greater vocal power exercised a progressively increasing, multi-faceted influence on technique and style; and (*b*) the breakdown of conventional forms gradually banished from new music many of the quasi-improvisatory skills that had depended on reliable regularity of function, and those skills began to atrophy.

These changes are in a sense epitomized by Wagner. In his mature operas there is little resembling a set piece or a cadenza, hardly any call for the skills of florid singing and no place for improvisation. Instead, there is an enormous orchestra that plays continuously under the guidance of an interpretative conductor; a symphonic accompaniment that would constantly surprise and thwart the singer who attempted spontaneous Bellinian rubato; a character to be interpreted whose behaviour could not be understood on the basis of dramatic 'type'. Over a century separates Handel's Rinaldo from Bellini's Romeo; less than 30 years separate Romeo from Tristan; yet the difference in what is required of (and possible for) the singer, even the difference in many practical considerations of execution, is far greater in the second comparison. In the last quarter of the 19th century, the great crusade in operatic performance was for the establishment of Wagner's operas in the repertory outside Germany; moreover, Italian composers found the way to continue after Verdi, and French after Gounod and Massenet, through the assimilation of values that were in large degree Wagnerian.

Thus it is far more necessary for the Romantic period than for the Classical to distinguish performance practices chronologically, almost decade by decade.

Sources

As sources, treatises on singing decrease in importance after the first half of the Romantic period, not so much in number as in relevance: methods and theoretical works came increasingly to concentrate on technical and physiological issues beyond the scope of this discussion. At the same time, the rapidly growing practice of publishing operas in complete piano-vocal scores gives us a richer surviving body of annotated performance material (if also one sometimes difficult to interpret, since a score in good condition could be passed down and written into by artists of successive generations). At the end of the period, moreover, a far more specific and illuminating type of evidence enters the picture in the form of sound recordings.

The most informative vocal methods from the standpoint of performance practice are those of Lanza (1809), Garaudé (the revised edition of 1825 gives especially useful treatment of some of the changes in the years since his first book in 1810), Ferrari (1818), Bacon (1824, but reflecting a comparatively 'Classical' point of view), Winter (1825; the performance information in this primarily technical collection is indirect, but copious), Nathan (1823, rev.1836), Marx (1826), Crivelli (*c*1840), Lablache (*c*1840–50, with a brief, intelligent overview of ornamental practice), Duprez (1845, especially informative for the emerging dramatic style closely associated with this singer and for the carefully attributed series of cadenzas by his contemporaries on the stage), García (1847 and frequent revisions; this is by far the most comprehensive and detailed statement on mid-19th-century style and technique), Faure (1870, with useful distinctions between French and Italian practices) and Delle Sedie (1876, valuable for its specific details of vocal inflection in the period dominated by the mature Verdi).[1]

The books of Sieber (1858), Lemaire and Lavoix (1881) and Alberto Bach (1883) are not vocal methods *per se* but historical overviews of singing style and technique;[2] they contain valuable stylistic information, with special emphasis on practices in Germany, France and England respectively. In addition, the reminiscences and other works of authors like John Ella and Castil-Blaze contain important accounts of performance practice supplemented by musical examples.[3]

Besides hundreds of unattributable but revealing notations of phrasing, ornamentation and dynamics, there survive in published form and in manuscript arias 'realized' or annotated by Rossini and Donizetti, and by (or after) singers including Velluti, Catalani, Rubini, Mario, Grisi, Malibran,

Finale of Act 3 of Meyerbeer's opera 'L'africaine', first performed at the Paris Opéra on 28 April 1865: engraving from 'L'illustration', 6 May 1865; the sinking of the ship on stage caused a sensation

Pasta, García (senior), Cinti-Damoreau, Naldi, Kemble, Viardot, Sonntag, Lind and others. There are also isolated cadenzas and ornaments by Verdi and by dozens of other singers.

Instrumental transcription came to be dominated by the free fantasias or virtuoso variations, reminiscences and paraphrases rather than the straightforward arrangements of the Classical period. But some of them continue to offer valuable information here and there – including those by Liszt, in which simple 'vocal' representations are always distinguishable from those pianistically conceived and varied.

Voice types

Voice categories became more pronounced in the 19th century as composers became more specific in their exploitation of particular vocal properties and operas became less subject to internal modification and transposition. The main changes in the first half of the century were the final disappearance of the castrato, the decline of the musico (as the female contralto who inherited the castrato's heroic roles was still called), and the emergence of the baritone as an independent type between tenor and bass. In the second half, the dramatic mezzo-soprano increasingly became a separate category, and separations of lighter and heavier voices (especially among sopranos) began to yield categories that would eventually, in the 20th century, become as different from one another in range and handling as tenor from baritone.

Technical aspects of Romantic singing

A full discussion of the accompanying technical changes in 19th-century singing would be out of place here, since a developed professional singer cannot simply shift technical procedures in the name of performance practice. But an overview is required to make the stylistic shifts intelligible. Singers will explore for themselves how far their techniques can accommodate period styles, and as awareness of those styles grows, some students will modify their technical development accordingly; this process is already underway.

One cardinal feature was the exploitation of the registers in which the greatest power was available. For male singers, this meant high notes, and above all the development of a powerful falsetto register in the tenor, little used before the height of the Classical period but routinely employed between about 1810 and 1845. Several theorists of this period describe the tenor voice as ranging generally up to d'' or e'', often with the specification of 'falsetto' on the notes above a'. John Braham sang at least to e'', Giovanni Mario to gb'' and Rubini to g'', though this most extreme register was employed generally in passage-work and cadenzas rather than sustained singing (the famous f'' in *I puritani* is an exception). Emphatic eb'''s, however, were written by Verdi for Mario and by Pacini for Verdi's favourite tenor, Gaetano Fraschini. This practice was halted by the still more powerful development of chest-voice high notes, taken as far as c'' by Gilbert-Louis Duprez in the 1830s. Verdi clearly preferred the chest-voice top, but did not count on it higher than a' or bb' for most of his career; only in *La forza del destino* and *Otello* does one find unavoidable chest-voice *bb*'s in his Italian scores. Wagner respected *a'* the limit for sustained singing.

Concurrently with this development, the high baritone came into his own. Though his part was notated in the bass clef (except sometimes in France), he was not simply a bass with further development of the top register; rather, he was jointly descended from the low tenor written for by Haydn (Orfeo), Rossini (many parts) and others and from the high bass. Several theorists call the baritone a 'low tenor' or 'mezzo-tenor', and he took on the tenor's role of antagonist in *opera seria* when the hero's part shifted from the musico to the tenor. The real separation probably came at the point when a top register based largely on head voice went out of fashion, The lower tenors, of whom Rossini could ask *A*'s, *Ab*'s and *G*'s and also head-voice roulades up to *cb"* and *db"*, were not easily able to accommodate *a"*s and *b*'s in chest, and emerged as baritones. (Lamperti writes of 'the *tenori serii*, who now sing the baritone', considering it a harmful development.)[4] There was a period of considerable flux. For instance, when Verdi's *Attila* was first given in London, the very high baritone part was performed with slight *upward* transpositions, while some low-tenor roles (notably Hérold's Zampa) were transmitted to later generations as baritone parts, even though they contained high head-voice notes that baritones had to omit. (Jean-Blaise Martin made his career as a baritone and gave his name to the French high-baritone type, but he himself retained the Rossini-tenor cultivation of top notes to at least the tenor's *db"*.) The baritones specialized in full-voiced sonority around and above *c'*. Verdi's preference for the upper part of this range was famously criticized late in the century by Bernard Shaw, but the abundance of brilliantly successful executants at precisely that period gives the lie to his protest; Shaw insisted, anachronistically, on thinking in SATB terms.

For female singers, the new demand for power involved not just an increased reliance on sustained *forte* top notes (before the advent of such 'groundswell' ensembles as the sextet in *Lucia*, sopranos were rarely asked to sustain a *bb"* over massed voices and/or full orchestra), but also a greater use of declamatory emphasis in the chest register, especially in Italy. The mezzo-soprano, still only loosely distinguished from soprano by the last quarter of the century, was often called upon to make her most telling effects in precisely the same pitch-range as the Verdian high baritone.

The female contralto voice as understood in England – functioning with ease below the treble staff and rarely rising above its top line – was never firmly established as an operatic type in the 19th century; the singers called contralto in Italy in the Rossinian period were so named largely for their specialization in heroic *travesti* roles, and their parts – written in the soprano clef – sometimes ranged up to *a"*, *b"* or even *c'''*.

A supporting development was the 'voix sombrée', associated with Duprez, in which full-voiced delivery was facilitated – and a novel artistic effect achieved – by a slight modification or darkening of vowel sounds, especially in the high range. As early as 1847 García recommended that a soprano modify the central vowel of 'Dio' towards the French 'u' when the word appeared on a sustained *bb"*. This practice is the ancestor of what eventually became known as 'covering' the tone.

Florid execution was emphasized less and less, in inverse proportion to the demands for power. Up to the end of the century it still formed the basis for improvised ornamentation, but the elaborate gracing found in Rossini is already replaced by something considerably less demanding in early Verdi, and by the 1890s most ornamental work relied on comparatively modest use of the *gruppetto* and a few simple cadential figurations. In Rossini's time, as before it, the florid aspect was more or less equal for all voice types; thereafter it declined faster and more decisively among the male singers than the female.

Vibrato increased gradually as an expressive device. Like 'di petto' (in chest), 'vibrato' is written as a special instruction at certain points in scores of Donizetti, Halévy, Meyerbeer and others. It was especially employed by the Italians and much criticized elsewhere; by the middle of the century, some Italians seem to have sung with an audible vibrato on nearly every sustained note.

Since all these developments have been continued, and in some cases steeply exaggerated, in the 20th century, it is worth pointing out that the priority given to sheer volume, sustained high notes, vowel modification and the like – as well as the neglect of florid technique – was still notably less at the turn of the century (as observed through phonograph recordings) than in, say, 1930 or 1950.

The solo scene

For the first half of the century, it is still most convenient to observe performance practices in terms of the formal scene that gave them their context in standard Italian opera. Many of the devices found their place also in solo stanzas of a duet or ensemble, or in recitative or *parlante* passages elsewhere. So although the discussion follows the shape of the solo scene, the examples are also drawn from other appropriate contexts. Many non-Italian scores follow the Italian forms more or less closely, and were similarly interpreted in many ways; some differences will be remarked upon as they arise.

RECITATIVE *Recitativo secco* declined quickly in the first quarter of the century, outlasting it only in *opera buffa* and even there only briefly. No notable changes in the style of delivery seem to have arisen. In orchestrally accompanied recitative, cantabile/arioso elements and ornamental vocalization continued to be important; composers increasingly wrote the ornaments into the score. Ex.1 shows part of Tancredi's opening recitative, as scored and then as realized for a singer by Rossini. Examination of this, along with recitative realizations by Rubini, García and other sources, shows that the greater floridity and greater variety of long and short note values observed in the recitatives of Verdi (especially the soprano recitatives up to the mid-1850s) reflect an increase not so much in elaborateness of recitative style as in the specificity of notating it. (Indeed, the actual elaboration of execution probably *decreased* somewhat, in contrast to the notational practice.)

Appoggiaturas – simple raised notes or other figures serving the same 'leaning' purpose – were still required on all feminine line endings, but

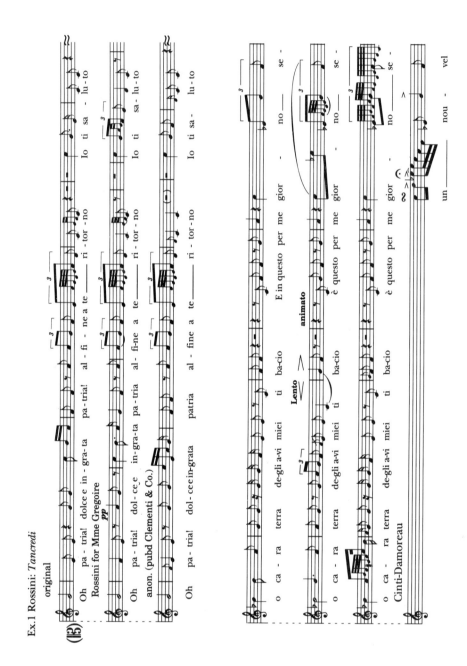

Ex.1 Rossini: *Tancredi*

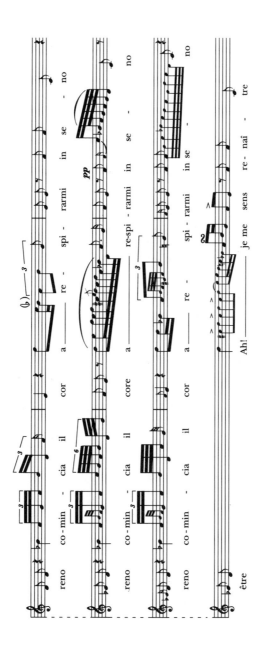

composers gradually began to write them into the score. The habit was not formed in strict chronological sequence: Cimarosa already marked his appoggiaturas in the 1790s; Weber, Rossini and Donizetti rarely did so; Beethoven and Schubert sometimes; Bellini and Verdi almost always; Wagner always. But towards the end of his career Verdi seems to have felt, along with the younger Italian composers, a desire for more naturalistic musical speech than the emphasis of the appoggiatura gives. Verdi's later operas, including *Otello* and *Falstaff*, have far more 'blunt endings' than his earlier ones, and Puccini seems never to have felt that the appoggiatura was obligatory at every feminine line ending.

The long-traditional vocal cadence of introductory recitatives – the falling fourth, tonic to dominant – continued to be employed as long as recitative and aria remained distinct, but the device underwent ornamental transformations. One of the most common was for the voice to move to the dominant on the penultimate syllable – often rising a fifth instead of falling a fourth – and to colour the note with figuration, often with minor-tinted neighbouring tones, or with an octave drop. Ex.2 gives the closing cadence of Pollione's first recitative in *Norma* with three realizations. (Bellini generally retained the falling-fourth notation, whereas Donizetti and especially Verdi often wrote out the decorated-dominant form of execution.)

Ex.2 Bellini: *Norma*

(a) original

In ram - men - tar - lo   io tre - mo

(b) Giovanni Mario

In   ram   -   men   -   (tar-lo) etc
(from Mario's score, Fondo Mario, *I-Rsc*)

(c) Vincenzo Massini
(Naples, before 1850)

In [ram - men - tar - lo io tre - mo]
(from Massini's score, Fondo Noseda, *I-Mc*)

(d) Covent Garden
prompter's score (? late *c*19)

In ram- men- tar - lo   io tre   -   mo
(from score in Royal Opera House archives)

Recitative in general gave way increasingly to the *parlante*, a kind of movement in which simple, declamatory vocal lines were sung over continuous orchestral music (often the orchestra carried the burden of the musical material). These were subject to the same conventions of appoggiatura that had prevailed earlier; the singer was necessarily somewhat less free to shape the rhythm of declamation, though by no means bound to the exact rhythmic values of the notation.

At least up to the last quarter of the 19th century, it was traditional for the recitative or dialogue portions of an opera to be adapted to the prevailing practice of the theatre in which it was given. The most familiar manifestation of this principle is the existence of so many French operas, including *Carmen* and *Manon*, in versions with or without spoken dialogue. Mozart's Da Ponte operas were long given in Germany with speech in place of the *secco* recitatives (according to Lilli Lehmann's autobiography, it was she who insisted on the restoration of the latter), whereas in London full string accompaniments (with a good deal of dramatic variety) were added to those in *Don Giovanni*. In many countries, meanwhile, recitatives were composed for *Fidelio*, *Der Freischütz* and *Die Zauberflöte*.

Ex.3 Cimarosa: *Il matrimonio segreto*

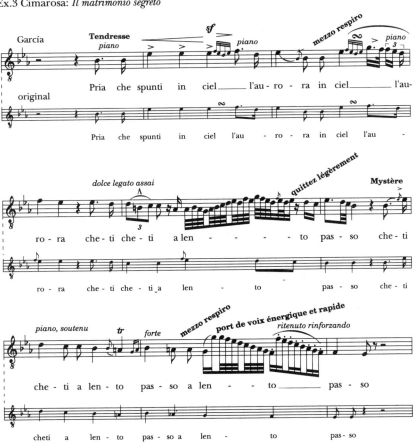

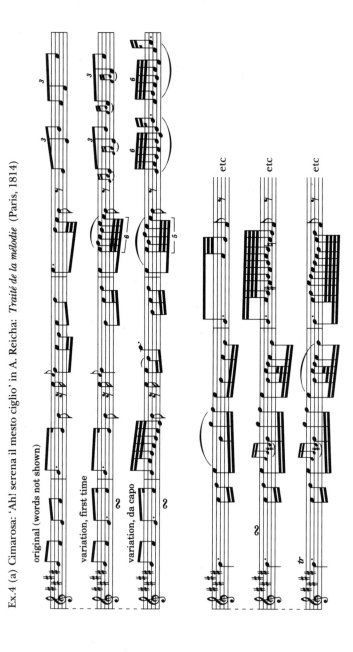

Ex. 4 (a) Cimarosa: 'Ah! serena il mesto ciglio' in A. Reicha: *Traité de la mélodie* (Paris, 1814)

(b)

ARIA CANTABILE The 'aria cantabile' – called variously the 'cantabile', 'andante' or 'largo', but not, as sometimes it is in modern usage, 'cavatina' – continued to be the principal locus for melodic embellishment. García, who is more explicit even than Corri, gives details of phrasing, dynamics and expression as well; ex.3 reproduces a section from one of his examples. The most basic units of ornamentation are passing notes, scales, *gruppetti* and elaborations thereof. Ex.4 shows shorter fragments of cantabile from (*a*) a collection of arias annotated by an anonymous Italian singing-master in London between 1834 and 1840, and (*b*) a simple piano arrangement of themes from *I masnadieri* by Enrico Truzzi, a Ricordi employee responsible for the piano–vocal reductions of several Verdi and Donizetti operas. The decrease in density of figuration is easy to discern (extending the examples backwards to, say, Catalani, and forward to the artists heard on early recordings, would show this to be a steady, continuous process). Also worth noting is the colouristic use of the flattened sixth in the major mode, which turns up quite often.

The fermatas of Classical arias are still found often in bel canto opera; even after they gradually fell out of use, the modulations and structural joints continued to be marked by rallentando and embellishment, often facilitated by the suspension of the accompaniment. Ex.5a shows several versions of the preparation ('deh, tu premia') and cadence in the dominant ('la mia fè') immediately preceding the reprise of 'Di piacer mi balza il cor' (Rossini, *La gazza ladra*). Ex.5b shows two cadences from the quartet in *Rigoletto* with the readings in Liszt's well-known transcription transferred to vocal notation.

Internal cadential points were often embellished with holds or ornaments even when the fermata did not appear in the score, and the accompaniment was often adjusted to accommodate this. Ex.5c shows an example of Donizetti carrying out this process himself. The vocal lines remain almost unchanged in these two versions of the *Lucrezia Borgia* finale, but the continuous movement of the accompaniment is altered to permit free vocal handling. Sets of orchestra parts all over Europe show similar adjustments in many scores. (The Donizetti example is also interesting for the implication of a chest-voice bb'' in the second example, written for Napoleone Moriani; the first need not have been so powerful.)

The final cadenza of the *andante* air underwent several mutations before vanishing in most music composed after about 1875. At the height of the Classical period it was in abeyance, since grand sonata-form arias closing with a cadenza in the tonic were on the way out with the castratos, and the *andante* component of the two-part rondo usually ended in or on the dominant, with a cadenza expressing a half-cadence or a transition. Early in the Romantic period (and occasionally before that, of course) the two parts of the aria became more independent, and the *andante* regularly came to end with a full close – still occasionally in the dominant up to the early 1820s, but later always in the tonic.

The usual cadenza form in the first quarter of the century consisted of two fermatas for successive roulade elaboration: one on the tonic 6-4, another, generally brief, on the dominant. Almost year by year one sees the burden of figuration shift from the former to the latter, a continuation of the process whereby the old cadenzas ending with supertonic trill gradually began to admit a dominant roulade at the end of the trill. Ex.13 in Chapter XV shows two of Lanza's 37 'various conclusions to shakes'; he goes on to say that, for a trill with fermata, one goes further and makes a series of more elaborate roulades – and here he shows what the Rossini generation would recognize as a standard dominant cadenza.

Ex.5
(a) Rossini: *La gazza ladra*

In German music the tonic 6-4 was often prepared by a secondary dominant (or sometimes a diminished seventh chord), a descendant of the familiar procedure in Classical da capo arias and concertos. As in those pieces, the voice often began the cadenza by sustaining the tonic. The tenor

(b) Verdi: *Rigoletto*

(c) Donizetti: *Lucrezia Borgia*

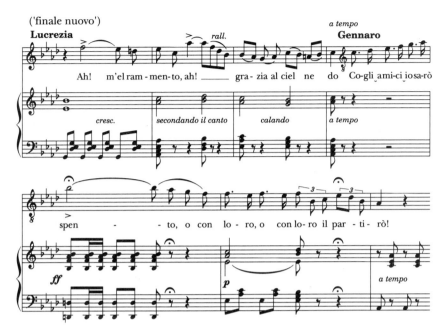

aria from Weber's *Freischütz* gives an example (ex.6*a*); three typical realizations are shown in Mendelssohn's *Frühlingslied* op.8 no.6 (ex.6*b*) and from Peter von Winter's *Singschule*, published in 1825 (four years after *Freischütz*) (ex.6*c*).

In ex.6*d*, in contrast, Winter starts the voice on the dominant and uses the preparation preferred in Italian music: II^6, with pause for vocal elaboration. Sometimes all three chords (the II^6, T^6_4, V^7) received vocal figuration (not shown here). Sometimes, as García explains,[5] one or the other of the first two chords – but never the dominant – was passed over without a melisma. (In the mid-aria cadenzas shown in ex.5*a*, the IIb/V and the V^7/V are elaborated, whereas the I^6_4/V is left plain.) Typically these cadenzas were sung on one or two words, and resolved to the tonic in a middle or low vocal range. Some theorists continue to cite the traditional prescription that the

Ex.6
(a) Weber: *Der Freischütz*

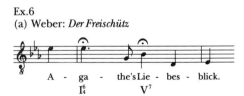

A - ga - the's Lie - bes - blick.
I^6_4 V^7

(b) Mendelssohn: *Frühlingslied* (op.8 no.6)

ein   Vei   -   -   ge - strauss.
       I^6_4 V^7

(c) Winter: *Vollständige Singschule*

(d)

cadenza be sung in one breath, but Rossini and several others acknowledge tacitly that this was no longer the rule. More typical seems to have been a breath between the tonic 6-4 figuration (if there was any) and the dominant seventh, with another breath possible at the end of the latter just before the final resolution to the tonic. García makes this explicit,[6] advising singers to reserve a word or syllable on which to make this final resolution, singing the melisma on 'ah' if necessary for that purpose (though this did not become customary until much later). Ex.7 gives examples from the Rossinian period. In the first two, all three chords are present. Velluti embellishes the tonic 6-4 and apparently adheres to the old rule about singing in a single breath. Rossini's cadenza for 'Il braccio mio' is all over the dominant chord, though the rising figure could be heard as either tonic or dominant (with appoggiaturas); Adelaide Kemble's is exclusively on the dominant, with a breath and brief ornament at the end. In the aria from *Ermione*, the II^6 has moving accompaniment, not a fermata, and the I_4^6 is omitted entirely; thus only the dominant seventh is available for the improvised cadenza.

In the next decade – the 1830s – elaboration on the 6-4 fell from use; Rossini had already bypassed it in some arias, and Donizetti only rarely gives occasion for it, while the II^6 is often still available for ornamentation. Bellini retains it more often, as in the examples shown in exx.7*d* and *e* (where the

Ex.7 (a) Rossini: *Aureliano in Palmira,* cadenza by Velluti for Arsace's solo in the duet 'Mille sospiri e lagrime' (published by Mechetti in Vienna, n.d.)

(b) Nicolini: 'Il braccio mio' (insert aria for *La donna del lago*)

Rossini (autograph in *F-Pn*)
bel cor del tu - o del tuo bel
Kemble (from her notebook, private coll.)
bel cor del tuo del tuo bel
original
bel cor del tu - o bel
ii 6 3 preparation I 6 4 V7

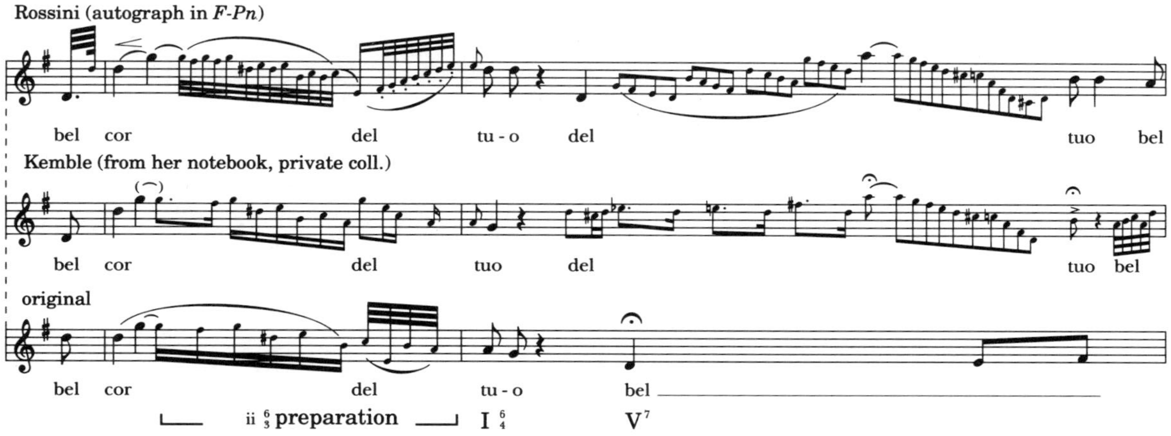

(c) Rossini: *Ermione,* cadenza by Rubini for aria inserted into *La donna del lago*

original
Rubini (published by Pacini in Paris, *c*1825)
Mer - - cè Mer - - - - cè
(V7) (I)

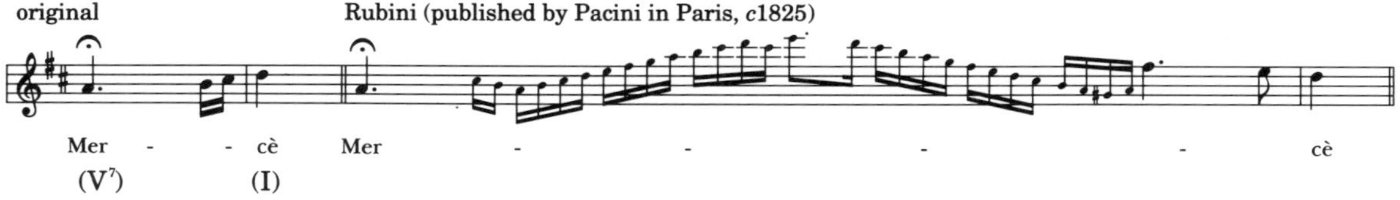

(d) Bellini: *Il pirata*, cadenzas by Mario for tenor solo
in the terzetto 'Vieni, cerchiam pe' mari'

(e) Bellini: *La sonnambula*

García, 1847 (after Malibran?)

Cinti-Damoreau (notebook in *US-BLl*)

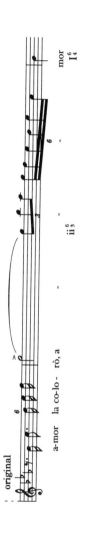
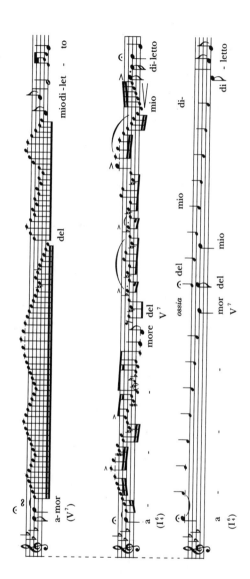

(f) Two attributed cadenzas from Duprez: *L'art du chant*

Pisaroni

Rubini

Ha

(g) Verdi: *Le trouvère*, cadenzas for 'La nuit calme' ('Tacea la notte')

Verdi's addition to role-book (for Mme Deligne-Lauters)

ah

ah! s'ouvrir les cieux

original
volonté

ah

s'ouv - rir les cieux

(h) Verdi: *Ernani*

Sieber (1858)

Mi do-ve-van gl'an-ni al-me-no far di ge- lo an-co - ra il cor, far di ge-lo an-co-ra il cor

Malibran–García version illustrates the practice of passing it by undecorated). The concentration was by then clearly on the dominant chord. By the time of early Verdi this process is complete; indeed, his codas in *andante* arias generally lack the II^6 harmony altogether, consisting instead of a simple I–V alternation (often in root position; occasionally even over a tonic pedal) leading to the fermata on V. These dominant cadenzas gradually came to be sung in two parts, as the portion after the breath became freer and more elaborate. The cadenzas attributed to Pisaroni and Rubini in ex.7*f* and that by Verdi in ex.7*g* are typical.

Concurrently, changes in the vocal style of the cadenzas were taking place. Florid passage-work gradually becomes less demanding after about 1835; declamatory exclamation, sometimes involving a whole line of text, supplements the melisma or even supplants it. This kind of cadenza, wrote García, 'is the recourse of comic singers and singers lacking flexibility'. At the same time, upward resolution – taking the tonic in an upper-middle part of the range – gradually began to appear, especially in Verdi, though this was still relatively rare until well after the time that cadenzas were no longer being composed.[7] Ex.7*h* gives a typical concluding portion of a cadenza from *Ernani* in this new style.

It is interesting that this migration of the cadenza did not end with its settlement upon the dominant seventh chord. Verdi, in his mature operas, often concludes arias with vocal figuration or arpeggios *on the final tonic* (see for instance 'O patria mia', 'O ma chere compagne', 'Il lacerato spirito'; the device was developed in ensemble numbers, where it occurs frequently). In some annotated scores and early recordings, one finds similar figures imposed anachronistically over the tonic postludes of Bellini or Donizetti.

In France it was a widespread practice to print final cadenzas and other 'points d'orgue' in vocal scores of the operas of Halévy, Auber, Thomas, Meyerbeer and others. They were shown in small print and with the designation 'variante', while on the main staff of the vocal part would appear a simple closing formula like those shown in Italian scores. These variants generally correspond to the earlier and more conservative Italian cadenzas, with a single roulade, and downward resolution. The cadenzas of several French singers, especially the renowned vocal improviser Laure Cinti-Damoreau, tend towards the later Italian practice of inserting a second, freer roulade (but not a syllabic sequence) after a breath.

CABALETTA From the time of Rossini, and until the dissolution of standard aria structures into the more flexible forms of the mature Verdi, the closing allegro in Italian arias was an independent quick movement called a 'cabaletta', consisting of a strophe, a ritornello, an exact repeat (occasionally abbreviated) and a coda whose length and complexity varied considerably. Rossini said in a letter to Clara Novello that 'The repeat is made expressly that each singer may vary it, so as best to display his or her peculiar capacities'.[8]

French and German arias, while including a closing *allegro*, did not regularly adopt the Italian strophe-and-repeat form of the cabaletta, preferring in general a simple sonata-like structure with a briefer element of reprise.

At first this movement succeeded the *andante* directly; increasingly in Donizetti, Bellini and early Verdi, librettists were called on to provide a 'distacco di pensiero' – a dramatic basis for changing the musical mood. This transitional passage (sometimes in recitative) was often concluded with a vocal flourish, which could sometimes recur between the strophes. These flourishes most often expressed a simple, unresolved dominant seventh. Several examples survive, including variants by Pauline Viardot (for a pupil) for the lead-in to 'Sempre libera' (*Traviata*) and one in the role-book for Azucena used to launch 'Deh, rallentate, o barbari' in the French version of *Il trovatore* in Paris (1857).

Ornamentation in the cabaletta itself is of three kinds: elaboration of fermatas which occur most often at the end of each strophe or during the coda; variation of the basic stanza upon repetition; and elaboration of the coda's stock cadential sequences, whose similarity from piece to piece facilitated free improvisation. The repeated stanza was the closest analogue in Romantic music to the old da capo air. In contrast to the usual gracings of cantabile, these cabaletta repeats took the form of genuine variations, freely altering the melodic shape at times. Orchestral doublings of the melodic line were very frequently removed to facilitate ornamentation, as can be seen from numerous sets of 19th-century parts including those used by Verdi for the première of *I masnadieri* with Jenny Lind. Ex.8 gives, as an example, a

Ex.8 Bellini: *Norma*

446

- tor - na del _____

tor - na del __ fi - do a - mor pri - mie - - ro, e con - tro il mon - do in-

-fe - sa __ a _____ te _____ sa -

-fe - - sa_a te _____ sa -

tie - ro _____ di - fe - sa __ a __ te sa -

concordance of five Pasta-related sources for part of Norma's 'Ah bello, a me ritorna'. None of them except the brief excerpt cited by García is described as offering Pasta's own variants, but the similarity of approach and Pasta's renowned association with the role suggests that her influence on the subsequent traditions of performing it were strong.[9]

Many other examples of cabeletta variation survive; Rossini's for several of his own cabalettas, and one each by Bellini and Nicolini have been published (with imperfect but decent fidelity) by Ricci.[10]

In Rossini, Bellini and Donizetti, the coda is based on the same chord sequence observed at the end of the cantabile, but this time in tempo and usually with accelerating harmonic rhythm, as (for example) in ex.9. This portion was elaborately and freely varied. García, Lanza and others give tables showing the multiple possibilities, and examples by Rossini and many singers exist.

Cabalettas continued to be embellished in early Verdi (Giulia Grisi's variations for *I due Foscari* survive in Rome). By the time he stopped writing them (his last orthodox solo cabaletta is in the 1863 version of *La forza del destino*; *Un ballo in maschera* (1858) is his first opera to have none at all), it had already become a frequent practice to omit the repeat in performance. Verdi wrote them in the repeated form as long as he wrote them at all, but in a letter of 1871[11] he endorses such cuts. It seems likely that the cabalettas were ornamented as long as they were repeated – but that the more forward-looking dramatic Verdian singers tended not to repeat them.

The very end of the coda is a problematic moment; up to, and probably throughout, Rossini's time, it seems to have been taken without rallentando, and with a burst of florid virtuosity, often concluding in the low register. But as the excitement of the held top note gradually assumed a greater role in vocal expression, it became customary to add one to the end of the cabaletta – either the tonic taken in a high register, or a held high dominant or supertonic, while the orchestra pauses or sustains a dominant chord, just before the final note. This is sometimes found in Verdi's scores, and was

Ex.9
(a) Rossini: *La donna del lago* 'O quante lagrime'

(mer-)cè, gra - ta mer - cè, gra - ta mer -

(b) Rossini: *Il barbiere di Siviglia*, 'Una voce poco fa'

(gio-)car, e cen-to trap - po-le fa - rò gio-car,   e__ cen - to trap-po-le fa - rò gio-

(c) Rossini: variants for (b)

(gio-)car, e cen-to trap-po - le fa-rò gio - car,_____ cen - to trap-po-le fa-rò gio-

occasionally applied in earlier ones, though it did not become a universal practice until much later, when cabalettas were no longer being composed. In general, the ending in tempo was the rule. Sometimes – increasingly, towards the end of the century – much or all of the coda was omitted; the singer proceeded from the final fermata of the strophe directly to the last few bars of coda or to the postlude.

The conclusions in ex.9 clearly envisage an ending in tempo. Ex.10 gives two more cabaletta conclusions; one by Naldi, clearly ending in tempo, and one by Viardot from *c*1880, showing a hold before the final note which is now

Ex.10(a) Rossini: *Torvaldo e Dorliska*, 'Ferma costante immobile'

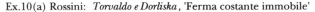

Naldi

original

(non) dà, no, no, non dà, no, no, non dà,___ no,___ no, non dà

(b) Verdi: *La Traviata*, 'Sempre libera'

Viardot

original

(pen-) sier, _____ il mio____ pen - sier

taken in the high register. Many sets of cabaletta variants break off at just this point, suggesting a conclusion more or less as in the score or with conventionalized elaboration, and many sources that are specific about accompaniment practice (above all García and Alary) show the conclusions of their cabalettas with no hint that the tempo was to be retarded. It should perhaps be noted that the practice of dropping out for several bars of the coda to save strength for a final annihilating top note is strictly a 20th century innovation, dating from after World War I.

Other forms

The various canzonettas, romanzas and serenades that alternate with formal aria structures in early 19th-century opera were frequently strophic and open to variation at the repeat. Donizetti provides 'realized' examples in, among others, 'Ah, non avea più lagrime' (*Maria di Rudenz*) and 'Com'è bello' (*Lucrezia Borgia*, first version; when a cabaletta was added to this scene the romanza was reduced to a single statement). That he expected the same procedure to be applied by performers in other instances is suggested by the existence of an ornamented copy of 'Una furtiva lagrima' in his hand at the Bibliothèque Nationale.

Adaptation

Throughout the Romantic period it continued to be understood that adaptations would often be necessary to suit a role to a particular voice, but the means for doing this became progressively more limited as continuity and unity of composition increased over the years. There are essentially four types of adaptation, discussed in decreasing order of magnitude. The first is the interpolation of new musical numbers – insert arias, either composed by the original author or another *maestro* specifically for the purpose, or lifted from other operas. Mario habitually added an aria (different ones at different times) when he sang the otherwise insufficiently prominent role of Rodrigo in *La donna del lago*; Pasta, Grisi and Malibran did the same in Rossini's *Otello*, adding an entrance aria for Desdemona. The most popular number of Rossini's *Le siège de Corinthe*, in its Italian translation as *L'assedio di Corinto*, was an interpolated duet cabaletta by Donizetti. Verdi wrote insert arias (to his own operas only) for Nicolai Ivanoff, Mario, Ignazio Marini and a few other singers, but put an end to this policy, with only one exception, after 1850.

A second expedient is simple omission without replacement of numbers, or parts of numbers, that were unsuited to the singer. Since cuts were so often made for other artistic or practical reasons, it is difficult to be specific about this, but one example is the traditional omission of the extremely difficult tenor arias in *Il barbiere di Siviglia* and *A Life for the Tsar*. Another is the pronounced (and artistically unfortunate) abbreviation of the role of Violetta that enabled Adelina Patti to continue singing the part in the last years of her stage career.

A third measure, transposition, continued to be extremely common throughout the 19th century, so much so that at Her Majesty's Theatre in

London the orchestra librarian had gummed labels specifying transpositions of a half or whole tone upwards or downwards with a blank for the date to be filled in; these were affixed to orchestral parts which were then transposed at sight by the players. For familiar operas, many houses kept sets of parts for the main arias in as many as four different keys. All the major composers readily transposed within their own operas in the first half of the century, but as internal continuity of scenes became the norm in the second half, the practice became increasingly inconvenient. Verdi protested against it in a letter shortly after the première of *Aida* (though that did not stop him from making a transposition to accommodate Francesco Tamagno in *Otello*).

An alternative way to effect agreement between the range of the singer and that of the role was called 'puntatura' ('pointing'), in which the accompaniment remained unchanged while the vocal line was judiciously recomposed to lie higher or lower, as needed. The more continuous the fabric of the opera, the more the balance tilts to this procedure as against transposition, but it was regularly practised in the era of number-opera too. Among the hundreds of surviving examples of *puntatura* are Rossini's adaptation of the final rondo of *La Cenerentola* for soprano (eliminating the low notes and generally raising the tessitura);[12] Mario's adjustment of the role of Pollione (written for Donzelli, a baritonal *tenore robusto*) to the higher range of the parts written for himself,[13] such as Ernesto in *Don Pasquale*; and a letter from Verdi approving and suggesting ways to eliminate the high notes from 'O don fatal' (*Don Carlos*).[14]

While our heightened awareness of the stylistic integrity of whole scores makes it unlikely that the interpolation of foreign arias will be much admired in revivals, judicious restoration of transpositions and *puntatura* could do much to improve the quality of operatic performances today, when so many singers sacrifice other musical values in an effort to conquer ranges and tessituras that do not come naturally to them.

The art song

Elucidation of performance practice for the great Romantic repertory of the art song is complicated by questions of context, since there was no strong tradition of public performance for any but the most popular or outwardly effective songs until quite late in the century. They were sung mostly in domestic concerts or private gatherings. We know something of Johann Michael Vogl's style in Schubert – highly declamatory, nuanced, rhythmically free, ornamental in varying degrees depending on the nature of the song[15] – but Vogl was an opera singer, and we also know that his style was criticized by the composer's friends.

Tempo and rubato

It was a song that prompted Beethoven's remark about a metronome indication being good only for the first bars, 'since feeling has its own tempo'. A hint of the extent to which feeling might vary the tempo can be gleaned from the very few publications that give metronome markings for internal tempo changes. One of the few is Tomášek's *Der Nachtigall letzter Gesang*

(op.77 no.2), a through-composed song in 2/4 time in which the opening
tempo ('Nicht zu langsam; sehr innig') is given the metronome mark quaver
= 88. After 23 bars, at the beginning of the poem's second stanza, this is
modified to 'Ein wenig bewegter' with the marking quaver = 126. (The
remaining instructions of the song, which have no metronome markings with
one exception, are 'Wie im Anfang', 'leidenschaftlich', 'wieder bewegter'
(quaver = 126), 'noch bewegter', 'zögernd bis zum Ende des Gesanges',
'ersterbend' and 'nach und nach immer langsamer'. Judging by the style of
the writing, it seems fair to suggest that these modifications did not represent
an exceptional case but rather were notations of conventional practices that
were more commonly left entirely in the interpreter's hands.

Opera outside Italy

French opera flourished throughout the 19th century, grand opera predomi-
nating in the first half, lyric comedy and lyric tragedy in the second. Its
impact on vocal norms was somewhat paradoxical. It is clear from the way in
which Rossini revised his Italian music for Paris that the norm there was less
florid than in Italy (despite the fact that the Paris operas were still liberally
embellished, as we know from Cinti-Damoreau and numerous other
sources). The strong penetration of the Italian repertory in the 1840s and
1850s by translated versions of Meyerbeer and Auber (to be followed later by
Gounod, Thomas and Massenet) led the way towards a simpler style of
impassioned lyricism in Italian singing (Giovanni Mario, regularly described
as being less brilliant than his predecessors in fioratura, was a leading
figure). Nevertheless, it was the French who maintained the old Italian skills
of florid singing rigorously to the end of the century. Paris at that time
boasted many basses, baritones and tenors who could have coped quite
respectably with Rossini's florid *opera seria* roles, had a revival of them been
attempted, while their Italian contemporaries had long simplified his *Otello*
and were beginning to do the same to the less demanding *Barbiere*.

In Germany and eastern Europe, a tension between the dominance of visiting
or resident Italians and emerging native styles was felt throughout the century,
with the Italians essentially ranged on the side of more freedom for the soloist,
less complication or symphonic surge in the orchestra, less dissonance in the
harmony and so forth. Composers in these countries could make the progress
they did partly because the native singers carried less weight with the public. By
the middle of the century in Germany, and by its end throughout Europe,
schools of singers had emerged as specialists in national repertory (eventually in
Wagner) – and in these singers the roots of what we know as 20th-century style
are found. However, in their preferences for tone production, the northern
countries prided themselves on maintaining classic Italian virtues that the
Italians themselves, in the view of many, were abandoning. In particular, they
resisted the introduction of continuous vibrato throughout the century.

Recordings by 19th-century singers

Though attention has always been paid to them, it is perhaps still not fully
realized how directly we can study singers of the late Romantic period on

recordings. They give us our best understanding of changes in performance style after about 1860. The first opera singer known to have made a surviving record is Peter Schram (1819–95), who sang serious and comic bass roles in Copenhagen from the early 1840s, appearing with Jenny Lind among others. In 1889 he sang two excerpts from his most popular role, Leporello in *Don Giovanni*, into a cylinder machine brought to Copenhagen by an Edison representative. They show a very free rhythmic treatment of the score, along with appoggiaturas and ornaments that correspond closely to practices observable in Mozart's own day. This record provides interesting testimony to the transmission of Classical music throughout the intervening years, but has little direct bearing on the performance of Romantic music. The few recordings made by Julius Stockhausen (1826–1906) are not known to have survived.

But seven singers born in the 1830s, and 24 born in the 1840s, also recorded, making over 400 sides or cylinders in all. These were artists who formed their style while the Wagnerian influence was still vestigial, well before that of the Italian verismists was even begun; they include collaborators of Brahms, Gounod, Verdi, Wagner, Grieg, Sullivan, Smetana and many others. Several dozen more, who were born in the 1850s and 1860s, left copious recordings.

This body of evidence brings the priceless opportunity to observe such things as the application of rubato and portamento, the details of vocal technique, and much else that has to be filled in by guesswork and extrapolation for all earlier music. They also point up important questions for future performance research, as they present some practices that would not have been guessed from the literature, and it remains to be shown just how far back those practices can be traced.

In the last quarter of the century one hears clearly that the national distinctions in vocal technique were marked. English, Scandinavian and German singers still cultivated a very narrow, regular vibrato, so fine as to strike some present-day listeners as indetectable on first hearing. Italians and Spaniards – with some of the Russians following their example – preferred a quick, intense, flickering vibrato that is most prominent in the records of the famous verismists Fernando de Lucia and Gemma Bellincioni. (Older Italians like Battistini and Patti did not do this; Patti was commended by Alberto Bach in 1883 for her judicious 'refusal to sing tremolos' in spite of the growing vogue for them.) In all of these cases, however, the vibrations were faster and narrower in pitch than has since become the norm. No singers born before the 1870s seem to have developed anything like the slow, wide vibrato we now call 'wobble' (or if they did, they were no longer invited to make any records, which makes the same point in a different way).

Portamento of the sort described a century earlier by Corri continued to be a prevalent expression of vocal legato. Lines were also shaped by what seems to modern ears very liberal application of rubato – both rallentando and accelerando, and occasionally a touch of the older kind of rubato in which voice and accompaniment are permitted to go out of phase. One habit very marked in the Italian singers is to accelerate in crescendos, passages of harmonic complication and impassioned cadential passages. In the latter, the singer would press ahead strongly until the last few notes of the passage were reached, then pull up sharp and make a fermata on the penultimate note. There are several 'senza affrettando' and 'senza accel.' markings in Verdi's later operas that make no sense whatever except in the light of this convention, which the composer clearly wanted to suspend for certain serene closes.

Ornamentation was still practised, mostly by Italian singers, but also by foreigners who made their careers in Italy or who became part of the budding 'international' scene in New York and London) and by some of the more old-fashioned artists based in France and Germany.

Ex.11 gives examples of passages recorded by singers born between 1843 and 1860, with transcriptions of ornaments, dynamics, portamento and rubato (necessarily 'impressionistic' except in the actual pitches) set against the original notation. Rubato is, almost by definition, nearly impossible to notate, but ex.11*b* attempts to show literally, even though it requires complicated notation, the displacements and tempo modifications in two lines from *La traviata* as sung by Gemma Bellincioni, whom Verdi is known to have admired in that opera.

The ornaments, as would be expected, are simpler and fewer than those in use earlier in the century. Most however were staples of ornamental practice

Ex.11

(a) Bellini: *La sonnambula*

(b) Verdi: *La traviata*

Gemma Bellincioni, 1903

original

going back at least to the Classical period: *gruppetti* of four or six notes, acciaccàturas, two-note slides, and the accented reiteration of the antepenultimate note of a cadence that García traces back to the castratos[16] and that was popularized by Rubini. For the music of Puccini and the *verismo* school, only the acciaccatura remained prominent as an improvised addition, though *gruppetti* were occasionally used by older singers.

All these ornaments were started on the main note, even the acciaccatura: though notated with a single 'small note' above the main note, it was uniformly executed as what we would now call an inverted mordent (unless approached by step from below, in which case it was sometimes sung in the 'modern' one-note fashion).

The only prominent ornament that is not found in earlier sources, and that seems to have developed in the second half of the century, is the extended acciaccatura figure seen in ex.11*d*; this was widely used in Verdi. French singers – less often Germans, almost never Italians – still introduced trills into their music, and executed the written trills with great clarity and elegant resolutions.

It is also to be noted on the early records that the preoccupation with interpolated high notes had not reached its later peaks; singers with good high notes often added them, but there are many recordings of the *Pagliacci* prologue, 'Largo al factotum', 'Sempre libera', 'La donna è mobile' and other favourite arias without the extra high notes that are so familiar today. These 'obligatory' notes, like the 'standard' coloratura variations of 'Una voce poco fa' and the *Lucia* mad scene, are mostly products of the 1920s and 30s, when Italian conductors and coaches set about the task of establishing more or less fixed texts for surviving Italian operas from the period of improvisation.

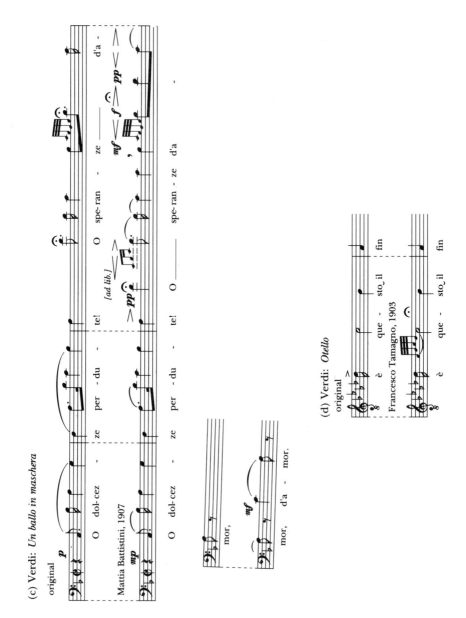

(c) Verdi: *Un ballo in maschera*

(d) Verdi: *Otello*

456

Voices

(e)
Thomas: *Le Caïd*

Leon Melchissedec, 1900

Andante Sostenuto ♪=112
original

dolce

En - fant ché - ri,   des dam - es, des gris - et - tes en - fant ga-

té   des bou- doirs, des guin- guet - tes, les fils d'or de ses é- pau-

let - tes sont moins brill- ant et moins nom- breux que ses   tri- om- phes a- mou - reux.

Notes

[1] G. Lanza, *The Elements of Singing* (London, 1809–13); A. de Garaudé, *Méthode de chant* (Paris, 1810, rev.); G. Ferrari, *A Concise Treatise on Italian Singing* (London, 1818); R. M. Bacon, *Elements of Vocal Science* (London, 1824); Peter von Winter, *Vollständige Singschule* (Mainz, 1825, 2/1874); I. Nathan, *An Essay on the History and Theory of Music, and on the Qualities, Capabilities and Management of the Human Voice* (London, 1823, rev. as *Musurgia vocalis*, 1836); D. Crivelli, *The Art of Singing and New Solfeggios for the Cultivation of the Bass Voice* (London, c1840, 2/1844); L. Lablache, *Metodo completo di canto* (Milan c1840–50); G. Duprez, *L'art du chant* (Paris, 1840); M. García *fils*, *Traité complet de l'art du chant* (Paris, 1840, 3/1851); J.-B. Faure, *La voix et le chant* (Paris, 1870); E. Delle Sedie.

[2] F. Sieber, *Vollständiges Lehrbuch der Gesangskunst* (Magdeburg, 1858); T. Lemaire and H. Lavoix, *Le chant, ses principes et son histoire* (Paris, 1881); A. B. Bach, *On Musical Education and Voice Culture* (Edinburgh, 1883).

[3] J. Ella, *Musical Sketches* (London, 1869); Castil-Blaze, *L'opéra italien de 1548 à 1856* (Paris, 1856).

[4] F. Lamperti, *Metodo di Canto* (London, 1877).

[5] Garcia, 1847, pt.ii, p.49.

[6] Garcia, 1847, p.48.

[7] See Crutchfield, 'Vocal Ornamentation in Verdi: the Phonographic Evidence', in *19th Century Music*, vii (1983–4), 3–54.

[8] Quoted in Mackenzie-Grieve, *Clara Novello* (London, 1955).

[9] Bochsa was a harpist who toured with the soprano; Kemble studied with her in Paris in the 1830s; Cinti, who never sang Norma, heard Pasta often and refers to her directly in connection with *Tancredi* ornaments preserved in the same notebook; Alary was a vocal coach in Paris for many years, and a collaborator of Grisi and Mario.

457

[10] Ricci, *Variazioni, Cadenze, Tradizioni per Canto*, aapx 2 (Milan, n.d.).

[11] Letter to Escudier, published in Verdi Newsletter no. 11 (March 1983).

[12] Autograph in *US-NYpm*.

[13] Entered in Mario's score, now in *I-Rsc*.

[14] Translation in Weaver and Chusid, *The Verdi Companion* (New York, 1979).

[15] Several of Vogl's versions are reproduced as appendixes to Walter Dürr's editions of the songs for the Neue Schubert-Ausgabe.

PART FOUR

The 20th Century

CHAPTER XXII

1900–1940

ROBERT PHILIP

The period 1900–1940 is different from the earlier periods discussed in this book in two important ways. First, it is the earliest one from which the most important primary source material survives. Recordings provide not just material *about* performance practice, but the performances themselves, often by the composers or by performers of whom they approved. This means that our knowledge of performance practice in the early 20th century can be more complete than is the case with earlier periods. Secondly, the period is recent enough to be regarded by most late 20th-century musicians as part of their own, rather than as a section of past history which warrants the investigation of performance practice. The main purpose of this chapter is to demonstrate just how different the performance practice of the early 20th century was from that of the late 20th century. Much of the chapter is based on the published writings of the period, but the evidence of recordings is used throughout to test the writings and to show how they relate to the actual practice of the time.[1]

String playing

VIOLIN PLAYING At the beginning of the 20th century, solo violin playing was dominated by the influence of Joachim and Ysaÿe, both of whom made a few recordings in the early years of the century. Later, the most influential violinist was Kreisler. Notable teachers included Leopold Auer, Otakar Ševčík, Jenő Hubay and Carl Flesch.

Many aspects of violin playing changed during the period, including bowing techniques and articulation, but the most important trends were the gradual adopting of the continuous vibrato and the gradual refinement of the portamento.[2] On the history of vibrato, Flesch writes:

> *Joachim's* medium of expression... consisted of a very close and quick tremolo. The same holds good for *Thomson. Sarasate* started to use broader oscillations, while *Ysaÿe's* vibrato, which followed closely every mood of his admirable personality, became the ideal goal of the generation around 1900. But it was *Kreisler* who... started a revolutionary change in this regard, by vibrating not only continuously in cantilenas like *Ysaÿe*, but even in technical passages. This fundamental metamorphosis has put his indelible stamp on contemporary violin playing ... our ears object already to the traditional gulf between the expressive theme and the unexpressive neutral passages.[3]

The most significant part of this extract is Flesch's statement that it was traditional in the early years of the century to distinguish between expressive themes, which might have a little vibrato, and 'neutral' passages, which would not. Recordings confirm this practice and the trend away from it.

461

Joachim's vibrato was very sparing, often hardly noticeable even on long notes.[4] Ysaÿe's vibrato, though more prominent, was still restricted to slow-moving passages, and many players of the first quarter of the century followed this selective use of vibrato, treating it almost as an ornament. By the 1930s, Kreisler's continuous vibrato had been adopted by most of the leading players; it had ceased to be an ornament and had become a constituent of fine tone.

This development defies neat analysis. Although Kreisler and, later, Heifetz were dominant influences in the use of continuous vibrato, they influenced some individual players more than others rather than establishing a 'school' of playing in the 19th-century sense. Nor do the prominent teachers of the early 20th century show a consistent influence on their pupils. Leopold Auer writes:

> remember that only the most sparing use of *vibrato* is desirable ... As a rule I forbid my students using the *vibrato* at all on notes which are not sustained, and I earnestly advise them not to abuse it even in the case of sustained notes which succeed each other in a phrase.[5]

Auer's approach to vibrato is consistent with the fact that he studied with Joachim in the 1860s. But his pupils included not only Zimbalist, who adhered to this traditional, sparing use of vibrato, but also Heifetz, who was a leading advocate of the modern, continuous vibrato. Ševčík's *Violin School* gives no advice about vibrato, and his pupils included Marie Hall, who used it sparingly in the traditional way, and Rudolf Kolisch and Wolfgang Schneiderhan, younger players with the modern approach to vibrato.[6]

The development of the continuous vibrato does not, therefore, follow a consistent pattern, and in the early years of the century it was a highly controversial topic. The following extracts are typical of the period: 'Exaggerated vibrato is ... to be condemned. Certain virtuosos abuse it, producing a ridiculous and tiring quavering',[7] and 'It is an embellishment very much overworked'.[8] *Grove 2* (1904–10) reprints an article on vibrato from *Grove 1* (1879–89): 'When the vibrato is really an emotional thrill it can be highly effective ... but when, as is too often the case, it degenerates into a mannerism, its effect is either painful, ridiculous, or nauseous, entirely opposed to good taste and common sense'.[9]

By the 1920s, however, teaching manuals were increasingly advocating the use of a continuous vibrato.[10] It is a sign of the times that *Grove 3* (1927–8) omits the earlier attack on vibrato, and comments instead, 'As an emotional effect produced by physical means it has obvious dangers, but no string-player's technique is complete without its acquirement'.[11] By 1930 Flesch was able to write, 'If we consider the celebrated violinists of our day, it must be admitted that in nearly every case they employ an uninterrupted (though technically unobjectionable) vibrato'.[12]

While the use of vibrato by violinists was gradually increasing, the routine use of portamento was falling out of favour. Here too, Flesch provides a useful historical guide. In *Violin Fingering* (completed 1944) he gives 200 examples from violin music illustrating the use of portamento, in many cases comparing the fingerings of his own day with late 19th- and early 20th-century fingerings which he considers old-fashioned.[13] His general observation is that the use of portamento became much more discriminating over the first four decades of the century. Earlier fingerings are often criticized by Flesch because they result in portamentos which are too frequent, which create false accents or which are for the player's convenience rather than the expressive shaping of the passage. 'I usually stigmatize the kind of audible portamento which is aesthetically inexcusable but technically convenient as "bus-portamento" – the cheapest and most comfortable way to move between positions.'[14]

This routine use of portamento is sometimes implied by writings of the early 20th century:

> To violinists the 'slide' is one of the principal vehicles of expression, and at the same time affording a means of passing from one note to another at a distance.[15]

By the 1920s, writers are frequently cautioning against excessive use of slides: 'we find that sliding is perhaps more abused than anything else in a violinist's outfit'.[16] Flesch emphasizes the need for care in the dynamic shading of portamentos. Remembering Joachim's old-fashioned crescendo during a portamento, he writes: 'This mannerism, quite attractive to Joachim's own generation, is considered offensive today and is used very rarely in concert performances'.[17]

Flesch distinguishes between three types of portamento: (*a*) an uninterrupted slide on one finger (ex.1); (*b*) a slide in which the beginning finger slides to an intermediate note, known as the 'B-portamento' (ex.2); and (*c*) a slide in which the last finger slides *from* an intermediate note, the 'L-portamento' (ex.3). Flesch states, and recordings confirm, that in the early

years of the century the continuous and the B-portamento were used with great frequency, but the L-portamento was rarely used. By the 1930s the L-portamento was accepted, though not used as frequently as the other portamentos (Heifetz used it particularly frequently). Recordings also show the extent to which the frequency, speed and shading of portamentos changed over the period.

Joachim's portamentos were frequent, generally slow, rarely disguised by a diminuendo and sometimes, as Flesch remembered, emphasized by a crescendo. Until the 1920s, the slow, undisguised portamento was still used though not as often as in Joachim's own playing. The change of fashion over the period 1900–1940 was, broadly speaking, a process of gradual refinement, with portamento becoming generally faster, less frequent and less prominent.

As with vibrato, the trend in the use of portamento seems to have been governed more by the response of individuals to fashion than by schools of playing or teaching. Auer writes, 'the *portamento* becomes objectionable and inartistic...when it is executed in a languishing manner, and used continually. The *portamento* should be employed only when the melody is descending, save for certain very exceptional cases of ascending melody.'[18]

Auer's most distinguished pupils ignored some or all of this advice. Some, such as Zimbalist, used slow portamento very frequently, while others, notably Heifetz, used faster and more selective portamento, but, contrary to Auer's advice, used it as often ascending as descending. The pupils of other teachers show similar inconsistencies. For example, of Hubay's pupils, Lener used much heavier and more frequent portamentos than Szigeti, and of Ševčík's pupils, Marie Hall used many more than Kolisch or Schneiderhan.

CELLO PLAYING Cello playing in the early years of the century, like violin playing, was generally sparing in its use of vibrato but made continual use of portamento. The English version of Carl Schroeder's *Handbook of Violoncello Playing* underlines the extent to which the vibrato was still regarded as an ornament by using the old term 'close shake'. 'A special sign for the close shake is not in general use, its employment being left to the player's taste.'[19] As to the portamento, Schroeder writes, 'If the notes are bound together to be played in one bow [at a shift], then the slide or portamento will be audible', though he cautions, 'The player must beware lest the portamento from one tone to another becomes exaggerated, and that the entire enharmonic scale lying between is not heard'.[20] E. van der Straeten writes: 'The student cannot be warned too earnestly against the abuse of the vibrato'. However, van der Straeten too cautions against excessive portamento: 'The portamento is a favourite ornamentation with singers, and the effect is very beautiful if applied sparing, and with discrimination'.[21] Despite such cautions, recordings show that frequent and slow portamentos were in general use among cellists through to the 1920s.

Hugo Becker was influential in the trend towards a more discriminating use of portamento. In his teaching manual[22] he distinguishes, like Flesch, between three types of portamento: the uninterrupted slide on a single finger, the interrupted slide on the starting finger (Flesch's B-portamento) and the interrupted slide on the second finger (Flesch's L-portamento). The first two types are 'more for the lyrical', the third is 'more for the heroic'. Becker identifies four general rules for portamento:

1. One should perform ... every portamento with a diminuendo.
2. The further apart the two notes to be joined lie, and the slower the sliding to be executed, the more essential the diminuendo.
3. One must never follow a portamento in one direction immediately with one in the opposite direction.
4. Vibrato should be used with the portamento when great passion ... is to be conveyed.[23]

The purpose of the vibrato, according to Becker, is the 'emotional enlivening of the tone', and 'The intensity and speed of the vibrato must be defined and applied solely in accordance with the specific emotional character [of the music]'.[24] Becker's selective approach to portamento, with emphasis on careful shading, and his view of vibrato as an ingredient of tone, contrast with the approach of cellists in the early part of the century.

But the outstanding cellist of the period, and the player who most influenced the next generation, was Casals. Like Becker he emphasized the importance of a flexible vibrato:

> The vibrato is one of the most active factors of the 'fullness' of tone-colour. The old school forbade its regular use...The vibrato is an expressive undulation [which] allows of the singing of a phrase, with the charm and intensity of a warm and well-coloured voice ... For weak sounds the vibrato should be spaced and supple. For full sounds the vibrato should on the contrary be rapid and nervous ... As a general rule one should abstain from using the vibrato only in certain rapid virtuoso passages, where it is absolutely out of the question to give an individual colour to each note, or again, in musical situations requiring, according to the taste of the player, a dull sonority.[25]

Casals's own playing was distinguished by the most subtle use of gradations of vibrato. As to portamento, he revolutionized cello fingering with the principal aim of enabling cellists to be more selective; he did this by the general use of extended fingering: 'this makes the playing easier and avoids a lot of shifts which are often detrimental to the music played'.[26]

The changing use of portamento is illustrated by ex.4, which shows an extract from Elgar's Cello Concerto, as played on recordings by W. H.

Ex.4 Elgar: Cello Concerto, 2nd movt

(1930) Squire   ———
(1928) Harrison - - - - -
(1945) Casals   - - - - -

Squire (an admired player of the old school, taught by Piatti), Beatrice Harrison (a pupil of Hugo Becker) and Casals. In this passage, Squire plays 23 portamentos, Harrison 16 and Casals 10. Squire's are usually slow, continuous and unshaped, whereas those of Harrison, and especially Casals, are generally faster, much more varied in type – sometimes continuous and sometimes interrupted – and often disguised by a diminuendo. Comparisons between violinists of this period often show similar differences between the older and newer styles.[27]

Some indications of this changing fashion in portamento are provided by editions of the period. Generally speaking, fingerings from the early part of the period provide more frequent opportunities for portamento than later fingerings. Published arrangements for strings of Liszt's *Liebestraum* no.3, for example, range from a cello version fingered by W. H. Squire in 1926 with 16 continuous slides, to a 1934 edition for violin fingered by Gustav Larsen with only two implied slides.[28] However, editions are not as helpful as they might be, because fingerings are often left to the choice of the player, and they are much less common in new works than in editions of earlier music. Specific indications of a portamento occur in certain passages in a number of early 20th-century works – such as Debussy's Violin Sonata, Ravel's Piano Trio and Bartók's Violin Sonata no.2[29] – but this must not be taken to imply that the rest of the work would have been played without portamentos.

STRINGS In the early years of the century gut strings were still used for all four strings of the violin and cello, and Italian gut was considered superior to German, English or French. The G string of the violin and the C and G strings of the cello were overwound with silver (copper was also used, but was considered dull in tone). Steel strings had been available since the turn of the century, but their tone was regarded as metallic and inferior.[30]

During the first three decades of the century steel strings greatly improved, so that by the 1920s Flesch was able to write, 'The difference in tone between gut and metal is hardly noticeable'. Flesch recommends a steel E string, aluminium-covered steel for the A, and a D of gut covered with aluminium.[31]

ORCHESTRAL STRING PLAYING The changing style of orchestral string playing during this period has been little documented, but recordings show that it broadly paralleled the trend among soloists.[32]

Orchestras were not recorded in the earliest years of the century, but from the many recordings made during the 1920s and 1930s we can hear that there was an almost universal trend among orchestras in Europe and America away from the conspicuous use of portamento. In the 1920s, portamentos were, in general, heaviest and most frequent in British orchestras, and lightest and most infrequent in some French and American orchestras. The trend to a 'cleaner' style is shown by the fact that, in the orchestras of London, Manchester, Paris, Vienna, Berlin, New York and Chicago, recordings made from the late 1930s onwards usually contain fewer and more discreet slides than those made in the 1920s.

A typical example is illustrated in ex.5a and b which shows extracts from Debussy's *Nuages*. Warm sliding, as indicated, is heard in the 1929 recording

Ex.5 Debussy: Nocturnes, *Nuages*

(a) 5th bar of fig.2   (b) fig.3

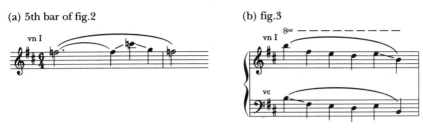

of the Paris Conservatoire Orchestra conducted by Gaubert. In the 1939 recording by the same orchestra under Coppola, there is only the slightest hint of sliding.

One necessary caution is that, when analysing recordings of orchestral portamento, it is not possible to tell how many of the players are sliding at any particular point. In some recordings of the 1920s, particularly British recordings, the placing of the portamentos seems so random as to suggest that different players are sliding at different times.

The extent to which vibrato was used by orchestral string players during the period cannot be readily assessed from recordings. String solos in orchestral works recorded before about 1930 tend to be played with little vibrato except on long notes, and it seems reasonable to assume that most orchestral players at that time played in much the same style as their section leaders. The Vienna PO cultivated a particularly 'straight' string sound with little vibrato, a style it preserved until World War II.

Recordings provide some clues as to the influence of particular conductors on orchestral string style. Two orchestras, the Concertgebouw Orchestra of Amsterdam and the Philadelphia Orchestra, continued, against the prevailing trend, to use prominent portamentos throughout the 1930s. Theirs were, however, selected and shaped with obviously rehearsed care, unlike some of the apparently random portamentos heard elsewhere in the 1920s. That this was encouraged by their conductors, Mengelberg and Stokowski respectively, is strongly suggested by the fact that the string styles of both orchestras changed considerably when their conductors changed, and their portamentos became much less conspicuous. Toscanini's recordings, with the New York Philharmonic SO and the BBC SO, tend to contain more frequent and prominent portamento in late Romantic works than in earlier music. This distinction in style is also found in Beecham's London PO in the 1930s, which played Delius and Elgar with much warmer portamentos than Mozart. Most other orchestras in the 1920s and 1930s made little distinction between different periods of music in their use of portamento.

Woodwind

FLUTE In the early years of the century, the wooden flute was still used in Britain, Germany and eastern Europe. The metal flute was already in general use in France, Belgium and Italy, and by some players in America.

The wooden flute was usually played without vibrato, or with no more than a slight, rapid tremor. This was true of British players until 1930, several of whom, notably Robert Murchie, continued in this style through the 1930s. The flautists of the Vienna PO, Berlin PO and Czech PO also played with little or no vibrato throughout the period. Richard Strauss's opinion in 1904 was that 'wooden flutes have a finer tone than metal ones (silver or gold), but the latter respond more easily'.[33]

The metal flute was associated with the French school of flute playing founded by Paul Taffanel (1844–1908), professor at the Paris Conservatoire, whose *Méthode* (with Philippe Gaubert) was published in 1923. The French style was distinguished from the wooden-flute tradition by a bright and silvery tone rich in upper partials, flexibility of phrasing and the use of vibrato. According to Louis Fleury, Taffanel stressed the importance of 'The search for tone, and the use, for this purpose, of a light, almost imperceptible *vibrato*' though in his own *Méthode* Taffanel argues against the use of vibrato.[34] Taffanel's pupils, including Philippe Gaubert, Georges Barrère, Louis Fleury and Marcel Moyse, dominated flute playing in France and profoundly influenced players in Britain and America. French recordings show that the vibrato, far from remaining 'almost imperceptible', had become quite prominent by the 1920s, and it was combined with phrasing of great flexibility, particularly in the playing of Marcel Moyse. In England the French instrument, with its vibrato and flexible phrasing, was first adopted by Geoffrey Gilbert in the 1930s (principal of the London PO), and his example was followed by other British flautists in the 1940s. French flautists in America early in the century included Georges Barrère (principal of the New York SO from 1905), and Barrère's pupils included the most influential American flautist, William Kincaid (principal of the Philadelphia Orchestra, 1921–60). Flautists of the French school during this period did not all play in the same style. Moyse's vibrato was quite fast and quite prominent, Gilbert's was slower and more discreet, and Kincaid's was extremely fast and constant. These differences have tended to characterize French, British and American flute playing in later years.

OBOE Like flute playing, oboe playing in the early 20th century was divided between French and German traditions. The oboes favoured in Britain, France and America were based on the late 19th-century French instruments developed by Triebert. German and Viennese oboists continued to use instruments derived from earlier 19th-century models, characterized by a wider bell and darker and less flexible tone. The Viennese oboe was based on J. Sellner's early 19th-century instrument, and his *Oboe School* was published in a revised edition in 1901.[35]

The tone of these different instruments was affected by the traditional 'scrape' of the reed, which varied from country to country and from player to player.[36] The most striking differences between players during this period, however, was in their styles of phrasing and vibrato. The oboists of Germany and Vienna played virtually without vibrato until after World War II, and their phrasing was generally broad and sustained. Oboe playing in France was usually more detailed in its phrasing, and almost all French oboists recorded during the 1920s and 1930s used a flexible vibrato. This tradition derives principally from the teaching of Georges Gillet, Taffanel's contemporary at the Paris Conservatoire, although Gillet himself was very sparing in his use of vibrato. As with Taffanel, it was the pupils who fully exploited the possibilities of vibrato.

The most influential oboist in America, Marcel Tabuteau (principal in the Philadelphia Orchestra, 1915–54), was a pupil of Gillet, and used an almost continuous, fast vibrato. Most other oboists in American orchestras during this period used vibrato, with varying degrees of flexibility and, as with American flautists, it tended to be faster than the vibrato of players in France.

Although most oboists in Britain had adopted the French instrument by the turn of the century, they generally played it in a more Germanic style than the French, with no vibrato (or at most a slight tremor) and with phrasing virtually devoid of dynamic nuances. The exception was Leon Goossens, who revolutionized British oboe playing by his introduction of a confident vibrato of moderate speed and exceptionally flexible phrasing. His style was to some extent inspired by the French school, and in particular by a Belgian oboist, Henri de Buesscher, who played in the Queen's Hall Orchestra 1904–13. A number of British oboists were influenced, to varying degrees, by Goossens after 1930, while others continued in the old British style throughout the 1930s.

The French tradition has had a great effect on oboe style later in the century, even in orchestras which still use the German or Viennese oboe. But in the early years of the century there were various opinions about French influence. Richard Strauss was certainly in favour of it. He complained (in 1904) that 'Some German "methods" try to produce a tone as thick and trumpet-like as possible, which does not blend in at all with the flutes and is often unpleasantly prominent. The French tone, though thinner and frequently tremulant, is much more flexible and adaptable.'[37]

By contrast, Henry Wood wrote in 1924:

> In England and France the oboes and bassoons, with their beautiful scales of even quality, have almost lost their 'bite'...Hence, when we go to Germany, the first thing which strikes us is the 'bite' of the oboes and bassoons, even while we dislike their 'throaty' quality.[38]

CLARINET National differences between clarinettists during this period were less striking than in the case of oboists and flautists, principally because vibrato did not become widespread. The French tone was bright and reedy, and a delicate, rapid tremor which was invariably much faster than the vibrato of flautists and oboists was in use by the 1920s. Vibrato was not in general use among clarinettists elsewhere in Europe, nor even in America, except among jazz clarinettists, despite the strength of French woodwind influence there. The Germans and Viennese favoured a broad style of tone and phrasing, and up to the 1920s British clarinet playing was also quite broad in style and used no vibrato. In the 1930s, however, Reginald Kell began to use a very flexible style of phrasing with a subtle, moderate-speed vibrato derived from the example of Leon Goossens, with whom Kell played in the London PO. No other British clarinettists on record used vibrato until the 1940s.

BASSOON The German Heckel bassoon was in general use in Germany and Austria by the turn of the century, and the first tutor for the Heckel bassoon, by Weissenborn, had been published in 1887. German and Austrian bassoonists did not use vibrato.

Elsewhere in Europe the French Buffet system bassoon was still preferred. In France, the clearer but less subtle tone of the German bassoon was considered greatly inferior to the French.[39] French bassoonists, like their clarinettists, favoured a reedier tone than the Germans (this was achieved both by the choice of instrument and by the scrape of the reed) and they played with a delicate, rapid vibrato and flexible phrasing. In Britain most players used the French instrument until the 1930s. At the turn of the century Hans Richter brought two Viennese bassoonists to the Hallé Orchestra, one of whom taught Archie Camden, the most celebrated British exponent of the German instrument. Camden's use of the German bassoon was not widely followed by other British players until the 1930s. The difference in tone and style between the French and German instruments in Britain was not as pronounced as the difference between native French and German players, because the tone of French instruments in Britain was neither as reedy nor as flexible as in France and because no British bassoonists used vibrato on either instrument. In America, both the French and the German bassoon were used by the 1920s, and a delicate, French-style vibrato was often employed.

The rarity of vibrato on woodwind instruments in the early 20th century, outside France and America, is suggested, if only by omission, in the writings of the time. In *Grove 2* (1904–10) the only reference to wind instruments in the article on vibrato is the statement that 'It is sometimes heard on the flute and cornet'.[40] Even in *Grove 3* (1927–8) this reference is only slightly broadened: 'The *vibrato* is obtainable to a limited extent on wind instruments, notably flute and cornet'.[41] This entry is reprinted unchanged in *Grove 4* (1940), although such a restricted view of woodwind vibrato was by then out of date. Many musical reference books of the first two decades of the century mention vibrato on voices and string instruments but make no mention of woodwind vibrato.

Brass

Styles of brass playing during the period 1900–1940 are more difficult to assess from recordings than woodwind styles, partly because of the rarity of brass solos in orchestral works compared with woodwind solos and partly because of the limitations of the recordings, which become unclear when the whole brass section is playing. There were, however, some important changes to the instruments used during the period, and significant differences in usage between countries.

HORN The narrow-bore 19th-century French horn was still in general use in the early years of the 20th century. The wide-bore German double F/B♭ horn came into use around the turn of the century in Germany, but met resistance elsewhere in Europe. Even in Germany Richard Strauss, whose horn parts were made considerably easier by the use of the B♭ crook, wrote, 'it requires practice to change the bright and sharp horn in B♭ into the soft and noble timbre of the horn in F'.[42] Some indication of opposition to the German horn in Britain is given by Cecil Forsyth, writing in 1914:

> The German instruments have very little resemblance to our own. Their tone-quality we should regard as more suitable to the Euphonium. It is somewhat coarse, thick, and 'open'. In lightness and brilliance they are inferior to the true French horns ... It must be added that they are much easier to play.[43]

French horns, and English instruments of French type, were the norm in Britain until the 1930s. The most distinguished horn player of the period, Aubrey Brain, continued to insist on French horns in the BBC SO throughout the 1930s, at a time when the London Philharmonic had already adopted the wider-bore German horns.

Most French players continued to use the French horn throughout the period, and in Vienna a narrow-bore Viennese horn was still in use. In America, conversion to the German double horn was led by Anton Horner, in Pittsburgh from the beginning of the century and in the Philadelphia Orchestra from 1930.

A light, fast vibrato was already in use in France and Czechoslovakia by the 1930s (not the wider vibrato which developed after World War II) and some American players used a similar vibrato. Vibrato was not generally used on the horn in other countries at this period.

TRUMPET AND TROMBONE As with the horn, the bore of the trumpet and trombone varied between countries, and there was a trend towards the adoption of wider-bore instruments during the period. Narrow-bore French trombones were used not only in France but also in British orchestras until the 1930s. Wider-bore American trombones, already in use in America, were adopted in Britain during the 1930s. German trombones were already wider-bore than the French early in the century.

The French and German trumpets in use during the early decades of the 20th century were narrower in bore than the modern instruments. Wider-bore trumpets began to be used in Germany and America during the 1930s, but the narrow-bore trumpet remained the norm throughout the period in England and France.

As with the horn, a light, fast vibrato was used by some trumpeters by the 1930s in France, Czechoslovakia, America and occasionally even in Britain.

The tone quality of the brass section as a whole is difficult to judge from recordings. However, there can be no doubt that the adoption of wider-bore instruments had the general effect of making the sound of the brass section thicker and more massive. By comparison, the narrower-bore earlier instruments produced an ensemble which was richer in upper harmonics, and therefore brighter and clearer.[44]

Rhythmic style

FLEXIBILITY OF TEMPO At the turn of the century, fluctuations of tempo within a movement were a traditional feature of performance practice. The ideas of Wagner and Bülow, who had advocated great flexibility of tempo, were still influential, and Wagner's essay *On Conducting* had recently been translated into English.[45] Mahler is reported to have said:

> All the most important things – the tempo, the total conception and structuring of a work – are almost impossible to pin down. For here we are concerned with something living and flowing that can never be the same even twice in succession. That is why metronome markings are inadequate and almost worthless; for unless the work is vulgarly ground out in barrel-organ style, the tempo will already have changed by the end of the second bar.[46]

Richard Strauss described Mahler as 'One of the few... who understand tempo modification'.[47]

Recordings show that many conductors, ensembles and soloists up to the 1930s habitually used changes of tempo to underline the contrasts between passages of different character. Elgar followed the practice of his time by varying the tempo of his own works much more than the indications in his scores suggest, and he wrote that he liked his music to be played 'elastically and mystically', not 'squarely & ... like a wooden box'.[48]

The trend towards a stricter control of tempo was led by Weingartner and Toscanini. Weingartner attacked the followers of Bülow as 'tempo-rubato conductors' with their 'continual alterations and dislocations of the tempo ... in no way justified by any marks of the composer'.[49]

Toscanini's firm control of tempo was highly influential on younger conductors. George Szell wrote that Toscanini 'wiped out the arbitrariness of the postromantic interpreters. He did away with the meretricious tricks and the thick encrustation of the interpretative nuances that had been piling up for decades'.[50]

Neither Weingartner nor Toscanini, however, was quite as strict in the control of tempo as has sometimes been supposed. Weingartner frequently adhered to the tradition of slowing down at lyrical themes, though more subtly than some of his contemporaries, and Toscanini's recordings from the 1920s and 1930s are often more flexible in tempo than his later recordings. The tradition of flexible tempo was refined, rather than abolished.

TEMPO RUBATO More detailed rhythmic flexibility – tempo rubato – presents a complicated picture during this period. It is found at its most extreme among pianists, and it was a controversial subject in the early years of the century.

Paderewski wrote that tempo rubato consists 'of a more or less important slackening or quickening of the time or rate of movement', and this is the sense in which many writers understood the term.[51] Tobias Matthay, an influential teacher, defined two forms of rubato:

> The most usual is that in which we emphasize a note (or a number of notes) by giving *more* than the expected Time-value, and then subsequently make-up the time thus lost by accelerating the *remaining* notes of that phrase or idea so as to enable us accurately to return to the pulse ... In the opposite form of Rubato ... we begin with a pushing-on or hurrying the time. This we must necessarily follow up by retarding the subsequent notes of the phrase.[52]

Matthay was one of a number of theoreticians who insisted that the time 'borrowed' must be 'payed back', to maintain what he called the 'Tempo outline'.[53] Paderewski, however, observed,

We duly acknowledge the high moral motives of this theory, but we humbly confess that our ethics do not reach to such a high level ... The value of notes diminished in one period through an *accelerando*, cannot always be restored in another through a *ritardando*. What is lost is lost.[54]

Some writers describe rubato in terms of detailed rhythmic adjustment rather than accelerando and ritardando. For example, 'Taking a portion of the time from one note of a melody and giving it to another, for the sake of expression',[55] 'Indicates that the music is not to be performed in strict time, certain notes being given more, others less, than their absolute value'.[56]

J. A. Johnstone regrets the rise of the 'curious artificial device' of the accelerando–ritardando rubato, and recommends a subtler kind of rhythmic adjustment: 'This device, which consists in the almost imperceptible lengthening and shortening of certain notes, this instrument of expressive beauty used invariably in the declamation of verse ... is astonishingly neglected by our pianists. Joachim produces wonderful effects by its use.'[57]

Fuller Maitland also praises Joachim's agogic accents, 'The kind of accent that consists, not of an actual stress or intensification of tone on the note, but of a slight lengthening-out of its timevalue, at the beginning of the bar, and at points where a secondary accent may be required'.[58]

A number of writers stress that rubato in a melody should not affect the accompaniment: 'any independent accompaniment to a rubato phrase must always keep strict time, and it is, therefore, quite possible that no note of a rubato melody will fall exactly together with its corresponding note in the accompaniment, except, perhaps, the first note in each bar'.[59] This description, from the turn of the century, is reminiscent of accounts of Chopin's and Liszt's rubato.

These three kinds of rubato – the use of accelerandos and ritardandos, the use of tenutos or agogic accents, and the rhythmic separation of melody and accompaniment – were all employed by instrumentalists, especially pianists, in the early decades of the 20th century. However, recordings reveal that, whatever some writers might have liked, practising musicians did not adhere strictly to one or other theory of rubato. In the 1920s J. B. McEwen demonstrated from a visual analysis of piano rolls by Busoni, Pachmann, Carreño and others, that these pianists did not apply the strict 'paying back' principle of Matthay, nor, where rubato in a melody became rhythmically separated from the accompaniment, did the accompaniment keep strict time.[60]

Although pianists did not adhere to the principle of keeping strict time in the accompaniment during melodic rubato, notes of a melody were often rhythmically separated from the accompaniment, frequently by delaying a note of a melody in order to create an accent, or sometimes to draw attention to an inner part. At the turn of the century, Oscar Bie wrote: 'the short pause, like the white mounting of a picture, raises the important note, giving to it its meaning, and with the meaning the due expression'.[61]

In this passage, Bie is writing not about 20th-century rubato, but about Couperin's *suspension*. But the confidence with which he does so suggests (and recordings confirm) that he was also describing a familiar device of his own time. The separation of melodic note and accompaniment was sometimes undisguised, at other times the separation was softened by spreading a chord. This practice is heard at its most extreme in pianists of the older generation and at its most subtle in younger pianists of the period.

Despite the assertion that it was 'astonishingly neglected by our pianists', the rhythmic adjustment of a phrase by the lengthening and shortening of individual notes (distinct from any accelerando or ritardando) was very common among pianists until the 1920s, and is also found in recordings of string players and singers. W. H. Breare advises singers that 'there is nothing more unattractive than the slavish observation of strict time. To execute any passage with grace, it becomes necessary to make a distinction between accented and unaccented notes'.[62] At its most extreme, this rhythmical adjustment goes so far as to create dotted or triplet rhythm from even note values. This is particularly common in the playing of Paderewski, although he makes no mention of it in his article on tempo rubato.

More subtle versions of this adjustment – a sort of momentary *notes inégales* – are found in the playing of many instrumentalists during the period. An important feature of this use of tenutos is that the lengthened note is immediately followed by a shortened note rather than by a gradual acceleration. It is this which distinguishes it from the rubato recommended by Matthay and from later 20th-century rubato. The effect is to emphasize a note without drawing out the phrase as a whole. Rakhmaninov, one of the most admired pianists of the period, makes frequent and subtle use of it. In ex.6, each tenuto is followed by a shortened note, so that the following bar is not delayed.

Ex.6 Rakhmaninov: Piano Concerto no.2, 1st movt, 2nd bar of 6 (Rakhmaninov, 1929)

Recordings show that there was a trend towards less extreme rubato during the period, and that by the 1930s the general use of agogic accents and the obvious dislocation of melody and accompaniment was becoming old-fashioned.

LONG AND SHORT NOTES, AND OVERDOTTING As well as specific rubato of these kinds, there was a general tendency in the early 20th century to lighten and hurry the short notes in patterns of long and short notes. This sort of 'throwaway' rhythmic lightness was the norm until the 1930s, and it can be heard (to a greater or lesser degree) in recordings of the most distinguished instrumentalists and ensembles of the time.[63]

One effect of this practice was to produce overdotted dotted rhythms. However, there are very few suggestions of this aspect of rhythmic style in the writings of the period. Arnold Dolmetsch, introducing rhythmic conventions of the 17th and 18th centuries, writes:

> In instruction books, be they old or new, we learn that 'a dot after a note makes it half as long again.' In spite of the intended modern precision there are still exceptions to that rule. In military marches, for example, figures like ♩♪ and ♫ are played ♩. *♪* and ♫, but such instances are rare.[64]

Instances of overdotting, and even double-dotting, were not as rare in the early 20th century as Dolmetsch supposed. In the march-like central section of Debussy's *Fêtes* (ex.7) the rhythm in the first and fifth bars is played as if it

Ex.7 Debussy: Nocturnes, *Fêtes*, fig.11, woodwind

were double-dotted in recordings of the Orchestra of the Berlin State Opera conducted by Klemperer (1925), the Philadelphia Orchestra under Stokowski (1928), the Paris Conservatoire Orchestra under Coppola (1939) and, in Ravel's arrangement for two pianos, by Josef and Rosina Lhevinne (1935). The Paris Conservatoire under Gaubert (1929) also overdots those bars. Such examples are not unusual, and instances of less drastic overdotting are very common indeed in recordings of orchestras, chamber ensembles and soloists.

There are some hints of this flexible attitude to dotted rhythms in the notation of the period. In ex.8, from Elgar's Enigma Variations, the duplet

Ex.8 Elgar: Enigma Variations, 'Nimrod', 2 bars before fig.37

and triplet semiquavers, which are theoretically of different lengths, were in practice played together. Ex.9, from Rakhmaninov's Piano Concerto no.3, is unplayable with strict observance of note values.

Among conductors, Weingartner and Toscanini, who led the trend towards stricter control of tempo, also encouraged unusually literal interpretation of dotted rhythms. As early as 1905, Weingartner insisted, in the

Ex.9 Rakhmaninov: Piano Concerto no.3, 1st movt, fig.20

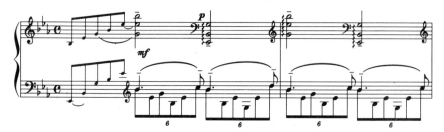

Ex.10 Beethoven: Overture 'Egmont', as quoted by Weingartner

rhythm from Beethoven's *Egmont* overture shown in ex.10, on 'preventing the last quaver of the first bar from being turned, as so often happens, into a semiquaver'.[65] By the late 1930s, a less 'casual' approach, not only to dotted rhythms but to rhythmical style as a whole, was generally discernible.[66]

The rhythmic style of the early 20th century often sounds casual, even careless, to modern listeners, but it cannot be dismissed as the result of incompetence or lack of rehearsal. It is certainly true that orchestral rehearsal time was often extremely limited. The deputy system, whereby a player could send a deputy to a rehearsal if more lucrative work called him elsewhere, was still in operation in the 1920s in London and Paris.[67] But by the late 1920s, recording sessions allowed for rehearsal time, involving, as Stravinsky observed, 'The frequent repetition of a fragment or even of an entire piece, [and] the sustained effort to allow not the slightest detail to escape attention, as may happen for lack of time at an ordinary rehearsal'.[68] Furthermore, the style is by no means confined to orchestras. The most admired soloists and chamber ensembles of the period show a similarly 'throwaway' rhythmic style. It was, therefore, part of the performance practice of the day, not just a symptom of low standards.

TEMPO The light rhythmic style of the early 20th century was often combined with very fast tempos in fast movements, compared with performances of the later 20th century. This applied not only to the standard repertory of 18th- and 19th-century music, but also to contemporary works, including those performed or approved by the composers. Recorded performances of the period by Rakhmaninov, Elgar, Richard Strauss, Bartók, Poulenc and Stravinsky are often faster than performances of a later generation, and sometimes faster than the composers' own published metronome indications.[69]

It was not unknown for performances to be speeded up so as to fit on to the records; but this practice was becoming uncommon by the late 1920s, and the countless examples of very fast performances on records which have room to spare make it clear that fast tempos were genuinely part of the performance practice of the time.

476

Even performances which are not exceptionally fast often seem so to a modern listener, because the seemingly casual lightness of unaccented notes gives an impression of haste.

Singers

Generalizations are more difficult to make about singers than about instrumentalists during the period 1900–1940, because of the great individual differences between singers. However, many of the practices which have been described above in relation to instrumentalists also apply to singers.

Writings on string playing of the period often refer admiringly to singers' use of portamento. For example, Auer writes: 'In order to develop your judgement as to the proper and improper use of the *portamento*, observe the manner in which it is used by good singers and by poor ones'.[70] The portamento was regarded by singers of the early 20th century not just as an occasional ornament, but as a necessary ingredient of good legato, as definitions of portamento in the early years of the century make clear: 'The passage across an interval by means of gliding with imperceptible gradations through all the intermediate tones in one continuous sound...Hence a legato style; so a singer is said to have a true *portamento*'.[71] Like string players, singers generally used heavier and more frequent portamentos in the early decades of the century than in later years, and the trend towards the 'cleaner' late 20th-century style was already discernible by the 1930s.

Vibrato was an even more controversial topic among singers than among string players in the early years of the century. There was also considerable confusion about it, some writers using 'tremolo' to mean a fluctuation in pitch and 'vibrato' to mean a fluctuation in intensity without a pitch change, other writers using the two terms synonymously to mean a pitch change, and yet others using one or other term without defining it.[72]

Many writers attacked the vibrato, in the sense of a fluctuation in pitch, and asserted that the best singers did not use it, except as an occasional effect expressive of extreme emotion. A typical essay of the first quarter of the century is 'The Vice of Vibrato and the Torture of Tremolo', in which the writer claims that 'There was never a suspicion of such a disfigurement in the singing of ... Patti ... Melba, Calvé, [or] De Reszke'.[73]

Studies of vocal vibrato at the Department of Psychology, University of Iowa, published in 1932, demonstrated that such claims, if taken literally, were unfounded. Distinguished singers on record were invariably found to use some vibrato, even though it was usually too fast and too shallow to be perceived as a fluctuation in pitch.[74] What is clear from recordings is that many singers of the early years of the century used a shallower vibrato than singers later in the century. In this respect, the trend in singers' vibrato parallels that in string playing, though there is less evidence of singers using vibrato so sparingly that it becomes an ornament.[75]

Allowing for substantial individual differences, what has been written above about rhythmical style applies, generally speaking, to singers as well as to instrumentalists. The relationship between vocal line and accompaniment often displays a rhythmic freedom analogous to the melodic rubato of pianists, and the use of tenutos, accelerandos and ritenutos was broadly in line with instrumental practice. Like instrumentalists, singers were tending towards a stricter and more literal interpretation of note values towards the end of the period.

Broadly speaking, performance practice in the early years of the 20th century was characterized by the following features: (*a*) the sparing use of vibrato by string players, and the general avoidance of vibrato on woodwind instruments except by French players; (*b*) the frequent use of prominent portamentos by string players and singers; (*c*) the use of tempo changes within movements, and the adoption of fast tempos; (*d*) a style of tempo rubato which included not only accelerando and ritardando, but also accentuation by lengthening and shortening individual notes, and the dislocation of melody and accompaniment; (*e*) a tendency, in patterns of long and short notes, to shorten short notes, and to overdot dotted rhythms; and (*f*) the continued use of narrow-bore brass instruments, wooden flutes (except by the French school) and French bassoons (except in Germany and Austria).

By the end of the period certain trends are clear: the spread of continuous vibrato on string instruments, its increasing prominence among singers, and its adoption by many flautists and oboists; the decreasing prominence and frequency of portamento, on both strings and voices; a trend towards stricter control of tempo, slower tempos in fast movements, more literal interpretation of note values, and more emphatic clarity of detail; the adoption of steel on the upper strings of string instruments, the increasing use of wider-bore brass instruments, the metal flute and the German bassoon.

Perhaps it is possible to summarize these changes by saying that, in the early years of the century, there was clearer and more detailed differentiation between levels of expression in a piece of music – between accented and unaccented notes, between long and short notes, between portamento and non-portamento, between vibrato and non-vibrato, and between faster and slower passages. The trend in later years, and continuing into the late 20th century, was towards greater evenness and regularity of expression – evenness of rhythmic emphasis and of tempo, regularity of vibrato, avoidance of disruptive portamento, and a style of rubato based on gradual flexibility rather than rhythmic distortion. National differences of style also tended to diminish, making styles early in the century more diverse, those later in the century more uniform. Add to this the fact that the tempos of fast movements were often faster in the early 20th century than in later years, then it is possible to characterize early 20th-century style as more volatile, responding rapidly to the rhetorical details of the music, and later 20th-century style as more deliberate, and more constant in expressive intensity.

The reasons for this stylistic trend are a matter for conjecture, but two developments might go some way towards explaining it. The first is the availability of recordings. By the late 1920s, performances of the finest instrumentalists, singers and orchestras were widely available in recordings of reasonable quality, and this must have contributed to the spread of new ideas and to the lessening of national differences. The ability of performers to analyse their own performances on record may also have encouraged greater attention to clarity of detail.

The second factor which may have influenced performance practice is the new music which performers were beginning to play during this period. Music which radically broke from conventional 19th-century structures and forms of expression must have encouraged a questioning of conventional performance practice. The complex and sharp-edged rhythms of Bartók and Stravinsky, for example, may have helped to lead to more literal and clear-cut interpretation of rhythms. The breakdown of traditional harmonic and melodic tensions may have encouraged the evening out of traditional expressive nuances. And the extreme difficulty of much of the new music of the period must have hastened the adoption of instruments which were more reliable and easier to play, notably German bassoons and wider-bore brass instruments.

Whatever the reasons for the stylistic changes in performance over the 20th century, one result of them is clear: performances in the early 20th century were often very different from the late 20th-century performances to which we are accustomed. There are countless recorded examples to illustrate the point, and they include, among the more striking instances: (*a*) the portamentos in Elgar's recordings, and in Beecham's recordings of Delius from the 1920s and 1930s; (*b*) Bartók's lightness of rhythm, and his subtle use of rubato and spread chords; (*c*) the vibrato-less woodwind style in Richard Strauss's German recordings; (*d*) the reedy tone of French bassoons and clarinets in Stravinsky's Paris recordings; and (*e*) Rakhmaninov's fast tempos, for example in the first movement of the Piano Concerto no.3.

Such examples illustrate the relationship of particular composers to the performance practice of their time; but this relationship is not without its complications. Consider, for example, the changing string style. Delius dedicated his First Violin Sonata to Arthur Catterall, a player of the old school in his attitude to vibrato and portamento, but dedicated his Second Violin Sonata to Albert Sammons, the leading British exponent of the new style. Similar contrast between older and later styles are found in the playing of Marie Hall and Yehudi Menuhin, with both of whom Elgar recorded his Violin Concerto, and much the same contrast applies to Samuel Dushkin and Joseph Szigeti, who were both associated with Stravinsky, Licco Amar and Szymon Goldberg, with whom Hindemith played, and Arnold Rosé and Rudolf Kolisch, who gave early performances of Schoenberg's works. In each case, the composer was accustomed to the old school of violin playing when it was the accepted style of the day, but happily accepted the new style when he encountered it. This is just one of many instances in which recordings demonstrate, more conclusively than indirect evidence can, that composers' views evolved as performance practice evolved, and that no composer had an unchanging idea of a 'right' way of performing his works.

Another complication, compounded rather than clarified by the existence of recordings, is the problem of establishing the status of the various practices of the early 20th century. For earlier periods, we can assemble the evidence for and against, say, double-dotting in a particular place and time, and even though the evidence may be contradictory or incomplete, make an informed judgment based on the opinions of the period. Recordings, however, reveal features of performance practice which are hardly mentioned in written sources. For example, subtle overdotting, and the general lightening of short notes, is a characteristic feature of early 20th-century performance, but most writers of the period were obviously unaware of it. This is presumably because it was such a normal, everyday detail of performance. Players of the early 20th century would probably not have been able to describe such a commonplace aspect of their style, any more than an Elizabethan English-man would have been able to describe his own style of speech. Detailed characteristics of performance are obvious to someone from a different place or time, but are unnoticed by their practitioners or accustomed audiences. This means that we cannot establish how important this lightness of rhythm was to the composers of the early 20th century, because they did not, on the whole, express an opinion on the subject. We are left to rely on our own unaided judgment of the recorded performances.

There are similar difficulties when trying to define the borderline between competence and style. Features of early 20th-century performance practice which now sound careless or sloppy cannot be assumed to have sounded like that at the time. For example, Stravinsky's Paris recordings of *The Rite of Spring*, *Petrushka* and *The Firebird* may, to modern ears, seem rhythmically slapdash compared with his later recordings. But they certainly did not seem so to Stravinsky when he made them, and he regarded them as 'documents which can serve as a guide to all executants of my music'.[76] Orchestras of the late 20th century may play Stravinsky with greater precision than they did in the 1920s and with a different kind of rhythmic clarity, but the difference is one of *style* as much as competence.

In a similar way, the routine use by string players of convenient porta-mentos in early 20th-century recordings, to which Flesch objected, can sound impossibly lugubrious to unaccustomed modern listeners. But recordings prove that it was an accepted practice until the 1920s, and it cannot be dismissed as old-fashioned carelessness.

If early 20th-century performance practice, with its lavish portamento, sparing vibrato, tempo changes, agogic rubato and casual rhythmic details, now seems old-fashioned, then the corollary is that late 20th-century style, with its sparing portamento, prominent vibrato, tempo control, more literal interpretation of note values and clarity of detail, can be seen as a recent development. This has implications not only for our view of the early 20th century, but also for our conjectures about the practices of earlier periods.

Notes

[1] For a discussion of orchestral recordings during this period, see R. Philip, *Some Changes in Style of Orchestral Playing 1920–1950 as Shown by Gramophone Recordings* (diss., U. of Cambridge, 1974).

[2] The relationship between early 20th-century and late 19th-century violin playing is discussed in C. Brown, 'Bowing Styles, Vibrato and Portamento in Nineteenth-Century Violin Playing', *JRMA*, cxiii (1988), 97.

[3] C. Flesch, *The Art of Violin Playing*, i (Berlin, 1923, 2/1929; Eng. trans., 1924, 2/1939), ii (Berlin, 1928; Eng. trans., 1930, 2/1939), i, 40.

[4] Writers confirm this, for example A. Rivardé, *The Violin and its Technique* (London, 1921), 27; for Joachim's own condemnation of habitual vibrato, see J. Joachim and A. Moser, *Violinschule* (Berlin, 1905), ii, 94.

[5] L. Auer, *Violin Playing as I Teach It* (New York, 1921), 24.

[6] Ševčík's writings include *Schule der Violin-Technik*, op.1 (Prague, 1881), and *Violin-Schule für Anfänger*, opp.6–9 (Leipzig, 1904–8).

[7] H. Chabert, *Le violon* (Lyons, 1900), 36.

[8] F. Emery, *The Violinist's Dictionary* (London and New York, 1925), 182.

[9] *Grove 1*, iv, 260.

[10] See S. Grimson and C. Forsyth, *Modern Violin-playing* (New York, 1920), 7–13; Rivardé, *The Violin*, 28.

[11] *Grove 3*, v, 494.

[12] *Art of Violin Playing*, i, 40.

[13] 329–70.

[14] *Art of Violin Playing*, i, 30.

[15] *Grove 2*, iv, 482.

[16] F. Thistleton, *The Art of Violin Playing* (London and New York, 1924), 127.

[17] *Violin Fingering*, 365.

[18] Auer, *Violin Playing*, 24–5.

[19] (Hamburg, 1889; Eng. trans., 1893), 67.

[20] ibid., 39.

[21] *Technics of Violoncello Playing* (London 1898, 4/1923), 137.

[22] H. Becker and D. Rynar, *Mechanik und Ästhetik des Violoncellspiels* (Vienna, 1929/R1971).

[23] 193–4.

[24] ibid, 199.

[25] D. Alexanian, *The Technique of Violoncello Playing*, with preface by Casals (Paris, 1922), 96–7.

[26] J. M. Corredor, *Conversation with Casals* (London, 1956), 199.

[27] See R. Philip, 'The Recordings of Edward Elgar (1857–1934)', *EM*, xii (1984), 482.

[28] Boosey, London, and Schott, Mainz, respectively.

[29] These and other examples are given in Flesch, *Violin Fingering*, 367–9.

[30] W. Honeyman, *The Violin: How to Master it, by a Professional Player* (Newport, Fife, 5/1892), 27–30; J. Dunn, *Violin Playing* (London, 1898), 11; C. Schroeder, *Handbook of Violoncello Playing* (Hamburg, 1889; Eng. trans., 1893), 12.

[31] *Art of Violin Playing*, i, 11.

[32] Philip, *Some Changes in Style of Orchestral Playing*, chaps. 1 and 2.

[33] Berlioz, *Treatise on Instrumentation*, rev. R. Strauss (Leipzig, 1904; Eng. trans., 1948), 227.

[34] P. Taffanel and L. Fleury, 'Flute' in *Encyclopédie de la musique et dictionnaire du Conservatoire*, ed. A. Lavignac (Paris, 1921–31), ii, 1523 but see Taffanel and P. Gaubert, *Méthode complète de flûte* (Paris, 1923), ii, 186.

[35] J. Sellner, *Theoretische-praktische Oboeschule* (Vienna, 1825, rev.2/1901).

[36] See D. Ledet, *Oboe Reed Styles* (Bloomington, 1981).

[37] Berlioz–Strauss, *Treatise on Instrumentation*, 183.

[38] 'Orchestral Colours and Values', in *A Dictionary of Modern Music and Musicians* (London, 1924), 364.

[39] See M. Letellier and E. Flament, 'Le Basson' in *Encyclopédie de la musique*, ed. Lavignac, II, 1595.

[40] iv, 260.

[41] v, 494.

[42] Berlioz–Strauss, *Treatise on Instrumentation*, 270.

[43] C. Forsyth, *Orchestration* (London, 1914), 109.

[44] More information about the bore of brass instruments in the early 20th century can be found in A. Baines, *Brass Instruments* (London, 1976), 219–66, and E. Tarr, 'Trumpet' in *Grove MI*, iii, 650.

[45] R. Wagner, *On Conducting* (Leipzig, 1869; Eng. trans., 1887).

[46] N. Bauer-Lechner, *Erinnerungen an Gustav Mahler* (Vienna, 1923), 25; Eng. trans., *Recollections of Gustav Mahler* (London, 1980), 46.

[47] M. Steinitzer, *Richard Strauss* (Berlin, 1911), 52. Quoted in E. Kravitt, 'Tempo as an Expressive Element in the Late Romantic Lied', *MQ*, lix (1973), 506.

[48] Letter dated 1903, in *Letters to Nimrod from Edward Elgar*, ed. P. M. Young (London 1965), 192. For examples of Elgar's tempo fluctuations, see Philip, 'The Recordings of Edward Elgar', 481–9; and E. Turner, 'Tempo Variation: with Examples from Elgar', *ML*, xix (1938), 308–23.

[49] F. Weingartner, *On Conducting* (Berlin, 1895, rev.3/1905; Eng. trans., 1906), 27–9.

[50] Quoted in H. Schonberg, *The Great Conductors* (London, 1968), 252.

[51] 'Paderewski on Tempo Rubato', in H. Finck, *Success in Music and How it is Won* (New York, 1909), 459.

[52] T. Matthay, *Musical Interpretation* (London, 1913), 70–71.

[53] ibid, 63.

[54] Finck, *Success in Music*, 459.

[55] R. Dunstan, *A Cyclopaedic Dictionary of Music* (London, 1908).

[56] A. Greenish, *Dictionary of Musical Terms* (London, 1917).

[57] J. A. Johnstone, *Essentials in Pianoforte Playing and Other Musical Studies* (London, 1914), 45.

[58] J. A. Fuller Maitland, *Joseph Joachim* (London and New York, 1905), 29–30.

[59] F. Taylor, *Technique and Expression in Piano Playing* (London, 1897), 73. See also F. Niecks, 'Tempo Rubato from the Aesthetic Point of View', *MMR*, xliii (1913), 29.

[60] J. B. McEwen, *Tempo Rubato or Time Variation in Musical Performance* (London, 1928).

[61] O. Bie, *Das Klavier und seine Meister* (Munich, 1898), Eng. trans., *A History of the Pianoforte and Pianoforte Players* (London, 1899/R1966), 57.

[62] W. H. Breare, *Vocalism: its Structure and Culture from an English Standpoint* (London, 1904), 108.

[63] See Philip, *Some Changes in Style of Orchestral Playing*, 237–334; and 'The Recordings of Edward Elgar', 484.

[64] A. Dolmetsch, *The Interpretation of the Music of the XVII and XVIII Centuries* (London, 1915, 2/1946/R1969), 53.

[65] Weingartner, *On Conducting*, 14.

[66] See Philip, *Some Changes in Style of Orchestral Playing*, 237–334.

[67] See I. Stravinsky, *An Autobiography* (New York, 1936/R1962), 148.

[68] ibid., 152.

[69] For examples from Elgar, see Philip, 'The Recordings of Edward Elgar', 484–5.

[70] Auer, *Violin Playing*, 24. See also van der Straeten, *Technics of Violoncello Playing*, 137, and 'Slide', *Grove 2*, iv, 482–3.

[71] R. Hughes, *Musical Guide* (London, 1903).

[72] For an example of the first, see 'Vibrato' and 'Tremolo' in *Grove 1* and 2, for an example of the second, see Dunstan, *Cyclopaedic Dictionary of Music*, 'Vibrato' and 'Tremolo'.

[73] Johnstone, *Essentials in Pianoforte Playing*, 81. For a selection of similar remarks, see M. Metfessel, 'The Vibrato in Artistic Voices' in *Studies in the Psychology of Music*, ed. C. Seashore, i (Iowa, 1932), 104–9.

[74] Seashore, *Studies*.

[75] For a study of singing styles during this period, see J. B. Steane, *The Grand Tradition* (London, 1974).

[76] Stravinsky, *An Autobiography*, 150.

CHAPTER XXIII

Since 1940

PAUL GRIFFITHS

This chapter will be a little different from those that have gone before in that it will be concerned more with questions than answers and more with ignorance than knowledge. This is partly for reasons of historical closeness. Students of performance practice in all ages will be aware that contemporary documents often expatiate on topics which are of marginal concern to the modern performer while remaining silent on exactly those matters that now seem most problematic; the chronicler's difficulty is one of distinguishing in the mass of current facts those that will be most useful to the future.

The task is, of course, made lighter by the availability of recordings, but the usefulness of these can be exaggerated, and they introduce almost as many problems as they solve. For instance, although the major works of Stravinsky, Britten, Copland and Stockhausen have nearly all been recorded in performances supervised by the composers, the authority that should be given these recordings is not certain. Stockhausen has indicated that his recordings are to be taken as adjuncts to the published scores, and in at least one case has even asked that the recording be understood as a correction.[1] But this begs many questions about the relationships between evidence in recorded sound and evidence in print, some of which will be considered in what follows. In many ways Stravinsky appears more realistic in his statement that he could not make any of his recordings 'the same way again',[2] implying that any performance is unique and therefore partial as a guide to practice. As he says elsewhere among these remarks:

> The fifty recordings of the Beethoven symphony are fifty different angles of distortion, but these distortions actually protect the scope of the work: the larger the variorum, the greater the guarantee that Beethoven himself will remain intact. The recording of the contemporary, on the other hand, lacking comparison, fixes the music at a single angle, and the gravest danger of this fixed angle, which is that the truly contemporary exists on the precarious edge of the comprehensible, is not obvious.[3]

Since any new artistic statement will draw nearer to what is not understood, Stravinsky suggests, a single approach may not be enough to capture its particular essence; instead it may be reduced to the level of what is known, or may instead fall in the other direction and become nonsense. The ideal, of course, would be that every major work (always assuming such could be distinguished) should be recorded by as many different performances as possible, but in the real world very few works indeed are likely to receive as many performances and recordings as had been enjoyed by *The Rite of*

Spring before the composer's death. And yet the central problem to which Stravinsky draws attention, that of defining the essence of the new, is hardly being lessened in an age of such multifarious musical activity.

The problem is, however, arguably reduced in those works that carry within themselves standards against which their qualities can be measured: works that evidently belong to some tradition. The nature of a Shostakovich symphony, for example, is perhaps more immediately apparent than is the nature of an orchestral work by Xenakis. Because more aspects of the music are shared with other music, the performer will more readily have a sense of which features are peculiar to the work in question. Performers will also be able to draw on their experience of playing other similar works, perhaps from quite different periods: one can imagine, for instance, that the experience of Haydn might be useful in the performance of Shostakovich, but not of Xenakis.

This assumption is not without its dangers. For one thing, the use of a past form, style or rhetoric may be ironical, implying not a similar manner of performance but a pretence at similarity, even a false similarity. In the case of Shostakovich, the tone of his heroic endings has been debated, both before and after the publication of purported memoirs that indicated his intentions were indeed ironic.[4] The assumption of traditional qualities, simply because a score looks traditional, is therefore a decision of performance, and has to be made awarely, especially in the case of much music written since 1970, where real or seeming traditionalism is often to be found. In that respect the works of high modernism, those produced by Stockhausen and Boulez in the 1950s for example, may be easier to perform than the post-modern works of David Del Tredici or Ligeti, for in the first case the difficulties are all at the surface level of technique, whereas in the second they are at the deeper level of intention. And so Shostakovich may after all be more problematic than Xenakis.

The difficulties at the level of technique, however, are certainly not to be underestimated, least of all in the music of Xenakis. Peter Hill, a pianist with Xenakis in his repertory, has stated that with this music 'the "victory" of playing all the notes exactly may only be attainable in slow motion, while the "defeat" of total incoherence is certain if exactness is attempted at the indicated speed'.[5] In the same article he goes further, and suggests ways in which the published text may be altered in the interests of practicability. Ex.1 shows a passage from *Evryali* which it is indeed hard to imagine being played 'correctly' (1*a*), together with Hill's 'performing solution' (1*b*). Other pianists have hotly contested the need for such simplifications,[6] but no one seems yet to have proved – as would be possible, given a recording and a patient accounter of notes – that such a work as *Evryali* can be played as notated.

Perhaps the test has not been made because of an awareness that it would not prove anything. The feasibility of literal performance is hardly evidence of musical quality. And if it proved impossible to find an accurate perform- ance of *Evryali*, then an apologist for Xenakis might argue that the work was intended to be impossible, and hence to stretch the technique of even the most accomplished virtuoso (Brian Ferneyhough has argued along these lines in excusing his highly complex notation),[7] or else that the work's

Ex.1 Xenakis: *Evryali*

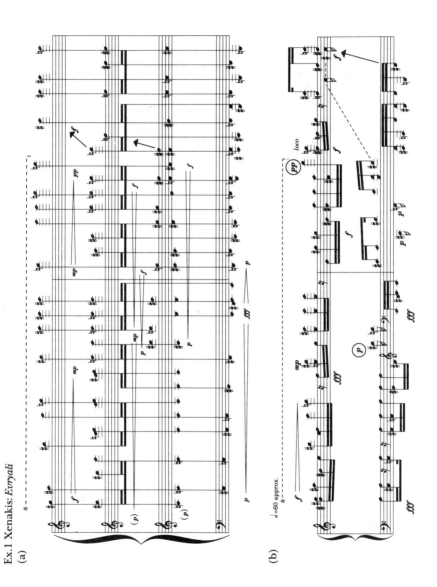

demands were simply beyond the scope of any living pianist and might conceivably be met in the future. Such an apologist might alternatively take the Cagean position, implicit in such works as *34' 46.776"* for piano, that 'impossible' notation serves to limit, and perhaps even eliminate, the scope for 'interpretation', and that this is not a 'fault' in the composition but an essential part of it. Possibly the only thing to be said with much certainty is that the idea of the score as representing some sounding ideal has been called into question, and that the question seems to be posed more acutely by the music of Xenakis (or Ferneyhough or Cage) than it is by that of Shostakovich.

But this is not a matter restricted to recent music; there would be no need for such a book as this if we still had complete trust in the score alone as the medium of musical intention. Developments in contemporary music may therefore only mirror general developments in the art, perhaps in the culture, even if they do so in an extreme fashion because present doubts have entered into the substance of creation. If the score is no longer a sufficient documentation of an intended performance then it may become something else: a challenge, as in Hill's view of Xenakis or Ferneyhough's view of himself, or a record of musical structures which have little or no possibility of expression in sound, or a graphic design. And while in extreme cases it may be any of these things absolutely, much more common are those hybrid instances where the score seems to combine old and new functions; the extremes, however, may illustrate these points more immediately.

Ex.2 shows a bar from Boulez's *Structure Ib* where it would seem beyond

Ex.2 Boulez: *Structures 1b*

dispute that the notation has gone over the bounds of relevance to performance. But the apparently excessive fastidiousness does turn out to be necessary to the deduction of the rhythmic structure at this point, and since this was a work in which Boulez was trying to lay the foundations of a new musical grammar, his notational exactitude has an obvious didactic function. Of course, there is no problem of performance practice here, but problems may well arise when the need to define a performer's activity is combined with the need to indicate some theoretical derivation which again may be irrelevant to performance. Conceivably this is the case with the example quoted from *Evryali*, in which case the player's 'performing solution' would have to take account not only of his view of practicality but also of his analysis of what is sonic intention in the music, and what is theoretical exposition. It is as if the player were required to make a translation into plain language of a paper in highly technical wording – with all the inevitabilities of mistranslation that are part of any such activity.

To raise this issue is to open the cloudy territory of the performer's commitment to the text, but perhaps one may suggest this commitment may be affected by the degree to which technical difficulties can be 'justified' as structural: the degree to which the theoretical exposition is identified with

the sonic intention. And it may be relevant here to quote from two more
piano works which rival *Evryali* in fearsomeness, the Cage work already
mentioned, his *34' 46.776"* (Ex.3), and Babbitt's *Post-Partitions* (Ex.4). The
large group in the Cage example occupies approximately a second and a half,

Ex.3 Cage: *34' 46.766"*

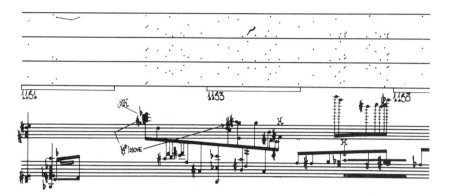

Ex.4 Babbitt: *Post Partitions*

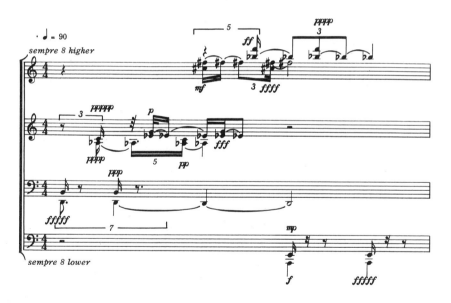

within which time the player must play two notes on the strings (those
marked 'H') and move the object used to prepare the *a♯'* between the two
appearances of that note. In addition, attention has to be given to the three
superior bands, indicating, from top to bottom, the force of attack (most at
the top), its distance (furthest from the keyboard at the top) and its speed
(slowest at the top). The Babbitt passage is perhaps more realistic in its

demands, though it should be noted that the distinction, say, between *pppp* and *ppppp* for the first notes on the second staff is crucial to the proper elucidation of the rhythmic organization.[8] Knowing as much, or at least knowing the aesthetic standpoints commonly associated with Xenakis, Cage and Babbitt, a performer may be inclined to feel that Xenakis's notation is designed to produce a general effect, Cage's to be absurdly challenging and Babbitt's to be aimed at an impossible ideal, relevant more to the reader than to the pianist. The grounds for such suppositions, however, would remain largely external to the actual works, and to a large degree suspect. They would offer the performer no assistance in dealing with a work by a composer whose background and opinions were unfamiliar.

The problem here might again be seen as that of discerning the intention contained within the printed score; but it is hard to maintain that view of performance when so much music seems to question the duality of message and medium. In the case of Cage, for instance, all his music since the late 1940s has been concerned with non-intention; there is, ideally, nothing behind the notes, and so perhaps the ideal performance would have to be no performance at all, unless one allowed the performer the paradoxical task of realizing a supposed intention of non-intention. Babbitt's position is super-ficially entirely different, but the very plethora of intentions in his scores produces a no less puzzling result. Whereas a performer of Mozart might justifiably assume a hierarchy of intentions, so that liberties with accent, dynamic level, phrasing and tempo would be more allowable than liberties with rhythm, and liberties with rhythm more allowable than liberties with pitch, in Babbitt there is no such hierarchy: as has been pointed out, a tiny distinction in dynamic nuance may be at the same level of meaning as a choice of pitch. A performer might argue that the 'meaning' here is more theoretical than practical, but such a view would be informed by an experience of Mozart rather than Babbitt: it would be a perpetuation of attitudes that may no longer be relevant. And again, the whole message of such a book as this is that the old view of a hierarchy of intention may not be justified in any music, that matters previously left to personal choice or tradition must be subjected to scrutiny in the light of documentary research, that the timbres of Mozart are indeed as important as the harmonies.

The endpoint of this attitude, in so far as it affects new music, might be the creation of electronic works on tape, and Babbitt has indeed suggested that he works with the RCA Synthesizer in order to avoid inaccurate performance.[9] The quandaries of performance practice then become merely those of sound reproduction. However, the weight of this argument rests on the asumption that the performer is or should be the channel for the realization of the composer's thought, that the performer's role is in essence no different from that of an amplifier and loudspeakers. And this assump-tion finds itself without any grounding once the notion of the score as representing sonic intention has gone: if the performer's duty is not that of actualizing some ideal embedded within the printed notes, then the relation-ship between composer and performer may become rather different.

One obvious alternative to the author–executant model is the facilitator–exhibitionist one: the score is created as a vehicle for virtuosities. This is, of course, a long-established way of working, though developments in notation during recent decades have enabled scores to record more outlandish feats than could be prescribed by Handel in writing for his singers (or indeed Britten in writing for his, Britten having remained among the large group of composers virtually to ignore new signs). Vast difficulties of performance practice result from such extensions; difficulties which it is beyond the scope of this chapter to survey. But one may note that the performance of the Sprechgesang in *Pierrot lunaire* remains a crux,[10] and that the lack of notational uniformity, even for relatively common effects like chords on solo woodwind instruments,[11] has acted against the evolution of a performing tradition. This alone makes it impossible to offer any general remark, other than that each score will require its own study. The problems here are again intimately connected with the evaporation of confidence in notation as a visual representation of an acoustic ideal. Some composers may have attempted to regain that traditional ground by using new symbols for new sounds, often providing a lengthy preface of instructions in the new code;[12] but this is to enter a vicious circle. If each effect requires its own symbol, then the notation rapidly becomes as complex as that already quoted from Xenakis, Cage and Babbitt, so that the possibility of an accurate rendering begins to recede.

One solution may be for the composer to avoid the imperfections of notation by working with a chosen group of performers. Reich, Glass and other minimalists, for instance, have at various times worked exclusively with their own ensembles, and Boulez became a conductor in the first place in order to secure adequate performances of his music. Yet even in his case, where the breakdown in the relationship between composer and performer is resolved by their being united in one person, his recorded performances have revealed profound difficulties.[13] For instance, both his recordings of *Pli selon pli* take a tempo at the start of 'Tombeau' which manifestly contradicts the score; yet in neither case does he observe, as in the Stockhausen case mentioned above, that the recording is to be taken as a correction. Perhaps this may be interpreted as a reversion to the old implicit theory of a hierarchy in musical values, so that tempo could be seen as a relatively malleable function. And yet Boulez's scores are remarkable for the precision with which this function is stipulated, suggesting the uncomfortable idea that score and performance are now so loosely linked as to be potentially dissimilar, and that there may be possibilities of performance which the score does not record. If the score has lost its authority to that extent, then there is no obvious reason why the composer's recordings should be presumed as carrying authority either, in which case future performers of *Pli selon pli* have nothing in which to place their trust.

Paradoxically, Boulez's recordings do not exploit one area in which the score of *Pli selon pli* exposes its lack of authority, for both performances choose the same ordering of events in the final section of 'Don'. More generally, however, aleatory notations have appeared to extend the variability of performance, and to recognize the dissolution of the authority of score and composer by making both more stimulators than directors of musical activity. The range of aleatory notations, like that of new symbols for new instrumental and vocal effects, became enormous during the 1960s, but the essential points may be made with reference to a rather extreme example,

Ex.5 Stockhausen: *Prozession*

Elektronium gibt $\begin{array}{|c|}\hline R \quad 8 \\ D \\\hline\end{array}$

Per	Per		Per	+	Per	Per		
		+						
+	+	+	+	+	+	+	+	+
		+						
				+				

from Stockhausen's *Prozession* (Ex.5), one of several works written for his own live electronic ensemble. This passage is from the tam tam part, and shows that the player must follow the lead of the electronium in register ('R') and duration ('D') for eight changes of event. The mathematical symbols are to be applied to the parameters of register, duration, volume and internal complexity, so that, for example, the fourth event may be higher and longer (or longer and louder, or higher and more subdivided, etc) than the third. The sign 'Per' indicates a movement towards regular periodicity.

Thus the score seeks to make possible 'chain reactions of imitation, transformation and mutation'[14] starting out from the players' memories of earlier Stockhausen works. Yet it must be obvious that, even given this experience, the notation defines the sounds only very loosely, and that performers could very rapidly move from the Stockhausen memories in any direction they wanted. Of course, performances by Stockhausen's ensemble have been under his direction, and with him controlling filters and potentiometers. But it is an open question whether performers should take his performances as a guide. If they do, then they are compromising what would appear to be the essential spirit of the work: the creation of a group musical activity feeding only from memory (of the specified earlier Stockhausen works) and momentary event. If they do not, then they may easily produce something entirely different from Stockhausen's recording.

The tendency in Stockhausen's works of this period, and in much other music at the time, was towards the intuitive, the improvisatory. Under such conditions, the identity of a work begins to break down, and there may be no meaningful sense in which a performance of *Prozession* is any longer possible; it was created for a particular group of people at a particular time, and even if Stockhausen himself were to take charge of another group, the result would be so different as hardly to justify the use of the same title. In as much as *Prozession* has any real identity at all, that identity is locked into the authorized recording; and so an ostensibly libertarian composition may turn out to be as fixed as a tape piece by Babbitt.

However, and more alarmingly, this view of works as sealed into some past is capable of further extension. Once again, it would seem to underlie the current of thought that has produced the science of performance practice, which rests on a mistrust of the notion of a 'work' as profound as that conveyed by *Prozession*. If the score has lost its sovereignty, requiring correctives and commentaries from the study of performance practice, then works are no longer as directly available as they once were. One cannot re-create the work; one can re-create only a contemporary performance of it. In effect this is a victory of realism, hinging on a doubt that there is some ideal behind the score that is accessible to the musical intellect. Given that doubt, it is not surprising that the creation of scores should itself have become dubious to composers during the very period, the 1950s and 1960s, when the restoration of contemporary performance practices began to become a goal for musicians. If, nevertheless, a great deal of music has continued to be written – and indeed the expression of doubt in aleatory notations has ceased to be necessary – that is not because any certainty has been found. Music can only be created now in the face of a strong suspicion that future performances will necessarily be antiquarian, and perhaps a greater optimism will come only when one can be optimistic that the performance of Bach may be continuous rather than retrospective.

Notes

[1] Note to recording of *Refrain*, Vox STGBY 638 (1969).

[2] I. Stravinsky and R. Craft, *Dialogues* (London, 1982), 121.

[3] ibid, 120.

[4] *Testimony: the Memoirs of Shostakovich*, ed. S. Volkov (New York, 1979).

[5] 'Xenakis and the Performer', *Tempo*, no.112 (1975), 18.

[6] See letters from Y. Takahashi and S. Pruslin in *Tempo*, no.115 (1975), 53–4, and Hill's reply in *Tempo*, no.116 (1976), 54–5.

[7] See for example the performance notes published with his *Cassandra's Dream Song* for solo flute.

[8] For an analysis of this bar see P. Griffiths, *Modern Music: the Avant-garde since 1945* (London, 1981), 156.

[9] See his 'On Relata I', *PNM*, ix/1 (1970), 22.

[10] See for example P. Boulez, *Relevés d'apprenti* (Paris, 1966), 262–4.

[11] The classic and highly influential text on these is B. Bartolozzi, *New Sounds for Woodwind* (London, New York and Toronto, 1967).

[12] See for example works by Luciano Berio, Hans Werner Henze, Peter Maxwell Davies and Brian Ferneyhough, particularly those from the late 1960s and early 1970s.

[13] See P. Griffiths, 'Le marteau de son maître, or Boulez selon Boulez', *Pierre Boulez: eine Festschrift zum 60. Geburtstag am 26. Marz 1985* (Vienna, 1985), 154–8.

[14] Note to recording of *Prozession*, Vox STGBY 615 (1969).

Bibliography of Sources

1. Keyboard

(a) General

J. Bermudo, *El libro llamado declaración de instrumentos musicales* (Osuna, 1555/*R*1957)

T. de Santa María, *Libro llamado arte de tañer fantasía* (Valladolid, 1565/*R*1972)

E. M. Ammerbach, *Orgel-oder Instrument Tablatur* (Leipzig, 1571, rev. 2/1583/*R*1984)

———, *Ein new künstlich Tabulaturbuch* (Leipzig, 1575)

A. de Cabezón, Preface to *Obras de música para tecla, arpa e vihuela de Antonio de Cabezón*, ed. H. de Cabezón (Madrid, 1578); ed. H. Anglés, MME, xvii (1966)

G. Diruta, *Il transilvano dialogo sopra il vero modo di sonar organi, et istromenti da penna* (Venice, 1593/*R*1978, 1983); ed. in BMB, 2nd ser., cxxxii (n.d.)

A. Banchieri, *L'organo suonarino*, op.13 (Venice, 1605, rev. 2/1611 as op.25; rev. 3/1622 as op.43); Eng. trans. D. E. Marcase, *Adriano Banchieri's 'L'organo suonarino': Translation, Transcription and Commentary* (diss., Indiana U., 1970)

C. Antegnati, *L'arte organica* (Venice, 1608); ed. R. Lunelli (Mainz, 1938, 2/1958)

M. Praetorius, *Syntagma musicum*, i (Wittenberg and Wolfenbüttel, 1614–15/*R*1959, 1968); ii (Wolfenbüttel, 1618, 2/1619/*R*1958, 1980; Eng. trans., 1962, 1986); iii (Wolfenbüttel, 1618, 2/1619/*R*1958, 1976)

S. Scheidt, *Tabulatura nova* (Hamburg, 1624), ed. M. Seiffert, DDT, i (1892, 2/1958); ed. C. Mahrenholz (Hamburg, 1953)

F. Correa de Arauxo, *Libro de tientos y discursos de música practica, y theorica de organo intitulado Facultad organica* (Alcalá, 1626/*R*1948)

J. Nenning [Spiridion], *Nova instructio pro pulsandis organis, spinettis, manuchordiis*, i–ii (Bamberg, 1669–71); iii–iv (Gerbstedt, 1675)

L. Penna, *Li primi albori musicali per li principianti della musica figurata* (Bologna, 1672, 4/1684/ *R*1969, 5/1696)

B. Bismantova, *Compendio musicale*, MS, Ferrara, 1677/*R*1978

Anon., *Vermehrter und nun zum zweytenmal in Druck berfördeter kurtzer jedoch gründlicher Wegweiser* (Augsburg, 1693)

H. Purcell, *A Choice Collection of Lessons for the Harpsichord or Spinnet* (London, 1696/*R*, 3/ 1699)

D. Speer, *Gründrichtiger . . . Unterricht der musicalischen Kunst oder Vierfaches musicalisches Kleeblatt* (Ulm, 1697/*R*1974); altered and expanded version of *Gründrichtiger . . . Unterricht der musicalischen Kunst* (Ulm, 1687); Eng. trans. in H. E. Howey, *A Comprehensive Performance Project in Trombone Literature* (diss., U. of Iowa, 1971)

?M. de Saint-Lambert, *Les principes du clavecin, contenant une explication exacte de toute ce qui concerne la tablature et le clavier* (Paris, 1702/*R*1974); Eng. trans. R. Harris-Warwick (Cambridge, 1984)

J. B. Samber, *Manuductio ad organum* (Salzburg, 1704)

?M. de Saint-Lambert, *Nouveau traité de l'accompagnement du clavecin, de l'orgue et des autres instruments* (Paris, 1707); Eng. trans. S. F. Burchill, *Saint Lambert's 'Nouveau traité de l'accompagnement': a Translation and Commentary* (diss., U. of Rochester, 1979)

F. Gasparini, *L'armonico pratico al cimbalo* (Venice, 1708/*R*1967); Eng. trans. F. S. Stillings, as *The Practical Harmonist at the Keyboard*, ed. D. L. Burrows (New Haven, 1963)

J. D. Heinichen, *Neu erfundene und gründliche Anweisung . . . zu vollkommener Erlernung des General-Basses* (Hamburg, 1711)

F. Couperin, *L'art de toücher le clavecin* (Paris, 1716, 2/1717; Eng. trans., 1933); ed. M. Halford (Port Washington, 1974)

Bibliography

J.-P. Rameau, 'Principes d'accompagnement' in *Traité de l'harmonie reduite à ses principes naturels* (Paris, 1722; Eng. trans., 1737); ed. and Eng. trans. P. Gossett (New York, 1971)

——, *Pièces de clavecin avec une méthode pour la mécanique des doigts* (Paris, 1724, rev. 2/1731 as *Pièces de clavecin avec une table pour les agréments*)

P. Prelleur, *The Harpsichord Illustrated and Improved* (London, c1730)

J.-P. Rameau, *Dissertation sur les différentes méthodes d'accompagnement pour le clavecin ou pour l'orgue* (Paris, 1732)

J. Mattheson, *Kleine General-Bass-Schule* (Hamburg, 1735)

F. A. Maichelbeck, *Die auf dem Clavier spielende ... Caecilia*, opp.1–2 (Augsburg, 1736–8)

J. Mattheson, *Der vollkommene Capellmeister* (Hamburg, 1739/R1954; Eng. trans., 1981)

L. Mizler, *Anfangs-Gründe des General-Basses nach mathematischer Lehr-Art abgehandelt* (Leipzig, 1739), 68

C. A. Thielo, *Tanker og regler fra grunden af om musik for dem, som vil laere musiken til sindets fornøjelse, saa og for dem, som vil gjøre fait af klaver, general-bassen og synge-kunsten* [Thoughts and rules providing an introduction for those who wish to learn music to delight the mind, as well as for those who wish to learn keyboard playing, thoroughbass and the art of singing] (Copenhagen, 1746)

M. Corrette, *Les amusemens du Parnasse, méthode courte et facile pour apprendre à toucher le clavecin avec les plus jolis airs à la mode où les doigts sont chiffrés pour les commençans ensemble des principes de musique* (Paris, 1749, enlarged 2/1779); repr. in C. G. Lister, *Traditions of Keyboard Technique from 1650 to 1750* (diss., U. of North Carolina, Chapel Hill, 1979)

F. W. Marpurg, *Die Kunst das Clavier zu spielen durch den Verfasser des critischen Musicus an der Spree* (Berlin, 1750, rev. and enlarged 4/1762/R1969; Fr. trans., Berlin, 1756/R1973, 2/1760 as *Les Principes du clavecin*; Eng. trans. E. L. Hays, *F. W. Marpurg's 'Anleitung zum Clavierspielen' (Berlin, 1755) and 'Principes du clavecin' (Berlin, 1756): Translation and Commentary* (diss., Stanford U., 1977)

J. X. Nauss, *Gründlicher Unterricht den General-Bass recht zu erlernen* (Augsburg, 1751)

C. Avison, *An Essay on Musical Expression* (London, 1752, rev. 2/1753/R1967, 3/1775)

C. P. E. Bach, *Versuch über die wahre Art das Clavier zu spielen* (Berlin, 1753–62, 2/1787–97/R1957); Eng. trans. ed. W. J. Mitchell, as *Essay on the True Art of Playing Keyboard Instruments* (New York, 1949)

F. Geminiani, *The Art of Accompaniment* (London, c1754)

F. W. Marpurg, *Anleitung zum Clavierspielen der schönen Ausübung der heutigen Zeit gemäss* (Berlin, 1755, 2/1765/R1969; Dutch trans., 1760/R1970); Eng. trans. E. L. Hays, *F. W. Marpurg's 'Anleitung zum Clavierspielen' (Berlin, 1755) and 'Principes du clavecin' (Berlin, 1756): Translation and Commentary* (diss., Stanford U., 1977)

J. Adlung, *Anleitung zu der musikalischen Gelahrtheit* (Erfurt, 1758/R1953, 2/1783)

N. Pasquali, *Thorough-Bass Made Easy* (Edinburgh, 1757, later edn., 1763/R1974 with preface by J. Churchill)

L. Frischmuth, *Gedagten over de beginselen en onderwijzingen des clavecimbaals* (Amsterdam, 1758)

N. Pasquali, *The Art of Fingering the Harpsichord* (Edinburgh, 1758)

G. S. Löhlein, *Clavier-Schule, oder kurze und gründliche Anweisung zur Melodie und Harmonie* (Leipzig and Züllichau, 1765, 6/1791 ed. J. G. Witthauer, 6/1804 ed. A. E. Müller, 8/1825 ed. C. Czerny, 9/1848 ed. F. Knorr)

M. J. F. Wiedeburg, *Der sich selbst informirende Clavier-Spieler* (Halle and Leipzig, 1765–75)

F. Bédos de Celles, *L'art du facteur d'orgues* (Paris, 1766–78/R1963–6; Ger. trans., 1793; Eng. trans., 1977); ed. C. Mahrenholz (Kassel, 1934–6, 2/1963–6)

J. S. Petri, *Anleitung zur praktischen Musik, vor neuangehende Sänger und Instrumentspieler* (Lauban, 1767, enlarged 2/1782/R1969)

J. Adlung, *Musica mechanica organoedi*, ed. J. L. Albrecht (Berlin, 1768/R1961); ed. C. Mahrenholz (Kassel, 1931)

J.-J. Rousseau, 'Doigter', *Dictionnaire de musique* (Paris, 1768/R1969)

V. Manfredini, *Regole armoniche, o sieno Precetti ragionati* (Venice, 1775, 2/1797)

J. P. Kirnberger, *Grundsätze des Generalbasses als erste Linien zur Composition* (Berlin, 1781/R1974), 3

A. F. Petschke, *Versuch eines Unterrichts zum Klavierspielen* (Leipzig, 1785)

E. W. Wolf, *Vorbericht als eine Anleitung zum guten Vortrag beim Klavier-Spielen* (Leipzig, 1785)

D. G. Türk, *Von den wichtigsten Pflichten eines Organisten: ein Beytrag zur Verbesserung der musikalischen Liturgie* (Halle, 1787/R1966, rev. 2/1838 by F. Naue)

————, *Clavierschule, oder Anweisung zum Clavierspielen für Lehrer und Lernende nebst 12 Handstücken* (Leipzig and Halle, 1789/*R*1962, enlarged 2/1802/*R*1967); Eng. trans. R. H. Haggh (Lincoln, Nebraska, 1982)

J. C. F. Rellstab, *Anleitung für Clavierspieler den Gebrauch der Bachschen Fingersetzung, die Manieren und den Vortrag betreffend*, op.62 (Rellstab op.4) (Berlin, 1790)

F. S. Sander, *Kurze und gründliche Anweisung zur Fingersetzung für Clavierspieler* (Breslau, 1791)

J. Blewitt, *A Complete Treatise on the Organ to which is added a Set of Explanatory Voluntaries* (London, *c*1795)

J. Gunn, *An Essay towards a more … Scientific Method of … the Study of the Pianoforte* (London, *c*1795)

J. H. Knecht, *Vollständige Orgelschule* (Leipzig, 1795–8)

J. L. Dussek, *Instructions on the Art of Playing the Piano Forte or Harpsichord* (London, 1796, and many later edns.; Fr. edn. as *Méthode pour le piano forte*, Paris, 1799; Ger. edn. as *Pianoforte-Schule*, Leipzig, 1802, 4/?1815)

A. E. Müller, *Anweisung zum genauen Vortrage der Mozartschen Clavier-Concerte* (Leipzig, 1796)

I. J. Pleyel and J. L. Dussek, *Méthode pour le piano forte* (Paris, 1796)

J. P. Milchmeyer, *Die wahre Art das Piano Forte zu Spielen* (Dresden, 1797)

L. Adam and L. W. Lachnith, *Méthode ou principe général du doigté pour le forte-piano* (Paris, 1798, 2/1814)

D. G. Türk, *Anweisung zum Generalbass-spielen* (Halle, rev. 2/1800/*R*1971)

M. Clementi, *Introduction to the Art of Playing on the Piano Forte* (London, 1801/*R*1974, rev.11/1826)

J. C. Kittel, *Der angehend praktische Organist* (Erfurt, 1801–8)

L. Adam, *Méthode nouvelle pour le piano* (Paris, 1802, 2/1805/*R*1974)

J. N. Forkel, *Über Johann Sebastian Bachs Leben, Kunst und Kunstwerke* (Leipzig, 1802/*R*1968; Eng. trans., 1820 and 1920)

A. Streicher, *Kurze Bemerkungen über das Spielen, Stimmen und Erhalten der Forte-Piano* (Vienna, 1802; Eng. trans., 1983)

L. Adam, *Méthode de piano du Conservatoire* (Paris, 1804)

D. Steibelt, *Méthode de pianoforte* (Paris, 1805)

J. B. Cramer, *Instructions for the Pianoforte* (London, 1812)

C. Czerny, *School of Extemporaneous Performance*, i–ii, opp.200 and 300 (Paris, ?*c*1816)

M. Clementi, *Gradus ad Parnassum, or The Art of Playing on the Piano Forte* (London, Leipzig and Paris, 1817–26)

F. Starke, *Wiener Pianoforte-Schule* (Vienna, 1819–21)

A. L. Crelle, *Einiges über musicalischen Ausdruck und Vortrag: für Fortepiano-Spieler* (Berlin, 1823)

J. N. Hummel, *Ausführliche theoretisch-practische Anweisung zum Piano-forte Spiel* (Vienna, 1828, rev. 2/1838; Eng. trans., 1829)

F. Kalkbrenner, *Méthode pour apprendre le piano-forte à l'aide du guide-mains*, op.108 (Paris, 1831, 3/1837; Eng. trans., 1866)

C. Montal, *L'art d'accorder soi-même son piano* (Paris, 1836/*R*1976)

C. Czerny, *Letters to a Young Lady on the Art of Playing the Pianoforte*, ed. and trans. J. A. Hamilton (New York, ?1837–41)

————, *Complete Theoretical and Practical Piano Forte School*, op.500 (London, 1839)

————, *Erinnerungen aus meinem Leben* (MS, *A-Wgm*, 1842; Eng. trans., *MQ*, xlii (1956), 302

A. Kullak, *Die Ästhetik des Klavierspiels* (Berlin, 1861; Eng. trans., 1893)

A. Marmontel, *L'art classique et moderne du piano* (Paris, 1876)

M. Jaëll, *Le mécanisme du toucher* (Paris, 1897)

(b) Organ, from c1800

H. Laag, *Anfangsgründe zum Clavierspielen und Generalbarr* (Osnabruck, 1774)

F. Schmoll, MS, *D-B* Mus.ms. 30196

J. Marsh, *Eighteen Easy Voluntaries*, [i] (London, 1791)

————, *Eight Voluntaries for the Organ … to which is prefix'd an Explanation of the Different Stops* (London, 1791)

J. Blewitt, *A Complete Treatise on the Organ* op.4 (London, *c*1795)

Bibliography

J. H. Knecht, *Vollständige Orgelschule für Angänger und Geübtere* (Leipzig, 1795–8)

F. Linley, *A Practical Introduction to the Organ* op.6 (London, 9/c1800)

S. P. Taylor, *Practical School for the Organ* (New York, c1800)

J. C. Kittel, *Der angehend praktische Organist* (Erfurt, 1801–8, 3/1831/R1981)

J. P. E. Martini, *Ecole d'orgue* (Paris, c1804)

J. H. Zang, *Der Vollkommene Orgelmacher* (Nuremberg, 1804, 2/1829)

F. Guthmann, 'Einige Worte über die Applikatur beym Choralspiel auf der Orgel und auf dem Pianoforte', *AMZ* (24 July 1805), 693–5

J. G. Werner, *Orgelschule* (Meissen, 1805–7)

J. C. H. Rinck, *Practische Orgelschule* op.55 (Bonn, 1818–21)

————, *Vorschule für angehende Organisten in gebundenen Spiele* op.82 (Bonn, 1827)

A. Hesse, *Nützliche Gabe für Organisten* (Breslau, 1830)

J. C. F. Schneider, *Handbuch des Organisten* (Haberstadt and Leipzig, 1830)

P. F. J. André, *Anleitung zum Selbstunterricht in Pedalspiel* (Offenbach, 1834)

J. C. A. Miné, *Méthode d'orgue* (Paris, c1836)

L. E. Gebhardi, *Theoretisch-praktische Orgelschule in Uebungen nebst Anweisung* (Brieg, 1837)

C. Czerny, *Complete Theoretical and Practical Piano Forte School* op.500 (London, 1839)

J. C. H. Rinck, *Die drei erste Monate auf die Orgel* op.121 (Bonn, 1839)

————, *Theoretisch-practische Anleitung zum Orgelspielen* op.124 (Darmstadt, 1839)

F. W. Schütze, *Practische Orgelschule* (Dresden and Leipzig, 2/c1839)

J. A. Hamilton, *A Standard Tutor for the Organ* (London, 1840, 2/1842, 3/1851, 4/1865, 5/1875)

P. F. J. André, *Kurzgefasste theoretisch-practische Orgelschule* op.25 (Offenbach, 1845)

A. C. Fessy, *Manuel d'orgue à l'usage des églises catholiques (Paris, c1845)

T. Loud, *The Organ Study* (Philadelphia, 1845)

F. Mendelssohn-Bartholdy, Prefatory Remarks, *Six Sonatas* op.65 (London, 1845)

J. C. Beckel, *Amateur's Organ School* (Boston, 1850)

J. Lemmens, *Nouveau journal* [two years] (Brussels, 1850–51)

J. C. F. Schneider, *Schneider's Practical Organ School* (Boston, 1851)

J. Zundel, Preface, *Two Hundred and Fifty Easy Voluntaries and Interludes* (New York, 1851)

W. T. Best, *Modern School of the Organ* (London, 1853)

C. Loret, *Cours d'orgue* op.19 (Paris, 1858)

————, 'Exercise Journalier', *La maîtrise*, ii (1858–9)

W. Volckmar, *Orgelschule* op.50 (Leipzig, 1858)

J. Zundel, *The Modern School for the Organ* (Boston, 1860)

H. Bönicke, *Die Kunst des freien Orgelspiels* (Leipzig, 1861)

J. Lemmens, *Ecole d'orgue* (Mainz, 1862)

J. G. Herzog, *Orgelschule* op.41 (Erlangen, 1867)

D. Buck, *18 Studies in Pedal Phrasing for the Organ* op.28 (New York, 1868, 1894)

E. F. Richter, *Katechismus der Orgel* (Leipzig, 1868, 3/1885)

E. Thayer, *The Art of Organ Playing* op.16 (Boston, 1870)

M. Lussy, *Traité de l'expression musicale* (Paris, 1874, 8/1904); Eng. trans. as *Musical Expression* (London, 1885)

F. Archer, *The Organ* (London, 1875)

J. Hiles, *Catechism of the Organ* (London, 1876, 2/1878, 3/1882, 4/1890)

D. Buck, *Illustrations in Choral Accompaniment and Hints in Registration* (New York, 1877)

J. Stainer, *The Organ* (London, 1877)

G. E. Whiting, Introduction, *20 Preludes, Postludes etc. for the Organ* (Boston, 1877)

E. Thayer, *Eugene Thayer's Complete Organ School* op.60 (Boston and New York, 1880)

G. Merkel, *Orgelschule* op.177 (Leipzig, early 1880s)

'Accentuation in Organ Playing', *Musical Record*, no.22 (16 Dec 1882), 207

M. Lussy, *Le rythme musical, son origine, sa fonction et son accentuation* (Paris, 1883)

H. Riemann and C. Fuchs, *Katechismus der Phrasierung* (Leipzig, 1886)

M. Hauptmann, *Die natur der Harmonik und Metrik* (Leipzig, 1853, 2/1873); Eng. trans. as *The Nature of Harmony and Metre* (London, 1888, 2/1893)

C. Locher, *Erklärung der Orgelregister* (Berne, 1887); Eng. trans. as *Dictionary of the Organ* (New York, 1914) and as *An Explanation of the Organ Stops* (London, 1888)

H. Riemann, *Katechismus der Orgel* (Leipzig, 1888)

H. Riemann and C. Armbrust, *Technische Studien für Orgel* (Leipzig, 1890); Eng. trans. as *Technical Studies for the Organ* (Leipzig, 1890)

'A Few Hints on Registration', *The Organ*, i/6 (Oct 1892), 127, 137

Bibliography

M. Reger, *Phantasie über den choral "Freu' dich sehr, O meine Seele"* op.30 (Leipzig, 1899)

C. M. Widor, 'Avant-Propos', *Symphonies pour orgue*, opp. 13, 42 (Paris, 1901)

M. Lussy, *L'Anacrouse dans la musique moderne* (Paris, 1903)

H. Riemann, *System der Musikalischen Rhythmik und Metrik* (Leipzig, 1903)

G. A. Audsley, *The Art of Organ Building*, (New York, 1905/R1965)

A. Schweitzer, *Deutsche und Französische Orgelbaukunst und Orgelkunst* (Leipzig, 1906/R1962, 2/1927)

W. H. Clarke, *How to Use Organ Stops and Pedals* (Reading, MA, 1908)

E. H. Lemare, 'The Art of Organ Playing', *The Musical Educator*, iv (London, c1910), pp. v–xv

A. Eaglefield Hull, *Organ Playing: its Technique and Expression* (London, 1911)

A. Cellier, *L'orgue moderne* (Paris, 1913)

C. M. Widor, Preface, *Jean-Sébastien Bach ... Oeuvres completes pour orgue: édition critique et pratique en huit volumes*, i (New York, 1914)

C. Eddy, *Pipe Organ Method* (Cincinnati, 1917)

W. Goodrich, *The Organ in France* (Boston, 1917)

E. M. Skinner, *The Modern Organ* (New York, 1917)

G. A. Audsley, *The Organ of the Twentieth Century* (New York, 1919/R1970)

E. Truette, *Organ Registration* (Boston, 1919)

N. Bonovia-Hunt, *The Church Organ* (London, 1920)

G. A. Audsley, *Organ Stops and their Artistic Registration* (New York, 1921)

C. Dickinson, *The Technique and Art of Organ Playing* (New York, 1922)

N. Bonovia-Hunt, *Modern Organ Stops* (London, 1923)

J. Huré, *L'esthétique de l'orgue* (Paris, 1923)

G. A. Audsley, *The Temple of Tone* (New York, 1925)

W. H. Barnes, *The Contemporary American Organ* (New York, 1930)

A. McCurdy, 'Lynnwood Farnam: a Few Reminiscences and an actual Example of Mr. Farnam's Minute Attention to the Details of Registration', *American Organist*, xiv/3 (March 1931), 149–51

C. M. Boyd, *Organ Accompaniment and Registration* (Philadelphia, 1932)

N. Bonovia-Hunt, *Modern Studies in Organ Tone* (London, 1933)

———, *The Organ of Tradition* (London, 1939)

A. Cellier, *Traité de la registration d'orgue* (Paris, 1957)

(c) Sources for fingering

(those cited in (a) above are given in the form J. Adlung (1758))

H. Buchner, *Fundament Buch, CH-Bu* F.i.8a

J. Bermudo (1555)

L. Venegas de Henestrosa, (*Libro de cifra nueva* (Alcalá, 1557)

T. de Santa María (1565)

E. M. Ammerbach (1571)

———, (1575)

A. de Cabezón (1578)

T. Tallis, 'Felix namque', *GB-Lbm* R.M.24.d.3

E. M. Ammerbach, *Orgel oder Instrument Tabulaturbuch* (Nuremberg, 1583)

G. Diruta (1593)

E. Bevin, 2 preludes, *GB-Lbm* Add.31403

J. Bull. 'Miserere', *GB-Och* 1207, *F-Pc* Rés.1186 bis ii; Preludes, *GB-Lbm* Add.31403, *Lcm* 2093, *Cu* Dd.4.22 8 et al; Pavans, almans, galliards, etc, *F-Pc* Rés.1185, *GB-Lbm* Add.36661 and R.M.24.d.3, *Cfm* 32.G.29

W. Byrd, 'Fortune', *GB-En* Panmure 9, *GB-Lbm* R.M.24.d.3; 'The Carman's Whistle', *GB-Lbm*, Add. 30486; 'Qui passe', etc, *GB-Lbm* R.M.24.d.3 and *My Ladye Nevells Booke*

Prencourt, 'Short, Easy & Plaine Rules', *GB-Lbm* Add.32351

A. Banchieri, Conclusioni nel suono dell'organo (Bologna, 1608)

O. Gibbons, 'Preludium', *GB-Och* 89, *F-Pc* Rés. 1186 bis ii, *GB-Hdolmetsch*; 'Fantasia', *GB-Och* 378, *F-Pc* Rés. 1186 bis ii; 'Whoop, do me no harm good man' etc, *GB-Och* 431, *F-Pc* Rés. 1186 *bis* ii and *Priscilla Bunbury's Virginal Book*; 'the Woods so Wild', 'The Italian Ground' etc, *GB-Lbm* Add.36661

A. Banchieri, *L'organo suonavino* (2/1611)

Bibliography

J. P. Sweelinck, Fantasias and toccatas, *D-Bds* Lynar Al

S. Scheidt (1624)

Anon., 'Courrante Lavigon', sarabandes, other dances, 'Engelendische Nachtigall', chorales etc [Danish, *c*1625], *Dk-Kk* Kgl. Saml. 376, 2°

F. Correa de Arauxo (1626)

R. Mesangeau, Allemande, *Dk-Kk* Kgl. Saml. 376, 2°

Anon., Diminutiones, Praeludia, suites [German, *c*1640], *D-W* Guelf 1055

G. Gentile, *Porta musicale*, *I-Rc* 2491

T. Tomkins, Prelude, Galliard etc, *F-Pc* Rés. 1122; 'For Edward' etc, *GB-Ob* mus. sch. c.93

W. Fabricius, 'Kürtze Praeambula vor Incipienten durch alle Claves', *Us-Cn*

G.-G. Nivers, *Livre d'orgue* (Paris, 1665)

J. Nenning [Spiridion] (1669–71)

L. Penna (1672)

B. Bismantova (1677)

J. H. Kittel, '12. Praeamb. durch all Claves auf clavichordien und Instrum.: zu gebrauchen', *R-BRm* 808

D. Speer (1687)

A. Raison, *Livre d'orgue* (Paris, 1688)

Anon., *Vermehrter und nun zum zweytenmal in Druck befördeter kurtzer jedoch gründlicher Wegweiser* (Augsburg, 1693)

H. Purcel (1696)

D. Speer (1697)

Anon., Preludes, voluntaries, 'The Canaries' [English, *c*1700], *GB-Lcm* 2093

————, 'Praelude oder Applicatio der rechten und lincken Hand', *D-LÜr* KN 149

D. Croner, 'Applicaturae', *R-BRm* 808

A. Scarlatti, 'Toccata primo' *GB-Lbm* Add.14244, *I-Nc* 34.6.31

?M. de Saint-Lambert (1702)

J. B. Samber (1704)

?M. de Saint-Lambert (1707)

F. Gasparini (1708)

J.-F. Dandrieu, *Pièces de clavecin courtes et faciles* (Paris, 1713)

F. Couperin (1716, 2/1717)

C. Graupner, *Partien auf das Clavier* (Darmstadt, 1718)

J. S. Bach, 'Prelude et Fugetta' BWV870a, *D-Bds* P 1089; 'Applicatio' BWV994 and Praeambulum BWV930, *Clavierbüchlein vor Wilhelm Friedemann Bach*, *US-NH*; 'Canzona' BWV588 etc, *D-Le* 7, part 21

G. F. Handel, 'Ciacona' HWV435, *GB-Lbm* Add.35177

D. Zipoli and anon., Minuet, *GB-Cfm* 57

J.-P. Rameau (1722)

————, (1724)

A. B. Della Ciaia, *Sonate per cembalo*, op.4 (Rome, 1727)

P. Prelleur (*c*1730)

J. G. Walther, *Gesammelte Werke für Orgel*, i; ed. M. Seiffert, DDT, xxvi (1906) [the sources of the fingerings have been lost or destroyed]

J. P. Rameau (1732)

M. Corrette, *Premier livre de pièces du clavecin* (Paris, 1734)

J. Mattheson (1735)

F. A. Maichelbeck (1735–8)

L. Mizler (1739)

C. A. Thielo (1746)

M. Corrette (1749)

Hartong [P. C. Humanus], *Musicus theoretico-practicus* (Nuremberg, 1749)

F. W. Marpurg (1750)

J. X. Nauss (1751)

C. P. E. Bach, *Achtzehn Probestück in sechs Sonaten* H70-75 (Berlin, 1753)

————, (1753–62)

F. W. Marpurg (1755)

————, (1756)

J. Adlung (1758)

L. Frischmuth (1758)

Bibliography

N. Pasquali (1758)

F. Gherardeschi, 'Elementi di contrappunto', *I-Bc*

G. S. Löhlein (1765)

M. J. F. Wiedeburg (1765–75)

C. P. E. Bach, *Kurze un leichte Klavierstücke mit veränderten Reprisen und beygefügter Fingerset-zung* H193–203, 228–3 (Berlin, 1766–8)

J. S. Petri (1767)

J.-J. Rousseau (1768)

V. Manfredini (1775, 2/1797)

J. P. Kirnberger (1781)

A. F. Petschke (1785)

C. P. E. Bach, *VI sonatine nuove* H292-97 (Hamburg, 1786, 2/1787)

D. G. Türk, *Klavierschule* (1789)

F. Sander (1791)

J. N. Forkel, 'Litteratur und Praxis der neuern Musik', *Allgemeine Litteratur der Musik* (Leipzig, 1792), 326, 331

J. H. Knecht (1795–8)

A. E. Müller (1796); see Löhlein (1765)

J. C. Kittel (1801–8)

J. N. Forkel (1802)

C. Czerny (1842); see also Löhlein (1765)

2. Voice

L. Zacconi, *Pratica di musica utile et necessaria si al compositore per comporre i canti suoi regolatamente, si anco al cantore* (Venice, 1592/*R*1967)

G. Caccini, *Le nuove musiche* (Florence, 1601/2/*R*1934); ed. H. W. Hitchcock in RRMBE, ix (1970); Eng. trans. by O. Strunk in *Source Readings in Music History* (London, 1950), 377

T. Coryat, *Coryat's Crudities* (London, 1611)

M. Praetorius, *Syntagma musicum*, i (Wittenberg and Wolfenbüttel, 1614–15/*R*1959, 1968); ii (Wolfenbüttel, 1618, 2/1619/*R*1958, 1980; Eng. trans., 1962, 1986); iii (Wolfenbüttel, 1618, 2/1619/*R*1958, 1976)

D. Friderici, *Musica figuralis, oder Newe Unterweisung der Singekunst* (1618, 4/1649); ed. E. Langelutje as *Die Musica figuralis des Daniel Friderici* (Berlin, 1901)

F. Rognoni, *Selva di varii passaggi secondo l'uso moderno per cantare e suonare con ogni sorte de stromenti* (Milan, 1620/*R*1970)

L. Zacconi, *Pratica di musica seconda parte* (Venice, 1622/*R*1967)

D. Hitzler, *Extract aus der Neuen Musica oder Singkunst* (Nuremberg, 1623)

V. Giustiniani, *Discorso sopra la musica* (Rome, 1628); Eng. trans. by C. MacClintock, MSD, ix (1962)

M. Mersenne, *Harmonie universelle: Livre sixième de l'art de bien chanter* (Paris, 1936–7/*R*1963)

G. B. Doni, *Annotazioni sopra il Compendio de' generi e de' modi della musica* (Rome, 1640); extracts ed. C. Gallico as 'Discorso sesto sopra il recitare in scene con l'accompagnamento d'instrumenti musicali', *RIM*, iii (1968), 286

J. A. Herbst, *Musica practica sive instructio pro symphoniacis, das ist Eine kurtze Anleitung, wie die Knaben . . . auf jetzige italienische Manier . . . unterrichtet werden* (Nuremberg, 1642, 2/1653 and 3/1658 as *Musica moderna prattica*)

C. Bernhard, *Von der Singe-Kunst, oder Maniera* (c1649); Eng. trans. in W. Hilse, 'The Treatises of Christoph Bernard', *Music Forum*, iii (1973), 1

J. Playford, *A (Breefe) Introduction to the Skill of Musick for Song and Violl* (London, 1654, rev. 7/1674/*R*1966, rev. 12/1694/*R*1973, rev. 19/1730)

J. Crüger, *Musicae practicae praecepta brevia et exercitia pro tyronibus varia. Der rechte Weg zur Singekunst* (Berlin, 1660)

J. Millet, *La belle méthode, ou l'art de bien chanter* (Besançon, 1666/*R*1963, ed. A. Cohen, and 1973)

B. de Bacilly, *Remarques curieuses sur l'art de bien chanter* (Paris, 1668/*R*1971, 4/1681); Eng. trans. by A. B. Caswell as *A Commentary Upon the Art of Proper Singing* (Brooklyn, 1968)

J. R. Ahle, *Brevis et perspicua introductio in artem musicam, das ist Eine kurtze Anleitung zu der lieblichen Singekunst mit etlichen Fugen und den gebräuchlichsten terminis musicis vermehret* (Mühlhausen, 1673); ed. J. G. Ahle as *Kurze doch deutliche Anleitung zu der lieblich- und loblichen Singekunst mit . . . nöhtigen Anmerkungen . . . zum Drukke befördert durch des seeligen Verfassers Sohn Johann Georg Ahlen* (Mühlhausen, 1690, enlarged 2/1704)

T. Mace, *Musick's Monument, or, A Remembrancer of the Best Practical Musik* (London, 1676); facs. with transcr. and commentary, ed. J. Jacquot and A. Souris (Paris, 1958/R1966)

W. C. Prinz, *Musica modulatoria vocalis oder Manierliche und zierliche Sing-Kunst* (Schweidnitz, 1678)

J. Rousseau, *Méthode claire, certaine et facile pour apprendre à chanter la musique* (Paris, 1678, 6/1707/R1976)

W. M. Mylius [Möller], *Rudimenta musices, das ist: Eine kurtze und gründrichtige Anweisung zur Singe Kunst* (Gotha, 1686)

G. Falck, *Idea boni cantoris, das ist Getreu und gründliche Anleitung* (Nuremburg, 1688)

P. Berthet, *Leçons de musique . . . pour apprendre à chanter sa partie à livre ouvert* (Paris, 2/1695)

S. de Brossard, *Dictionaire de musique, contenant une explication des termes grecs, latins, italiens et françois* (Paris, 1703/R1964)

J. B. Peyer [Beyer], *Primae lineae musicae vocalis* (Freiburg, 1703, 2/1730)

M. H. Fuhrmann, *Musicalischer-Trichter, dadurch ein geschickter Informator seiner Informandis die Edle Singe-kunst nach heutiger Manier . . . einbringen kan* (Frankfurt an der Spree, 1706, rev. 2/1715 as *Musica vocalis in nuce, das ist Richtige völlige Unterweisung zur Singekunst*)

B. Marcello, *Il teatro alla moda, o sia Metodo sicuro e facile per il ben comporre ed eseguire l'opere italiane in musica all'uso moderno* (Venice, c1720); Eng. trans. in R. Pauly, 'Il teatro alla moda', *MQ*, xxxiv (1948), 371; xxxv (1949), 85

P. F. Tosi, *Opinioni de' cantori antichi e moderni, o sieno Osservazioni sopra il canto figurato* (Bologna, 1723/R1968; Eng. trans. by J. E. Galliard, 1742, 2/1743/R1969 as *Observations on the Florid Song: or Sentiments on the Ancient & Modern Singers*)

P. Prelleur, *An Introduction to Singing: The Modern Musick-Master, or The Universal Musician*, pt.i (London, 1731, 2/1735/R1965)

F. David, *Méthode nouvelle ou principes généraux pour apprendre facilement la musique et l'art de chanter* (Paris, 1737)

J. Mattheson, *Der vollkommene Capellmeister* (Hamburg, 1739/R1954; Eng. trans., 1981), pt.1 chap.6; pt.ii chaps.1, 3 and 11

P. Denis, *Nouveau système de musique pratique* (Paris, 1747, rev. 2/1760 as *Nouvelle méthode pour apprendre . . . la musique et l'art de chanter*)

C. Buterne, *Méthode pour apprendre la musique vocale et instrumentale* (Rouen, 1752)

J.-A. Bérard, *L'art du chant* (Paris, 1755); Eng. trans. with commentary by S. Murray (Milwaukee, 1969)

J. Blanchet, *L'art ou les principes philosophiques du chant* (Paris, 1756)

J. F. Agricola, *Anleitung zur Singekunst* (Berlin, 1757; trans. with additions of P. F. Tosi's *Opinioni de' cantori antichi e moderni*, 1723; both R1966 ed. E. R. Jacobi)

M. Corrette, *Le parfait maître à chanter, méthode pour apprendre facilement la musique vocale et instrumentale* (Paris, 1758, enlarged 2/1782)

J. Lacassagne, *Traité général des éléments du chant* (Paris, 1766/R1972)

Lécuyer, *Principes de l'art du chant* (Paris, 1769)

J. A. Hiller, *Anweisung zum musikalisch-richtigen Gesange* (Leipzig, 1774, enlarged 2/1798)

——, *Exempelbuch der Anweisung zum Singen* (Leipzig, 1774)

G. Mancini, *Pensieri, e riflessioni pratiche sopra il canto figurato* (Vienna, 1774, rev. and enlarged 3/1777 as *Riflessoni pratiche sul canto figurato*; part repr. in A. Della Corte, *Canto e bel canto*, Turin, 1933); Eng. trans. in E. Foreman, *Masterworks on Singing*, vii (Champaign, 1967)

V. Manfredini, *Regole armoniche, o sieno Precetti ragionati* (Venice, 1775)

C. Burney, *A General History of Music from the Earliest Ages to the Present Period*, i (London, 1776, 2/1789); ii (1782, repr. 1811–12); iii–iv (1789); ed. F. Mercer in 2 vols. with the 1789 text of the orig. vol.i (London, 1935/R1957)

J. Hawkins, *A General History of the Science and Practice of Music* (London, 1776, repr. 1853/R1963, 1875/R1969)

D. Corri, *A Select Collection of the Most Admired Songs, Duetts* (Edinburgh, c1779)

J. A. Hiller, *Anweisung zum musikalisch-zierlichen.Gesange* (Leipzig, 1780)

S. Arteaga, *Le rivoluzioni del teatro musicale italiano dalla sua origine fino al presente* (Bologna, 1783–8, rev. 2/1785; Ger. trans., 1789; Fr. trans., 1802)

Bibliography

G. Aprile, *The Modern Italian Method of Singing, with a Variety of Progressive Examples and Thirtysix Solfeggi* (London, 1791)

J. P. Martini, *Mélopée moderne, ou l'arte du chant reduit en principes* (Lyons, 1792)

J. B. Lasser, *Vollständige Anleitung zur Singkunst* (Munich, 1798)

J. F. Schubert, *Neue Singe-Schule oder gründliche und vollständige Anweisung zur Singkunst in 3 Abtheilungen mit hinlänglichen Uibungsstücken* (Leipzig, 1804)

A. de Garaudé, *Méthode de chant* (Paris, 1809, rev. 2/1811, 3/1854)

G. Lanza, *The Elements of Singing* (London, 1809–13)

Celoni, *Grammatica, o siano regole de ben cantare* (Rome, 1810)

D. Corri, *The Singer's Preceptor* (London, 1810)

A. Benelli, *Regole per il canto figurato* (Dresden, 1814)

A. Reicha, *Traité de la mélodie* (Paris, 1814); ed. C. Czerny as *Vollständiges Lehrbuch der musikalischen Composition*, ii (Vienna, 1832)

G. G. Ferrari, *Breve trattato di canto italiano* (London, 1818; Eng. trans., 1818)

J. B. Roucourt, *Essai sur la théorie du chant* (Brussels, 1821)

I. Nathan, *An Essay on the History and Theory of Music, and on the Qualities, Capabilities and Management of the Human Voice* (London, 1823, 2/1836 as *Musurgia vocalis*)

R. M. Bacon, *Elements of Vocal Science* (London, 1824)

P. von Winter, *Vollständige Singschule* (Mainz, 1825, 2/1874)

A. B. Marx, *Die Kunst des Gesangs, theoretisch-praktisch* (Berlin, 1826)

N. Vaccai, *Metodo pratico di canto italiano per camera divisio in 15 lezioni, ossiano Solfeggi progressivi elementari sopra parole di Metastasio* (London, 1832)

A. Panseron, *Méthode complète de vocalisation, Recueils de vocalises* (Paris, 1839)

D. Crivelli, *The Art of Singing and New Solfeggios for the Cultivation of the Bass Voice* (London, c1840, 2/1844)

Escudier [*frères*], *Etudes biographiques sur les chanteurs contemporains, précédées d'une esquisse sur l'art du chant* (Paris, 1840)

M. García [*fils*], *Traité complet de l'art du chant* (Paris, 1840, 3/1851; Eng. trans., enlarged, 1894)

L. Lablanche, *Metodo completo di canto* (Milan c1840–50)

A. Belgiojoso, *Breve osservazioni sull'arte del canto* (Milan, 1841)

G. Duprez, *L'art du chant* (Paris, 1845)

G. A. Perotti, *Guida per lo studio del canto figurato* (Milan, 1846)

F. Casella, *Compendio dell'opera sulle teorie per l'arte del canto* (Rome, 1848)

L. Cinti-Damoreau, *Méthode de chant composée pour ses classes du Conservatoire* (Paris and London, 1849)

Castil-Blaze, *L'opéra italien de 1548 à 1856* (Paris, 1856)

J. Mainvielle-Fodor, *Réflexions et conseils sur l'art du chant* (Paris, 1857)

J. Wass, *Complete Singing Method* (London, 1857)

F. Sieber, *Vollständiges Lehrbuch der Gesangskunst* (Magdeburg, 1858)

F. Chiaramonte, *L'art de phraser et de cadencer* (Paris, 1865)

G. Carulli, *Méthode de chant* (Paris, 1868)

S. de la Madelaine, *Etudes pratiques de style vocale* (Paris, 1868)

J. Ella, *Musical Sketches* (London, 1869, 3/1878)

F.-J. Fétis, *Méthode des méthodes de chant* (Paris, 1869)

J.-B. Faure, *La voix et le chant* (Paris, 1870)

H. Panofka, *Voix et chanteurs* (Paris, c1870)

J. Audubert, *L'art du chant* (Paris, 1876)

E. Delle Sedie, *Arte e fisiologia del canto* (Milan, 1876); abridged in *A Complete Method of Singing* (New York, 1894)

V. Cirillo, *Vocal Method* (Boston, 1878)

G. Bozzelli, *Breve considerazioni sull'arte del canto* (Menaggio, 1880)

F. Coletti, *La scuola di canto in Italia* (Rome, 1880)

E. Delle Sedie, *Riflessioni sulle cause della decadenza della scuola di canto in Italia* (Paris, 1881)

T. Lemaire and H. Lavoix, *Le chant, ses principes et son histoire* (Paris, 1881)

A. B. Bach, *On Musical Education and Voice Culture* (Edinburgh, 1883)

E. Delle Sedie, *L'estetica del canto e dell'arte melodrammatica* (Paris, 1886); abridged in *A Complete Method of Singing* (New York, 1894)

S. Reeves, *On the Art of Singing* (London, 1900)

Bibliography
3. Strings

P. Jambe de Fer, *Epitome musical des tons, sons et accords, es voix humaines, fluestes d'alleman, Fluestes à neuf trous, Violes & Violons* (Lyons, 1556); repr. in *AnnM*, vi (1958–63), 341

R. Rognoni, *Passaggi per potersi essercitare nel diminuire terminatamente con ogni sorte di instromenti* (Venice, 1592) lost; MS copy by F. Chrysander, *US-SFsc*

S. Cerreto, *Della prattica musica vocale e strumentale* (Naples, 1601, 2/1611; *R*1979)

A. Agazzari, *Del sonare sopra 'l basso con tutti li stromenti e dell'uso loro nel conserto* (Siena, 1607, 2/1608 in *Sacrae cantiones*); repr. in O. Kinkeldey, *Orgel und Klavier in der Musik des 16. Jahrhunderts* (Leipzig, 1910/*R*1968); facs. edns. (Milan, 1933, Bologna, 1969); Eng. trans. in O. Strunk, *Source Readings in Music History* (New York, 1950), 424

M. Praetorius, *Syntagma musicum*, i (Wittenberg and Wolfenbüttel, 1614–15/*R*1959, 1968); ii (Wolfenbüttel, 1618, 2/1619/*R*1958, 1980; Eng. trans., 1962, 1986); iii (Wolfenbüttel, 1618, 2/1619/*R*1958, 1976)

F. Rognoni, *Selva di varii passaggi secondo l'uso moderno per cantare e suonare con ogni sorte de stromenti* (Milan, 1620/*R*1970)

M. Mersenne, *Harmonie universelle* (Paris, 1636–7/*R*1963); Eng. trans. of the book on instruments by R. E. Chapman (The Hague, 1957)

A. Maugars, *Response faite à un curieux sur le sentiment de la musique d'Italie, escrite à Rome le premier octobre 1639* (Paris, *c*1640); modern edn. in E. Thoinan, *Maugars, célèbre joueur de viole . . . sa biographie suivie de sa response* (Paris, 1865/*R*1965); Eng. trans. in C. MacClintock, *Readings in the History of Music in Performance* (Bloomington, 1979), 116

J. A. Herbst, *Musica practica sive instructio pro symphoniacis* (Nuremberg, 1642; 2/1653 and 3/1658 as *Musica moderna prattica, oveso maniera del buon canto . . . sonderlich aber für die Instrumentisten auff Violin und Cornetten zugebrauchen*)

G. Zanetti, *Il scolaro . . . per imparar a suonare di violino, et altri stromenti* (Milan, 1645)

A. Kircher, *Musurgia universalis, sive Ars magna consoni et dissoni* (Rome, 1650/*R*1970, 2/1662, 3/1690)

J. Playford, *Musick's Recreation on the Lyra Viol* (London, 1652, rev. 4/1682/*R*1960)

————, *A. (Breefe) Introduction to the Skill of Musick for Song and Violl* (London, 1654, rev. 7/1674/*R*1966, rev. 12/1694/*R*1973, rev. 19/1730)

C. Simpson, *The Division-Violist* (London, 1659, rev. 2/1665/*R*1965 as *The Division-Viol*, 3/1712)

Du Buisson, [Rules for Bowing], MS, *US-Wc*; Eng. trans. in G. J. Kinney, 'Writings on the Viol by Dubuisson, De Machy, Roland Marais and Etienne Loulié', *JVdGSA*, xiii (1976), 19

T. Mace, *Musick's Monument, or A Remembrancer of the Best Practical Musik* (London, 1676); facs. with transcr. and commentary, ed. J. Jacquot and A. Souris (Paris, 1958/*R*1966)

De Machy, [*Sieur*], 'Avertissement' to *Pièces de violle en musique et en tablature* (Paris, 1685); transcr. in H. Bol, *La basse de viole du temps de Marin Marais et d'Antoine Forqueray* (Bilthoven, 1973); Eng. trans. G. J. Kinney (1976)

M. Marais, 'Avertissement' to *Pièces à une et à deux violes* (Paris, 1686/*R*1972); repr. and trans. in M. Marais, *The Instrumental Works*, i, ed. J. Hsu (New York, 1980)

Danoville, *L'art de toucher le dessus et basse de violle* (Paris, 1687/*R*1972)

J. Rousseau, *Traité de viole* (Paris, 1687/*R*1965)

G. Falck, *Idea boni cantoris, das ist Getreu und gründliche Anleitung* (Nuremberg, 1688)

J. Lenton, *The Gentleman's Diversion, or the Violin Explained* (London, 1693, 2/1702 as *The Useful Instructor of the Violin*)

Anon., *Nolens Volens, or you shall learn to play on the violin whether you will or no* (London, 1695)

Anon., *The Self-Instructor on the Violin* (London, 1695, 2/1697 as *Instructor on the Violin*)

S. de Brossard, *Fragments d'une méthode de violon* (MS, *F-Pn*, *c*1695)

D. Merck, *Compendium musicae instrumentalis chelicae, das ist: kurtzer Begriff welcher Gestalten die Instrumental-Music auf der Violin, Pratschen, Viola da Gamba, und Bass gründlich und leicht zu erlernen seye* (Augsburg, 1695)

E. Loulié, *Eléments ou principes de musique* (Paris, 1696, 2/1698; Eng. trans. with suppl., 1965/*R*1971)

D. Speer, *Gründrichtiger . . . Unterricht der musicalischen Kunst oder Vierfaches musicalisches Kleeblatt* (Ulm, 1697/*R*1974); altered and expanded version of *Gründrichtiger . . . Unterricht der musicalischen Kunst* (Ulm, 1687); Eng. trans. in H. E. Howey, *A Comprehensive Performance Project in Trombone Literature* (diss., U. of Iowa, 1971)

G. Muffat, 'Premiers observations de l'auteur sur la maniere de jouer les airs de balets a la françoise selon la méthode de feu Monsieur de Lully', in *Florilegium secundum* (Passau, 1698); ed. H. Rietsch, DTÖ, iv, Jg.ii/2 (1895/*R*); Eng. trans. K. Cooper and J. Zsako, 'Observations on the Lully Style of Performance', *MQ*, liii (1967), 20

B. Hely, *The Compleat Violist* (London, 1699)

E. Loulié, *Méthode pour apprendre à jouer la violle* (MS, *F-Pn*, *c*1700); transcr. in A. Cohen, 'An Eighteenth-Century Treatise on the Viol by Etienne Loulié', *JVdGSA*, iii (1966), 17

G. Muffat, Foreword to *Ausserlesene Instrumental-Music* (Passau, 1701); ed. E. Luntz, DTÖ, xxiii, Jg.xi/2 (1904/*R*); lxxxix (1953); Eng. trans. in O. Strunk, *Source Readings in Music History* (London, 1950), 449

M. P. de Montéclair, *Méthode facile pour apprendre à jouer du violon* (Paris, 1711–12)

P. Dupont, *Principes de violon par demandes et réponce* (Paris, 1713, 4/1740)

J. Mattheson, *Das neu-eröffnete Orchestre* (Hamburg, 1713)

T. B[rown], *Compleat Musick-Master* (London, 3/1722)

P. Prelleur, *The Modern Musick-Master, or The Universal Musician* (London, 1731/*R*1965, 4/1738/*R*1965)

E. Titon du Tillet, *Le Parnasse françois* (Paris, 1732/*R*1971)

M. Corrette, *L'école d'Orphée, méthode pour apprendre facilement à jouer du violon dans le goût françois et italien avec des principes de musique et beaucoup de leçons*, 1–2 violins, op.18 (Paris, 1738/*R*1973, enlarged 2/1779, ?3/1790)

H. le Blanc, *Défense de la basse de viole contre les entreprises du violon et les prétentions du violoncel* (Amsterdam, 1740/*R*1975); reprinted serially in *ReM*, ix (1927–8); Eng. trans. in B. G. Jackson, 'Hubert Le Blanc's "Défense de la Viole"', *JVdGSA*, x (1973), 11, 69; xi (1974), 17; xii (1975), 14

R. Marais, *Regles d'accompagnement pour la basse de viole de Roland Marais* (MS, *NL-DHgm*, *c*1740)

M. Corrette, *Méthode théorique et pratique pour apprendre en peu de tems le violoncelle dans sa perfection* (Paris, 1741/*R*1972, 2/1783); Eng. trans. in C. D. Graves, *The Theoretical and Practical Method for Cello by Michel Corrette* (diss., Michigan State U., 1971)

C. Tessarini, *Gramatica di musica: insegna il modo facile, e breve per bene imparare di sonare il violino sù la parte* (Rome, 1741); Eng. trans. as *An Accurate Method to Attain the Art of Playing Ye Violin* (London, *c*1765) and *A Musical Grammer which Teaches an Easy and Short Method of Learning to Play to Perfection on the Violin* (Edinburgh, *c*1765)

J. D. Berlin, *Musikalske elementer* (Trondheim, 1744)

M. Corrette, *Méthode pour apprendre facilement à jouer du par-dessus de viole à 5 et à 6 cordes* (Paris, 1748); Eng. trans. in C. R. Farrar, *Seven String Instrument Treatises of Michel Corrette, Translation and Commentary* (diss., North Texas State U., 1978)

R. Bremner, *The Compleat Tutor for the Violin Concerning the Best and Easiest Instructions for Learners to Obtain a Proficiency* (London, *c*1750)

R. Crome, *The Fiddle new Model'd or a useful Introduction for the Violin Exemplify'd with familiar Dialogues* (London, *c*1750)

F. Geminiani, *The Art of Playing on the Violin* (London, 1751/*R*1952)

C. Avison, *An Essay on Musical Expression* (London, 1752, rev. 2/1753/*R*1967, 3/1775)

J. Herrando, *Arte y puntual explicación del modo de tocar el violín* (Paris, 1756); Eng. trans. M. H. Jasinski, *A Translation and Commentary on José Herrando's 'Arte y puntual explicación'* (diss., Brigham Young U., 1974)

L. Mozart, *Versuch einer gründlichen Violinschule* (Augsburg, 1756/*R*1976, 2/1769–70, enlarged 3/1787/*R*1956, 4/1800; Dutch trans., 1766/*R*1965; Fr. trans., 1770; Eng. trans., 1939 [?1948], 2/1951/*R*1985)

L'abbé le fils [Saint-Sévin], *Principes du violon pour apprendre le doigté de cet instrument, et les differens agrémens dont il est susceptibles* (Paris, 1761/*R*1961, 2/1772)

S. Lanzetti, *Principes ou l'application de violoncelle par tous les tons* (Amsterdam, before 1770); Eng. trans. in C. D. Graves, *The Theoretical and Practical Method for Cello by Michel Corrette* (diss., Michigan State U., 1971)

J. B. Tillière, *Méthode pour le violoncelle contenant tous les principes nécessaires pour bien jouer de cet instrument* (Paris, 1764; Eng. edn., London, *c*1795 as *New and Compleat Instruction*, rev. 4/1901, by I. Danbe); Eng. trans. in Graves, *The Theoretical and Practical Method* (1971)

R. Crome, *The Compleat Tutor for the Violoncello, Containing the Best & Easiest Instructions for Learners* (London, 2/*c*1765/*R*1971 in Graves, *The Theoretical and Practical Method*)

C. R. Brijon, *Méthode nouvelle et facile pour apprendre à jouer du par-dessus de viole* (Lyons, 1766)

J.-B.-A. Forqueray, [Letter to Friedrich Wilhelm of Prussia, *c*1767], repr. in Y. Gérard, 'Notes sur la fabrication de la viole de gambe et la manière d'en jouer. D'après correspondance inédite de Jean-Baptiste Forqueray au Prince Frédéric de Prusse', *RMFC*, ii (1961–2), 168; Eng. trans. J. Rutledge, *JVdGSA*, xiii (1976), 12

G. Tartini, 'Lettera [dated 1760] del defonto Sig. Giuseppe Tartini alla Signora Maddalena Lombardini', *L'Europa letteraria*, v/2 (Venice, 1770; Eng. trans., 1771/*R*1967)

————, *Traité des agréments de la musique* (Paris, 1771), ed. E. Jacobi (1961) [incl. Eng. and Ger. trans. and facs. of orig. It. MS in *I–Vc*]

F. Cupis, *Méthode nouvelle et raisonnée pour apprendre à jouer du violoncelle* (Paris, 1772); Eng. trans. in C. D. Graves, *The Theoretical and Practical Method for Cello by Michel Corrette* (diss., Michigan State U., 1971)

M. Corrette, *Méthodes pour apprendre à jouer de la contre-basse ... de la quinte ou alto et de la viole d'Orphée* (Paris, 1773/*R*1977); Eng. trans. in C. R. Farrar, *Seven String Instrument Treatises of Michel Corrette, Translation and Commentary* (diss., North Texas State U., 1978)

J. B. Baumgartner, *Instructions de musique, théorique et pratique à l'usage du violoncelle* (The Hague, *c*1774); Eng. trans. in C. D. Graves, *The Theoretical and Practical Method for Cello by Michel Corrette* (diss., Michigan State U., 1971)

G. S. Löhlein, *Anweisung zum Violinspielen ... mit 24 kleinen Duetten erläutert* (Leipzig and Züllichau, 1774, enlarged 3/1797, ed. J. F. Reichardt)

H. Azaïs, *Méthode de basse contenant des leçons élémentaires* (Paris, *c*1775); Eng. trans. in C. D. Graves, *The Theoretical and Practical Method for Cello by Michel Corrette* (diss., Michigan State U., 1971)

J. Reichardt, *Ueber die Pflichten des Ripien-Violinisten* (Berlin and Leipzig, 1776)

M. Corrette, *L'art de se perfectionner dans le violon où l'on donne à étudier des leçons sur toutes les positions* (Paris, 1782/*R*1973)

A. Lolli, *L'école du violon en quatuor* (Berlin and Amsterdam, *c*1784)

J. Gunn, *The Theory and Practice of Fingering the Violoncello*, with *A Treatise on the Origin of Stringed Instruments* (London, 1789)

F. Scripiani, 'Principii da imparare a suonare il violoncello e con 12 Toccate a solo' (MS, *I–Nc*)

F. Galeazzi, *Elementi teorico-pratici di musica con un saggio l'arte di suonare il violino analizzata, ed a dimostrabili principi ridotta*, i (Rome, 1791, rev. 2 as *Edizione seconda ricorretta, e considerabilmente dall'autore accresciuta coll'aggiunta di molte, e nuove tavole in rame, e specialment di quattro gran prospetti concernenti l'arte dell'arco*, Ascoli, 1817); ii (Rome, 1796)

J. A. Hiller, *Anweisung zum Violinspielen* (Leipzig, 1792)

R. Kreutzer, *40 études ou caprices pour le violon* (Paris, ?1796)

J. B. Cartier, *L'art du violon* (Paris, 1798, 2/1801, enlarged 3/*c*1803/*R*1973)

M. Woldemar, *Méthode pour le violon* (Paris, 1798, rev. 2/*c*1800 as *Grande méthode ou étude élémentaire pour le violon*)

P. Gaviniès, *Les vingt-quatre matinées* (Paris, *c*1800)

J. Müntzberger, *Nouvelle méthode pour le violoncelle* (Paris, 1800)

D. Bideau, *Grande et nouvelle méthode raisonnée pour le violoncelle* (Paris, 1802)

P. Baillot, P. Rode and R. Kreutzer, *Méthode de violon* (Paris, 1803/*R*1974)

P. Baillot, J. H. Levasseur, C.-S. Catel and C.-N. Baudiot, *Méthode de violoncelle* (Paris, 1804/*R*1974; Eng. trans., *c*1850)

J.-B. Bréval, *Traité du violoncelle*, op.42 (Paris, 1804); partial Eng. trans. (?1810)

M. J. Gebauer, *Méthode d'alto* (Paris, *c*1805)

P. Rode, *24 caprices en forme d'études* (Berlin, *c*1815)

A. B. Bruni, *Méthode pour l'alto-viola contenant les principes de cet instrument suivis de 25 études* (Paris, *c*1816)

B. Campagnoli, *Nouvelle méthode de la mécanique progressive du jeu de violon ... distribuée en 132 leçons progressives pour deux violons, et 118 études pour un violon seui*, op.21 (Leipzig, 1824; It. trans., n.d.; Eng. trans., 1856)

C. N. Baudiot, *Méthode de violoncelle* (Berlin, 1826–8)

J. Fröhlich, *Kontrabass-Schule* (Würzburg, 1829; Eng. trans., ?1840)

K. Guhr, *Ueber Paganinis Kunst, die Violine zu spielen* (Mainz, 1829)

J.-F. Mazas, *Méthode de violon, suivi d'un traité des sons harmoniques ... après le système de Paganini* (Paris, 1830), ed. G. Enescu (Paris, 1916)

J. J. F. Dotzauer, *Violoncellschule*, op.165 (Mainz, 1832); ed. J. Eckhardt, *Die Violoncellschulen von J. J. F. Dotzauer, F. A. Kummer, und B. Romberg* (Regensburg, 1968)

L. Spohr, *Violinschule* (Vienna, 1832/*R*1960; Eng. trans., 1843)

P. Baillot, *L'art du violon: nouvelle méthode* (Paris, 1834)

Bibliography

J. J. F. Dotzauer, *Violoncellschule für den ersten Unterricht nebst 40 Übungsstücken*, op.126 (Vienna, 1836)

F. A. Kummer, *Violoncello-Schule*, op.60 (Leipzig, 1839); ed. J. Eckhardt, *Die Violoncellschulen von. J. J. F. Dotzauer, F. A. Kummer, und B. Romberg* (Regensburg, 1968)

B. H. Romberg, *Méthode de violoncelle* (Berlin, 1840); ed. J. Eckhardt, *Die Violoncellschulen von J. J. F. Dotzauer, F. A. Kummer, und B. Romberg* (Regensburg, 1968)

F. Habeneck, *Méthode théorique et pratique de violon* (Paris, c1840)

J.-J.-B. Martinn, *Méthode élémentaire d'alto*, ed. J. Frey (Paris, 1841)

J.-D. Alard, *Ecole de violon: méthode complète et progressive* (Paris, 1844)

P. A. F. Chevillard, *Méthode complète de violoncelle* (Paris, c1850)

J. Hindle, *Der Contrabass-Lehrer* (Vienna, ?1850)

C. Dancla, *Méthode élémentaire et progressive pour violon*, op.52 (Paris, c1850)

C.-A. de Bériot, *Méthode de violon*, op.102 (Paris, 1858)

F. David, *Violinschule* (Leipzig, 1864)

————, *Die hohe Schule des Violinspiels* (Leipzig, 1867–72, 2/1903)

G. Bottesini, *Metodo completo per contrabbasso* (Milan, n.d.; Fr. trans., 1869; Eng. trans., ?1870, 2/1876)

J. J. F. Dotzauer, *Praktische Schule des Violoncellspiels*, op.155 (Hamburg and Leipzig, ?1870)

F. Simandl, *Neueste Methode des Contrabass-Spiels* (Vienna, 1874; Eng. trans., 1903/R1964)

G. Quarenghi, *Metodo di violoncello* (Milan, 1876)

L.-A. Vidal, *Les instruments à archet* (Paris, 1876–8/R1961)

G. Banger, *Praktische Violoncellschule*, op.35 (Offenbach, 1877)

H. Léonard, *Méthode de violon* (Paris, 1877)

G. Braga, *Metodo per violoncello* (Milan, 1878)

A. Piatti, *Method for the Violoncello* (London, 1878)

O. Ševčík, *Schule der Violintechnik*, op.1 (Prague, 1881)

B. Brähmig, *Praktische Bratschenschule* (Leipzig, c1885)

A. Pougin, *Viotti et L'école moderne de violon* (Paris, 1888)

J. de Swert, *The Violoncello* (London, c1890)

O. Ševčík, *Schule der Bogentechnik*, op.2 (Leipzig, 1895)

H. Klingenfeld, *Viola School for Violin Players* (Leipzig, 1897)

A. Wilhelmj and J. Brown, *Modern School for the Violin* (London, 1898)

K. Courvoisier, *The Technics of Violin Playing on Joachim's Method* (London, 1899)

J. Joachim and A. Moser, *Violinschule* (Berlin, 1902–5, 2/1959, ed. M. Jacobsen)

4. Wind

G. M. Artusi, *L'Artusi, overo Delle imperfettioni della moderna musica ragionamenti dui* (Venice, 1600/R1969)

A. Virgiliano, *Il dolcimelo* (MS, c1600, facs. edn., 1979)

S. Cerreto, *Della prattica musica vocale e strumentale* (Naples, 1601, 2/1611; R1979)

A. Agazzari, *Del sonare sopra 'l basso con tutti li stromenti e dell' uso loro nel conserto* (Siena, 1607, 2/1608 in *Sacrae cantiones*); repr. in O. Kinkeldey, *Orgel und Klavier in der Musik des 16. Jahrhunderts* (Leipzig, 1910/R1968), 216; facs. edns. (Milan, 1933; Bologna, 1969); Eng. trans. in O. Strunk, *Source Readings in Music History* (London, 1950), 429

C. Bendinelli, *Tutta l'arte della trombetta* (MS, 1614; facs. with commentary by E. H. Tarr, DM, 2nd ser., v, 1975; Eng. trans., 1976)

M. Praetorius, *Syntagma musicum*, i (Wittenberg and Wolfenbüttel, 1614–15/R1959, 1968); ii (Wolfenbüttel, 1618, 2/1619/R1958, 1980; Eng. trans., 1962, 1986); iii (Wolfenbüttel, 1618, 2/1619/R1958, 1976)

F. Rognoni, *Selva di varii passaggi secondo l'uso moderno per cantare e suonare con ogni sorte di stromenti* (Milan, 1620/R1970)

G. Fantini, *Modo per imparare a sonare di tromba* (Frankfurt, 1638/R1934, 1972; Eng. trans., 1976)

M. Mersenne, *Harmonie universelle* (Paris, 1636–7/R1963); Eng. trans. of the book on instruments by R. E. Chapman (The Hague, 1957)

P. Trichet, *Traité des instruments de musique* (F-Psg 1070, c1640); ed. F. Lesure, *AnnM*, iii (1955), 283–387; iv (1956), 175–248; edn. pubd separately (Neuilly-sur-Seine, 1957)

B. Bismantova, *Compendio musicale*, MS Ferrara, 1677/R1978

Bibliography

J. Hudgebut, *A Vade Mecum for the Lovers of Musick, Shewing the Excellency of the Rechorder* (London, 1679)

J. Banister, *The Most Pleasant Companion or Choice New Lessons for the Recorder or Flute* (London, 1681)

————, *The Sprightly Companion* (London, 1695)

D. Speer, *Gründrichtiger...Unterricht der musicalischen Kunst oder Vierfaches musicalisches Kleeblatt* (Ulm, 1697/*R*1974); altered and expanded version of *Gründrichtiger...Unterricht der musicalischen Kunst* (Ulm, 1687); Eng. trans. in H. E. Howey, *A Comprehensive Performance Project in Trombone Literature* (diss., U. of Iowa, 1971)

J. P. Freillon Poncein, *La véritable manière d'apprendre à jouer en perfection du haut-bois, de la flûte, et de flageolet* (Paris, 1700)

G. Muffat, Preface to *Ausserlesene Instrumental-Music* (Passau, 1701); ed. E. Luntz, DTÖ, xxiii, Jg.xi/2 (1904/*R*); lxxxix (1953); Eng. trans. in O. Strunk, *Source Readings in Music History* (London, 1950), 449

J. Hotteterre, *Principes de la flûte traversière, ou flûte d'Allemagne. De la flûte à bec, ou flûte douce, et du haut-bois* (Paris, 1707/*R*1982, 4/1721/*R*1973, 6/*c*1728/*R*1941; Dutch trans., 1728); Eng. trans. of 1st edn. by D. Lasocki as *Principles of the Flute, Recorder, and Oboe* (New York, 1968)

Anon., *Complete Tutor to the Hautboy* (London, *c*1715)

J. Hotteterre, *L'art de préluder sur la flûte traversière, sur la flûte à bec, sur le haut-bois, et autres instruments de dessus* (Paris, 1719/*R*1966)

J. C. Schickhard, *Principes de la flûte* (Amsterdam, *c*1720)

F. Bonanni, *Gabinetto armonicò pieno d'istromenti sonori indicati e spiegati* (Rome, 1722, rev. and enlarged by G. Ceruti with 151 plates engraved on copper by A. van Westerhout, 1776)

Abbé de la Salle Démoz, *Méthode de musique selon un nouveau système très-court, très-facile & très-sûr* (Paris, 1728)

Anon., *Instructions and Tunes for the Treble Recorder* (London, *c*1731)

P. Prelleur, *The Modern Musick-Master, or The Universal Musician* (London, 1731/*R*1965, 4/1738/*R*1965)

J. F. B. C. Majer, *Museum musicum theoretico practicum* (Schwäbisch Hall, 1732/*R*1954, 2/1741)

J. P. Eisel, *Musicus autodidaktus* (Erfurt, 1738)

M. Corrette, *Méthode pour apprendre aisément à joüer de la flûte traversière avec des principes de musique et les brunettes*, 1–2fl (Paris, *c*1742/*R*1978, enlarged to include ob, cl, 2/1773, ?4/1781/*R*1977); Eng. trans. in C. Farrar, *Michel Corrette and Flute-Playing in the Eighteenth Century* (Brooklyn, New York, 1970)

C. Avison, *An Essay on Musical Expression* (London, 1752, rev. 2/1753/*R*1967, 3/1775)

J. J. Quantz, *Versuch einer Anweisung die Flöte traversiere zu spielen* (Berlin, 1752, 3/1789/*R*1952); Fr. trans., 1752; Dutch trans., 1754); Eng. trans. by E. R. Reilly as *On Playing the Flute* (New York, 1966)

A. Mahaut, *Nieuwe manier om binnen korten tyd op de dwarsfluit te leeren speelen* [*Nouvelle méthode pour apprendre en peu de temps à jouer de la flûte traversière*] (Amsterdam, *c*1759/*R*1977)

C. Delusse, *L'art de la flûte traversière* (Paris, *c*1761/*R*1973)

V. Roeser, *Essai d'instruction à l'usage de ceux qui composent pour la clarinette et le cor* (Paris, 1764/*R*1972)

L. C. A. Granon, *Plain and Easy Instructions for Playing on the German-flute* (London, 1770/*R*1976, 4/1766)

L. Heron, *A Treatise on the German Flute* (London, 1771)

A.-F. Cajon, *Les éléments de musique, avec des leçons à une et deux voix* (Paris, 1772)

?J. C. Fischer, *New and Complete Instructions for the Oboe or Hoboy* (London, *c*1772, 4/1802)

L. J. Francoeur, *Diapason général de tous les instrumens à vent* (Paris, n.d., 2/1772); ed. E. A. Choron as *Traité général des voix et instruments d'orchestre principalement des instruments à vent à l'usage des compositeurs* (Paris, 1813)

P. Jaubert, ed., *Dictionnaire raisonné universel des arts et métiers ... nouvelle édition* (Paris, 1773)

A. Lorenzoni, *Saggio per ben suonare il flauto traverso* (Venice, 1779)

Anon., *The Clarinet Instructor* (London, *c*1780)

J.-B. de La Borde, *Essai sur la musique ancienne et moderne* (Paris, 1780/*R*1972)

J. J. H. Ribock, *Bemerkungen über die. Flöte, und Versuch einer kurzen Anleitung zur bessern Einrichtung und Behandlung derselben* (Stendal, 1782/*R*1980)

J. G. Tromlitz, 'Neuerfundene Vortheile zur bessern Einrichtung der Flote', *Miscellaneen artistischen Inhaltes* (Erfurt, 1785)

Bibliography

A. Vanderhagen, *Méthode nouvelle et raisonnée pour le clarinette* (Paris, 1785/*R*1972)

E. Ozi, *Méthode nouvelle et raisonnée pour le basson* (Paris, *c*1787)

——, *Méthode de basson ... avec des airs et des duos* (Paris, 1788)

O. J. Vandenbroek, *Méthode nouvelle et raisonée pour apprendre à donner du cor* (Paris, *c*1789)

Anon., *The Compleat Tutor for the Hautboy* (London, *c*1790)

J. G. Tromlitz, *Ausführlicher und gründlicher Unterricht die Flöte zu spielen* (Leipzig, 1791/ *R*1973)

A. Vanderhagen, *Méthode nouvelle et raisonée pour le hautbois* (Paris, *c*1792/*R*1971)

J. Wragg, *The Flute Preceptor* (London, *c*1792)

F. Devienne, *Nouvelle méthode théorique et pratique pour la flûte* (Paris, 1794/*R*, later edns. incl. 1795, 1800/*R*1977)

J. Gunn, *The School of the German Flute* (London, *c*1794)

O. Vandenbroek, *Traité général de tous les instruments à vent à l'usage des compositeurs* (Paris, *c*1794/*R*1973)

J. E. Altenburg, *Versuch einer Anleitung zur heroisch-musikalischen Trompeter- und Pauker-Kunst* (Halle, 1795/*R*1972); Eng. trans. E. H. Tarr as *Essay on an Introduction to the Heroic and Musical Trumpeters' and Kettledrummers' Art* (Nashville, 1974)

G. Punto, *Seule et vraie méthode pour apprendre facilement les élémens des premier et second cors ... composée par Hampl et perfectionnée par Punto, son élève* (Paris, *c*1795, 3/1798)

F. Blasius, *Nouvelle méthode de clarinette et raisonnement des instruments principes et théorie de musique dédiés aux élèves du Conservatoire* (Paris, 1796/*R*1972)

Anon., *New and Compleat Instructions for the Clarionet* (London, *c*1798)

A. Vanderhagen, *Nouvelle méthode de clarinette divisée en deux parties* (Paris, 1798/*R*1972)

J. G. Tromlitz, *Über die Flöten mit mehrern Klappen* (Leipzig, 1800/*R*1973)

V. Michel, *Méthode de clarinette* (Paris, *c*1800)

J. G. H. Backofen, *Anweisung zur Klarinette nebst einer kurzen Abhandlung über das Basset-Horn* (Leipzig, *c*1802)

F. Chalon, *Méthode pour le cor anglais* (Paris, 1802)

F. N. Duvernoy, *Méthode pour le cor* (Paris, 1802)

F.-J. Garnier [*l'aîné*], *Méthode raisonnée pour le haut-bois* (Paris, 1802)

H. C. Koch, *Musikalisches Lexikon, welches di theoretische und praktische Tonkunst, encyclopädisch bearbeitet, alle alten und neuen Kunstwörter erklärt, und die alten und neuen Instrumente beschrieben, enthält* (Frankfurt am Main, 1802, 2/1817); abridged as *Kurzgefasstes Handwörterbuch der Musik für praktische Tonkünstler und für Dilettanten* (Leipzig, 1807)

X. Lefèvre, *Méthode de clarinette ... adoptée pour le Conservatoire* (Paris, 1802/*R*1974)

E. Ozi, *Nouvelle méthode de basson adoptée par le Conservatoire* (Paris, 1803/*R*1973)

A. Hugot [*le jeune*] and J.-G. Wunderlich, *Méthode de flûte du Conservatoire* (Paris, 1804/*R*1975)

C. F. D. Schubart, *Ideen zu einer Ästhetik der Tonkunst*, ed. L. Schubart (Vienna, 1806/*R*1969)

H. Domnich, *Méthode de premier et de second cor* (Paris, 1807/*R*1974)

M., 'Ueber die Klarinette', *AMZ*, x (1807–8), no.24, cols.369–75, and no.25, cols.385–91

J. Fröhlich, *Vollständige theoretisch-praktische Musikschule* (Bonn, 1810–11)

——, *Fagottschule* (Bonn, 1811–12)

A. Choron, *Traité général des voix et des instruments d'orchestre, principalement des instruments à vent, à l'usage des compositeurs; par L. J. Francoeur ... Nouvelle édition revüe et augmentée des instruments modernes* (Paris, 1813)

G. Vogt, *Méthode de hautbois* (MS, *F-Pn*, after 1813)

C. Nicholson, *Nicholson's Complete Preceptor, for the German Flute* (London, *c*1816)

A. Reicha, *Cours de composition musicale ou traité complet et raisonné de l'harmonie pratique* (Paris, ?1816–18; Eng. trans., 1854/*R*1977); ed. C. Czerny as *Vollständiges Lehrbuch*, i (Vienna, 1832)

A. T. Berbiguier, *Nouvelle méthode pour la flûte* (Paris, 1818)

J. Wragg, *Seventeenth Edition of Wragg's Improved Flute Preceptor for an Eight Key'd Flute* (London, 1818)

A. Vanderhagen, *Nouvelle méthode pour la clarinette moderne à douze clés, avec leur application* (Paris, 1819)

C. Baermann, 'Ueber die Natur und Eigenthümlictikeit des Fagotts', *AMZ*, xxii (1820), no.36, cols.601–7

C. Almenraeder, *Abhandlung über die Verbesserung des Fagotte* (Mainz, 1822–3)

G. Braun, 'On the Character and Treatment of the Oboe', *The Harmonicon*, i (1823), 163–4

L. F. Dauprat, *Méthode pour cor alto et cor basse* (Paris, 1824)

W. Gutteridge, *Introduction to the Art of Playing on Gutteridge's New Patent Clarinet* (London, 1824)

I. Müller, *Méthode pour la nouvelle clarinette et clarinette-alto* (Paris, 1825)

J. Sellner, *Theoretisch-praktische Oboeschule* (Vienna, 1825, rev. 2/1901; It. trans., *c*1827)

A. B. Fürstenau, *Flöten-Schule* (Leipzig, *c*1826)

H. Brod, *Grande méthode de hautbois* (Paris, *c*1826–30)

W. N. James, *A Word or Two on the Flute* (Edinburgh and London, 1826/*R*1982)

L. Drouet, *Méthode pour la flûte* (Paris, *c*1827)

T. Lindsey, *The Elements of Flute Playing* (London, 1828)

P. J. Meifred, *De l'étendue, de l'emploi et des ressources du cor* (Paris, 1829)

Anon., *Metzler and Son's Clarinet Preceptor* (London, *c*1830)

I. P., 'On the Oboe and Bassoon', *The Harmonicon*, viii (1830), 192–3

G. Catrufo, *Des voix et des instrumens à cordes à vent et à percussion, ouvrage à l'usage des personnes qui veulent écrire la partition* (Paris, 1832)

H. Brod, *Méthode pour le hautbois*, ii (Paris, *c*1835)

J.-L. Tulou, *Méthode de flûte progressive et raisonnée* (Mainz, Paris, Milan and London, *c*1835, 2/?1851/*R*1973; edn., Kassel, 1965)

F. Berr, *Méthode complète de basson* (Paris, 1836)

———, *Méthode complète de clarinette* (Paris, 1836)

———, *Traité complet de la clarinette à quatorze clefs* (Paris, 1836)

G. Hogarth, 'The Flute', *The Musical World*, iii/36 (1836), 145–50

———, 'Musical Instruments: the Oboe, Bassoon and English Horn', *Musical World*, iii/38 (1836), 178–81

C. Nicholson, *A School for the Flute* (New York, 1836, 4/1875)

G. Kastner, *Traité général de l'instrumentation* (Paris, 1837, enlarged 2/1844)

J. Sellner, *Theoretisch Praktische oboe Schule* (Vienna, 1837)

V. Coche, *Examen critique de la flûte ordinaire comparée à la flûte de Boehm, présenté à MM les Membres de l'Institut* (Paris, 1838)

G. Kastner, *Cours d'instrumentation* (Paris, 1839, 2/1844)

G. MacKintosh, *New and Improved Bassoon Tutor* (London, 1840)

P.-J. E. Meifred, *Méthode pour le cor chromatique ou à pistons* (Paris, 1840, rev. 2/1849)

C. Almenraeder, *Die Kunst des Fagottblasens* (Mainz, 1843)

H. Berlioz, *Grand traité d'instrumentation et d'orchestration modernes*, op.10 (Paris, 1843, 2/1855; Eng. trans., 1855)

H. E. Klosé, *Méthode pour servir à l'enseignement de la clarinette à anneaux mobiles* (Paris, 1843, enlarged 1868)

J.-B.-J. W. Bordogni, *Méthode complète pour le basson à l'usage des Conservatoire* [sic] *Royaux de Musique de Paris et de Bruxelles* (Paris, *c*1844)

Anon., *A Complete Course of Instruction for the Boehm Flute* (London, 1845)

J. F. Gallay, *Méthode complète pour le cor* (Paris, *c*1845)

E. Jancourt, *Grande méthode pour le basson* (Paris, 1847)

A. M.-R. Barret, *A Complete Method for the Oboe* (London, *c*1850, 2/1862)

C. Baermann, *Vollständige Clarinett-Schule* (Munich, 1864–75)

Mémoires de Hector Berlioz (Paris, 1870; ed. and Eng. trans. by D. Cairns, 1969, 2/1970); ed. P. Citron (Paris, 1969)

J. Radcliff, *School for the Flute, a Practical Instruction Book by Charles Nicholson . . . Altered and Adapted* (London, 1873)

R. Tillmetz, *Anleitung zur Erlernung der Theobald Böhm'schen Cylinder- und Ringklappen-Flöte, mit konischer Bohrung* (Leipzig, 1890)

M. Schwedler, *Katechismus der Flöte und des Flötenspiels* (Leipzig, 1897)

W. Heckel, *Der Fagott* (Biebrich, 1899, rev. 2/1931)

L. Bas, *Méthode nouvelle de hautbois* (Paris, n.d.)

5. Pitch

A. Schlick, *Spiegel der Orgelmacher und Organisten* (Speyer, 1511/*R*1959); ed. E. Flade (Mainz, 1931, 2/1951)

P. Aaron, *Thoscanello de la musica* (Venice, 1523/*R*1969, rev. edn. with suppl. as *Thoscanello in musica* 1529/*R*1969, 1539/*R*1971, 1562; Eng. trans. collating all edns., 1970)

Bibliography

S. di Ganassi dal Fontego, *Regola rubertina* (Venice, 1542)

M. Praetorius, *Syntagma musicum*, ii (Wolfenbüttel, 1618, 2/1619/*R*1958, 1980; Eng. trans., 1962, 1986)

G. B. Doni, *Annotazioni sopra il Compendio de' generi e de' modi della musica* (Rome, 1640); extracts ed. C. Gallico as 'Discorso sesto sopra il recitare in scena con l'accompagnato d'instrumenti musicali', *RIM*, iii (1968), 286

G. Muffat, *Florilegium secundum* (Passau, 1698), introduction, §4, III; ed. in DTÖ, iv, Jg.ii/2 (1895/*R*)

C. Douwes, *Grondig ondersoek van de toonen der musijk* (Franeker, 1699); ed. P. Williams (Amsterdam, 1971)

J. Mattheson, *Das neu-eröffnete Orchestre* (Hamburg, 1713)

B. Taylor, 'De motu Nervi tensi', *Philosophical Transactions of the Royal Society*, xxviii (London, 1713), 26

J. Sauveur, 'Rapport des sons des cordes d'instruments de musique, aux fleches des cordes; et nouvelle détermination des sons fixes', *Histoire de l'Académie royale des sciences* [1713] (Paris, 1716), *Mémoires*, 324

J. Mattheson, *Critica musica* (Hamburg, 1722–5/*R*1964)

P. F. Tosi, *Opinioni de' cantori antichi e moderni, o sieno Osservazioni sopra il canto figurato* (Bologna, 1723/*R*1968; Eng. trans. by J. E. Galliard 1742, 2/1743/*R*1969 as *Observations on the Florid Song: or Sentiments on the Ancient & Modern Singers* [see also Agricola, 1757]

L. Euler, *Dissertatio physica de sono* (Basle, 1727)

J.J. Quantz, *Versuch einer Anweisung die Flöte traversiere zu spielen* (Berlin, 1752, 3/1789/*R*1952; Eng. trans., 1966, as *On Playing the Flute*), xvii, vii, 6–7

J. F. Agricola, *Anleitung zur Singekunst* (Berlin, 1757; trans., with addns. of Tosi, 1723); facs. of both ed. E. R. Jacobi (Celle, 1966)

J. Adlung, *Anleitung zu der musikalischen Gelahrtheit* (Erfurt, 1758/*R*1953, 2/1783), 387

D. Bernoulli, 'Recherches physiques, méchaniques et analytiques, sur le son & sur les tons de tuyaux d'orgues différemment construits', *Mémoires de l'Académie Royale des Sciences* [1762] (Paris, 1764), 431–85

F. Bédos de Celles, *L'art du facteur d'orgues* (Paris, 1766–78/*R*1963–6); Ger. trans., 1793; Eng. trans., 1977); ed. C. Mahrenholz (Kassel, 1934–6, 2/1963–6)

J. Adlung, *Musica mechanica organoedi*, ed. J. L. Albrecht (Berlin, 1768/*R*1961), i, 193, 210f; ii, 55

J. H. Lambert, 'Observations sur les flûtes', *Nouveaux mémoires de l'Académie Royale des Sciences et Belles-Lettres* [1775] (Berlin, 1777), 13–48

C. Gervasoni, *Scuola della musica* (Piacenza, 1800)

A. J. Ellis, 'On the History of Musical Pitch', *Journal of the Society of the Arts*, xxviii (1880), 293

6. Tuning

Guido of Arezzo, *Micrologus*, ed. J. Smits van Waesberghe, CSM, iv (1955)

W. Odington, *Summa de speculatione musicae*, ed. F. F. Hammond, CSM, xiv (1970)

H. Spechtshart, *Flores musicae*, 1332–42, ed. K.-W. Gümpel (Wiesbaden, 1958); Renaissance ed, *Flores musice omnes cantus Gregoriani* (Strasbourg, 1488)

Ugolino of Orvieto, *Declaratio musicae disciplinae*, ed. A. Seay, CSM, vii (1959–62)

G. Anselmi, *De musica*, 1434; ed. G. Massera (Florence, 1961)

H. Arnaut de Zwolle, *Les traités*, ed. G. le Cerf and E. R. Labande (Paris, 1932)

F. Gaffurius, *Theoricum opus musicas disciplinae* (Naples, 1480)

Euclid, *Elementa geometriae*, trans. Johannes Campanus (Venice, 1482)

B. Ramos de Pareia, *Musica practica* (Bologna, 1482, 2/1482/*R*1969)

J. Hothby, *Ires tracatuli contra Bartholomeum Ramun*, ed. A. Seay, CSM, x (1964)

N. Burtius, *Musices opusculum* (Bologna, 1487/*R*1969)

F. Gaffurius, *Theorica musicae* (Milan, 1492/*R*1934, 1967)

G. de Podio, *Ars musicorum* (Valencia, 1495); ed. A. Seay, (Colorado Springs, 1978)

F. Gaffurius, *Practica musicae* (Milan, 1496; Eng. trans., 1968; MSD, xx, 1969; 2/1497; rev. It. trans., 1508, as *Angelicum ac divinum opus musicae*)

A. Schlick, *Spiegel der Orgelmacher und Organisten* (Speyer, 1511/*R*1959); ed. in *MMg*, i (1869), 77–114

H. Grammateus, [Schreyber], *Algorithmus proportionum una cum monochordi generis dyatonici compositione* (Kraków, 1514)

508

Bibliography

F. Gaffurius, *De harmonia musicorum instrumentorum opus* (Milan, 1518; trans. C. Miller, 1977)

H. Grammateus [Schreyben], *Ayn new kunstlich Buech* (Nuremberg, 1518)

F. Gaffurius, *Apologia adversum Ioannem Spatarium* (Turin, 1520)

G. Spataro *Errori de Franchino Gafurio da Lodi* (Bologna, 1521)

P. Aaron, *Thoscanello de la musica* (Venice, 1523/*R*1969; rev. with suppl. as *Toscanello in musica*, 1529/*R*1969, 1539/*R*1971, 1562; Eng. trans. collating all edns., 1970)

G. M. Lanfranco, *Scintille di musica* (Brescia, 1523/*R*); Eng. trans., B. Lee (diss., Cornell U., 1961)

O. Finé, *Epithoma musice instrumentalis* (Paris, 1530)

M. Agricola, *Rudimenta musices* (Wittenberg, 1539)

S. di Ganassi dal Fontego, *Regola rubertina* (Venice, 1542–3/*R*1970)

P. Aaron, *Lucidario in musica* (Venice, 1545/*R*1969), fol. 35*v*

M. Agricola, *Musica instrumentalis deudsch* (Wittenberg, 5/1545); facs. edn. (Leipzig, 1896)

J. Bermudo, *El libro llamado declaración de instrumentos musicales* (Osuna, 1555/*R* 1957)

N. Vicentino, *L'antica musica ridotta alla moderna prattica* (Rome, 1555/*R*1959, 2/1557)

G. Zarlino, *Le istitutioni harmoniche* (Venice, 1558/*R*1965, rev. 3/1573/*R*1966)

G. B. Benedetti, *Diversarum speculationum mathematicarum, & physicarum liber* (Turin, 1565), 282

T. de Santa María, *Libro llamado arte de tañer fantasia* (Valladolid, 1565/*R*1972)

E. N. Ammerbach, *Orgel- oder Instrument-Tabulatur* (Leipzig, 1571, rev. 2/1583/*R*1984)

G. Zarlino, *Dimostrationi harmoniche* (Venice, 1571/*R*1966, 2/1573, rev. 1588)

F. de Salinas, *De musica libri septem* (Salamanca, 1577, 2/1592)

V. Galilei, *Dialogo della musica antica et della moderna* (Florence, 1581/*R*1968)

G. Zarlino, *Sopplimenti musicali* (Venice, 1588/*R*1966)

V. Galilei, *Discorso intorno all'opere di Messer Gioseffo Zarlino da Chioggia* (Florence, 1589, repr. 1933)

C. Schneegass, *Nova & exquisita monochordi dimensio* (Erfut, 1590)

G. M. Artusi, *L'Artusi, overo Delle imperfettioni della moderna musica ragionamenti dui* (Venice, 1600/*R*1969)

S. Stevin, *Van de spiegeling der singconst*, *c*1600, ed. D. Bierens de Haan (Amsterdam, 1884); ed. A. Fokker in *The Principal Works of Simon Stevin*, v (Amsterdam, 1966), 413

G. M. Artusi, *Considerationi musicali* (Venice, 1603) [bound with his *Seconda parte dell'Artusi*]

A. Reinhard, *Monochordum* (Leipzig, 1604)

G. P. Cima, *Partito di ricercari, canzoni alla francese* (Milan, 1606[15]); ed. C. G. Rayner, CEKM, xx (1969)

P. Cerone, *El melopeo y maestro* (Naples, 1613/*R*1969)

M. Praetorius, *Syntagma musicum*, ii: *De organographia* (Wolfenbüttel, 1618, 2/1619/*R*1958 and 1980; Eng. trans. 1962, 1986)

G. B. Doni, *Compendio del trattato de' generi e de' modi della musica* (Rome, 1635)

M. Mersenne, *Harmonicorum libri, in quibus agitur de sonorum natura* (Paris, 1635–6)

———, *Harmonie universelle* (Paris, 1636–7/*R*1963; Eng. trans., 1957)

———, Letters, ed. C. de Waard and others as *Correspondance du P. Marin Mersenne* (Paris, 1932–)

G. B. Doni, *Annotazioni sopra il Compendio de' generi e de' modi della musica* (Rome, 1640)

J. Denis, *Traité de l'accord de l'éspinette* (Paris, 1643, 2/1650/*R*1969)

G. B. Doni, *De praestantia musicae veteris libri tres* (Florence, 1647)

D. R. van Nierop, *Wis-konstige musyka* (Amsterdam, 1659) [bound with his *Mathematische calculatie*]

I. Newton, unpubd MSS on music, 1665 (*GB-Cu* Add.4000)

L. Rossi, *Sistema musico, overo Musica speculativa* (Perugia, 1666)

C. F. Milliet de Chales, *Cursus seu Mundus mathematicus* (Lyons, 1674)

J. Zaragoza, *Fabrica, y uso de varios instrumentos mathematicos* (Madrid, 1674, 2/1675)

A. Werckmeister, *Orgel-Probe* (Frankfurt am Main and Leipzig, 1681, 2/1698/*R*1970 as *Erweiterte und Verbessere Orgel-Probe*, 5/1783)

W. C. Printz, *Exercitationum musicarum theoretico-practicarum curiosarum tertia de Quinta* (Frankfurt and Leipzig, 1687)

C. Huygens, writings on music, ed. in *Oeuvres complètes*, xx (The Hague, 1940)

T. Salmon, *A Proposal to Perform Musick in Perfect and Mathematical Proportions* (London, 1688)

J. Ozanam, *Dictionaire mathématique* (Amsterdam, 1691)

A. Werckmeister, *Musicalische Temperatur* (Frankfurt am Main and Leipzig, 2/1691/*R*1983)

509

Bibliography

M.-A. Charpentier, *Règles de composition*, ?c1692, *F-Pn*, nouv. acq. fr.6355, 6356

L. Chaumont, *Pièces d'orgue sur les 8 tons* (Huy, 1695); ed. J. Ferrard, Le pupitre, xxv (Paris, 1970)

W. C. Printz, *Phrynis mitilenaeus* (Dresden and Leipzig, 1696)

A. Werckmeister, *Hypomnemata musica* (Quedlinburg, 1697/*R*1970)

E. Loulié, *Nouveau sistème de musique* (Paris, 1698)

J. Wallis, 'A Letter of Dr. John Wallis to Samuel Pepys Esquire, Relating to some Supposed Imperfections in an Organ', *Philosophical Transactions* (1698), no.242, p.249

A. Werckmeister, *Die nothwendigsten Anmerckungen und Regeln, wie der Bassus continuus oder General-Bass wol Könne tractiret werden* (Aschersleben, 1698, 2/1715)

C. Douwes, *Grondig ondersoek van de toonen der musik* (Franeker, 1699/*R*1970))

A. Werckmeister, *Cribrum musicum* (Quedlinburg and Leipzig, 1700/*R*1970)

S. de Brossard, *Dictionaire de musique* (Paris, 1703/*R*1964, 2/1705)

J. Sauveur, 'Système general des intervalles des sons, et son application à tous les systêmes et à tous les instruments de musique', *Histoire de l'Académie royale des sciences* [1701] (Paris, 1704), *Mémoires*, 297–364

T. Salmon, 'The Theory of Musick Reduced to Arithmetical and Geometrical Proportion', *Philosophical Transactions of the Royal Society*, xxiv (1705), 2077

J. G. Neidhardt, *Beste und leichteste Temperatur des Monochordi* (Jena, 1706)

A. Werckmeister, *Musicalische Paradoxal-Discourse* (Quedlinburg, 1707/*R*1970)

J. Sauveur, 'Methode generale pour former les systêmes temperés de musique, et du choix de celui qu'on doit suivre', *Histoire de l'Académie royale des sciences* [1707] (Paris, 1708), *Mémoires*, 203

K. Hensling, 'Specimen de novo suo systemate musico', *Abhandlungen der Berliner Akademie* (Berlin, 1710)

J. Mattheson, *Das neu-eröffnete Orchestre* (Hamburg, 1713)

B. Le B. de Fontenelle, ed., *Histoire de l'Académie royale des sciences* [1711] (Paris, 1714)

J. Sauveur, 'Table generale des sistemes temperez de musique', *Histoire de l'Académie royale des sciences* [1711] (Paris, 1714), *Mémoires*, 309

C. A. Sinn, *Die aus mathematischen Gründen richtig gestellete musicalische temperatura practica* (Wernigeroda, 1717)

'Eclaircissement d'un problème de musique practique', *Mèmoires pour l'histoire des sciences et des beaux arts* (Trevoux, 1718), 310

J. Mattheson, *Réflexions sur l'éclaircissement d'un problème de musique pratique* (Hamburg, 1720)

——, *Critica musica* (Hamburg, 1722–5/*R*1964)

P. F. Tosi, *Opinioni de' cantori antichi e moderni* (Bologna, 1723/*R*1968; Eng. trans., 1742, 2/1743/*R*1969 as *Observations on the Florid Song*)

P. Nassarre, *Escuela música, según la práctica moderna* (Saragossa, 1723–4)

J. G. Neidhardt, *Sectio Canonis Harmonici, zur völligen Richtigkeit der Generum Modulandi* (Königsberg, 1724)

J.-P. Rameau, *Nouveau système de musique théorique* (Paris, 1726)

J. G. Meckenheuser, *Die sogenannte: Allerneuste, musicalische Temperatur* (Quedlinburg, 1727)

J. P. A. Fischer, *Kurt en grondig onderwys* (Utrecht, 1728)

J. D. Heinichen, *Der General-Bass in der Composition* (Dresden, 1728)

J. Mattheson, *Grosse General-Bass-Schule* (Hamburg, 1731/*R*1968; Eng. trans., 1981)

P. Prelleur, *The Modern Musick-master*, v: *The Art of Playing on the Violin* (London, 1731/*R*1965)

J. G. Neidhardt, *Gäntzlich erschöpfte mathematische Abtheilungen des diatonisch-chromatischen temperirten Canonis Monochordi* (Königsberg, 1732, 2/1734)

J.-P. Rameau, *Génération harmonique* (Paris, 1737); ed. and trans., D. Hayes (diss., Stanford U., 1974)

J. C. Petit, *Apologie de l'excellence de la musique* (London, c1740)

J.-J. Rousseau, *Dissertation sur la musique moderne* (Paris, 1743)

G. A. Sorge, *Anweisung zur Stimmung und Temperatur* (Hamburg, 1744)

——, *Vorgemach der musicalischen Composition* ii–iii (Lobenstein, 1746–47)

G. A. Sorge, *Gespräch zwischen einem musico theoretico und einem studioso musices* (Lobenstein, 1748)

Extraits des registres de l'Académie royale des sciences (10 Dec 1749)

R. Smith, (iii) *Harmonics, or the Philosophy of Musical Sounds* (London, 1749, 2/1759)

G. A. Sorge, *Ausführliche und deutliche Anweisung zur Rational-Rechnung* (Lobenstein, 1749)

F. Geminiani, *The Art of Playing the Violin* (London, 1751/*R*1952)

Bibliography

J. le R. d'Alembert, *Elémens de musique* (Paris, 1752)

M. Corrette, *Le maître de clavecin pour l'accompagnement: méthode théorique et pratique* (Paris, 1752/*R*1970)

G. Tartini, *Trattato di musica secondo la vera scienza dell'armonia* (Padua, 1754/*R*1966; Ger. trans., 1966)

B. Fritz, *Anweisung, wie man Claviere, Clavecins, und Orgeln, nach ein mechanischen Art, in allen zwölf Tönen gleich rein stimmen könne* (Leipzig, 1756, 5/1829)

F. Marpurg, *Principes du clavecin* (Berlin, 1756)

G. A. Sorge, *Anweisung Claviere und Orgeln behörig zu temperiren* (Leipzig and Lobenstein, 1758)

J. B. Romieu, 'Mémoire théorique et pratique sur les systèmes tempérés de musique', *Histoire de l'Académie royale des sciences* [1758] (Paris, 1763), *Mémoires*, 483–519

C. P. E. Bach, *Versuch über die wahre Art das Clavier zu spielen*, ii (Berlin, 1762/*R*1969)

G. Riccati, *Saggio sopra le leggi del contrapunto* (Castelfranco, 1762)

G. B. Doni, *Lyra Barberina amphieordos: accedunt eiusdem opera*, i–ii, ed. A. F. Gori and G. B. Passeri (Florence, 1763/*R*1975)

V. Roesner, *L'art de toucher le clavecin* (Paris, *c*1765)

J. J. Rousseau, *Dictionnaire de musique* (Paris, 1768/*R*1969; Eng. trans., *c*1775, 2/1779/*R*1975)

F. Bédos de Celles, *L'art du facteur d'orgues*, ii–iii (Paris, 1770/*R*1965)

G. A. Sorge, *Der in der Rechen- und Messkunst wohlerfahrne Orgelbaumeister* (Lobenstein, 1773)

J. H. Lambert, 'Remarques sur les tempéraments en musique', *Nouveaux mémoires de l'Académie royale des sciences et belles-lettres* (Berlin, 1774)

G. F. Tempelhof, *Gedanken über die Temperatur des Herrn Kirnberger* (Berlin and Leipzig, 1775)

F. W. Marpurg, *Versuch über die musikalische Temperatur* (Breslau, 1776/*R*)

J. B. Mercadier de Belesta, *Nouveau système de musique théorique et pratique* (Paris, 1776)

J. P. Kirnberger, *Die Kunst des reinen Satzes in der Musik*, ii/3 (Berlin and Königsberg, 1776–9/*R*1968, 2/1793)

F. Vallotti, *Della scienza teorica a pratica della moderna musica* (Padua, 1779)

J. J. Engel, *Über die musikalische Malerey* (Berlin, 1780)

H. P. Bossler, *Elementarbuch der Tonkunst* (Speyer, 1782)

C. F. Cramer, ed., *Magazin der Musik*, ii (Hamburg, 1784/*R*1975)

W. Jones, [of Nayland] *A Treatise on the Art of Music* (Colchester, 1784, 2/1827)

T. Cavallo, 'Of the Temperament of those Musical Instruments, in which the Tones, Keys, or Frets, are Fixed, as in the Harpsichord, Organ, Guitar, &c.', *Philosophical transactions of the Royal Society of London*, lxxviii (1788), 238

F. W. Marpurg, *Neue Methode allerley Arten von Temperaturen dem Claviere aufs Bequemste mitzutheilen* (Berlin, 1790/*R*1970)

A. Suremain-Missery, *Théorie acoustico-musicale* (Paris, 1793)

C. Gervasoni, *La scuola della musica* (Piacenza, 1800)

T. Young, 'Outlines of Experiments and Inquiries Respecting Sound and Light', *Philosophical Transactions*, xc (1800), 106–50

J. Robison, 'Temperament', *Encyclopaedia Britannica* (Edinburgh, 3/1801)

D. G. Türk, *Clavierschule* (Leipzig and Halle, enlarged 2/1802/*R*1967)

T. Cavallo, *The Elements of Natural or Experimental Philosophy* (London, 1803)

A. F. C. Kollmann, *A New Theory of Musical Harmony* (London, 1806, rev. 2/1823)

C. Stanhope, 'Principles of the Science of Tuning Instruments with Fixed Tones', *Philosophical Magazine*, xxv (1806), 291

J. W. Callcott, *Plain Statement of Earl Stanhope's Temperament* (London, 1807)

W. Crotch, *Elements of Musical Composition* (London, 1812, 2/1833)

C. Gervasoni, *Nuova teoria di musica* (Parma, 1812)

H. Liston, *An Essay on Perfect Intonation* (Edinburgh, 1812), 23

B. Asioli, *Osservazioni sul temperamento proprio degl'istromenti stabili* (Milan, 1816)

G. Serassi, *Sugli organi, lettere a G. S. Mayr, P. Bontichi e C. Bigatti* (Bergamo, 1816)

A. Fisher, 'Essay on Musical Temperament', *American Journal of Science*, i (1818), 9, 176

P. Lichtenthal, *Dizionario e bibliografia della musica* (Milan, 1826)

J. N. Hummel, *Ausfuhrlich theoretisch-practische Anweisung zum Piano-Forte Spiel* (Vienna, 1828; Eng. trans., 1829)

J. Jousse, *An Essay on Temperament* (London, 1832)

Index

Entries marked in bold indicate music examples.

515

Index

516

Index

Index

Index

Index

viola d'amore, 47, 330
viola bastarda, 93
viola da gamba, 119, 165
  in accompaniment, 10
  repertory, 41
viole d'arco, 173
viol family, 67–71, 75, 173
  bass, 46, 48, 67
  contrabass, 46–7, 77n
  violone da gamba, 46, 77n
  violone del contrabasso (violono grosso, violone, double bass viol),46, 65, 77n
  role of, 67
violin, 46–8, 212
  bowing, 50–54
  construction, 239, 329, 397
  frets, 77n
  repertory, 240–1
  styles, French, 289, 394–5, 407n; Brussels, 394, 407n
violin family, Baroque construction 45–7
  alto, 46
  bass, 46, 67 *see also* violoncello
  contralto, 46
  Quinte de violon, 46
  violino piccolo, 47
  'violino piccolo alla francese' [Monteverdi], 47
violoncello, 46, 48
  construction, 239
  German cello school, 394
  · in accompaniment, 10, 122
  in continuo, 63
  repertory, 240–41
  'violoncello', term used in Baroque, 46 *see* violin family; bass violin
  violoncello piccolo, 47
  'violoncino', term used in Baroque, 46
violone, in accompaniment, 10
  Venetian, 16
  'violone' *see* double bass, violoncello, viol family: violone da gamba, violone del contrabasso; ambiguity of term, 46–7
violone da gamba, *see* viol family
violone del contrabasso, 77n
Viotti, Giovanni Battista, 239, 241, 394, 401
  violin concertos, no.19, **402**,; no.24, **404**
  Violin method, 241
  'Viotti' bowing, **248**, 404
Virgiliano, 93
virginal, 30, 32
  English school 35, 42
Vitali family, 5
Vitruvius, *Dieci libri d'architettura*, 18n
Vivaldi, Antonio, 61, 89
  bassoon concertos, 88
  concertos for two horns, 92
  flute concerto op.10, 85
  Juditha triumphans, 4
  oboe concertos, 87

vocal performance
  improvised ornamentation, 212–13, 424–5, 431, 432–4, 438–43, 444–8, 451, 452–5
  technical basis, 295–6, 427–9
  chest and head voices, 106–7, 112–13, 295, 428
  vocal divisions, 106–7
Vogel, Harald, 119
Vogl, Johann Michael, 317, 449
Vogler, Georg Joseph, 184, 375, 377, 378, 382, 383
Vogt, Gustav, 254–5
voice
  recordings, 331, 425–6, 450–55
  tuning and intonation, 173–4
  types, 110–115, 294–5, 427
Voirin, François Nicolas, 397
'voix sombrée', 428
volata, 295
Volckmar, Wilhelm, 376, 379
Vořišek, Jan Václav, *Sonata quasi una Fantasia*, op.20, 352
Vorspiel, to songs, 287
Vuillaume, Jean-Baptiste, 330, 397

Wagenseil, Georg Christoph 240–41
Wagner, Richard, 207, 325, 338, 379, 395, 399, 424–5, 428, 471–2
  criticism, 336
  Lohengrin, 418
  Mein Leben, 335
  Parsifal, 417
  Rheingold, Das, 420
  Rienzi, 417, 420
  Ring des Nibelungen, Der, 419
  Tristan und Isolde, 418
  Über das Dirigieren, 336, 472
Wagner tuba, 420
Walter, Anton, 228, 348, 363
Walther, Johann Gottfried 18n, 53–54, **54**, 55, 60
  Hortulus Chelicus, 58, **59**, 60
  Musicalisches Lexicon, 33, 46
Washington, Smithsonian Institution, 371
Weber, Carl Maria von, 324, 328, 336, 395, 430
  clarinet concertos, 329
  Der Freichütz, **411**, 432, 436, **437**
Weckmann, Matthias, 93
Weidinger, Anton, 262–3
Weigl, Joseph, 256
  Concertante in E♭, 264n
Weingartner, (Paul) Felix, 336, 475
Weiss, Silvius Leopold, 73, 74
Welte-Mignon, player piano, 331
Welte Philharmonie, 331
Werckmeister, Andreas, 181, **182**, I, 66
Wesley, Samuel Sebastian, 333
Westhoff, Johann Paul von, 55

532

Index